Blogging

ALL-IN-ONE

3rd Edition

**by Amy Lupold Bair
and Susan Gunelius**

for
dummies®

A Wiley Brand

Blogging All-in-One For Dummies®, 3rd Edition

Published by: **John Wiley & Sons, Inc.,** 111 River Street, Hoboken, NJ 07030-5774, www.wiley.com

Copyright © 2023 by John Wiley & Sons, Inc., Hoboken, New Jersey

Published simultaneously in Canada

No part of this publication may be reproduced, stored in a retrieval system or transmitted in any form or by any means, electronic, mechanical, photocopying, recording, scanning or otherwise, except as permitted under Sections 107 or 108 of the 1976 United States Copyright Act, without the prior written permission of the Publisher. Requests to the Publisher for permission should be addressed to the Permissions Department, John Wiley & Sons, Inc., 111 River Street, Hoboken, NJ 07030, (201) 748-6011, fax (201) 748-6008, or online at http://www.wiley.com/go/permissions.

Trademarks: Wiley, For Dummies, the Dummies Man logo, Dummies.com, Making Everything Easier, and related trade dress are trademarks or registered trademarks of John Wiley & Sons, Inc. and may not be used without written permission. All other trademarks are the property of their respective owners. John Wiley & Sons, Inc. is not associated with any product or vendor mentioned in this book.

For general information on our other products and services, please contact our Customer Care Department within the U.S. at 877-762-2974, outside the U.S. at 317-572-3993, or fax 317-572-4002. For technical support, please visit https://hub.wiley.com/community/support/dummies.

Wiley publishes in a variety of print and electronic formats and by print-on-demand. Some material included with standard print versions of this book may not be included in e-books or in print-on-demand. If this book refers to media such as a CD or DVD that is not included in the version you purchased, you may download this material at http://booksupport.wiley.com. For more information about Wiley products, visit www.wiley.com.

Library of Congress Control Number: 2023931507

ISBN 978-1-119-98901-1 (pbk); ISBN 978-1-394-16195-9 (ebk); ISBN 978-1-119-98902-8 (ebk)

SKY10046287_042223

Table of Contents

BOOK 2: NICHE BLOGGING 81

CHAPTER 1: Understanding Niche Blogging 83

CHAPTER 2: Benefiting from a Niche Blog Approach 99

Introduction

Each person who creates a blog is unique, and therefore, each blog is unique. There are almost no boundaries to entering the *blogosphere* (the online blogging community made up of bloggers from around the world, creating user-generated content as part of the social web), and everyone is welcome to the party. Blogging is an amazing way to connect with people, promote a business, establish yourself as an expert in your chosen field, make money, or simply share content with friends and family. The choice is yours!

The blogosphere might be open to anyone, but many people are still confused and intimidated by the terminology, technology, and rules of the blogosphere. Truth be told, most bloggers dive in and learn as they go, but if you prefer to have a guide on hand to walk you through the theories, tools, and processes to create, publish, and maintain a blog, *Blogging All-in-One For Dummies*, 3rd Edition offers exactly that — a complete guide to blogging, all in one place.

About Blogging All-in-One For Dummies

Blogging All-in-One For Dummies, 3rd Edition provides a clear and concise introduction to all the terms, theories, and processes you need to understand to not only join the blogosphere but also meet your individual goals for your blog. The following list highlights some of the information you can better understand and apply to your blogging experience as you read this book — you find out how to

>> Find blogs to read.

>> Choose a topic and write blog posts.

>> Pick a domain name and identify the parts of a blog.

>> Follow the rules of the blogosphere.

>> Create a niche blog.

>> Develop a business blog.

>> Select a blogging platform, using detailed descriptions of the most popular blogging applications — WordPress, Blogger, Medium, and Wix.

- » Write with search engine optimization in mind.
- » Analyze your blog's performance.
- » Find and edit images for your blog.
- » Create and distribute a podcast.
- » Stay organized while blogging.
- » Include video content in your blogging strategy.
- » Promote and grow your blog.
- » Make money from your blogging efforts.
- » Develop your blog's brand on social media platforms.

Blogging can be fun. It can also be lucrative and help you meet a wide variety of goals, from growing a business to building relationships with a global audience. The choice is yours, and *Blogging All-in-One For Dummies,* 3rd Edition can help you get started on the path to blogging success, regardless of your personal or professional goals.

Foolish Assumptions

Blogging All-in-One For Dummies, 3rd Edition is written primarily for a beginner audience — people who have never blogged. However, I'm assuming that you know a few things before you start reading this book:

- » You know how to access and surf the Internet using a web browser on your computer.
- » You know how to download an app on your mobile device.
- » You have a general understanding of what a blog is, or you've seen a blog online.
- » You want to start your own blog, or you want to find out more about blogging to enhance your existing blog.

Understand that if you're a skilled blogger with a deep understanding of the tools and theories of the blogosphere, many of the topics discussed in this book are likely to be rudimentary for you. However, even the most seasoned bloggers admit they don't know everything about blogging and the social web, or at the very least, they haven't thought of something in a certain way. For example, you may have been blogging for years, but now you want to learn more about a different tool or niche. In other words, even skilled bloggers can find plenty of tips and techniques in this book that could come in handy or make their lives easier.

What You Don't Have to Read

Blogging All-in-One For Dummies, 3rd Edition is divided into eight individual Books. Each Book (and each chapter within a Book) is capable of standing on its own. Therefore, you can pick and choose to read specific Books or specific chapters to meet your needs and skip those Books and chapters that don't apply.

It's important to point out that reading cover to cover gives you a complete introduction to blogging and positions you to start your blog successfully and with fewer problems in the future. However, it's entirely up to you to decide how you want to use this book. Just as there really is no wrong way to blog, there's no wrong way to read this book.

How This Book Is Organized

Blogging All-in-One For Dummies is divided into eight Books. Each Book tackles a broad topic related to blogging. From discovering what a blog is to monetizing a blog — and everything in between — this book has a section on nearly every blogging subject. Here's a description of each Book so that you can identify the ones that are likely to be most helpful to you.

Book 1: Entering the Blogosphere

Book 1 starts from the beginning with an introduction to the fundamental principles of blogging. You find out what blogs are and why people blog. You also get guidance on finding blogs to read and making the decision to start your own blog.

After the introduction, you start to get your hands dirty. This Book explains how to pick a blog topic, write blog content, choose a domain name, and understand the bits and pieces that make up a blog. Importantly, you also find out the written and unwritten rules and ethics of the blogosphere. If you want to be a welcome member of the blogosphere, make sure you know and follow the rules discussed in this Book.

Book 2: Niche Blogging

Niche blogging has become more and more popular in recent years as the blogosphere gets more crowded. Book 2 explains what niche blogs are, how to choose a niche, and how to start your own niche blog. You also find out how to write content for a niche blog. Although many of the guidelines of writing a blog discussed in Book 1 apply to niche blogs, niche bloggers need to think about even more considerations when they write blog posts. This Book tells you how to set up your niche blog for success.

Book 3: Corporate and Non-Profit Blogging

Blogging for an organization has become a strategic imperative for large organizations and a competitive differentiator for small companies. No matter what business you're in, a blog can help you with both tangible and intangible benefits. This Book teaches you how starting a company blog can benefit your corporation or non-profit organization. You also find out about companies that are effectively using business blogs so that you can benchmark them for your own efforts. Furthermore, you find out how to create your own business blog marketing plan, choose business bloggers, and write your business blog. Finally, you discover how to blog safely to keep yourself and your organization out of trouble.

Book 4: Figuring Out Blogging Platforms

With so many blogging platforms and tools to choose from, it can be hard for beginner bloggers to know where to begin. This Book explains what blogging applications and blog hosts are and helps you select the best choices for you to meet your goals. You also get a more detailed introduction to four of the most popular blogging applications — WordPress, Blogger, Medium, and Wix.

Book 5: Blogging Tools

You can use a never-ending list of blogging tools to extend and enhance your blog. This Book introduces you to some of the most commonly used tools to help you with handling search engine optimization, analyzing your blog's performance, enhancing blog post content, and staying organized on your blogging journey.

Book 6: Promoting and Growing Your Blog

Many bloggers have goals to develop a popular and well-trafficked blog. If you're one of those bloggers, Book 6 is a Book you need to read! You find out the secrets of blogging success and how to build a community and market your blog through social networking, social media, guest blogging, and content distribution.

Book 7: Making Money from Your Blog

If you want to make money from your blog, Book 7 is for you! This Book tells you all about blog advertising, including contextual ads, text link ads, impression ads, affiliate ads, feed ads, and direct ads. This Book explains publishing ads on your blog as a monetization tactic as well as publishing sponsored content, selling merchandise, and a variety of indirect monetization opportunities.

Book 8: Moving Beyond Writing Blog Posts

While blogging has historically been a written-word medium, many bloggers now branch out and create content beyond writing blog posts. This Book runs you through a variety of ways to flex your creative muscles and take your content creation to a new level. From creating and editing visual content to diving in to the world of online video, this Book encourages you to reach new audiences and provide fresh, new content to your existing blog community. Book 8 also takes a look at podcast creation and how to use social media platforms to create additional blog-related content.

Glossary

Not sure what a word used in this book means? Check the glossary for simple definitions of many common terms used by members of the blogosphere.

Icons Used in This Book

All *For Dummies* books include helpful icons that highlight valuable information, tips, tricks, and warnings:

Points out helpful information that's likely to save you time and effort.

Alerts you to lurking danger. This icon tells you to pay attention and proceed with caution.

TECHNICAL STUFF

Highlights techie-type information nearby. If you're not feeling highly technical, you can skip this information; if you're brave, the information next to the Technical Stuff icons throughout this book can be very helpful.

REMEMBER

Marks a point that's interesting and useful, which you probably want to remember for future use.

Beyond the Book

In addition to the material you're reading right now, this product also comes with some goodies on the web. Check out the free Cheat Sheet at www.dummies.com; just search for "Blogging All-in-One For Dummies Cheat Sheet."

Where to Go from Here

It's up to you! You can read this book in any order you choose. Because each chapter is modular, each chapter can stand on its own. Of course, reading the book from start to finish provides you with a complete and thorough introduction to blogging, but, depending on your goals and experience, the number of chapters you read and the order in which you read them will vary.

Bottom line: Blogging is fun, and each blogger's goals are completely different. Just because someone else is doing XYZ on their blog doesn't mean that XYZ is right for your blog. Use this book as a guide to help you understand the theories, tactics, strategies, and tools of the blogosphere, and then apply them to your blog in the best way to meet *your* needs.

Now it's time to start blogging!

1

Entering the Blogosphere

Contents at a Glance

IN THIS CHAPTER

» **Discovering what makes a blog a blog**

» **Following the history of blogging**

» **Uncovering the reasons why people blog**

» **Finding blogs to read**

» **Deciding to start a blog**

Chapter **1**

Joining the Blogosphere

The term *blog* has become part of common vernacular. What was once thought a fad has become an integral part of the social, media, and business worlds. It seems like everyone knows someone who writes or reads a blog. In fact, many people read blogs and don't even realize it! Today, blogs can look just like traditional websites. Some of the most popular online destinations are blogs, which shows just how far the fad has actually come.

According to Earthweb.com, an online tech news site, there are currently over 600 million blogs on the Internet. That number continues to grow each day as new bloggers and existing writers launch new content.

Why? It's simple. There are virtually no barriers to entry. Just about anyone can create a blog, for free and with very limited technical abilities, and have a place on the web to publish anything they want. (Of course, there are unwritten rules of the blogging community, called the *blogosphere,* which you can find out about in Chapter 4 of this Book.)

The inherent draw of blogging is the opportunity it provides for anyone with access to the Internet to publish content online and join a community of existing bloggers. The content can be made available to a global audience or to a select few, and the topic of a blog is only limited by the creator's imagination! Again, when you start a blog, you become the owner of your own mini media outlet.

As you read on, keep in mind that different people have different goals for their blogs, and for that reason, not all blogs are alike. You find out more about why people blog later in this chapter. For now, just remember, a blog is what its author makes of it, and that's where this book is your guide. It's time to dive in and join the blogosphere!

Getting to Know the Blogosphere

Blogs have arguably been around since 1994, but they've come a long way since their inception when someone named Justin Hall wrote about HTML on Links. net. In the early days of the Internet, websites were fairly static destinations containing information. As new ways evolved for people without extensive technical knowledge to develop their own web presences, blogging was born.

The term *blog* is a shortened version of the word *weblog*, coined in 1997 by Jorn Barger to describe "logging the web" or "web logging." Originally, blogs were simple online diaries, personal homepages where people chronicled specific events, data they wanted to track, or even the daily events of their lives. In the early days of blogging, people wrote primarily for themselves or for a very small audience. Over time, some began to write journal-type blogs to keep friends and family connected. For example, a woman might update her online diary with information about her journey through pregnancy to share the events with her family and friends across long distances. Just as the telephone brought people closer than ever a century earlier, blogs brought people from around the world together at the end of the 20th century.

In the beginning

Blogs began as very rudimentary web pages that looked like little more than a lengthy narrative of text, sometimes with entry dates acting as content separators, appearing much like the pages of a hard copy diary or journal. Early blogs didn't include the social element that today's blogs offer through the commenting feature, which allows two-way conversation to take place, or create a sense of community by integrating social media platforms. In those days there was no such thing as social media! In this sense, early blogs were literally a one-sided log of information on the web.

Not only was the layout of the content simple, but the overall design was as well. A higher level of technical knowledge was required to create a blog in 1994, such as HTML coding skills and access to expensive software that would allow people to create their own web pages. Therefore, some folks might argue that blogging, as we know it today, didn't actually begin until 1999, when hosted blogging applications — such as LiveJournal.com and Blogger.com — debuted and made blogging accessible, easy, and free to the masses.

It wasn't until 2002–2003 that blogging became popular among broad audiences. According to Technorati's State of the Blogosphere 2008 report, the number of active blogs grew from under 200,000 in 2003 to over 184 million in 2008. Suddenly, what was originally viewed as a tool for personal communication turned into an alternative media channel: Journalists, politicians, businesses, and experts in a wide variety of industries and fields started their own blogs and gained notoriety and popularity because of those blogs.

Blogs today

What was once an ancillary or fun way to get online has turned into an essential tool to many. Today, blogs compete with mainstream media in delivering news and information faster and more accurately than ever before.

One of the first and best examples of this shift occurred when the news of Michael Jackson's death first appeared on a celebrity gossip blog, TMZ.com. (Figure 1-1 shows the article on TMZ.com.) Traditional news media organizations, such as CNN.com, were hours behind the blog in verifying the accuracy of the TMZ.com report.

FIGURE 1-1:
The news of Michael Jackson's death was first reported by the TMZ blog.

Similarly, news of rebellion in Iran that followed the 2009 presidential election in that country spread through individuals updating the world from inside Iran via the micro-blogging social media platform Twitter, not from traditional news media. A scheduled shutdown of Twitter.com for routine maintenance was cancelled so as not to interrupt the spread of information through the site about the fallout from the Iranian election. Today, blogs and social media have become valuable sources of real-time news and information, from earthquakes in California to political uprisings around the world.

Blogs have come a long way in terms of design and use. No longer are they always simple online diaries. Today, blogs are used for a myriad of reasons, from sharing information with friends and families, to spreading political news, to promoting a business, to making money, and everything in between. The opportunities are endless.

In fact, many business websites are built using a blogging application, such as WordPress.org, rather than traditional web design techniques because business owners can update and modify blogs easily without incurring huge investments in redesigns. Blogging applications are so easy to use and customize that users can create just about any kind of website they want with them — not just online diaries.

What is a blog?

REMEMBER

Today's blogs can have many different forms, and many would be unrecognizable as blogs to some of the original bloggers. However, it's worthwhile to take a look at the elements that make up the traditional model of a blog:

>> **Posts:** A traditional blog is a website that consists of entries (called *posts*) that appear in reverse chronological order, so the most recent appears at the top of the page.

>> **A commenting feature:** A blog includes a comment feature that allows readers to publish their own comments on the posts they read. Comments provide interactivity, discussions, and relationship-building opportunities between bloggers and their communities of readers.

>> **Links:** The links in a blog allow readers to find more information either within the blog or on other blogs and websites. Links provide another interactive tool and allow the blogger to build relationships with other bloggers and website owners by sending traffic to their sites.

>> **Categories:** Blog posts can be sorted by thematic categories, allowing the reader to locate all of the blog's content relating to that category with just one click.

>> **Archives:** A blog includes an archive of all posts published on that blog since its inception, making it very easy to find older posts. Blogs also typically allow readers to peruse the blog archives through a search tool.

Blogs have evolved to come in many forms and undoubtedly will continue to change and grow over time. For example, blogs originally included only written entries, but today blogs can also consist of photo entries, video content, and audio content. In fact, blogs can include a combination of *each* of those types of entries.

Finding and Reading Blogs

TIP

One of the best ways to determine whether you truly want to join the blogosphere is to find and read other blogs. If you don't enjoy spending time reading blogs, chances are that you won't enjoy spending time writing a blog!

Paramount to being a good blogger is understanding what other people are saying and doing across the blogosphere, particularly within the topic you ultimately choose to blog about.

Why read other blogs?

While reading about what makes a blog a blog is helpful, it is still important to dive in and take a look at some of the other millions of blogs on the Internet.

TIP

You should find out how blogging works and take a look at what else is going on around you in the blogosphere. Check out your surroundings with these questions:

>> Which blogs do you enjoy reading?

>> Which blogs seem to receive a lot of comments or shares on social media?

>> Which blogs are attractive to the eye and make you want to keep scrolling?

>> Which blogs are tough to read and make you want to click away?

Take some time to look around, read blogs, see what you like and what you don't like, and then apply those techniques to your own blog.

As with anything else in life, a book and proper instruction can take you only so far until you finally do have to jump in and get started. Just make sure you're prepared first. Think of this book as your life preserver, but be sure to take the time to actually jump into the water.

Finding blogs

With what will soon be upwards of a billion blogs on the web, it should not be surprising that there is no longer one clear way to locate a blog on the Internet. Gone are the days of comprehensive blog directories and search engines. There are simply too many blogs popping up every day to keep them all organized in such a manageable way.

But take heart! Just because you can't pull out the Yellow Pages and flip through to find the best blogs to read, that doesn't mean that blogs are hard to find.

Blog search engines

While blog search engines are highly imperfect at best, they are one place to start when looking for blogs to read. Blog search sites that no longer exist, such as Technorati and Google Blogs Search, used to provide a one-stop shop to search the blogosphere. Bloggers could register their blogs with these search engines and indicate their blog's topical focus. With both of these giants of blog searching gone, there is no longer one central location where most bloggers register to participate in searches.

Fortunately, several other search tools are available to help you find some blogs about the topics of your choice:

>> **BloggingFusion.com:** Blogging Fusion allows blogs and websites to submit listings to a directory for a fee. Visitors can then search listed sites by keywords or browse by category or region.

>> **Bloggernity.com:** Much like the original blog search pages of the early days of blogging, Bloggernity allows bloggers to submit their blogs to the search engine directory. You can also peruse lists of blogs under categories such as hobby blogs and humor blogs.

>> **Ontoplist.com:** This is another blog search engine where bloggers are able to submit their blogs for inclusion in a directory. The directory is then searchable by keyword. The site also provides a list of what they categorize as "best blogs."

>> **Bloggeries.com:** This includes a directory page where visitors can search for blogs by topics including the arts, politics, travel, and technology. You can also search a keyword to locate related blogs.

Additional ways to locate blogs

Blog search engines are not the only way to begin browsing the blogosphere and likely not even the best.

Don't discount these other great ways to find and read blogs:

» **Word of Mouth:** You may be surprised how many suggestions you receive if you ask your friends to share their favorite blogs!

» **Google Search:** While Google's blog search engine no longer exists, that doesn't mean that you can't use Google to locate wonderful blogs. Simply type in a topical keyword search and add the word "blog" to get started, as shown in Figure 1-2.

» **Through Other Blogs:** The more time you spend reading other blogs, the more cool blogs you'll stumble upon accidentally, and that's where the power of links and networking across the blogosphere becomes apparent. Bloggers often link to one another in their posts or on their blog's *sidebar* (the narrow column that runs along either the right or left side of the blog page).

» **Social Media:** One thing bloggers love to do is share their content! Search your favorite hashtags on your favorite social media platforms and you will surely find links to related blog posts.

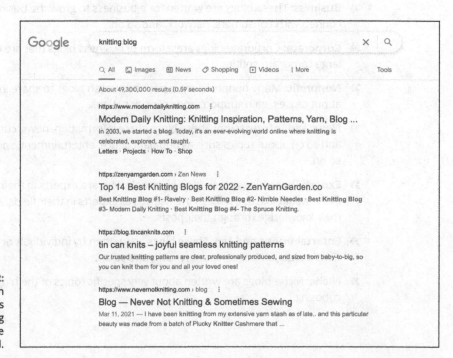

FIGURE 1-2:
A Google search of the keywords knitting and blog helps locate blogs to read.

Understanding Why People Blog

The best part about blogging is anyone can do it! If you have a desire to get your voice heard online, whatever the reason, you can do it with a blog. You are your own boss when it comes to your blog.

Blogs can be written on just about any subject. They can be written in a multitude of languages, and they can be updated as often as you want. Of course, if you have goals to make money, build your business, increase web traffic, and so on with your blog, you ought to know some tricks of the trade that can help you be a successful blogger (I mention some at the end of this chapter), but for now, it's important to understand the open nature of the blogosphere.

Some of the most popular topics being blogged about are fashion, food, and travel, but you can write on any topic of your choosing. You'd be surprised how many people around the world are interested in the same things that you love!

There are many different types of blogs, including but certainly not limited to:

>> **Journal:** A bit like a diary, these blogs are written by individuals about topics of a personal nature such as their likes and dislikes, hobbies, opinions, and so on.

>> **Business:** These blogs are written for a business to grow the business, connect with consumers, network, and so on.

>> **Corporate:** Corporate blogs are a form of business blogs that are owned by large corporate entities.

>> **Nonprofit:** Many nonprofit organizations publish blogs to share information about causes, gain support, and solicit donations.

>> **News and information:** These blogs share information, news, current events, and so on about topics such as popular culture, entertainment, sports, and so on.

>> **Expert:** These blogs are written by people who are experts in their fields, or those would like to establish themselves as experts in their fields, and share their knowledge through their posts.

>> **Entertainment and fan:** These blogs are written by individuals or organizations about celebrities, sports, music, and so on.

>> **Niche:** Niche blogs are written about *very* specific topics of the blogger's choosing.

The uniqueness of blogs comes from the voices of the writers. Additionally, how creators use the blogging application's functionality and tools can help a blog stand out from the crowd. Nonetheless, a blogger's creativity typically stems from why they blog in the first place.

Blogging for fun

Millions of blogs are written by people who have few goals for their blogs other than to have fun. They might just be connecting with family and friends or using the blogosphere as a place to share their opinions simply because they love to write those thoughts down somewhere. Interestingly, many blogs that people write just for fun become incredibly popular, turning the bloggers behind them into online influencers and sometimes transitioning their hobby into their full-time job!

Bloggers like Jenny Lawson, of TheBloggess.com (shown in Figure 1-3); Darren Rowse, of ProBlogger.com; and Gary Vaynerchuk, of Gary Vaynerchuk.com all started their blogs for fun, because they loved the topics they wrote about or simply wanted to document a part of their lives or opinions. Today, all three are well-known and successful both online and offline.

FIGURE 1-3: Jenny Lawson's popular blog, The Bloggess, has led to multiple best-selling books.

Blogs written for fun are typically very personal in nature, and people often write about the following topics on personal blogs. But remember, the topic you blog about is entirely up to you. In fact, the topic you choose to focus on may not yet exist in blog form! Here are some topics to get you started:

>> **Entertainment:** Celebrity gossip, fan clubs, movie reviews, book club discussions, music, personal writing, personal videos, personal photos

>> **Sports:** Favorite teams, local sports, children's sports, exercise

>> **Parenting:** Pregnancy, homeschooling, humor, raising children

>> **Photography:** Travel, people, landscape

>> **Personal health:** Dieting, medical battles, pain management, nutrition

>> **Creativity:** Your own writing, art, music

>> **Travel:** Documenting your vacations and other travels locally and around the world

>> **Current events:** Your views on current events of any kind

>> **Hobbies:** Cooking, crafts, auto maintenance, home repairs

>> **Pets:** Your own pets, breeding, competitions, grooming

REMEMBER

The list of blog topics could go on and on, but the takeaway is this: Any blog topic is okay as long as you're passionate enough about the subject to want to keep writing about it. Of course, it also helps if you have at least a basic knowledge of your blog's topic.

Check out Chapter 2 in this book to find out more about choosing a blog topic.

Blogging for networking

Many people decide to start a blog to meet or bring together other people with similar interests. This type of networking can be for personal or professional reasons. People who blog to network with others often define their success by the communities that develop around their blogs through comments, links, social media connections, emails, and even in-person events.

The Leaky Cauldron (www.the-leaky-cauldron.org), shown in Figure 1-4, is an example of a blog written to link the blog's creator with other people online who have a similar interest (in this case, *Harry Potter*). The site has grown into a vibrant online community of *Harry Potter* fans where readers can comment, submit content, and connect with one another.

FIGURE 1-4:
The Leaky Cauldron is an online hub for all things *Harry Potter*.

Another example is MacRumors.com. Founded in 2000 by Arnold Kim, MacRumors.com is a one-stop shop for discussions of upcoming Apple product news and guides to existing products. Users can read blog posts, how-to guides, study a buyer's guide, and connect with other Apple product users on online forums, as shown in Figure 1-5.

Blogging for exposure

Many entrepreneurs blog to increase their online exposure and get the word out that they are an expert in a specific field. In other words, the primary goal of these bloggers is to get their names in front of wider audiences than they could achieve with static websites (or no web presence at all). These blogs often include updates about each blogger's career or business, with some promotional content peppered in between knowledge-based or opinion posts.

For example, Speak Schmeak (www.speakschmeak.com) is the blog of Lisa Braithwaite, a professional public speaker and consultant. Her blog posts, shown in Figure 1-6, provide free tips and tricks of the trade while providing visitors with the option to hire her for one-on-one coaching.

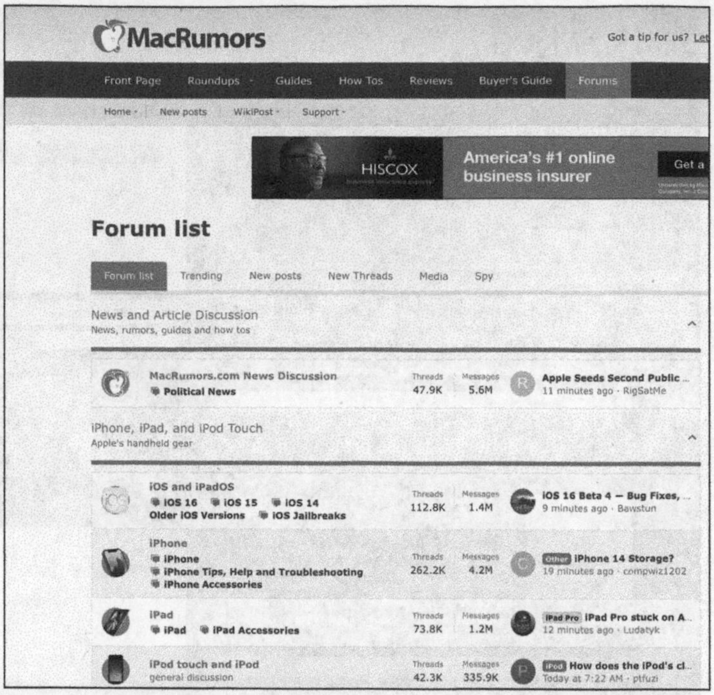

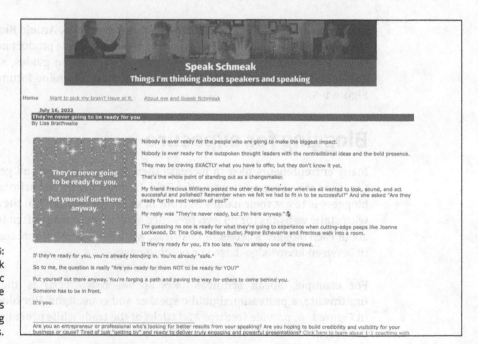

FIGURE 1-5:
Visitors to
MacRumors.com
can connect with
one another via
the site's forums.

FIGURE 1-6:
Speak Schmeak
provides public
speaking advice
and offers
consulting
opportunities.

Blogging for business

You can find many types of business-related blogs on the web. Whether a blogger is trying to share their knowledge of business, boost sales, or indirectly promote their business, a blog is a great way to reach those goals. I discuss business blogging in detail in Book 3.

SucceedAsYourOwnBoss.com, shown in Figure 1-7, is the home of small business expert, author, and speaker, Melinda Emerson. Her blog walks readers through a variety of topics related to small business ownership while pointing visitors to her other online properties, including podcasts and products.

FIGURE 1-7: Melinda Emerson blogs all things small business related at SucceedAsYour OwnBoss.com.

Blogging for branding

Many people view their blog more as a jumping off point for other endeavors than as a final destination or goal. For many, maintaining what appears to be a personal blog is actually done with the purpose of creating a consistent brand or persona.

For example, Martha Stewart is a household name with myriad product lines, television shows, and books. She gathers all of her interests and business pursuits in one place at MarthaStewart.com, which features her personal blog. Martha Up Close and Personal (www.themarthablog.com), shown in Figure 1-8, looks very much like an old-school blog from the original days of blogging and is updated regularly with her latest harvest, behind-the-scenes sneak peeks, and product news, providing readers with brand updates that maintain a personal and intimate feel.

Deciding to Start a Blog

To many people, the decision of whether to start a blog is a difficult one because it seems like a daunting task and a big commitment. Truth be told, starting a blog is a quick and easy pursuit as long as you don't allow yourself to become overwhelmed by all that it *can* entail. Instead, start small, and you'll be surprised how quickly you get up to speed, grow your blog, connect with new people, and start enjoying yourself.

The key is to define the reasons you want to start a blog so you can then determine the best path to meet your goals. Read on to find out about the pros and cons of blogging before you decide to become a blogger.

Blogging benefits

Ask any two bloggers what they think are the benefits to publishing their blogs, and it's highly likely that you'll get two very different answers. That's because all bloggers have their own reasons for blogging and derive their own benefits from it.

The following are ten ways blogging can benefit you, depending on your goals:

>> **Have fun and express yourself.** If you have something that you want to say, blogging is an enjoyable way to do it.

>> **Connect with people.** Whether you want to communicate with family, friends, colleagues, or strangers, a blog can make it happen.

>> **Find people like you.** Maybe you just want to find people who share your views on life or a specific subject. You'd be surprised how many other people are traveling across the blogosphere waiting to be found.

>> **Have a creative outlet.** If you love painting, photography, architecture, or any other creative activity, a blog is a great place to share your work and ideas.

>> **Learn.** A big part of blogging is reading other blogs, communicating with people, and publishing updated content. What better way is there to make the learning process fun and ongoing?

>> **Make a difference.** If you feel strongly about a particular issue, then a blog is a great place to talk about it and gather people to rally around it with you.

>> **Help people.** If you have specific knowledge on a topic, why not share it and help other people learn and grow?

>> **Promote yourself or your business.** If you have a product, service, or business, a blog is a perfect place to talk about it directly or indirectly.

>> **Establish yourself as an expert.** Blogging is a great way to share your knowledge in a field or industry in which you want to be known as an expert. Whether you're looking for a career boost or trying to pick up speaking engagements, a blog offers a destination to share your expertise with the world.

>> **Make money.** Many people blog simply to make some extra money through advertising, reviews, and more.

Blogging repercussions

Like anything in life, blogging isn't all sunshine and happiness. There are negatives to joining the blogosphere, and you should consider them before you start a blog.

Check out the following list of blogging cons:

TIP

>> **Privacy issues:** Unless restricted, blogs are visible to everyone with access to the Internet.

It's highly probable that anyone can find out your address, phone number, and more by doing a simple Google search. Therefore, as long as you're not publishing anything too personal or slanderous to another person or entity on your blog, it's unlikely that you have to worry about privacy issues simply because you write a blog. However, it's important to remember that public blogs are visible to anyone. You might not want to publish those pictures of you and your friends partying on a blog that your boss can find. With that in mind, publish content with the knowledge that a wider audience than you can imagine might stumble upon your blog.

>> **Time commitment:** Successful blogging can require a major time commitment. You have to find subjects to write about, update your blog regularly, respond to comments, read other blogs and contribute your own comments, and more. Of course, your success is dependent on that time commitment, so you need to determine how much time is enough to invest toward reaching your blogging goals.

>> **Technological demands:** The blogosphere, the Internet, and technology are constantly changing. Although blogging doesn't require a degree in computer science, you'll find greater success if you continue to learn and adopt new tools.

>> **Writing requirements:** Blogging requires writing, so if you don't like to write, blogging will undoubtedly be a grueling chore for you. Furthermore, people don't like to read blogs that are poorly written. You don't need to be Shakespeare, but you should be able to put together a coherent, grammatically correct sentence. If you can't, brush up on your writing skills before you start blogging.

>> **Patience concerns:** Blogging success doesn't happen overnight. You need to be prepared to make a long-term commitment to your blog. Without patience, you're likely to abandon your blog too soon.

>> **Social pressures:** Blogging is a two-way street. If you don't interact with your audience members, they'll leave and find someone who values their input. It's not much fun to blog alone.

>> **Some people won't like you:** The online world is filled with all kinds of people, and they won't all like you. Unfortunately, many of those people never learned the old adage, "If you don't have anything nice to say, don't say anything at all." To make matters worse, some people, often called *trolls,* enjoy visiting blogs and making nasty comments for no reason other than to stir up trouble. As a blogger, you need to be prepared to read negative things said about you on your blog and on other sites without getting overly concerned about them.

Blogging success secrets

The preceding section tells you about the repercussions and negatives of blogging, but how can those very same things be turned around into the secrets of successful blogging? It's simple! Take a look at the following list to see what I mean.

REMEMBER

Successful bloggers . . .

>> **Write a lot:** The best blogs are updated frequently with fresh, relevant, and interesting content.

>> **Are passionate:** That passion and their unique personalities shine through in their writing styles.

>> **Love to read:** The best bloggers spend a lot of time surfing the web and reading (and commenting) about their blog topics.

>> **Are very social:** The best bloggers care about their audience and take time to interact with them and show them that their opinions are truly valued.

>> **Are thick-skinned:** Insults roll off the best bloggers' backs and are forgotten quickly.

>> **Like to take risks:** New technology means new opportunities, and the best bloggers dive right in.

>> **Love to learn:** The best bloggers realize they don't know it all.

>> **Are comfortable speaking their minds:** The best blogs are written by people who aren't afraid to express their opinions to the online audience and then discuss those opinions in an open and professional manner with both proponents and opponents.

Setting your goals

Now that you know the good, the bad, and the ugly about blogging, it's time to think about what you want to get out of your blogging experience. Consider both the short- and long-term objectives for your blog because they can have a significant effect on the path you take in joining the blogosphere.

Start by creating a plan to get your blog up and running, but don't try to do everything at once. Take your time, learn as you go, and in no time at all, you'll be an active and welcome member of the blogosphere!

IN THIS CHAPTER

» **Picking your blog topic**

» **Writing in your own voice**

» **Knowing what to write about**

» **Writing blog posts that readers will enjoy**

» **Finding topics to write about**

» **Understanding blogging frequency and trends**

Chapter 2

Preparing to Start and Write a Blog

After you make the decision to start a blog, you need to take some time to do some planning. What do you want to blog about? How often should you publish posts? What writing style should you use? These are all questions that every blogger needs to consider. This chapter walks you through the basics so you can start with a confident plan of action in mind.

Of course, if you're simply blogging for fun, your planning process doesn't have to be as detailed as it would be if you intend to blog to build your business, make money, or establish yourself as an expert in your field or industry. However, if you have greater goals than simply blogging for personal enjoyment, investing time into understanding the *process* of blogging before you get started can save both time and frustration later.

Choosing a Topic

The first step to starting a blog is choosing your blog's topic. Most blogs are dedicated to a particular subject. For example, you can find blogs about entertainment, crafts, sports, business, and many other topics. Chapter 1 of this Book provides a variety of blog topic ideas, some of which I discuss later in this chapter as well.

Take some time to surf the blogosphere and find out what kind of blogs are already out there. Does it matter to you, based on your long-term blogging goals, if there are already a lot of popular blogs written about your topic of choice? Or are you most interested in blogging because you're passionate about a specific topic, no matter the competition to attract readers? Does competition for traffic affect your objectives? Or will blogging primarily be a hobby for you? You need to ask yourself these questions before you finalize your blog topic selection.

For example, food is an extremely popular blog topic. From recipes to tips and tricks, some of the most popular blogs online are a foodie's paradise, such as Skinnytaste (www.skinnytaste.com) and Smitten Kitchen (www.smittenkitchen.com), which is shown in Figure 2-1. If you're considering cooking and recipes as the topic of your blog, you need to decide whether that kind of heavy-hitting competition is a problem for you before you start your blog.

TIP

Even though popular blog topics provide a lot of competition for views, those topics also provide a lot of readers looking for new content!

FIGURE 2-1: Smitten Kitchen is one of the most popular blogs about food and cooking.

Reviewing popular blog topics

The list of the most popular blog topics is constantly in flux, but there are certainly some leading areas of focus that provide a great place to begin your analysis of popular blog topics.

TIP

Don't waste time reinventing the wheel. Instead, stop by popular blogs to find out what draws people to them. Consider incorporating what you love most from your favorite blogs into your own blog (as appropriate, of course).

Some of the most popular blog topics include:

>> **Food:** Recipe searches bring readers to some of the most popular blogs day after day as readers hope to find delicious new meal ideas.

>> **Health and Fitness:** You can imagine that health and fitness blogs receive the most traffic shortly after people make their New Year's resolutions, but they are also well-read throughout the year.

>> **Lifestyle:** Lifestyle blogs cover a huge range of topics from home décor to hobbies and sports. Check out Cup of Jo, shown in Figure 2-2, for one example of a popular lifestyle blog.

>> **Fashion and Beauty:** If you've ever searched online for a hair how-to or a beauty tutorial, you're well aware of the vast number of fashion and beauty blogs online.

>> **Photography:** Not only are blogs a great place to learn about photography, but many photographers also find them to be the perfect platform to share their work with the world.

>> **Parenting:** This popular blog topic encompasses the full range of the parenting experience from favorite products to parenting advice and more.

>> **Crafting and DIY:** Have a knack for knitting, a penchant for painting, or maybe you're far more than so-so with a sewing machine? You are not alone! The blogosphere is the place to be for crafting and DIY lovers.

>> **Personal/Journal:** Before the blogosphere exploded into hundreds of millions of sites, blogs were most often simply online journals of personal interests or day-to-day diary entries. For many writers, blogging is still just that!

>> **Business:** There is certainly always plenty of content for those wanting to chronicle the ins and outs of the business world from the latest news to hot takes on big business.

>> **Travel:** Whether people travel professionally or just for fun, or even if they simply wish they could travel, the blogosphere provides them with a place to talk about it.

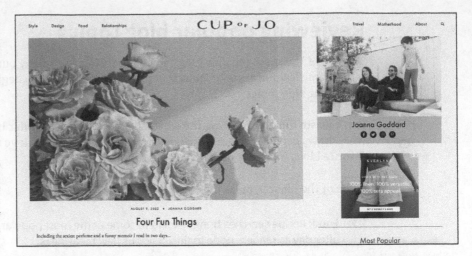

FIGURE 2-2:
Cup of Jo, started
by blogger
Joanna Goddard,
describes itself
as a women's
lifestyle site.

Determining the best topic for your blog

Contemplating all the topics you could write about on your blog can be an over-whelming task. But take heart! Here are some ways to narrow down the best topic for you to write about on your blog.

Blog about a topic you love

What is your passion? What subjects and areas most interest you? If you plan to write regularly on your blog, you will need to be able to write about that topic *a lot*. That means you shouldn't pick a subject area that you're likely to get bored with quickly. There's not much point in starting a blog that you're going to abandon in three months because you're already tired of the subject matter. Instead, pick a topic that you know you'll be able to write about for many, many months (and possibly years) to come.

Blogging takes a lot of effort and a major time commitment if you want to become successful. With that in mind, you need to be certain that you truly love your cho-sen topic before you get started.

Blog about a topic you like discussing with other people

An inherent and powerful feature of blogs is the commenting feature, which invites readers to provide their own thoughts related to the posts you publish. To be a successful blogger, you need to engage your readers by showing them you value their opinions. Whether or not they agree with you, you need to actively join the conversation by responding to their comments and creating an ongoing dialogue.

In simplest terms, if you don't want to debate with anyone about your blog topic and don't want to hear anyone else's opinions but your own, you may need to look for another topic. Many bloggers define success by the community that develops around their writing, and that community grows through the conversations that take place on the blog.

WARNING

Unfortunately, the commenting feature inherent to blogs opens up your blog to spam and rude comments. You should delete these comments in order to ensure the user experience on your blog is a positive one. (For more about handling comments, see Chapter 2 of Book 6.)

Blog about a topic you enjoy researching

An important part of being a successful blogger is staying abreast of what's happening with your blog topic, especially if you're hoping to use your blog as a way to establish yourself as an expert on that topic. You need to be willing to keep reading and discovering new things about your chosen area. Doing so will give you ideas for blog posts, keep your blog fresh, help you network with other bloggers, and help you build relationships with your readers and other bloggers.

Many of the best bloggers don't claim to know all there is to know about their blog topics and instead make it clear that they are open to learning. That's why they embrace the social aspect blogging provides by actively engaging in conversations with their readers and other bloggers through the commenting and linking features that blogs offer.

Going broad or staying focused

As the blogosphere gets more crowded, there are more writers competing for views from the same readers. It's important to determine whether you want to blog about a broad topic, which could mean your blog will have a lot of competition from similar sites, or whether you want to blog about a more specific subject, which could mean a smaller potential audience. Only you can choose which option will better help you meet your blogging goals.

Black Yoga Society (www.blackyogasociety.com), shown in Figure 2-3, is an example of a blog with a highly focused topic: blog posts written by Black contributors around the topic of wellness fields such as yoga, crystals, and African spirituality. The site, and now online community, was born out of one blogger's struggle to locate Black-owned yoga studios or wellness products in the spring of 2020. Sometimes narrowly focused blogs are created specifically because they meet a need or fill an online vacuum.

You can find out more about blog specificity (called *niche* blogging) and the pros and cons of focused versus broad blogging in Book 2.

FIGURE 2-3:
Black Yoga Society was created to fill a need discovered by the site's founder.

Finding Your Voice

One reason that people enjoy writing and reading blogs is the personality behind them. Each blogger has a unique writing style and personality — often called the blogger's *voice* — that shines through their blog posts. Your voice is something you need to consider before you begin writing your own blog.

Do you want the tone of your blog to be professional or humorous? Do you want a journalistic tone or a personal diary tone? The answers to these questions determine the writing style you should use on your blog. For example, you can write in a highly professional manner, as if you're writing business communications. Alternatively, you might write in a personal manner, exactly the way that you speak. You may even decide to combine both extremes and find a happy medium. The choice is yours, but your style should stay consistent in every post and match your blog's topic and content.

The next step is to inject your personality into that style. That's what makes your blog stand out from the crowd. Of course, you could fabricate the persona you take on in your blog completely, and that's just fine. Daniel Lyons, author of the retired The Secret Diary of Steve Jobs blog (`www.fakesteve.net`), shown in Figure 2-4, did exactly that. He wrote his blog as if he were Steve Jobs, and readers loved it for its satirical humor (and just to be clear, he's *not* Steve Jobs!).

Together, writing style and personality define your blog's unique voice, and it's that voice, coupled with great content, that keeps readers coming back for more.

REMEMBER

A specific personality should shine through your writing, connecting your readers to you and making them feel like they know you personally.

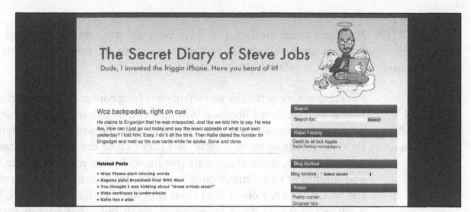

FIGURE 2-4:
The Secret Diary of Steve Jobs blog had a unique and humorous voice.

Selecting Suitable Topics

After you've chosen your blog's topic, you need to decide what to write about in your blog posts. It's your blog, so you can write about whatever you want. Of course, keep it within reason and be sure to read the cautionary information later in this chapter. The key to success is choosing subjects that you're passionate about, letting your personality shine through, and writing in a way that invites readers to be interested, too!

Deciding what to write about

Don't be afraid to get creative, and don't feel bound to your blog's topic. Although relevant content should certainly dominate your blog posts, it's acceptable to inject an unrelated post on occasion. Doing so lets your readers get to know you a little bit better by introducing them to another aspect of your life or another subject that interests you.

Read "Understanding Types of Blog Posts" and "Avoiding Blogger's Block and Finding Blog Post Ideas" later in this chapter for more information about what to write about on your blog.

Knowing what not to write about

Although the rules of the blogosphere are primarily unwritten, there are topics and content you might want to consider not writing about on your blog. For example, if you're not up for debate and name-calling, you should avoid blog topics that invite that kind of behavior. For example, highly political blogs often lead to passionate dialogue, and any blog post that expresses an extremely strong opinion is likely to be met by equally passionate comments.

REMEMBER

Manners count online, too. Just because you can hide behind your computer doesn't mean you should forget to be courteous, polite, and professional on your blog and in related communications.

WARNING

Exercise some caution as you write your blog content. Avoid writing anything that might be considered libelous. Whether you mention another person, a product, or a company on your blog, keep in mind that the world can see what you publish. Providing your opinion is okay, but don't cross the line into defaming anyone or anything. Also, think about sensitive topics before you write about them. Although you might not think much about religion, for example, millions of people around the world are very devoted to their religions. Think twice before you write about a subject that you don't know much about but other people are passionate and vocal about.

Writing Great Blog Posts

An essential part of your blogging success is publishing great content, and this holds true no matter what type of blog you write or what goals you have for your blog. (You can find some specific tips for writing posts for niche blogs and business blogs in Chapter 4 of Book 2 and Chapter 4 of Book 3, respectively.) That means your posts must be well written, interesting, and entertaining.

The first step to writing great blog content is injecting your personality into your posts. (Read the earlier section, "Finding Your Voice," for details.) Your blog post should not only interest your readers, but it should also encourage them to engage with you and other readers by leaving a comment, writing about, and linking to your post from their own blogs, or sharing a link to your post via social media.

Writing meaningful and interesting content

Select blog post topics that are meaningful and interesting to your blog's audience. If people aren't interested in the posts you're writing on your blog, they're unlikely to keep reading or ever return. Before you write a new blog post, always consider your audience.

Staying consistent

Consistency matters in terms of both your post topics and your writing voice. People will return to your blog time and time again because they want to hear more from you. Readers are building a relationship with you and each other in the comment section of your blog posts because they like both what you have to say as well as how you say it. Want to try a different style of post or take a different tone? Consider changes carefully and play around with any new writing styles before hitting publish. Be sure that you are completely ready to change directions before springing a totally different topic or tone on your readers who have come to know what to expect from your blog.

Being honest

Always be honest in your blog posts. Not only is it important for readers to feel comfortable trusting your blog's content, but people online have a way of figuring out quickly when someone is being dishonest. Don't ruin the future of your blog — and your credibility as a blogger — by being dishonest in your writing!

Citing sources

Cite your sources, link to them, and build relationships with them if possible. Doing so is not only the right thing to do ethically, but it also helps you network with peers and give your readers more sources for great content. The blogosphere has plenty of room for healthy competition. Sharing useful sources with your readers is a good thing. If you continue to write great, consistent content, you shouldn't have to worry about losing readers to the sources you cite in your own blog posts.

Using images

Use images as appropriate, always cite their source, and only use them if you have permission to do so. Images make your posts, and your blog in general, more visually appealing, drawing readers in to read more of your content. Just be sure to use images that are clear, the appropriate resolution for online use, and actually relevant to your content. (For more information about copyrights, see Chapter 4 in this Book.)

Writing for the web

Writing blog posts is not the same as writing a high school research paper no matter how serious or factual your content! Be sure to write blog posts that are easily consumable online — especially via a mobile platform. That often means writing in short paragraphs, using headings to separate text, and providing visual relief in the form of bulleted or numbered lists. Webpages with a lot of white space are far easier to read (or even skim) than text-heavy pages. Your goal is to get people to read your content (skimming is perfectly fine, too), not click away because they're bombarded with more text than they can process. This also means keeping in mind how long it will take for the average reader to read an entire post.

TIP

Many bloggers actually include the total time it will take to read a post at the top of the post to help readers decide if they've got time to read the content now or should bookmark it for later!

Understanding Types of Blog Posts

Blog posts come in many flavors, some more popular than others. It's your blog, so you can write any type of post you want, including posts that aren't highlighted in the following list! However, it's good to make yourself familiar with some of the most popular types of blog posts in order to give yourself a starting point as you launch your blog.

Types of blog posts include (but are very certainly not limited to) the following:

>> **Listicles:** People love a good list! A *listicle*, shown in Figure 2-5, is simply a blog post written in the form of a numbered or bulleted list. They may have catchy titles such as "Ten Ways to Have a Successful Staycation" or "Fifteen Reasons to Adopt a Dog Today."

>> **Current events/news:** Do you love to keep your finger on the pulse of what's happening in the news today? Consider writing commentary posts or news wrap-ups in response to what's going on in the world around you. These posts can have a global, national, or even a local focus.

>> **Tips and thought leadership:** Many bloggers use their blogs as a way to flex their expert muscles and establish themselves as an authority in a particular topic. If you have a specialized knowledge in an area, share it through a blog post where you provide that knowledge as a series of tips or an explanatory post that showcases your leadership in the field.

>> **Reviews:** Bloggers are considered online influencers and a powerful source of word-of-mouth marketing. The reason is simple. Research shows that people trust other people more than they trust traditional advertising. You can review anything related to your blog topic in your blog posts, and your readers are likely to be happy to read that content and possibly share it with other people. Just be sure to disclose if you have received a product or service for free in exchange for your published review (check out Chapter 4 of this Book for more information about blogging best practices and disclosures)!

FIGURE 2-5:
Buzzfeed (www.buzzfeed.com) makes frequent use of the popular listicle blog post format.

>> **Recommendations:** Similar to reviews, recommendation posts allow you to share your favorites or preferred things related to your blog topic without providing complete reviews.

>> **How-tos and tutorials:** Blog readers often look to the Internet to learn how to do something, making how-to posts and tutorials very popular.

>> **Polls and surveys:** Get your readers involved by creating a poll and asking them to vote. People love polls! Use a tool such as Crowd Signal (www.crowdsignal.com) or SurveyMonkey (www.surveymonkey.com) to create polls about anything you want.

>> **Interviews:** Not an expert on a topic, but know someone who is? Interested in publishing another perspective on your blog's topic? You can reach out to others to request their participation in an interview to be published on your blog. You'd be surprised how many people will welcome the exposure your interview can bring them.

>> **Contests:** Many blog readers love to enter contests, so contest blog posts are often very popular.

>> **Visual media and podcasts:** Sick of typing your thoughts? Consider recording and sharing a video, uploading a podcast episode, or publishing a post made up entirely of photographs.

>> **Checklists and printables:** One of the main reasons readers turn to the blogosphere is to locate resources for everything from preparing to take your child to college to packing for a vacation. Consider creating useful checklists and printables for your readers.

>> **Roundups:** Roundup posts highlight a series of related content either from your own blog or from around the blogosphere with headlines, content previews, images, and links.

Avoiding Blogger's Block and Finding Blog Post Ideas

Blogger's block, just like your run-of-the-mill writer's block, occurs when a blogger is struggling to come up with new content ideas. It's very common, and every blogger experiences it at one time or another. Some days you just feel less inspired than others. Don't despair; see the nearby sidebar for tips to get past blogger's block.

If you are still finding it difficult to move beyond blogger's block, you may need to invest more time in finding and planning post ideas. Fortunately, there are many sources available to bloggers to help find blog post fodder.

TIP

The following list suggests some popular ways to find blog post ideas:

>> **Visit online communities and forums.** Sites such as Reddit (www.reddit. com) provide people with places to share online content and launch related discussions with other members of the online community. Many online readers turn to these communities to have their questions answered and find great content on any topic you can imagine.

>> **Look at Google Trends.** Google Trends (www.google.com/trends) provides a continually updated list of the most-searched-for search terms, as shown in Figure 2-6. If people are searching for a term, it's safe to assume they're interested in the topic, which could make a great blog post idea!

>> **Read news sites.** Review news sites (local, regional, national, or global), which may have breaking stories related to your blog topic that you could write about on your blog.

>> **Search social media.** Conduct a keyword or hashtag search on your favorite social media site, such as Twitter or Instagram, to see what people are talking about right now related to your blog's subject matter.

TRICKS TO CURE BLOGGER'S BLOCK

It's inevitable. One day you'll sit down at your computer to write a blog post, and you won't have any ideas for what to write. Try the following tricks to cure blogger's block:

- **Walk away from your computer.** Simply do something else for a while! When you return to your computer later, refreshed and in a different frame of mind, you might find that blog post ideas are easier to come by.

- **Spend some time surfing the blogosphere and reading other blogs.** Keep in mind that the advice here is not to steal someone else's blog post idea but simply to find inspiration!

- **Chat with friends or family.** I can't begin to tell you how many times a blog post idea of mine resulted from a conversation I had with friends, both online and off, or with my spouse and children.

- **Grab a quick shower.** I would love to find a way to blog in the shower because some of my very best ideas over the years have come while I'm singing along to the radio or washing my hair!

- **Work out.** Many bloggers swear by deep-breathing exercises, exercise such as yoga, or even a brisk walk to regain their focus and get the mind flowing freely again.

- **If all else fails, pop on over to the kitchen and grab a snack.** Maybe your blogger's block is just trying to tell you that you're hungry or need to drink more water!

FIGURE 2-6: Google Trends provides a snapshot of the most-searched-for terms on Google.

Determining How Often to Publish Blog Posts

How frequently you publish new content on your blog is completely up to you! There are no rules for number of posts per month, week, or even per day. If you're blogging for fun and aren't trying to reach a specific goal, such as number of readers or income generated, you can publish as frequently or infrequently as you want. However, if you want to grow your blog and become a successful blogger, you need to publish with some sort of regularity.

The quality of your content is certainly critical to your blog's success, but without fresh content, people won't have much incentive to return to your blog or tell other people about it. One great post just doesn't get the job done if you want to grow your blog. The more frequently you publish good blog posts, the more reason there is for people to return again and again, and the more likely it is that your readers will share your content with others.

Frequent blog updates can also help with search engine optimization (which I discuss in Chapter 1 of Book 5) because each new blog post is a new entry point for search engines to find your blog. More entry points give people more chances to find your blog through a Google search, for example.

When you know how much you want your blog to grow and how quickly, you can determine how often you need to publish new blog posts. Some bloggers publish new content more than one time a day, but it's a more reasonable goal to try to publish fresh content once a day. If growth isn't that important to you, but you don't want to be the only person reading your blog, try to publish a new blog post every few days so you have fresh content up two to three times per week. Finally, if growing your readership isn't the focus of your blog and instead you just want to write for your own enjoyment, you can publish new blog posts whenever you want and as infrequently as you want.

REMEMBER

Blogging success is directly tied to your goals for your blog and your commitment to investing time into your blog. Write great content in your own voice, be social, and make sure your content is fresh.

Following Blogging Trends

Congratulations! You've spent some time perusing the blogosphere, you've selected the focus for your blog, you've made a plan for how often to write and what to write about — but don't get too cozy. The blogging world is always changing and updating what's new and what's next. Part of preparing to start a blog is figuring out how to put your finger on the pulse of what's happening in the world of blogging.

I'll give you a head start by taking a look at some of the latest blogging trends:

>> **Visual content:** Visual content such as photos, infographics, screenshots, and videos top the current trend list for what is popular in the world of blogging. Don't be afraid to move beyond the written word! Book 8 takes a closer look at how to do this well.

>> **Long-form content:** While it may seem counterintuitive to write lengthy content for the web, the fact is that deep-dive content for the more critical-minded reader is very popular.

>> **Mobile-first blog format:** When deciding how to format your blog, keep in mind that many people will be accessing your content via their phones. Many bloggers have decided to focus on reaching those readers by selecting a blog format that focuses on mobile readability.

>> **Estimated reading times:** Remember those critical thinkers who enjoy long-form writing? They also like to know how much time they'll need to invest to get to the end of a post. Bloggers are finding that their readers really like having an estimated reading time posted at the top of each blog post.

TIP

Keep in mind that the average person reads 200 to 250 words per minute.

>> **TL;DR summaries:** Have you ever seen TL;DR and wondered what it means? It stands for "too long; didn't read." If you decide to follow the trend of writing lengthy, wordy blog posts, consider adding a TL;DR summary at the start of each piece highlighting your main points for those who don't have time — or won't make time — to read every word.

>> **Daily posts:** Earlier in this chapter I discussed frequency of posting. Bloggers have found that posting once a day seems to be the sweet spot for return on investment.

>> **Utilizing guest posts:** Don't feel like every post needs to be written by you! It is very popular to welcome guest posts on your blog. Just be sure to vet the writing before accepting it so that the content aligns with the rest of your blog.

>> **Interactive content:** Perhaps the wave of the future, interactive content is making a splash in the blogosphere. This includes quizzes, polls, and even shoppable *lookbooks* (digital content that combines the trends of interactive and visual content by allowing readers to virtually flip through pages and click to make purchases).

IN THIS CHAPTER

» **Getting your blog underway**

» **Understanding domain names**

» **Selecting a domain name**

» **Buying a domain name**

» **Getting to know the parts of a blog**

Chapter **3**

Blogging Basics

Congratulations! You've committed to starting a blog, and now it is time to take a closer look at the next steps to joining the blogosphere. Launching a blog takes more than just a good idea. It's important to understand the basic aspects of blogging from selecting a name to identifying the components of a typical blog.

This chapter teaches you everything you need to know from how to hit the ground running to the ins and outs of domains to how to identify the typical parts of a blog so that you're completely educated and ready to get into the nitty-gritty technical part of creating your blog.

Launching Your Blog Quickly

Once you've got your blog topic selected, you may want to move immediately from first considering writing a blog to actually publishing and sharing content on the web. Good news! It is absolutely possible to launch your new blog quickly and share your ideas with the world as the latest new online content creator.

REMEMBER

Taking your blog from idea to reality generally includes the following basic steps:

1. **Choosing a blog topic:** Covered in depth in Chapter 2, selecting a topic for your blog is the key to moving forward with your decision to write a blog. After all, you've got to know what it is you'll be writing!

2. **Choosing a blog name:** Grab a paper and pen and start brainstorming creative titles. What really speaks to your inspiration to blog in the first place? Do you love puns and creative titles? Maybe you prefer to be more serious when selecting a blog name. Whatever is right for you, be sure that you love your blog's name before moving on to the next step because your blog's name is the first thing your new readers will see when they visit your site.

3. **Choosing a domain name:** In the following section, I look at what it means to choose your blog's domain name and URL (Uniform Resource Locator). A URL is essentially your blog's home address on the web. This step, like selecting your blog's name, requires careful consideration. Once you've created your blog's URL, it is easy to move quickly to the next step.

4. **Choosing a hosting platform:** The content that you create for your blog needs a place to "live" on the Internet. That is where a blog hosting platform comes into play! Book 4 takes a much closer look at what it means to select a hosting platform while also previewing a variety of platform options.

5. **Selecting a theme:** A blog's theme is the design of the blog from the appearance to readers to the functionality behind the scenes. There are free themes as well as very expensive themes that come with all the bloggy bells and whistles. Blog platforms tend to offer basic — often free — themes to get you started quickly.

6. **Writing and publishing a post:** You've selected your blog topic and name, you've found a great domain name and blog platform, you've chosen the theme for your blog — it's time to start writing! You can spend as little or as much time on writing and editing a blog post as you like.

   TIP

   Want to get started quickly? Consider starting by writing an introduction post telling readers a bit about yourself and your inspiration for creating your new blog.

7. **Sharing a link to your content:** Now it is time to share your wonderful new blog with the world! Many bloggers share a link to their site by posting on various social media platforms or emailing friends and family to spread the word.

Choosing a Domain Name

Your blog's domain name is the unique part of your blog's URL, which is connected to your blog only. Your URL is your blog's complete web address that people type into their browser search bars to find your site. Take a look at the format of the following URL:

```
http://www.google.com
```

The parts of the URL are as follows:

1. **Access protocol:** The `http://` represents the access protocol, Hypertext Transfer Protocol, in the above URL example used to send and retrieve information across the web.

2. **Domain name:** `www.google.com` represents the domain name in the URL example — a unique identifier and extension. In the example, `www.` stands for World Wide Web, `google` is the unique identifier, and `.com` is the domain name extension.

In the early days of the Internet, `.com` was one of the only domain name extension options, representing commercial websites. Additional extensions such as `.gov`, `.org`, and `.edu` came along to help distinguish between different types of websites that debuted online: government, nonprofit, and education/schools, respectively.

Before you can begin publishing online content on your blog, you need to choose a domain name in order to create your blog's unique URL or web address. The type of domain and the process you follow to get it depends partly on the blogging platform you choose, which is covered in depth in Book 4.

Regardless of how you go about getting a domain name for your blog or which blogging platform you choose, you need to select or create a domain name before you can begin blogging. It is a good idea to brainstorm a list of options before launching into your search for a domain because it is possible that your first choice will already be taken. There's a chance that your most clever domain name idea was someone else's most clever domain name idea first, and many people purchase domains for the sole purpose of selling them for a profit in the future. This means that some of the best domain names are already taken even if they're not currently in use by a website. Don't give up! The right domain name for your wonderful new blog is out there.

REMEMBER

Each domain name is unique to that particular website just like a home's street address. If the domain name you have in mind for your blog is already taken, you will have to come up with a new idea!

Understanding the types of domain names and extensions

If you decide to use a blogging platform that provides hosting for your blog, meaning you don't have to purchase a hosting account through a separate company to store your blog data, choosing a domain name is a simple part of the blog set-up process. Your blogging platform will walk you through the steps to select your domain name. However, if you host your blog content through a third-party web host, you need to purchase your own domain and associate it with your hosting account and blog. Book 4 discusses in detail domain names as they relate to specific blogging applications.

For now, take a look at the following list of popular domain name extensions in the United States because choosing the unique identifier for your domain name is only part of the domain name selection process.

TIP

Bloggers outside of the United States have different domain extensions available to them, typically identified by a letter combination that represents their country.

>> .com: In spite of the ever-increasing number of options, this is still the most common and most well-known domain extension. As such, it's typically the first extension people add to domains when they type them into their browser search bars. This doesn't mean that you shouldn't consider other domain extensions! It can be difficult to find an available domain that includes your first choice for a domain name with the .com extension, but it's not impossible if you get creative.

>> .net: This domain extension is a popular second choice behind .com. Short for network, .net is used by many popular blogs and websites focusing on network-based technology. However, the .net extension is not exclusively used by bloggers writing on topics related to technology, as shown in Figure 3-1. Anyone may purchase and use a blog URL with a .net extension!

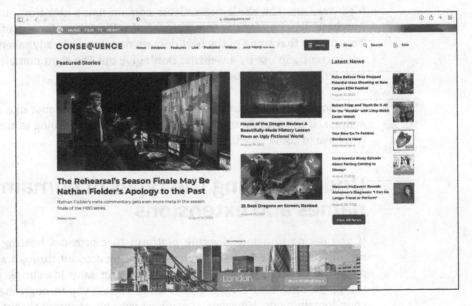

FIGURE 3-1:
Consequence, a blog focusing on music, television and film, uses the .net domain extension.

>> `.org`: Although this extension was once restricted to nonprofit organizations, today, anyone can register a domain using `.org`.

>> `.info`: Unfortunately, spammers have a tendency to target blogs using this extension, so you might want to check the availability of your chosen domain using other extensions before you settle on `.info`.

>> `.co`: Originally `.co` was created as a ccTLD, or country code top level domain, assigned to the country of Colombia. However, use of the extension is not exclusive to any location. Many websites now use `.co` to represent "company" or corporation," and some bloggers select this extension in order to have access to a domain name that is not available with a `.com` domain extension.

>> `.us`: As you may have guessed, `.us` is the ccTLD for the United States and is exclusively available to residents of the U.S..

>> `.xyz`: This extension has been available since 2014, and like `.co`, `.xyz` is often used with the `.com` a blogger would like to use is no longer available.

>> `.ly`: The `.ly` domain extension was created as a ccTLD for Libya, but it is often used in creative ways by website owners around the world, as shown in Figure 3-2.

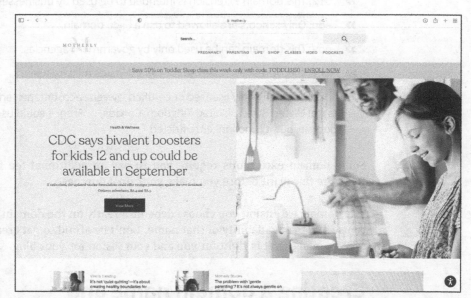

FIGURE 3-2:
The blog
Motherly cleverly
uses the .ly
extension
to create the
`www.mother.ly`
web address.

>> `.me`: This domain extension was created as a ccTLD for Montenegro, but anyone may use it. It is sometimes used by those looking for a very personal-sounding domain name and may be a fun idea for someone planning a journal blog.

- » **.site**: Able to be used by anyone, this domain extension is popular and used by many looking for a versatile alternative to .com.

- » **.blog**: This domain extension is a great choice to consider for a website that is exclusively a blog.

- » **.io**: Created as a ccTLD for the British Indian Ocean Territory, the .io extension has come to be associated with tech companies and business startups rather than with a geographical area.

- » **.shop**: Planning to include an online store as part of your blog? Consider the .shop domain extension!

- » **.online**: This is an option if the domain name that you are interested in using is not available with other domain extensions.

- » **.name**: This domain extension is intended for people who want to register their own names only. If you register a name with the .name extension that doesn't belong to you, you might be required to give up that domain in the future.

- » **.tv**: This domain is typically used by websites and blogs that publish video content.

- » **.biz**: This domain extension is intended to be used by businesses.

- » **.edu**: Only schools are allowed to use a .edu domain.

- » **.gov**: This domain can be used only by government agencies.

- » **.mil**: This domain is reserved for United States military use.

- » **.pro**: Originally only licensed or certified lawyers, accountants, and engineers in the United States, United Kingdom, Canada, or France could use this domain, but it is no longer restricted.

WARNING

Some domain extensions require you to pay an additional fee for registration. Read the fine print before you make your final purchase.

The domain extension you choose depends greatly on the domain name you want to use and the availability of that name. Don't be afraid to get creative to find the domain name that is right for you and your vision for your blog.

Creating a domain name and making sure it's available

When it comes to naming your blog, you have to balance two factors: the creative factor of coming up with a great name and the practical factor of making sure the domain name is available for you to use.

Bloggers primarily choose one of two distinct paths when setting up their blogs and selecting their domain names:

>> **Hosted account domain name:** If you blog with WordPress.com, Blogger, Wix, or another provider that both provides a blogging platform and hosts your online content, you aren't required to purchase your own domain name. Instead, a free domain name is available to you, which uses the provider's extension by default (for example, *domainname*.wordpress.com, *domainname*.blogspot.com, or *domainname*.typepad.com). You *do* get to choose the unique name that appears before the domain extension.

>> **Purchased domain name:** If you aren't blogging with a provider that also hosts your content, you need to purchase your own domain name through a third-party domain registrar.

TIP

Keep in mind that you can give your blog a boost in credibility by demonstrating that you're committed enough to your blog to spend money and effort on obtaining your own unique web address for it.

If you need to or want to purchase your own domain name for your blog, start by creating a list of domain names you'd like to use. After you make your list of favorite domain names, consider the alternative extensions you'd accept or maybe even prefer if .com is not available. Also, think of ways you can creatively enhance your chosen domain name to make it unique and thus more likely to be available. Most domain name registrars offer a search tool that delivers both the availability of your chosen domain as well as alternative domain options. I discuss several domain name registrars in detail later in this chapter.

Your domain name should fit well with your blog's name, although depending on availability they may not match exactly. Just be sure that the domain name you choose represents your blog well and is somehow memorable. After all, once you've found a new reader, you want them to be able to find you again, too!

WARNING

Just because a domain name exists doesn't mean you should use it! However, if the blog name you've got in mind is already in use, don't use the following suggestions for domain name creation to try to get around trademarks. The last thing you want is to start your blogging journey off with a legal dispute with an existing blog or business!

Following are suggestions to enhance your domain name to broaden your search and increase the odds of the name being available for use with a common extension such as .com or .net. People are most familiar with those extensions and likely to use them when searching for your blog if they aren't already aware that your domain uses a less common extension.

» **Get creative.** If the domain name you want that is no longer available is intuitive and obvious, consider using something more creative. During this stage of the creative process, anything goes! Jotting down a couple of crazy ideas may lead you to the perfect domain name in the end.

» **Add prefixes or suffixes.** Sites such as Engadget (www.engadget.com) and Friendster (www.friendster.com) are examples of domains that add prefixes and suffixes to common words to make them unique.

» **Use a superlative.** Try using such words as *best* or *fastest* in your domain name.

» **Add an adjective.** Just as you can try using superlatives, try adding descriptive words into your domain name. My personal blog Resourceful Mommy (www.resourcefulmommy.com), for example, uses the adjective "resourceful," as shown in Figure 3-3.

» **Add a hyphen.** If your desired domain is more than one word, try adding a hyphen between those words.

» **Use plurals.** Is there a word in your domain that you can change from singular to plural? Give it a try!

FIGURE 3-3: Consider adding an adjective to create your domain name as in Resourceful Mommy.

>> **Make up a word.** Many blogs, websites, and businesses use words that aren't in the dictionary, such as the exceptionally popular global marketplace, Etsy (www.etsy.com), which is shown in Figure 3-4. If you find yourself at a dead end, make up your own word and use it in your domain and as your blog's title. If nothing else, your blog will have instant branding!

FIGURE 3-4:
Etsy is an example of a website with a name and corresponding domain name that isn't in the dictionary.

WARNING

After you choose your domain name, changing it can cause a lot of problems. Old links to your blog won't work, your Google search rankings will drop, and loyal readers may not know where to find your content. Pick your domain name with great care and be sure it's one you can live with for the life of your blog in order to avoid problems later.

Finding a domain name that you like can be challenging. Even if you use a blogging application that doesn't require you to purchase your own domain name, finding an available domain through those sites is still a challenge. For example, millions and millions of blogs are hosted on Blogger, which means millions and millions of domain names with the provided .blogspot.com extension are already taken. Be patient, don't get frustrated, and be prepared to not get the first, second, or even the tenth domain name of your choice. Eventually though, you'll find a domain name that's available and suitable for your blog.

Buying a domain name

A *domain name registrar* is a website that enables you to purchase your own, unique domain name. Many sites allow you to purchase a domain name, but not all domain name registrars are alike. For example, they charge different fees that can vary based on the length of your contract or the domain name extension you choose. Be sure to read all the fine print before you make your final purchase, and do some comparison shopping before you commit to a vendor.

Keep an eye out for the following:

>> **Add-on services:** You may want to use your selected domain registrar only for purchasing your domain name, but it may be that you'd like the option for add-on services including hosting.

>> **Domain expiration policies:** What happens if your credit card expires and you forget to update your information with your domain registrar? Do you lose the domain name forever, or does the registrar allow for a grace period to buy the domain back?

>> **Domain transfer:** The ability to transfer a domain may be important to you in the future if you move your blog from one platform to another or if you sell your blog or domain name.

>> **Pricing:** The price of a .com is often lower than the price of a specialized domain extension. Some domain names are also priced higher due to expected popularity. Look closely before purchasing your domain name!

>> **Registration period:** Before selecting a domain name registrar, be sure to check on how long you will own that name. A price that seems low may come with a shorter registration period.

When you do find an available domain name that you're happy with, be prepared to purchase it immediately. It's not uncommon to find an available domain name one minute and then find it's gone a few minutes later. With that in mind, do your research on current pricing plans and discounts *before* you actually search for available domain names, or you could waste a lot of time. Select the domain registrar you want to make your purchase through and then conduct your search on that site.

Following is a brief list of popular websites where you can search for and purchase domain names. This list is *not* exhaustive, and companies and offers change all the time. Do your research when you're ready to find your domain so you're certain to get the best deal from the best company at that time.

>> **Bluehost** (`www.bluehost.com`): Bluehost is not only a domain registrar, but it is also a popular blog hosting company. Many users find that they like the simplicity of registering their domain and hosting their blog with the same company.

>> **Domain.com** (`www.domain.com`): Domain.com offers typically low prices, but you may need to pay a higher rate after a period of time. Be sure to look at the entire pricing list.

>> **DreamHost** (`www.dreamhost.com`): Similar to Bluehost, DreamHost is known primarily as a site hosting company, but it also offers domain registration.

>> **Google Domains** (`domains.google.com`): This is a simple, straightforward option if you only want to register your selected domain and are not interested in any additional bells and whistles.

>> **GoDaddy** (`www.godaddy.com`): GoDaddy is a service that's been around for a long time and a popular site for hosting and domain name registration. Take a look at Figure 3-5 to see how easy it is to search for a domain name from the GoDaddy home page.

>> **HostGator** (`www.hostgator.com`): While HostGator is another commonly used site for purchasing both blog hosting and domain names, keep in mind that it does not offer some premium domain extensions.

>> **NameCheap** (`www.namecheap.com`): As the name implies, NameCheap is known for low prices on domain names with popular, generic domain extensions.

>> **Network Solutions** (`www.networksolutions.com`): Network Solutions is one of the longest-running domain registration services and some of their pricing reflects that standing.

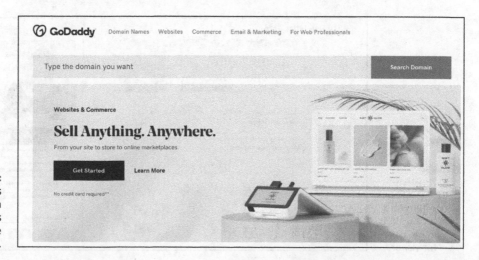

FIGURE 3-5:
GoDaddy makes it easy to search for domains directly from the site's home page.

Check all the pricing and check it again before you commit to purchasing a domain name. Compare pricing from several providers to ensure you're getting the best deal.

Identifying the Basic Elements of a Blog

Although the content and look of every blog is unique, most blogs have several specific elements in common. Of course, as with most aspects of blogging, there are exceptions to every rule: Even though most blogs include elements such as sidebars, footers, and archives, those elements aren't mandatory. It's up to individual bloggers to choose and include the blog elements that provide the user experiences they want to deliver.

Furthermore, blogs vary in the way they're laid out. In other words, the design of the blog can affect where elements appear on your screen. The flexible layout is one of the best parts about blogging and allows you to really flex your creative muscles! The look and feel of your blog is entirely up to you.

Homepage

Your blog's homepage is your blog's primary landing page where readers first arrive after typing in your domain name. In other words, it's the most popular starting point for a readers' journey through your blog's content. Figure 3-6 shows an example of a blog home page, JUST is a Four Letter Word (www.justisafourletterword.com), where it's easy for readers to navigate to the other standard blog elements without feeling lost.

FIGURE 3-6: JUST is a Four Letter Word offers a useful home page for visitors.

Traditionally, most-recent blog posts typically appear first on a blog's home page with remaining posts appearing in reverse chronological order. Blogs are usually divided into columns of content (two- and three-column blog formats are most common) with blog posts appearing in the widest column. Additional content on the home page may include links and the various elements described throughout the remainder of this chapter.

Blogs can use home pages that replicate popular news sites' layouts (sometimes referred to as *magazine layouts*), or specific layouts for portfolios or photography. For example, in the example shown in Figure 3-6, the blog post categories food, travel, and holidays are highlighted as image links near the top of the page to draw attention to them. Bloggers have more choices than ever, so don't be surprised if a blog you visit doesn't have a simple home page layout or looks more like a website than a blog.

TECHNICAL STUFF

As a beginner blogger, you should strongly consider keeping things simple in terms of your blog's home page layout. More complicated blog layouts often require more work in terms of formatting, updating, and so on. Unless you're prepared for those technological challenges, stick with more traditional two- or three-column blog layouts.

The important point to remember when creating your blog is that your home page is your blog's welcome page. Think of its function in much the same way as the exterior of a home. It can either have curb appeal, welcoming readers to stay awhile, or it can turn visitors away.

WARNING

Don't try to fit every piece of information you want to share with your visitors on your home page or it will get cluttered and become difficult for your audience to read. Instead, try to create a clean home page with useful information and easy-to-follow links.

About or profile page

The About page of your blog is simply a biography or description of who you are and why you're writing your blog. Readers like to know more about the person behind the blog, particularly if your blog offers advice or professional opinion. Your audience needs to believe that you're qualified to write your blog.

TIP

Planning to write a more topical and less personal blog? Your About page may focus more on the history of the site than on its author.

Remember that an essential part of becoming a successful blogger is developing relationships with your readers. The strength of a blog often comes from the community that evolves around it. Take the time to write a thorough profile page that shares information about your experience, credentials, and reasons for taking the time to write your blog.

Some bloggers' profile pages are very long with professional and personal information included in rich detail. Others are short and to the point. Either approach can work depending on your goals for your blog. Figure 3-7 takes a look at the About page for the JUST is a Four Letter Word blog.

FIGURE 3-7:
Andrea Updyke uses a simple, effective About page on her blog.

It's also important that your profile page is easily accessible. Don't make your readers try to hunt down information about you. Reach out to them and make it easy for them to get to know you by making your profile page a prominent part of your blog.

TIP

Keep in mind that some blogs have two About pages. One talks about the blog itself, and the other talks about the blogger. It's up to you to decide whether you want two About pages or one, but most blogs use the single-About-page approach.

Posts

Each entry that you write and publish on your blog is called a *post*. Those posts are typically displayed on your blog's home page in the order that you published them with the most recent appearing at the top of the page.

A certain number of posts appear on the home page, depending on the settings you choose within your blogging application. You can find older posts by clicking a link that appears at the bottom of the posts on the home page and each subsequent page. (The link is usually labeled *Previous Posts, Previous Entries,* or something similar.) You can also find older entries by using the archive and category features of your blog, as described later in this chapter.

All blogs include posts. The exception occurs when someone uses a blogging application to create a more traditional website, but then it could be argued that those sites aren't really blogs at all. The essential element that makes a website a blog is the post feature, therefore it's safe to say that all blogs, in the traditional sense, include posts.

Your blog posts typically include a few common elements, including an author byline, date, title, the post content, links, images, and comments. A sample blog post is shown in Figure 3-8, showing the various elements in detail.

FIGURE 3-8:
Andrea's site includes an example of a typical blog post including an author byline and date.

TECHNICAL STUFF

The blog post column traditionally takes up about 75 percent of the width of your blog's screen space.

Comments

Comments help make a blog interactive and foster a sense of community among your readers and between your readers and you. It may be surprising because bloggers typically write content alone, but blogging is generally meant to be social. If it were intended to be one-sided, it wouldn't be much different from a traditional website.

Comments appear at the end of a blog post. Most bloggers allow anyone to leave a comment, using the comment moderation tool in their blogging applications to filter inappropriate and spam comments before they're actually published. You can read more about comment moderation in Chapter 2 of Book 6.

People like to offer their own opinions, and blog commenting allows them to do exactly that. Commenting helps readers feel involved and part of the community on your blog. That's a powerful thing when it comes to growing your blog, especially because you want your readers to share your content with others. It's important to acknowledge the people who leave comments on your blog and show them you value them by responding to those comments and engaging the people who leave them. That's how you build relationships with your readers.

As your blog grows, so too will the number of comments your posts receive. Figure 3-9 shows an example of a blog post with comments. Don't be discouraged if your blog doesn't get a lot of comments, especially in the beginning. If you stay committed, keep writing, share your content regularly, and continue interacting with the people who do leave comments on your posts, eventually more comments should come. Patience is key to your blog's success and growing your blog's community.

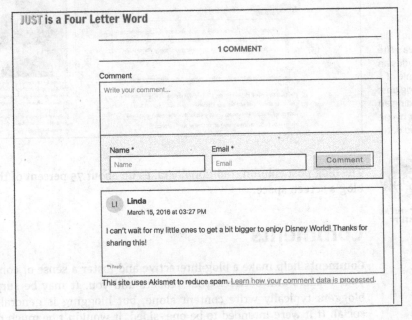

FIGURE 3-9:
JUST is a Four Letter Word includes a comments section at the end of each post.

Categories or labels

Depending on the blogging application that you use, you might be able to categorize your blog posts (as WordPress lets you do) or attach labels to them in an informal categorization system (as with Blogger). Regardless of the specific functionality available to you, the end result is similar. Categories (or labels) create an easy way for readers to find old content related to specific topics.

Most bloggers include a list of categories (or labels) in their blog's navigation bar, either across the top of the blog or along one side, making it extremely easy for readers to find additional content of interest. The list of categories at the top of Andrea's blog in a format called a horizontal navigation bar is shown in Figure 3-10. This category list guides readers to posts about recipes, travel, and holidays.

FIGURE 3-10: Andrea's blog categories focus on the topics of recipes, travel, and holidays.

Make sure you take the time to categorize or label your blog posts well so readers have no trouble finding older blog posts.

TECHNICAL STUFF

Use labels and categories that are intuitive. Consider what term you would search for in order to find the type of content in your blog posts and then label or categorize your content to match.

Sidebar

Sidebars give your blog flexibility. Although you can have a blog with just one column containing your blog posts, it's not common. Bloggers typically use a two- or three-column format where sidebars appear to the left and/or right of the blog post column. It's easy to fall into the trap of filling your sidebars with as many elements as you can possibly squeeze into them, such as ads, links, and so on. However, your sidebars should offer information and links that are truly useful to your readers. If an element doesn't add value to the user experience, leave it out of your sidebar.

TIP

Just because you have space that can be filled in your blog's sidebar, that doesn't mean you have to fill it. Less is more.

Perhaps the biggest trap bloggers fall into when creating their blogs' sidebars is related to advertising. If you decide to include ads in your blog's sidebar to make money, then it's easy to clutter your sidebar with every kind of ad you can get access to. That's a huge mistake though. Blogs that are covered in ads create a negative user experience. Instead, try testing just a few ads in your sidebars. Analyze the results and then choose the advertising opportunities that make the most sense for your blog, your audience, and your revenue goals. You can learn all about blog monetization, including advertising, in Book 7.

So what should go in your blog's sidebar? The following is a list of some of the most common sidebar elements that bloggers use, which you might want to include in your own blog:

>> **A link to your About (or profile) page**

>> **Your picture**

>> **Link to the best way to connect with you**

>> **Links to your blog's social media profiles**

>> **Your blog's subscription information**

>> **A list of blog post categories or labels**

>> **Links to your blog archives by date**

>> **Ads**

>> **A *blogroll* (essentially, a list of links to other blogs you like)**

>> **A list of links to your recent blog posts**

>> **A list of links to your popular blog posts**

Figure 3-11 shows a partial view of the sidebar on the JUST is a Four Letter Word blog, which includes a sign-up window to receive the blog's newsletter via email as well as links to recommended blog posts.

FIGURE 3-11:
The sidebar on JUST is a Four Letter Word includes a place for readers to sign up for emails.

Header

Your blog's header can be loosely compared to a newspaper masthead. The area stretches across the top of every page of your blog and typically includes your blog's name, an image or logo, and possibly a slogan or short description of your blog. Your blog's header is what brands your blog and tells readers where they are when they arrive on your site. Think about it: Would you know you were on the *New York Times* website if the header at the top of the page didn't tell you so? Most people wouldn't know. The same principle holds true for your blog.

That's why taking the time to create a great header is important. Try to make your header distinct and in line with your blog's brand or distinct identity. Branding is covered in more detail in Book 7, but the basic idea is for reader's to easily identify your blog's name and identity. Use a font that's easy to read and an image that you own or are allowed to use based on its copyright license, described in more detail in Chapter 4 of this Book.

Depending on the template that you use to create your blog, or if you hire a designer to help you create your blog, you may be able to include additional elements in your blog's header. Some people include a search bar, subscription area, or ads in their blog's header. Figure 3-12 shows the header for JUST is a Four Letter Word (www.justisafourletterword.com), which includes links to blog post categories, an email sign-up, a link to the About page, a link to the blog's shop, and a place to search blog content.

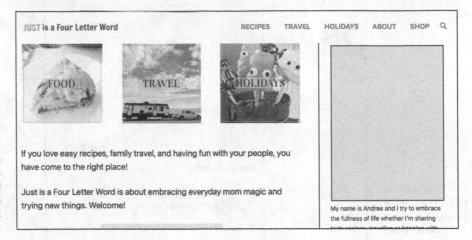

FIGURE 3-12:
The JUST is a Four Letter Word header features more than just the blog's title.

REMEMBER

Your blog's header appears at the top of every page on your blog and is the primary element people notice first anytime they visit your blog. Make it unique so people remember it and grow to recognize it.

Footer

A blog footer typically spans across the bottom of the screen on all pages of your blog. Although it's not essential to include a footer in your blog's design, it's a great place to put copyright information. In fact, some people use the space in their footer for far more than just disclaimers and legalese.

Following are some suggestions of elements to include in your blog's footer:

>> **Copyright and disclaimer statements**

>> **Links to terms and conditions of use and privacy statements**

>> **Link to your email address**

>> **Your contact information, such as your phone number or address** (primarily useful for business blogs)

- **>> Ads**
- **>> Links to other resources within or outside of your blog**
- **>> Links to your social networking, bookmarking, and Twitter profiles**
- **>> Feeds from other blogs you write or enjoy**

As always, it's important to keep in mind that there are no set rules related to formatting a blog footer. Use that space to help you meet your blogging goals and create a better user experience.

TIP

Not all of your blog readers are going to scroll through to the bottom of your blog pages to find and read your footer information. Therefore, don't put critical information that you really want your readers to see in your blog's footer. Save that space for ancillary information you want to share that isn't essential to meeting your goals.

Blogroll or links

Depending on what blogging application you choose, you have the option to include a blogroll or list of links in your blog's sidebar (or footer, depending on your blog's template layout). A blogroll (or link list) is a list of links to other blogs that you like and recommend to your readers.

In the early days of blogging, blogrolls were powerful tools that directly led to increased traffic. There were a few reasons for this phenomenon. First, getting your blog's link listed on other blogs meant that other people who read those blogs might notice the link, follow it, and start reading your blog, too. If the blogger linking to you in their blogroll has a popular, well-trafficked blog, the number of click-throughs to your blog could be quite high. Second, each incoming link to your blog is weighted as a positive in Google's search algorithm. In other words, having more incoming links (particularly from popular websites and blogs) means your blog is ranked higher by Google, driving your pages up higher in related keyword searches. Higher rankings provide the potential for more search traffic.

Today, the power of blogrolls isn't what it once was. For example, there are companies that pay for links in blogrolls, which diminishes the value of them to readers. Many blogrolls are created and forgotten — making the links in them less than useful to people as time passes — and links break or the content on blogs becomes outdated. Also, originally, adding links to a blogroll was considered a reciprocal practice. If you added someone's blog to your blogroll, you could contact them to let them know, and they would almost always link back to you. It was an unwritten rule of blog etiquette. That rule doesn't necessarily apply today. In fact, many blogs don't even include blogrolls anymore.

However, blogrolls can still be a good networking tool, and if you're truly sharing links to blogs that you think your readers can benefit from and enjoy, it's an element you can provide as an added benefit. In other words, a useful blogroll certainly can't hurt your blog, and it may even help it.

Many bloggers call their blogrolls by an entirely different name these days. For example, you might see a list of links referred to as a blogroll a few years ago now labeled Resources or Helpful Links.

Trackbacks, backlinks, and pingbacks

In simplest terms, a *trackback, backlink,* or *pingback* are virtual shoulder taps telling other bloggers that you linked to one of their posts in one of your own posts. If you want your blog to grow and be successful, it's important that you take the time to turn on the trackback or backlink functionality within your blog settings and then actively use it. Doing so lets other bloggers know you like their content enough to link to it, thereby promoting it on your blog, too. By linking to another blogger's content, you can help to boost their traffic *and* yours because the process automatically leaves a reciprocal link on the blog post you linked to (assuming the other blogger has the functionality activated on their blog as well).

You can find out more about trackbacks and backlinks as they relate to specific blogging applications in Book 4.

Tags

In WordPress, tags are used for search engine optimization purposes as well as blog post categorization. In simplest terms, when you write a new blog post using WordPress, you can input keywords as *tags,* which sites use to index your content. Additionally, because tags appear as links on your blog post, Google includes them in its indexing process. Either way you look at it, tags can only help your blog posts get found — so long as you don't overstuff keywords in your blog post tags that is. Figure 3-13 shows what tags look like at the end of a blog post.

TECHNICAL STUFF

Depending on the blog template design, tags can appear in different locations, such as at the top or bottom of a blog post. Some bloggers choose not to display them at all.

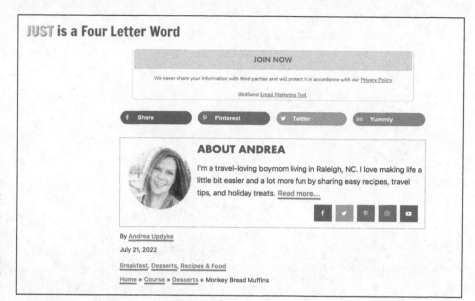

Template or theme

Every blog is built on a template, which designers and bloggers customize to create their own blogs' unique looks. Depending on the blogging application you use, your blog's layout could be called a *template* (Blogger) or a *theme* (WordPress), but either way, the concept is the same.

Many free templates are available to bloggers, which anyone can use. You can also find premium templates that are offered for a fee, making them rarer than the scores of free templates available online and, typically, more customizable and better coded. Some bloggers invest in having a custom template created so their blogs look completely original.

Templates usually include one, two, or three columns, with the blog posts taking up the majority of the space (approximately 75 percent). There are also unique templates for magazine-style sites, portfolios, and more. Long story short, you have what may overwhelmingly feel like unlimited choices when it comes to blog design. The template you ultimately use depends on your technical skills for updating as well as your budget.

Remember, the type of template you decide to use on your blog is entirely up to you. Choose a template that provides the basic look and feel you want your blog to communicate to readers. You can find out more about finding and choosing a template for your blog based on your chosen blogging application in Book 4.

Chapter **4**

Blogging Best Practices

Although you won't find any formal rules and regulations related specifically to blogging, there are laws that extend to your blog's content and widely accepted practices that you should be aware of and adhere to throughout your life as a blogger. Those guidelines can extend from common courtesy and avoiding doing things that can be perceived as spam all the way to acts punishable by law, such as plagiarism and failure to disclose sponsored content.

This chapter points you in the right direction by highlighting some of the biggest things you should avoid related to blogging as well as offering tips for how to do things the right way (or at least the way that other bloggers and blog readers prefer).

REMEMBER

Understanding the topics in this chapter will not only help you avoid blogging headaches and pitfalls, it will also guide you to becoming a respectful member of the blogging community.

Avoiding Blogging Don'ts

Just as in life in general, it is important in the blogosphere to mind your manners. Like magazine or newspaper publishers, the information you publish online through your blog must follow similar ethical and legal codes of conduct. Those codes relate to plagiarism, libel, and more.

WARNING

Many bloggers argue that laws related to free speech give them the right to write and publish anything they want on their blogs. However, don't use freedom of speech as an excuse to publish content that could be hurtful to another person or entity. That's where bloggers need to dance the fine line between staying within the law and within ethical limitations while still freely publishing their thoughts and opinions. Remember your manners, and you should be okay.

With that in mind, the blogging don'ts that I discuss in the following sections are some of the biggest. Violate them at your own risk!

Don't plagiarize

Get permission! Just as your teacher told you in your high school English class, plagiarism is wrong and punishable by law. Don't copy content from any other source and simply republish it on your blog. If you find another blog post or article online or offline that you want to write about on your blog, write your own original content about that subject.

TIP

If you believe someone has copied content from your blog, you can test your suspicions by using a site like Copyscape (www.copyscape.com), shown in Figure 4-1, which allows you to enter the URL of a page on your blog and do a search to determine whether the text on that page appears anywhere else online.

If you decide to copy a portion of another blog post or article on your blog or use an image that you find elsewhere on the web within one of your blog posts, it's likely that you'll need to obtain permission to do so based on the type of copyright license attached to that content or image. (I discuss copyrights later in this chapter in detail, in the section "Understanding Copyright and Fair Use.") The safest route to take if you're not certain whether you're allowed to republish content or an image on your blog is to contact the owner and request permission to do so. Look for a contact form or email address, often found on the site's About page, to know how to best reach out to the content creator. If you can't obtain written permission, don't use the content or image.

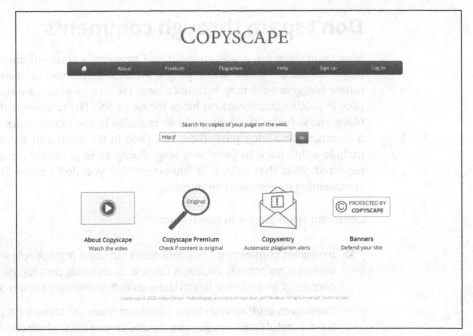

FIGURE 4-1:
Copyscape allows you to determine whether your blog content has been copied elsewhere on the web.

Don't commit libel against someone or something

Publishing libelous statements about another person or entity is illegal.

In simplest terms, *libel* is written words that are intended to destroy or negatively impact a person or entity's reputation in front of a broad audience. Although your blog is your own place in the online world and it's permissible to publish your opinions on your blog, it's not okay to publish hateful or highly disparaging content, which could be considered libelous.

Most blogging applications include rules of conduct within their terms of use agreements notifying bloggers that blogs including libelous, hateful, or similar content will be deleted (if they're found or someone reports them). Similarly, search engines try to find and eliminate from indexing processes those sites with this kind of content on them. Long story short, a blog with content that could be construed as libelous might not have a long life and could lose all search traffic — not to mention the fact that the blogger could get in trouble with the law. The best course of action is to keep your more extreme opinions to yourself.

WARNING

Many bloggers have been fired from their jobs because of negative content published on their personal blogs about their employers. Be careful what you write about on your blog! You never know who might be looking.

Don't spam through comments

Blog comments are a way to build and promote a sense of community on your blog. Commenting on other people's blogs helps you to connect with your fellow bloggers and may introduce new readers to your content. In fact, many people publish comments on blogs for no reason but to drive traffic to their own blogs and websites through the links included in their comments. When you leave a comment on a blog post, there is a field in the comment form where you can include a link back to your own blog. Doing so is perfectly acceptable and even expected. With that said, it is important that you don't move from appropriate commenting to comment spamming.

Comment spam comes in two flavors:

>> **Irrelevant comments:** Comment spam can come from people who leave useless or completely irrelevant comments on a blog post for the sole purpose of getting their link to show up in the comment section of the post.

>> **Comments stuffed with links:** Comment spam can come from people who leave a useful comment but also include several links, which could be relevant or irrelevant. Leaving an additional useful link within a comment is perfectly acceptable, but stuffing comments with a list of links isn't, whether or not those links are related to the topic of the corresponding post. Some comments stuffed with links are quite obviously spam, such as the one shown in Figure 4-2.

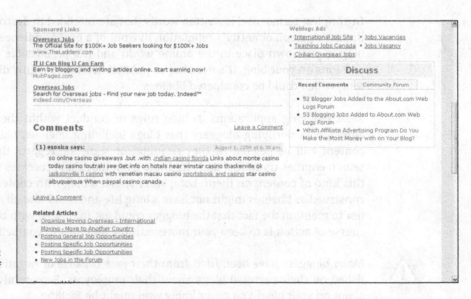

FIGURE 4-2:
An example of comment spam.

Be sure to avoid leaving comments on other blog posts that could be viewed as spam. Doing so can get you blacklisted within the minds of other bloggers who will think of you as little more than a spammer.

It's also important to reduce comment spam on your own blog to enhance the user experience by creating a comment policy, as discussed in the "Creating a comment policy" section later in this chapter. Also, you can reduce spam through comment moderation, which I discuss in Chapter 2 of Book 6.

Don't publish spammy posts

Just as blog comments can be spam, so can blog posts or entire blogs. If your blog posts include nothing more than one promotional message after another or if your blog is covered in ads with little to no useful information, readers (and search engines) will identify it as spam. Readers have no reason to return to a blog that offers no meaningful content. Just as you wouldn't want to sit in front of a television all day and watch nothing but commercials, no one wants to read a blog that includes nothing but ads or promotional posts.

It's absolutely fine to include ads and promotional posts on your blog, but they must be identified as such for full transparency and disclosure (check out Chapter 4 of Book 7 to read more about the need for proper disclosure of paid relationships). Paid content should also be limited in quantity or integrated well into quality content. Don't mindlessly cut and paste promotional copy from paying clients. Take the time to create posts your readers will enjoy and appreciate while also highlighting advertising partners. The part of your blog that will convince people to return again and again is the content that you write, not the ads that you publish.

Don't steal bandwidth

Bandwidth is a measure of digital data consumption. Stealing bandwidth happens when you publish something on your blog, such as an image, without uploading that image to your own blog hosting account first. Instead, you simply publish the link code from the original blog or website where you found the image. Doing so allows the image to appear in your blog post, but that image data still resides on the originating site's hosting account. Anytime the image loads on your blog, the originating site serves it, meaning your blog is using the originating site's bandwidth each time a visitor views the image on your blog.

For every piece of content (written, image, audio, video, and so on) that you publish on your blog, a bit of space is used up from your hosting account. Most blogs and websites have a limited amount of hosting space that the blogger pays for each month (or uses up each month, in the case of some free blogging accounts). Bloggers and website owners can be charged more if the number of times that their content is accessed increases dramatically (such as when other bloggers use images without saving them to their own hosting accounts first).

Long story short, you wouldn't like it if you had to pay extra because other people were stealing your bandwidth, so don't do it to other bloggers and website owners. Instead, copy the picture you want to use (being certain you have permission to do so first), save it to your hosting account, and then insert it into your blog post. (See Book 4 for details on how to make a blog post.)

Providing Attribution

When you find a great article or blog post and write about it on your blog, you should provide attribution to your source. Not only is it ethical to do so, but if you cite and provide a link to the original source, that other blog or website could get a trackback or backlink (as described in Chapter 3 of this book). The blog or website owner can also see traffic coming from your blog through their own research into their site statistics (discussed in Chapter 2 of Book 5). Either way, providing attribution to sources within your blog posts could put your blog on another blogger's radar screen and lead to additional traffic to your blog. You can provide attribution by simply linking text within your blog post to your source, or you can provide a more formal attribution at the end of your blog post.

Furthermore, if you copy a specific quote from another source, it's imperative that you identify the quote as such and attribute the original source to avoid being accused of plagiarism. The same holds true for using images that you find from other sources. You should obtain permission to use them (unless they have a copyright license attached to them that allows you to republish them without first obtaining permission) and provide appropriate attribution to the source within your blog post.

Figure 4-3 shows an image used on a blog with permission and proper attribution.

JOURNAL   FAMILY & HOME   FAITH   SOCIAL GOOD   TRAVEL   DISNEY   BLOGGING & SOCIAL MEDIA   PARTIES & GIVEAWAYS

Photo courtesy of Disney Parks (Caitlyn McCabe, photographer)

Outdoor Kitchens Feature Fresh Food and Drink

Guests can embark on a mouth-watering journey around the park to experience a smorgasbord of options, with more than 20 delectable stops to choose from. Each Outdoor Kitchen offers a specialty menu of creative cuisine and libations to savor and sip. New options this year include:

- **EPCOT Sunshine Griddle**, offering Avocado Toast, Shrimp and Grits, Corned Beef Brisket Hash and more
- **EPCOT Farmers Feast**, featuring Spring Onion Soup, Duck Confit and more
- The Lavender Honey Mustard-marinated Chicken Flatbread at **The Honey Bee-stro Hosted by National Honey Board**
- Impossible Sausage and Kale Soup at **Trowel & Trellis Hosted by Impossible Foods**

FIGURE 4-3:
Always provide attribution to your sources.

Understanding Copyright and Fair Use

The rules of copyright are a bit blurred in the online world, but the safest path to follow is one that errs on the side of being more conservative. Copyrights protect an author, artist, photographer, musician, or creator from having their original work stolen or misused without permission.

WARNING

If there is a piece of content on your blog that you didn't create, someone else holds the copyright to it. Copyrights are enforceable by law, so before you use text, images, video, or audio on your blog, be certain a copyright license is attached to it that allows you to use it without asking formal permission to do so. If you're uncertain, ask permission before you use it.

The blurred lines of copyright come into play around the concept of *fair use* as it applies to copyright laws. If you're republishing content on your blog that some-one else owns for the purpose of providing criticism, commentary, education, reporting, training, or research, you may not be required to seek permission to reuse that material on your blog thanks to a legal loophole called *fair use*. How-ever, the lines of fair use are highly debatable. The safest course of action is to ask permission if you're unsure whether you can republish content on your blog within the bounds of copyright law, and of course, always provide attribution to your source, as described in the preceding section.

Using Creative Commons Licenses

Creative Commons licenses are designed to give the owners of original work a way to share that work more freely (and allow other people to build on that work) by protecting the owner of the original licensed work without applying a full and highly restrictive copyright to it. In other words, a Creative Commons license allows other people to use the owner's work, but restrictions can be attached depending on the type of Creative Commons license the owner applies to that work. The licenses were created by the nonprofit organization Creative Commons (http://creativecommons.org).

Six types of Creative Commons licenses exist, and each has different rules of use attached to it as well as attribution requirements. Following are brief descriptions of each license type:

>> **CC BY:** This is the most permissive Creative Commons license. It allows anyone to distribute, remix, adapt, or build upon an original work both noncommercially and commercially. The only requirement is that the license owner is provided proper credit for the original work. Bloggers can do this by citing the source.

>> **CC BY-SA:** This license is similar to CC BY in that it allows anyone to distribute, remix, adapt, or build upon an original work both noncommercially and commercially as long as the original creator receives attribution. The only difference is that modified material created must also be attributed under the original terms.

>> **CC BY-NC:** This license is similar to CC BY except that the work may only be used for non-commercial purposes.

>> **CC BY-NC-SA:** This license is similar to CC BY-SA, in that the modified material created must also be attributed under the original terms, except that the work may only be used for non-commercial purposes.

>> **CC BY-ND:** This license only allows for the work to be copied and distributed in unadapted form only with attribution given to the creator of the work. This license allows for commercial use of the work.

>> **CC BY-NC-ND:** This license is similar to CC BY-ND except that the work may only be used for non-commercial purposes.

It is also possible for a creator to label their work as CC0, or *Creative Commons Public Domain*. This means that the creator has given up all copyrights to their work and is allowing the work to become part of the worldwide public domain, able to be used and redistributed without restriction.

In Figure 4-4, you can see the About Licenses page of the Creative Commons website (http://creativecommons.org/about/licenses) and the four icons that represent how the different licenses work.

TIP

Consider obtaining a Creative Commons license for your blog content and then include information about that license in your blog's footer. You can get started at https://creativecommons.org/share-your-work/.

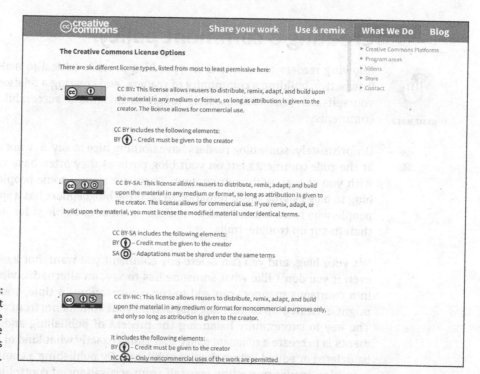

FIGURE 4-4:
The About Licenses page of the Creative Commons website.

Disclosing Your Policies

Creating policies for your blog is a good way to set reader expectations and protect yourself from unlikely but possible legal entanglements. For example, if someone plagiarizes your content or accuses you of selling their email address, having clear and published policies that show how you handle copyright and privacy issues could be very important.

Following are three of the most common policies published on blogs:

>> **Comment policy:** Describes what comments are inappropriate and how they're moderated.

>> **Disclaimer and Disclosure page:** Includes information about sponsored content, affiliate links, and the like.

>> **Privacy policy:** Describes what information is collected about visitors and how that information is used.

>> **Terms and Conditions of Site Use page:** Describes legal information about your blog, such as copyrights, availability, and warnings.

Creating a comment policy

REMEMBER

Allowing readers to comment on your blog posts is critical to making your blog interactive, building a community of readers, and creating a relationship between yourself and your readers. It is tough to imagine a successful blog with no comments!

Unfortunately, some blog readers have nothing nice to say. Try not to take offense at the rude comments left on your blog posts as they often have very little to do with you or even with your content. There are simply some people who go from blog to blog leaving mean remarks. In fact; the blogosphere has a special name for people who leave hateful and obnoxious comments on blogs for no reason other than to stir up trouble: *trolls.*

It's your blog, and you can delete any comment you want, but keep in mind that even if you don't like what someone has to say, an alternative viewpoint (stated in a courteous manner) can add to the conversation. In time, your loyal readers might even step up to the plate and defend your statements from your opponents. The key to successfully balancing the process of publishing and deleting comments is to create a *comment policy* that states exactly what kind of comments will be deleted or edited before they're published. By publishing a comment policy on your blog, you're protecting yourself from accusations of controlling the conversation on your blog.

You can write your blog comment policy in a friendly or professional tone as long as your rules are clear. You may want to cover the following points in your comment policy for *any* sort of blog:

>> **Hateful or attacking language:** You can include a rule that says comments that are hateful in nature or attack other visitors will be deleted.

>> **Spam:** Be sure to include a statement that says all comments that are considered to be potential spam will be deleted.

>> **Editing and deleting:** Include language that says you reserve the right to edit or delete all comments that are off-topic, offensive, or detract from the blog community discussion.

Sometimes it's hard to tell whether a comment is legitimate. If you prefer to err on the side of caution, delete comments that could be spam even if you're not certain. By including a reference to how *potential* spam comments are handled on your blog, you're protecting your right to delete those comments and warning readers to be sure to write useful comments that can't be perceived as spam. To make your guidelines related to spam comments even clearer, you can include examples of the types of comments that you consider spam and could be deleted within your comment policy.

The following are some other items you might want to cover in your comment policy, but these items depend more on the type of blog you have and want to maintain:

>> **Profanity:** You can include a statement saying comments that include profanity will be edited to remove potentially offensive language.

>> **Links:** You can include a statement warning visitors that comments containing more than a specific number of links (such as three links) will automatically be detected as spam and deleted. (Typically, you can configure this setting within your blogging application.)

These lists are by no means complete. I recommend reading comment policies from different blogs to see whether you can find other points that you want to add to your own.

The comment policy page on Copyblogger (www.copyblogger.com/comment-policy/), shown in Figure 4-5, shows one example of a fairly standard blog comment policy page.

Disclosing paid content

Many bloggers create their blogs with the hope of earning income, which is a wonderful goal! However, it is important to note that not only do you need to be careful not to spam readers with too much sponsored content as mentioned earlier in this chapter, but you also need to disclose to your readers that your content has been sponsored.

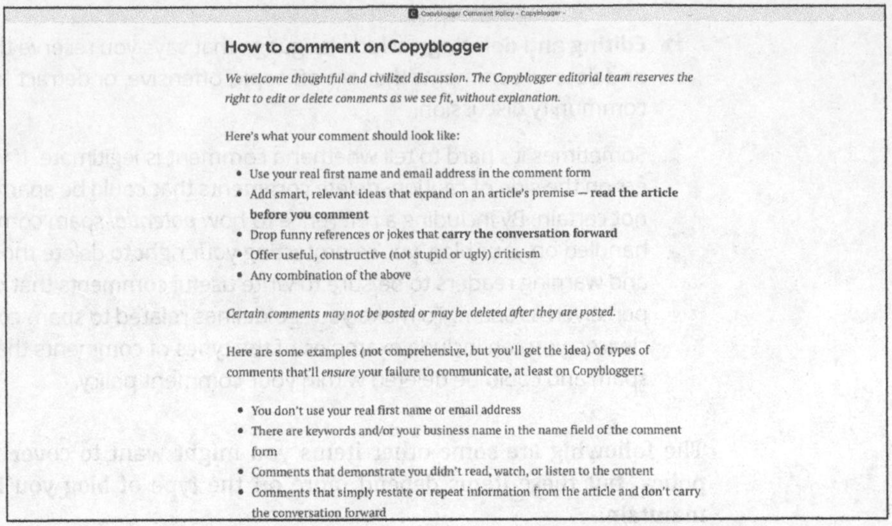

How to comment on Copyblogger

We welcome thoughtful and civilized discussion. The Copyblogger editorial team reserves the right to edit or delete comments as we see fit, without explanation.

Here's what your comment should look like:

- Use your real first name and email address in the comment form
- Add smart, relevant ideas that expand on an article's premise — **read the article before you comment**
- Drop funny references or jokes that **carry the conversation forward**
- Offer useful, constructive (not stupid or ugly) criticism
- Any combination of the above

Certain comments may not be posted or may be deleted after they are posted.

Here are some examples (not comprehensive, but you'll get the idea) of types of comments that'll *ensure your failure to communicate*, at least on Copyblogger:

- You don't use your real first name or email address
- There are keywords and/or your business name in the name field of the comment form
- Comments that demonstrate you didn't read, watch, or listen to the content
- Comments that simply restate or repeat information from the article and don't carry the conversation forward

FIGURE 4-5:
Copyblogger sets up expectations for readers on its comment policy page.

WARNING

The Federal Trade Commission, or FTC (www.ftc.gov), requires bloggers by law to make it explicitly clear to readers if written content has been sponsored by an advertiser, if products reviewed have been provided to the blogger at no cost, and if links to items for purchase are affiliate links, generating revenue for the blogger if a purchase is made.

While it's a best practice to disclose sponsored content, free product, or affiliate links at either the very beginning or very end of each related blog post, many bloggers also publish a disclosure page laying out their blog's policy regarding this type of content. Figure 4-6 is an example of a disclosure page on Amy Ever After (www.amyeverafter.com), informing readers of ways in which blogger Amy Oztan receives payment as a result of her blog.

Writing a privacy policy

It's a good idea to include a privacy policy on your blog, particularly if you display ads. A *privacy policy* is intended to communicate to blog readers how their behavior on your blog (paths taken, links clicked, and so on) will be tracked and how any personal information provided on your blog (such as email addresses in comments or forms and so on) will be used. It is very typical to provide a link to your privacy policy in your blog's footer. The policy can provide details about any information that's collected about visitors and their behaviors on your blog, confirmation that you won't sell any private information given on your blog, and acknowledgement that your site tracks visitors' behavior through the use of an automated web tracking tool called *cookies*. (If you participate in ad programs or track your blog usage statistics as described in Chapter 2 of Book 5, your blog probably uses cookies for tracking.)

FIGURE 4-6:
Amy Ever After
includes a blanket
disclosure that
applies to her
entire blog.

Basically, you want readers of your blog to know that any personal information they provide won't be sold to marketers who will start cluttering their email inboxes with offers. You also want to warn them that their behavior on your blog (links they click, the amount of time they spend on your site, and so on) is recorded. Figure 4-7 shows a blog privacy policy example from Neil Patel's blog (www.neilpatel.com/privacy/).

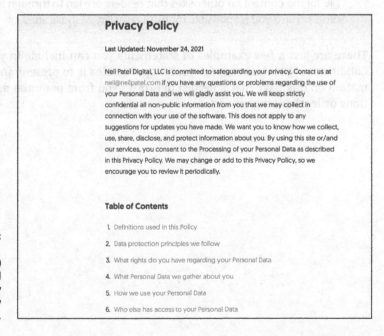

FIGURE 4-7:
Neil Patel (www.
neilpatel.com)
uses a detailed
and regularly
updated privacy
policy on his blog.

Developing a Terms and Conditions of Site Use page

A *Terms and Conditions of Site Use* page is the right place to provide disclaimers and warnings about your blog. It's a way to protect yourself and your blog's content from potential problems such as copyright infringement. A Terms and Conditions of Site Use page isn't a requirement, but if you do decide to use one, a common place to link to it is in your blog's footer.

Your blog's Terms and Conditions of Site Use page can include the following elements:

>> **Copyright information:** Include both *your* blog's copyrights as well as information on who to contact if a reader finds content on your blog that he believes violates copyright laws.

>> **Site availability:** Include information that protects you if, for some reason, your blog is unavailable at any given moment. For example, sometimes your blog hosting company could have a server problem, or you might need to disable your blog for maintenance.

>> **Warnings:** Include warnings as appropriate. For example, you might want to include a warning for visitors under 18 years of age if your blog uses profanity or material offensive to children.

>> **Link responsibilities:** Include language that tells readers you're not responsible for the content on other sites that readers are led to through links on your blog, nor are you responsible for the availability of those sites.

These are just a few examples of statements you can include in your Terms and Conditions of Site Use page for your blog. The idea is to present any and all information on this page that's needed to protect you from potential negative accusations or legal entanglements.

2
Niche Blogging

Contents at a Glance

Chapter 1

Understanding Niche Blogging

The blogosphere is a crowded place with millions of blogs and bloggers competing for readers, advertising dollars, and links every day. How can a brand-new blogger compete with bigger, established blogs? Certainly, blog marketing and promotion, relationship building, and reader engagement are ways to boost your blog traffic, but before you even start your blog, you might consider another strategy to becoming a successful blogger: defining your blog's niche.

This chapter explains how to find a niche, decide whether niche blogging is right for you, and position your niche blog for success.

Determining What Makes a Niche Blog

A *niche blog* is one that focuses on a very specific topic. That topic needs to be popular enough to be capable of drawing a sufficient audience to make maintaining the blog worthwhile to the blogger, but it also needs to be specific and refined enough to keep it out of the fray of competition with the larger, well-established blogs that cover more general topics.

Niche blogs can grow to be very popular simply because the bloggers behind them provide specific information that a highly targeted audience wants. They usually fill a void that other, larger blogs are missing but audiences want.

Because a niche blog is highly focused on a specific topic, you need to be certain you're very passionate about that topic to ensure you'll be able to write about it for a long period of time without getting the content becoming boring or repetitive. (See Chapter 2 of this Book for more about finding your focus.)

Understanding what a niche blog is

A niche blog is highly focused — all content and conversations center on a single, specific subject. The audience for a niche blog is typically very connected to the topic and often quite vocal about it. In short, niche bloggers deliver content gems that people want but struggle to find among all the information on broad-topic blogs, and their readers reward them by enthusiastically supporting their blogs.

Niche bloggers understand their audiences. They know readers come to their blogs for specific content, and they don't disappoint. Niche bloggers strive to continually meet the expectations of their audiences, keeping track of what other bloggers who write about their subject matter in a broader sense are publishing, and filling in the gaps. Niche bloggers also tend to build a strong community with other bloggers within their niche, partly because it's by definition a small group and partly because they tend to be very passionate about their focus area.

In the same way that niche bloggers bring great enthusiasm to their writing, niche blogs have an amazing opportunity to attract and create very loyal readers because the audience is already connected to and passionate about the subject matter. If readers like the blogger's voice and content as it relates to that subject matter, the blogger is poised for success.

Differentiating what a niche blog is not

Niche blogging is sometimes a term used to discuss blogs created solely for the purpose of Internet marketing and making money. These websites tend to appear quickly and often look rather rudimentary. Rather than focusing on great content and a visually appealing positive reader experience, this type of blog tends to be covered in advertisements and filled with links.

Sometimes called a *splog*, or a spam blog, these sites are set up specifically to earn income quickly through direct advertising and affiliate links. To be clear, that is not the type of niche blogging covered here.

Visiting Niche Blogs

Before taking on the unique challenge of creating a niche blog, spend some time perusing existing niche blogs to achieve a better understanding of what makes a niche blog. While it may initially seem that locating a niche blog is a bit like looking for a needle in a haystack, the truth is that searching for niche blogs is actually very easy because you can search for them using traditional blog search tools and very specific keyword phrases. Instead of sifting through hundreds of pages of search engine results for a broad search term such as *parenting,* you can find niche blogs about a more specific subject using a search term such as *parenting triplets* or *potty training multiples.* The more specific you get with your search terms, the better your chances are of finding a blog about the niche you have in mind.

Because your future blog readers will find your blog about a specific subject in exactly the same way, it's important for you to do some keyword research before choosing your blog's niche in order to get an idea of the topic's popularity. You can find out about keyword research as it relates to niche blogging in detail in Chapter 3 of this Book.

The following sections provide examples of five different kinds of niche blogs related to five very different and highly focused subjects: knitting/crocheting, big family travel, small town business, purses, and Mustang restoration. Take a look at the examples to see how researching existing niche blogs can provide you with new insight into the opportunities niche blogging presents in terms of creativity, readership, networking, and monetization.

Petals to Picots

Petals to Picots, shown in Figure 1-1, is a great example of a niche blog focusing on a popular hobby and providing resources for that hobby community. Author Kara Gunza is personally passionate about crocheting, so much so that she's received a Masters of Advanced Stitches and Techniques from the Crochet Guild of America. She has taken this passion and poured it into her site, which contains everything from video tutorials to free patterns available for readers to download.

Petals to Picots (www.petalstopicots.com) includes posts and tutorials about knitting, crocheting, and other fiber arts. It also provides readers with opportunities to sign up for email newsletters and to shop an online store.

Petals to Picots
CROCHET, KNIT, CREATE .

CROCHET   KNIT   CREATE   TUTORIALS   RESOURCES   BROWSE   SHOP   ABOUT

Get What You
Love at Etsy

Crochet   Knit   Create

FIGURE 1-1:
Petals to Picots
is a niche
blog focused
on knitting,
crocheting, and
fiber arts.

Six Suitcase Travel

There's no shortage of blogs focused on the broad topic of travel. However, there are far fewer blogs focused on the unique challenges of traveling with a large family.

Six Suitcase Travel (www.sixsuitcasetravel.com/blog), shown in Figure 1-2, fills that gap for families struggling to find travel accommodations for a family with more than four people. Born out of the author's own struggle finding travel accommodations for her family, Six Suitcase Travel features posts and resources hyper-focused on families of five, six, seven, or eight people.

Small Biz Survival

There are many blogs online about small businesses. How can a blogger turn such a broad topic into a niche blog? Simple: Choose a very specific subject within the broader topic of small businesses.

Small Biz Survival (www.smallbizsurvival.com), shown in Figure 1-3, is an example of doing exactly that. Rather than trying to cover all aspects of small businesses, Becky McCray and her team of bloggers focus on rural and small-town small businesses.

FIGURE 1-2:
Six Suitcase Travel is a niche blog focused on travel for families with more than four members.

FIGURE 1-3:
Small Biz Survival turns the broad topic of business into a niche blog.

The Purse Blog

Fashion and beauty are incredibly popular blog topics, but there are many ways to find a niche within those broader topics. The Purse Blog (www.purseblog.com), shown in Figure 1-4, provides a great example. This blog, online forum, and shop is dedicated to purses — everything and anything related to luxury-brand handbags. This blog has a large, focused audience for the content as well as profitable niche advertising opportunities.

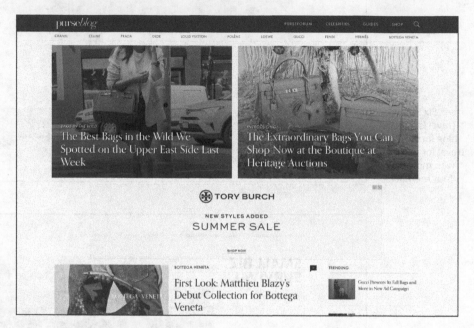

FIGURE 1-4:
The Purse Blog is all about handbags and nothing else.

67 Mustang Blog

Many blogs are written about cars, and many blogs are written about specific brands of cars. Car enthusiasts are typically very loyal to their favorite make and model and are looking for great blogs about those car makers.

Figure 1-5 shows the 67 Mustang Blog (www.67mustangblog.com), which takes the niche blogging concept a step further by focusing on the blogger's journey to restore his 1967 Ford Mustang with a bit of broader Ford Mustang-related content thrown in for flavor.

FIGURE 1-5:
The 67 Mustang
Blog follows
the restoration
of a blogger's
beloved car.

Finding Out What Makes
Niche Blogs Successful

The success of niche blogs comes primarily from the voices of the bloggers behind
them. Typically, the niche blogger is an expert in their niche or feels strongly
about it, which gives their blog a unique perspective. However, it doesn't matter
how strongly you feel about a topic: Your blog won't succeed if there aren't other
people in the world who are equally interested in that topic.

REMEMBER

The key to writing a successful niche blog is finding a topic you love that other
people are equally passionate about.

For example, many people write blogs about animals. Fewer bloggers write blogs
about dogs, and fewer write blogs about a specific breed of dog such as the basset
hound. Going a step further, even fewer blogs are written about training basset
hounds. Notice how the subjects of the blogs I describe here get more and more
focused and thus become about more and more specific niches. You can use the
same strategy in identifying the right niche topic for your blog. Take a look at
the broader topic and keep narrowing it down until you find the best niche for
your blog. You can find out more about choosing a niche blog topic in Chapter 3
of this Book.

TIP

Successful niche bloggers position themselves as the go-to people for their specific topics. Establishing yourself as an expert in your blog's topic could be as easy as listing your education, experience, and other credentials in your profile or biography published on your blog. For example, if you write a blog about pregnancy and you're an obstetrician, your authority is easy to establish.

If you don't have any official credentials, don't despair. You can still position yourself as an expert by publishing authoritative content that's both meaningful and useful. Also, take some time to showcase your knowledge off on your blog. You can do this by writing guest posts or articles about your blog topic on other blogs and websites and by participating in online forums and social networks where you can share your expertise with more people. Consider teaching courses or speaking at events where your knowledge can be highlighted. In other words, if you don't have credentials when you start your niche blog and you want your blog to grow and be successful, you should make an effort to create them. Don't be afraid to think outside of the box and pursue unique opportunities to establish your expertise both on- and offline.

TIP

Patience is paramount when it comes to building a niche blog. Successful niche bloggers start small in terms of topic and scope. Over time and with patience and persistence their reputation and blog traffic grow.

A great example of a niche blogger's success comes from Gayla Baer-Taylor, the former owner of a blog called MomGadget, who started her blog in 2000 as a step in building a career working from home. Her blog evolved to focus sharply on reviewing and discussing gadgets that make parents' lives easier. Gayla got the idea for her blog after attending a baby shower and seeing how excited she and the other attendees got about the various gadgets the expectant parent received to ease the transition to parenthood.

The origins of Gayla's success can be attributed to her ability to recognize a niche, capitalize on it, and develop her online presence as an expert in her blog's topic with a large audience of followers. By establishing her niche, she was ultimately able to grow in a new direction just as businesses broaden their product lines after they find success in their core competencies.

Over the years, MomGadget grew in scope to include content about broader family-related topics as well as working-from-home tips based on her own blogging experience; however, without establishing her niche audience first, it would have been extremely difficult for Gayla to find success competing against broader topic blogs with deeper pockets and wider reach. By developing her core audience first, she was able to introduce new topics to her loyal followers while continuing to meet their existing expectations, thereby growing her blog exponentially and enabling her to ultimately sell it. The trick is to find your niche and build a following around it *before* you try to expand in broader directions.

Benefiting from the Positives of Niche Blogging

As with any online endeavor you pursue, niche blogging offers both positives and negatives. It's critical that you take the time before you start your blog to weigh those positives and negatives and make an educated decision as to whether niche blogging is right for you and your goals. Don't just think of your blogging goals today or next month. Instead, look a few years into the future and determine where you want your blog to take you between now and then. Your blog topic could greatly affect your ability to reach those goals.

The following sections give you a good idea of the primary advantages of niche blogging, but don't stop there. Also read the later section, "Identifying the Drawbacks to Niche Blogs," so you're aware of the negatives, too.

Loyal readers and community

The people who find your blog and like what they read on it are more apt to return and become loyal readers simply because they're likely to have a stake in the subject matter. The reason is simple. If visitors are interested in your niche topic and know they can count on you to write relevant posts in a voice they enjoy time and again, they'll want to come back and read more from you. It follows the principle that if you give people what they want, they'll want more from you.

There's a reason why bloggers who write about specific celebrities (and write frequent, relevant posts) typically draw large and loyal audiences: People who are interested in those specific celebrities can never get enough information about them. They want to talk about those celebrities and share their thoughts about those celebrities with other people. You can use the same principles to create loyal readers on your own blog by focusing on a niche people feel strongly about.

REMEMBER

Loyal readers who are passionate about your blog topic will also naturally create an online community within the pages of your blog. While this community typically begins in the comments section of blog posts, it doesn't need to stop there. Many niche bloggers also add a forum function to their site so that readers can become members and interact with one another in a more organized way. (Find out more about blogger communities in Chapter 2 of Book 6.)

Less competition

As discussed earlier in this chapter, niche blogs have less competition for traffic by nature of the fact that there are simply fewer blogs related to niche blogs than there are more generalized blogs. Larger, successful blogs typically don't focus on a specific subject that's likely to attract a smaller, targeted audience. Instead, their focus is on providing broad content and attracting a wide audience. However, many people visit broad-topic blogs looking for specific types of information. That's where the power of niche blogs comes into play — in providing that specific content consistently, accurately, and in a way that's easier for readers to find!

Think of it this way — if you want to find information about college football teams in Florida, would you visit a blog that covers *all* college football teams, where you're likely to have to sort through dozens of unrelated posts to find what you're looking for? Or would you prefer to visit a blog that is dedicated to talking about college football teams *only* in the state of Florida? Most likely, you answered the latter because you'd save time and find more relevant information on that niche blog than you would on the broad-topic blog. You can apply the same principles to your own niche blog by identifying the specific segments of the broader audience and delivering the information that one of those segments is looking for.

REMEMBER

The blogosphere is a big and wide-open place. Instead of competing with other blogs, particularly popular blogs, find your niche and make the most of it. Network with those bigger bloggers and become the go-to person for your niche.

Long-tail search engine optimization

Search engine optimization (SEO) is discussed in detail in Chapter 1 of Book 5, but I would be remiss if I didn't mention it here. *Long-tail* search engine optimization is based on very specific keyword phrases made up of three or more words. These keywords and phrases are searched less often and tend to have fewer results as well. For example, instead of simply searching for *Italian recipes* in your preferred search engine, you could search for a targeted phrase such as *easy Italian meatballs recipes*, which would yield comparatively specific, and fewer, results.

Because a niche blog focuses on a specific topic, you can optimize your posts and pages for those targeted keyword phrases and drive more targeted traffic to your blog. People who are searching for a specific keyword phrase that matches the content on your site are far more likely to be satisfied when they find your blog, read more content there, and return later than they would be if they arrived there following a broad search.

Many large websites and blogs spend a lot of money trying to derive benefits from long-tail search engine optimization. Those opportunities are inherent in niche blogging.

Opportunities beyond the blog

As a niche blogger, your name may become closely associated with your blog's topic. Many niche bloggers intentionally use their blogs as an online platform, serving as a jumping-off point for other opportunities. Once you are established through your blog as being highly knowledgeable on that topic, you may find opportunities including but not limited to:

>> Consulting

>> Media appearances and interviews

>> Quotes in print media

>> Speaking engagements

>> Guest blogging

>> Book writing

>> Product creation or endorsement

Figure 1-6 shows the Shop page on the previously mentioned blog, Petals to Picots (www.petalstopicots.com). Site owner Kara Gunza established herself as a crochet expert through her blog and as an online pattern resource through her blog's free crochet patterns. Her online shop takes that to the next level by offering additional patterns at a nominal fee.

Many broad-topic bloggers try to be everything to everyone, but few succeed. By virtue of being a niche blogger, you potentially position yourself as an expert in your field.

Targeted advertising opportunities

Niche blogs attract targeted audiences, and smart advertisers want to match their ads with those targeted audiences. That means niche blogs can be very attractive to advertisers who share similar consumer audiences for their products. Not only do advertisers want to purchase ad space on blogs where they can connect with a targeted audience, they're often willing to pay more for that space.

FIGURE 1-6: Petals to Picots includes an online shop where readers can purchase crochet patterns.

Think of it this way: If Mattel wants to advertise a new Barbie product, and the company had the choice to advertise to a smaller audience on a blog for parents of grade school children or a blog about parenting in general, which is likely to offer a better return on their investment? Certainly, the larger, broader site might lead to more people clicking the ad overall, but the smaller, niche site is more likely to lead to more sales per click. At the end of the day, more sales per click are often worth far more to advertisers than more clicks with fewer sales.

Identifying the Drawbacks to Niche Blogs

Now that you understand the positives of niche blogging, it's time to look at the negatives. As with anything, not every aspect of niche blogging is a positive, but if you understand the potential drawbacks before you dive in, you can better position yourself for success as a niche blogger in the long term. By no means are the negatives of niche blogging insurmountable. On the contrary, they can all be overcome with dedication and patience.

Lower traffic and a smaller audience

By nature of the word *niche*, niche blogs appeal to a smaller audience than broad-topic blogs. That's not necessarily a bad thing though, as you discover in previous sections. However, it can be difficult for new bloggers to make that distinction. Many bloggers join the blogosphere with dreams of attracting thousands of visitors to their blogs each month. The truth of the matter is that it takes the vast majority of bloggers a long time to attract that kind of traffic to their blogs.

Furthermore, niche blogs can have difficulties achieving high rankings on search engines for broad and common search phrases because the competition for those broad search phrases is so high. Trying to compete with big sites for higher search rankings on common search terms can be a daunting and time-consuming task. Investing your time into maximizing your niche search term traffic is often a more successful strategy to pursue.

On the flip side, when you attract large numbers of visitors to your blog, it's likely that many of them won't stay long, and they're even less likely to return. The key to developing a successful blog is attracting and retaining a loyal audience of readers. Niche blogs might appeal to a smaller audience, but they're typically a very loyal audience. If you can live with a smaller audience, niche blogging might be right for you.

The startup curse

As with all new things, a niche blog might be niche today, but it could become the cool, popular thing next month. Remember when Twitter wasn't even a real word? Today, tweeting is a word used in mainstream conversation and every major company and brand has an official Twitter account. What started as a niche tool for the early adopters and tech nerds grew into a must-use tool at record speed. The same thing can happen with niche blog topics.

For example, you might have an idea to write a blog about a specific niche topic that no one else is currently writing about online. Sure, other bloggers might mention your niche topic in their broad blog, but no one is covering it exclusively. You recognize the opportunity and jump on it only to find in six months that your niche topic has become the cool, popular thing online. Competition soars before you have a chance to truly position yourself as the go-to place for information related to your niche topic. Other bloggers with greater influence, reach, and time usurp your position and become the go-to places for your niche, leaving you and your blog behind. That's a risk that all niche bloggers take, and it's up to you to determine how much effort you're willing to put into your blogging success and into creating contingency plans in case this happens to you.

The disappearing niche

A hot niche today could become obsolete tomorrow. Make sure you choose a niche that has staying power. For example, blogs about popular television shows that go off the air may have been hot while the program was going strong, but what happens to them when the show ends? What does the blogger do then? If you're looking for long-term blogging success, it's best not to tie your fate to a topic that might not be around one day. Instead, make sure you're in control by choosing a niche topic that is timeless or can morph into something else if the key element fades.

Niche fan blogs are perfect examples of "here today, gone tomorrow" blog topics. For example, blogs about upcoming sporting events, such as the next Olympic Games, can become obsolete as soon as the event is over. As another example, consider *The X-Files*, which was a highly popular television show with a strong fan following. Many of these fans created blogs to share their love of the program. When *The X-Files* went off the air in the late 1990s, the conversations died and so did most of the blogs.

Fewer advertising opportunities

Although niche blogs can attract targeted advertisers who are willing to pay more to connect with the specific audiences niche blogs attract, fewer advertising opportunities are available to niche bloggers overall. There is a very simple reason for this.

Many advertisers (particularly small and mid-size company advertisers) don't understand that the return on investment in connecting with a highly targeted audience that matches their best customer's demographic profile will be higher than the return on investment they get from connecting with a larger, less-targeted audience (if their goal is to make sales rather than just raise awareness of their products and services).

Because niche sites attract fewer visitors overall than larger, broad-topic blogs, it can be harder for an advertising manager to convince their leadership team of the value of advertising on a more targeted site than it is to sell them on the benefits of advertising on one of those larger blogs. It's unfortunate, but it's a gap in thinking that can be difficult for advertisers to overcome.

As such, even though your site might attract 1,000 readers who are obviously extremely interested in your niche topic and might be the *perfect* audience for an advertiser's messages, that advertiser might still choose to place its ad on a broad site that receives 10,000 visitors instead. The reason for this is simply that the decision makers on the advertiser's side can't get beyond the traffic numbers to fully understand who the audience members behind those numbers are and what they want and need.

The best option for niche bloggers is to test advertising opportunities and rates. Research what your competitors are doing (if you can find any) and test similar advertising opportunities. In time, you'll find a mix that works for you, and as your traffic increases thanks to your persistence and patience, additional advertising opportunities will undoubtedly present themselves to you.

Chapter 2

Benefiting from a Niche Blog Approach

S tarting a niche blog and staying both inspired and focused on a single topic for the lifetime of that blog can be challenging. It's easy to get bored or sidetracked as time goes by. Naturally, your blogging voice and content will evolve over time, but the heart of your blog, your niche, should always remain the cornerstone of your content. That's what readers will grow to rely on. So long as you stay true to your core niche, your readers will be likely to follow you on your journey as a blogger.

Always remember that to be a successful blogger, your relationship with your readers is a vital part of your blogging experience. Keep them happy by providing the kind of content they expect and enjoy from you. If you fail to meet their expectations, they might just look elsewhere for a blogger who does.

This chapter helps you find your focus as a niche blogger, grow your niche blog audience, and establish yourself and your blog as the go-to place online for information and commentary about your niche topic. You find out how to leverage relationships with other bloggers and your own readers to catapult your niche blog to success. Read on and get ready to be a niche blogger!

Finding Your Focus and Keeping It

All bloggers have days where they wake up feeling less motivated than they do on other days. You can find ideas on how to get over blogger's block in Chapter 2 of Book 1, but the challenge of staying focused and inspired can be even more difficult for niche bloggers. No matter how passionate you are about your chosen niche, boredom can be an inevitable part of writing about the same subject day in and day out. Because niche bloggers write about highly specific topics, there might appear to be less room for creativity in your writing. Some bloggers erroneously think that niche blogging is too confining or limiting, but that assumption couldn't be further from the truth.

Niche bloggers zero in on the specific subtopic of a broader subject, but that doesn't mean they need to become prisoners of their self-selected niches. Don't believe me? Take a trip around the blogosphere and start reading niche blogs on a wide variety of targeted subjects. Analyze what those bloggers are writing about and determine how you can creatively use similar ideas to enhance your own niche blog content.

One way to get creative while remaining focused on your niche is to categorize the types of information you want to share on your blog related to your niche. Think of categories within a niche blog as even more focused topics within an already highly focused subject! Blogging lends itself well to categorization through the tools built into common blogging platforms such as WordPress and Blogger, as shown in Figure 2-1.

For example, My Halal Kitchen (www.myhalalkitchen.com) by Yvonne Maffei breaks the niche topic of halal cooking and eating down to the following categories as shown in Figure 2-2:

>> Food

>> Travel

>> Life

>> What is halal cooking?

>> Shop

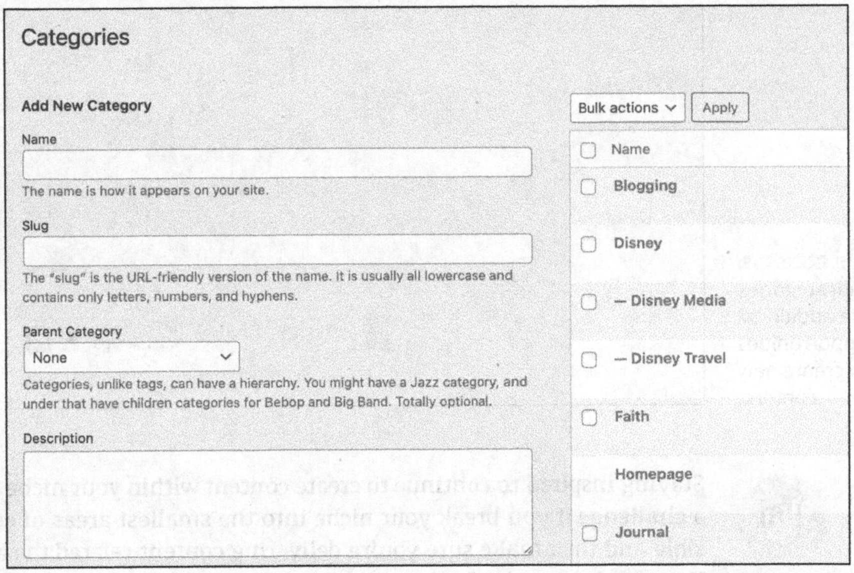

FIGURE 2-1:
Utilize existing blog platform tools to help build categories within your niche topic.

FIGURE 2-2:
My Halal Kitchen includes categories to break the topic of halal cooking down into smaller topics.

The author takes the categorization of her blog's content even further by breaking categories down into subcategories. For example, the category of Food is refined to the following topics, as shown in Figure 2-3:

» Cooking techniques and kitchen tips

» Entertaining

» Recipes

Many subcategories are broken down even further to include more refined subtopics within the blog's niche. The lesson is this: Instead of trying to think of broad topics to fit your niche blog, think of narrower topics and write posts about those more focused topics.

FIGURE 2-3: Subcategories create additional opportunities to create new content.

REMEMBER

Staying inspired to continue to create content within your niche doesn't have to be a challenge if you break your niche into the smallest areas of concentration possible and then make sure you're delivering content related to each of those areas. You may be surprised at how many subtopics relate to your blog's larger focus and how easy that makes it to keep the creative juices flowing!

Generating Traffic and Capturing an Audience

Bloggers who aspire to be successful are usually overly concerned with traffic early in the lives of their blogs. To build *real* traffic to your blog (meaning, traffic that lands on your blog for the right reasons and turns into loyal readers), you need to be prepared to invest time and remain patient. However, you can take steps to speed up the process of building an audience for your blog.

Search engine optimization

Search engine optimization, or SEO, refers to steps bloggers take to appear near the top of search engine keyword searches. SEO is covered in depth in Book 5, Chapter 1.

Niche blogs offer both negatives and positives when it comes to search engine optimization:

>> **The bad news:** It's difficult for niche bloggers to compete for high search rankings for common, broad search terms (although not impossible). The

problem is that broad search terms are very competitive. A small, beginner blogger has a hard time fighting for high search rankings for common keywords when so many strong, established websites and blogs are fighting for the exact same thing.

>> **The good news:** Niche blogs can rank very high for very specific search terms. As mentioned in Chapter 1 of this book, such traffic is said to come from *long-tail* search engine optimization benefits, and many bloggers work diligently to capitalize on that long-tail traffic by optimizing their posts with very specific keyword phrases in mind.

Think of it this way: If you can't compete for a search term like *Hawaii*, you might be able to appear near the top of a search for a specific search phrase such as *restaurants in Kaanapali Hawaii*. And there would be your niche! Instead of writing a blog and posts about Hawaii in general, a topic that's covered over and over across the Web and blogosphere, why not corner the market on the topic of dining in one of the most popular tourist cities on the island of Maui? Suddenly, your competition for that specific phrase is much smaller than it would be for the broader term, and that's how long-tail search engine optimization, that is, optimizing your site for very specific keywords that attract a highly targeted audience, can benefit a niche blog's traffic growth exponentially.

Link benefits

As you publish more and more posts on your blog, your archive of content will grow. At the same time, your blog traffic will grow through steps such as networking with other bloggers and optimizing your posts with targeted keyword phrases. Congratulations! More visitors to your site means more people who might like your content enough to mention it on their own blogs where they can link to it and drive more traffic to it.

To learn more about links from one blog to another, visit Book 5, Chapter 1. Your blog readers may also decide to share links to posts they enjoy through their social media accounts, such as Facebook or Twitter.

REMEMBER Each link to one of your blog posts could mean more traffic to your blog.

Furthermore, with each new link to your blog, your blog's search engine rankings could get a boost. Search engines takes incoming links to your blog seriously when determining which sites appear in search results, so when your blog attracts a lot of incoming links, particularly from popular websites and blogs, your blog's search engine ranking goes up. Appearing higher in search rankings will drive more traffic to your blog.

WARNING

Not all incoming links are equal. Search engines, such as Google, weigh incoming links from popular sites high, but links from spam sites and links that are paid for can actually get your blog removed from Google search rankings entirely. Organic, real growth is far more valuable to your blog's success than quick, manufactured growth.

Organic growth

Organic growth is a long-term blog-traffic-growth strategy that happens naturally as the amount of content on your blog grows and your efforts at engaging in conversations across the blogosphere boost your online exposure. The key to achieving organic growth is to continually publish great content, particularly content that no one else is writing about or with your own unique spin. Use your unique voice and become a vocal, contributing member of the blogosphere by networking and building relationships with other bloggers and blog readers. In time, your blog traffic will grow slowly but steadily as a result of your efforts. You can find out more about the methods of increasing organic growth through the section "Networking with Other People in Your Niche," later in this chapter.

Establishing Yourself as an Expert

As a niche blogger, you have the opportunity to become recognized as an authority on your subject matter. This is true particularly if you have credentials such as an education or work experience related to your niche blog topic. However, a passion for and deep knowledge of your subject could be enough to establish you as an expert. The recognition of your expertise depends partly on the content you publish on your blog as well as the tone with which you write. Even a blog that's based completely on opinion could become an online go-to place for information on a specific subject. Again, it depends in part on your writing style and the type of information or opinion you publish on your blog.

Consider these two blogs: a blog about California state politics written by a person who works for a member of the state government versus a blog about California state politics written by an unhappy citizen who publishes little more than personal rants and complaints. Which blogger is likely to become known in the online community as an expert in his particular niche and become the go-to person for information related to California state politics? Of course, the answer is the former example — the blogger who works within the California state political scene every day. Alternatively, the opinion blogger *could* become considered an expert if his blog was written in a more professional tone, rather than rants and complaints. A personal opinion blogger can be recognized as an expert, but the tone needs to match that of an expert rather than a complainer.

WARNING

The bottom line is that blogging provides a unique opportunity for people to become recognized as knowledgeable within their fields of expertise or interest. However, not every blogger earns the reputation of being an expert that people can rely on for great information. If you want to become known as an expert in your niche blog topic, your content needs to match that intent.

Gaining Online Exposure

Online exposure is quite simply being seen and recognized throughout the Internet. While some bloggers joke that working for the chance of exposure doesn't pay the bills, it *can* lead to money-making opportunities! You can boost your online exposure and drive traffic to your blog in many ways. Networking and building relationships are discussed in detail in the next section, but you can also pursue other online tactics to boost your online exposure. Take a look at the following list to get some ideas:

>> **Write articles.** Many websites offer repositories of articles and content written by people from all walks of life. Some sites even offer a form of payment for the content you contribute, and all offer ways for you to link that content back to your blog for added exposure and traffic.

WARNING

Be sure to read the terms and conditions of article sites to ensure the copyright and payment terms match your current and future goals.

>> **Create videos.** Video offers a great way to boost traffic to your blog through the use of another medium. Create videos and upload them to popular video-friendly social media sites such as YouTube, Instagram, and Facebook.

>> **Create podcasts.** Audio is another medium that people enjoy online, and it provides another way to drive traffic to your blog. You can start an online radio show on a site, such as BlogTalkRadio (`www.blogtalkradio.com`), or create podcasts, which you can publish on your blog as well as on audio sites such as iTunes (`www.apple.com/itunes`).

>> **Share presentations.** SlideShare (`www.slideshare.net`), shown in Figure 2-4, offers a great way for people to upload and share presentations — a perfect way to further establish yourself as an expert and provide links to your blog.

>> **Share pictures.** If you write a niche blog that lends itself to visuals, upload them to picture-sharing sites such Flickr (`www.flickr.com`) with links back to your blog.

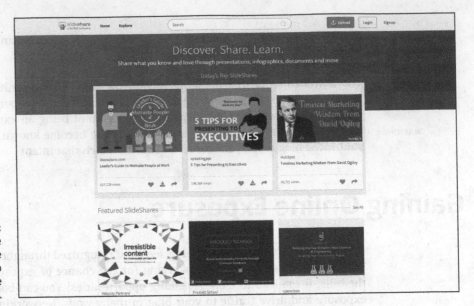

FIGURE 2-4:
SlideShare offers a place for people to upload and share presentations.

The opportunities for increasing your online exposure and driving traffic to your blog are virtually limitless. Don't be afraid to get creative, test new tactics, and find the right mix for you and your blog. Learn more about opportunities for bloggers off of their blogs in Book 8.

Networking with Other People in Your Niche

Perhaps the best way to increase niche blog traffic and attract loyal readers is networking both on and off your blog. You can use both formal and informal methods to network and build relationships with people online in order to grow your blog. Take a look at some of the following suggestions to get started on your journey to boost your blog's readership:

>> **Respond to comments on your blog.** Take the time to respond to all comments left on your blog. Doing so shows your readers that you value their opinions and provides the opportunity to get to know them better and build relationships with them.

Relationships lead to loyalty, and loyalty leads to increased blog readership over time.

REMEMBER

» **Leave comments on other blogs in your niche.** Visit other blogs in your niche and take the time to leave useful comments on posts you enjoy. Ask questions and follow up to keep the conversation going. Be sure to include your blog's URL in the appropriate field of the blog comment form to drive traffic back to your blog. The blogger will get to know you, and a relationship will develop naturally. Once you're on other bloggers' radar screens, they're more likely to follow your blog, leave comments on your posts, and link to your blog, thereby driving traffic to it.

» **Connect with people on social networking sites.** Take the time to find and connect with people who write and work in your niche on Facebook, LinkedIn, and other social networking sites. Then share content with them and build relationships with them, and as a result, your blog traffic might just grow organically over time.

» **Write guest posts for other blogs in your niche.** Reach out to other bloggers who write about your niche or write about broader subjects related to your niche and offer to write guest posts for them. Busy bloggers are likely to welcome a guest post from you, and it's a great way to not only build relationships with those bloggers but also get your name in front of their established audiences. Be sure to include a link to your blog in your guest post or bio.

» **Send emails to other bloggers in your niche.** Find other blogs about your niche or about a broader subject related to your niche and reach out directly via email to the bloggers who write them. Introduce yourself and the idea of working together to promote and support one another!

» **Attend blogging conferences or events related to your niche.** You'd be amazed at the number of people you can meet and the networking you can do at conferences and events related to blogging or your niche topic.

There are not only conferences related to blogging in general — many conferences and events exist for niche blogs. For example, TBEX (www. tbexcon.com), shown in Figure 2-5, is a yearly conference aimed at travel bloggers and industry professionals.

» **Join forums and groups related to your niche and get involved.** Because so many online forums and groups are available online, one is bound to be related to your blog's niche. Take some time to find them and then join and start posting comments, questions, and answers to other members' questions. Forums are a great way to build relationships with other people who are interested in your niche topic and to lead them to your blog for more information and conversation.

FIGURE 2-5:
TBEX is a yearly conference focused on the niche of travel blogging.

Branching Out Beyond Your Blog

A successful and well-received blog is the perfect jumping off point for other related endeavors. The sky's the limit in thinking about what's next once you've put in the work to create great content and draw in a loyal community of readers.

TIP

The following are just a few ideas of beyond-the-blog benefits of establishing yourself in the niche blogging community:

>> Blogging for a niche-related brand

>> Product creation

>> Online store

>> Writing books

>> Speaking at events

>> Creating podcast or video content

>> Working offline in a related field

>> Creating pay-to-download printables or resources

Myquillen Smith, better known to her readers and fans as The Nester, started out in the blogging world writing about attainable ways to create a cozy home at her site, Nesting Place (www.thenester.com). After achieving incredible success within the home design niche, she expanded into books (as shown in Figure 2-6), classes, and even in-person events.

FIGURE 2-6:
The Nester is a great example of a blogger moving beyond the pages of their niche blog.

TIP

Want to learn more? Book 8 looks closely at a variety of ways to move beyond creating content on your blog. You can also find out much more about growing your blog in Book 6, but do take the time now to consider how you can follow some of the suggestions provided in this chapter to find people who are likely to be interested in your specific niche blog topic. Then start engaging them where they already spend time online. Lead them to your blog with *useful* links, but don't over-promote. You don't want to be viewed as someone who is only looking for traffic to your blog. The key to blogging success is marrying great content with strong relationships. The combination is unstoppable.

Chapter **3**

Choosing Your Niche

Choosing your niche can be a challenge. Some bloggers have a singular passion, a hobby, or area of expertise that clearly takes center stage in their lives. Most people, however, have a variety of interests that could all make for great blog content. When there are so many subjects to choose from, how do you know which is the right niche for you? How do you narrow that subject down into a niche that will inspire you to write passionately? And how can you determine which niche will help you meet your blogging goals for exposure, traffic, and monetization?

Fear not! This chapter gives you the information and tools you need to confidently select a niche topic for your blog.

One of the biggest mistakes you can make as a blogger is choosing a topic that you have no business writing about. Doing so makes it more likely that you will give up before your blog has had a chance to succeed. Even if you do stay the course, choosing the wrong blog niche offers far more chances for failure than success. Remember, blogging success comes from a combination of the fantastic content you publish on your blog coupled with your unique voice and perspective on your blog's subject. If you don't know enough about a subject to write well and often about it, and you don't feel strongly enough about it to write with passion, you need to select a different niche topic.

Determining Your Niche Blogging Goals

Choosing your blog's niche topic is dependent partly on your goals for your blog. Naturally, if you're writing your blog solely for pleasure and not defining success in terms of traffic or money-making opportunities, you can choose any niche that interests you. How much time you dedicate to writing your blog or the tone you use matters only to you and your readers if you're writing it only for yourself and your community.

However, if you have objectives for your blog that include growing your readership, becoming recognized within the larger audience of your blog's topic, or making money, the niche topic you choose is absolutely essential to increasing your chances of attaining those objectives. Writing a niche blog comes with unique opportunities to find success both on and off your blog. To help you get started in creating your own goals for your niche blog, the remainder of this section teaches you about five of the most common objectives niche bloggers strive to achieve.

TIP

Don't choose your blog's niche topic until you determine your short- and long-term goals for your blog. Those goals could greatly affect the niche topic that you ultimately write about on your blog. You can find out more about setting blogging goals in Chapter 2 of Book 1.

Building your expertise

Many people start blogging because they view it as a low-cost way to build their online platforms and establish themselves as experts across a wide audience they can't otherwise reach. The blogosphere attracts readers from around the world and from all walks of life. If you want to establish a reputation as an expert in a particular area, you can do so through blogging. This is particularly true of niche bloggers who focus their content on specific topics and become the go-to sources in their areas of expertise. Over time, bloggers who earn reputations as experts often find themselves called upon for national news media coverage, book writing, and more.

As you might expect, your success in establishing yourself as an expert in a specific area comes not only from your background experience and education but also from the content you write on your blog. In a crowded blogosphere, the bloggers who focus on niche areas can fill the gaps left by the jack-of-all-trades bloggers and corner the market on their topics.

For example, rather than writing a blog all about blogging, Lorelle VanFossen knew her area of expertise was in the WordPress blogging platform, and she created a niche blog where she writes with knowledge and passion for her subject. Her blog, Lorelle on WordPress (http://lorelle.wordpress.com), is shown in Figure 3-1.

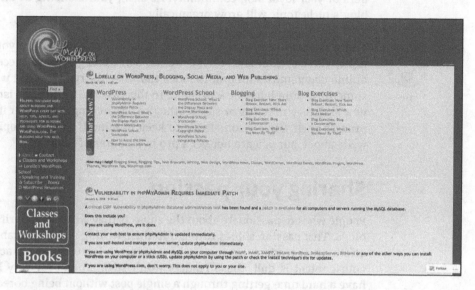

FIGURE 3-1:
Lorelle
VanFossen owns
a niche blog
about WordPress.

Today, Lorelle is known across the web as one of the key people for information, tips, and education about using WordPress. She has written books on the subject, contributes to other high-profile blogs about blogging, and frequently speaks at industry events. What started as a niche blog has not only established Lorelle as an expert in her field but also opened new doors of opportunity to her.

Of course, you can't expect to start a blog on any specific subject and become known as the expert in the subject matter automatically. A niche blogger can attract and retain readers only if they write about a topic about which they have both experience and knowledge. Readers can see through a blog written by a person who lacks knowledge or experience. This is one area where the old adage "fake it until you make it" does not apply! The mark of a successful niche blogger is a thorough understanding of the subject matter based on first-hand experience, which enables them to speak intelligently and authoritatively.

Think of it this way: If you need to find information about building a deck onto the back of your house, would you rather read a blog on the topic written by a master carpenter or one written by a novice wood-working hobbyist? I don't know about you, but I'd like my new deck to be structurally sound! Certainly, the former blogger would provide more authoritative content and could more easily establish themselves as an expert in their blog's niche topic than the latter blogger.

Choosing Your Niche

The same principle holds true for your own niche blog. When you contemplate niche topics, consider why you should be *the* person writing a blog on that subject. Determine what makes your blog stand out from others on the same or similar subjects. Decide what unique content or perspectives you have that can attract readers and make them want to build relationships with you and turn into members of your loyal blog community. As such, your standing as an expert in your blog's niche topic will grow organically.

TIP

There is one caveat to the guideline that you should come to your blog's niche topic with a certain level of experience. Some bloggers have successfully created online communities around the idea that they're trying — and writing about — something completely new to them. In this case the niche topic isn't so much the new skill they're trying or subject they're researching, but rather it is the learning process itself. This is something to keep in mind if there's a topic you'd love to write about, but you are not yet a pro in that area of interest!

Sharing your passion

People who are passionate about the subjects they write about write the best niche blogs. That passion shines through in their writing and both grabs and holds the attention of readers. No matter how successful you are at attracting readers, if your content is dull, those readers won't stick around for very long. If readers have a hard time getting through a single post without being bored, your blog has little chance for success.

REMEMBER

Niche blogs are different from broader topic blogs because the authors behind them typically have made conscious decisions to focus on a topic they love rather than attempting to cover a large range of topics. If this applies to you, don't hold back in your writing. It is a common mistake for bloggers to write posts they believe will be the most successful rather than writing what they're most inspired to write. Let your passion for your blog's topic spill out onto the screen! Don't let your words die a quick death because they're torturously boring. Instead, let your passion for your niche subject shine through, and readers will get caught up in your enthusiasm, too.

Prescott Perez-Fox (www.scottperezfox.medium.com) is a wonderful example of a blogger who unapologetically allows his passion to shine through in every aspect of his writing. Shown in Figure 3-2, his blog provides insight into the topic of branding, offering a unique perspective on the popular marketing subject. As he writes in his About page (www.perezfox.com), he is "proud to be an oddball and sideways thinker." His passion for his subject along with his experience and knowledge make his blog stand out from the crowd of blogs about branding.

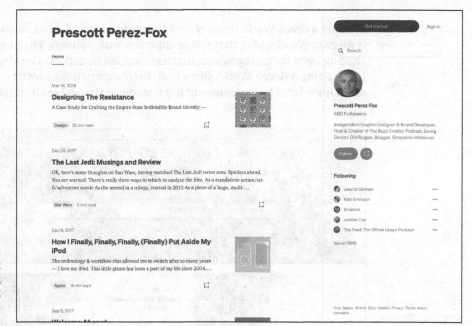

FIGURE 3-2:
Prescott Perez-Fox's blog about branding is insightful and unique.

In other words, if you're very passionate about a topic, that could be the perfect subject for your niche blog! At the very least, that topic offers a great place for you to start your quest to select a niche blog topic.

Offering your opinion and sharing your knowledge

If you're educated or experienced in a specific subject, or even if you just hold strong opinions about that subject, it could be a good choice for your niche blog topic. Niche bloggers who are very knowledgeable in their subject matter provide authoritative content and can easily become recognized across the blogosphere as experts. Alternatively, people with strong opinions on a specific subject can gain reputations as pundits, as long as their opinions are expressed as authoritative commentary rather than mere complaints or rants.

Readers look for blogs written by people with both experience and knowledge as well as by people who simply have strong opinions. While many bloggers write blogs about topics related to their work, there are also plenty of blogs that have nothing to do with the writer's day job and instead focus on an outside area of interest. Both types of bloggers can find audiences across the blogosphere. The trick is to understand which type of blogger you are (or want to be), choose a topic that matches your level of experience or opinion, and then stick to it.

Crafting a Green World (`http://craftingagreenworld.com`), shown in Figure 3-3, is an example of a blog that mixes expertise with opinion. The blog is dedicated to sharing ideas for craft projects that use recycled materials. The bloggers who write for Crafting a Green World share both their experience in testing crafts and their opinions related to environmentally friendly crafts and craft-related products.

FIGURE 3-3: Crafting a Green World focuses on a very specific niche topic.

In fact, many hobby bloggers write niche blogs based on their love of a particular activity. They may not be experts in that activity, and they may not have even been participating in that activity for very long. However, they feel passionately about it and want to share their opinions and thoughts about it with a wider audience. Strong opinions for a specific subject can translate into a successful niche blog just as easily as vast experience or knowledge can.

TIP

What do you love? That could be your blog's niche topic!

Networking and building relationships

Many bloggers start their blogs to find other people with similar interests for personal or professional networking. The blogosphere provides a place for you to interact with people from across the globe and forge relationships with them that can be helpful in terms of sharing ideas and learning from each other as well as boosting your online exposure and driving traffic to your blog.

Networking and building relationships start with writing great content on your own blog that invites comments and discussion. By responding to comments left on your blog *and* leaving comments on other blogs about your niche, you can start to create your own network of online relationships. Many bloggers find great success thanks to the community that forms around their blogs as well as the relationships that they make with people on other blogs, social networking sites, forums, and more. For example, there are many online forums and groups dedicated to more topics than you could possibly imagine. From Harley Davidson owners to work-at-home moms (see Figure 3-4 for a popular work-at-home mom's forum at `www.wahm.com/forum`) and everything in between, there's probably a forum or group for it.

FIGURE 3-4: WAHM.com is a popular forum for work-at-home moms.

Basically, you should fully leverage every opportunity you have to interact with your peers and audience. There is perhaps no other medium that allows *anyone* to become a vocal, contributing member as easily as blogging. Use it to your advantage and build strong relationships that boost your online exposure *and* create loyal readers of your own blog.

REMEMBER

Growing your niche blog is easier if you already have relationships and networking contacts related to that niche topic that you can tap into to build an early audience and start conversations on your blog.

Making money

The number of people who start blogs with high aspirations of making lots of money grows every day. Unfortunately, making money from your blog is challenging and often takes a lot of time and patience. However, you can speed up the process, or at least increase your chances of success, by choosing a niche topic that's easier to monetize. You can find out more about choosing a niche to make money later in this chapter. For now, it's important to understand that it's possible to make money from a niche blog.

If you hope to earn an income from your niche blog, you need to be sure there are moneymaking opportunities available that are at least somewhat related to your blog's subject matter before selecting that blog topic. Irrelevant sponsored content and ads are unlikely to be useful to your audience, and that could potentially drive readers away. Fewer readers means fewer clicks and less traffic, which in turn leads to fewer advertisers interested in purchasing ad space on your blog.

Bottom line, if you want to make money from your blog, you need to choose a niche that has a built-in audience, but you also need to be certain that relevant advertising programs and opportunities are available for your niche. If making money is important to you, be sure to read Book 7 for all the details about monetizing your blog that you need to get started on the right path to success.

Identifying Niches That Might Work for You

The best way to choose your blog's niche topic is to start broad and slowly narrow your topic down until you end up with a list of possibilities. The following steps can help you get your thought process flowing:

1. **Think of a broad topic that you're passionate and knowledgeable about.**

   Here's an example: After much thought, you determine that you're both passionate and knowledgeable about writing, but a lot of blogs and websites are dedicated to the broad topic of writing already.

2. **Narrow down the broader topic into smaller categories.**

   You can divide writing into categories such as book writing, article writing, copywriting, freelance writing, writing for pleasure, fiction writing, nonfiction writing, screenplay writing, and much more.

3. **Choose a few of those categories that you're interested in and break them into even smaller segments.**

   Using the category of fiction writing, you can break it down by genre or audience as fantasy writing, memoir writing, children's writing, young adult writing, and so on.

4. **Select some of those subcategories and break them down even further.**

   For example, the young adult writing segment could be broken down into writing how-to guides, reviews, and specific genres to start.

5. **When you have your categories broken down to small enough segments, choose the ones that interest you the most and which you think you can write about passionately, intelligently, and frequently for a long time to come.**

   You might choose a niche category for your blog, such as young adult fiction, and focus your content on strategies, trends, success stories, reviews, and how-to's, as they all relate to writing young adult fiction.

TIP

To get those creative juices flowing, consider the following popular broad topic areas and then begin the refining process:

- ❯❯ Education
- ❯❯ Favorite offline hobbies
- ❯❯ Finding shopping deals
- ❯❯ Frugal living
- ❯❯ Home design and décor
- ❯❯ Parenting
- ❯❯ Personal journaling
- ❯❯ Political commentary
- ❯❯ Popular culture and celebrity news
- ❯❯ Sports
- ❯❯ Technology news and review

Keep in mind that you want a subtopic that's broad enough to attract an audience of more than a handful of people. You also want a subtopic that fills a gap in the online world or allows you to add your unique perspective to differentiate it from everything else that's already out there.

After you select a blog topic niche, take some time to write out a list of blog post ideas. Find other blogs, websites, or forums related to your niche topic and determine whether there's an existing audience of readers interested in the topic and peers that you can build relationships with.

Determining the Audience Potential for a Niche Blog

A niche blog's success depends in part on the potential audience size for that niche. For example, no matter how much a person might love the topic of teaching parrots to do tricks, only so many people in the world are also interested in that topic. Therein is the struggle for a blogger who wants to successfully create an online community around their blog or turn their blog into a money-making opportunity.

With that in mind, you need to determine the audience potential for your niche blog topic. Of course, if your only goals are to blog for fun with no plans to build your online exposure or make money, it won't matter to you how many other people are interested in your niche blog topic. If that is you, then feel free to skip past the following sections and dive right in with your chosen topic! However, the vast majority of bloggers *do* want to build an audience of readers, establish themselves as experts, or make money from their blogs. If you're one of those bloggers, you need to do some research before you make your final niche topic choice.

You can start your research by finding and spending time on other blogs that are either broadly or specifically related to your potential niche blog topics. This is one way to get a good idea of what people are interested in and talking about, and you'll have a chance to find any gaps or unique angles on the topic that you can bring to your own blog. Next, you need to do some keyword research. These steps help you identify the potential traffic your blog could draw over time.

WARNING

Nothing is guaranteed with blogging. The research you do now only tells you the *potential* for your niche blog; it doesn't guarantee success. Instead, success comes from your hard work, dedication, and passion for blogging.

Researching existing niche blogs

There are two primary reasons for researching existing niche blogs as part of your process to choose your own niche topic:

>> You can learn from other niche blogs. Even if they're written about a topic unrelated to anything you're familiar with, you can still learn from them in terms of content, conversation, and community.

>> You can research both the potential audience and existing competition when you seek out and read other blogs related to your niche topic.

The following sections cover great sources for doing your research.

Google Alerts

Google offers a great tool called Google Alerts that provides a way for you to keep track of what's being published online related to your niche blog topic. When you set up a Google Alert for a specific search term, you receive an email notifying you when new content is published online with that search term. To set up your own Google Alert, follow these steps:

1. **Visit Google Alerts at www.google.com/alerts.**

   The Google Alerts page, shown in Figure 3-5, opens.

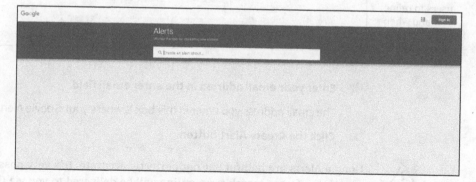

FIGURE 3-5:
The Google Alerts allows users to monitor specific terms on the Internet.

2. **Enter your search term in the Search Query text box.**

   This step tells Google Alerts that you want to be notified anytime a blog or website uses that search term.

3. **Select Show Options in order to customize your search (Figure 3-6).**

   Within the options menu you are able to select your preference in the following areas:

   - Frequency of notifications
   - Sources
   - Language
   - Geographic region
   - How many results

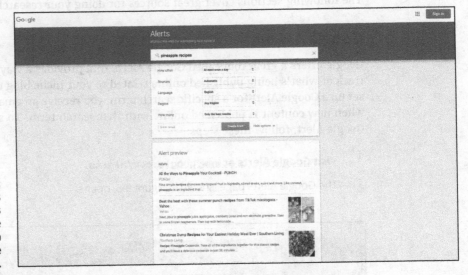

FIGURE 3-6: The options menu allows users to refine how and when they receive Google Alerts.

4. **Enter your email address in the enter email field.**

   The email address you enter in this box is where your Google Alerts are sent.

5. **Click the Create Alert button.**

WARNING

Google Alerts are helpful but not perfectly accurate. It's very possible that not all mentions of your search term online will be delivered to you via Google Alerts. In other words, it's a useful tool, but not an exact science.

Social media searches

Conversations about niche blog topics don't only occur on those blogs. Social media searches are a great way to get a sense of the potential audience for your selected niche blog topic. For example, if you search for the term *pineapple reci-pes* while considering launching a blog focused primarily on that subject and the results returned are few and far between, you may want to go back to the drawing board before launching your site.

TIP

To get started, take a look at the following platforms when gauging potential interest in your blog's topic:

- » Pinterest
- » Facebook
- » Instagram
- » Twitter
- » LinkedIn
- » Reddit

A quick search of Facebook, shown in Figure 3-7, displays recent posts related to our sample search phrase, *pineapple recipes*. Good news! There are recent public posts on the topic, and by scrolling through the results I'm able to see that there seems to be enough interest in the topic to make this niche blog idea worth further consideration.

FIGURE 3-7:
A Facebook search helps gauge interest in a potential topic.

Performing keyword searches

Keyword research is critical to determine whether the niche you want to write about is something that people are actually looking for through search engines.

The reality of blogging is that a lot of your blog's traffic comes from search engine keyword searches. If you have goals to draw a lot of visitors to your blog, you need to be sure that not only are people looking for keywords related to your niche, but also that your content is optimized for those keywords.

REMEMBER

Much of your blog's traffic will come from online searches, particularly in the early life of your blog before readers begin to share your content through social media.

Chapter 1 of Book 5 takes a closer look at available keyword search tools, both paid and free. During the process of selecting your niche blog's topic, it makes the most sense to stick to the tools that offer free accounts, but as you dive in more to blogging and the use of keywords, consider upgrading if you're serious about keyword analysis.

Google search

An easy place to begin looking at the popularity of a keyword search is to simply conduct a traditional search on Google using keywords you would use if you were looking for the type of content you plan to publish on your blog. Think like a reader would and use the keywords they would be likely to use. After you conduct your keyword search, scroll to the bottom of the first page of search results provided by Google (as shown in Figure 3-8) and notice the list of keyword phrases under the "Related searches" section. This is a list of other popular search terms that Google identifies as being similar to your search term, and this list can give you great ideas of the ways people are searching for the type of content you provide on your blog!

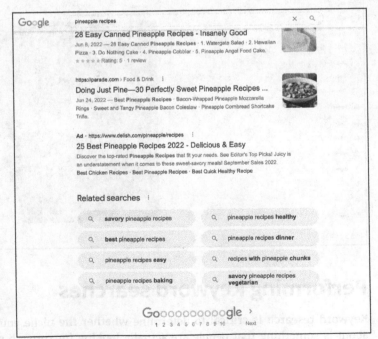

FIGURE 3-8:
Additional keyword suggestions from a Google search shows what topics are important to potential readers.

Want additional keyword information but in a different format? About the middle of the first page of Google search results you will find the "People also ask" section, as shown in Figure 3-9. These questions are real searches that Google search engine users have performed that are related to your keyword or phrase.

FIGURE 3-9: Google shares what questions users are asking related to your keyword or phrase.

Another way to utilize Google search when selecting the niche topic for your blog is to make note of the number of pages of results returned when you perform a Google search for that topic. For example, a search of *Schuylkill County Kosher Restaurants* only returns six pages of results, as shown in Figure 3-10. This is a helpful clue that perhaps a blog focused entirely on restaurant reviews of places serving kosher food in Schuylkill County, Pennsylvania, would not be highly trafficked or able to provide very much content.

Google Trends

Google Trends (trends.google.com) is a tool provided free by Google that shows a list of the most popular search terms on Google at any given time. If your niche blog topic is particularly timely, Google Trends just might be a good place to get an idea of exactly how people are searching for your topic right now. For example, Figure 3-11 shows the top recently trending search terms according to Google Trends at the moment I'm writing this chapter.

FIGURE 3-10:
Pay attention to
how many pages
of search results
are returned.

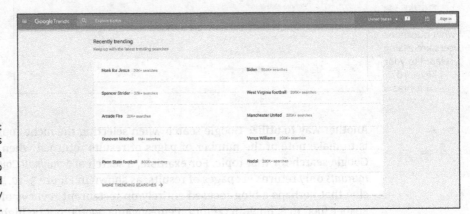

FIGURE 3-11:
Google Trends
provides a
glimpse into
popular keyword
searches at any
given moment.

REMEMBER

Keep in mind that the keyword analysis described in this chapter tells you only what's happening online right now. It's possible your niche might be growing in popularity, and you could be one of the first bloggers to stake a claim in that niche. It's also possible that a topic that's hot right now might decline in popularity in the future.

Chapter 4

Writing for Your Niche

I n many ways, creating content for a niche blog isn't much different from writing for a broader topic, but niche blog content does need to stay focused on the specific topic of the blog. This brings with it a unique set of challenges. Readers visit a niche blog for targeted content about a subject they're interested in. If your niche blog content steers off course significantly with irrelevant content, readers will become confused and look elsewhere to find the targeted content they want and need.

Consider a blog about classic rock that suddenly contains content about classical music. How do you think the blogger's audience of classic rock enthusiasts would react to this type of inconsistency in content? It's unlikely that they would be happy about it. In fact, they might turn their backs on the blogger and seek another source for the information, opinions, and conversations they're looking for about classic rock music.

Writing about a niche topic doesn't mean you need to limit yourself, but it does mean you need to find creative ways to expand your subject while sticking to your niche. You can find ways to tie unrelated subjects to a niche blog, but it takes a bit of ingenuity. This chapter helps you find ways to write content for your blog without feeling confined by your niche topic.

Creating Content

A phrase used often among bloggers is "content is king," meaning the content you publish on your blog is far more important than anything else you do during your life as a blogger. This is absolutely true. No one is going to read your blog if the content is terrible. But how many times can you talk about the same subject before your niche blog becomes repetitive and boring? The creativity you need to produce great content for your niche blog comes from thinking outside of the box and stretching the limits of your subject matter, which is something you can do with a bit of direction and thought.

Keep reading for tips and suggestions about the type of content you can create on your niche blog and how to keep that content interesting by getting creative.

Writing different types of posts

The easiest way to breathe life into a niche blog is by varying the types of posts you publish. Although you need to create your own unique style and voice that readers will associate with your blog, that doesn't mean you need to adhere to a stringent style guide. Sometimes you can even present the exact same idea in a different way using a different type of blog post, appealing to a different segment of your audience without sounding repetitive.

As an example, consider a blog post on a young adult fiction blog about writing dialogue that teens actually believe. You can write a post called *Young Adult Dialogue: The Good, The Bad, and The Ugly*, where you provide examples of good and bad dialogue to help readers learn the difference. Alternatively, you can publish a post called *10 Tips for Writing Great Young Adult Dialogue* where you provide ten very specific tips to help your blog readers learn to write compelling dialogue for their intended audiences. Both posts focus on the same aspect of writing for young adults but with very different approaches, making them unique and able to add value to your readers' experiences on your blog.

Following is a short list of types of posts you can write on your niche blog to keep the content fresh without straying too far from your niche topic:

>> **Listicles:** Everyone loves lists. From *Top 10 Tips* to *10 Steps* and everything in between, listicles — short *for list articles* — are always popular blog posts for any blog, niche or not. For niche bloggers, the key is to create very specific lists that tie directly to your niche topic.

>> **How-to:** Providing step-by-step tutorials to teach your readers how to accomplish a task is another way to present content that people love. How-to posts work very well on niche blogs because you can provide very detailed instructions about a specific topic your audience is certain to be interested in already. There's also a good chance that your readers have a basic understanding of the related broader topic, allowing you to go in-depth with your how-to posts.

>> **Don'ts:** Just as people like to read tips and how-to's, they also like to know what they should avoid. Tell them in a blog post and be specific!

>> **Videos:** Turn your readers into viewers by including video content on your site. Create your own videos or embed videos other people create so you can share them with your readers and provide your opinions related to them in order to enhance your own content. Remember to stay relevant to your niche topic to meet reader expectations.

Interested in learning more about including video in your blogging? Visit Book 8, Chapter 2.

TIP

>> **Polls:** Everyone likes to give their opinion. Invite them to do so in a poll that you publish in a blog post. People who read niche blogs typically have strong opinions on the narrow topic and are highly likely to jump into the conversation if they're asked to do so.

>> **Reader questions:** Blog readers often email questions or leave questions within the comments section of your blog posts. Those questions can become great blog posts where you provide the answers! For niche bloggers, this is particularly helpful because the content of your blog is very focused. Chances are good that if one person has a question about the niche topic, a lot of other readers have similar questions!

>> **Reviews:** Help your readers with important information about niche-related products and services by providing your own reviews that are very closely related to your niche topic. Although it might be tempting to review unrelated products and services, especially if they're provided for free, niche bloggers need to pay close attention to meeting reader expectations. Unhelpful reviews aren't likely to meet those expectations. In fact, they can confuse and even annoy your readers.

If you choose to review products that have been provided to you for free, be sure to disclose to your readers that you received the product in exchange for your review post! Learn more about this type of disclosure in Chapter 4 of Book 7.

WARNING

>> **Links:** Publishing blog posts that include links (sometimes called *link round-ups*) of posts from other blogs that you enjoy is a great way to grow your

Writing for Your Niche

online network and drive traffic back and forth between your blog and other blogs that you like or recommend. For niche bloggers, link roundups are like mining gold. Find the best bloggers in your niche or up-and-coming bloggers and link to them to start a relationship. Bloggers understand that helping each other through sharing content and links can help both blogs grow.

» **News:** What's going on in the world related to your niche blog topic? You can write about it on your niche blog! Don't just report the news, though. Be sure to add your own opinion, knowledge, or experience to your posts to ensure readers receive added value from your blog beyond the information they can find elsewhere online. Take the opportunity to demonstrate your knowledge or expertise in your niche within your commentary.

» **Trends:** If you know of new or interesting trends related to your blog topic, write about them on your blog and start discussions about what those shifting trends might mean to your topic, to you, and to your audience. Again, trend posts are a great way to further establish your expertise, passion, and knowledge in your niche topic.

» **Success stories:** Research other people who have achieved great success in some way related to your niche topic. Such stories can be both educational and motivational to readers. Offer links and request quotes when possible, which helps you build relationships with influential and interesting people while also further building your reputation in your niche area.

» **Interviews:** Contact successful individuals who can share useful knowledge about your niche topic and request to interview them. Then publish the interviews on your blog so your readers can learn from them. Again, this is a great way to build relationships with key influencers and further establish your own reputation within your niche.

» **Guest blog posts:** Contact others who have knowledge of your topic and ask them to write a guest blog post for you. Your readers are likely to enjoy hearing a different perspective from time to time, and it's a great way to get a conversation going on your blog as well as put you on the radar screens of influential people and bloggers. Guest blogging is a win-win for you and the guest blogger. Not only does the guest blogger receive exposure on your blog, but you also have an opportunity to build a relationship with that person.

These ideas are just a taste of the ways you can vary your style of content to very effectively keep your niche content fresh and interesting. Keep in mind that these types of posts work on a broad-topic blog as well, as discussed in Chapter 2 of Book 1.

TIP

Any blog post topic can become the subject of multiple blog posts without becoming repetitive or boring. For example, think of a topic for a blog post you could write about and then take a look at the types of posts listed in this section. How can you take that post topic using those types of posts and morph it into multiple posts? After you answer that question, you can publish the posts together as a series or separately over time.

Choosing your voice and style

Whether you write a broad topic blog or a niche blog, your blog's voice and style make it unique and set it apart from other blogs and websites. This is particularly true of niche blogs that are highly focused on a specific topic because the uniqueness of the blogger's voice sets the blog apart in spite of the similar content from blog to blog.

REMEMBER

No matter how great your content is, no one will want to read your blog if it's written in an unappealing voice and a style that's disconnected from the topic. I've stumbled across many blogs over the years that appear to offer great content, but the writing style, grammatical errors, and ineffectual voice have caused me to click away and look for an alternative source for the same kind of information. You don't want that to happen to your blog, so take the time to determine what your voice should be on your blog and then stick to it. Also, brush up on your writing skills to ensure your content is well written. Most importantly, remember your niche, from your topic to your content to your voice and stick to it!

One of the aspects of the blogosphere that makes it so easy to join is that bloggers don't have to be trained writers to publish a blog. This fact holds true for niche bloggers just as much as it does for broad-topic bloggers. Most blogs are written in a conversational tone rather than a strictly professional or academic tone. That's because the blogosphere is rooted in conversations and relationships. If blog readers wanted to find an institutional, formal writing style, they would turn to textbooks and professional journals, not blogs. Even the most professional blogger can write in an informal and inviting voice that encourages conversation and relationships. The last thing you want to do on your niche blog is intimidate your readers by writing with a voice that doesn't match your topic, and because niche blog topics are always very specific, your voice needs to be equally specific and on target with your topic.

TIP

After you determine the niche topic for your blog, you need to choose the specific voice that will dominate your blog posts. By staying consistent in terms of your writing tone and style, your audience will feel comfortable visiting your blog and interacting with you, which leads to loyalty and relationships — the goal of many bloggers.

Writing for Your Niche

For example, popular faith blogger Ann Voskamp (www.annvoskamp.com), shown in Figure 4-1, has grown to celebrity status thanks in part to her highly recognizable writing style and unique voice. Her kind, thoughtful, and reflective tone matches her topic, and her loyal readers respond strongly to her. Her readers feel so connected and loyal to her writing, in fact, that they've made her a best-selling author and sought-after public speaker. If Ann suddenly began writing with a sarcastic, biting wit or a deeply formal and serious tone, her readers would surely find themselves with a bad case of whiplash! It wouldn't be long before her blog started to lose traffic and her books began to drop in sales — or no longer be published at all.

FIGURE 4-1:
Ann Voskamp's consistent and recognizable tone and style keep readers coming back for more.

Linking

Links are an extremely important component of any blog if you have goals to grow your blog's readership and moneymaking potential. Following are the two primary reasons for the importance of incoming links:

>> **Traffic from search engines:** More incoming links (particularly from popular blogs and websites) translate into a higher ranking on search engines. Higher search engine rankings lead to more incoming traffic and higher advertising rates. Sites such as Google rank pages with more incoming links from authoritative sources (as opposed to spam sites and sites with low-quality content) higher because the automated algorithm used to find and return search results assumes pages with more incoming links are better than those without incoming links. The theory is that no one would link to an inferior page, but many will link to a great page.

>> **Traffic from the links themselves:** More incoming links means more potential traffic to your blog from the blogs and websites that publish those links.

In short, incoming links provide more entry points for people to find your blog, so writing great content that other website owners and bloggers want to link to is very important to the success of your niche blog. This is particularly important when you're first establishing yourself online and don't yet have the power or funds to invest in search engine optimization, advertising, and other marketing strategies. But how do you get people to link to your blog? No matter how much great content you write, no one will link to your blog if they don't know it exists. That's where creating content with outgoing links can be helpful to growing your blog's audience.

When you write a blog post, be sure to link to your sources, provide links to additional information and related content. Turn on the trackback or backlink function in your blogging application (described in detail in Chapter 3 of Book 1), so other bloggers are notified via a pingback when you publish a post on your blog that links to their blog. Also, once you've published new content, click through each link in your blog post once to make sure they work. As your readers click those links, the website owners or bloggers that you link to will see those links within their own blog traffic statistic reports (Chapter 2 of Book 5 discusses traffic analytics), which puts you on their radar screens. This situation sets the ball in motion for you to start a relationship with those other site owners and bloggers. When they visit your blog and see the great content you publish, they may decide to use your blog as a source for their own posts, which can lead to more traffic to your blog in the future.

TIP

It only takes a few seconds to provide links to sources and additional information within your blog posts. Be sure to do so, because outgoing links can lead to indirect blog traffic just as incoming links can lead to direct blog traffic.

Finding inspiration for new content

Expanding the post possibilities for your niche topic can sometimes take additional work in terms of reading and researching. That's because it's easy to have blogger's block when you're writing about a very specific and narrow topic like you do on a niche blog. It's reasonable to assume that you won't be motivated to write great posts every day, but for your blog to grow, you need to publish content frequently and consistently. With that in mind, take a look at the following suggestions to get your creative juices flowing and come up with new post ideas. You can also find out more about avoiding blogger's block in Chapter 2 of Book 1:

>> **Read other blogs and websites.** Visit other blogs and websites that publish content related to your niche topic and find out what they're writing about.

>> **Check Google Trends.** Using Google Trends, you can find the search terms that are currently the most popular on Google. If people are searching for a term related to your niche topic, not only could it make for an interesting blog post, but you could get some of that search traffic! The process of using Google Trends is described in detail in Chapter 3 of this Book.

>> **Check your Google Alerts.** Set up a Google Alert for keywords related to your blog's niche topic using the steps in Chapter 3 of this Book. Then check your Google Alerts messages to find the recent related content people are publishing on other websites and blogs.

>> **Conduct a social media search.** If people are talking about your niche blog topic on social media, you might find ideas for posts there! Follow the steps in Chapter 3 of this Book to search your favorite platforms for keywords related to your niche.

>> **Conduct a YouTube (www.youtube.com) search.** You never know what kinds of videos people are uploading to YouTube. Conduct a search on YouTube using keywords related to your niche topic and see what comes up. You just might find an interesting video that you can either embed or link to in your own blog post or that gives you inspiration for a new blog post.

WARNING

Never republish content on your blog that you find on another website or blog. This is a violation of copyright laws (if you don't obtain permission to do so first). It can also hurt your search traffic over time because search engines such as Google downgrade sites that lack original content and might even blacklist them as spam.

Branding Your Blog

After you have chosen your blog's niche topic, take some time to think about your blog's branding. In simplest terms, your blog's *brand* is a representation of who you are and what you do that becomes easily recognizable to your readers and other bloggers. You can create tangible representations of your blog's brand by creating a unique header and logo as well as a specific color scheme, font, and overall design aesthetic. Consistent visual elements can go a long way when it comes to building your online brand.

Although a corporate blog has a built-in brand to create a blog around, a niche blogger has to create their own brand from scratch. Don't be intimidated. Building a brand is fun! Start by thinking of what you want your blog to represent. What will your blog's content communicate to readers on a high level? Will your blog be serious or fun? Do you anticipate your audience will be made up primarily of men or women, teens or senior citizens, local or global readers? Consider your message and your audience members and what you want to provide to them on your blog. In other words, what can you promise your audience that they can be sure to find on your blog every time they visit? That's your brand promise. Then choose the unique design, header, colors, and voice that best represent and communicate that brand promise to your audience and stick to it!

TIP

Branding isn't just about images. It can also be about words! Some blogs include a tagline as part of their blog name or header image. Play around and see what you come up with that's a fit for your blog.

The Hispana Global (`www.hispanaglobal.net`), shown in Figure 4-2, provides a great example of a well-branded blog. The colors and images are consistent throughout, which immediately sends a message that the blog is well-organized and that the blogger has given the blog time and attention. Additionally, images of blog author, Jeannette Kaplun, are easily visible in multiple locations on the blog's landing page making it clear who is behind this beautiful blog. Right in the middle of the blog's landing page is a brief explanation of what readers can expect: "beauty, recipes, travel & tips for busy women." The button in the middle of the page labeled Hispana Global En Español alerts readers to the fact that this is a bilingual blog.

FIGURE 4-2:
Hispana Global is a well-branded blog.

It's important to understand that much of successful brand-building comes less from the tangible symbols of a brand and more from the intangible elements. For example, no one cared much when Walmart changed its logo in 2009, but they would care if Walmart shifted its brand promise from low prices to something like luxury shopping. Consumers would be unlikely to accept that change because they have expectations for the Walmart brand that they have come to rely on. When Walmart consistently meets those consumer expectations, the company's brand value grows, and consumers feel a sense of security with it. That security leads to brand loyalty, repeat business, and word-of-mouth marketing from a powerful group of consumer-brand advocates.

The same process holds true for your blog. Your content, your voice, your style, and your visuals should consistently communicate your brand message, image, and promise. If you fail to do so, your readers will become confused and might abandon you and your blog in lieu of another that meets their needs time and again. There are a lot of blogs out there, and even the smallest niche blog has competition within the blogosphere. Don't let your readers get away by disappointing them. Remember, your blog's brand extends beyond your blog design. It's inherent in your content as well. Be consistent.

The rule of brand consistency applies to your online activities that occur off of your blog as well. From the comments that you leave on other blogs and in forums to the guest posts that you write for other blogs, and everything in between, successful bloggers develop an online persona (or brand) that follows them everywhere they go and in everything they do. That's how you build a powerful online brand that helps you build your online presence, establish yourself as an expert, drive traffic to your blog, and build relationships.

TIP

To truly understand branding, pick up a copy of *Branding For Dummies* (John Wiley & Sons, Inc., 2014), by Bill Chiaravalle and Barbara Findlay Schenck, and start to familiarize yourself with the tools and techniques experts use to create powerful brands.

Networking and Commenting

You might be surprised to find out that you can directly *and* indirectly find ideas for content to publish on your own blog by networking with other bloggers and commenting on their blogs, particularly blogs related to your niche topic. First, reading other blogs is one of the best ways to keep up with the online conversation about your niche topic. By reaching out to the bloggers who write blogs about similar topics to your own, you can interact in a dialogue that might spark creative ideas for your own blog. It's very possible that those other bloggers might begin sending tips to you and sharing news, opinions, and more, which can provide further content for your blog.

Networking is critical to niche blogging success because you're writing about a very narrow topic and competing against much larger blogs and websites. Without deep pockets and extensive manpower, the typical niche blogger has to rely on building relationships to grow their blogs. That's not a bad thing. In fact, it's probably a very good thing, because relationships can far outlast short traffic boosts that ads and promotions can deliver to larger blogs.

Writing great content for your niche blog comes from your ability to write interesting, original content, but it also comes from networking, joining conversations, and finding out what people want from your blog and your niche topic in general. As your reputation grows in relation to your blog topic, other bloggers will turn to you for your opinions as the expert in your niche. This is another way you can find more content for your blog.

Much of a blog's success comes from the open community and the relationships built within that community among people who share each other's content, talk about it, and drive traffic to it. Don't underestimate the power of online relationships and conversations in terms of growing your blog. Instead, create content that enhances those conversations and relationships.

Of course, a lot of your blog content will be related to your personal opinions, experiences, and knowledge, but it's equally important to understand *all* the content your potential audience is looking for related to your topic. If you want your blog to grow, your job is to deliver a balance of content that matches your needs for your blog as well as your audience's. After all, a blog is nothing more than a one-man show if there's no audience reading it and starting dialogues around it.

Creating Off-Blog Content for Your Niche Blog

As discussed earlier in this chapter, the most successful bloggers (even broad-topic bloggers) don't hide out on their own blogs. Instead, they're active, participating members of the larger blogging community. In other words, if your goal is to become a successful blogger, you need to spend as much time participating in activities off of your blog as you do on your blog. Remember, blogging is part of the social web. Notice the word *social*? If you want to grow your blog, particularly a niche blog that caters to a narrower audience by definition, you need to be social.

A lot of the time you spend off of your blog is in participating in direct and indirect promotional activities and relationship-building efforts. Commenting on other blogs and on forums related to your blog's niche are both off-blog activities that can help you build relationships and drive traffic to your blog. Additionally, you can pursue specific promotional efforts to grow your blog, which are discussed in detail in Book 6.

Niche blogs are the perfect type of blog to grow through off-blog content — the content you create and share using other tools than your blog. Take a look at the examples in the following sections and start thinking how you can apply them to your own niche blog. Depending on your niche topic and the audience you build around it, targeted off-blog content tactics can work very well in helping you to meet your blogging goals. Be sure to read *Digital Marketing All-in-One For Dummies*, by Stephanie Diamond (John Wiley & Sons, Inc., 2019).

Email campaigns

Many niche bloggers conduct their own publicity campaigns by creating a list of subscribers and emailing information to them as appropriate. For example, bloggers email updates, guest post submissions, articles for republishing, interview submissions, invitations to webinars, and more in an effort to further build relationships using content published outside of their blogs. If you send information that is truly useful to the people on your email list, they're more likely to appreciate receiving it.

Try to make sure your emails are personalized. No one wants to receive mass emails from people who don't take the time to get to know their needs and preferences. That's the technique spammers use, and bloggers call it *blog blasting*. You don't want to be grouped in the same category as spammers!

TIP

Think like a public relations professional and create emails that are valued by the people you send them to. The last thing you want is to look like an email spammer. If you don't inundate your email list with messages and only send useful information, you should get positive feedback.

Newsletter subscriptions

Similar to email campaigns, many bloggers send formal newsletters to their subscribed readers on a weekly, biweekly, or monthly basis. Unlike email campaigns, the format of these newsletters is typically the same from one mailing to the next. They are sent on a consistent, predictable schedule rather than on an as-needed basis.

Your newsletter can include content that isn't on your blog as well as links to content that is published on your blog. The key to creating a useful newsletter isn't simply republishing the content that readers can already find on your blog. Including links and excerpts to that content is fine, but your newsletter content should be original and enhance the content on your blog.

Life with Tanay (www.lifewithtanay.com), shown in Figure 4-3, provides a good example of promoting a blog newsletter by offering a sign-up window on the blog's homepage.

FIGURE 4-3:
Life with Tanay offers a newsletter subscription for readers when they arrive on the site.

You can use a number of email tools that are available online to create and send newsletters. For example, Constant Contact (www.constantcontact.com), which is shown in Figure 4-4, is one of the most popular tools for creating standardized email campaigns such as newsletters.

Other options include but are not limited to:

» MailChimp (www.mailchimp.com)

» Sendinblue (www.sendinblue.com)

» Aweber (www.aweber.com)

» HubSpot (www.hubspot.com)

» MailerLite (www.mailerlite.com)

» Emma (www.myemma.com)

» iContact (www.icontact.com)

» Vertical Response (www.verticalresponse.com)

» Moosend (www.moosend.com)

Each tool offers similar features. Be sure to compare the current offerings on each site before you commit to using a particular tool. Learn more about distributing content in Chapter 4 of Book 6.

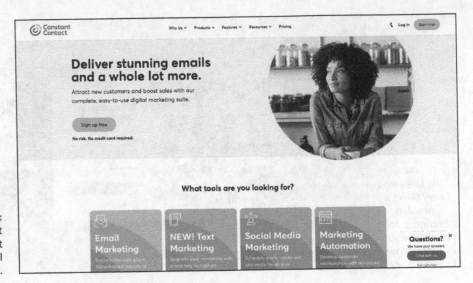

FIGURE 4-4:
Constant Contact is one of the most popular email tools.

TIP

Most email tools offer free trials or free services to people who need to send small volumes of emails. Be sure to look for these offers.

E-books and printables

A *printable* is downloadable digital content that a reader prints out at home after downloading a file from a blog, website, or email newsletter. Printables are sometimes available to readers for free. However, bloggers who utilize printables to enhance and add to their online-only content tend to create at least some printables that can only be downloaded after the reader pays a small fee.

Typically, a printable is helpful in some way such as to be used for home organization, learning, or holiday planning. They almost always include graphic design elements as well as text. Printables are especially useful to niche bloggers because they offer an additional way to highlight and share highly focused content. For example, an education niche blogger may create printables such as sticker design sheets, lesson plan calendars, educational worksheets, or coloring pages and activities.

TIP

Creating printables that can be downloaded and shared is a great way to add value to your blog posts and encourage your readers to share links with their friends and families who may benefit from downloading and printing the content as well.

E-books are digital books that anyone can write. Readers download them from the Internet, but unlike printables, they are not meant to be printed out after downloading. E-books have become one of the hottest promotional tools that a blogger can add to their marketing arsenal. Of course, you need to write a great e-book, with content your audience actually finds useful, or it won't be successful. You can check out the nearby sidebar for tips on writing and promoting an e-book, but first you need to determine your objectives for writing an e-book. Some bloggers use e-books as a way to further establish themselves as experts in their fields, but others use them solely to earn money by charging a price for them. These are two very different e-book strategies, but both can work depending on your goals for your niche blog.

If your blogging goal is to broaden your online presence or establish yourself as an expert in a field related to your niche topic, an e-book can help. E-books have a reputation for going viral, meaning people like to share the best ones. They talk about great e-books and pass them on to their friends. This viral tendency works perfectly to support a strategy of growing your online presence and establishing yourself as an expert. As more people get their hands on your e-book, more people will recognize your name and blog and associate them with being sources for authoritative information on your niche subject.

If those are your goals, your e-books should be made freely available to anyone who wants to download them to ensure maximum sharing and exposure. Provide a Creative Commons license on your e-book so people know they can share it freely with proper attribution. (Chapter 4 of Book 1 provides details about Creative Commons licenses and copyrights.)

For maximum exposure of your e-book, don't put a *gateway* in front of it. In other words, don't require people to provide their email addresses or any other information to access your e-book. If you want to maximize exposure, putting up a deterrent before a person can even see the contents of the e-book will ruin your hard work in writing a great e-book. Also, make sure that everyone visiting your blog immediately knows that you have made an e-book available for them to download and read. For example, Simply Stacie (www.simplystacie.net) offers a free e-book, which visitors see immediately on her blog's landing page (see Figure 4-5).

REMEMBER

E-books that are free and available for sharing are downloaded significantly more often than e-books that require email address submission or payment prior to a person downloading them.

FIGURE 4-5: Simply Stacie offers a free e-book at the bottom of her blog's homepage.

If your goal for your blog is to make money, then you probably care less about how much your e-book is shared and more about how you can maximize earnings from it. If that's the case, then you should charge a fee for people to access your e-book with the understanding that the number of people willing to pay for your e-book could be very small unless you've already established yourself as an expert in your niche topic with something very unique and useful to say. Set a reasonable price for your e-book ($4.99–9.99 is a common price range, depending on your expertise and how well known you are within your niche), and include copyright and disclaimer information indicating that the content of your e-book may not be shared. You can set up a free account with PayPal to accept payments so that people can download and read your e-book for a fee.

TIP

Promote your e-book through links and images in your blog's sidebar, within your blog posts, emails, newsletters, and social media pages. The key to generating downloads of your e-book is to raise awareness of it and make people understand why it will be useful to them.

Don't feel like you have to stop with e-books and printables. Although e-books and online printable tools are amazing promotional tools in terms of establishing your expertise and growing your blog audience, many bloggers, particularly niche bloggers who successfully establish themselves as experts in their fields through their blog content and activities, are able to pursue other writing opportunities as well. Don't be afraid to think big!

TIPS FOR WRITING AND PROMOTING E-BOOKS

When you sit down to write an e-book, you need to follow a few basic guidelines to ensure your final product will meet readers' expectations.

For example, your e-book shouldn't look like a typical document typed in a common word-processing application such as Microsoft Word. Instead, you need to make sure your e-book is visually appealing. Use images and diagrams to break up text-heavy pages and write in short paragraphs as well as bulleted lists to add white space to your pages.

Because people read e-books on their phones or computer screens, use a larger font as well as a typeface that is easier to read onscreen than the common 10-point or 12-point Times New Roman. Save your e-book in PDF format so that people can easily view and download it with the free Adobe Acrobat Reader software.

Your e-book should offer information that's truly useful to readers. Consider their needs and create an e-book that addresses them just as you would if you were developing a new product — that's what your e-book is after all. Write in an inviting tone rather than a highly professional one. Your e-book should be easy to read yet packed with meaningful information.

To promote your e-book, contact the bloggers you have relationships with as well as others who blog about topics related to your niche. Offer to send them a copy of your e-book, telling them they can feel free to offer a link to it on their blog. Offer to write a guest post or provide an excerpt for them to publish on their own blogs.

Talk about your e-book on social networking sites and invite your readers to do the same. Include a link to your e-book in your email signature and anywhere else that you can provide a link.

Most importantly, make sure your e-book is available without requiring information from your readers, such as asking for an email address before the download is available. Offer your e-book for free with a Creative Commons license that invites people to share it across the web, if your goal is to boost your online exposure, blog traffic, and status as an expert in your niche topic.

Social networking and content sharing

Social media and content sharing offers a variety of ways that niche bloggers can share content both on and off their blogs to gain exposure and traffic. Depending on your blog's niche topic, some opportunities might work better than others in helping you reach your blogging goals. The similarity between the various methods of sharing content off of your blog through social media platforms and content sharing sites is making your content freely available for others. That's where the term *viral* comes from — when a piece of online content spreads across a wide audience through sharing from one person to the next. It's a powerful thing that you can leverage for your blog's success. The following sections highlight a few easy tools you can use to share the off-blog material supporting your blog in order to give that content, you, and your blog added exposure and recognition, which just might lead to more traffic and moneymaking opportunities.

YouTube videos

YouTube (www.youtube.com), shown in Figure 4-6, is the most popular website for uploading and sharing videos with people from around the world. To begin sharing video content with the world, simply sign-up for a free YouTube account and start uploading your own videos! Be sure to include a link back to your blog in your videos or YouTube profile and video description areas. Make sure you upload your videos so they're available for the public to both view and share by linking and embedding them into their own blogs and websites. That's the only way a video can truly go viral — if there are no barriers to sharing it. You can find out more about creating and uploading content to YouTube in Book 8.

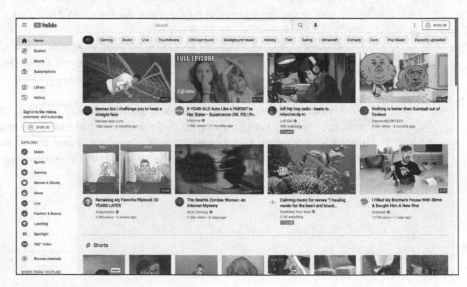

FIGURE 4-6:
YouTube provides an opportunity for niche bloggers to upload and share video content.

Facebook and LinkedIn groups and pages

Facebook (www.facebook.com) and LinkedIn (www.linkedin.com) are two of the most popular social networking sites online. Facebook has a global audience of billions — yes, billions — of subscribers who come from all walks of life. You can create a personal profile on Facebook as well as a Facebook Group and Page for your blog brand or business. As an example, Figure 4-7 shows the Facebook Page for my personal blog, Resourceful Mommy.

The audience of LinkedIn users is typically focused on more professional, business-related people and networking opportunities. With LinkedIn, you can share content by answering questions and setting up your profile notifications to let your connections know when you upload new content to a wide variety of social sites such as SlideShare (discussed in the next section). You can find out more about social networking in Chapter 3 of Book 6.

SlideShare presentations

SlideShare (www.slideshare.net) is a website where you can upload presentations, either from a file location on your computer or from an online cloud platform such as Google Drive, in order to share that presentation content with the online audience around the world. It's particularly useful for people who write niche blogs related to business or academics because they can upload additional content that their readers are likely to be interested in and that further establishes them as experts in their subjects. You can see an example of content uploaded to SlideShare in Figure 4-8.

WARNING

Be careful when you create and upload content such as videos and presentations where you use images or audio. You should be certain you have permission to use all images and audio in your content, unless you can clearly claim that the content used is protected under the terms of fair use, which are described in detail in Chapter 4 of Book 1.

Flickr

Flickr (www.flickr.com), shown in Figure 4-9, is undoubtedly the most popular sites for uploading and sharing images publicly. Whether you want to share a photograph or an image of a diagram, flowchart, or cartoon, you can do so on a photo-sharing site such as Flickr. Be sure to apply a Creative Commons license to your uploaded content and upload only images that you own. A large audience of bloggers and website owners search photo-sharing sites every day looking for royalty-free images that they're allowed to use on their blogs. Depending on your blog's niche topic, image sharing can be an effective way to drive traffic to your blog, build relationships, and expand your online exposure.

TIP

Embed your blog's URL in your uploaded images as a watermark to ensure your blog is always referenced as the copyright owner and source.

Self-published books

Moving from writing online only to writing for print is a natural progression for many bloggers. Ask a room full of bloggers if they've ever dreamed of authoring a book and you'll see a lot of hands in the air. This is an especially natural path for niche bloggers because they focus so heavily on just one area and often become experts in that field through their years of researching, posting, and networking with others passionate about the same subject matter.

REMEMBER

While using a blog as a jumping off point for a book deal is a dream of many, the fact is that it is sometimes an unattainable goal. Even the most popular blog may not be an easy sell to a publishing house who needs their books to be profitable once on the shelves. That's where the self-publishing industry comes into play. Many bloggers, especially those already creating off-blog content such as a product or pay-to-print resources, turn to self-publishing to create additional content in the form of self-published books. With existing connections in the area of their blog niche and a ready-made community of readers, a blogger interested in writing a book related to their niche blog topic may find that marketing and selling that book is an easy next step. If you're involved in offline communities related to your blog's topic such as affinity groups or conferences, you've got additional markets in which to distribute your printed content.

Don't give up on your dream of writing a book if working with an outside publisher turns out to be an unreachable goal!

3
Corporate and Non-Profit Blogging

Contents at a Glance

Chapter **1**

Starting a Business Blog

Business blogging has moved from being an edgy way for corporations to interact with customers to being a standard practice in some industries. Huge corporations, solo entrepreneurs, and every business in between recognize the power of the blogosphere and online conversation in boosting both customer relationships and sales. For-profit companies, non-profit companies, government agencies, and NGOs have all discovered the benefits of blogging. However, to some business owners and CEOs, blogging can still seem like an unnecessary effort as they struggle to make the connection between traditional marketing and the opportunities blogging provides. This chapter helps you understand why companies blog, which companies are blogging well, and how a business blog can benefit you or your place of employment.

Any business can benefit from a company blog in some way. I built my entire post-teaching career from the idea of building an online writing portfolio while staying home with two small children. Today, I have a thriving independent writing and social media marketing business, and it's all thanks to the power of blogging and the online conversation that happens on the social web. My story is not unique. Many business owners around the world have already realized blogging offers a potential opportunity to build their businesses, and many have achieved great success from that knowledge and a lot of effort. The best part about blogging is that you can do it, too.

REMEMBER

Business blogging isn't exactly the same as personal blogging. You have to deal with more unwritten rules and do's and don'ts related to business blogging simply because what is published on a business blog has a direct impact on a company's brand and future sales. Don't worry. You find out all the do's and don'ts in Chapter 5 later in this Book. Right now, focus on the why's and why not's and save the do's and don'ts for later, when you have a better understanding of business blogging overall.

TIP

Don't start a business blog out of a sense of obligation or because everyone else is doing it. A successful business blog requires deep commitment in terms of time and passion. Set your goals and understand what you're getting yourself into before you jump into business blogging.

Revealing Why Organizations Blog

Companies large and small start business blogs for countless reasons. Frequently, companies have goals to generate sales directly or indirectly from their web presence, and a blog appears to be a natural extension of reaching those objectives. Following are several reasons why companies blog (note that this list isn't comprehensive):

>> To build brand awareness

>> To network with other businesses and experts

>> To build relationships with existing and potential customers

>> To boost sales

>> To communicate marketing messages and promotions

>> To learn more about their customers

>> To launch and promote fundraising campaigns and charity initiatives

>> To manage their reputation by debunking rumors and nudging conversations in the desired direction

>> To seem real and human in consumers' eyes rather than as an untouchable entity

There's much more to business blogging than trying to boost sales or raise funds. In fact, a business blog that focuses entirely on marketing and promotion is unlikely to be successful. Instead, the secret to publishing a business blog that has a chance for success is to write content that's truly useful and meaningful to the consumers who are likely to want and need your products and services.

REMEMBER

The most successful business blogs are written for consumers, *not* for companies. That's the first shift in thinking you need to make before you can start planning your business blogging strategy.

With that in mind, companies blog for more reasons than just to generate sales. Perhaps the most powerful thing a business blog can deliver is a chance to build relationships with consumers both locally and around the world. In the 21st century, companies have realized that the most powerful brands and businesses are those that have built strong relationships with consumers. Relationship brands, such as Apple and Harley Davidson, which allow consumers to experience the brands in their own ways or with larger groups and develop deep loyalty to them, are some of the strongest brands in the world, thanks primarily to the loyal group of consumers who band together in support of those brands.

REMEMBER

A business blog offers a perfect way for companies to do more than just talk *at* consumers. By using a blog, companies can talk *with* customers and build the powerful relationships that brand managers covet. For some companies, a blog is a key component of their customer service strategy!

Furthermore, business blogs provide the opportunity for companies to start conversations about their products, services, and brands. They can nudge those online conversations in the right direction and then let them flourish. Loyal consumers who have built relationships with a company and brand will talk about it and defend it, particularly in the online community. Leverage that conversation by providing a venue for it and by getting involved to keep it going. You can do it with a blog.

A business blog is an incredible marketing tool for several reasons. You can

>> **Display your expertise.** Establish your business as *the* source for information related to the types of products and services you provide.

>> **Reward your fans.** Present special offers and discounts to thank your loyal readers.

>> **Shown another side of your brand.** Invite customers in to get to know your brand better and see another side of your company.

>> **Get to know your customers.** Listen to and respond to your customer's comments.

The best part about publishing a business blog is that the monetary investment is negligible in comparison to traditional marketing initiatives. You can't beat it! My response to clients who ask me whether they should have blogs for their businesses is always the same: "The question isn't why should you have a business blog, but why *shouldn't* you have a business blog?"

Unfortunately, the blogosphere contains a lot of spam and highly personal blogs, which can give some people a skewed interpretation of what blogging can actually do for a business. The truth of the matter is that spam is just a fact of life on the Internet. As much as everyone online wishes spam would go away, that's not going to happen anytime soon or likely ever. That doesn't mean that a business blog will automatically come across as spammy or that companies shouldn't try to utilize the platform. In terms of personal blogs, they're also a fact of life in the online world because the blogosphere is open to just about anyone. To counter the stereotype that blogs are created for personal reasons only, you need to make sure your business blog is well-designed, written, and managed in a professional way, and is distinctly different in design and content from a personal blog. You can find out more about designing a business blog and creating content in Chapters 2 and 4 of this Book, respectively.

Finding Companies That Do It Right

A lot of companies have blogs, but many of them aren't fully leveraging the opportunities that the blogosphere offers because they're not publishing the kind of content they should be, and they're not engaging their readers. The strength of a blog comes from interesting, unique content written in a voice that captivates an audience and makes them want to join the conversation. If your business blog posts read like press releases or corporate rhetoric, no one is going to feel compelled to return after the first visit.

Before you get to know the do's and don'ts of writing great content for your business blog, take some time to peruse the blogosphere and start reading company blogs. Read business blogs from large and small companies and blogs within your industry and outside of it. Find blogs from businesses you're actually interested in and start reading and leaving comments. What do you like about those blogs as a consumer? What do you dislike?

Chances are good that if you don't like something about a business blog, you're not alone, and the same concept holds true for your own business blog. You can discover more about finding business blogs to bookmark and understanding your blog's audience in Chapter 2 of this Book. In the meantime, take a look at the examples of blogs that follow to understand what business blogging is truly about. These companies each offer great content that consumers are interested in and *believe*. And that's where successful business blogging begins.

Southwest Airlines

Southwest Airlines is known as one of the first companies to publish a blog from the employees' perspectives — Nuts About Southwest, shown in Figure 1-1. The Nuts About Southwest blog's debut was revolutionary because it gave employees an opportunity to engage the consumers they work for every day. Naturally, employees had some rules they had to follow, but the free flow of information and conversation between Southwest bloggers and the consumers who read the Nuts About Southwest blog made a significant difference in helping the airline grow and develop relationships with its consumers.

FIGURE 1-1: The original Southwest Airlines blog was a bit nutty, in a good way, included social networking, media sharing, and Twitter links.

Over the years the Nuts About Southwest blog grew and evolved into a larger Southwest online community with a blog as one component, shown in Figure 1-2, rather than the star of the show. This evolution into a community was natural on the heels of such a successful, ground-breaking blog. Southwest Airlines achieved this goal by providing multiple ways for members of the online community to engage with its primary brand.

You can see exactly how much the leaders of Southwest Airlines understand the power of the blogosphere as a tool to build relationships and share information by reading the community's welcome message (shown in Figure 1-2, or by visiting https://community.southwest.com and selecting "Welcome to the Community!" at the top of the page). Within the text, the company makes this knowledge very clear by saying, "We think you'll like it here. The Southwest Airlines Community is full of people just like you, who enjoy low-cost travel and great Customer Service. This is where they tell their stories and share their knowledge, and we're inviting you to join in."

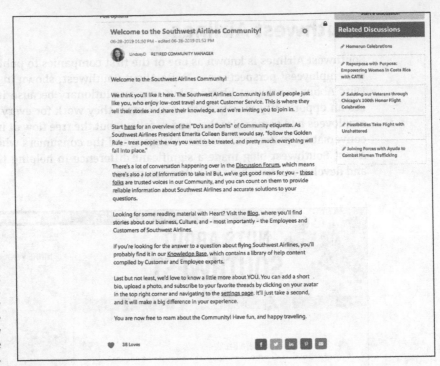

Welcome to the Southwest Airlines Community!

06-28-2019 01:50 PM - edited 06-28-2019 01:52 PM

LindseyD   RETIRED COMMUNITY MANAGER

Welcome to the Southwest Airlines Community!

We think you'll like it here. The Southwest Airlines Community is full of people just like you, who enjoy low-cost travel and great Customer Service. This is where they tell their stories and share their knowledge, and we're inviting you to join in.

Start here for an overview of the "Do's and Don'ts" of Community etiquette. As Southwest Airlines President Emerita Colleen Barrett would say, "follow the Golden Rule – treat people the way you want to be treated, and pretty much everything will fall into place."

There's a lot of conversation happening over in the Discussion Forum, which means there's also a *lot* of information to take in! But, we've got good news for you – these folks are trusted voices in our Community, and you can count on them to provide reliable information about Southwest Airlines and accurate solutions to your questions.

Looking for some reading material with Heart? Visit the Blog, where you'll find stories about our business, Culture, and – most importantly – the Employees and Customers of Southwest Airlines.

If you're looking for the answer to a question about flying Southwest Airlines, you'll probably find it in our Knowledge Base, which contains a library of help content compiled by Customer and Employee experts.

Last but not least, we'd love to know a little more about YOU. You can add a short bio, upload a photo, and subscribe to your favorite threads by clicking on your avatar in the top right corner and navigating to the settings page. It'll just take a second, and it will make a big difference in your experience.

You are now free to roam about the Community! Have fun, and happy traveling.

38 Loves

Related Discussions

Homerun Celebrations

Repurpose with Purpose: Empowering Women in Costa Rica with CATIE

Saluting our Veterans through Chicago's 100th Honor Flight Celebration

Possibilities Take Flight with Unshattered

Joining Forces with Ayuda to Combat Human Trafficking

FIGURE 1-2:
Southwest Airlines builds community with a welcome message for new readers and site users.

The welcome page also succeeds in setting reader expectations related to participation, encouraging everyone to follow the Golden Rule and linking to a set of community do's and don'ts, shown in Figure 1-3.

Finally, the welcome page introduces users to the option to personalize their experience in settings so that Southwest Airlines can get to know a little bit about them as well. Overall, it's well done and shows exactly how much the people at Southwest Airlines understand how a blog community should work and how the content within it should be written.

TIP

If you want your employees to write about your business, take a look at the content on the Southwest Airlines blog to get ideas for the types of posts that make an employee-written blog interesting.

Dell

Dell's company blog (www.dell.com/blog), shown in Figure 1-4, focuses on providing the following through a blog format:

>> Company updates

>> Product information

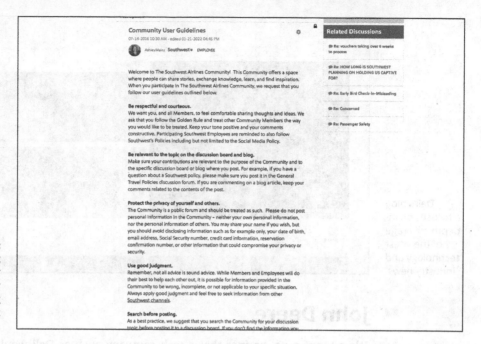

FIGURE 1-3:
Southwest Airlines sets clear expectations for readers engaging with their content and community.

» Technology solutions

» Services and support

Articles are industry-focused and written by technology professionals, either employed by Dell or as a Dell consultant. Blog content is not written with the average consumer in mind, but the service and support section provides a bridge between the general customer and the professional support they may need.

Dell had some blogging troubles in the past, though. After being caught in an attempt to quash a blog post that painted Dell's sales process in a negative light, when an employee shared secrets of getting discounts at Dell with the popular blog The Consumerist (http://consumerist.com), Dell has since put a lot of effort into using the blog as a more effective social media tool. Dell received a huge amount of negative press and backlash for trying to bury this negative conversation about its brand and business. Since then, the company has made a conscious effort to revamp its social media strategy, including its blog content, in order to encourage online conversations rather than stop them. The current Dell blog and social media profiles are intended to be more transparent and offer more customer service and meaningful content than they did in the past.

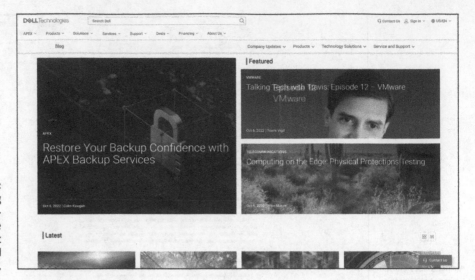

FIGURE 1-4:
Dell's blog focuses on in-depth coverage of the latest technology and industry news.

John Deere

It's a bit of a no-brainer that a tech company such as Dell would dive into the blogging world, but what about companies that you might not expect to be leading the online charge? John Deere, known for their big green tractors, has not one but *six* online publications:

>> **John Deere News (www.johndeere.com/news):** The online source of the latest John Deere news including community impact stories, employee pieces, company value statements, and more.

>> **The Furrow (https://www.deere.com/en/publications/the-furrow):** Shown in Figure 1-5, the online version of the magazine for farmers John Deere has been publishing since 1895!

>> **The Dirt (https://www.deere.com/en/publications/the-dirt):** An online magazine focused on construction industry news and stories.

>> **The Landing (https://www.deere.com/en/publications/the-landing):** An online magazine with content primarily written about the logging industry.

>> **The Worksite Journal (https://www.deere.com/en/publications/the-worksite-journal):** An online magazine focused on providing practical tips and success stories.

>> **Power Connect (https://www.deere.com/en/stories/power-connect):** Online stories of how customers are using John Deere products to find solutions.

FIGURE 1-5:
The Furrow is John Deere's online magazine for farmers.

Each one of John Deere's online publications invites the reader and customer to connect in a variety of ways. Customers are invited to submit their own related stories for consideration, as shown in Figure 1-6 on The Dirt's landing page. Each individually themed blog also allows the reader to sign up to receive content via email. Every publication keeps the end goal of sales at top of mind — and at the top of the page — with links to products and the Find a Dealer tool.

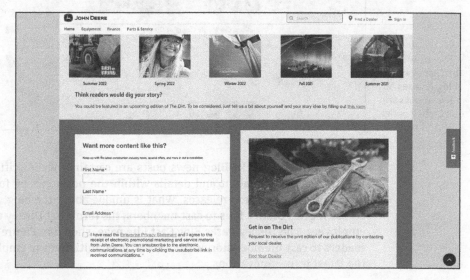

FIGURE 1-6:
John Deere draws customers in with content then connects with them via email and dealer information.

Disney Parks

Disney Parks, part of the Walt Disney Company, jumped into the blogging and social media game fairly early, engaging with online influencers and bloggers and then creating an in-house blog of their own. Disney fans, sometimes known as Disneyphiles, are some of the most brand-loyal consumers in the world. It made perfect sense for the Disney Parks to create an online destination where customers could receive company news and engage with the content through comments and social shares.

The Disney Parks Blog (www.disneyparks.disney.go.com), shown in Figure 1-7, provides the latest news about all of the Disney parks and resort destinations as well as the travel company, Adventures By Disney. Rather than reading like boring press releases, each news item comes across more like an interesting story in blog post format.

FIGURE 1-7:
The Disney Parks blog focuses on news about various Disney parks and resorts.

While the Disney Parks Blog news posts are certainly well-written and popular with readers, the content and details within the posts can be found on a variety of sites due to press releases. What is unique about the blog, however, is the access it gives Disney fans to cast members, the term that Disney uses for its park employees. The Disney Parks Blog Cast Life page, shown in Figure 1-8, introduces readers to cast member stories from social good initiatives to employee profiles to the latest team innovations.

FIGURE 1-8:
The Cast Life page gives Disney fans a look at employee stories.

The blog provides readers with more than just stories to read, offering up video content and interactive content, such as the quiz page, shown in Figure 1-9. The blog also invites readers to connect on a variety of platforms by linking in the right sidebar to the Disney Parks social media properties.

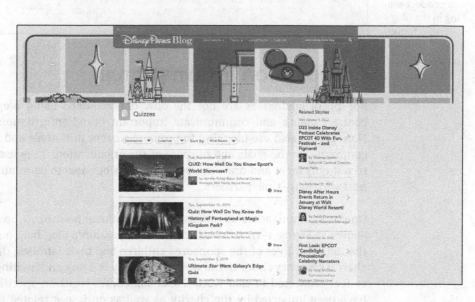

FIGURE 1-9:
The Disney Parks Blog offers interactive content.

Disney utilizes the footer of each page (shown in Figure 1-10) to focus on the call to action, which is to bring readers into the parks! There are vacation planning tools for the Disney Cruise Line, the Disney Parks, Adventures By Disney, as well as other Disney resorts such as Aulani in Hawaii. There are also links for guests to be able to visit Shop Disney, an online store.

FIGURE 1-10: Disney moves from story-telling to product selling in the blog's footer.

Compassion International

For-profit businesses are not the only organizations using blogs as a way to connect online and communicate important brand information with readers. Non-profits also use blogging to promote current initiatives and campaigns and communicate the goals and purpose of the organization. They use their websites to not only meet and draw in new supporters but also to communicate and connect with long-time partners.

One such organization is Compassion International (www.blog.compassion.com), shown in Figure 1-11. Stories found on Compassion's blog help paint a picture of the impacted lives of the sponsored children and their families, drawing existing charity sponsors closer to the work the charity is doing and inviting new sponsors to feel connected to that work. Posts sometimes focus on specific children who have been impacted by the charity as well as on issues related to the Christian non-profit from prayer to the role of the community pastor. The blog also keeps readers up to date on how current affairs are affecting the work Compassion is doing around the world.

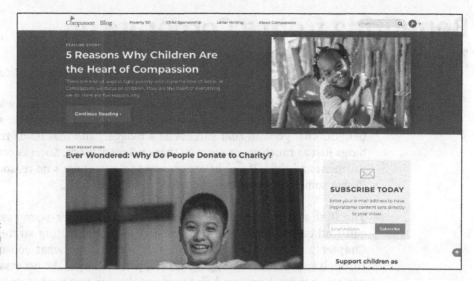

FIGURE 1-11:
The Compassion
International
blog.

Like most successful company blogs, the Compassion International blog includes a call to action, inviting readers to sponsor a child. This invitation is found in the horizontal navigation bar across the top of every page of the blog (see Figure 1-12). The site also contains areas focused on other important goals such as encouraging current sponsors to write letters to their sponsored children, explaining the history of Compassion, and answering questions about the work the organization is doing.

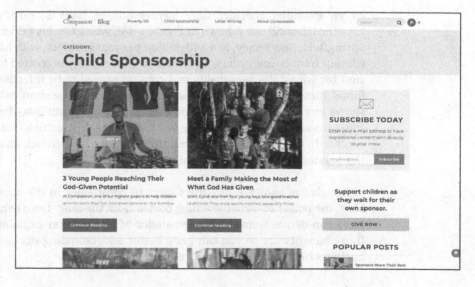

FIGURE 1-12:
Readers are
invited at the
top of the blog
to sponsor a
child through
Compassion
International.

Benefiting from a Corporate or Non-Profit Organization Blog

The benefits to publishing a business blog can be as big and wide as you want them to be. The truth is that you're in control of creating your success and the benefits that go with that success as a blogger, and that holds true for business blogs just as much as, or more so than, personal blogs. Success comes from commitment and time. If you have those two things, there's no reason that you can't derive some benefits and success from a business blog.

The first step is to determine what your goals are for your business blog. You can find out all about creating a business blog marketing strategy and goals in Chapter 2 of this Book. When you fully understand what you want to achieve through your business blogging efforts, you can target the necessary steps to help you reach them. However, before you get that far, you need to understand some of the most common benefits of business blogging. For many businesses and non-profits, the first objective that comes to mind is to increase sales or recruitment of donors, and a blog can certainly help both directly and indirectly in that area with links to your online store, special promotions and discounts, and current charity initiatives and campaigns. But business blogging is about so much more than increasing sales and raising money. In fact, if you look at business blogging as simply a tool to boost revenue, you're missing immeasurable opportunities to grow your business in the long term.

As an example, consider Gary Vaynerchuk of Wine Library TV, at `http://tv.winelibrary.com` (shown in Figure 1-13), who grew his father's wine store in Springfield, New Jersey, to a $50 million per year business, with half of those sales coming from online orders, all thanks to a video blog he created to share his passion for wines. His personality and content proved to be infectious, and he soon found himself called upon to speak at events and appear on national television shows as a social media expert. He even signed a multimillion-dollar book deal to share his social media experience and knowledge. If you think that a business blog can't help you grow your business, think of Gary Vaynerchuk and get inspired by the possibilities business blogs offer.

Although you can certainly use tactics to boost sales in the short term on your blog, the power of a business blog comes from the long-term benefits your company can derive from it. The remainder of this chapter explains what some of those benefits are so you can get a better understanding of the potential that a business blog can offer to your company.

FIGURE 1-13:
Gary Vaynerchuk's Wine Library TV blog helped him grow his business to $50 million per year.

Building an online presence

Blogging opens the doors for businesses to build online presences that are more expansive than anyone could have dreamed 10 or 20 years ago. With a blog, even the smallest business or organization can create a low-cost, professional-looking website and provide an online destination for readers to learn about the company, products, and purpose. By publishing frequent blog posts to that site, the business owner can build relationships with consumers, boost search engine optimization and search traffic, provide customer service, publicize promotions, recruit new supporters, establish the business and employees as experts, and sign up new non-profit volunteers. Truly, the opportunities are limited only by your own creativity.

REMEMBER

Many company websites run on the WordPress blogging platform. You'd be surprised at how many business websites are powered by a blogging application. Gone are the days of investing tens of thousands of dollars on web design and maintenance. This is especially helpful for start-ups, small business, and non-profits. Today, business owners can handle most of the technical aspects of their websites by themselves if those sites are built on an easy-to-use blogging platform.

TIP

Hiring a blog designer to help you create your business website and blog typically costs a lot less than it does to hire a web designer and developer to create a traditional website. When your blog and website are designed, you'll save money in the long run because, unlike a traditional website, you need very little technical knowledge to maintain and modify a website built on a blogging platform.

Because a blog is updated frequently, your business blog offers you more chances to connect with consumers both on and off your website because you always have something new to point people to and talk about. Unlike a static website that offers little to no fresh content for conversational purposes, blogs allow businesses to reach out to consumers and create a new way to interact with them that offers significant value over the one-sided informational and transactional websites that dominated the web in the past.

Marketing and publicity

A business blog is an amazing marketing tool. While there are certainly still business owners who remember the days before the Internet, many companies today take for granted the ease of heading online to promote their businesses. Long gone are the days of relying on *Yellow Pages* and newspaper ads to market your company. In fact, those types of marketing tactics are getting closer to obsolescence every day. In the 21st century, the majority of consumers turn to the Internet to find information about businesses, charities, products, and services. That's why it's critical that your business has a website, even if you don't actually sell any products online on an eCommerce platform. Today's Internet is an informational, transactional, and social place, and your business needs to join the conversation and be represented accordingly.

However, a fine line exists between publishing promotional content on your business blog that is useful and valued by readers and publishing so much promotional content that your blog is viewed as all marketing and no substance. At the core of your blog should be substance. Using the classic 80–20 rule, wherein it's estimated that typically 80 percent of a company's business comes from just 20 percent of its customers, you can apply the same percentages to your business blog content. Try to write 80 percent content that's useful, interesting, and meaningful to readers (substance) and 20 percent about discounts, publicity, and so on (promotional).

REMEMBER

Gauge your readers' reactions to your content mix over time and adjust as necessary to ensure you're meeting their expectations for your business blog. Remember, interaction is the key to business blogging success!

A company that does a good job of providing substance in its business blog is the Moz blog, at www.logodesignworks.com/blog (shown in Figure 1-14). While Moz offers a suite of products and services primarily focused on SEO (search engine optimization; see Book 5 Chapter 1 for more on this), their blog provides seemingly endless free tips and tools to readers. At the end of the day, Moz would like to convert readers to customers, but there's never a hard sell. Instead, the blog comes across as a helpful tool regardless of if you're planning on signing up for paid tools while you're there.

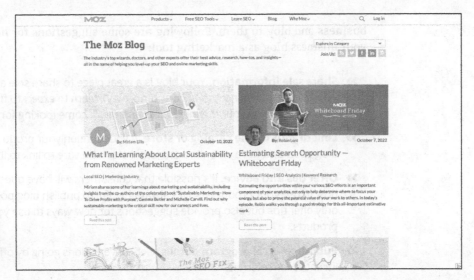

FIGURE 1-14:
The Moz blog provides free tools and resources to readers.

One of the most powerful aspects of business blogging is the potential to generate word-of-mouth marketing from the content you publish. If you can engage your audience members and get them talking about your business, products, charity, and services *outside* of your website, you've hit marketing gold. Blogs are a perfect tool to achieve that goal because they're conversational in nature. They're also filled with personality (at least the good ones are) that encourages readers to participate and build relationships with the bloggers and businesses behind them. Relationships drive customer loyalty and create vocal brand advocates who want to talk about the brands they love and are willing to defend those brands from criticism. This can be especially true for non-profit organizations whose blog readers unite around a common goal or initiative. When that conversation moves off your blog and turns into an online buzz, you've achieved another goal that marketing managers dream of.

The power of the social web comes from the conversations and buzz that occur on it. With a business blog, you have a chance to start those conversations, nurture them, and let them grow. As a marketer by profession, I think we live in the most incredible time because the power of the social web and blogging provides more opportunities for businesses to connect with consumers and drive word-of-mouth marketing wider and louder than ever!

TIP

Start thinking about the types of promotions and public relations posts that you can publish on your own business blog that would actually help your readers and put smiles on their faces. You don't want to bore them with promotional information. Instead, you want to make them feel like they're special because they take the time to read your blog. For instance, you can thank them for their loyalty by publishing exclusive discounts for blog readers only, further connecting your business and blog to them. Following are some suggestions for how you can use your business blog as a marketing tool:

>> **Share sale information.** Your blog is a great place to share sale and discount information with consumers. Over time, they'll learn to *expect* to find this type of information on your business blog, and they'll come looking for it.

>> **Link to your online catalog or store.** If you mention your products in your blog posts and have an online catalog or store, be sure to link to it!

>> **Offer tips and advice.** It's possible that consumers will have questions about how to use your products, so it's always helpful to publish blog posts that not only offer tips but also provide suggestions for new ways to use your products.

>> **Publish referral program details.** Get conversations going by offering an incentive for referrals.

>> **Hold a contest.** People love to win prizes. You can take advantage of that by holding contests on your blog. For example, hold a contest on your blog and offer a gift card for a future purchase from your business as the prize, or offer products as prizes. When you send the product to the winner, ask whether they'd like to write a review of the product for your blog or whether you could interview them about their experience using it.

>> **Answer questions.** Engage your blog readers by asking them to send questions to you, and then you can answer them on your business blog. If one person has a question, chances are good that they aren't the only one.

>> **Solicit customer stories.** People love to see their names and photos in lights, so to speak. Ask your customers to send in stories about their use of your products and publish them on your blog. It's likely each person you talk about on your blog will want to share the post with their friends.

>> **Share impact stories.** Let readers know how your non-profit is already impacting the lives of others and why their support is needed to continue the work.

>> **Include social sharing links on your posts.** Be sure to include a link or button that allows readers to share posts they enjoy through social networking sites as well as email. It's an easy way to foster an online buzz.

>> **Respond to all comments.** Make sure your readers feel valued! Respond to every comment left on your blog and keep the conversation going.

The possibilities are practically endless. Don't be afraid to think outside the box and be creative about using your business blog as a marketing tool. You can find out more about writing content for your business blog in Chapter 4 of this Book.

Brand building

A *brand* is the message, image, and promise that your business, product, or service consistently, persistently, and repeatedly communicates to consumers. Branding should include recognizable features such as a logo, tagline, image, color scheme, and even a specific tone or voice used in communications.

A blog is an amazing tool for building your brand. Not only does it give you the opportunity to put a voice to your brand, which allows you to develop and meet customer expectations for your brand, but it also allows you to extend your company's web presence exponentially. Each new blog post you publish on your business blog becomes another entry point, and each new entry point provides the potential for more traffic. As the traffic to your business blog increases, so will the number of loyal readers your blog attracts, the number of incoming links your blog receives, and the extent of your business' online presence. That increased traffic leads directly to building the awareness of your brand to a wider audience who could talk about it, link to your content, tell friends about it, and so on.

REMEMBER

Much of the power of a business blog as a marketing tool comes from the long-term brand-building effects that the blog presents. The longer you maintain and grow your online presence, the higher up your brand will appear in search engine results and the more new readers — and potential customers — will find you. There is no secret to achieving that kind of success. It's just a matter of investing time and sweat into writing great content, interacting with people both on and off the blog, and keeping focused on the long-term benefits of blogging as a tool to build a brand and business.

Your business blog content must offer the same level of brand consistency as all your other marketing communications do. From your content to your voice and everything in between, a strong brand is one that is consistently presented to consumers. Inconsistency leads to confusion.

Another critical element of brand building is persistence. You need to give readers the opportunity to develop expectations for your brand, which happens organically through persistent (and consistent) brand communications and experiences. After those expectations develop, you must continue to communicate your brand's messages, images, and promises in order to keep satisfying consumers. You can't give up. The unfortunate truth is that consumers are fickle, and they won't hesitate to leave you if you can't meet their expectations. By building a brand and consistently and persistently meeting consumers' expectations for it, you develop a relationship with them that translates into brand loyalty and brand advocacy, which are both essential to developing effective online marketing communications.

Online conversations about your brand can have far-reaching effects. The goal of building your online brand is to start those conversations and keep them going so there are more and more opportunities for people to find your brand online. After all, there isn't much point to maintaining a web presence if no one can find it. That's like paying for advertising space in a magazine that no one buys. Why waste your time and money unless you're willing to commit to the long-term brand-building benefits that a business blog can provide? Instead, focus on the long term when you develop your business blog marketing strategy (discussed in detail in Chapter 2 of this Book) and use short-term marketing tactics to enhance that strategy.

Customer relations versus customer service

A blog is an excellent tool to enhance customer relationships. I caution against publishing a blog for the sole purpose of answering individual customer service–related questions because each individual customer service issue is personal and unique. It's hard to appeal to the members of a wide audience when they have to scroll through a lot of content that doesn't apply to them. Also, you don't want your business blog to become a complaint destination. That type of content doesn't help you build relationships with your readers, network across the social web, and boost your business. However, publishing some customer service–related posts can be helpful to your readers and provide a good forum for conversations that affect broad consumer groups.

TIP

If you choose to deal with customer service complaints away from your company's blog, I suggest placing a disclaimer on your blog in a place where visitors can easily see it. Don't just delete personal customer service questions and complaints. Instead, answer them if the topic would be helpful to the general blog audience. If not, take the time to direct the commenter to the proper place to get an answer to his personal questions or problems. The worst thing you can do on a business blog is try to stop the conversation or hide the negative comments people leave.

Although it's perfectly acceptable to delete hateful comments or edit comments to remove profanity, you don't want to be accused of trying to cover up negative conversations. (See the earlier section, "Dell," for the story about what happened when the company tried to quash an online conversation that painted the company in a negative light.)

Of course, as with any tool that allows people to voice their opinions, some people will leave comments on your business blog strictly to start arguments and say rude things. It's an unfortunate reality of publishing a blog. As long as you're honest, forthright, and transparent in your writing and commenting, your loyal readers and the majority of new visitors can tell the difference between a *troll* (someone deliberately trying to cause social friction) and a person who is commenting for the right reasons. (You can find out more about responding to negative attacks on your business blog in Chapter 5 of this Book.)

REMEMBER

The success of your business blog as a customer service tool is to set reader expectations so they know what kinds of customer service discussions are appropriate for the blog. In other words, although your blog is not the forum for discussing personal customer service issues, it's a fine place to discuss topics that your customer service team would usually talk to consumers about, such as new payment options, recalls, and so on, which help you build *relationships* with your customers. Provide information that's useful and helpful to them related to customer service issues rather than individual problems.

Give your readers the credit they deserve. In time, you'll find them coming to your defense for you when attacks do occur. That's because blogs are truly a better customer *relationship–building* tool than a customer *service* tool. Building relationships with customers is where a business blog can become a vital part of your marketing plan.

Employee retention

When most people think of a business blog, they often think of only the external blogs that companies publish to promote their products and services. Business blogs offer a lot more than a promotional opportunity. They can also boost employee morale and retention, particularly when employees are given the chance to write blogs for and about the company and their areas of expertise in their own voices.

Of course, if employees have to write adhering to a stringent set of guidelines, and if every post has to be approved by a dozen departments and lawyers, you can forget the part about boosting morale and retention. When that happens, business blogging becomes another annoying item on employees' annual reviews, and it's more of a burden than something they can feel passionate about. Instead, make sure your business bloggers are given the opportunity to express themselves, inject their personalities, and converse with readers as themselves, not as a spokesperson from the public relations department. Readers can tell the difference, and they're unlikely to enjoy the corporate rhetoric that comes when employee bloggers aren't given the opportunity to write from their hearts. You can find out more about setting blogger guidelines in Chapter 3 of this Book.

STAFF ONLY! USING INTERNAL BLOGS

Business blogging for employee retention doesn't stop with a company's external (public) blogs. Instead, companies can also publish internal blogs that are available to employees only, to share company information, news, employee stories, and more with staff members.

Internal blogs are a great way to boost the communication process with employees and make them feel like they're knowledgeable rather than just another number on the employee roster.

The key to writing a successful internal business blog is to get employees involved. Allow them to publish posts, share their opinions freely, and then respond to them. Transparency is vital on an internal blog when it comes to using it for employee retention purposes.

Make your employees feel valued and essential to your company's team by inviting them to participate, listening to them, and giving them the information that they want.

Employee referrals and new hiring

Business blogs are useful tools not only for existing employees and volunteers but also for potential team members. Consider using your blogs to publish open job announcements or calls for volunteers, both long-term and for specific one-time charity events. For an internal business blog, include referral bonuses in job postings. In other words, get the readers of your business blogs actively involved in helping you find great talent. As your business blog grows, your job postings are likely to get noticed by other bloggers in your industry, who will link to your postings and share them on their social media profiles. You should do the same to help spread your posts to the widest audience possible. You'd be amazed at the incredible talent out there that's actively participating in the social web.

Remember, many people use the social web as a tool to build their online presences and establish themselves as experts in their fields. Don't wait for them to actively look for and find your job posting on job listing sites or social media platforms such as LinkedIn. Instead, blog about it, too, and give your job posting the chance to spread to audiences you never dreamed possible.

You can also reach out directly to other bloggers in your industry and ask them to help spread the word about your job openings. It's likely that other bloggers would be happy to share the news about a great job opportunity with their own audiences. And keep in mind that each incoming link to your job postings means more incoming links to your blog overall, which translate into more entry points for people to find your business blog and a boost in Google search rankings.

Knowledge, experience, and expertise

If your employees are knowledgeable in your industry and enjoy writing, blogs offer another incredible opportunity. Millions of people publish blogs as a tool to boost their online presences and establish themselves as experts in their fields. Many of them become the go-to people for their subject matters. With that in mind, a business blog written by your expert employees or volunteers can link your brand closely with topics related to your industry and put your company on the map. Suddenly, your business blog can attract a wider audience than ever because people seeking thought leadership content might be very different from your typical consumer blog readers. By offering different ways for people to experience your brand and interact with you online, you expose a more diverse audience to your brand, business, products, and services, which can lead to an indirect boost in sales over time.

Many CEOs and presidents of small and mid-size businesses write blogs and establish themselves as experts in topics related to their companies. For example, one of my favorite small-business blogs is written by Drew McLellan, Top Dog at McLellan Marketing Group, a marketing company he owns in Iowa. Through his blog, Drew's Marketing Minute (www.drewsmarketingminute.com), shown in Figure 1-15, Drew has established himself as a marketing thought leader who writes in a personable voice that draws in both marketing novices and marketing pros. As a result, the conversations on his blog are lively, and he has developed relationships with a broad audience around the world. Undoubtedly, his business blog has led to new and repeat business for McLellan Marketing Group as he became known across the blogosphere as one of the go-to guys for marketing and branding expertise.

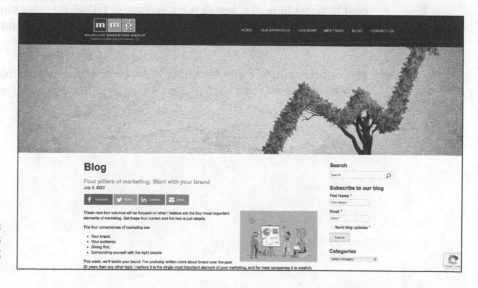

FIGURE 1-15: The Drew's Marketing Minute blog.

TIP

Think of the kinds of information your consumer audience would be interested in learning about from an expert from your company as well as the content wider audiences would look for from an expert. Then find the right person with the necessary knowledge and experience within your company to write a blog that delivers the information that people want and need.

Search engine optimization

Blogs provide a unique and measurable way to boost your company's search rankings on search engines such as Google, because with each new post, you create a new *entry point*, or way for search engines to find you. If you write those posts with keywords in mind, as discussed in Chapter 1 of Book 5, you can boost your search rankings even higher. That means when people conduct a search on Google (or their preferred search engines) using the keywords that your posts are optimized for, your blog posts are likely to appear higher on the list of results returned for those searches.

But that's not all! Blogs that are updated frequently with amazing content are often linked to by other website owners and bloggers who like the content and want to share it with their own audiences. Great blog posts are also likely to be shared on social media platforms. All of that sharing means more and more incoming links to your blog. Google uses a proprietary algorithm to rank the results it finds for keyword searches, and that algorithm ranks pages with many incoming links higher than pages without incoming links. The reason is because Google believes that people will want to link to great content, so a page with lots of links is assumed to include great content and therefore to be worthy of a higher ranking than a page with few or no links. If you publish interesting content on your business blog that people want to share or talk about, your blog will get more incoming links, which boosts traffic directly through clicks and indirectly through higher search rankings. What's not to like about business blogs?

You can check how many incoming links are pointing to your blog at any time with free backlink tools such as Moz's Link Explorer (https://analytics.moz.com), shown in Figure 1-16.

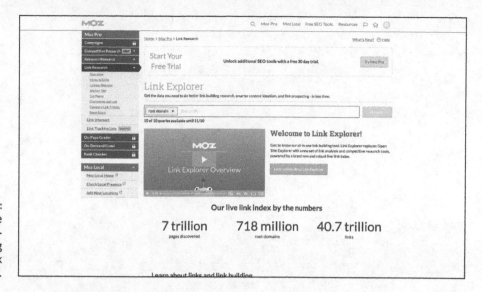

FIGURE 1-16:
Checking the number of incoming links to a blog using Moz Link Explorer.

WARNING

Be careful about paying for incoming links to your blog or website. Google sees paid text links as a tactic that artificially inflates a site's search ranking and may downgrade your site if you pay for text links, or it may even remove your site from search results entirely.

IN THIS CHAPTER

» **Finding and analyzing your competition**

» **Differentiating your business blog**

» **Getting to know your audience and their needs**

» **Defining your business blog marketing strategy**

» **Setting goals for your business blog**

» **Developing a team blog with multiple contributors**

Chapter **2**

Developing a Blog Plan

C reating a business blog plan is a similar process to creating any blogging plan. You need to know who your competitors are and what they're doing in the same online space where your blog will live, and you need to know who your audience members are and what they want from your blog. You need to determine what goals you have for your blog as well as how you want your blog to look and sound. You can't create a strategy until you do some research. Only then can you create goals that are focused and attainable. In other words, you need a well-crafted plan before you can leverage the full potential of the blogosphere for your business or non-profit organization.

This chapter shows you how to create your company blog's plan before you launch your new online presence. Joining the blogosphere can be exciting, but don't rush into anything. Launching a blog that's poorly designed, written, and developed can do more harm than good for your business. In short, you don't want people to find your blog, be disappointed in what they find there, and never return. Do the prep work first!

As you read through this chapter, remember that the most successful business bloggers are creative, not just in the design of their business blogs but also in the content, conversations, and promotions related to those blogs. Because the blogosphere is constantly changing, you never know what might work. Also, you need to continually provide content that your audience likes. Certainly, doing the same thing every day can get boring very quickly. The same is true of your blog content. If you publish the same type of information every day, advertise on the same sites all the time, and your marketing plan never evolves, your blog will quickly get stuck in a rut.

Researching the Competition

Long gone are the days when only the most cutting edge and innovative companies had blogs. Now it's common for everyone from famous global brands to community charity organizations to include a blog component on their websites. Just as in the personal blogging world, the word "competition" is used in reference to company blogs to describe the quest for page views. You need to find out whether you're creating a blog that will not only attract an audience but hold their attention once they arrive there — and keep them coming back for more!

Keep in mind that your list of competitors' blogs isn't limited to business blogs published by companies in your industry or offering the same products and services that your business offers. Depending on the type of information you decide to publish on your business blog, competition can come from a wide variety of blogs. Think of it this way: If you own a local hardware store, your business blog competes with all of the following:

» Blogs written by big corporations such as home improvement chain stores, Walmart, and more

» Local business competitor blogs

» Blogs written by builders, handymen, home improvement enthusiasts, and so on

With that in mind, the hardware store's business blog strategist should research *all* of these types of blogs and bloggers to determine what makes them unique and what drives conversations. Then you can use your discoveries to craft a business blog strategy in order to provide valuable content that is different from what's already out there. Try to create a blog that meets a need that other blogs have not already met!

TIP

As you research your blog's competition, be sure to analyze the designs of those blogs. Your design must not only be a fit for your goals but also compete with your competitors' designs. If your competitors' blogs are highly professional and look amazing, you might want to invest in hiring a blog designer to ensure your blog looks as good or even better!

Finding business blogs to benchmark

The first step in developing your business blog's plan is to find other blogs that are delivering the type of information that your target audience is interested in reading. This is a time-consuming task if you're thorough about it, and being thorough is essential to developing a blog strategy. You need to not only find blogs related to your industry, but you also need to read them, keep track of the comments and conversations happening on those blogs, and analyze the types of content and posts that pique readers' interests and dialogue.

TIP

Following are several tips for finding business blogs to benchmark:

» **Visit your competitors' websites.** As a business owner, you undoubtedly have a list of your primary competitors. Find their websites and look for links to associated blogs.

» **Do a Google blog search.** You can search blog content on www.google.com to find blogs that mention keywords related to your business as described in Chapter 1 of Book 1.

» **Follow post links.** As you find blogs related to your business through Google searches, take a look at the links included in the blog's posts. Many of them just might lead you to *more* blogs related to your business.

» **Follow blogroll links.** Visit blogs related to your business' subject matter and look for a section included in many blogs' sidebars called *Blogroll, Useful Links,* or something similar. Bloggers include links to other blogs they like and recommend in their blogrolls, which may lead you to more content for research and benchmarking.

Start a notebook and jot down notes as you spend time on business blogs that will compete with your own. What do you like about them? What do you dislike? What content sparks conversation? What kind of information does the blogger focus on? What information is missing? Find the gaps and opportunities, which you can use to create your own blog marketing plan.

Furthermore, you can seek out blogs that are indirectly related to your business. These blogs provide the opportunity for you to offer additional value to those bloggers' audiences through link exchanges, guest posts, and other collaborations. Indirect marketing is an important part of a successful business blog plan. Using the hardware store example that I mention earlier in this chapter, you can partner with a business blog published by a landscaping company. Although the landscaping company isn't your business's direct competitor, your companies have an indirect relationship because consumers have expressed an interest in home improvement by hiring a landscaping company, and they're likely to need hardware supplies now or in the future. Thinking outside the box like this can help you better understand how your business blog can fit into the online community while adding value and drawing in readers.

Differentiating your organization's blog from the competition

When you know who the competition is for your business blog, you need to analyze the content and conversations on those blogs as I mention earlier in this chapter. That's the only way you can accurately find gaps and weaknesses and develop a blog marketing plan that capitalizes on those opportunities. Conducting this competitive research allows you to position your blog in consumers' minds just as well-known brands position themselves against their competition.

You want your business blog to own a space in your target audience's minds just as brands own a space, such as a word or phrase, in consumers' minds.

A business blog that's exactly like every other blog published about a similar line of business is a fairly useless effort unless your only goal is to provide customers with information solely about your product. The most successful brand blogs go beyond that type of content to provide additional value. Why should people leave a blog that they're already reading to get the exact same information elsewhere? Readers have no incentive to visit your business blog if it doesn't add new value to an audience's online experience. After you research competitor blogs and fully understand what they publish and what works for them, you can determine which parts of their strategies you want to emulate and which you want to change or add to.

For example, if Joe's Hardware Store focuses on providing content related to product reviews and new product trends, your hardware store blog might also include that type of information, but your greater focus should be on another niche topic such as providing tutorials and videos showing readers *how* to use those products and accomplish specific tasks. Naturally, there will be some overlap in content between your blog and your competitors' blogs. However, it's important to find a way to distinguish yourself in the minds of your readers and customers.

If your blogging application and host allow it, get your own domain name for your blog. Doing so helps not just in brand building and search engine optimization, but also in making your blog seem more professional than a generic domain name with a hosted extension (such as wordpress.com, blogspot.com, or typepad.com).

Understanding Your Readers and Delivering Content They Want

Your business blog has no chance of successfully providing value and meeting your goals if it doesn't provide the content that your target audience wants and needs, just as a product will fail if no one wants or needs it. Of course, you can create a perceived need for your business blog as marketers often do with products and services. However, it's a lot easier to take the time to discover what your audience actually wants and needs from your business blog and then deliver that information consistently.

REMEMBER

Your business blog is another tool in your marketing toolbox. It's an excellent place to provide marketing messages, build relationships, and create brand loyalty, but none of that will happen if you're not publishing the right messages. That's why your blogging plan development process needs to include audience research.

TIP

As you begin to develop your blogging plan, take time to think about your blog's potential audience, which may be made up of the following groups:

>> Consumers

>> Distributors

>> Business partners

>> Potential clients

>> Potential customers

>> Non-profit volunteers

>> Partner non-profits

>> Service recipients

>> Brand fans

Naturally, it's difficult to provide content that interests diverse readers who want and need very different information from you. That's where focus becomes key to your business blog's success. Remember, your blog can't be all things to all people. Instead, you need to do your research and determine which audience to build your business blog for. That's not to say you can't publish content on your blog that will interest segments of your target audience. However, you do need to choose your core audience — the one that will help you achieve your business blogging goals — and focus the majority of your blogging efforts around that audience.

Setting blog goals and purpose

If you're reading this book, chances are that you've already decided that a blog will be beneficial to your business or organization. Even if you're all in on the idea of blogging, it is still incredibly important and helpful to be able to articulate your blog's goals and set a purpose for creating the blog. This is especially true if you need to sell the idea of a company blog to a supervisor or owner of the organization where you work.

You may have a seemingly endless number of goals and purposes when setting out to create a blog for your company. Some places to start include:

>> Providing resources related to your product or service

>> Creating a place for current customers to learn about new products or services

>> Establishing yourself or your company as an industry expert

>> Fostering community around your brand in order to create brand loyalty

>> Drawing in new customers who have not yet discovered your product or service

>> Keeping current donors informed about your organization's work and how resources are being used

>> Making supporters aware of upcoming charity events that require volunteers

REMEMBER

Your brand blog can't be all things to all people! You only have a limited amount of time and resources to devote to your new site or website functionality, so while it would be great to create the most productive company blog of all time, the truth is that it's more realistic to start with a narrow focus and set of goals. This will also make it easier to monitor and determine if you are meeting those goals.

Determining tone

Once you've determined your main goals for your new company blog, it's time to decide what tone you want your blog to convey. It has become very popular in recent years for brands to take a humorous tone on their social media accounts, often interacting with one another in a tongue-in-cheek competitive way. While that tone is not as common on company blogs, it's not unheard of.

Your tone will most likely be determined by a number of factors including your type of company or non-profit organization as well as the goals for the blog. For example, you may not want to take a joking tone if your goal is to establish yourself as an expert in your area. Likewise, if you're hoping to build a sense of community or a connection between the consumer and the brand, a highly serious or technical tone may not do the trick.

The Slack blog, found at `https://slack.com/blog`, sets the tone right from the start with the blog name: Several People are Typing (shown in Figure 2-1). While the blog provides tons of great content, the reader knows immediately that this is not a company that takes itself so seriously that it isn't relatable to its customers and readers.

FIGURE 2-1: Slack sets the tone early with the blog's name.

TIP

If you have multiple people writing for your brand's blog, be sure that they're all writing with the same style and tone in order to maintain consistency on your site. Check out the later section, "Blogging with Multiple Writers," for more on briefing your writers.

Finding your customers online

While it's important to plan your blog content strategy around what your target audience might want to read, it is also important to be able to find that audience. Finding your audience is easy if you put yourself in your customers' shoes and search the web just as they might. Conduct blog searches just as you did for your competitor research discussed earlier in this chapter, in the section "Finding business blogs to benchmark." For example, blogs with a lot of comments might be places where your audience is spending time. Next, search social networking sites, such as Facebook, for groups and fan pages related to your business. Don't forget to do a hashtag search on all of your favorite social media platforms.

Take some time to search for online forums related to your business or organization. Active forums and groups often represent online destinations where customers like to ask questions and help one another.

Follow these steps to find groups on LinkedIn:

1. **Visit** www.linkedin.com.

2. **Enter a keyword or keyword phrase in the search box.**

LinkedIn results that match your keywords are returned to you, as shown in Figure 2-2.

FIGURE 2-2:
The results of a LinkedIn keyword search.

3. **Locate related groups by clicking Groups in the horizontal navigation bar.**

Groups related to your keyword search will appear in a list, as shown in Figure 2-3.

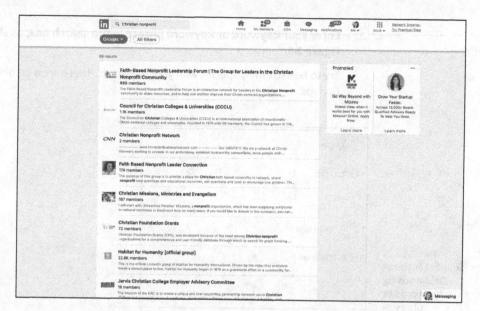

FIGURE 2-3:
Locate LinkedIn
Groups related to
your business or
organization.

You can perform a similar process using Facebook Groups, as follows:

1. Visit www.Facebook.com and log in to your account.

2. Click on Groups on the left sidebar, as shown in Figure 2-4.

FIGURE 2-4:
Facebook Groups
are located on
the left sidebar.

3. **Enter your keyword or keyword phrase in the search box, as shown in Figure 2-5.**

   Try to be extremely specific with your keywords. There are a lot of Facebook Groups!

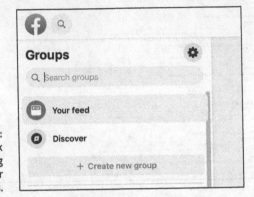

4. **Click on Groups on the left sidebar of the results page, as shown in Figure 2-6, to narrow results.**

Weighing cost and benefit of communities and forums

What you'll discover through audience searches on LinkedIn, Facebook, and other social media platforms is that online conversations are occurring around the topic of your cause, product, or service. You have the option of finding those conversations and joining in as appropriate, but there is also the option of creating an online community right on your company's blog. Many blogging platforms either offer the ability to include a forum page on your blog right out of the box or integrate well with plugins that provide that next level of functionality.

TECHNICAL STUFF

So what is a forum? *Online forums* are message boards where members can engage in conversations through a series of threaded posts. Long before there were social media platforms, Internet forums existed as a place for like-minded people to gather and discuss the topics that interested them. Some popular forums, like the Disney fan forum Disboards (www.disboards.com, shown in Figure 2-7), now also exist on social media platforms in the form of pages and groups. But forums remain popular with those looking for highly focused conversations within an online community. Many online communities that are attached to blogs use forum software to provide the functionality necessary for the conversations to occur.

FIGURE 2-7: Disboards is a popular online forum around the topic of Disney.

REMEMBER

While the idea of moving online conversations related to your business onto your brand's website sounds like a fantastic idea, there are both costs and benefits that should be weighed before you make the decision to give forums a try. Benefits of including a forum on your company's blog include:

>> **Customer service opportunities:** An online forum is a window into the mind of the consumer. Monitoring conversations occurring in the forum gives you the opportunity to step in and rectify any customer service issues or concerns.

>> **Customer engagement:** Consumers love to feel connected to their favorite brands and causes. Joining in with the conversation in the forum helps customers feel even more connected to your company.

>> **Drive, start, or redirect conversations:** Impacting conversations happening about your brand can be very difficult, even when they're occurring in public settings such as social media platforms. Conversations in a forum on your company blog can be driven, redirected, or even started in the first place by you, the brand.

>> **Hear directly from customers:** Forums offer another way for you to hear directly from your customers, meeting their needs and answering their questions. In many ways forums act as an online focus group!

>> **Boost for SEO:** An active forum is a great boost for a site's search engine optimization.

>> **Draws people to your site:** Even the most loyal customer may not have a reason to visit their favorite company blog often. A forum is another way to draw people in to your website.

WARNING

On the flip side, there are certainly reasons to not include discussions beyond post comments on your company's blog. While I'm sure brands who have attempted to include forums and changed their minds could write an even longer list than this one, the cons of building a forum feature into your site include:

>> **Need to create rules and employ moderators:** Just as you need to set guidelines for blog interaction and comments, you will need to create rules for your forum and make sure they are stated clearly where all users can find them easily. You'll also need to enforce those rules by employing a moderator to monitor conversations and delete inappropriate content as needed.

>> **Time consuming:** It's probably no surprise that offering a forum functionality on a blog is time consuming when done right. You'll need to come up with conversation starters, monitor conversations, and engage with users as appropriate. Forums are even more time consuming when they play a role in customer service.

>> **Empty room issue:** If there are few or no comments on a blog post, it is not always readily apparent because the focus is on the content itself. Not so on a forum. The focus of a forum is the conversation and the conversation alone. No company wants to launch a forum on their company blog only to have it sit empty for all the world to see.

>> **A shift in resources:** There are only so many hours in the day, and every small business or organization owner knows that there are already too many tasks to accomplish than there is time. Spending time creating and monitoring a forum means time not doing something else.

>> **Spam attracter:** The only thing worse than an empty blog forum is one filled with spam.

>> **Tough for customers to use:** Even the least tech-savvy person has likely been able to figure out how to use a favorite social media platform or customer contact form, but forums require additional steps such as account creation. For some customers, this may be frustrating.

Ultimately, it depends mostly on your goals for your blog as well as your time, resources, and tolerance for bumps in the road whether or not you choose to add a forum or community feature to your blog. If you are highly risk averse, it might not be a fit for you. But if your brand is always looking to try new things, there could be a huge payout!

Researching what consumers talk about and want from your blog

You can begin doing some research about your customers by following their conversations and discovering what matters most to them after you've successfully found where they spend their time online or have added forum functionality to your website. In other words, you can begin researching the type of content your audience wants and needs by analyzing your competitors' blogs first, as discussed earlier in this chapter, and identifying the types of posts that generate a lot of comments and buzz.

If you're lucky enough to find forums, LinkedIn Groups, and Facebook Groups related to your business, join them and get involved. The conversations that occur on these social sites can be very indicative of the type of information your customers would be happy to find on your business blog. Look at the questions being asked and the answers users provide on these sites. Then consider ways that you can take those questions and answers a step further on your blog so it earns a reputation as being *the* place online for that kind of useful content.

Don't forget the possibilities that offline customer research can provide for you. There may be an audience of consumers who don't realize they can get great content on a business blog. Ask your existing customers and supporters what kind of information they'd like to read. After all, no one knows better than them! Hand out a survey or send one by email or through social media asking your customers, clients, donors, and volunteers to provide their opinions. That's one way to be certain you know exactly what your audience wants and needs.

Getting involved in the online conversation

After you find the target audience for your business blog online, you need to begin connecting with them and engaging in conversations with them. That's where the power of the social web comes from, and it's the conversations that happen through the social media that drive traffic to your blog, help you build relationships that lead to customer loyalty, and boost your business.

Successful bloggers get to know their audience members and build relationships with them both on and off their blogs. The same rule holds true for business bloggers. Think of the rule as it applies to personal relationships — you can't always expect everyone to always come to the party at *your* house. Unless you have the coolest house around, you have to visit them at their own homes or hangout spots sometimes, too. That's what makes it a two-sided relationship. Now replace *house* with *blog* in the previous scenario because the rule applies to online relationships, too.

Building from the steps I discuss earlier in this chapter, getting involved in the online conversation related to your business is easy. Visit the blogs, forums, groups, public social media profiles, and so on where topics related to your business are discussed, and join in! It's that easy. The social web is typically a very open place where anyone with intelligent commentary to add is welcome to the conversation. If you provide useful answers and interesting information, you'll be very welcome on most blogs and in most groups and forums.

Don't leave your audience hanging. Turn on the comments feature within your blogging application and let the conversation begin! If the dialogue slows, put on your thinking cap and get it going again just as if it were an awkward moment of silence in a face-to-face conversation.

Answering consumer demand with meaningful content

As you get to know more members of the online community, you'll get a better understanding of the kind of content they want and need from you and your business blog. Remember that your business blog shouldn't be about you. Instead, the content has to be written for and about your consumers. You must deliver the information they want and need to make them want to visit again and again and build a relationship with you and your business.

Every post you publish on your organization's blog should add some type of value to your target audience or there's little reason for them to return. Of course, you can be creative when writing your posts (as discussed in detail in Chapter 4 of this Book), but first you need to take the fundamental step to develop a blogging plan by fully understanding the type of content that will be meaningful and useful to your target audience. Take your time in doing the necessary competitor and consumer research before you start blogging to ensure you're heading down the path to success.

Driving consumers to your blog

Business blog traffic-building techniques are very similar to personal blog traffic-building techniques. First, you need to publish amazing content. When you have a repository of great blog posts, you need to start spreading the word about your blog. Following is a brief list of blog promotion tactics to get you started, but for more details, be sure to read Book 6.

>> **Leave comments on related blogs.** One of the best ways to start driving traffic to your business blog is by leaving useful comments on other blogs related to your business. Be sure to include your blog's URL in the appropriate comment form field, so readers who like your comments can follow the link to your blog to read more.

>> **Link to great content on other blogs.** When you link to content on another blog from one of your blogs, the other blogger can be notified via a trackback or backlink or through their blog analytics tools. Getting your blog on the radar screens of other influential bloggers in your niche is a great way to prompt them to check out your blog and to build relationships with them.

>> **Include your blog's URL everywhere you can.** Put your blog's URL on your business cards; email signatures; Facebook, LinkedIn, and Twitter profiles; invoices; receipts; promotional items; and anywhere else you can think of.

>> **Use search engine optimization techniques.** Be sure to write each of your blog posts using keywords and search engine optimization tips discussed in Chapter 1 of Book 5 to increase your rankings for keyword searches via search engines such as Google.

>> **Share your content on social media platforms.** Publish links to your best content on sites such as Facebook, LinkedIn, and Twitter.

>> **Hold a contest.** People love contests. You can hold blog contests to boost comments, increase subscribers, build incoming links, and more!

WARNING

The opportunities to increase traffic to your business blog are limited only by your imagination and time constraints. Just be careful not to cross the fine line between useful promotion and over-promotion, which can get you blacklisted as a spammer by members of the blogosphere and by search engines.

Creating a Blog Marketing Strategy

After you complete your competitor and audience research, you can begin thinking about your larger blog marketing strategy. Remember, the online world moves quickly, and what makes sense for your business blog today may be very wrong for it tomorrow. You must be flexible enough to change your business blog marketing strategy as new opportunities arise and existing opportunities fall out of favor. With that said, be prepared to continually review and revise your blog's marketing strategy. No one has the recipe for blog marketing success mastered because the environment is constantly evolving. That means you need to be willing to test new tactics and strategies and learn from them, even if they don't meet your expectations.

TIP

Don't get sucked into experimenting with every new blog tool. Instead, choose the ones that get great reviews and seem to be capable of truly adding value to your blog. Consistency is key in building a business blog, and that rule holds true for functionality just as much as it does for content.

Setting long-term goals

A business blog is most effective in helping you achieve long-term goals for your business for the simple reason that it's rare for a blog to become popular quickly. It takes time to generate awareness of your blog, recognition of it, and eventually traffic. You can speed up the process by investing time in short-term marketing tactics to boost growth of your business blog, but more often than not, business blogging success comes from patience and persistence.

Your long-term goals for your business blog should include

>> Developing relationships with your audience and building brand loyalty (the most important goals!)

>> Achieving specific traffic volumes

>> Reaching specific numbers of published posts

>> Achieving specific numbers of subscribers

Notice that besides the first item, these long-term goals are tangible and measurable. Setting measurable goals will help you stay on track in terms of publishing great content and growing your blog organically over time.

TIP

The majority of your long-term goals for your business blog are easier to achieve if you publish amazing content frequently and engage in the conversations that occur on your blog.

Developing short-term promotional campaigns

After you set your long-term goals for your blog, you can develop short-term marketing tactics to help you reach those long-term goals. For example, to help you reach your one-year traffic goals, you can hold a blog contest that provides each person who subscribes to your blog's feed with an entry to win a prize from your business such as a discount or product. Alternatively, you can publish guest posts on other blogs to build your incoming links, which typically leads to an increase in blog traffic.

If an initiative doesn't help you reach your short- or long-term goals, you need to think long and hard about whether it's worth your while. The amount of time you spend on initiatives that don't help you meet your goals for your business blog takes away from the time you could be spending creating great content and engaging with your audience — both of which are guaranteed ways to help you build your blog and your business.

REMEMBER

The marketing rule that tells us it's cheaper to retain existing customers than it is to find and attract new ones holds true for blogging, too. Don't waste time on short-term tactics that simply inflate your traffic artificially with people who aren't likely to return. Instead, focus on targeted initiatives that attract and retain the audience that wants and needs the information found on your business blog.

For example, don't hold a blog contest strictly to boost your blog's traffic in the short term. With proper promotion, a blog contest for a great prize can generate a lot of traffic, but the important consideration for a business blog is how much of that inflated traffic is likely to return to the blog after the contest is over. If the answer is "not many," you should reconsider investing time and effort into that particular promotional tactic.

Jumping on advertising opportunities

You can pursue many low-cost opportunities to grow your business blog's readership. Always keep in mind, though, that it's very possible to grow your blog's audience without spending a penny on advertising. However, doing so takes time, and your business might not have the time to wait for organic growth. If that's the case for your business, following are a few cost-based advertising opportunities that you can pursue to find and attract your blog's target audience:

>> **Place Google AdWords ads.** You can join the Google AdWords (https://ads.google.com) advertising network, shown in Figure 2-8, and create contextual ads that are published on blogs and websites, which contain related content.

>> **Try Facebook ads.** Facebook offers a low-cost advertising program (www.facebook.com/business) that you can use to drive targeted traffic directly to your blog.

FIGURE 2-8:
The Google Ads landing page.

>> **Use traditional image and text ads.** You can contact other blogs and websites where your audience spends time and discuss advertising rates for image and text ads.

WARNING

Beware! Paying for text link ads could be considered spam by Google, who might downgrade your blog or eliminate it from search results entirely.

>> **Obtain reviews.** Reach out to other bloggers or influencers regarding review opportunities. Be certain to require that reviews include a link back to your blog.

>> **Join ad networks.** There are many affiliate programs and ad programs that bloggers can join and use to drive traffic to their business blogs. Read Book 7 for specific examples and details.

The most important thing about growing your business blog is getting the word out and motivating your target audience members to visit for the first time. If your content is useful to them, they're likely to return or tell someone else about your blog. Your goal as a business blogger is to seek out and leverage every opportunity available to you to increase the awareness and recognition level of your blog among your primary audience. Then you can motivate the audience to take action, just as you would with any other marketing initiative.

Branding across social media

Deciding to take your company or non-profit organization into the blogosphere involves far more than simply adding a blog page to your existing brand website. If you don't already have social media properties related to your brand claimed and managed, now is the time to focus on doing so and roll that work right into your business blog marketing plan. It is incredibly important for your brand to establish a presence on social media making it easier for customers, clients, and supporters to find and connect with you.

Social media accounts offer additional opportunities to establish your brand's identity with consumers. What are you hoping to convey through your blog posts, tweets, and Facebook page? Is your brand's personality one that is personable and relatable? Are you hoping to establish your brand as a thought leader in the space, an expert in a particular field? Is your charitable cause the focus and that is the only message that matters? It's important that your company's blogging goals and social media presence align and are always consistent. Readers and followers need to always know what to expect when they interact with your company on the social web.

One company that has become well-known for branding across social media is the restaurant chain, Wendy's, shown in Figure 2-9. If one day Wendy's Twitter account suddenly became serious instead of humorous, no one would believe it was the same brand. This clear branding has helped build the Wendy's Twitter following into the millions.

FIGURE 2-9:
Wendy's consistently takes a humorous tone on social media.

Within the figure:

Wendy's ✓
222.3K Tweets

Wendy's ✓
@Wendys

We like our tweets the way we like our fries: hot, crispy, and better than anyone expects from a fast food restaurant.

🔗 wendys.com   📅 Joined July 2009

444 Following   **3.9M** Followers

Follow

Blogging with Multiple Writers

Many business blogs successfully recruit employees, business partners, customers, and paid writers to contribute content to the blog. Having multiple writers contribute blog posts is a great way to increase publishing frequency, keep readers engaged, and boost entry points and search traffic to your business blog.

Blogs written by multiple contributors are often referred to as *team* blogs. Contributors can write posts, provide video content, publish photos, and more. However, you shouldn't recruit a bunch of writers, set them loose, and expect your business blog to be a success. You need to take some steps to develop a team blog that has a chance to attract and retain readers.

Keeping a consistent voice

Just as it is important to keep consistent branding across your company's blog and social media platforms, each member of your team of writers must keep a consistent voice and tone, too. Certainly, every writer will approach blogging a little differently to everyone else. In fact, those different approaches, skill sets, and expertise are part of what makes taking a team approach to blogging so great. However, you should still establish guidelines early on regarding the general voice that the company blog is going to have.

For example, decide before the first post is written how you feel about things such as sarcasm and snark. Will your company's blog keep a serious and professional tone or is the goal to be more personable and relatable? You don't want one author to write a humorous piece only to have the next post be a lengthy deep dive into a complex aspect of the industry.

You may also want to decide what blog post formats are acceptable to be included in your company's blog content. For example, decide if all of the posts should look the same with headers and paragraphs or if lists and interactive content should be included.

Developing a team blog

As mentioned in the previous section, one of the most important keys to success in developing a team blog is making sure everyone is on the same page from day one. From there, keep team members in the loop with frequent communication and truly set them up for success with clear feedback and expectations.

TIP

Follow these steps to develop a team blog correctly:

>> **Communicate the team blog's focus and goals.** Educate every team member about the blog's focus and the specific goals you want to achieve through the business blog. Don't assume that team members know what you want to do, how you want them to write, what you want them to write about, or why you want them to contribute content. Clarify your goals so that team members support them and understand what they're contributing and why.

>> **Develop a team blog style guidelines document.** Ensure that there's no room for confusion and that all content is written and published consistently by creating a comprehensive team blog style guidelines document. Style guidelines are discussed in detail in Chapter 3 of Book 3.

>> **Choose the appropriate team blog tool.** Some blogging applications are much better for team blogs than others. Use a blogging application that offers (at minimum) author pages, author bios, and tiered security access. See the next section in this chapter, "Choosing a team blogging application," for more details.

>> **Hire a team blog editor.** With multiple contributors, your business blog needs a single point of contact who manages writers and edits content for consistency. This person should also schedule post publishing. In other words, hire a team blog editor.

>> **Create an editorial calendar.** The best team blogs are focused and consistent. An editorial calendar helps to keep all contributors on track to ensure that the content is always relevant and useful to the target audience. Editorial calendars also help to leverage seasonal and timely content opportunities.

>> **Offer contributors access to communication and collaboration tools.** You have to stay in contact with all contributors, and using a communication and collaboration tool that's specifically created to manage virtual teams can make the process easier for everyone. These tools are discussed in detail in Chapter 3 of Book 3.

>> **Provide ongoing feedback to contributors.** You also need to provide direct feedback to every person who contributes content to your business blog. This should be done in a private setting outside of the team communications. Use email, phone calls, or online meeting tools to provide feedback, praise, direction, and suggestions. Make sure that your team members feel valued, and provide them with the information they need to be successful.

Don't forget to ask your contributors to provide feedback to you, too. Two-way feedback is vital to ensuring that the entire team reaches its full potential.

Choosing a team blogging application

A number of blogging applications offer the features and capabilities needed to develop a successful blog written by multiple authors. The platform you choose to use for your team blog can be a traditional blogging application or a more advanced content management system (CMS) that provides even more features for managing and publishing content in a blog format.

The best choice for group blogging is installing the WordPress blogging software on a self-hosted server. The self-hosted WordPress application is more of a content management system than a simple blogging application. It offers a variety of features, including tiered user access roles. Where WordPress truly stands out is the huge number of third-party plugins that add a wealth of additional capabilities, including those specifically related to managing a group blog. WordPress.org is very easy to use, so creating and managing your own team blog is quick and extremely cost-effective.

Another platform option worth considering is Drupal. With Drupal you get a powerful content management system that's free to use. You can create a team blog with Drupal as well as a website, forum, social networking site, eCommerce site, intranet, and more. As you might expect with all these features, Drupal has a much steeper learning curve than WordPress.org. However, for the technically savvy, it's a great choice for a team blog.

Many businesses like the highly advanced features offered through Drupal, but for businesses that have neither the technical staff nor the time or budget to learn how to use Drupal, WordPress.org is still the best choice for a multiauthor blog. To read more about blogging platform options, check out Book 4.

IN THIS CHAPTER

» **Looking internally for bloggers**

» **Finding external bloggers**

» **Defining rules and guidelines**

» **Training bloggers**

» **Providing feedback**

Chapter 3

Choosing Bloggers

After you define your blog's content plan and marketing strategy, you need to find someone to write content for it on an ongoing and frequent basis. If you'll be the only blogger publishing content on your blog, then you're in charge, and you can get started right away. However, if your plan for your organization's blog will take more time than you're able to dedicate to it — responding to comments, creating content, and creating an active community on your company's blog — you should look for help.

Fortunately, several avenues are open to you to find great blogging talent. In fact, you might already have someone working for you who not only would be happy to write your business blog, but would also do a great job at it because they already have writing and social media experience.

Alternatively, many people around the world blog for a living. You can hire a blogger to become your employee or independent contractor. This chapter helps you find bloggers, pay them, and set guidelines for them.

Knowing When You Need Outside — or Inside — Help

Hiring a professional blogger who is familiar with the unique experience of writing for a blog can give your site an immediate leg up on the competition. That's because professional bloggers who are very knowledgeable and experienced know how to write content that people want to read. They know how to start online conversations and use multiple tactics to drive traffic to your blog. In fact, the difference in hiring a professional blogger to write your blog rather than an employee with no blogging experience is significant.

TIP

Finding an existing employee who also has blogging experience is the best of both worlds!

Depending on the type of content you want your organization's blog to contain, the learning curve a professional blogger has to get over in order to understand your business may be minimal, but the learning curve a social web novice would have to get over is long and filled with tricks that only experienced bloggers know. I'm not saying the tricks and techniques can't be learned. They absolutely can be, and reading this book is an excellent place to start! However, it takes time to figure out all the do's and don'ts of the blogosphere. An experienced, knowledgeable blogger already knows how the social web works and can dive into creating great content and driving traffic to your business blog.

REMEMBER

Your budget, existing depth of employee talent, and short- and long-terms goals for your blog are the factors that help you determine whether you can use a current staff member to write your business blog or you need to seek external help.

The blogosphere is a popular place, and it's very likely that one or more people who already work for you might be very well versed in the details of the social web. They might write personal blogs or spend a lot of time on social media sites such as Facebook. Regardless of exactly where they spend time online, finding a person who understands how the blogosphere works and *already* knows your business is like finding a golden needle in a haystack. If you can find that person, you've hit the jackpot!

Following are two main reasons why finding an internal candidate who understands the social web is great for your business blog:

>> The candidate already understands how to build relationships online.

>> The candidate knows about your product, service, or cause.

The key to get started is identifying who the right people are for the job. Send out an internal communication asking employees if they would be interested in writing for your company's new blog. Make sure you look at any blogs they already write as well as their social networking profiles to ensure they actually know their stuff and can write well. The best blogger you can find has a passion for the subject matter and the skills to make the company's blog the best it can be. They'll understand that the goal is to connect with your audience, and they'll be happy to work towards that goal.

REMEMBER

The most important thing you need to keep in mind when you recruit an existing employee to write your business blog is that it takes a significant time investment to create a successful blog. Although your employee might not have to spend eight hours per day working on your business blog at first, the time commitment will grow as your blog grows. Also, the more time the blogger invests into creating content, engaging in conversations, and promoting the blog, the faster it will grow. With that in mind, you need to determine whether taking the employee away from other tasks so they can work on your blog makes sense financially and in terms of meeting your overall business goals.

On the other hand, you can recruit a team of internal bloggers to write your business blog, which can help spread the workload. For example, the Whole Foods Whole Story (see Figure 3-1) blog, which now exists as an online archive (`http://blog.wholefoodsmarket.com`), was written by employees who created posts in addition to their regular roles on the Whole Foods Market staff. Over time the blog evolved and grew to include dozens of employee contributors.

FIGURE 3-1:
The Whole Story blog from Whole Foods Market.

Having multiple writers can be a good thing and a bad thing. Remember, many people return to a blog again and again because they like the voice and personality of the person writing that blog. The overall voice of a blog can get confusing when multiple authors contribute content. However, multiple authors can work together cohesively, and readers often find the specific bloggers within the larger team whose content they enjoy the most. Think of your blogging team as an ensemble cast that works together to provide individual perspective with a common focus.

Knowing the Skills to Look for When Hiring a Blogger

When you make the decision to recruit a blogger, you need to make sure your candidates have a strong understanding of not just the technical aspects of using blogging tools, but also how the social web works. Of course, you can hire someone strictly to write content for your blog, and you can handle the promotion yourself or internally. That way, you can cut some costs while ensuring your content will be well written, search engine optimized, and written in a voice that's likely to attract and retain visitors and incoming links.

Once you know your budget, you can determine the type of blogger or blogging team you need to hire and the skills and qualifications they need to possess. The following sections discuss several skills a professional blogger should have.

Confirming blogging experience

Writing content for a blog is unlike any other type of writing. The best bloggers know how to marry great content, a personable voice, and traffic-building techniques in the posts they publish for you. Have candidates provide you with links to blogs they currently write or have written in the past, and take the time to read the content they published, the comments and conversations that related to those posts, and the linking and search engine optimization used within those posts. In addition, analyze the frequency with which they published new content and the depth of that content in terms of longevity, diversity, and interest.

Assessing ability to use blogging applications and tools

Experienced bloggers know how to use the tools of the blogosphere, including blogging applications such as WordPress and its associated tools. They know how to perform tasks such as inserting videos and images, and they understand how to name and link those files to boost search engine optimization. Typically, they know enough HTML and CSS to ensure your blog posts publish correctly and are visually appealing, and they know how to use functionality within blogging applications that can improve your blog's performance, boost the reader experience, and drive traffic.

Checking writing skills

The blogger you hire must be able to write coherently using proper grammar rules. Furthermore, they need to be able to write in a tone that's appropriate for the conversational style for which the blogosphere is so well known. If their posts all sound like press releases, marketing pitches, or corporate rhetoric, and if they're filled with grammatical and spelling errors, you don't want that person to write your organization's blog content. After all, your company's blog is one of the faces of your organization and brand. It's an online destination that can create a first impression *and* reader expectations for your company. If consumers arrive on your blog and find content that's difficult to read, they are unlikely to return. Your blog content should not sound like a commercial or be overloaded with industry jargon. Posts should also be free of misspellings and grammatical errors, which don't inspire confidence in the writer or the brand.

Taking advantage of social personality

A key component of successful blog promotion and growth is the conversation that happens on your blog through the commenting feature. If the blogger you hire needs to build relationships with consumers and people on and off your business blog, they need to bring a social personality with them. A good blogger is happy to be a part of online discussions both on and off your blog with appropriate compensation for their time.

Understanding search engine optimization

Search engine optimization (SEO) is essential to driving traffic to your blog. For most blogs, the majority of their traffic comes from search engines. The best bloggers know how to write posts using keywords, embed links, and create content that organically helps your blog's search rankings without violating any of the unwritten rules of the blogosphere and algorithms of search engines such as Google. Most professional bloggers have enough SEO knowledge and experience to be capable of publishing content on your blog that leverages the opportunity to increase search traffic to your business blog. You can find out more about search engine optimization in Chapter 1 of Book 5.

Existing social networking experience

Experienced bloggers should have established presences on social networking sites, such as Facebook and LinkedIn. Ask for their usernames on these sites, and connect with them so you can take a look at their profiles and find out how they're already using these tools. The best bloggers also have presences on a range of social media types to show their ability to create and engage with a variety of content types such as video on YouTube and visual content on Instagram.

Demonstrating knowledge about finding and attracting visitors to your blog

Good bloggers know how to find people who might be interested in the content on your blog and entice them to visit your blog to get that information. It will take them time to build an audience, but experienced bloggers know how to do it. Ask candidates what steps they would take to drive traffic to your blog and then read Book 6 and compare their answers with the techniques to the information shared there. At the very least, an experienced blogger will list the techniques presented in Book 6!

Showing self-motivation and dependability

Most bloggers work virtually and with little to no supervision. That means the blogger you hire must be self-motivated and dependable, so the content you and your audience need is published consistently and your requirements for the blog are met.

Understanding your business or industry

Although it's not essential for a blogger to understand your business to the same degree as other employees within the company, it does shorten the learning curve and make for more compelling content faster if the blogger you hire already understands your business, industry, products, customers, or services.

Publicizing Your Open Blogger Job

Next, you need to spread the word about your open blogger job. Fortunately, there are a number of blogs and websites that allow you to publish blogger job postings. Some require that you pay a small fee, but others are completely free. When you publish your blogger job opening on some of the more popular sites and blogs, people will share the link to your job posting on other blogs and social media platforms. In fact, if you publish your blogger job opening on some of the most popular sites that bloggers use to find positions, you may get hundreds of responses, many from very qualified bloggers.

The following list includes some of the most popular locations to publish your blogging job posting. Be sure to check each site before you submit a job posting to confirm the current fees:

>> **The ProBlogger Jobs Board (http://jobs.problogger.net):** This online jobs board, shown in Figure 3-2, is one of the most popular places for bloggers to seek work. You have to pay a fee to publish a job posting on here, but you're guaranteed to get a lot of qualified applicants when you do.

FIGURE 3-2:
The ProBlogger
Jobs Board.

>> **Indeed (www.indeed.com):** This job listing site is one of the most popular online and a great place to find writers looking for work.

>> **Freelance Writing Jobs (www.freelancewritinggigs.com):** One reason that this blog is popular for freelance writers, including bloggers, is its job postings. You can publish an open blogger job posting on Freelance Writing Jobs for a fee.

>> **BloggingPro (http://bloggingpro.com/jobs):** Splashpress Media, the same company that owns the aforementioned Freelance Writing Jobs blog, also owns BloggingPro. You can publish a blogger job posting there for free, or pay for a featured listing.

>> **Freelance websites:** Many websites allow companies to publish job postings. Freelancers visit these sites and conduct searches to find open positions that match their qualifications, and then they submit bids for those projects. Alternatively, you can search for freelancers who have created profiles on these sites to find someone whose skills match your needs and then invite them to submit a bid for your project. Most freelance websites charge fees — either membership or flat fees *or* a percentage of the freelancer's pay goes directly to the website. Examples of freelance websites where you can post open blogger jobs are Upwork (www.upwork.com) and Guru (www.guru.com).

WARNING

Be sure to read all the terms and conditions on these sites before you publish a job posting on them.

Hiring a Blogger

After you decide to hire a person to write and manage your business blog, you need to consider some personnel-related issues. For example, you need to define the requirements the blogger has to meet and the skills they need to have in order to meet those requirements successfully so you can write a detailed job description. You also need to review your budget to determine how much you can pay a blogger that you hire. The following sections highlight some of the most important factors you need to consider before you start your search for a business blogger.

Defining employment status

First, you need to determine whether the blogger should be an employee of your company or work for the company as a freelance contractor or vendor. Each employee status warrants a slightly different payment and taxing structure. You should consult with your accountant to determine which employee status and payment method is best for your business. Following is a brief overview of the three most common employee statuses that bloggers typically hold:

>> **Employee:** Many bloggers are full- or part-time employees of the companies they blog for. In the United States, they're paid as W-2 employees with taxes and other withholding deducted from their paychecks.

>> **Contractor:** The majority of bloggers are paid as independent contractors. In the United States, that means they aren't considered employees of the companies for which they provide services. As such, taxes aren't withheld from their pay, and they're taxed as 1099 contractors.

>> **Vendor:** Some bloggers provide services through their own companies, in a vendor-client relationship, with payment and taxes flowing through the vendors' companies and taxed as company income.

Establishing a pay model

After you determine the employment status that your blogger will hold, you need to determine how much you can pay them for their work. The pay structure you choose depends on the tasks and responsibilities the blogger will have to perform. For example, a blogger who is only required to publish posts would be paid differently from a blogger who is required to publish posts, respond to comments, and promote the blog through other websites.

Following are some of the most popular blogger pay structures to give you a place to start as you develop your own pay plan:

>> **Pay per post:** Many bloggers are paid a flat amount for each post they publish. Depending on the experience of the blogger you hire, you may pay anywhere from $50 per post to $250 and up. As you might expect, the best bloggers charge higher rates per post. Payment might also depend on the post length and other requirements, such as images and linking.

>> **Flat monthly rate:** Some bloggers are paid a flat rate each month and are required to perform certain tasks in order to earn that pay, such as publishing a specific number of posts, answering a specific number of comments, and creating a certain number of links to the blog from other sites. The payment amount varies greatly depending on the requirements the blogger must meet. Playing a flat rate typically works out to a lower rate per post than paying for one post at a time.

>> **Pay per post or flat monthly rate *plus* traffic bonuses:** Some bloggers are paid either per post or a flat monthly rate and have the opportunity to earn bonuses if they exceed certain goals, such as the number of pageviews, comments, or incoming links. As such, the payments these bloggers earn vary significantly.

>> **Pageviews or traffic only:** Some bloggers are paid a specific amount based on the traffic or pageviews a blog receives each month. For example, a blogger may earn a specific amount for every 1,000 pageviews the blog receives each month.

>> **Revenue sharing:** Some bloggers are paid only when the blog owner makes money based on ad impressions, clicks, donations, or affiliate ad purchases.

WARNING

Publishing ads on a business blog can make your blog appear less professional and damage the user experience.

>> **Combination pay models:** Some bloggers are paid using a combination of pay models, such as pay per post *plus* a pageviews bonus *plus* revenue sharing when a sale is made or ads are clicked.

The pay model you choose to follow or reinvent in order to pay your business blogger is up to you and depends very much on your goals for your blog and your budget. For example, if you want to hire a blogger who can write great content *and* drive traffic to your blog, and you're willing to pay them to invest time and energy into promoting your blog to the fullest extent, you need to be willing to pay significantly more than if you only need a blogger to publish posts on your blog.

REMEMBER

Most freelance bloggers wear many hats. Unless you hire a freelancer on a full-time basis and with full-time pay, it's very likely that the blogger you choose to write your business blog has other projects and clients as well. In fact, the best candidates *should* have existing clients. As such, bloggers tend to work unusual hours that fit their hectic schedules. Keep this in mind when you set expectations for your new blogger. You might have to be flexible in terms of the times a blogger actually performs work for you.

Defining Blogger Guidelines

It's important that you create written *blogger guidelines* that tell bloggers what they can and can't do on your company blog. At the same time, it's essential that your bloggers have the opportunity to write from their hearts and with passion so their unique voices and personalities shine through. That's how bloggers build relationships with readers, and relationships lead to purchases, word-of-mouth marketing, and brand loyalty.

The first step you can take to create blogger guidelines is to read Chapter 5 of this Book and discover some of the ways you can promote a business blog while ensuring your company stays out of trouble at the same time. Then communicate those do's and don'ts to your bloggers. Also, take the time to get specific in your guidelines. For example, if bloggers shouldn't mention your competitors in a negative way, make sure to include that in the guidelines. If you don't want bloggers to mention certain prices or talk about certain employees, you need to tell them that.

Following are a few suggestions for blogger guidelines to get you started on creating your own:

>> **Don't mention customer names without written permission.**

>> **Don't discuss individual customer service issues.** Instead, direct specific questions to the customer service phone number or contact form.

>> **Remain professional at all times.** Don't write negative information about your competitors or their products.

>> **Always use brand names correctly.** This is particularly important for companies that have specific capitalization or punctuation requirements related to their trademarks.

>> **Don't use offensive language.** Personal anecdotes and commentary are welcome, but remain professional in your language and content at all times. We don't want to offend anyone, but we do want your personality to shine through.

>> **Don't publish anything you might regret.** If you're not sure whether it's okay to post something, ask your supervisor. Once something is published online, it can spread faster and wider than you can imagine and then there's no taking it back!

It's important to start somewhere, but don't worry about creating a comprehensive list of guidelines right away. Instead, it's better to understand that your blogger guidelines will change over time as new situations occur on your blog and you learn from them.

REMEMBER

While moderation is important, don't try to control the conversation that happens on your blog too much. Instead, allow readers to take control while your bloggers gently nudge the conversation in the direction you want.

Writing a Style Guide

A *style guide* is a document that outlines the specific requirements that bloggers need to follow when they create content for your business blog. A style guide usually includes information about voice and formatting to ensure that all posts sound like they're consistently coming from the same company.

Consistency is essential to effectively build a brand, so use the following suggestions to create a comprehensive style guide for your contributors.

Crafting title guidelines

Writing great blog post titles is important for two reasons. First, blog post titles can appear across the web on social media platforms, in email messages, and in texts. They need to be intriguing enough to motivate people to click them and visit your blog to read more. Second, they should be written with search engine optimization in mind to boost incoming search traffic to your blog. That means blog post titles should include keywords whenever possible. You can read more about search engine optimization in Chapter 1 of Book 5.

Cover the following areas in your blog style guide:

- **Title length:** Specify requirements related to the number of words and characters used in blog post titles.

- **Format:** Describe the types of blog posts that should be used whenever possible, such as lists, questions, how-to, and so on.

- **Keywords:** Provide instructions for how, when, and where to use keywords in post titles.

- **Capitalization and punctuation:** If you have any requirements related to the use of title case and punctuation in post titles, include them in your style guide.

- **Grammar:** Any grammar requirements should also be provided. For example, include instructions related to using words or numerals for numbers and contractions.

Including body guidelines

The body of each blog post is where the most inconsistency can happen on team blogs. It's the heart of each blog post, so this section of your style guide is likely to be the longest.

Be certain to address the following points in your blog style guide:

- **Lead and closing:** Indicate whether you require that bloggers create a specific type of introduction at the beginning of posts or a summary at the end of posts.

- **Voice:** Explain how you want the voice and tone of the content published on your business blog to sound. For example, do you want your blog to use a casual tone to be more relatable, or a formal tone for a professional audience? Is it okay to use humor or sarcasm?

- **Length:** Indicate specific blog post length requirements related to word count.

- **Links:** Explain what type of anchor text should be used with links, how many links are too many or too few for a post, when to link internally to other posts, links to avoid, and how links should open when visitors click them (in the same window or a new window).

- **Images:** Give details for where to find images that can be used on the blog as well as where and when to use images within each post. Also, provide instructions for image size, positioning, alignment, and titles.

>> **Formatting:** Blog posts are easiest to read when paragraphs are short (no more than a few sentences), headings are used to break up text, and bulleted and numbered lists are used to make posts easy to scan. Include specific instructions related to formatting for all contributors to follow.

>> **Attribution:** Provide an example of exactly how all sources (for text, quotes, and images) should be cited in all posts.

>> **Categories and tags:** Most blogging applications allow bloggers to categorize or label posts and add keyword tags to them. Make sure your style guide includes instructions for tagging and categorizing posts. For example, state the maximum number of categories and tags each post can include.

>> **Keywords and SEO:** Provide directions for evaluating and selecting keywords, using them within the post body, and writing posts with SEO best practices in mind. Also, explain all SEO mistakes that bloggers should avoid.

>> **Grammar and punctuation:** Include information related to how you want bloggers to use brand and company names, how to format quotes, and how to use acronyms and abbreviations.

>> **Original content:** It's a good idea to include a section in your style guide that reiterates the requirement for all posts to be original content that have not been copied from any other source nor will be republished on any other website or blog.

Highlighting additional tasks, tools, and features

If bloggers are expected to perform any additional tasks or use any additional tools or features when they write and publish posts on your business blog, provide detailed directions within your blog style guide.

Additional topics that are often included in blog style guides are described in this list:

>> **Plug-ins:** If your blog uses any *plug-ins* or *extensions* — add-ons with features that extend functionality — explain what they are and how to use them. For example, many blogs built using WordPress.org use third-party plug-ins that require bloggers to fill out forms within the blog post editor or plug-ins that require bloggers to select featured images, and more.

>> **Scheduling:** If bloggers are allowed to schedule their own posts for publishing on your blog, provide any requirements related to when they can set their posts to go live.

>> **Social media:** If you require that bloggers promote their posts through their social media profiles and accounts, explain what you expect them to do.

>> **Commenting:** If you're paying bloggers to respond to comments on their own posts, comment on posts written by other bloggers on your blog, or comment on posts published on other blogs, provide all of the requirements and an explanation for how their comments should be tracked.

REMEMBER

Your blog will change and grow; therefore, your style guide needs to be flexible so that it can evolve with your blog.

Training Bloggers

It's absolutely imperative that you take the time to train your bloggers. If they're internal employees, you need to make sure that they understand how to use the tools of the blogosphere in order to meet the goals you set for them and your blog. If they're freelancers, you need to make sure that they understand your business, your customers, your cause community, and your competitors.

It's your job to provide your bloggers with rules and guidelines as discussed in the previous section. Don't assume they know what you want them to do. Every blog owner has different objectives for their blogs and styles they prefer for the content that's published on their blogs. You need to clearly communicate your objectives and preferences to your bloggers.

TIP

Create an electronic training manual (be sure to include your blogger guidelines and style guide discussed earlier in this chapter) that your bloggers can refer to at any time for direction and that you can update on the fly whenever it's necessary (and it will be).

If you have specific requirements for your business blog, you should have your bloggers submit posts to you for review during the first month or so that they write for your blog. This way, you can work with each blogger to revise posts to meet your vision for the blog's content *before* those posts are published for the world to see. In time, your bloggers will get a better understanding of what you want and need from the blog's content, and you'll become more confident that each blogger can meet your expectations.

REMEMBER

Most professional bloggers expect each of their clients to have varied and sometimes very specific likes and dislikes in relation to the content published on their blogs. They expect you to provide them with feedback and guidance so they can better meet your objectives. Don't be afraid to give them some direction. You'll both be happier and more satisfied in the end if you communicate well from the beginning.

Communicating and Collaborating with Bloggers

A business blog written by multiple contributors has little chance for success if everyone's efforts are disjointed and incongruous. That's why ongoing communication and collaboration is vital to the health of a team blog. Even a business blog written by a single blogger is limited in terms of growth potential if the blogger operates in a silo with no feedback from the business.

If you want your business blog to grow and your bloggers to be happy so their passion and enjoyment is evident in their posts, then you need to create a 360-degree loop of communication that's nonthreatening.

Knowing what to communicate and why

Much of the information you need to communicate to your blogging team on an ongoing basis should be related to performance, topic holes that need to be filled, ideas for future content, and acknowledging successes.

Use your team communications as a platform to

>> **Solicit ideas and information from your bloggers.** Find out what's working for your bloggers and what improvements they might need you to make. For example, your team members might have great ideas for topics that aren't adequately covered on your blog yet. Give them the freedom to voice their opinions.

>> **Keep your team members informed.** Discuss the blog's growth and how your team's efforts are affecting the overall business. Mention tactics that need to be modified and warn bloggers about upcoming changes. For example, if you're introducing a new tool, make sure your contributors understand why and how it will affect their jobs.

>> **Understand who your bloggers are.** Bloggers bring specific skills and experience to the table. Collaborating with them and learning from them, rather than just dictating to them, is particularly important, especially when the bloggers you hire are experienced professionals.

>> **Publicly acknowledge your contributors.** Most importantly, thank them for their effort and make sure you understand that you value their efforts. For example, if a particular post is picked up and shared by a popular site, your site will receive a great deal of traffic. You should not only thank the blogger personally and publicly in your team forum, but also think of incentives for

your top performers. For example, you can create monetary bonuses for exceptional performance, such as rewarding bloggers for big traffic numbers to their specific posts.

Using tools for communication and collaboration

Whether your business blog is written by a team of internal employees or writers located around the world, you need some way to communicate and collaborate with them. Fortunately, a variety of tools make managing teams virtually extremely easy, and most of them are very affordable (or free).

These tools can be accessed regardless of location or time zone, making it far easier to manage a team of diverse bloggers than traditional meetings during regular office hours provides.

The following list describes a variety of popular communications and collaboration tools that are perfect for managing teams of bloggers:

>> **Forums:** Many free and paid forum tools make it extremely easy for teams of bloggers to communicate and collaborate. vBulletin (www.vbulletin.com), phpBB forums (www.phpbb.com), and bbPress (http://bbpress.org) are all popular options.

>> **Groups:** You can create a group for collaboration using Facebook Groups. Invite your blog contributors to join the group, and you're ready to go. Since most bloggers already know how to use these tools, there is little to no learning curve for team members.

>> **Teambox** (www.teambox.com): This collaboration tool for online teams and project management is easy to use, and it operates similarly to a social network with activity streams, threaded conversations, inbox management, alerts, RSS feeds, and more.

>> **Basecamp** (www.basecamp.com): This is one of the most popular online collaboration tools. Team members can upload and share documents, have discussions, create calendars, and more.

IN THIS CHAPTER

» **Understanding types of blog posts for company blogs**

» **Turning a business blog into a sales tool**

» **Following success tips**

» **Avoiding things customers don't like**

» **Engaging your audience**

Chapter **4**

Writing an Organization's Blog

Your organization's blog has no chance at success if it's not well-written, but that applies to more than just the grammatical correctness of your blog's content. It also applies to the *kind* of content that you publish on your company blog. To be successful and attract and retain an audience, your business blog posts have to be interesting, entertaining, informative, and conversational. In other words, they need to provide value to the reader. Different readers will surely find value in different types of content. But the bottom line is still the same: If your content isn't quality, no one will want to read your blog.

This chapter focuses on the actual writing of your business blog posts, showing you how to write content that your audience members want and that can motivate them to join the conversation. Remember, the power of your blog as a business tool is building relationships with readers. You can't build a relationship with someone unless you use your blog as an interactive location for two-way conversation.

Discovering the Types of Corporate and Non-Profit Blog Posts

The only limit in terms of the types of posts you can publish on your business blog is your own creativity. By thinking outside the box, you can create a wide variety of blog posts to keep your content fresh and unique. By writing with your own voice and allowing your personality to shine through, your blog posts are innately unique.

To get started on your path to creating excellent business blog content, take a look at the short list of types of posts you could publish as follows (you can get additional details about these post types and more in Chapter 2 of Book 1):

>> **New product information and reviews:** If you have a new product, talk about it on your blog!

>> **How-to's:** Teach your readers how to use your products. Consider video posts for this type of content!

>> **Trends:** Discuss trends related to your industry. What's changing? What are the latest predictions for the future? Add your own insight to your posts to remind readers that you're knowledgeable and trustworthy.

>> **New charity initiatives:** Introduce new ways that your organization is making a difference.

>> **Answer questions:** Your blog is a great place to answer consumer questions related to your products and services.

WARNING

Be careful with this type of post unless dealing with customer service concerns is part of the goal of your blog. Even if you don't invite questions related to complaints, you will likely receive them!

>> **Interviews:** You can interview happy customers, distributors, employees, industry experts, and organization volunteers.

>> **Videos and podcasts:** Mix things up by publishing video and audio posts. Publish a video demo of your product in action or film a behind-the-scenes video that shows your employees doing their jobs to make your business seem more human to your blog audience. Interview a customer or employee and publish it on your blog as an audio post. Get creative and have fun!

>> **Photos:** Take pictures around your office or at company events and share them in a blog post so people can see what's happening behind the scenes. Photos can be especially compelling for non-profit organizations. Tell your story!

>> **Contests and discounts:** Make your audience feel special by holding contests and announcing special discounts for your products and services on your blog before anyone else hears about them, or make the contests or discounts for your products and services exclusive to people who find them on your blog.

>> **Insider perspectives:** A great way to build relationships with your audience members is to give them an idea of who is behind the company and what it's like to work at the company. As such, publish posts that talk about the daily activities of your employees or volunteers. What motivates them? What keeps them loving what they do?

>> **Tips, secrets, and lists:** People love list posts, and you can create a list about almost any topic. For a business blog, you can publish helpful lists that give people ideas about how to use your products. You can also get creative and publish entertaining posts such as *10 Things You Never Knew about the CEO,* or informative posts such as *10 Ways Your Charity is Making a Difference*. The key is to offer useful information about your business and build relationships by letting your audience get to know you, your employees, and your business a bit better.

>> **Guest posts:** Invite industry experts and customers to write guest blog posts and offer new perspectives for your audience.

>> **Polls and questions:** Ask questions and publish polls on your blog for informal market research and information sharing. People love polls!

>> **Industry news:** Give your audience an education about your industry by talking about it on your blog. Add your own commentary to news about current events to help your readers understand how it applies to them and can affect their lives.

>> **Company news:** Share exciting news about your company but don't write the news so that it reads like a press release. Keep it conversational.

TIP

Don't always publish the same types of blog posts. Mix up your content for variety or your audience will lose interest.

Canva is one of the leading online design websites. The brand maintains a blog (www.canva.com/learn), shown in Figure 4-1, where the writers talk about a wide variety of topics from how to maintain your calendar to lists of inspirational quotes, but those posts are all cleverly tied back to Canva's core purpose — design.

An example of this is a listicle titled *10 Common Myths About Graphic Design*. The post cleverly tackles a Canva-related topic that is educational and serves the reader while embedding invitations to click through to Canva's design tool within the post, as shown in Figure 4-2.

FIGURE 4-1:
Canva's blog provides content on a variety of topics.

FIGURE 4-2:
Canva provides useful content while linking to their design tools.

Turning a Business Blog into a Direct Sales Tool

Your business blog can be an effective tool in driving sales both directly and indirectly. The first thing that probably comes to mind when thinking about using your blog as a sales tool is publishing posts that hype your products and services.

This is absolutely something you should do on your business blog, but you need to exercise restraint. You don't want your business blog to read like one marketing pitch after another. Remember, your business blog isn't an advertising medium but rather a medium for interaction, building relationships, and driving word-of-mouth marketing. However, you can apply short-term marketing tactics to your business blog strategy by occasionally publishing new product announcements, reviews, and special discounts.

Many small business owners do this very well on their company blogs by mixing useful, informative posts with announcements of events they'll be speaking at or attending. That's a great way to establish yourself as an expert in your industry and offer people places where they can network with you in person. Long story short, if your promotional posts are useful and interesting to your blog's audience, then by all means publish them.

As an example, The Moz Blog (`www.moz.com/blog`), shown in Figure 4-3, regularly publishes helpful and informative content related to the services they offer — SEO. This is a great way to share useful information *and* remind readers of the expertise you offer through your business.

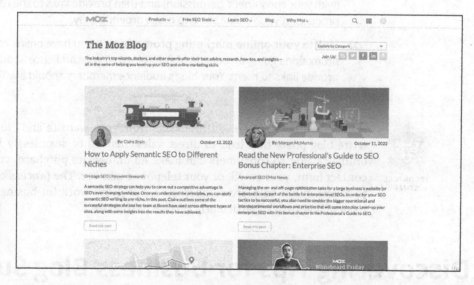

FIGURE 4-3:
The Moz Blog offers informative content related to the service they sell.

You can turn your business blog into a sales tool in a number of specific ways. Some suggestions follow, but remember, your business blog is *always* an indirect catalyst to sales because it provides you the opportunity to build your brand, engage your target audience members, and develop relationships with them in a manner that wasn't possible before the creation of blogging and social media. Use that ability to connect with consumers to your advantage, but don't abuse it.

(I tell you how to avoid abuses in the later section, "Avoiding Things Blog Readers Don't Like.")

» **Publish exclusive discounts and promotions.** Your blog audience should be rewarded for taking the time out of their busy schedules to read your content. Make them feel special and valued by providing exclusive discounts and information on your blog that no one can hear about *unless* they read your blog.

» **Provide links to your online catalog.** Don't be afraid to get creative in order to publish links to products you want to push on your blog posts. For example, publish product demonstration videos or tutorials and tips related to one of your products, and be sure to include links to that product in your online store to make purchasing it as easy as possible.

» **Send newsletters with links to your blog.** Email newsletters to your customer email list with links to your useful blog content. Make sure some of those links lead to posts that hype a product or offer an exclusive discount to entice readers to make a purchase.

» **Ask consumers to write reviews.** Publish consumer reviews as blog posts (with your consumers' permission) and then provide links to the reviewed products in your online store to make ordering easy.

» **Link to your online marketing promotions.** If you have online marketing promotions going on outside of your blog, tell your audience about them and provide links to them. Your blog's audience members should always feel like they're in the know.

TECHNICAL STUFF

If your business operates offline aside from your website and blog, you can still write blog posts that lead to direct sales. Instead of seamlessly linking to your online catalog so consumers can make an immediate purchase, you can link to a contact form, your email, or your telephone number. The process consumers have to follow might be more cumbersome, but it can work for businesses that don't have online stores, particularly service businesses.

Discovering Tips for Business Blog Success

You can do many small things when you write your business blog posts to position your blog for success. Most of them don't take long to implement but can have a big impact on your blog's growth. Many of these tips apply for personal blogs, too. Take a look at the following list to put your blog on the path to success:

>> **Write often.** Each new blog post represents a new entry point for search engines to find your blog. The more you post, the more potential search visitors you can attract.

>> **Write well.** No one wants to read a blog that's poorly written and filled with grammatical and spelling errors. Furthermore, great content will pull in traffic over time.

>> **Be social.** Show your audience members you value them by responding to comments and emails and making them feel like they're part of the community.

>> **Use links.** Include outbound links to great content on other blogs. Don't just hyperlink words like *look here.* Instead, use keywords for linking to boost your search engine rankings.

>> **Get incoming links.** Visit other blogs and start leaving comments. Offer to write guest blog posts for other bloggers, and be sure to include links back to your blog.

>> **Remember your brand.** Blogs are powerful brand-building tools. Be sure to present your brand consistently and persistently.

>> **Write for your audience.** Your biggest priority is writing content that will help your readers. Put yourself in their shoes and then create the kind of content they want and need.

>> **Don't fall for get-traffic-quick schemes.** More often than not, people who guarantee big traffic in a short amount of time are using techniques that could get you banned from Google search.

>> **Don't buy text links.** Google doesn't like them because they artificially increase the number of incoming links that a site gets, which Google uses to rank search results. If Google catches you paying for text links, your blog may be removed from Google searches entirely.

>> **Don't be a hermit.** For your blog to be successful, you need to spend time outside of your blog networking and promoting your amazing content. The blogosphere doesn't work like *Field of Dreams.* If you build it, they *won't* necessarily come.

Avoiding Things Blog Readers Don't Like

Your blog is an interactive tool that thrives on personality and conversation. Blog posts that sound like your legal department wrote them won't attract or retain visitors. In fact, they'll drive visitors away. Instead, your blog content has to be inviting and devoid of the corporate style that many businesses use in their customer communications. Blog posts should be easy to read, highly scannable, and interesting, as opposed to being excruciating to read, so complex they require a legal dictionary to understand, and utterly boring. Again, put yourself in your target audience members' shoes and publish the type of content they want and need written in a friendly voice that invites them to hang out for a while.

TIP

Take a step back from your blog and read the content as if you were attending a party and the blog posts are stories that another party guest is telling you. Would you want to keep talking to this person, or would you want to escape and avoid him for the rest of the night? The answer to that question should tell you whether or not you're writing the kind of content that attracts and retains visitors to your blog.

It can take time for your blogging style and personality to evolve, but you can help the process by avoiding some of the fundamental don'ts of the blogosphere. The following sections tell you how to avoid doing some of the things that blog readers don't like. Commit these wrongs at your own risk.

Avoiding a blog that reads like an employee manual

Your business blog shouldn't be written like an employee manual, a press release, a legal document, a technical paper, a training guide, or anything similarly difficult to read. Blog posts are meant to be highly consumable, in other words, easy to read. Posts should sound conversational, written to sound as much the way someone would talk as possible. Would you rather read a manual from your company's human resources department or personable blog posts written in a conversational and inviting tone? With any luck, you answered the latter, because that's what the vast majority of blog readers want.

The team from the WooCommerce blog (www.woocommerce.com/blog), shown in Figure 4-4, offers a great example of writing business blog posts in a human voice that's conversational, inviting, and tells a story.

Humanizing an impersonal tone

This tip goes along with the "Be human" tip. Your blog posts must be written in a conversational tone that allows your personality and unique voice to shine through. Often a blogger's passion for their subject and personal viewpoint is what keeps readers coming back to read more. Yours might be a business blog, but that doesn't mean it has to be written like a business communication. Instead, inject your personality into every post.

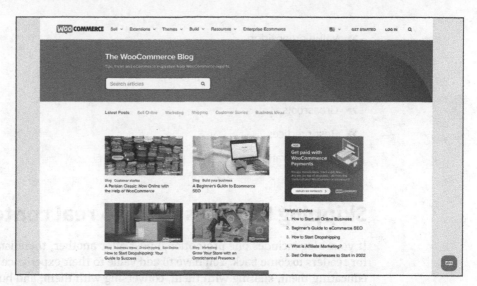

FIGURE 4-4:
The WooCommerce blog is written in a conversational tone.

Uncovering a blog that lacks transparency

In today's world, transparency is more important than ever. Companies that are honest and forthcoming with information are valued higher in consumers' minds than those that try to hide information or tell only part of a story. With that in mind, your blog posts should be written with honesty and candor without giving away any company secrets. People can see through a blog that's written in half-truths and will leave your blog with the perception of your company being untrustworthy if that's the only kind of content they find. That's a reputation you don't want to spread!

Ditching the corporate rhetoric

Jargon and buzzwords have no place in a business blog unless your target audience is business-to-business readers who understand those words and phrases. Consider your audience before you use an acronym in your blog posts.

WARNING

Following are just ten of the many words that the online community often refers to as *gobbledygook* because they do nothing to enhance writing. Try to avoid these words unless they truly are appropriate for your specific audience:

» Scalability

» Best in class

» Methodology

» Paradigm

- » Value proposition
- » Synergy
- » Organic
- » Grassroots
- » Best practices
- » Next generation

Skipping PR posts with no real content

If your blog includes one promotional post after another, there isn't much reason for readers to come back. You have to add value to their experience on your blog by educating them, sharing with them, conversing with them, and building relationships with them as opposed to just speaking *at* them by publishing one PR pitch after another. Would you want to watch television if all you saw was one commercial after another? The same question can be asked about your blog. Would you want to read a blog that includes one promotional post after another? Your business blog should include at least 80 percent useful posts and 20 percent promotional posts to strike a good balance that will keep readers interested without frustrating them.

Engaging with Your Audience

The power of a business blog comes from the interactivity it provides between the company publishing the blog and the consumers reading it. It's an opportunity to build relationships with consumers that every business owner can leverage because the barriers to entry into the blogosphere are negligible. Keep in mind that the way your audience engages with you through your blog can often coincide with the types of blog posts you write, as discussed earlier in this chapter. In other words, your content can often prompt and steer the ongoing conversation that happens on your blog. The following sections review some of the ways you can interact with your audience to create conversation and build relationships with them.

Providing content the audience wants

The best way to strike up a conversation is to talk about something other people are actually interested in. If your side of the conversation is boring, chances are good that no one else will join in. However, if your side of the conversation is informative and interesting, other people are much more likely to join in.

Responding to readers in a timely manner

The goal of any blog, corporate or personal, is to create a conversation between the reader and the blogger as well as between the readers. Be sure to include guidelines for your team bloggers or for yourself around how quickly comments should both be moved out of moderation and responded to. There's nothing more frustrating than finding great content from a favorite brand, asking a question that's important to you, and not receiving a response.

REMEMBER

Comments should be responded to in a matter of days at the longest, not a matter of weeks. And while it is important to block spam left in the comments section of your blog, don't abandon legitimate posts in comment purgatory! Pop in often to read and approve comments so that readers don't wonder what happened to that gem they left in response to your great post.

Encouraging comments

Remind readers that they're invited to join the conversation by asking for their opinions. Ending your blog posts with a simple sentence, such as, "Leave a comment and tell us what you think," can do wonders in terms of prompting people to join the conversation. Want to take it to the next level? Instead of asking open-ended questions, considering asking a question that is more pointed and relates directly to the content of the post.

Solving reader problems

As much as readers love a well-written, engaging blog post, you know what they love even more? They love feeling like stopping by a blog resulted in their problem being solved!

This may look like how-to videos or tutorials, helpful product reviews with tips, or work arounds for known issues with a product. You may even want to include a special section that provides content solely with the purpose of helping readers solve issues they're facing related to your business or content area.

REMEMBER

Decide from the beginning if you want your blog to play a role in customer service. If that is outside of the scope of your goals or simply would require too many resources at this time, be sure to make that clear on your site so that your readers don't come to your blog to seek help with customer or client concerns.

Making the audience feel special or exclusive

As I mention earlier in this chapter, there are many ways you can create blog posts that make your audience feel special or exclusive. For example, you can publish special discounts for your blog audience only. The goal is to thank your audience for reading your blog and show them how much you value them. If you ignore them, they're not as likely to stay loyal to your brand. Instead, make sure you remind them how important they are to you by publishing unique posts that make them feel special.

Creating relationships with key influencers

One of the best things you can do for your business blog is to find and connect with key online influencers. These influencers might be other industry bloggers, consumers, journalists, industry experts, or even customers and volunteers. The key is to find people who can be your vocal brand advocates and spread the word about your products and blog by creating an online buzz.

For example, if you sell technical equipment, connecting with gadget bloggers who have large and loyal audiences of their own would be a major coup for you. When those influencers know your blog exists and you publish great content, they might link to your content. Alternatively, you can approach them to write product reviews, or write a guest blog post for their blogs. But first, you have to build relationships with them or your requests are likely to get lost in the email clutter popular online influencers have to sort through every day.

Leveraging word-of-mouth marketing

After you find online influencers, you can leverage their reach to boost word-of-mouth marketing about your blog, business, products, and services. Additionally, you can tap your own blog audience members and ask them to write about your business or share your best posts with the larger online community through social media platforms. The key is to jump-start the online sharing process so the online buzz and word-of-mouth marketing have a chance to grow and spread.

Furthermore, take time to interact with people outside of your blog. You can start an online buzz through conversations that happen on other blogs and websites just as easily as you can start them on your own blog. The key is to be patient and persistent. In time, your efforts *will* pay off, but blogging success very rarely happens overnight. For most bloggers, it can take months or years to build a successful blog. Be prepared to invest your time and energy into achieving long-term success with short-term boosts along the way.

IN THIS CHAPTER

» **Following the rules of the blogosphere**

» **Staying within the law**

» **Keeping private information private**

» **Responding to negative attacks**

» **Leveraging search engine reputation management**

Chapter **5**

Keeping Yourself and Your Organization Out of Trouble

ecause anyone with Internet access can see your organization's blog, you must follow both the rules of the blogosphere *and* the rules of law in order to avoid trouble. Although a blog might seem more casual and flexible than traditional business publications, and it should be, that doesn't mean you can violate established rules and laws. This is particularly true for public companies that are subject to strict insider trading regulations. The best path to follow is one of caution. It's better not to publish something you're unsure of than it is to risk getting in trouble for something you publish on your company's blog.

Trouble isn't restricted to the content you publish on your blog. It can also come from the *conversation* that happens on and off your blog. Unfortunately, some people travel around the blogosphere trying to incite arguments and stir up trouble by publishing comments for the sole purpose of igniting passionate responses. You need to be aware of that potential problem when you publish a brand blog, and you should have a plan to avoid or deal with negative publicity when the time comes.

This chapter provides an overview of the primary areas where business bloggers can find themselves at the center of trouble as well as specific rules and guidelines you need to follow to avoid attracting a negative buzz and unwanted turmoil related to your company and brand.

Learning Rules and Laws

You've undoubtedly heard of copyright infringement and privacy laws. Both can be applied to the content you publish on your company's blog. Furthermore, you're probably familiar with terms such as *spam* and *attribution*. All of these terms represent rules and laws you need to be aware of and adhere to as you publish content on your blog. Just because you're hiding behind your computer as a blogger doesn't mean that you're above the law. The rules still apply to you.

Many rules and guidelines apply to all bloggers, but you also need to take time to consider how your online behavior and activity affect your brand based on the industry you're in, who your customers are, and where and what you sell. Non-profit and NGO bloggers also need to be aware of the guidelines that pertain specifically to their organizations. It's very possible that you need to follow industry-related rules in addition to the blanket guidelines and laws that apply to the blogosphere and online publishing.

TIP

When in doubt, either don't publish questionable content or consult with an attorney to ensure that you can safely publish that content on your organization's blog. It's always better to be safe than sorry because, in the eyes of the blogosphere or in a court of law, you can't simply claim ignorance and walk away unscathed when you do something wrong.

Following blogosphere rules

The rules of the blogosphere deal primarily with ethics. In other words, the blogosphere simply asks you to publish content in an ethical manner.

WARNING

Following are some of the primary rules you need to adhere to as a blogger:

>> **Publish original content.** Don't copy content and republish it as your own.

>> **Provide attribution.** Always link to your sources. You can do this in a variety of ways so long as the method you choose is clear and easy to locate. For example, you might include a photo attribution in the image caption, as

shown in Figure 5-1, which is from my personal blog Resourceful Mommy (www.resourcefulmommy.com). Remember to ask for permission before using content that is not your own.

English Tea Garden Presented by Twinings of London in the United Kingdom pavilion, which also offers a Self-Guided Tea Tour.

» Don't publish spam. Don't leave comments on other blogs that are filled with links and viewed as spam.

» Play nice. Don't attack other people or organizations on your blog in a hateful manner.

In other words, act politely.

Staying within the law

Many laws apply to online publishing, and unfortunately, many personal bloggers don't know what they are. You can't afford *not* to fully understand those laws and apply them to your company or organization's blog. The last thing you want to elicit from your blog is a legal entanglement. With that in mind, it's a good idea to publish a Terms and Conditions document on your blog so your audience understands the legalities surrounding their participation on your blog. Your blog should also have a clearly stated and easy to find privacy policy. You can learn more about these types of disclosure statements in Chapter 4 of Book 1.

To be safe, always publish content on your business blog with the following legal issues in mind:

TIP

>> **Copyrights:** Every piece of published content is owned by the person who created it under copyright law. That means you can't simply find an image on the web and republish it on your business blog. Don't violate copyright laws. Either create original content or seek written permission to use someone else's content before you publish it on your blog.

Read Chapter 4 of Book 1 for more blogging rules and details about Creative Commons copyright licenses and fair use.

>> **Plagiarism:** Simply republishing content that someone else created is considered to be plagiarism and is punishable by law. Instead of republishing someone else's words, link to your source and then write about the content and inject your own voice, opinions, and expertise to make it your own.

>> **Permissions:** Don't use images, graphs, charts, texts, or any other content on your blog unless one of these exceptions applies:

- You have written permission to do so.

- You know the content is copyrighted under a Creative Commons license that allows for its use.

- You know it's appropriate for you to use that content under the laws of fair use.

You can communicate to your readers that content is republished with permission by including a simple phrase such as "used with permission" and linking back to your source as appropriate.

>> **Citations:** Always, always, always cite your sources and link to them if possible.

>> **Libel:** Avoid publishing content on your business blog that can be construed as libelous. In other words, don't publish content that's malicious or can damage another person's or business's reputation, credibility, and livelihood.

>> **Insider information:** If your company is public, you must adhere to laws related to insider trading and sharing information that might affect the company's stock price. Be sure that any content you publish on your business blog is information that's freely available to the public.

>> **Confidentiality agreements:** If your company has signed confidentiality agreements with any business partners, your blog content must adhere to the restrictions listed in those agreements.

Maintaining private information

As an organization, you likely have access to personal information about your volunteers, donors, customers, employees, and business partners. Privacy laws get stricter every day. Don't risk violating them. Instead, avoid publishing personal or private information on your blog unless you get written permission to do so first. This applies to written content, quotes, pictures, and anything else that might violate either a person or a business's privacy.

WARNING

Don't share private information about your blog's audience unless you get explicit permission to do so.

It's a good idea to publish a privacy policy on your blog, so visitors understand what information you collect from them during their visit (such as the path they travel as they navigate your blog — accessed via your web analytics tool, as discussed in Chapter 2 of Book 5). You can see an example of a privacy policy in Chapter 4 of Book 1.

TIP

Consider hiring an attorney to write your business blog's privacy policy and Terms and Conditions document to ensure you and your business are fully protected.

Knowing when to hold your tongue

Because the blogosphere is an open medium, people will stumble upon your content and might leave irrelevant, erroneous, or hateful comments on your business blog. It's important that you understand that these types of comments are inevitable and prepare for responding to them. The worst thing you can do is react in a negative way to negative online conversations about your organization or blog. Instead, act professionally and represent your business the best way you can by deleting irrelevant, hateful comments, communicating in a professional tone, and trying to steer conversations back on track without arguing.

TIP

Creating and posting a clear comment policy helps to avoid complaints or accusations of burying negative feedback should you need to delete comments from trolls. If you've let readers know up front what you will and will not tolerate in the comments, they are less likely to complain when you enforce those rules.

The same theory holds true for the content you publish on your blog. Always make sure the topics you write about are relevant and useful to your audience. Although it's important to inject your personality into your business blog posts, don't write your business blog like it's your personal blog. In other words, although there are some topics you can write about freely on your personal blogs, those topics might not be appropriate for your business blog.

For example, most professional bloggers steer clear of writing about religion and politics on their blogs unless those topics relate specifically to their organization because they know those topics can affect their brand and can incite passionate conversations that often turn into arguments and become irrelevant to the business behind the blog. It's up to you to determine which topics and conversations are relevant to your blog and then write content that's appropriate for those topics.

REMEMBER

If your organization deals directly with content areas that are more likely to attract trolls looking to start trouble in the comments or even just well-intentioned readers who are overzealous, it is especially important to find a blogging team well-equipped to handle your unique readership. For example, if your organization is a religious-based charity, create clear guidelines for how your blogging team should respond and react to comments that are outside the scope of what is important on your company's blog. And make it very clear to readers what will and will not be published in comments.

TIP

If someone leaves an irrelevant comment on one of your blog posts that isn't spam but also isn't helpful, you can try to steer the conversation back on track by responding with a new comment pointing readers back to the topic at hand.

Responding to Negative Comments and Attacks

The day will come during the lifespan of your company's blog that you or your business will become the subject of negative comments or the target of attacks. This negative publicity can happen on or off your blog, so it's important that you keep track of what's being said about your business and brand online by implementing a strategy for search engine reputation management (SERM), as discussed later in this chapter. At the same time, you need to have a strategy in place to respond to negative comments and attacks.

You can employ a number of tactics to respond to a negative buzz about your business online. Each situation is unique, and each business has its own goals for its online presence that can affect its response strategies. Take the time to prepare yourself for the inevitable negativity that will come as a result of your business blog so you can react in a timely and professional way when that day comes.

REMEMBER

Bloggers must be thick-skinned. There may come a time when someone will say something online that's particularly cruel about you as a person. Don't take it personally, and try to remember that people forget their manners when they're hiding behind their computers. Don't feed into their power delusions by spending any time thinking about them.

Ignoring the negative

Believe it or not, sometimes responding to negative comments just adds fuel to the fire. In time, your loyal blog audience might come to your defense, so you won't have to participate in a negative conversation at all. I caution against ignoring relevant negative comments on your company's blog, though. Remember, transparency and honesty are essential elements of a successful business blog. By professionally responding to relevant negative comments, your audience is likely to respect your forthrightness and like you more for it. You may even find that the negative comments are helpful for your organization's growth, by showing that you are able to receive critical feedback and adapt accordingly. A once-disappointed customer who has been won over by your organization's efforts to make a situation better has the potential to become your biggest fan!

However, you can take a different approach to handling highly negative comments that address personal complaints and add little to the conversation on your business blog. By responding with a comment that directs the visitor to the appropriate source for answers to their personal problems or questions, you can keep private conversations off of your business blog while being responsive and showing you value *all* visitors at the same time.

TECHNICAL STUFF

Don't be afraid to delete hateful or off-topic comments that detract from the conversation on your blog. You can also edit comments to remove profanity. Remember, just be sure to publish a comment policy on your blog to set visitor expectations, as discussed in Chapter 4 of Book 1!

Defending the business

The natural response to negative comments and attacks is to defend yourself and your business. Naturally, you should defend your company against false statements, but be careful. You don't want to come off as completely defensive. Instead, you need to *listen to* and *acknowledge* what people are saying in their comments — even if those comments are negative. Doing so demonstrates to your audience that you value all your visitors and understand that their thoughts, opinions, and experiences matter to you and your company.

When you defend your organization against negative comments and attacks, do so in a professional manner. Be open to opposing viewpoints and allow debates and discussions to happen on your blog, knowing that your role is to provide accurate information and a forum for dialogue while reeling in conversations that veer off topic. Instead of jumping up and saying, "That's not true!" in response to a negative comment, ask the commenter why they feel that way or what happened to give them that perception so you can work to make things right or help clarify the issue for them.

Blogging is all about building relationships. Even if you disagree with someone, their opinion is valid and should be acknowledged accordingly. Chances are good that if one person feels negatively about an aspect of your business, they are not alone. Rather than telling them they are wrong, discuss the issue with them, and your larger audience will respond positively to your openness, honesty, and willingness to listen to and work with your customers. In short, don't try to squash the negative. Instead, try to turn negatives into positives through the social conversations that blogs offer. You may find that your openness and willing to change turns a negative commenter into one of your biggest brand supporters!

Engaging the source and audience

Often, negative comments are made about you or your business off of your blog. You need to be aware of those conversations and reach out to the people who start them to set the record straight. Proceed professionally so the originating blogger or commenter understands you're not defensive or attacking them in return. You want to extend an olive branch and try to work with them to resolve problems and correct wrongs. Point them in the direction of accurate information online, offer to follow up via email or phone, or provide them with the accurate contact information where they can get the help they need.

REMEMBER

Make it clear from the start, both to your readers and your blogging team, if your company's blog is going to be a tool in your organization's customer service toolbox. If that is not the purpose of your blog, don't get lost in the weeds of trying to handle customer service issues within the comments of your blog posts. Instead, create and follow a policy of redirecting customer service conversations to the appropriate channels.

The same process holds true on your own blog. Over time, you'll notice that your loyal audience will do some of the talking for you both on and off your blog. As your loyal brand advocates, they'll jump to your defense, sometimes better than you can do yourself!

Understanding Search Engine Reputation Management (SERM)

Search engine reputation management (SERM) is tied to online brand building. When you search Google or your preferred search engine for your business or brand name, what comes up? Are the results you find the kind of results that you want your customers to find? Those links are the ones people will click to learn about you, your business, and your brand, so the content found through those links will define your online reputation. *Search engine reputation management* is the process of working to make sure that search engine results related to your business offer links that accurately reflect your brand.

As an example, look at Figure 5-2, which shows an old Google search results page for the keyword phrase *target blog*. At the time this search was conducted about a decade prior to the publishing of this book, the second result on the page was a blog written by a disgruntled consumer. In fact, official Target business pages didn't appear at all within the first page of results. If you were to recreate that Google search today with the same keywords, you would find a very different result, no doubt as a result of efforts by Target to improve their search engine reputation.

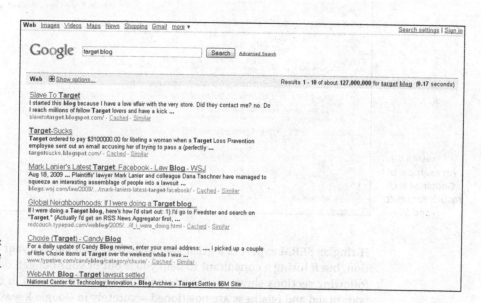

FIGURE 5-2:
Negative Google search results for *target blog.*

Another excellent example is one found during the writing of the first edition of this book. When the author entered the keyword phrase *Levitt and Sons* into the Google search bar, as shown in Figure 5-3, the top result was a blog written by a highly disgruntled consumer. Additional negative results were listed before any listings that led directly to the builder's site appeared in the search results. Levitt and Sons went bankrupt not long after this search was conducted. However, this blog came up at the top of the search results *before* Levitt and Sons closed its doors. This search was conducted in 2007 when the author was looking at new home construction and builders, and after finding this result, decided not to pursue purchasing a home from this builder. Of course, it's just one person's experience, but the content published on his blog was compelling and greatly tarnished the company's brand. Levitt and Sons may not have been able to save its business by making search engine reputation management a priority, but it certainly could have helped.

WARNING

You do *not* want this to happen to your business, and that's why ongoing search engine reputation management is absolutely vital.

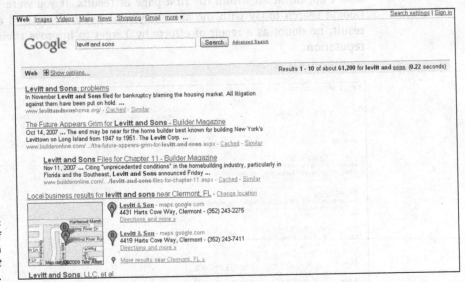

FIGURE 5-3:
An example of Google search results for *Levitt and Sons.*

Hiring an SERM expert is a great way to analyze and perfect your online reputation, but if hiring a consultant to help you is out of your budget, don't worry. The following sections show you how to conduct SERM initiatives in order to ensure your brand and business are positioned accurately in Google keyword searches.

Responding to and acknowledging mistakes

One of the first things you can do to preserve your search engine reputation is to respond to negative comments and attacks where they happen. For example, if someone writes a negative comment about your company on another blog, leave your own comment in response to offer help or provide accurate information. People who find the negative comment via search engines are likely to also see your proactive and helpful response.

You don't want people to read only one side of a story, particularly when that story paints your business in a negative light. Get involved at the source, engage the original publisher, and redeem yourself and your business where conversations are happening.

Burying the untrue or reputation threats

One of the best ways to control your search engine reputation is to publish great content constantly. The more great content you publish, the more quickly that deeply negative or untrue content published by other people gets buried. Unless that negative content appears on a blog or site that's better search engine optimized for relevant keywords than your own blog, you should be able to bury negative content by flooding the web with your own content.

With that in mind, don't spend a lot of time responding to negative comments and attacks. Acknowledge them and set the record straight as appropriate, but remember that the more content you publish related to that negative attack, the more chances it has to rise to the top of search rankings. The last thing you want is for the buzz to spread about that negative content, which may draw a lot of incoming links to it, making it harder to bury.

Building an audience of brand advocates and brand guardians

Over time, your blog readers will become loyal to you, your business, and your brand. As such, they'll become vocal brand advocates who want to talk about your organization. They represent a powerful form of word-of-mouth marketing that can give your brand a significant boost. Furthermore, they're likely to become brand guardians who will defend your business against negative comments and attacks.

There's no stronger form of word-of-mouth marketing than consumer brand advocates who talk about the brands they love, defend those brands, and try to convert people into brand advocates just like them. Leverage their willingness to talk about you and your business and let the online conversation flow.

REMEMBER

Don't be afraid to give up control. Although it's important that you stay aware of what's being said about you and your organization online, you shouldn't try to stop conversations. Instead, try to guide them in the right direction, correct inaccuracies, and make yourself available to the wider online community. That's how your blog, as a marketing tool of the social web, can drive your online reputation and your business to new heights.

Using SERM techniques

To keep track of what's being said online about you, your business, and your brand, you need to stay on top of the conversations taking place on the web and the content being published. You can keep track of your online reputation in a number of ways. Following are some of the free techniques you can use:

» **Google Alerts:** Set up Google Alerts (www.google.com/alerts) for your business and brand names as well as keywords people are likely to use to search for your products and services. You can find instructions to set up a Google Alert in Chapter 3 of Book 2.

» **Google search:** Conduct a daily Google search using the Advanced Search feature (www.google.com/advanced_search), shown in Figure 5-4, so you can look for specific search strings found within a specific time period, such as within the past 24 hours.

Google

Advanced Search

Find pages with...		To do this in the search box
all these words:		Type the important words: tricolor rat terrier
this exact word or phrase:		Put exact words in quotes: "rat terrier"
any of these words:		Type OR between all the words you want: miniature OR standard
none of these words:		Put a minus sign just before words you don't want: -rodent, -"Jack Russell"
numbers ranging from:	to	Put 2 periods between the numbers and add a unit of measure: 10..35 lb, $300..$500, 2010..2011

Then narrow your results by...		
language:	any language	Find pages in the language you select.
region:	any region	Find pages published in a particular region.
last update:	anytime	Find pages updated within the time you specify.
site or domain:		Search one site (like wikipedia.org) or limit your results to a domain like .edu, .org or .gov
terms appearing:	anywhere in the page	Search for terms in the whole page, page title, or web address, or links to the page you're looking for.
SafeSearch:	Show explicit results	Tell SafeSearch whether to filter sexually explicit content.
file type:	any format	Find pages in the format you prefer.
usage rights:	not filtered by license	Find pages you are free to use yourself.

Advanced Search

FIGURE 5-4:
The Google
Advanced
Search page.

» **Incoming links to your blog:** Using your web analytics tool, follow incoming links to your blog and read what those publishers are saying about you. You can find out more about web analytics in Chapter 2 of Book 5.

You can also find incoming links to your blog by using Google Search Console (`https://search.google.com/search-console`) as shown in Figure 5-5.

FIGURE 5-5:
Research
incoming links
with Google
Search Console.

The key to managing your search engine reputation is persistence and consistency. The more amazing content you publish that's optimized for your target keyword search phrases and your business or brand name, the more control you'll have over your online reputation.

4

Figuring Out Blogging Platforms

Contents at a Glance

Chapter **1**

Choosing a Blogging Platform

A blogging *platform* is the program used by bloggers to create and maintain blogs. Blogging platforms are also sometimes called *blogging applications* or *blogging software*.

Choosing a blogging platform that allows you to meet your goals for your blog is critical to your long-term success in the blogosphere. Each blogging platform offers similar functionality, but the nuances that exist among platforms can have a significant impact on what you can and can't do with your blog. For example, if your goal for your blog is to increase your web presence or make money, you need to take time to do some research up front to make the best choice to achieve that goal.

This chapter introduces you to what blogging platforms and applications can do for you and defines the types of platforms and applications available, so you can begin your research with an educated base of knowledge about the primary tools of the blogosphere.

Getting Familiar with How Blogging Applications Work

Before taking a look at what blogging platforms are and how to select one, it's best to begin by talking about blogging applications. The primary function of all blogging applications (also called *blogging software*) is the same: to provide users with a way to create a web presence on a blogging platform.

In essence, blogging applications are web-based content management systems (read the sidebar for more information about content management systems) that allow users to create and publish content in the form of a blog without knowledge of Hypertext Markup Language (HTML) or other programming or markup languages. When blogging applications launched in the 1990s, the online world changed. Suddenly, anyone could have a website. Today, many of the most trafficked and popular websites — including non-blog sites — are built using a blogging application as a content management system.

All types of blogging applications offer several consistent features:

>> **Blog posts:** This content is published on the blog.

>> **Blog comments:** Comments are the conversation that happens around each blog post.

TECHNICAL STUFF

WHAT ARE CONTENT MANAGEMENT SYSTEMS?

A *content management system* (CMS) is an application used to store and publish documents. Content management systems typically offer archive functionality as well as collaborative functionality for creating and editing content.

Document management systems are used to manage documents such as news articles, company documents, financial and legal documents, manuals, and more. These documents can be in digital or printed form. When companies use a document management system, it's often referred to as an *enterprise content management system*.

Web content management systems are used to manage the content published online. Most web content management systems don't require users to have online programming knowledge such as HTML, Extensible Markup Language (XML), or cascading style sheets (CSS) coding abilities. WordPress, Joomla!, and Drupal are examples of popular web content management systems.

>> **Easy-to-use content creation and editing tools:** A simple What You See Is What You Get (WYSIWYG) editor, as shown in Figure 1-1, is the hallmark of most blogging applications because that's what allows users to publish posts through an interface similar to word processing software, rather than through extensive coding.

>> **Archives:** The older content that's stored for easy online access is referred to as a blog's *content archive*.

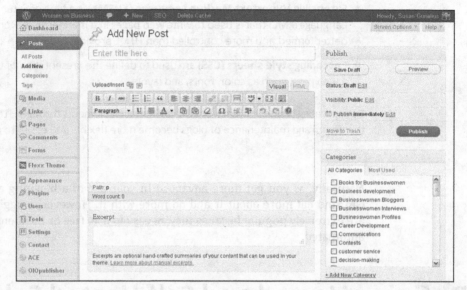

FIGURE 1-1:
The WordPress blogging application features a WYSIWYG post editor.

Blogging applications are amazing tools for web publishers because they use WYSIWYG editors and drag-and-drop tools to help nontechnical users create professional-looking websites and blogs. Although it can be helpful to know programming languages such as HTML and CSS to leverage the full functionality of a blogging application, it isn't necessary to do so. Take a look at the sidebar to find out more about how HTML and CSS are used to create blogs.

Blogging applications also automate a number of useful functions that website owners had to do manually in the past. For example, when a new post is published using a blogging application, that post is automatically included in the blog's archives. Additionally, search engines are pinged, notifying them that new content is available. You just have to click the Submit or Publish button within your blogging application, and everything else is done for you!

Naturally, as you get more advanced in your use of a blogging application, you can find out more about it and do more with it. However, blogging applications are extremely popular because they're easy to use, free or inexpensive, and highly automated.

Defining Hosted and Self-Hosted Solutions

While the blogging application or software does the heavy lifting for the creation of your blog's content, that application needs to live somewhere. Blog applications either run as part of or are downloaded to a *blogging platform*.

Your blog content has to be *hosted* somewhere, meaning it has to be stored somewhere. Blogging applications can be found on two types of blog platforms: *hosted* or *self-hosted*:

>> Hosted blogs are websites that include the blogging platform, or software required to blog. These host sites often offer blogging accounts for free that include an already-installed blogging application.

>> Self-hosted blogs are hosted on a server provided by a paid web host and require a blogging platform, such as WordPress, to be selected and downloaded by the blogger.

Both options have benefits and drawbacks. The following sections provide an introduction to both forms of hosting.

Hosted blog

Hosted blog platforms are a great way for a new blogger to get their blog up and running quickly and easily!

Many blogging application developers, such as WordPress and Blogger, offer an option for you to host your content on the developer's platform.

REMEMBER

By selecting that particular blogging platform, you are also choosing that type of blogging application. In other words, if you choose to blog on the WordPress.com blogging platform, your blog will be created using the WordPress application.

Some blogging application developers provide hosting services free of charge while others require you to pay a fee (typically a monthly fee, which could be based on the amount of content the developer is hosting for you). Blogs hosted through an application developer usually include an extension on the blog's URL such as .wordpress.com, .blogspot.com, or .typepad.com.

By hosting your blog on the blogging application developer's platform, you benefit from a consistently high *uptime*, meaning your blog will be live and functional when people look for it. Hosted blogs also offer lower costs and fewer maintenance hassles, which is appealing to many beginning bloggers. Of course, even developer-hosted blogging platforms can have problems, but going this route significantly reduces the potential for issues *and* makes it incredibly easy for a nontechnical person to have a web presence.

Self-hosted blog

Rather than hosting your blog content on the blogging application developer's platform, many people choose to use a separate web host to store their data. This is referred to as *self-hosting* your blog.

A *web host* is a company that provides Internet connectivity and makes space on its servers available to individuals and organizations for a fee, where those people can store data for their websites and blogs. Web hosts do not exclusively provide blogging platforms. Instead, they provide server space where customers can host any number of applications, including blogging applications.

The self-hosting option is best for people who aren't afraid of technology and are willing to pay a bit more for greater flexibility and functionality for their blogs.

REMEMBER

By self-hosting your blog, you benefit from complete control of your blog in terms of design, content, and functionality. Unlike hosted platforms where you must use the blogging application that comes with the platform, self-hosting allows you to select your own blogging application and change it if you decide you don't like it! If you self-host your blog, you must find and pay for your own domain name. Domain names are inexpensive and provide consistency for people to find your site in the long term as well as unique branding for your blog.

TECHNICAL STUFF

Depending on the blogging application and hosting type you choose, the platform options and features vary. Read Chapters 3–6 of this Book for more details about some of the most common blogging platforms.

Considering the Types of Blog Hosts

The two primary hosting options are discussed in the previous section of this chapter, but the subject isn't quite that cut and dried. The types of blog hosts can actually be split up even more, which can also affect your choice of a blogging application. Take a look at the types of blog hosts that follow to ensure you understand the various options available to you:

>> **Free:** Everyone loves things that are free, and free blog hosts actually offer a great deal of functionality. Free blogging platforms, such as WordPress and Blogger, provide both the blogging application *and* host the online space to store your blog content. However, there are typically restrictions related to the amount of space your blog can take up on the developer's servers, the amount of advertising you can publish on your blog in order to make money, and your ability to customize your blog's appearance. With that said, free blog platforms are a good choice for beginner bloggers as well as anyone who wants to keep their blogging costs to a minimum.

>> **Shared:** A shared blog host is one where space on a server is shared by multiple users. A shared blog host generally has the lowest price tag attached to it, next to the free option. If you use a shared blog host, your blog content is stored on the same server as other customers of the blog hosting company. That means your costs are kept down, but you may still have restrictions in terms of space, uptime, and the speed of loading your pages. You may be able to upgrade your account for a higher fee and access more storage space when you need it. Shared blog hosts are used by the majority of bloggers and small business owners because the offerings are fairly comprehensive despite the reasonable costs.

>> **Reseller:** Some people, known as *resellers,* buy server space from a blog host or company and then rent that space to bloggers. It's essential that you research a reseller before you commit to hosting your blog through one. It's *very* likely that you can get the same features, functionality, and pricing if you work directly with a blog hosting company.

>> **Dedicated server:** Blogs that get a lot of traffic and/or need consistent uptime are often hosted on a dedicated server, meaning they don't share server space with any other blogs or websites. That means the price tag is higher, but storage space and transfer speed are also higher. Typically, you receive little benefit by paying for a dedicated server host rather than a free or shared server host unless your blog is extremely large and trafficked. Liquid Web (www.liquidweb.com), shown in Figure 1-2, is an example of a company that offers dedicated server hosting for blogs and websites.

The vast majority of blogs are hosted on free blogging platforms or on shared server platforms.

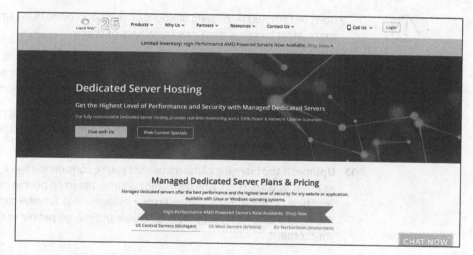

FIGURE 1-2: Liquid Web provides blog hosting services on dedicated servers.

Finding and Choosing a Web Host for a Self-Hosted Blog

Now that you know the primary functions of blog platforms and the most common types of blog hosts, you need to decide which option (free, shared, or dedicated) is best to help you meet your blogging goals.

WARNING

Changing from one blog platform to another rarely works seamlessly. To avoid problems later, take the time to choose the best blog hosting option for you now!

Comparing web hosts

You can use the following five comparison points to evaluate blog host options:

TIP

WARNING

TIP

>> **Fees:** Review the features available from different types of blog hosts and platforms described in the previous section (free, shared, or dedicated) and then determine whether investing in a paid blog host can benefit you in the long run.

Web hosting prices and packages change frequently. Be sure to review pricing right before you commit to purchasing web hosting services, so you're not surprised by a sudden price change.

>> **Space:** It's important to know whether a blogging platform provides enough space to meet your needs at a price you're willing to pay.

Don't be tempted by hosting discount offers that provide huge amounts of space. Most bloggers don't need terabytes of space.

>> **Transfer speeds and limits:** You need to know that the platform you commit to using provides a data transfer rate that's fast enough *and* can accommodate all the content on your website that's viewed by every person who visits.

You can upgrade your web host account to include higher transfer limits as your blog grows in popularity and traffic. Don't overpay for features and functions you don't need when you're first starting your blog.

>> **Uptime:** If the blogging platform or host you're considering has a reputation as one that doesn't provide consistent uptime, meaning people can access your blog online without getting error messages, look for alternative hosting! You need a blog host that provides reliable uptime, so people can always read your content.

>> **Support:** This is the area where some web hosts excel and others fail. The blog platform you use should have a reputation of providing excellent customer service and support. If you have a problem with your blog at any time during the day or night, you need to know you can pick up the phone, send an email, or start an online chat session to get help quickly and easily.

Identifying popular web hosts for self-hosting your blog

In Chapter 2 of this Book 1 outline various blogging platforms and their related applications, including free and fee-based platforms. This section deals only with self-hosted servers where bloggers can pay for space to host their blogging application and content data.

Web hosts come and go all the time, which is why it's important to choose a web host that has an excellent reputation and staying power. The following list offers several of the most popular web hosts to get you started on your research into finding the best blog host for you:

>> **Bluehost (www.bluehost.com):** Known for affordable costs as well as consistent uptime, features, and support.

>> **GoDaddy (www.godaddy.com):** Has been in business for a long time and has a reputation as a reliable source for blog hosting.

>> **HostGator (www.hostgator.com):** Has a reputation for reliability and great support.

>> **SiteGround (www.siteground.com):** Known to be able to support complex sites for well-established bloggers.

>> **DreamHost (www.dreamhost.com):** Shown in Figure 1-3, DreamHost is known for offering competitive pricing.

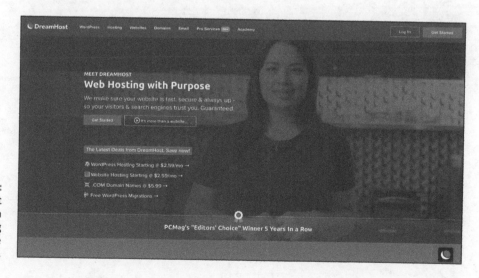

FIGURE 1-3: DreamHost has a reputation for offering competitive pricing.

Selecting a web host

After you've compiled the facts about the features, price, and support offered by several self-hosting companies, look at them side by side and determine which offers the functionality you need for the best price.

You can always upgrade to a package that provides more space and speed as your blog grows. It's an easy process to upgrade from one package to another from the same hosting company, but it can be a hassle to move from one hosting company to another.

That's not to say it's impossible to move from one hosting company to another. It just takes a bit more technical knowledge to make sure everything transfers without any glitches. However, transferring from using a free hosting platform to self-hosting your blog on a web host creates its own set of problems. Foremost, it's very likely that you'll have to change your domain name (for example, to drop the .wordpress.com, .blogspot.com, or .typepad.com extension) when you move from a free host to a web host. This can hurt your search engine rankings and cause you to lose your search engine traffic.

REMEMBER

Bottom line: It's absolutely critical that you set your goals, do your research, and choose the best blog hosting service that will help you over the long term, rather than selecting the quick-and-easy short-term option.

IN THIS CHAPTER

» Setting your goals

» Introducing popular blogging platforms

» Comparing popular blogging platforms

» Reviewing other blogging platform options

» Choosing the best blogging platform for you

Chapter 2

Finding the Right Blogging Platform

Choosing the right blogging platform is almost as an important decision as choosing to blog in the first place! Although it's true that the popular blogging platforms, such as WordPress and Blogger, offer similar functionality, the nuances among them are great enough that you need to do some research and thinking before you start your blog, in order to ensure you pick the right tool.

For example, if you choose to blog on the free platform WordPress.com, the types of ads you can display on your blog are extremely limited. If making money from your blog is important to you, WordPress.com is likely not a good choice for your blog. The less-obvious differences like this one can greatly affect your blog in both the short and long term. This chapter helps you understand the blogging platforms that are available to you so you can make the best decision possible.

Determining Your Goals and Needs

As with all aspects of joining the blogosphere, the blogging platform you choose depends on your goals and needs for your blog. Each blogger has a unique set of reasons to start blogging, and those reasons will impact which blog application is best for you and on which blog platform. Yes, you can publish blog posts, allow comments, and store archives using any blogging application, but there's more to blogging than just writing posts.

If your plans for your blogging experience extend beyond publishing written entries, you must consider the factors included in the following sections before you choose where and how to blog.

Growing your blog

If you have dreams of growing your blog into a popular, highly trafficked online destination, you need to choose a blogging platform that offers enough storage space and bandwidth to ensure the user experience is both streamlined and fast. As your blog traffic grows (or if your blog includes a lot of photos and images), your blog needs enough storage space to hold all the new content you create as well as a higher bandwidth to ensure pages load quickly. As mentioned in Chapter 1 of this Book, blogs that require a large amount of storage space are best served by a self-hosted platform.

Customizing your blog

Not all blogging applications are equal when it comes to customizing your blog's design and functionality. For example, some free blogging platforms provide significantly limited customization and functionality in comparison with blogs that use the WordPress application on a self-hosted platform, which offers you maximum customization and control.

TIP

It is possible to "hack" or change the HTML code on some free blogging platforms in order to customize your blog beyond what the customization menu offers. However, many bloggers decide that it's easier to move to a self-hosted platform once their customization needs are no longer being met, rather than take the risk of breaking the code and disabling their blog.

Branding your blog

Branding is a representation of who you are and what you do that becomes easily recognizable to your readers and other bloggers, and it encompasses both tangible (color palette, logo, header image, and other design elements) and intangible (your voice, content, and style) elements, which together create audience expectations for your blog. A well-branded blog typically uses a custom design that differentiates the blog from its competitors. Personalized domain names and customization options are less flexible on some blogging platforms than on others. Furthermore, blogs that use personalized domain names devoid of the standard extensions that free blogging platforms append to them are instantly viewed as more professional. Visitors look at this personalized domain name and recognize that the blogger actually invested money in the blog.

Maintaining your blog

Different blogging applications require different levels of technical knowledge in order to maximize the potential they offer. Because some blogging platforms only allow the use of one type of blogging application, it's important to know how much technical know-how you bring to the table — or are willing to learn — before selecting a blogging platform. Although you can publish content easily using any blogging application, modifying design and functionality, for example, is accomplished with less technical knowledge in some blogging applications than in others.

Investing money into your blog

Some blogging applications require that you pay a monthly fee to use them. Others are offered for free, such as WordPress.org, but require you to pay to store your blog's content through a self-hosted platform, such as Bluehost or GoDaddy, which offers maximum functionality and customization. And other blogging applications are completely free but offer limited functionality and customization. The amount of money you're willing to invest in your blog directly affects your choice of blogging applications.

Making money from your blog

Not all blogging platforms allow you to include ads and other monetization initiatives on your blog. If you want to make money from your blog, you need to be certain that you choose a blogging platform that allows you to use your blog as a money-making tool.

Blogging with multiple authors

If multiple people contribute content to your blog, then you need to choose a blogging application that enables a team of bloggers to publish blog posts securely. Some blogging applications make it easy for you to add authors and set a variety of security permissions to each person's account. Even if you don't have multiple bloggers writing content on your blog initially, there may come a time when your blog grows and additional writers are needed. Make sure the blogging application you choose is capable of growing with you as your blog grows.

Taking a Look at the Most Popular Blogging Platforms

While certain platforms, such as WordPress.com and Blogger, have remained popular for nearly as long as blogging has existed, the list of top blogging platforms is constantly shifting and changing as new platforms gain in popularity and new blogging capabilities and features become popular. These platforms provide bloggers access to blogging applications that are well-developed and quick to integrate new updates and functionality as the blogosphere evolves. They're also easy to use and offer excellent support resources.

That's not to say that other blogging platforms aren't good. In fact, you can find out about some blogging platform alternatives later in this chapter. It just means that the reputations and reliability of the applications listed here have driven their popularity.

WordPress.com

www.wordpress.com

WordPress.com, shown in Figure 2-1, is a free blogging platform that uses the WordPress blogging application. Typically, people refer to blogging on WordPress. com as "hosted WordPress" versus "self-hosted WordPress" (see the next section if you'd like to "self-host" using WordPress). Because blogs published on WordPress.com are hosted by WordPress, rather than self-hosted, they include the domain extension .wordpress.com, unless you pay a premium fee, in which case you can use your own domain name. WordPress.com bloggers are limited in terms of the functionality they can add to their blogs. For example, you aren't allowed to display ads on a WordPress.com blog unless they're part of the WordPress WordAds program, and the design templates (called *themes* in WordPress) you can use to customize your blog are limited unless you pay a fee to access premium features.

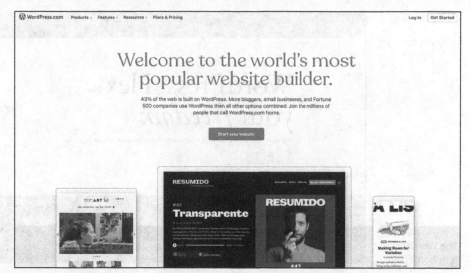

FIGURE 2-1:
The WordPress.com homepage.

On the other hand, WordPress.com is very easy to use, and you can have a blog up and running within minutes. WordPress.com does offer some useful features, including automatic pinging of search engines such as Google as well as a comment spam–blocking plug-in (Akismet), post labeling, categorization, trackbacks, and more.

You can find out more about the WordPress blogging applications in Chapter 3 of this Book.

WordPress.org

www.wordpress.org

WordPress.org, shown in Figure 2-2, is a popular blogging application offered for anyone to download and use for free. However, you need to have a place to install the "self-hosted WordPress" application, which means purchasing your own domain name and hosting platform account through a web host. (You can find out more about web hosts in Chapter 1 of this minibook.) Additionally, WordPress.org requires some technical knowledge or, at the very least, a lack of fear of technology. That's because to use WordPress.org, you need to be able to upload the application to your web hosting account and customize it yourself. This isn't hard to do, particularly because most web hosts offer tools that make installing WordPress very simple. However, it's a process that some bloggers prefer to avoid.

FIGURE 2-2:
The WordPress.
org homepage.

When you use WordPress.org as your blogging application, you have complete control and maximum flexibility. Developers around the world create tools, called *WordPress plug-ins,* that make it easy to add new features to your blog, and custom designs are simple to create. Additionally, you can use any kind of moneymaking tools on your WordPress.org blog that you want.

REMEMBER

Of all the popular blogging applications, WordPress.org is the most flexible and works closest to a true content management system without being technologically overwhelming.

Blogger

www.blogger.com

Blogger, shown in Figure 2-3, is owned by Google. It was one of the first blogging platforms to gain widespread appeal and continues to be one of the most popular blogging platforms for several reasons. It's completely free to use, and it offers enough customization that many small- and mid-size blogs work very well on the platform.

Over the years, Google has added several new features to Blogger that make it competitive with WordPress.org, such as the ability to use your own domain name. However, what sets Blogger apart from other blogging applications is its free price tag coupled with the lack of restrictions related to monetization. In other words, you can publish ads and make money through a free Blogger blog.

FIGURE 2-3:
The Blogger
homepage.

Blogger is the first platform I used when I began blogging well over a decade ago. It is a great starter blogging platform for anyone who wants to dive right in and get a website up and running quickly and with very little effort. Even though Blogger works well for beginning bloggers, there are some bloggers who choose to stay with Blogger as their platform of choice throughout their blogging career.

You can get details about Blogger in Chapter 4 of this Book.

Squarespace

www.squarespace.com

Squarespace, shown in Figure 2-4, is a fee-for-service blogging platform with prices beginning at $16 a month. Squarespace is popular with eCommerce businesses and bloggers alike in part because of its unique drag-and-drop interface that sets it apart from Blogger and WordPress, both hosted and self-hosted. Squarespace allows for easy blog customization and offers a free trial for bloggers interested in giving a different sort of platform a try.

The Squarespace blogging platform is not only *mobile-responsive*, meaning that the blog is easily read via mobile devices and not just on computer screens, but it's also easily able to be edited via a mobile device. If you're someone who likes to share your thoughts quickly and on the go via your phone, Squarespace may be a good fit for you!

FIGURE 2-4:
The Squarespace blogging homepage.

Tumblr

www.tumblr.com

Tumblr, shown in Figure 2-5, is a bit different from the other blogging applications described here, but it remains wildly popular with its users thanks to its ease of use and social features. Tumblr blogs, referred to as *Tumblogs*, are used for quickly publishing and sharing text, audio, video, and image content. The social aspect comes from the sharing and "tumbling" of content among the community of Tumblr users.

FIGURE 2-5:
The Tumblr home page.

Many people refer to Tumblr as a cross between a blogging application and a social media platform. Depending on your blogging goals, it might offer just the right functionality for you.

Comparing Popular Blogging Platforms

WordPress.com, WordPress.org, and Blogger all offer similar basic features, but each has its own nuances that can affect your decision in terms of which blogging application will suit you over the long term. Remember, changing from one blogging platform to another can be done, but it can cause problems discussed later in this chapter. Position yourself for success from the start by comparing the most popular blogging platforms before you join the blogosphere.

REMEMBER

Table 2-1 provides a visual comparison of the most popular blogging applications.

TABLE 2-1   **Comparing Blogging Applications**

Feature	WordPress.com	WordPress.org	Blogger
Price	Free (Premium features are available for a fee.)	Free (Web hosting and domain are required, which include fees.)	Free
Functionality	Limited (Additional functionality is available for a fee.)	Extensive	Limited
Monetization	Limited (Additional monetization is available for a fee.)	Yes	Yes
Technical Knowledge Required	Little	Moderate	Little
Branding	Limited (Additional features, such as personal domains, are available for a fee.)	Yes	Yes

(continued)

TABLE 2-1 *(continued)*

Feature	WordPress.com	WordPress.org	Blogger
Customization	Limited (Additional customization options are available for a fee.)	Extensive	Limited
Author and Blog Quantity Limits	Limited number of authors, unlimited number of blogs	Unlimited number of authors, unlimited number of blogs	Limited number of authors, unlimited number of blogs

An additional note on functionality: WordPress.org offers the most functionality, although many of those features come from third-party plug-ins and require a bit of technical knowledge to install and use. Blogger offers a good amount of functionality given its free price tag.

Also keep in mind that WordPress.org provides the highest level of customization. Blogger users also have a lot of customization options, but the open-source community of developers who create plug-ins and themes for WordPress.org users put it above any other blogging application in terms of customization.

WARNING

Visit the websites for each blogging platform you're considering using to check the most recent information about features and functionality as well as pricing. Blogging platforms are updated frequently, so you need to review the most current offerings before you choose your blogging platform.

Considering Other Blogging Platforms

Although WordPress and Blogger are undoubtedly two of the most popular blogging platforms, you have what can seem at times like endless other options. No two bloggers are exactly alike, nor are two blogging applications. That's why there are many platforms to choose from and happy, loyal users of each. Following is an overview of some of the less-popular-but-still-loved blogging applications.

LinkedIn

www.linkedin.com

If you're like most people, blogging is not the first thing to come to mind when you hear the platform name LinkedIn. Primarily a home for professional networking and career development opportunities, an online resume of sorts, LinkedIn is also home to posts published by its many users.

All LinkedIn profile accounts have the ability to publish posts, much like a traditional blog, on their profile page. In fact, LinkedIn users could publish a complete blog directly to their LinkedIn homepage (shown in Figure 2-6). While that may seem like a crazy idea, keep in mind that visitors are coming to LinkedIn hungry for well-written, professional, helpful information and connections making it the perfect place for thought-pieces and how-to posts, for example.

FIGURE 2-6:
The LinkedIn
homepage.

Medium

www.medium.com

Medium, shown in Figure 2-7, is part social media platform and part blogging tool. Anyone is able to create their own Medium profile page and immediately begin writing and posting. Many of the first steps for blogging that exist on every other platform simply don't apply to bloggers writing on Medium. For example, there's no reason to create a memorable logo, buy a domain address, or think about branding because you'll have a profile page on an already branded and named site rather than a site of your own. The trade-off is that you'll also get a built-in community of readers who are hungry for new content to read and follow.

Jekyll

www.jekyllrb.com

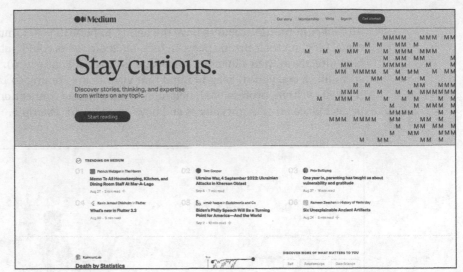

FIGURE 2-7:
The Medium homepage.

Jekyll (shown in Figure 2-8) is the opposite of a sign-up-and-go platform. Perfect for experienced coders who are looking for a place to flex their creative muscles, Jekyll is a blogging application that works with GitHub Pages (www. pages.github.com) to provide free blog hosting and custom domain names.

TIP

If you have some coding knowledge and decide to build a blog using Jekyll, it's a good idea to find a Jekyll-specific tutorial to get started. After that, the sky's the limit on how you can customize your new blog!

FIGURE 2-8:
The Jekyll homepage.

Weebly

www.weebly.com

Another option for those interested in blogging on a free platform, Weebly (shown in Figure 2-9) is great for beginners, especially those looking to get up and running quickly. Once your blog is established and you decide you'd like to make some upgrades, Weebly offers accounts in a range of monthly price points, each with its own set up add-ons.

TIP

Weebly is owned by and therefore integrates well with Square, the mobile credit card payment solution, making this platform an ideal choice for bloggers who plan to add an eCommerce component to their site.

FIGURE 2-9:
The Weebly
homepage.

Drupal

www.drupal.org

Drupal, shown in Figure 2-10, is an open-source CMS, or content management system, that allows users to create a wide variety of websites such as blogs, communities, eCommerce, podcasting, networking, and more. As such, Drupal has a more challenging learning curve than popular standalone blogging applications such as WordPress and Blogger. With that said, if you take the time to understand and learn how to use Drupal, you will find that the out-of-the-box tools and features are exceptional compared to easier to use starter blog platforms.

FIGURE 2-10:
The Drupal homepage.

Joomla!

`www.joomla.org`

Like Drupal, Joomla!, shown in Figure 2-11, is an open-source web content management system, and it allows users to create simple to elaborate websites with complete flexibility and control. Therefore, it's far more challenging to learn Joomla! than it is to learn how to use standalone blogging applications such as WordPress and Blogger. It does, however, have exceptional features without the need for upgrades and provides more opportunities for your blog to grow and evolve to your changing needs.

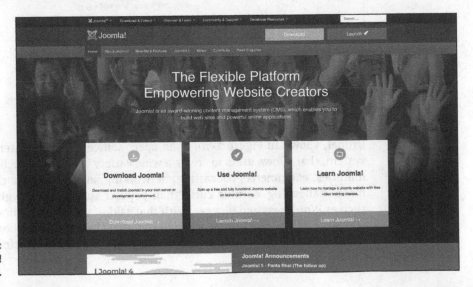

FIGURE 2-11:
The Joomla! homepage.

Write.as

www.write.as

Write.as is, in many ways, the opposite of so many other blogging platforms, especially those that feature the ability to code and design your way to an elaborate website. Write.as is for bloggers who want a simple words-on-the-page look to their blog and also want to be able to get started quickly and with little technical ability.

At the time of publication, Write (shown in Figure 2-12) .as was no longer accepting new free accounts, but paid accounts begin at as low as $6 a month. If you begin blogging and fall in love with the Write.as, additional platforms exist in the studio of products including Snap.as (www.snap.as) for online photography portfolios without the clutter of other platforms.

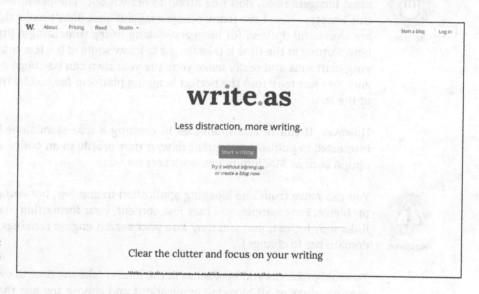

FIGURE 2-12:
The Write.as homepage.

Choosing the Right Blogging Platform for You

With all these blogging application choices and so many more, how do you know which is the right one for you? The easiest way to come to the best choice for you is to take the time to define your goals for your blog, as discussed earlier in this chapter. Once you feel confident about your blogging goals, you can select the blogging platform that you're technically adept enough to feel comfortable using and that helps you reach those goals at a price you can afford.

The most important factors to consider are price, ease of use, and functionality. If you're a beginner blogger joining the blogosphere for fun and have minimal goals for your blog aside from personal enjoyment, then a free blogging application is all you need. WordPress.com or Blogger should work well for you. If you want to be able to monetize your blog as well, Blogger is a good choice.

Alternatively, if you have plans to grow your blog significantly or need complete customization control over your blog for business branding or other purposes, you need a more flexible blogging application. WordPress.org on a self-hosted platform is an excellent choice for people who want to grow their blogs or create blogs for business purposes. If you aren't afraid to learn a bit of technology (or invest a bit of money to hire a blog designer or developer to help you get past the technical steps), WordPress.org is the way to go.

REMEMBER

While WordPress.com, Blogger, and WordPress.org provide all the options that most bloggers need, don't be afraid to branch out. The platforms mentioned in this chapter — and the many others available that didn't make this finite list — are wonderful options for bloggers looking to try something a little different or new. Putting in the time it takes to get to know some of the less mainstream blogging platforms and really make your site your own can pay huge dividends in the end. You just may find the perfect blogging platform for you by thinking outside of the box!

However, if you're less interested in creating a true standalone blog and more interested in publishing content to your user profile in an online community, an option such as Medium might work best for you.

WARNING

You can move from one blogging application to another, but doing so may cause problems. For example, you may lose content, your formatting may change, your links may be lost, and you may lose your search engine rankings (if your blog's domain has to change).

To avoid problems and headaches in the future, take the time to evaluate the current offerings of all blogging applications and choose the one that will not only help create the perfect blog for you, but also position it for long-term success.

Chapter **3**

Taking a Look at WordPress

WordPress is an excellent blogging platform choice for anyone joining the blogosphere. The platform offers the flexibility bloggers need to start a blog without much technical knowledge as well as the features needed to grow and customize their blogs in the future for the ultimate blogging experience.

WARNING

WordPress remains one of the most popular blogging platforms, particularly for people who have goals for their blog beyond a casual hobby. Before you choose to use WordPress, be aware that the WordPress blogging application comes in more than one form, which can be confusing. It's important to understand the differences between them before you start your WordPress blog.

This chapter shows you what WordPress can do, the differences between the two forms of WordPress, and how to start your blog and publish posts using WordPress. For more detailed information and advanced instruction about WordPress, be sure to read *WordPress For Dummies,* 9th Edition (John Wiley & Sons, Inc., 2020), by Lisa Sabin-Wilson.

Finding Out What WordPress Is

In simplest terms, WordPress is a blog publishing application that makes it incredibly easy for anyone to start a blog without any computer programming knowledge. WordPress uses What You See Is What You Get (WYSIWYG) editors that allow you to write and publish posts similarly to how you create documents using word-processing software such as Microsoft Word. Additionally, WordPress uses widgets, or additional computer applications within the WordPress software, to make adding features to your blog as easy as pointing and clicking or dragging and dropping. WordPress is also known for its flexibility in terms of customization. You can find a myriad of free and premium WordPress themes online and within the blogging application, which anyone can use to change both the look and functionality of their WordPress blog.

With WordPress, you can have ultimate control over the function and design of your blog. In fact, WordPress can even be used as a content management system (CMS) to create non-blogging websites, which is particularly useful for small businesses and nonprofit organizations with limited budgets. However, many of the most popular blogs and also many non-blogging websites are created using WordPress, including *TIME Magazine* (www.time.com) and even the Rolling Stones' website (www.rollingstones.com), shown in Figure 3-1!

FIGURE 3-1: A WordPress blog can look like a non-blogging website.

Understanding the Two WordPress Options

Perhaps the most confusing aspect of WordPress derives from the fact that WordPress comes in two different forms: WordPress.com and WordPress.org. The two forms have many differences, and you need to be certain that you understand them before choosing one of them for your blog. Both options allow users to create blogs, but the features, functionality, fees, and technical skills required for the options differ significantly.

Checking out the differences

The confusion between WordPress.com and WordPress.org is commonly felt by new bloggers. Typically, the nuances are explained in technical language that doesn't help sort out the differences unless you're a seasoned blogger. Members of the blogosphere also tend to simply refer to each platform as WordPress, making it unclear to which they are referring. This section describes the differences between WordPress.com and WordPress.org.

» **WordPress.org:** The WordPress blogging application launched in 2003 as an open-source application, meaning developers can create tools (which have come to be known as *plugins*) that users can integrate seamlessly into WordPress to enhance functionality. Open-source application code is freely available to anyone who wants to create enhancements and modify it to meet their needs. As such, WordPress.org requires some technical knowledge to utilized fully but offers great flexibility in terms of adding functionality and customization.

  WordPress.org is free, but users have to upload the application to their own, separate web hosting accounts to be able to use it. This requires an investment in web hosting and a domain name as well as additional technical knowledge, making WordPress.org a bad option for those hoping to launch a blog for free. Although the technical skills required to use WordPress.org are minimal unless you plan to handle your own extensive customization, people who aren't comfortable with technology might find this path challenging.

» **WordPress.com:** Because WordPress.com provides both the blogging software and the platform on which to operate it, blogs are hosted by WordPress.com are free. That means there are no hosting or domain name fees. The technical knowledge requirements are minimal, so if you can use a word-processing application and navigate the Internet, you should have no issues using WordPress.com. The features and functionality available to WordPress.com users are more limited than those using WordPress.org, but premium services to enhance your blog can be purchased.

Table 3-1 provides a breakdown of the primary differences between WordPress.com and WordPress.org.

TABLE 3-1: WordPress.com versus WordPress.org

	WordPress.com	WordPress.org
Price	Free, with the option to pay for premium features.	Free, but you must pay for hosting through a third party as well as for a domain name.
Technical Skills Required	Easy to use if you know how to use a word-processing application and can navigate the Internet.	Requires more technical skills or a willingness to learn because you need to obtain your own web host then upload and configure the application to your host.
Functionality	Offers sufficient but limited functionality with the option to pay for additional features.	Offers maximum functionality through the use of plugins and themes that you can add to your blog, often for free.
Domain Names	Uses the .wordpress.com domain extension, but you can pay a fee to use your own domain that you purchase separately.	Use domains that you purchase separately.
Customization	Offers limited free customization with the option to pay for additional customization such as HTML and CSS modifications.	Offers nearly unlimited customization.
Monetization	Only allows restricted advertising through WordPress' WordAds program or the WordPress VIP program for qualifying highly trafficked blogs.	Allows monetization of any kind.
Authors	Limits the number of authors for each blog.	Has no author limits.
Storage	Offers limited storage space (though it's usually enough for most beginner and intermediate-level bloggers).	Storage dependent solely on your contract with your web host and not limited at all by the blogging application.

Choosing between WordPress.com and WordPress.org

With your new knowledge of the differences between WordPress.com and WordPress.org in mind, review your blogging goals and priorities to determine which version of WordPress will best help you reach those goals. The biggest considerations are the following:

- » Blog functionality
- » Customization options
- » Cost of operation
- » Monetization opportunities and rules
- » Technical skills needed to operate

REMEMBER

Changing from WordPress.com to WordPress.org after your blog has been established can be done but may cause problems such as lost data, lost links, or formatting issues. Also, if your domain name has to change, you'll lose incoming link traffic and search engine traffic.

If you plan to create a blog for personal enjoyment with limited long-term growth and monetization goals, WordPress.com should work well for you. If you want to create a blog that grows in popularity to the point of becoming a money-making endeavor, WordPress.org is a better choice. Alternatively, if you want to use the WordPress blogging software to create a business or nonprofit website, WordPress.org is an excellent choice.

TECHNICAL STUFF

The technical skills required to use WordPress.org aren't difficult for most people to learn. Additionally, many freelance blog designers and developers offer help at reasonable prices, and many blogs and forums are dedicated to helping people with WordPress.org, as discussed later in this chapter in the section "Getting Help and Finding Resources." If you would like to try to blog using WordPress.org, you may find that it is easier than it sounds at first glance!

Creating a Free Blog at WordPress.com

If starting a free blog with limited free functionality is all you need to meet your blogging goals, WordPress.com is a good choice for your blogging application. In fact, creating a blog with WordPress.com takes a matter of minutes. As soon as your blog is live, you can publish posts using the simple WYSIWYG post editor. It just couldn't get any easier!

REMEMBER

Your goals for your blog may be wildly different than someone else's goals, but that doesn't make them any less important. It may, however, make achieving those goals less expensive. Sometimes more is just more, not better. If your goal is simply to create a beautiful home on the web where you can freely write, a free blog at WordPress.com may be the perfect way to meet the mark!

Opening a new account and creating a blog using WordPress.com require only a few steps:

1. **Visit www.wordpress.com (Figure 3-2) and click the Get Started button in the upper-right corner of your screen.**

   This step takes you to the new account creation page.

FIGURE 3-2:
Get started
creating a
free blog at
WordPress.com.

2. **Complete the signup form on the new account page, shown in Figures 3-3, or opt to sign-up for a WordPress.com using an existing Google or Apple account. and then click the Create Blog button at the bottom of the form.**

3. **Click the Create your account button.**

4. **Optional: Create a domain name for your blog.**

   At this stage of the account creation process, you have the option to select an available domain name for your blog. Your options include:

   - Register a domain name entirely for free, which will include the wordpress.com extension as part of your blog's URL.

   - Register a domain name without the wordpress.com, which will be free for the first year. Following that year, you will need to pay a fee in order to keep the same domain name.

Let's get started

First, create your WordPress.com account. Have an account? Log in

Your email address

Username

Choose a password

By creating an account you agree to our Terms of Service and have read our Privacy Policy.

Create your account

OR

G Continue with Google

 Continue with Apple

If you continue with Google or Apple, you agree to our Terms of Service and have read our Privacy Policy.

FIGURE 3-3:
Sign-up for a WordPress.com account by providing information or logging in to an existing Google or Apple account.

WARNING

Look closely at the fees associated with the domain that you select! While WordPress.com provides account holders with a domain name for free for one year, the fee in the following years varies significantly based on the URL's extension. For example, a .com domain name is far less expensive than a .movie domain name. Choose wisely! You can:

- Use a domain that you already own.

- Skip this part of the process for now and choose a domain name later.

Chapter 3 of Book 1 discusses brainstorming ideas for blog names and domain names. Now is the time to pull out that list and select your favorite domain name, as shown in Figure 3-4.

5. **Optional: Select a paid account plan, as shown in Figure 3-5, or select "start with a free site."**

REMEMBER

For many new bloggers, the best feature of hosting a blog on WordPress.com is the ability to blog totally for free! The sign-up process can confusingly make it appear as though you need to pay a fee to blog at WordPress.com. Don't panic! The free blog option is still available.

Taking a Look at WordPress

6. **Customize your experience further by selecting your goals from your blog from a pre-determined list, as shown in Figure 3-6, or opt to go straight to your blog's Dashboard.**

7. **Congratulations! You are now the owner of your very own WordPress. com blog. You may now customize your new site on your Dashboard, as shown in Figure 3-7.**

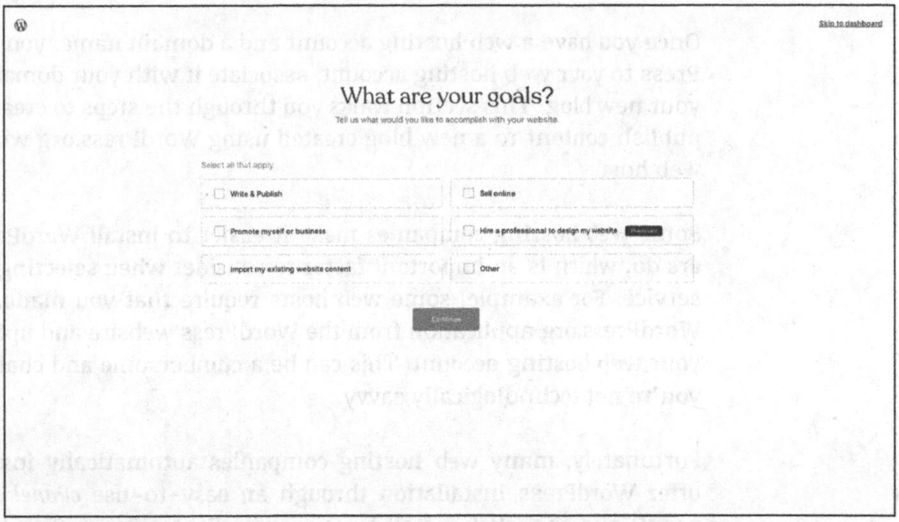

FIGURE 3-6:
You may
indicate your
goals for your
new WordPress.
com blog.

FIGURE 3-7:
Welcome to your
new WordPress.
com blog's
Dashboard.

Installing WordPress.org

WordPress.org requires more work up front to create a new blog than WordPress.com does. First, you need to obtain a web hosting account to store your blog's data. There are many web hosting companies, and some are described in Chapter 1 of this Book. After you obtain a web hosting account, you need to purchase a domain name for your new blog, which is described in Chapter 3 of Book 1.

Taking a Look at
WordPress

Once you have a web hosting account and a domain name, you can upload WordPress to your web hosting account, associate it with your domain name, and start your new blog. This section walks you through the steps to create, customize, and publish content to a new blog created using WordPress.org with Bluehost as the web host.

Some web hosting companies make it easier to install WordPress.org than others do, which is an important factor to consider when selecting your web hosting service. For example, some web hosts require that you manually download the WordPress.org application from the WordPress website and upload all the files to your web hosting account. This can be a cumbersome and challenging process if you're not technologically savvy.

Fortunately, many web hosting companies automatically install WordPress or offer WordPress installation through an easy-to-use *cPanel* (short for control panel) and one-click install tools such as Fantastico or SimpleScripts. With the simple click of your mouse on an icon in your web hosting account cPanel, you can install WordPress to your chosen domain in seconds.

TIP

If you're not technically adept, be sure to choose a web host that includes a user cPanel and offers one-click installation of WordPress through Fantastico or SimpleScripts.

Following are the simplest steps to install WordPress to a new domain that has already been purchased using Bluehost:

1. **Log in to your Bluehost web hosting account and click My Sites, as shown in Figure 3-8.**

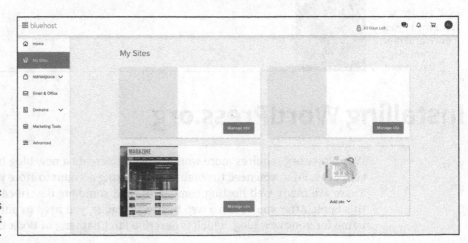

FIGURE 3-8:
Select My Sites
from the left
sidebar.

2. **Click "Add site" and select Create New Site, as shown in Figure 3-9.**

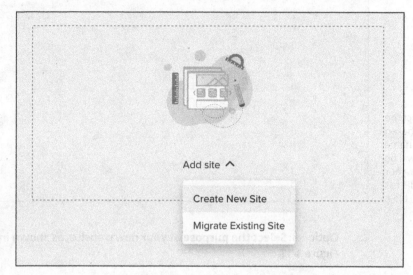

FIGURE 3-9:
Select Create
New Site to begin
setting up your
new self-hosted
WordPress blog.

3. **Type your blog's name and tagline, as shown in Figure 3-10.**

Create a new WordPress site

Site Name

Simply Delicious Pastries

Site Tagline

Happiness starts here

Advanced

Cancel   Next

FIGURE 3-10:
Name your
new blog.

4. **Select the domain associated with your new blog, as shown in Figure 3-11.**

   At this point, Bluehost offers to automatically install selected free plugins. You may choose to install them or decline at this time.

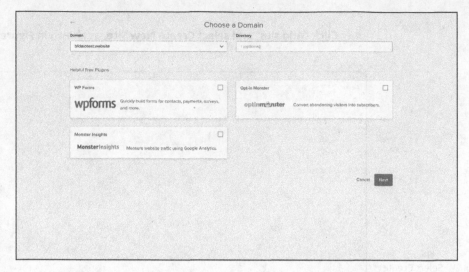

FIGURE 3-11:
Select the purchased domain name that you will be using for your new WordPress blog.

5. **Optional: Select the purpose of your new website, as shown in Figure 3-12.**

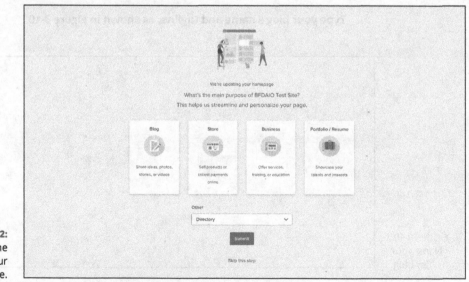

FIGURE 3-12:
Select the purpose of your new site.

6. **WordPress has now been installed on your new site (Figure 3-13), and you may log in to your Dashboard.**

   You may want to log in and customize your password to something you will remember before proceeding any further.

   Your new blog is now live using the default WordPress theme and information!

FIGURE 3-13:
WordPress has
now been
automatically
installed on your
Bluehost blog.

Reviewing the WordPress Dashboard

The WordPress.com and WordPress.org dashboards work very similarly. However, the WordPress.org dashboard offers more options and controls. The remainder of this chapter uses the WordPress.com dashboard for reference, but note that some of the features shown aren't available on the WordPress.com dashboard. If you use WordPress.com, you can skip the features listed in the remainder of this chapter that don't apply to you. In short, if you don't see a feature discussed in this chapter on your WordPress.com dashboard, it's either not available to you or available only if you pay for premium features.

TECHNICAL STUFF

Depending on your blog host and the manner in which you install WordPress to your account, you might be using a different version of WordPress than the version shown in the figures within this chapter. Note that the majority of the functionality is the same, but the layout of your WordPress dashboard might look a bit different than the images shown in this chapter.

When you log in to your WordPress account, your WordPress dashboard opens, as shown in Figure 3-14. This is where you can access all the features and functions to create content and customize your blog.

The majority of your screen is taken up by boxes (referred to as *modules*) that make accessing commonly used features quick and easy. For example, you can see recent comments, incoming links, and so on. To access all features available to you in WordPress, click each item listed in the left sidebar to view a flyout submenu or to fully expand each menu, as shown in Figure 3-15. You can also return to the main WordPress dashboard page at any time while you're logged into your WordPress account by clicking the Dashboard link at the top of the left sidebar.

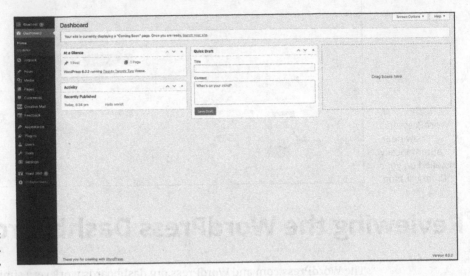

FIGURE 3-14:
The WordPress.
org dashboard.

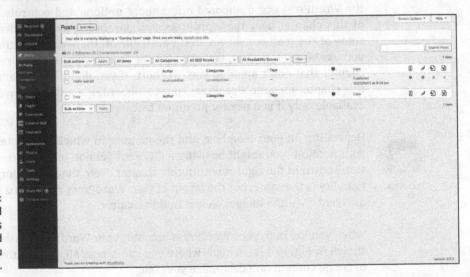

FIGURE 3-15:
Expanded
WordPress
dashboard
sidebar menu
item.

The WordPress dashboard sidebar typically provides the following menu items, which can all be expanded:

- » **Posts:** The links under the Posts heading allow you to edit existing posts, add new posts to your blog, and add new tags and categories. Tags and categories can also be added at the time a post is created. You can get instructions for creating a new post later in this chapter.

- » **Media:** The links under the Media heading allow you to view all images and media that you've already uploaded to your media library or add new images. You can also add images directly from within a new blog post.

- » **Pages:** The links under the Pages heading allow you to edit existing pages on your blog and create new ones. For example, you can create an About page or use WordPress to create a more traditional website with the Pages feature. Adding pages works just like adding posts, as described later in this chapter, except that instead of tagging and categorizing pages, you select where they should be published based on your site's page hierarchy using a simple drop-down list in the sidebar of the page editor.

- » **Comments:** The Comments link allows you to view and moderate comments left on your blog posts. From the Comments page, you can approve, delete, edit, and respond to comments as well as mark comments as spam that the built-in comment spam plugin, Akismet, misses.

- » **Appearance:** From the Appearance section of your WordPress dashboard, you can modify the visual aspects of your blog including theme and color scheme, for example.

- » **Plugins:** Use the Plugins section of your WordPress dashboard to extend the functionality of your blog. Here you can search for, install, activate, deactivate, update, and uninstall plugins.

- » **Users:** From the Users section, you can add, delete, or edit individuals who can access your WordPress dashboard to publish content or manage the site.

- » **Tools:** From the Tools section of your WordPress dashboard, you can access your blog's default tools including the ability to import content to your blog and export content away from your blog to a new site or platform.

- » **Settings:** Configure all of your WordPress site's reading, writing, discussion, media, and other settings from this area. Several of these settings are discussed in the Configuring Settings section of this chapter.

Creating posts and pages, adding media and links, and moderating comments are made extremely easy using the simple WordPress interface. Just fill in the text boxes and select options using the provided drop-down menus, and you're done! For specific details on using WordPress, be sure to read *WordPress For Dummies*, 9th Edition (John Wiley & Sons, Inc., 2020), by Lisa Sabin-Wilson.

Configuring Settings

Because the first thing you should do when you start a new blog is configure its settings, the following sections walk you through some of the most important settings you need to consider before you begin publishing content on your blog.

TIP

Take the time to look through all the pages and options available through the WordPress dashboard. Although the configuration suggestions included in this section are considered to be the most important, you should review all options to ensure your blog works exactly the way you want it to.

Profile

The Profile Settings page is where you can configure the settings that define and describe you and your blog as follows:

1. Click the Users link on the WordPress dashboard, shown in Figure 3-16.

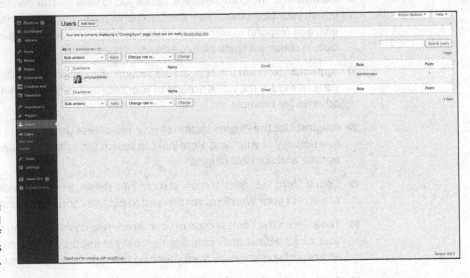

FIGURE 3-16:
The expanded Users section of the WordPress dashboard.

2. Click on your profile.

3. Scroll down to enter the requested profile information in the boxes provided as shown in Figure 3-17.

4. Click the Update Profile button at the bottom of the page to save your changes.

A Profile Updated message appears near the top of your screen when your data is saved.

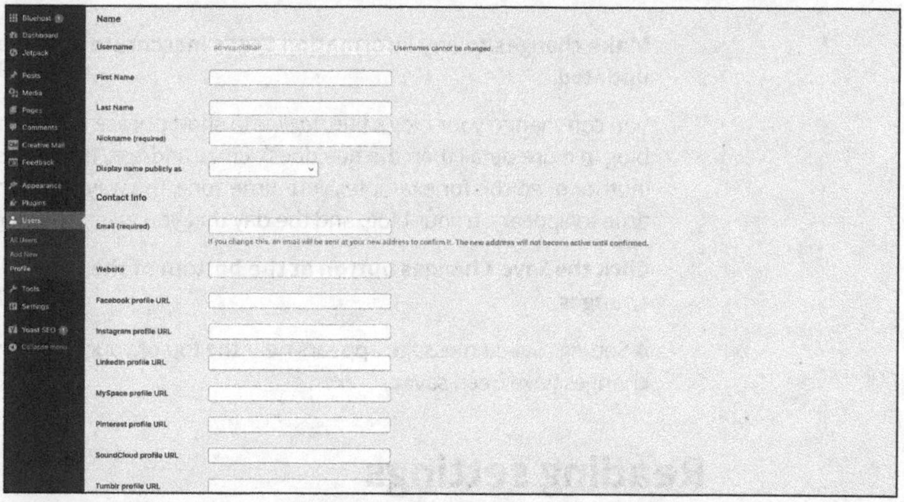

FIGURE 3-17:
The Profile configuration page.

You can change these settings at any time, but it's a good idea to configure them up front.

TIP

General settings

The General Settings page is where you can configure the broad settings that affect your entire blog as follows:

1. Click the General link under the Settings heading in the left sidebar of your WordPress dashboard as shown in Figure 3-18.

This step opens the General Settings configuration page.

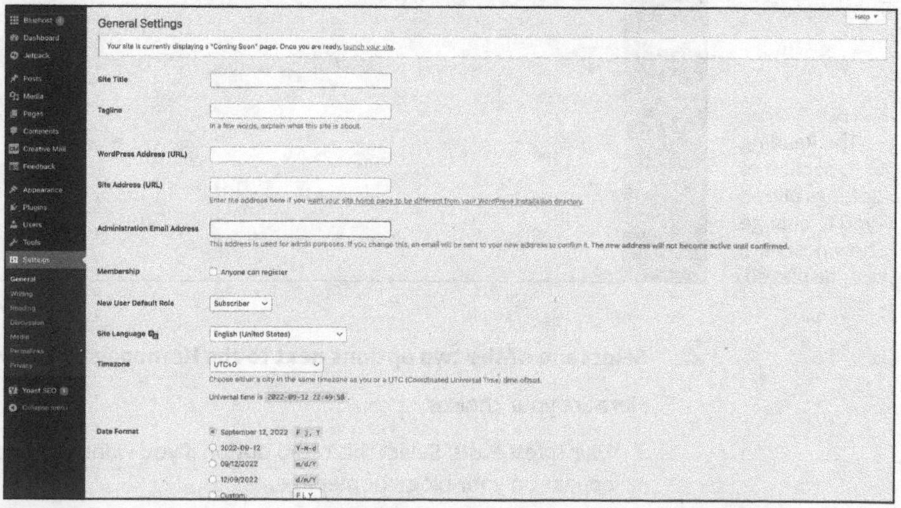

FIGURE 3-18:
The General Settings allow you to change or update basic settings for your blog.

2. **Make changes to any information that's inaccurate or needs to be updated.**

   You can change your blog's title, *tagline* (a short phrase that describes your blog in more detail than the title does), email address, new users' default roles (author or editor, for example), your time zone, the way you want the date and time to appear on your blog, and the day that you want new weeks to start on.

3. **Click the Save Changes button at the bottom of the page to save your changes.**

   A Settings Saved message appears near the top of your screen when your changes have been saved.

Reading settings

The most important settings you need to configure for your new blog are related to your blog's front page and post settings as follows:

1. **Click the Reading link under the Settings heading in the left sidebar on the WordPress dashboard as shown in Figure 3-19.**

   The Reading Settings page opens.

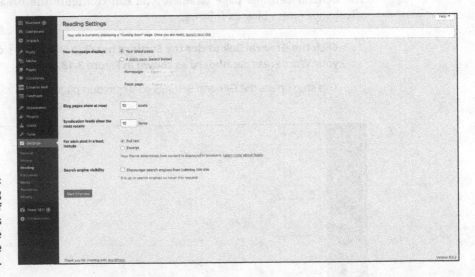

FIGURE 3-19:
The Reading section of Settings allows you to change how posts are displayed.

2. **Select one of the two options next to the Homepage displays heading.**

   Here are your choices:

   • *Your Latest Posts:* Select this radio button if you want your blog posts to appear on your blog's homepage.

- *A Static Page:* Select this radio button if you want a static homepage to be your blog's front page so it looks more like a traditional website. Then select the page you want to use from the drop-down lists.

  If you want to use a static page for the main page of your blog, the page must already be created so you can select it from the drop-down lists.

3. **Next to the Blog Pages Show at Most heading, select the number of posts you want to appear on your blog's homepage.**

4. **Next to the Syndication Feeds Show the most recent heading, select the number of posts you want your blog to display in syndicated form.**

5. **Click the Save Changes button at the bottom of the screen.**

   A Settings Saved message appears near the top of your screen when your changes have been saved.

Discussion settings

The discussion settings are very important because this is where you determine how comments are handled on your blog posts as follows:

1. **Click the Discussion link under the Settings heading in the left sidebar of your WordPress dashboard as shown in Figure 3-20.**

   The Discussion Settings page opens.

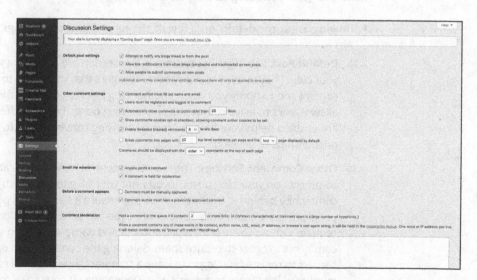

FIGURE 3-20:
The Discussion section of Settings determines how you handle blog comments.

2. **Review the preconfigured discussion settings and make any desired changes related to comments and trackbacks including the following:**

- Allow blogs to be notified when you've linked to them in a post.

- Allow trackbacks to appear on your posts.

- Allow readers to comment on your posts.

- Notify you via email when a reader has commented.

- Hold comments from new commenters in moderation until approved.

TIP

Learn more about trackbacks in Chapter 3 of Book 1.

It's important to note that these are the general settings for every post on your blog. Should you want to change the settings on one particular post, you are able to do so. For example, you may write a blog post that is especially personal or controversial and decide not to allow comments on that post only.

3. **Click the Save Changes button at the bottom of the screen.**

A Settings Saved message appears near the top of your screen when your changes have been saved.

TIP

The predefined discussion settings are the ones most bloggers use, but you're free to make any changes you want. For example, when your blog gets popular, you might not want to receive an email every time someone leaves a comment on your blog, or you would be inundated with email! You can find out about using comments to grow your blog in Chapter 2 of Book 6.

Following are some details on a few of the most common settings:

>> **Default Post Settings:** The settings in this section are important for growing your blog. They're used to notify other bloggers that you linked to their content and to notify you when another blog links to yours. Furthermore, they allow visitors to leave comments on your blog posts. Ensuring these settings are enabled helps your blog to grow by allowing conversations to flow and relationships to develop.

>> **Other Comment Settings:** These settings control how people can leave comments on your blog posts. If you want your blog to grow with a strong community behind it, the best option is to ensure it's as easy as possible for people to leave comments. For example, you can select the option that requires visitors to enter an email address and name in order to submit comments in order to reduce spam. Selecting the configuration option to ask readers to register and log in to leave a comment, however, will reduce the number of legitimate comments, too. Depending on your goals for your blog, that might not be something you want to do.

>> **Email Me Whenever:** The settings in this section are intended to help you keep track of the conversations happening on your blog, and you can configure them in the manner that suits your preferences best.

>> **Before a Comment Appears:** These settings affect how much control you have over publishing comments on your blog. You can choose to approve *all* comments manually before they can be published, or you can choose to have to approve comments only when a new user writes one; after a user's initial comment has been approved by you, any further commenting by this user will be approved automatically. This is entirely up to you.

>> **Comment Moderation:** The comment moderation section allows you to automatically hold comments that meet your specified criteria for moderation. For example, you can configure your blog so comments with more than two links are always held for moderation or so comments that are flagged as potential spam are always held for moderation.

>> **Disallowed Comment Keys:** Just as you can configure your blog so comments are held for moderation if they contain certain words, you can also blacklist specific words and automatically relegate them to your comment spam folder.

The Discussion Settings page in your WordPress dashboard also includes an area where you can configure avatar settings. An *avatar* is a small image that people use to identify themselves online and can appear next to comments they leave on avatar-enabled blogs. For example, you can use a photograph of yourself as your avatar.

If you'd like to allow avatars to appear along with comments that people leave on your blog, you can configure that option within the Avatar Settings section of the Discussion Settings page. You can also configure settings for the types of avatars that are allowed on your blog (using a simple ratings scale that determines audience-appropriateness levels), and you can choose the images to publish when a commenter doesn't have a preconfigured avatar.

Privacy settings

To access the Privacy Settings page, click the Privacy link under the Settings heading in the left sidebar of your WordPress dashboard, as shown in Figure 3-21. The Privacy Settings page is where you can create a privacy policy to display on your blog.

TIP

It is best to include a privacy policy page on your blog, especially if you plan to make money with your site. Your privacy policy will let your readers know how their time on your blog is being tracked and how it is being used. To learn more about blog privacy policy pages visit Chapter 4 of Book 1.

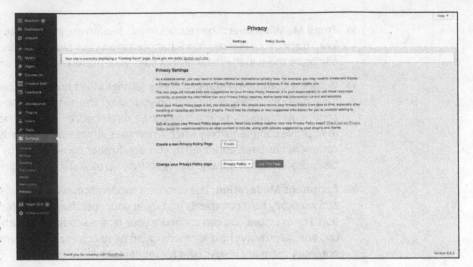

FIGURE 3-21:
The Privacy Settings page allows you to create a privacy policy for your blog.

Permalink settings

A *permalink* is the permanent URL, or web address, of each individual blog post. The Permalink Settings page is overlooked by most beginner bloggers, but configuring the settings on this page before you begin writing is actually very important because they can greatly affect the amount of search engine traffic your blog gets. This is also a setting that you should not alter once you've established your blog as changes made will impact your readers' ability to find old posts as well as your standing in search engine results. Follow these steps to adjust the settings:

1. **Click the Permalinks link under the Settings heading on the WordPress dashboard as shown in Figure 3-22.**

   The Permalink Settings page opens.

2. **Select the radio button next to the post link structure that you prefer.**

   Selecting a permalink structure that adds your post title to your blog posts links gives them better search engine optimization opportunities because your post names might include useful keywords that search engines look for in their indexing algorithms.

3. **Click the Save Changes button at the bottom of the page.**

   A Settings Saved message appears near the top of your screen when your changes have been saved.

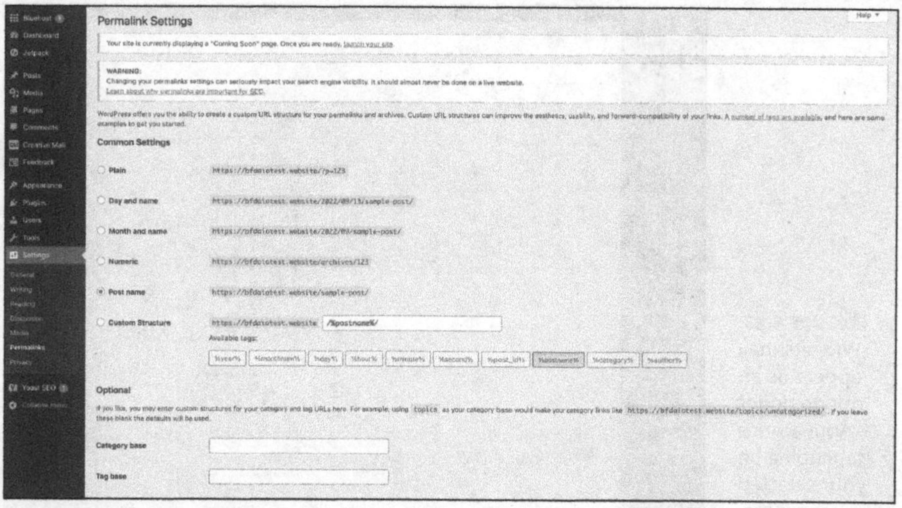

Figure 3-22 shows the Permalink Settings page.

Permalink Settings

FIGURE 3-22:
Visit the Permalink Settings page to configure how future post links will be written.

Understanding Widgets

Depending on the theme you have selected for your blog, you may find widgets by clicking the Widgets link under the Appearance heading in the left sidebar of your WordPress dashboard, as shown in Figure 3-23. Widgets are used in Word-Press to make adding features and functions easy. Rather than rewriting HTML or CSS code to alter your blog's appearance, widgets are built into most Word-Press themes, including some of the default WordPress themes, which allow you to simply drag and drop widget boxes to your blog. Looking at Figure 3-23, you can see how the Widgets configuration page is set up in your WordPress dash-board. You can simply click and drag widgets from the Available Widgets module on the left side of your screen to your site in the center of the screen to add to your blog's appearance and functionality. Similarly, you can remove widgets by dragging them from the right side of your screen back to the Available Widgets (to reset them) or Inactive Widgets (to save them for later) area of your screen.

After you drag a widget to your blog using the WordPress dashboard Widgets page, you might be given the option to click a drop-down arrow to the right of the wid-get's name to further customize the content in the widget.

TIP Don't be afraid to play around with the widgets available to you. You can't break anything, and if you don't like a change, you can simply drag the widget out of your sidebar from the widgets configuration page to remove it.

FIGURE 3-23:
Widgets may
appear as an
option under
Appearance
depending on
your selected
theme.

Personalizing Your Blog

The best part about using WordPress.org as your blogging application is the wide variety of customization options that are available to you. Even if you use WordPress.com, you can choose from a number of themes, and you can modify colors and other settings, but WordPress.org truly leads the pack in terms of customization.

TECHNICAL STUFF

Most of the appearance customization changes you can make on your blog depend on the theme you're using because some themes offer more customization options than others.

Themes

You can access the Manage Themes page by clicking the Themes link under the Appearance heading in the left sidebar of your WordPress dashboard. Here you can access the themes that are preloaded with WordPress and change your blog's appearance simply by activating one of the new themes listed on this page. You can even preview your blog using the new theme with the Preview link provided.

Add new themes

You can access the Add Themes page, shown in Figure 3-24, by clicking the Add Themes tab at the top of the Themes page (accessible under the Appearance heading in the left sidebar of your WordPress dashboard). This is where you can find the true flexibility of WordPress design.

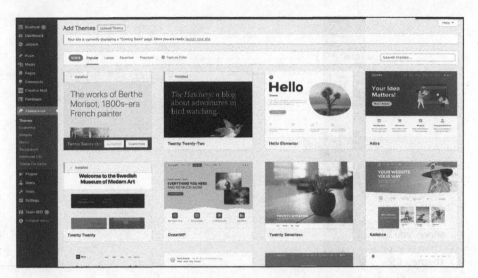

FIGURE 3-24: The Add Themes page allows you to install new themes to your blog's Dashboard.

Using WordPress.org, you can access a wide variety of free themes directly from this page (try the Popular, Latest, Favorites, and Search areas near the top of the page to help you find themes you like), or you can upload one of the many free themes available online. You can also purchase a premium theme and upload it to your WordPress account. Using a premium theme requires a small investment, but premium themes are typically well-tested and provide a more unique look for your blog than frequently used free themes do. I tell you where you can find WordPress themes later in this chapter, in the section "Finding themes."

Editor

You can open the cascading style sheets (CSS) editor shown in Figure 3-25 for your active WordPress theme by clicking the Theme File Editor (this may have a slightly different name depending on your selected theme) link under the Appearance heading in the left sidebar of your WordPress dashboard. If you know CSS, this editor is extremely powerful and allows you to modify any part of your WordPress theme.

Cascading style sheets is the programming language used to create web page presentation, including WordPress blogs. CSS tells the web browser how to display the Hypertext Markup Language (HTML) elements that make up the page content. In broad terms, HTML is used to create the page content, and CSS is used to create the presentation, layout, and design of that content.

WARNING

Proceed with extreme caution! Always copy the content of the editor text box and paste it into another document before you make any changes. If something doesn't work the way you want it to after you make your edits, you can simply copy and paste the original CSS code back into the editor text box as if nothing was ever changed.

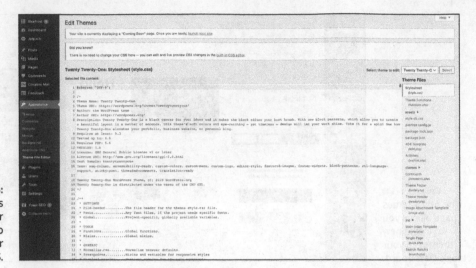

FIGURE 3-25:
The WordPress theme editor allows you to change your theme's CSS.

Choosing a theme

Looking online, you will find what seems like an endless variety of themes for WordPress.org blogs. Some themes are free, but others, called *premium* themes, are available for either a one-time fee or a yearly subscription fee. The primary differences between free and premium themes are as explained in Table 3-2.

TABLE 3-2   ## Free versus Premium Blog Themes

	Free Themes	Premium Themes
Price	They're, well, free!	They typically cost between $10–$200.
Reliability	Anyone can create free themes, so you can't be completely sure that they work well until you try them (unless you know the reputation of the developer).	Premium themes from respected developers are far more likely to work the way they're supposed to and typically offer more functionality.
Support	Free themes usually come with no support.	Premium themes often offer support for a fee or through a community forum.
Originality	Free themes can be used by anyone, so your blog might not look unique if you select a popular free theme.	Premium themes offer greater customization and because they have a cost associated with them, fewer people use them, giving your blog a better chance of looking unique.

Finding themes

Perhaps the best place to begin when searching for the right theme for your blog is on your WordPress Dashboard! Selecting the Feature Filter on the Add Themes setting page, as shown in Figure 3-26, allows you to customize exactly what you're looking for in a theme.

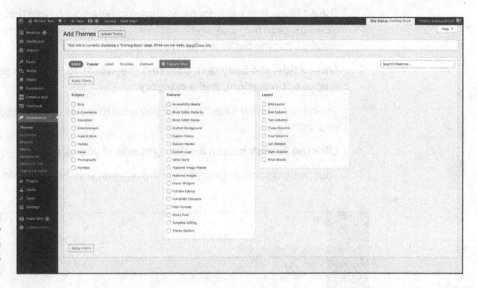

FIGURE 3-26:
Search for a new theme within your WordPress Dashboard.

A variety of sites offer WordPress themes, both free and paid. Following are a few of the popular sites to find free WordPress themes:

>> **Theme Forest** (www.themeforest.net)

>> **WPBeginner** (www.wpbeginner.com)

>> **WPHub** (www.wphub.com)

>> **WooCommerce** (www.woocommerce.com)

>> **Elegant Themes** (www.elegantthemes.com)

>> **StudioPress** (www.studiopress.com)

Publishing a Post

Publishing a post using WordPress is extremely easy:

1. **Click the Add New link under the Posts heading on your WordPress dashboard.**

   The Add New Post page opens, as shown in Figure 3-27. Note that your Add New Post page may look slightly different depending on the theme you have installed, but the basics will be the same.

2. **Enter a title, the body text, post *tags* (keywords to help with search engine optimization), and a category.**

   Select the Add New Category link if you need to create a new category for your post.

3. **Click the Publish button on the right side of your screen.**

   Your new blog post appears as the top entry on your blog. It's that easy!

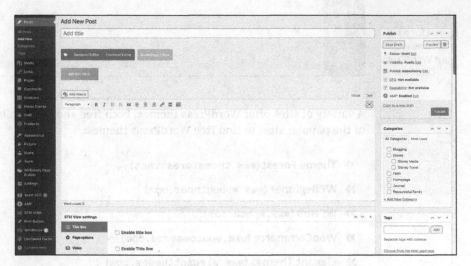

FIGURE 3-27:
Create a new post from the Posts section of your WordPress dashboard.

Take some time to hover your mouse over the various icons in the visual editor box to see the pop-up text explaining what each icon does. Most of these tools work the same way in WordPress as they do in word-processing applications. You can add bold to text, create links, and insert images using these icons.

To reveal more options for managing your post, click the Screen Options dropdown arrow in the top right of your screen to reveal options to display and modify the post author, a post excerpt, and more.

TIP

Create a test post and play with the various icons in the visual text editor to see what they do. You can use the Preview button on the right side of your screen to see the results or publish the post. (You can delete it right away by clicking the Edit link under the Post heading on your WordPress dashboard.)

Making Sense of WordPress Plugins

WordPress plugins are created by individual developers who want to add functionality to WordPress.org. You can install plugins to your WordPress account, activate them, and then use them on your blog. For example, some plugins allow you to create online forms and site maps, add social networking icons to your blog posts for sharing, and more.

TIP

You can search for plugins from your WordPress Dashboard or visit `http://wordpress.org/extend/plugins` to search the official repository of WordPress plugins.

Plugins are easily installed through your WordPress dashboard:

1. **Click the Add New link under the Plugins heading on the right side of your WordPress dashboard.**

    The Add Plugins page shown in Figure 3-28 opens.

    From this page, you can search for plugins to install using the search box or upload a plugin you already downloaded to your computer's hard drive using the Upload link.

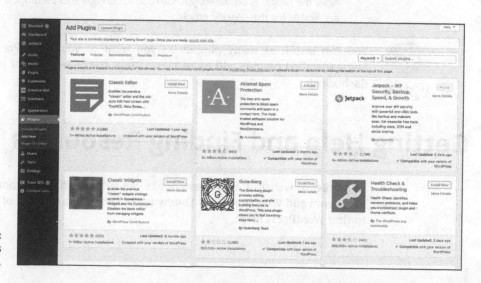

FIGURE 3-28:
The WordPress
Add Plugins page.

2. **Enter keywords to search for a plugin or select the Upload link at the top of the page and follow the steps to upload the plugin.**

When you find a plugin you want to install through a search, simply click the Install Now link under the plugin name to instantly install it to your WordPress dashboard.

If you uploaded the plugin from your computer, the plugin appears in the Plugins page on your WordPress dashboard (shown in Figure 3-29), which you can access by selecting the Installed Plugins link under the Plugins heading on the left side of your WordPress dashboard.

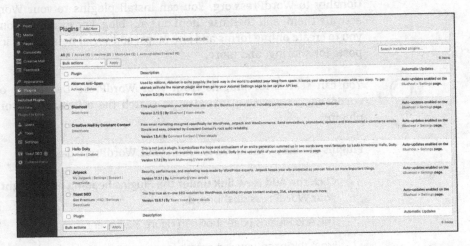

FIGURE 3-29:
The WordPress
Plugins page.

3. **Click the Activate link to activate the plugin.**

After the plugin is activated, you can use it, configure its settings, and so on as applicable for the specific plugin.

TECHNICAL STUFF

You can install as many plugins as you want to your WordPress.org account. Some installed plugins add more menu items to the left side of your WordPress dashboard.

Getting Help and Finding Resources

A number of websites, blogs, and books can help you find out more about Word-Press.com and WordPress.org. Following is a short list of some of the best places to find WordPress help:

>> **WordPress For Dummies:** Lisa Sabin-Wilson wrote this guide to WordPress. com and WordPress.org, which is available through most booksellers.

>> **WordPress.org** (`www.wordpress.org`): This is the online guide to everything and anything WordPress.org-related.

>> **WordPress.com Support** (`www.wordpress.org/support`): You can find online support for WordPress.com here.

>> **WordPress.com forums** (`www.wordpress.org/forums`): This is the online forum for WordPress.com users to ask questions and discuss their blogs.

>> **WP Modders** (`www.wpmods.com`): This is an excellent blog to learn about WordPress themes and news and access helpful tutorials.

Chapter 4

Using Google Blogger

Blogger was originally launched by Pyra Labs in 1999 as one of the first dedicated blogging applications. In 2003, Google purchased Blogger, and since then, the application has grown more popular as new features have been introduced and other Google applications have been seamlessly integrated into the Blogger user interface. Today, Blogger remains one of the most popular blogging applications, and because it is free to use, remains a favorite among beginning bloggers.

This chapter teaches you what Blogger can do, how the basic functions work, and where you can find more help. Joining the blogosphere can be overwhelming, but Blogger remains popular for several reasons — it's easy to use, feature-rich, and budget-friendly. That's all many bloggers need, and Blogger delivers.

Discovering Blogger

Blogger is a wildly popular, free blogging platform using a What You See Is What You Get (WYSIWYG) editor. Like WordPress, covered in depth in Chapter 3 of this Book, Blogger's WYSIWYG editing format makes writing and publishing content on your blog as easy as it is to type a document using your preferred word-processing software.

Blogger also provides gadgets that make adding enhanced functionality and features to your blog as easy as pointing and clicking. Although Blogger started out as a fairly limited blogging application, enhancements over time made it easy for bloggers to accomplish common blogging tasks such as scheduling posts for the future, adding videos to your blog, and sharing via social media platforms. It's even possible to make custom alterations to Blogger code to change your blog's appearance entirely. The Blogger of today is a far cry from its early days! That's why even though WordPress is a dominating platform in the world of blogging, many top blogs are still powered by Blogger. Even the highly popular Althouse blog (www.althouse.blogspot.com), shown in Figure 4-1, runs on Blogger.

FIGURE 4-1: The Althouse blog has been hosted on Blogger since its launch in 2004.

One of the primary benefits to using Blogger as your blogging application is that it allows you to run any ad that you want to monetize your blog. Not only can you add multiple revenue streams such as direct ads, pay-per-click ads, pay-per-impression ads, affiliate ads, sponsored reviews, text ads, and more to your blog, but Blogger makes it extremely easy to integrate one of the most popular monetization opportunities for bloggers: Google AdSense. You can find out more about making money from your blog in Book 7.

Creating a Free Blog at Blogger.com

If you want to start your blog using a blogging application on a free platform that offers a lot of functionality and flexibility, Blogger is an excellent choice. Starting a new blog using Blogger takes just a few minutes, so you can publish content and start monetizing your blog (if making money is one of your blogging goals) almost instantly. And when you're ready to take your blog to the next level, Blogger offers a number of more advanced features to help you reach your goals.

TIP

Google adds new features and functions to Blogger all the time. You can read about past changes to Blogger and learn about new updates by reading the Blogger Buzz blog at `http://buzz.blogger.com`.

To create a new blog using Blogger, take the following steps:

1. **Direct your browser to `www.blogger.com`.**

2. **Click Create Your Blog in the middle of the page, as shown in Figure 4-2.**

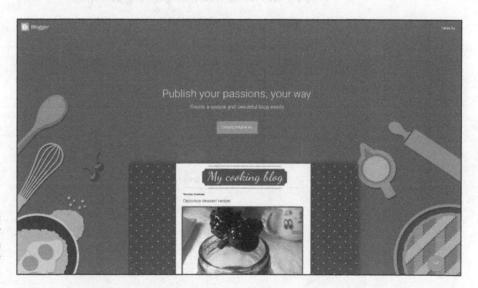

FIGURE 4-2:
Click Create Your Blog to begin setting up your new Blogger blog.

3. **Sign in to an existing free Google account or create a Google account, as shown in Figure 4-3.**

    Your Google account will be used to sign in to and manage your blog content.

    If you already have a Google account, that's great and saves time. Simply sign-in to your account and continue to Step 4.

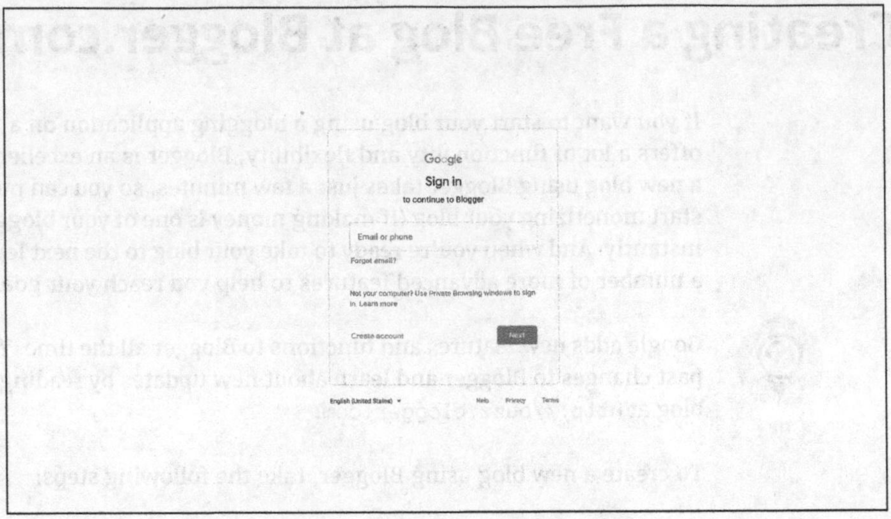

Creating a Free Blog at Blogger.com

FIGURE 4-3:
A free Google account is required to create a blog on Google's Blogger platform.

If you don't have a Google account, click the create account, as shown in Figure 4-3. You will then be prompted (Figure 4-4) to:

- Fill in the required information.

- Accept the terms of service.

- Click next.

FIGURE 4-4:
The Create a Google Account page.

The Blogger blog creation screen where you will name your new blog now appears, as shown in Figure 4-5.

4. **Enter a name for your new blog and click next.**

   It's important to note that if you aren't yet sure of your new blog's name, you have the option to skip this step. It is also possible to change the name to something else later. This decision isn't permanent!

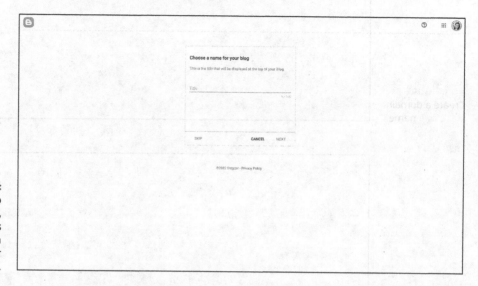

FIGURE 4-5:
After signing in to a Google account, Blogger prompts you to create a name for your new blog.

5. **Create a domain name for your blog and click next, as shown in Figure 4-6.**

   If your first choice for a domain name is already taken, try alternative names until you find one that is available. It may take a few tries — don't give up!

   TECHNICAL STUFF

   As outlined in Chapter 2 of this Book, Blogger domain names all end with blogspot.com. To learn more about domain names visit Chapter 3 of Book 1.

6. **Choose the display name that readers will use to identify you as the author of your blog and click finish, as shown in Figure 4-7.**

   How would you like to be identified? You may choose to create a a fancy pen name or write your blog as yourself. Some bloggers use initials only or perhaps a variation of their given name. It's entirely up to you!

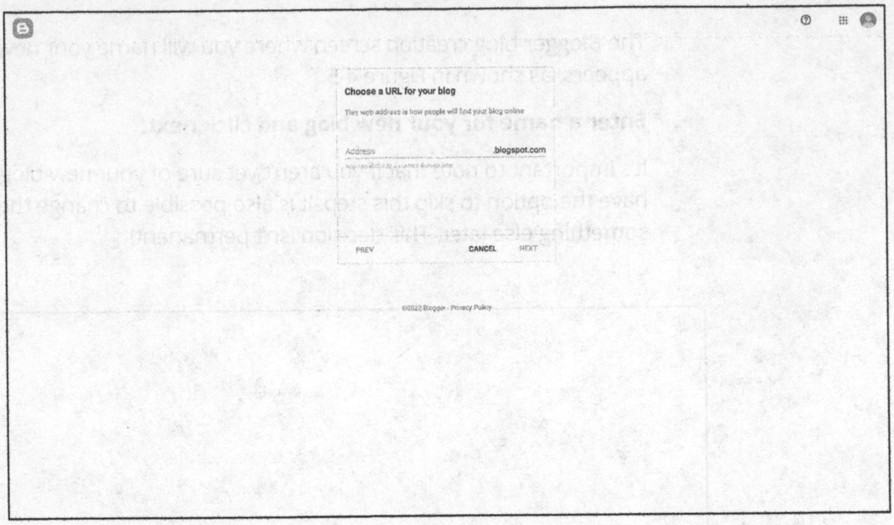

FIGURE 4-6:
Create a domain
name.

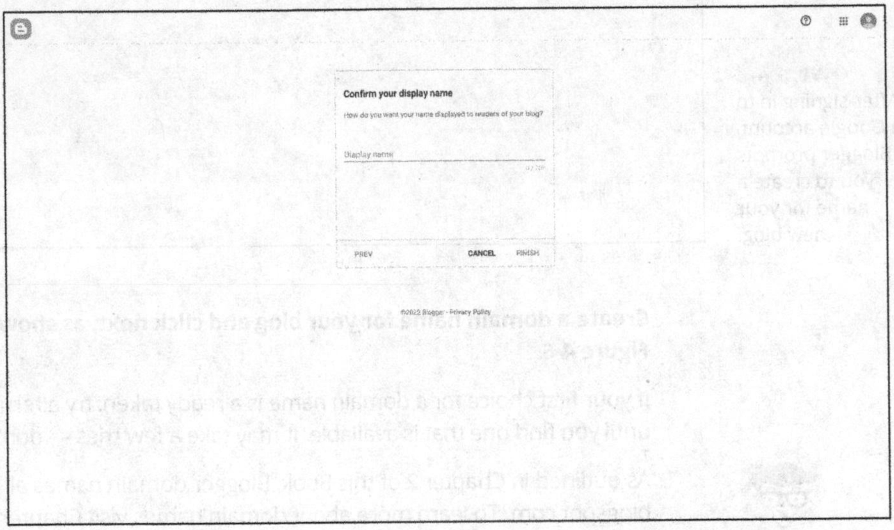

FIGURE 4-7:
Decide what
author name
you would like
displayed to your
readers.

Congratulations! You are now the owner of a brand-new Blogger blog! Once you've clicked Finish on the last step of the creation process, the Blogger dashboard will appear, as shown in Figure 4-8.

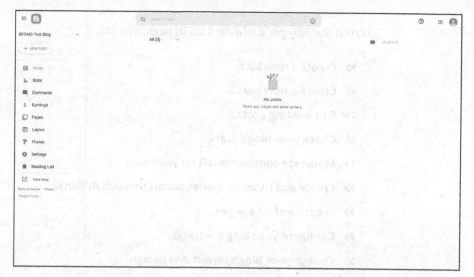

FIGURE 4-8:
The Blogger
dashboard.

Reviewing the Blogger Dashboard

The Blogger dashboard is where you access all the functions, features, and controls for your new blog. You can add new posts, edit old posts, add enhancements to your blog, change your blog's design, and much more from your Blogger dashboard.

TIP

Don't rush into creating content on your blog until you take the time to click through the many sections accessible through your Blogger dashboard. Reviewing each section helps you find out more about what you can do to personalize and configure your blog so it looks and works exactly how you want it to.

Review the following sections to see what kinds of tools are available from the various navigation tabs on your Blogger dashboard.

The Blogger dashboard main page

To access your Blogger dashboard at any time, direct your browser to www. blogger.com and click Sign-In in the upper righthand corner. Sign in to the Google account associated with your Blogger blog, and the dashboard will appear, as shown in Figure 4-8.

From the Blogger dashboard main page, you can

>> **Create a new blog.**

>> **Create a new post.**

>> **Edit existing posts.**

>> **Check your blog's stats.**

>> **Moderate comments left on your blog.**

>> **Create and manage monetization through AdSense.**

>> **Create and edit pages.**

>> **Configure your blog's settings.**

>> **Change your blog's layout and design.**

>> **View and edit your profile.**

>> **Edit your photo.**

>> **Access your Google account.**

>> **View blog posts from blogs in your reading list.**

>> **View how your blog appears to readers.**

All of the features are accessible through the links, drop-down menus, and buttons found on the main page of your Blogger dashboard.

Account link

In the top-right corner of your Blogger dashboard (shown in Figure 4-8) is the display name and Google account email you selected while creating your blog. Click this icon to access a submenu where you can edit your account or profile at any time.

New Post button

Click the New Post button near the top of your Blogger dashboard (refer to Figure 4-8) to add a new post. The New Post button is likely to be a section of your Blogger dashboard that you access often, assuming that you publish new content frequently on your blog.

Posts button

Click the Posts button (a stack of papers icon) shown in Figure 4-8 to view and access all posts published on your blog. This is a quick way to find older posts that you want to edit or delete.

Stats button

Click the Stats button to access data about everything from the number of comments on your blog to the number of visitors. You can learn about data for individual posts or your entire blog as well as individual pages you've created on your site.

Comments button

Once you've posted content and readers have begun engaging with your writing and each other, comments will appear in this section of your dashboard. To learn more about building a community through comments, visit Chapter 2 of Book 6.

Earnings button

Ready to begin monetizing your Blogger blog by creating a Google AdSense account? This is where you will find all you need to sign-up, manage your AdSense account, and receive payments. For more on Google AdSense, see Book 7.

Pages button

Once you have created individual pages on your blog, you can go to this section of your dashboard to edit those pages.

Layout button

Clicking the Layout button allows you to customize the look and functionality of your blog through the use of what Google calls gadgets. To learn more about all that you can do in this section of your dashboard, read "Understanding Blogger Gadgets" later in this chapter.

Theme button

Like the Layout button, the Theme button also allows you to customize the look and reader experience for your Blogger blog. Learn more later in this chapter in the section, "Personalizing Your Blog."

Settings button

The Settings button, explained in depth in the following section, allows you to configure settings related to everything from your author profile to your blog's comment experience. Take some time to read through and customize this section of your dashboard before beginning to post content and develop a community of readers. You can always come back and make changes later, but it's best to start by putting the time in up front.

Reading List button

In this section of your dashboard you can find the blogs that you've chosen to follow. To get you started, Blogger has added the Blogger Buzz blog to your Reading List.

Configuring Settings

Before you publish a new post on your blog, you should configure a number of settings to ensure your blogging experience goes as smoothly as possible and your readers enjoy the best possible experience when they visit your blog. The following sections walk you through some of the most important settings you should configure before you publish your first blog post.

REMEMBER

Your blog is yours, which means you can configure its settings any way you want to meet your blogging goals. The suggestions included in the following sections are the settings most bloggers who want to grow their blogs use, but you can choose your own settings. Also, you can change your blog's settings at any time, so you're not locked into the settings you choose when you start your blog.

Profile

Your blog's profile is where you describe who you are and why you're writing your blog. Take the time to write a complete profile so your blog's readers can get to know you and understand why you're the right person to be writing a blog on your chosen subject. Follow these steps to create your blog's profile page:

1. **Click the Settings button in the dashboard menu on the left side of the screen.**

2. **Scroll all the way to the bottom of the Settings page to locate and click on User Profile, as shown in Figure 4-9.**

   The Edit User Profile page opens, as shown in Figure 4-10.

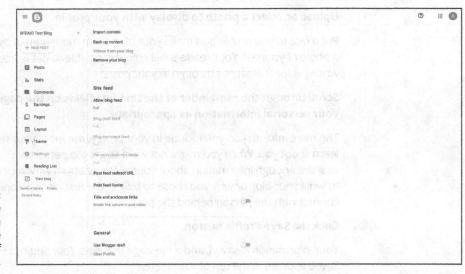

FIGURE 4-9:
The User Profile settings option is located at the very bottom of the Settings page.

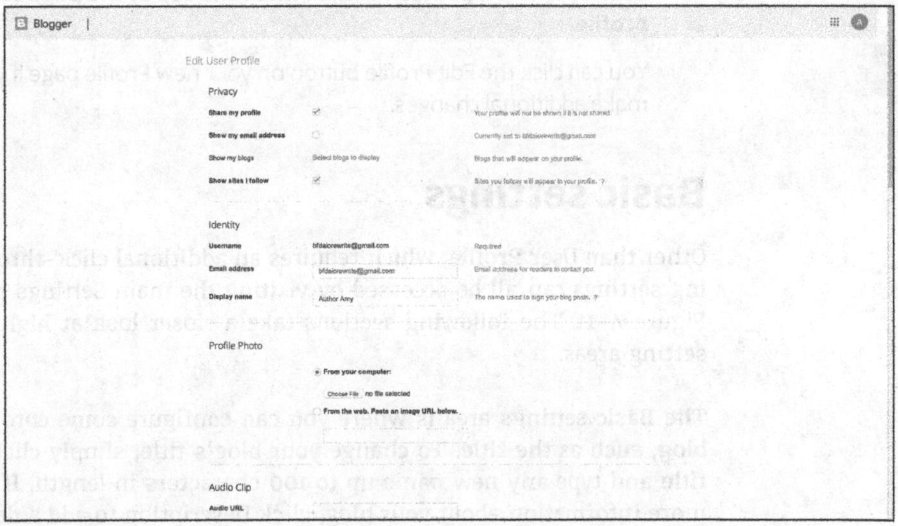

FIGURE 4-10:
The Edit User Profile page allows you to customize your profile information.

3. **Make sure the Share My Profile check box is selected and click the Select Blogs to Display link next to Show My Blogs to choose which of your blogs (if you have more than one Blogger blog) that you want to include in your profile.**

TIP

There are very few anonymous popular bloggers. If you want to grow your blog, the best choice is to tell your audience who you are in your blog's profile. If maintaining anonymity is important to you, consider creating a pen name!

4. **Upload or select a photo to display with your profile.**

Put a face to you profile and make your blog seem more human by uploading a photo of yourself. Your readers will enjoy being able to put a face to the writing voice that shines through in your posts!

5. **Scroll through the remainder of the text box fields on the page and enter your personal information as appropriate.**

The more information you include in your profile, the more your readers will learn about you. While you might not want to get too personal, it's a good idea to share enough information about yourself to establish why you're qualified to write your blog or why you chose to blog in the first place. People like to connect with the person behind the post.

6. **Click the Save Profile button.**

Your information is saved, and a message that says Your Settings Have Been Saved appears at the top of your page.

7. **Click the View Updated Profile link at the top of the page to review your profile.**

You can click the Edit Profile button on your new Profile page if you need to make additional changes.

Basic settings

Other than User Profile, which requires an additional click-through, the remaining settings can all be accessed by visiting the main Settings page, as shown in Figure 4-11. The following sections take a closer look at highlights from those setting areas.

The Basic settings area is where you can configure some core settings for your blog, such as the title. To change your blog's title, simply click on your current title and type any new name up to 100 characters in length. If you'd like to add more information about your blog, click Description to add a description of what your blog is about up to 500 characters in length.

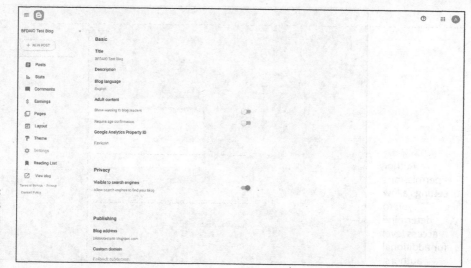

FIGURE 4-11:
The main Settings page allows you to customize a variety of blog settings.

Privacy

While your blog's first readers will likely find you through links that you've shared with friends, family, and followers on social media platforms and elsewhere, the long-term goal is for search engines to drive traffic to your blog through search results. In order for that to happen, you need to make sure that your privacy setting is set to allow search engines to find your blog.

REMEMBER

If you want your blog to grow and attract more visitors, it needs to be visible to search engines. Most blog traffic comes from search engine keyword searches, so you're missing a huge opportunity to expose new visitors to your blog if you exclude your content from search engine indexing processes. Don't be afraid to put your great content out there for the world to see!

Permissions

Unless you're starting a blog with a group of friends or coworkers, you will likely be your blog's only author when you begin blogging. However, many blogs have multiple authors or even guest authors for time to time. Your Permissions settings allow you to determine what level of access additional authors have to your blog. Figure 4-12 shows where author permissions can be changed to determine if secondary authors have access to do more than write and edit new content. If you invite additional authors and give them Admin level access, they will be able to do everything on your blog from changing the appearance to moderating comments. You can also invite new authors from this settings area.

FIGURE 4-12:
Author
permissions
settings allow
you to
determine
access level
for additional
authors.

Another setting under Permissions is Reader Access, shown in Figure 4-13. This is a default setting that applies to your entire blog, so unless you really only want a select few to read your blog, be sure that this setting is set to Public.

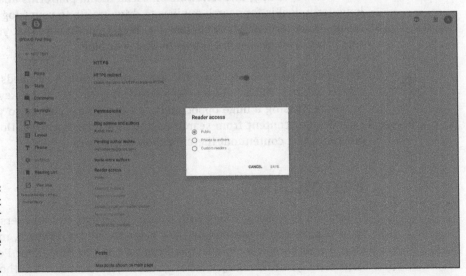

FIGURE 4-13:
Be sure to select
Public under
Reader Access
to allow anyone
to read your
content.

TIP

If you are starting a blog with a group of authors, you can use this setting to give permission to view posts to authors only until a determined period of time when you decide to launch your blog to the public. Then simply pop back in to these settings and change the permissions to Public!

Posts

The Posts section of the settings allows you to determine a couple post-related pre-sets that will apply to your entire blog, including the number of posts to allow on the main page. Depending on the design theme that you select, discussed later in this chapter, you may want to limit the number of posts on the main page. Your readers are more likely to want to click through to page two than they are to want to scroll indefinitely through post after post.

You can also use this setting to select to use a post theme on every future blog post. This is especially useful if you plan to include a specific element in every blog post such as:

>> a logo

>> an image

>> a standard introduction

>> a signature

>> social media links

>> a disclosure statement

In order to use this setting, you must first create a new post that contains the element you would like to include in every post. Later in this chapter you can take a closer look at how to create posts in Blogger. Once you've created a new post with the theme you'd like to use, click on the pencil icon in the upper left-hand corner in order to switch to HTML view, as shown in Figures 4-14 and 4-15.

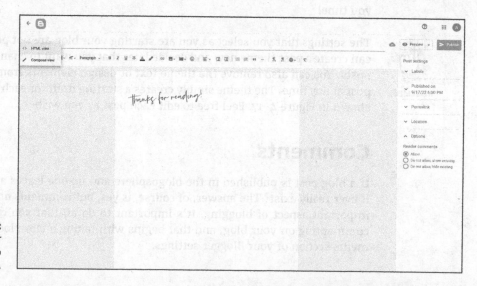

FIGURE 4-14:
Switch your post editor to HTML view.

In this example, I inserted a standard signature that I'd like to appear at the end of every future blog post. The HTML is the programming code that determines what readers see when they visit your blog. Don't be concerned if this looks like a confusing mess to you. That's okay! You can use this feature of Blogger settings without understanding HTML. Simply select and copy the code that appears.

FIGURE 4-15: Copy the HTML from the new post with the design or text elements you would like to include in every future post.

Once you have copied that HTML code, return to the Settings area of your Blogger dashboard. It's time to put that code to use! Paste that HTML code into the Post Theme area of settings and click save, as shown in Figure 4-16. Every future New Post will now automatically include that text or design element, ideally saving you time!

REMEMBER

The settings that you select as you are starting your blog are not permanent! You can create a post theme now and decide later that you want to change it for future posts. You can also remove the theme text or design elements from an individual post at any time. The theme simply creates a starting draft for each future post, as shown in Figure 4-17. Feel free to edit each post as you wish.

Comments

If a blog post is published in the blogosphere and no one leaves a comment, did it ever really exist? The answer, of course, is yes, but comments *are* an incredibly important aspect of blogging. It's important to do all that you can to facilitate commenting on your blog, and that begins with taking a close look at the Comments section of your Blogger settings.

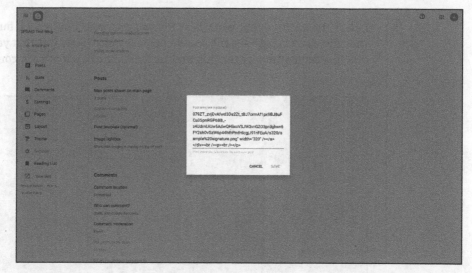

FIGURE 4-16:
Place the copied HTML code into the Post Theme settings area and click save.

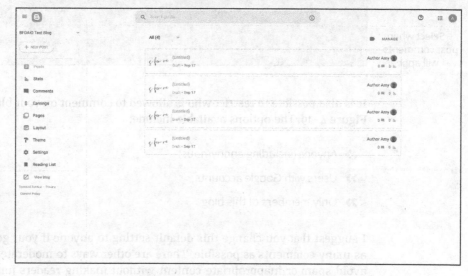

FIGURE 4-17:
The Post Theme setting determines what is included in all future drafts unless changed.

There are four available options (shown in Figure 4-18) for comment locations, including:

>> **Embedded:** This setting allows readers to comment directly on the post with comments appearing on the same page as the post content.

>> **Full page or popup window:** Both of these options take the reader to a new page, away from the original post, to see the comments displayed.

>> **Hide:** Selecting to hide comments does not delete comments. Rather it hides the comments from view and can be changed to display them at any time.

TIP

Select the settings that work best for you and your blog goals, but keep in mind that the easier it is to see the comments, the more likely it is that your readers will create a community by reading and responding to each other's comments.

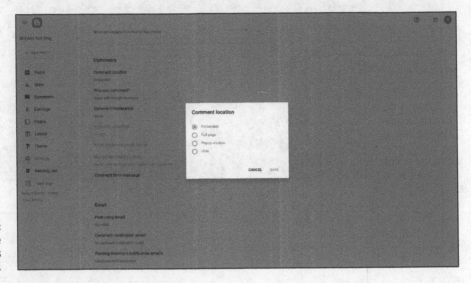

FIGURE 4-18:
Select where
post comments
will appear.

It is also possible to restrict who is allowed to comment on your blog, as shown in Figure 4-19. The options available include:

» Anyone (including anonymous)

» Users with Google accounts

» Only members of this blog

I suggest that you change this default setting to anyone if your goal is to receive as many comments as possible. There are other ways to moderate comments and avoid spam or inappropriate content without making readers jump through the hoops of signing in with a Google or member account.

If you would like to hold comments in moderation, not publishing them until you've read and approved them, select the always option under Comment moderation, as shown in Figure 4-20.

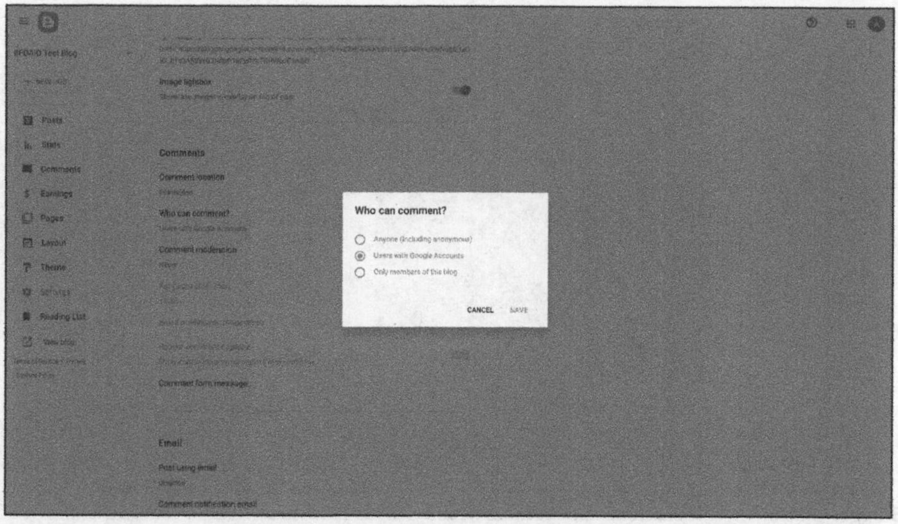

FIGURE 4-19:
Select who is
allowed to
leave a comment
on your blog.

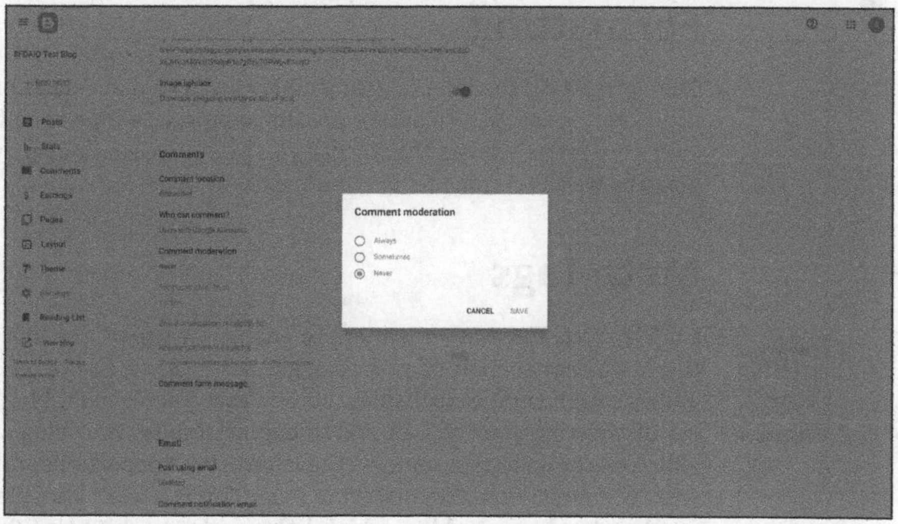

FIGURE 4-20:
Select always in
order to hold all
future comments
in moderation.

Email

The Email section of Settings allows you to change the settings related to email in various areas including comment moderation. One important note is that this section of settings is where you can elect to allow posting to your blog via email. For those who love to write on the go and post from a mobile device, this is a fantastic option. Be sure to select to either publish posts via email immediately or save emails as post drafts. Once selected, you can create a secret email address (shown in Figure 4-21), which you can use exclusively for the purpose of blogging via email.

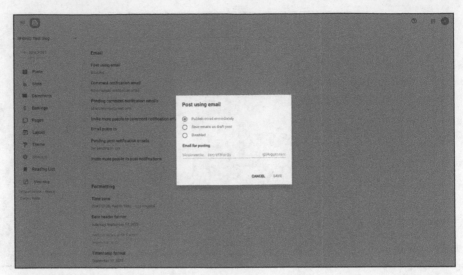

FIGURE 4-21:
You can blog
via email on the
Blogger platform.

Formatting

The Formatting section of Settings allows you to make decisions about date and time. Use this section to determine the appropriate time zone for timestamps on your content as well as the format you prefer to use to display the date of your posts as well as comments on your posts.

Meta Tags

REMEMBER

I highly recommend that you opt to enable the use of a search description under the Meta tags section of your Blogger settings, as shown in Figure 4-22. This allows search engines to display a brief description of your blog to potential read-ers discovering your blog in search engine results. Your blog search description, which can be up to 150 characters in length, is an opportunity to tell future readers what to expect when they visit your blog. This is also an ideal place to include key-words related to your blog, which helps with Search Engine Optimization (SEO). To learn more about SEO visit Chapter 1 of Book 5.

TIP

Take a look at each of the additional settings to determine if you want to change anything to get started. Keep in mind that you can return to these settings at any time to change them or change them back. What's covered here are the areas that are most important to set before launching your blog, but they are not the only settings available to you. One area of note is the section under Manage Blog that allows you to edit all of the video content on your blog in one place, as shown in Figure 4-23. To learn much more about video content, check out Book 7.

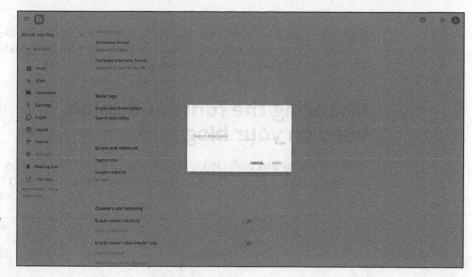

FIGURE 4-22:
Use the Meta
tags section of
Settings to write a
brief description
of your blog.

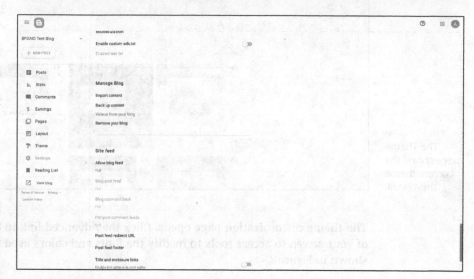

FIGURE 4-23:
View and edit
all of your blog's
video content in
one location.

Personalizing Your Blog

The many free Blogger design and layout themes, previously referred to as themes, that are available can give your blog a more personalized look, depending on your tastes. You can access many free themes through your Blogger dashboard, or you can download free and paid themes from a variety of websites, some of which are listed later in this section.

If you're happy with your blog's theme but just want to change the fonts and colors used in your blog, you can do that through your Blogger dashboard, too, and the best part is that you don't have to know HTML to do it!

Changing the fonts and colors used on your blog

Click the Theme link in the left sidebar of your Blogger dashboard and then click the Customize button under the thumbnail of your current as shown in Figure 4-24.

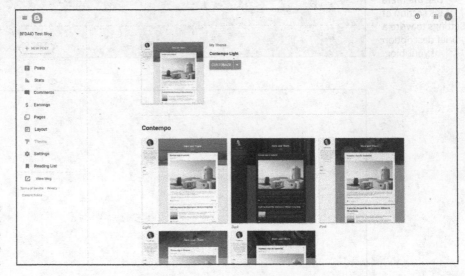

FIGURE 4-24:
The Theme page shows the current theme thumbnail.

The theme customization page opens. Click the Advanced link in the left sidebar of your screen to access tools to modify the fonts and colors used on your blog as shown in Figure 4-25.

From the Advanced settings page of the Theme customizing tool, you can select the various elements that you want to customize within your blog's theme from the list on the left side of the screen, as shown in Figure 4-26. After you select an element, you can use the color and font selection tools below to select the settings you want to use for that element on your blog. You can even see how your edits will look on your blog. If you don't like a change that you make, just click the clear advanced changes link.

WARNING

If you change your blog to a different Blogger theme, your font and color changes will be overridden with the default settings for the new theme.

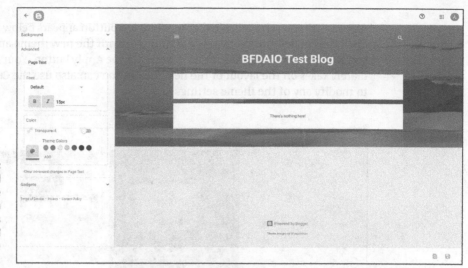

FIGURE 4-25:
The Advanced theme customization settings page is where fonts and colors can be changed.

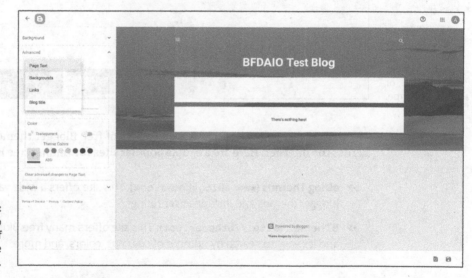

FIGURE 4-26:
Click Page Text to see the areas of font that can be customized.

Finding and choosing themes

It's easy to change your blog's entire color scheme and layout simply by choosing a different theme to use as the skeleton of your blog. To change your blog's theme, just click the Theme link in the left sidebar of your Blogger dashboard, and scroll down to select a theme from the free ones provided by Blogger as shown in Figure 4-24.

As you click on each available theme, a Preview button appears below it (Figure 4-27). Click the Preview button to preview your blog with the new theme applied to it. After you find the theme you like, select it and click the Apply button. Your live blog immediately takes on the layout of the new theme. You can also use the Customize button to modify any of the theme settings.

FIGURE 4-27:
Click a new theme in order to preview, customize, or apply that theme.

If you'd prefer, you can access a wide variety of free Blogger themes from sources across the Internet. Here are a couple popular sites for finding free Blogger themes:

>> **eBlog Themes** (www.eblogthemes.com): This site offers a wide variety of free Blogger themes and includes user ratings.

>> **BThemes:** (http://bthemes.com): This site offers many free Blogger themes, and it's easy to search by number of columns, colors, and more.

Understanding Blogger Gadgets

You can personalize your Blogger blog and add enhanced functionality to it through the handy gadgets available through your Blogger dashboard. Each Blogger gadget represents a different feature you can add to your blog, such as a list of links, text, a video, a poll, and more. Adding gadgets to your blog is as simple as pointing and clicking.

To add a gadget to your blog, click the Layout link in the left sidebar of your Blogger dashboard, which opens the Layout page shown in Figure 4-28.

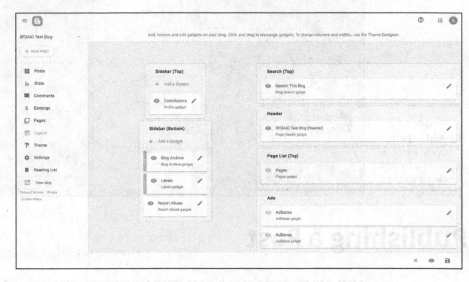

FIGURE 4-28:
The Layout page
on the Blogger
dashboard.

The Layout page shows a *wireframe* image (a visual representation without content) of your blog's layout with each element already included in your blog's layout represented as a box such as your header, blog posts, and footer. You can drag and drop each of these elements to a different position. You can remove or hide elements by clicking the pencil icon within a box and following the instructions provided. (Note that not all elements can be deleted from your blog's layout.) Additionally, you can edit the configuration of any element included in your blog by clicking the pencil icon within a box and following the instructions provided.

You can also add more elements to your blog by clicking the Add a Gadget link, which opens the Add a Gadget popup window shown in Figure 4-29.

Take your time selecting each gadget and reviewing the options included for each to determine which you'd like to add to your blog. Most gadgets are added to a blog's sidebar. For example, you can use the Search Box gadget to add a handy search tool to your blog, which helps visitors find posts related to specific keywords. Alternatively, you might like to add a list of links to other sites and blogs you own or recommend, which you can do in just a few steps by using the Link List gadget.

You can always delete a gadget after you add it, so don't be afraid to test out the gadgets available to you!

TIP

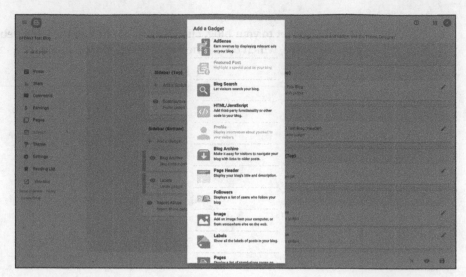

FIGURE 4-29:
The Add a Gadget popup window allows you to add new gadgets to your blog layout.

Publishing a Post

After you configure your blog to work the way you want it to and you set up your blog's layout and functionality to meet your preferences and needs, you're ready to publish your first post. Don't worry! Publishing posts using Blogger is a snap if you already know how to use a word-processing application such as Microsoft Word. That's because the visual editor available in Blogger works extremely similarly to a word-processing application. Even the icons in the visual editor toolbar are similar to the ones you're probably already familiar with from your word-processing application!

To publish a post on your new Blogger blog, simply follow these steps:

1. **Click the New Post button on your Blogger dashboard page (shown earlier in Figure 4-8) to open the New Post page, as shown in Figure 4-30.**

    TIP

    Take some time to hover your mouse over the icons in the visual editor toolbar to see what they do.

2. **Enter a title for your post in the Title text box and type the body of your post in the large text box in the middle of the page.**

3. **(Optional) Click the Labels link in the right sidebar, and enter labels into the text box that appears in order to categorize your post.**

4. **If you want to schedule your post to go live at a future time, click the Schedule link in the right sidebar to reveal the scheduling options.**

    From here, you can change the date and time when you want your post to go live. You can also disallow comments on a specific post from here.

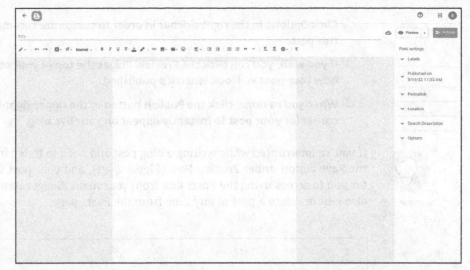

FIGURE 4-30:
The New Post page is where you create a Blogger post.

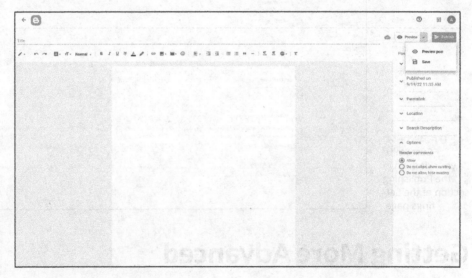

FIGURE 4-31:
Save your post by clicking Preview Post and selecting Save.

5. **Click the Permalink link in the right sidebar if you would like to customize your post's permalink.**

6. **If you would like to tag your post with a location, click the Location link in the right sidebar.**

7. **Click Search Description in the right sidebar to enter up to 150 characters, which will appear in search engine results as a brief post description.**

8. Click Options in the right sidebar in order to customize comments on this post.

9. If you wish, you can click the Preview link at the top of your screen to see how your post will look when it's published.

10. When you're done, click the Publish button in the upper right-hand corner for your post to instantly appear on your live blog.

TIP

If you're interrupted while writing a blog post and need to finish it later, just click the Save button under Preview Post (Figure 4-31), and your post will be available for you to access using the Posts link from your main Blogger dashboard. You can also edit or delete a post at any time from the Posts page.

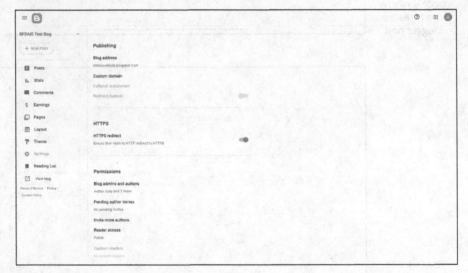

FIGURE 4-32:
Customize your domain in the Publishing section of the Settings page.

Getting More Advanced

Blogger has earned a reputation as a beginner's blogging application, but over the years, many new features have been added, making it a suitable choice for advanced bloggers, too. One of the most popular features is the ability to use a purchased domain and host your blog through a web host.

Many bloggers don't like having the .blogspot.com extension appended to their blog's domain names. Instead, they want to brand their blog with a personal domain name, and they're willing to invest some money to do so. If you want to purchase your own domain and associate it with your blog, you can, and Blogger makes it easy to do right from your Blogger dashboard, as follows:

1. **Click the Settings link on your main Blogger dashboard.**

   The Basic settings page opens as shown in Figure 4-11.

2. **Scroll down to the Publishing section of the settings, as shown in Figure 4-32.**

3. **Select Custom Domain and a popup window appears allowing you to enter a domain that you already own or buy a domain, as shown in Figure 4-33.**

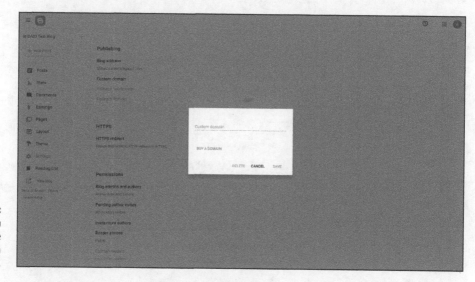

FIGURE 4-33: Input a custom domain name or purchase a new one.

4. **After you find an available domain, follow the registration and payment instructions to purchase your new domain.**

   Your .blogspot.com domain will automatically redirect to your newly purchased domain name.

Getting Help and Finding Resources

You can take advantage of many resources to find out more about using Blogger. Some of the most popular follow:

>> **Blogger Help** (https://support.google.com/blogger): The official Blogger help site offers a lot of information to help you create your blog.

>> **Blogger Blog** (https://blogger.googleblog.com): The official Blogger blog provides updates about new Blogger features, problems, and more.

>> **Blogger Help Community** (https://support.google.com/blogger/community): The official Blogger Help Community allows you to learn from and receive support from other Blogger bloggers.

Chapter **5**

Understanding Medium

Medium (www.medium.com) is a blogging platform unlike any other. While other blog platforms provide the software needed to blog, and in some cases also provide the online hosting, Medium is a digital publishing space that not only provides writers with a place to create content, but also provides them with people to read that content. With over 100 million monthly readers, Medium is an interesting option for new bloggers looking to get started quickly and build a loyal following of readers. What makes Medium an even more enticing option is that for the writers, Medium is entirely free to use!

In this chapter, you find out how to start a new blog using Medium, configure the most important settings, personalize your blog, and publish content to it.

Finding Out about Medium

Medium, shown in Figure 5-1, is different from all other blogging platforms to the point that some wouldn't even call writing on Medium blogging. The fact is that with the rapidly increasing popularity of the platform for online content creators searching for community — in other words, bloggers — there's no way to deny that Medium has made a huge splash in the blogging world, traditional blogging platform or not.

WARNING

While there are many positive reasons to select Medium as the location of your new blog, there are also downsides to be aware of. In the following sections, we'll take a look at both.

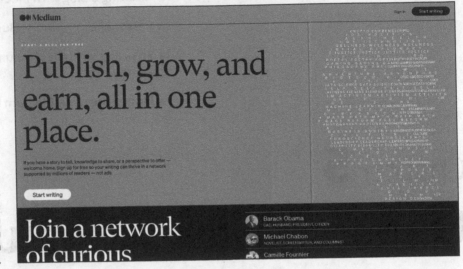

FIGURE 5-1:
Medium is growing in popularity with bloggers as a blogging platform option.

Discovering Medium's best qualities

REMEMBER

Blogging on Medium is incredibly different from traditional platforms, which brings with it a variety of unique and positive qualities. If you're looking to start a typical blog on a fairly standard platform, then this chapter is not for you. That's okay! I suggest you take a closer look at the chapters on WordPress and Blogger and select between those two tried-and-true blogging platforms. There is much to love about traditional blogging.

But if what you're looking for is something a little different, then consider the following, all very positive — and I think interesting — aspects of Medium:

>> **No need to worry about site SEO:** SEO, or *search engine optimization*, refers to taking steps to make a website more likely to appear in search engine results, all with the goal of driving more traffic to that site. For most bloggers, SEO can take up a lot of time from the creation of their website to the writing of their content. Many bloggers install website plugins, often with an associated cost, to help boost their blogs in search engine result pages. The bloggers most serious about maximizing SEO turn to outside experts for website SEO analysis and assistance. While bloggers on Medium can take some steps to help with SEO for their individual posts, they have no control over the SEO of

the website — it's handled completely by the platform. Plus, because the website is well established, search engines are automatically more likely to include Medium posts in their results pages. To learn more about SEO, visit Chapter 1 of Book 5.

» **Free to writers:** For many beginning bloggers, start-up costs are a major determining factor when selecting where to blog. At Medium, bloggers write for free! There are paid account options, but a paid account is not necessary to write on the site. There are paid as well as free options for readers, making it more likely that people will join and read the content on the site.

» **Ready-made audience:** Speaking of readers, Medium boasts upwards of a hundred million monthly active users at the time of this book's printing. While there's certainly no guarantee that those readers will show up on your new blog's content immediately, it does mean that there's an audience in place and ready to find you if you provide the right content to draw them in.

» **Known and respected platform:** New bloggers often take a while to establish themselves as worthy of a reader's time and attention. However, Medium is already a known and respected online writing platform, making it more likely that a new blogger's content will be given more than a passing glance. How known and respected is the platform? Consider that former United States President Barack Obama writes on the platform (Figure 5-2).

FIGURE 5-2: Bloggers on Medium share the platform with a variety of famous members.

» **Writers can get paid to write:** Not only is it free to blog on Medium's platform, but it is also possible to get paid for your writing. Bloggers are able to earn money based on the popularity of their content, including the amount of time readers spend on each post. To learn more, visit the section on monetizing at the end of this chapter.

» **Content can be re-used:** Many well-established bloggers and authors have decided in recent years to start a Medium blog along with their other writing outlets. Part of the reason why is because writers are allowed to re-use content from their other platforms on their Medium blog. The only rule regarding re-using your own content is that you are not allowed to re-publish content on Medium that you have already published on that site. If you have another blog, a WordPress.com blog for example, and you would like to pull together old content to re-purpose on your new Medium blog, that is permitted by the platform. Some bloggers have found that Medium is a way to breathe new life into an old post, all while reaching the eyes of new readers!

» **Easy to get started:** Not only is it free to write on Medium, but it is also very easy to get started. This is one of the most exciting aspects of the platform for many writers who are hungry to get started putting their content out there to the world. Unlike other platforms that require numerous steps to join and the changing of one setting after another before the first post can even be written, Medium gets new bloggers up and running in no time. I take a closer look at the exact steps required later in this chapter.

» **Connect with like-minded community:** Medium is more than a digital publishing platform. It also considers itself a social media platform. There are a variety of engagement tools built into the platform that go beyond the basic blog comment, and these tools help not only readers to connect with writers, but also help writers to connect with one another. And because of the popularity of the platform, it's easy for new bloggers to find others blogging around the same topic or interest areas.

» **Perfect for niche bloggers:** Because Medium bloggers grow much of their readership by drawing in existing Medium members to their content, bloggers tend to keep their writing focused on one topic or closely related topics. It's easier to grow a following on Medium when your content is consistent and predictable. This is perfect for niche bloggers who already plan to keep their writing highly focused. To learn more about niche blogging, check out Book 2.

» **Opportunity to establish expertise:** One of the benefits of writing highly focused content is the opportunity to establish yourself as an expert in a specific area. Robert Roy Britt, for example, is an independent journalist with over two decades of researching and writing experience. His blog on Medium (robertroybritt.medium.com, shown in Figure 5-3) has grown to a following of over 100,000 readers and is part of his branding as an expert in the fields of health and science.

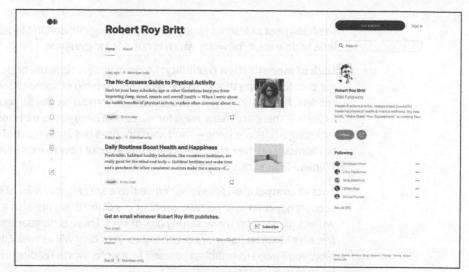

FIGURE 5-3:
Medium provides
bloggers with an
opportunity to
establish them-
selves as experts
in a field.

Understanding Medium's downsides

With a long list of positives, it may seem that Medium is the perfect blogging platform. But like all blogging applications, there are some downsides to consider. The key to choosing the perfect blogging platform is to choose the platform that is perfect for *you*, so take a look at the following cons for this particular site to see if they are a dealbreaker for your wonderful new blog:

>> **Medium owns the site traffic:** Much like a blog on WordPress.com (see Chapter 3 of this Book) or Blogger (see Chapter 4 of this Book), bloggers who write on Medium do not own their site traffic. That means that if their Medium blog grows to have a huge following, drawing in a large number of readers each month, that blogger cannot decide to capitalize on that growth by selling the platform. It is simply not theirs to sell the way a self-hosted blog would be.

>> **Readers need to pay for some content and features:** The large number of existing readers is one of the best aspects of Medium, but not all of the readers are paid members, meaning they cannot see all of the content or interact with it in the same way. The best way to connect with readers and grow a following is to make it as easy as possible for your readers to find you and engage with your content. The need to have a paid account may be a deterrent to some people trying to read your content.

>> **Lack of control:** While some bloggers may love the fact that aspects of the site such as SEO are completely taken care of and out of their control, that is not the case for everyone. When I first began blogging, one of my favorite things to do was play around with the HTML code to change the appearance and the features on my site. I often did things wrong at first and experienced

the fulfillment of learning and growing as a blog owner. On Medium, there is little to do except for write, which is not a fit for everyone.

>> **Lack of monetization flexibility:** Medium writers have the opportunity to get paid for writing thanks to the paid membership of some of the site's readers. For many bloggers, this is a dream come true. But as you'll discover in Book 7, there are many ways for successful bloggers to earn money — including a full-time living — and Medium does not allow most of those ways to monetize on their platform. Learn more about how to monetize on Medium later in this chapter.

>> **Lots of competition for views:** While there are certainly a lot of existing readers eager for shiny new content on Medium, there are also a lot of writers, all vying for those same pairs of eyes. There is no guarantee that just because Medium has a large readership, your blog will as well. Like any new blog, you'll need to establish yourself as a writer worth reading in order to bring in those pageviews.

>> **Extensive rules to follow to avoid suspension:** On many blog platforms, especially those that are self-hosted through a paid server account, there are very few rules restricting what you can do on your blog. Medium, however, has a long list of standards that all of their writers must follow in order to not have their blogs suspended. This may feel too restrictive for some bloggers.

>> **Need to follow a prescribed format in order to find success:** Similar to the long list of rules that Medium needs to follow, there is also a fairly standard and defined blog post format that Medium writers who find success tend to follow. The focus on Medium is on consistently well-written content. If you would prefer to experiment and think outside the box, then Medium may not be the best blogging platform for you.

Creating a Medium Account

Getting started with Medium — both as a writer and as a reader — begins with creating an account. Non-member visitors to Medium will find themselves prompted often to sign-in or create an account (shown in Figure 5-4), and having a Medium account is the first step to being able to write on the platform. There are two types of accounts on Medium — free and paid. Let's take a look at how to create both types of accounts.

FIGURE 5-4:
Readers at Medium are asked to create a free account in order to access certain content.

Participating in Medium for free

In order to create a free Medium account, take the following steps:

1. **Point your favorite web browser to www.medium.com, as shown in Figure 5-5.**

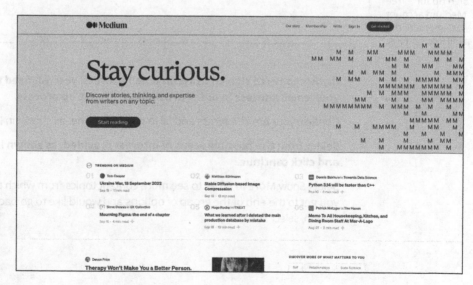

FIGURE 5-5:
Go to www.medium.com to create a free account.

2. **Click Get Started and a popup window with three sign-up option appears, as shown in Figure 5-6.**

New account holders have the option to create an account using one of the following three sign-in methods:

- Sign up with Google

- Sign up with Facebook

- Sign up with email

FIGURE 5-6:
Sign up for a free
Medium account
using one of the
available options.

3. **If you choose to sign up using an email address, you will need to confirm your email address in order to complete the set-up process.**

Confirm your email address and fill in your full name, as shown in Figure 5-7.

4. **Select from the possible areas of interest provided, as shown in Figure 5-8, and click continue.**

Select Show More in order to see more content topics from which to choose. If you get to the end of the group of options and would like to go back to the first screen, select Start Over.

FIGURE 5-7:
Provide your full name in order to finish creating your email-based account.

FIGURE 5-8:
Select the areas of content that most interest you.

Paying for a Medium account

You may notice that immediately upon creating your free Medium account, you will be given the option to upgrade to a paid member account. In order to do so, take the following steps:

1. **Point your web browser to www.medium.com and click Membership, as shown earlier in Figure 5-5.**

2. **Select Get Unlimited Access, as shown in Figure 5-9.**

FIGURE 5-9:
Select Get
Unlimited Access
to begin creating
a paid member
account.

3. **Sign in to an existing free Medium account or create a new account, as shown in Figure 5-10.**

FIGURE 5-10:
Sign in to a
Medium account
in order to create
a paid member
account.

4. **Select from one of the two paid account options, as shown in Figure 5-11:**

    ● Monthly account costing $5 USD per month

    ● Yearly account costing $50 USD per year

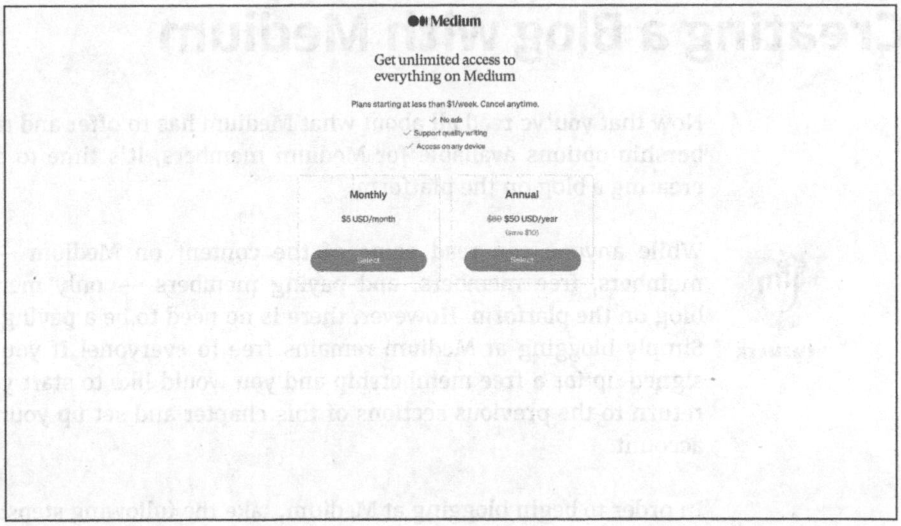

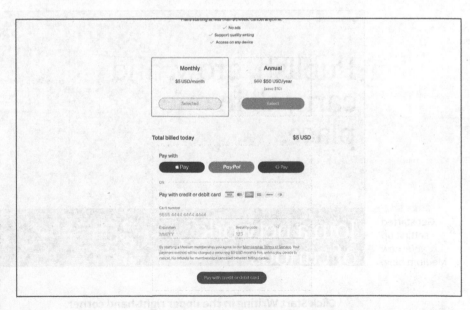

FIGURE 5-11:
Paying Medium
members may
select from two
price options.

5. **Fill in your selected payment information in order to complete your paid account sign up, as shown in Figure 5-12.**

FIGURE 5-12:
Provide your
payment
information in
order to
complete the
sign-up process.

REMEMBER

It is not necessary to create a paid member Medium account in order to create a Medium blog!

Creating a Blog with Medium

Now that you've read all about what Medium has to offer and the multiple membership options available for Medium members, it's time to dive in to actually creating a blog on the platform!

REMEMBER

While anyone can read some of the content on Medium — including non-members, free members, and paying members — only members are able to blog on the platform. However, there is no need to be a paying member to do so. Simply blogging at Medium remains free to everyone! If you have not already signed up for a free membership and you would like to start your Medium blog, return to the previous sections of this chapter and set up your free membership account.

In order to begin blogging at Medium, take the following steps:

1. **Point your favorite web browser to www.medium.com/creators, as shown in Figure 5-13.**

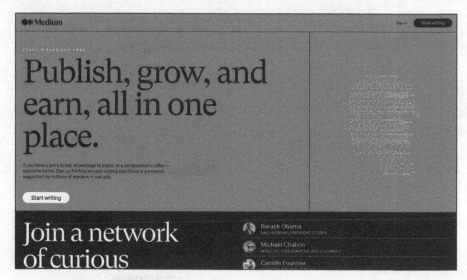

FIGURE 5-13: Get started setting up your new Medium blog.

2. **Click Start Writing in the upper right-hand corner.**

3. **Sign in to your account in order to be taken to your new blog.**

   You are now able to begin writing and publishing content on Medium, as shown in Figure 5-14!

FIGURE 5-14:
Dive right in by creating your first Medium post.

TIP

Unlike most other blogging platforms, there is no need to come up with a clever blog name or find an existing domain name if you don't want to! Your new Medium blog is automatically named after the full name that you provided during your account sign up, and the domain name is the following: `www.medium.com/@ yourname`. The following sections walk you through steps to customize your blog's name and domain name if you wish.

Configuring your Medium settings

Once you have created an account in order to blog on Medium, there are a number of settings that can be configured to your preferences. In the following sections, we'll take a closer look at a number of the available settings. To get started, go to `www.medium.com/me/settings`, as shown in Figure 5-15.

Profile

Once on your Medium profile settings page, scroll to Profile to take a look at the following areas:

>> **Name:** Your name will appear not only on your Profile page, but also in your blog posts as a byline and as the name of the person responding to reader engagement. You must provide a name in this field, although some people choose to use a pen name.

FIGURE 5-15:
Customize your
Medium settings.

>> **Short bio:** Your short bio may be up to 160 characters in length and will appear as part of your Profile page for readers reading one of your blog posts.

>> **Photo:** The photo that you upload will appear not only on your Profile page, but will also appear along with each one of your blog posts.

>> **About page:** This section of your profile allows for more detail than the short bio, providing readers with more information about you and your writing.

>> **Username & URL:** You will be assigned a username and blog URL upon the creation of your blog. You may edit those assigned names within this section of your profile.

>> **Medium subdomain:** This section allows you to change your URL from www.medium.com/@yourname to the subdomain www.yourname.medium.com. Changing to a subdomain may impact how quickly your content appears in search engine rankings. A subdomain does not benefit as much from the established Medium.com domain SEO.

>> **Custom domain:** Like many other blogging platforms, it is possible to upgrade your Medium blog to a custom domain of your choosing. This option is for paid Medium members only.

Design

While Medium blogs are not able to be customized nearly to the extent of other platforms, that doesn't mean that you don't have any control at all over the look of your blog. Scroll down your settings page to Design and click Design your profile. A Design customization page for your blog will open, as shown in Figure 5-16.

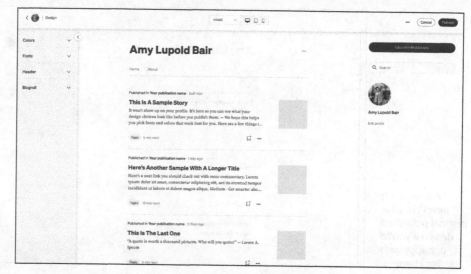

FIGURE 5-16:
Customize the
appearance of
your blog.

Navigate to the top of the screen to determine which area of the blog you are editing, as shown in Figure 5-17. You can choose to edit the appearance of your Medium blog homepage or the appearance of each individual post, which Medium calls a Story. You can also click the device icons to preview how your changes will appear on a desktop screen, a tablet, and a phone.

FIGURE 5-17:
You can edit
the design of
either your blog
homepage or
your individual
stories.

TIP

Your changes are saved automatically as you work, but don't worry about regretting your design choices. Don't like what you've chosen? Simply click the three dots in the upper right-hand corner, as shown in Figure 5-18, to return your design to its previous settings or to the default settings.

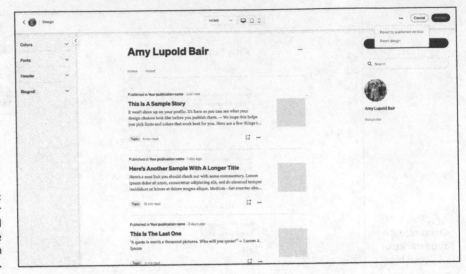

FIGURE 5-18:
Revert to your
original published
design if you're
unhappy with
design changes.

The following areas are able to be customized:

» **Colors:** Change the color of your blog's background as well as the accent color for your blog.

» **Fonts:** Change the selected fonts for blog titles, details, and body.

» **Header:** Change the look and color of the words in the header or upload a header background image, as shown in Figure 5-19. You can also upload a logo under this setting, which will replace the name of your blog, as shown in Figure 5-20.

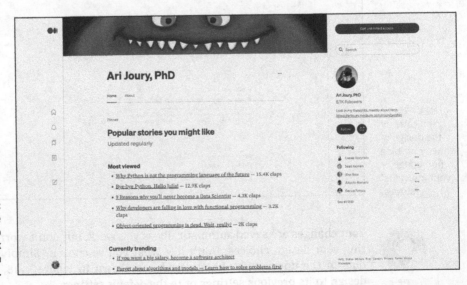

FIGURE 5-19:
Upload an image
to the header to
change the look
of your Medium
blog.

>> **Blogroll:** Select to either display or not display a blogroll of the most recent posts of the Medium blogs and publications you follow.

Audience development

The Audience development section of your settings allows you to customize the following areas:

>> **Tipping:** This section allows you to collect tips from readers through a third-party platform such as PayPal.

>> **Email subscriptions:** Manage how and if readers are able to subscribe via email to your blog updates by clicking Promote subscriptions, which takes you to the Promote Email Subscriptions page shown in Figure 5-21.

>> **Import email subscribers:** This setting is only available to established Medium writers.

>> **Export email subscribers:** Export a list of your current subscriber emails.

Email settings

In this section you can customize what emails you receive from Medium and to which email address. Options include Medium content, site updates, social media notifications, and more. You also have the option to opt-out of receiving any emails from Medium.

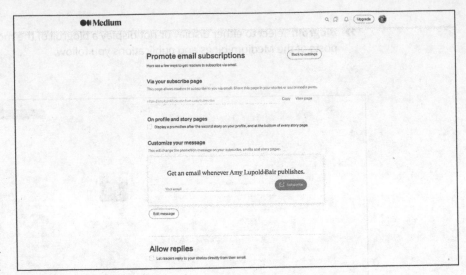

FIGURE 5-21:
Customize how
readers are able
to subscribe via
email to your
blog updates.

Connections

Connect social media accounts to your Medium blog through this section of the Settings page. You can also choose to display a link to your Twitter account on your Medium profile page.

The previous sections take a closer look at the areas of your Settings page that you are most likely to use as you are starting your blog. From your settings page it is also possible to take a number of other steps including upgrading your membership, blocking specific users, and even deleting your account entirely. You can also access this settings page from www.medium.com directly at any time by clicking on your profile picture in the bottom left-hand corner and clicking Settings, as shown in Figure 5-22.

Publishing a post

Now that you have all of your blog settings customized to your preferences, it's time to write your first post! First, let's get to know your Medium homepage, including the left sidebar and its navigation tools.

1. **Point your favorite web browser to www.medium.com.**

    If you are signed in to your account, you will see a feed of stories about the subject areas you selected during your account creation. To the left you will see a sidebar with icons. Let's take a moment to click on each icon and get to know what it does.

FIGURE 5-22:
Access your
profile settings
at any time from
Medium.com

2. **Click on the house icon, as shown in Figure 5-23.**

The house icon is how to always return back to this home screen.

FIGURE 5-23:
The house icon
returns you to
your Medium
home screen.

3. **Click on the bell icon, as shown in Figure 5-24.**

Clicking this icon will take you to your notifications page. This is also where you
will access your blog stats page, which will tell you how many visitors and
pageviews your content has received.

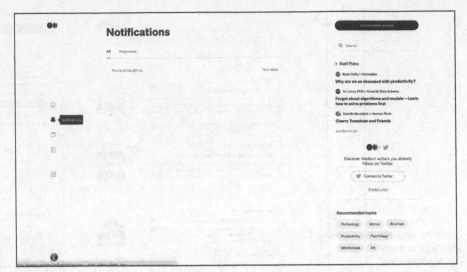

FIGURE 5-24:
The bell icon
takes you to your
notifications and
stats pages.

4. **Click on the bookmark icon, as shown in Figure 5-25.**

   This icon takes you to your lists where you have organized content that you
   would like to read.

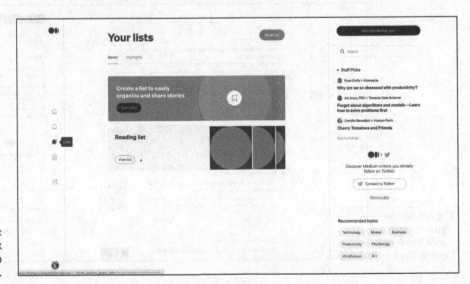

FIGURE 5-25:
The bookmark
icon takes you to
your saved lists.

5. **Click on the page icon, as shown in Figure 5-26.**

This icon takes you to all of your published and draft stories, which as a reminder is what Medium calls blog posts. You can also manage your comments or responses to your stories from the page. This is also where you can import a blog post that you've written on another platform and re-publish it — with edits, if you like — on your Medium blog.

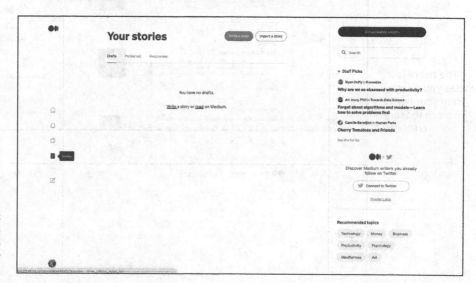

FIGURE 5-26: The page icon allows you to manage your blog content.

REMEMBER

Only import posts to your Medium blog that *you* have written and own the rights to.

From the Your stories page, you can write a story by clicking the green Write a story button near the top of the page. You can also write new content by taking the following steps:

1. **Click on the pencil icon in the left sidebar of your home screen, as shown in Figure 5-27.**

The story creation page will appear, as shown in Figure 5-28.

2. **In order to fill in text to either the title or the body of the Story, simply click on that field and type.**

FIGURE 5-27:
The pencil icon takes you directly from your home screen to Story creation.

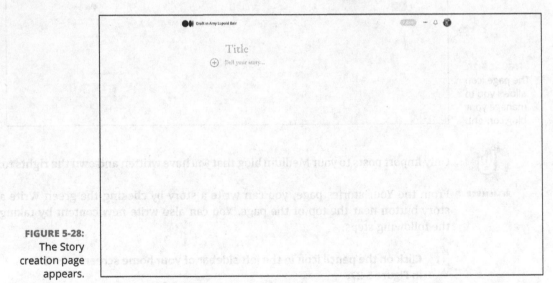

FIGURE 5-28:
The Story creation page appears.

3. **To add content other than text, click on the plus sign inside the circle to reveal the menu, as shown in Figure 5-29.**

   The menu options that appear include:

   - Camera: Add an image from your computer.

   - Magnifying lens: Add an image from Unsplash, a free image source.

   - Play button: Add a video.

- Angle brackets: Embed content.
- Line break: Break Story content into a new part.

FIGURE 5-29:
Clicking the plus sign inside the circle reveals the menu.

4. **In order to format existing text, select and highlight it, as shown in Figure 5-30.**

   The formatting menu allows you to do the following with existing text:

   - Change to bold
   - Change to italics
   - Add a hyperlink
   - Change to heading text
   - Revert back to body text
   - Format as a quote
   - Create a private note related to the text

5. **If appropriate, mention other Medium writers in your post by using the @ symbol and they will be notified once you publish that post.**

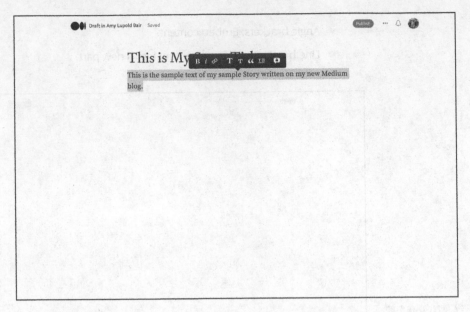

This is My

This is the sample text of my sample Story written on my new Medium blog.

FIGURE 5-30:
Highlight text to format.

6. **Click on the three dots at the top of the page (Figure 5-31) to access additional menu items, including:**

   - Add to publication
   - Share draft link
   - Share to Twitter
   - Manage unlisted setting
   - Change featured image
   - Change display title/subtitle
   - Change topics
   - See revision history
   - More settings

   From this area you can also receive more hints and shortcuts as well as look for more help.

7. **Click on More settings at the bottom of the three dots menu in order to access the following Story Settings (Figure 5-32) while writing a post:**

   - **Story Preview:** The Story Preview area allows you to see your post as it will appear once published. This is also where you can pin a post to appear at the top of your Medium blog or profile.

FIGURE 5-31:
There are additional Story menu items available at the top of the Story editing page.

- **Author:** In this area you are able to both check your Partner Program status as well as apply to be a member of the program. Read more on the Partner Program later in this chapter.

- **Reader Interests:** The Reader Interests section of Story Settings allows you to indicate up to five topics that you believe relate to this post. Remember the interest areas you selected when you opened your Medium account? Those are examples of topics that people fill in in this section of their post settings.

- **SEO Settings:** This is the area where you have a bit of control over the SEO of your Medium blog! If you wish to, fill in an SEO-friendly title and description for your post that will appear in search engine results and hopefully draw readers to click through to your content.

- **Promotion:** In this area you have access to a link that you can provide to friends and family to allow them to read your content for free even if it is behind a paywall for other readers.

- **Content Licensing:** Use this setting to edit your licensing for your content to alert readers that they may not copy or redistribute your content without permission.

- **Advanced Settings:** This setting allows you to customize the link depending on if the content was originally published on another site. This is also where you can delete a post from your blog.

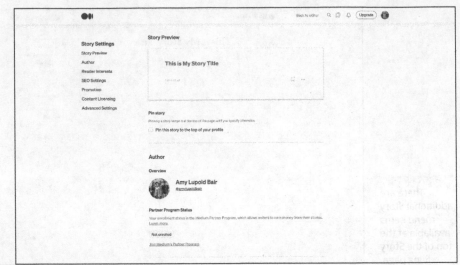

FIGURE 5-32:
The Story Settings
page provides
you with
additional
Story tools.

Finding Success as a Medium Writer

If you've made it this far into the chapter, you've likely realized by now that blogging on Medium is different than many other blogging platforms. That can be a dealbreaker for some writers, but for others, it's exactly what draws them in. If you're intrigued and want to give becoming a Medium blogger a try, the following sections are for you. They contain tips and tricks to find success as a writer on the Medium platform.

Following best practices

Medium is a digital publishing platform with a fairly consistent and standardized platform from profile to profile. While some bloggers choose to personalize their pages with color scheme tweaks, header images, or logos, there's not a lot of visual difference going from one blogger's content to another. The same can also be said about the content itself, not just the design of the page.

TIP

In order to find success as a Medium blogger, it's best to stick to a few best practices. Keep these guidelines in mind when writing on Medium:

>> **Be as consistent as possible:** In order to help your content on Medium make it onto the screens of potential readers, write consistently. Posting a few days a week for a month and then stopping completely for a month will not work on this platform. Select a number of times per week to post and then stick to that as much as possible.

- » **Take the time to write good titles:** Medium rewards good title writing! Don't write your blog posts titles as an afterthought. Take the time to write eye-catching titles for every post you publish.

- » **Write regularly and often:** Beyond just writing on a consistent schedule, be sure to write often. Some Medium bloggers suggest that it's best to post every single day if possible.

- » **Follow the general Story format:** Blog posts on Medium all look very similar to one another regardless of who is writing the post. Following that format is a path to success!

Take the time to read other content on Medium before you write your first word. Get to know the typical format for a Story, including using headers, images that are appropriate and helpful to the content, and post lengths that aren't too short and also aren't too long. Read Story titles paying particular attention to those that seem to be popular with readers and try to discern what it is that is drawing readers in to a post.

Avoiding getting suspended

If you're a think-outside-the-box sort of person who doesn't enjoy following rules, then Medium is likely not the platform for you. That's okay! There are plenty of blogging applications in the sea. Swim around until you find the one that is right for you. But if you're ready to dive in, be sure that you're swimming with the current and following the rules or your blog will be suspended by the site.

WARNING

The rules are somewhat subjective, meaning that Medium maintains the final say on whether or not to suspend an account after review. However, they do make it clear that the following areas, among others, are non-negotiable in order to remain on the platform:

- » No threats of violence and incitement
- » No hateful content
- » No harassment, bullying, and targeting
- » No breaching of someone's privacy or attacking someone's reputation
- » No promotion of controversial, suspect, or extreme content
- » No graphic content
- » No duplicate content from Medium to Medium

>> No advertising or third-party sponsorships

>> Affiliate links must be disclosed

To read more, including the full list of rules, visit `https://policy.medium.com`.

Being curated

As mentioned earlier in the chapter, Medium receives over 100 million visitors a month looking for great content to read. But how do you make sure that those readers are viewing *your* content? One of the best ways is to have your Story curated by the Medium curation team.

Being *curated* means that your content is being included in areas such as the Medium homepage or reader newsletter. It means that it may appear when people click on a topic heading as well. In short, being curated on Medium means that your content is being promoted by the platform. You can find out if your content has been curated by checking your Stats page, as shown earlier in Figure 5-24.

REMEMBER

While Medium says that all content is eligible for distribution beyond your followers and subscribers, the content that is selected by the curation team receives more promotion and therefore more traffic. The curation team is looking for the following, among other qualifications:

>> Quality content

>> Stories that follow the rules

>> No clickbait Story titles

>> No calls to action within posts

>> No links within headings

To learn more visit `https://help.medium.com` and click on Distribution, as shown in Figure 5-33.

Writing for publications

Similar to having a piece selected by Medium for distribution beyond your followers, it is possible to reach a larger audience by writing for what Medium refers to as a publication. Figure 5-34 shows an example of one of the most popular publications on the Medium platform, The Mission.

FIGURE 5-33:
Learn more about Medium's content distribution system.

FIGURE 5-34:
The Mission is one of the most followed publications on Medium.

Publications are shared spaces, collections of Medium stories that all focus on a central topic or theme. They can be written by multiple authors or all by the same author. There are publications that are run by Medium staff as well as those run by members of the Medium community. Each Medium publication includes these defining characteristics:

>> A dedicated, customizable home page

>> A single owner with the potential for a team of editors

>> The ability to be distributed via email newsletter

>> A custom URL following the format medium.com/your-publication-name

Anyone who writes on Medium and has a paid account can create a publication following these steps:

1. Once signed in to your account at www.medium.com, click your profile picture in the lower left-hand corner, as shown in Figure 5-35, and select Manage Publications.

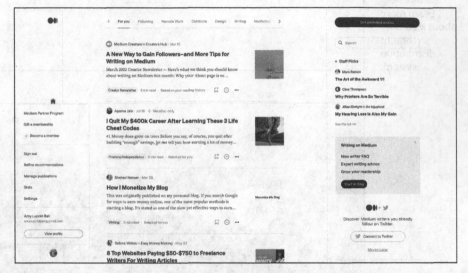

FIGURE 5-35:
Access Manage Publications from your Medium home page.

2. Select New Publication, as shown in Figure 5-36.

3. Fill in all of the required fields, clicking Next and then Create when you are finished.

Medium bloggers may create up to seven unique publications, but can submit their writing to as many publications as they wish. This is, perhaps, the best way to reach new readers and gain new followers — writing for an existing publication. If you find a publication that is a fit for your writing and your topic, reach out to the editors and request to write for them. Once approved, you will be able to start submitting Story drafts for review and consideration, as shown earlier in Figure 5-31.

Engaging with the community

As mentioned previously, Medium considers itself not only a digital publishing platform but also a social media platform. You can connect your existing Twitter and Facebook social media accounts to your Medium blog, but there are also ways to interact with readers and other writers within the Medium platform that go beyond the traditional blog comment. Interacting with a Medium author and their content includes the following options:

>> **Follow an author:** If you like an author's content and want to follow everything that they publish, you can have the option to select Follow under their profile on the right sidebar, as shown in Figure 5-37.

>> **Subscribe via email:** Similar to following, you have the option to subscribe to a particular author's content via email, also shown in Figure 5-37.

There are a variety of ways to engage that are all included in a horizontal navigation area just below the Story content, as shown in Figure 5-38. They include:

>> **Share content:** Click to share content to other social media platforms.

>> **Save content:** Add a Story to your saved content.

>> **Respond to content:** Respond to a Story, which other blogging platforms refer to as commenting.

>> **Clap for content:** Provide a Story with a clap, which is similar to a like or thumbs up on other platforms.

FIGURE 5-37: Medium allows readers to follow an author by clicking Follow on their profile.

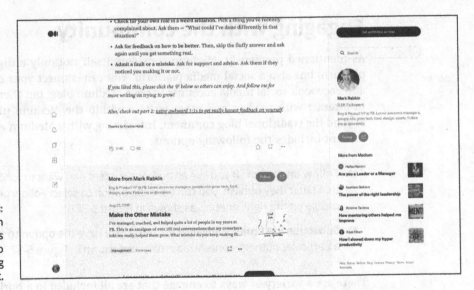

FIGURE 5-38: Medium encourages readers to engage with blog post content.

Another way to engage with a reader's content is called a Highlight. If you find a passage of writing in a Story that particularly interests you, you have the option to select and highlight just that passage. Passages that you have highlighted will be seen by your followers, and the author will also receive a notification that their Story has been highlighted. Figure 5-39 shows that once you have highlighted a passage, you can choose to simply highlight by clicking the pencil icon, leave a response with the highlight included by clicking the speech bubble, or share via Twitter by clicking the Twitter symbol. If you decide to remove your highlight, simply click and select the same passage and click the pencil icon to undo your original highlight.

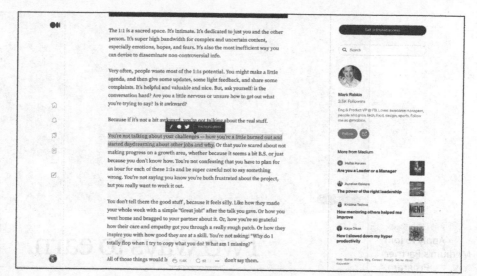

FIGURE 5-39: Highlighting is a way to engage with other Medium content.

Monetizing Your Medium Blog

One of the aspects of blogging on Medium that gives many new bloggers pause is the fact that monetizing on the platform is so heavily restricted. There are no sidebar ads or sponsored posts, no calls to action allowed. However, the most successful Medium bloggers have managed to turn writing on Medium into a full-time salary. Let's take a look at the two main ways to monetize on Medium.

Taking advantage of affiliate programs

Making money with an affiliate program simply means that when you write about a product or service, you use a custom link to that product or service in your content. When a reader clicks through that custom link to purchase or subscribe to that product or service, you receive a percentage of that sale. Affiliate programs exist for everything from huge online stores such as Amazon to small start-ups. The key is to write authentically about the things you love and to build a large following of readers who trust your advice and feedback about purchases. Learn more about affiliate programs in Chapter 3 of Book 7.

Participating in Medium's Partner Program

Another way that many successful Medium bloggers earn money is through the Medium Partner Program. Writers can earn money based on the amount of time paying Medium readers spend on their content. Writers wishing to apply to join the Partner Program should go to https://medium.com/earn, as shown in Figure 5-40.

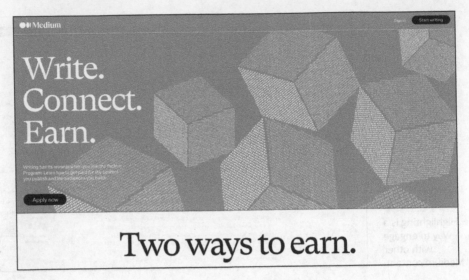

FIGURE 5-40:
Apply to join
Medium's Partner
Program.

In order to be eligible for the Partner Program, you must meet the following requirements:

» Live in an eligible location.

» Be aged 18 years or older.

» Have at least 100 followers on Medium.

» Have at least one published Story on Medium.

Once approved to join the Partner Program, members earn money based on how much time a paying reader spends on their stories as well as how many non-paying readers have converted to paying readers on one of their posts. Only stories that are behind a paywall, meaning a reader has to pay in order to read that content, are eligible to earn money. Once you have been approved to join the program, you can put both new content behind a paywall as well as existing content.

IN THIS CHAPTER

» **Discovering Wix**

» **Creating a Wix blog**

» **Personalizing your blog**

» **Navigating the Wix dashboard**

» **Publishing content**

Chapter **6**

Blogging with Wix

While WordPress and Blogger were the two biggest players in the blogging platform world for the beginning years of the blogosphere, much has changed over the years. Many other blogging platforms have emerged to compete with the most popular applications both for number of users and for website traffic. Wix (www.wix.com) is one of the top competitors that has become a favorite with many in the blogosphere.

This chapter shows you how to start your own Wix blog, customize it, personalize it, and publish content on it. With over 200 million Wix users at the time of publishing, you'll be in good company! Getting started with Wix is quick, easy, and free, so you have no reason not to see for yourself what the buzz is about.

Checking Out Wix

Wix, shown in Figure 6-1, is easy-to-use cloud-based blogging software providing bloggers with a free blog platform option. Wix utilizes a drag-and-drop website builder, which means that Wix is:

» Easy for anyone to use.

» Great for brand new bloggers.

>> A perfect quick-start blog platform option.

>> Ideal for bloggers who are not especially tech savvy.

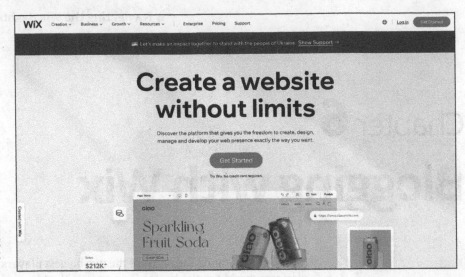

FIGURE 6-1:
The Wix blogging platform is great for beginners.

While Wix is certainly popular for a reason and has many positive features, like any blogging application, it may not be the right platform for everyone. Let's take a look at some of the pros of blogging on Wix as well as some of the cons.

Understanding what's great about Wix

Perhaps the absolute best aspect of Wix is that it's one of the best blogging platforms available for anyone whose priority is to get their blog up and running as quickly as possible. I'll discuss the actual steps to starting a Wix blog in later sections, but it's important to know that Wix blogs are built using drag-and-drop tools. It is very easy to create an account and publish a website in a matter of minutes rather than weeks, days, or even hours.

Another positive is that Wix, much like WordPress.com and Blogger, provides a free-to-use account option. Should you choose to upgrade your account, Wix offers a variety of premium account packages depending on needs ranging from a custom domain name to the creation of an eCommerce site. It is also possible to monetize your Wix blog, even while keeping a free account. Wix is compatible with the Google AdSense advertising system, and unlike some blogging platforms such as Medium, Wix does not restrict other monetization strategies such as selling products or services from your blog.

Similar to WordPress plugins, Wix offers something called Wix Apps in the Wix App Marketplace (www.wix.com/app-market), shown in Figure 6-2. There are apps available for free as well as at a cost, and they allow Wix bloggers to do everything from analyze site traffic to connect social media accounts to their blog.

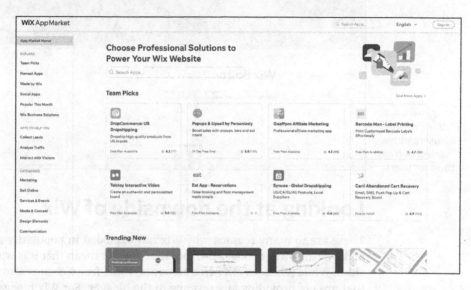

Wix also provides a long list of Wix Features that are free to account holders (www.wix.com/features/main), shown in Figure 6-3. Wix Features include but are certainly not limited to the following:

>> Over 100 fonts available and the option to upload your own fonts

>> Built-in SEO tools

>> An app-development platform called Velo

>> A contact management system to organize email subscriptions

>> A store manager for eCommerce sites built on the platform

>> A booking system to facilitate booking client work

>> A free logo maker

FIGURE 6-3:
Wix provides users with a variety of free tools for users.

Looking at the downside of Wix

There are so many reasons why Wix has exploded in popularity among bloggers and website owners in general, but that doesn't mean that it is without its downsides. While Wix does offer free accounts, those free websites also include Wix ads that are not providing any revenue to the blogger. For Wix bloggers who want to switch to a premium account (shown in Figure 6-4) in order to remove the site ads, the cost can be prohibitive with prices starting at $16 a month. If you want to move from a domain name that is a subdomain of Wix.com and instead use a custom domain, you will have to pay for that domain name on top of the monthly premium account fee.

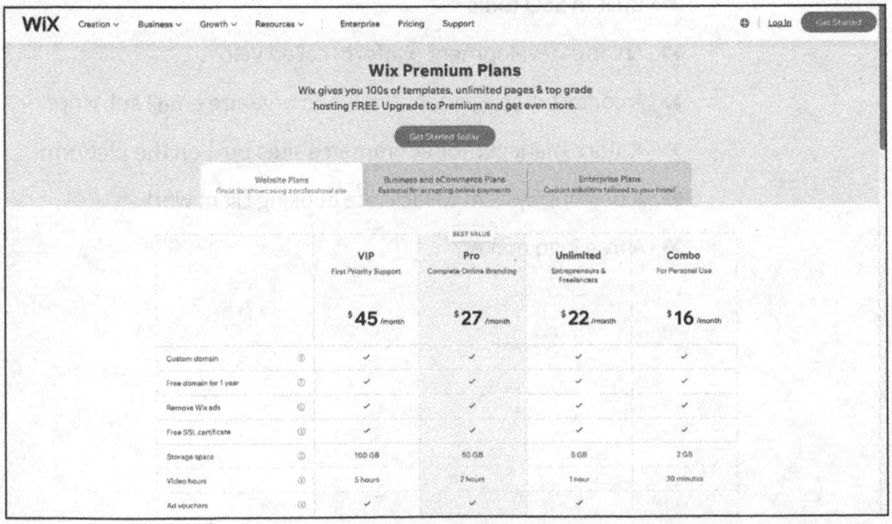

FIGURE 6-4:
Wix offers the option of upgrading to a paid premium account.

WARNING

The drag-and-drop blog building platform and variety of beautiful free templates are reasons that many bloggers love Wix, but a word of caution! Once you have selected your template and published your site, you are not able to go back and change your template. This is very different from platforms such as WordPress and Blogger where you can change your theme as often as you wish. This is just one of the ways that Wix is less flexible than WordPress. For bloggers who want to get started quickly and not worry about technical details such as coding or style-sheets, Wix is great. But for bloggers who want to have the complete flexibility to change their site as often as they like, and however they like, Wix is not a great choice of blogging platform.

Finally, much like blogging on a platform such as Medium, discussed in Chapter 5 of this Book, blogging on Wix means that you do not own your site. The website that you build and promote is owned by Wix. For some bloggers, this lack of autonomy and ownership are a deal-breaker when it comes to selecting a blogging platform.

Creating a Free Blog with Wix

If you've decided that Wix is the right platform for your new blog, then it's time to get started! As mentioned, creating a blog with Wix is a quick, easy, and straight-forward process. Follow the instructions throughout the remainder of this chapter to create and configure your Wix blog.

Follow these steps to start your new Wix blog:

1. **Visit the Wix home page.**

   Enter the URL www.wix.com (shown in Figure 6-1) into your browser, and click the Get Started button in the upper right corner. The Wix Sign-Up page opens, as shown in Figure 6-5.

2. **Sign-Up using one of the three following options:**

   - An email address

   - A Facebook account

   - A Google account

   If using an email address to sign up, you will be sent an email verification email with a link to click to verify your email address.

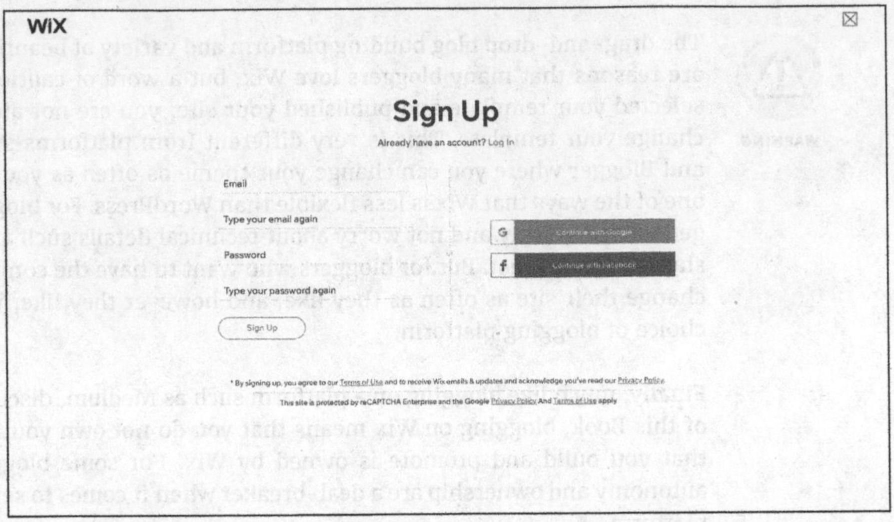

WiX

Sign Up

Already have an account? Log In

Email

Type your email again

Password

Type your password again

[Sign Up]

G Continue with Google

f Continue with Facebook

* By signing up, you agree to our Terms of Use and to receive Wix emails & updates and acknowledge you've read our Privacy Policy.
This site is protected by reCAPTCHA Enterprise and the Google Privacy Policy And Terms of Use apply.

FIGURE 6-5:
Create a new
account on the
Wix Sign-Up page.

3. **A page will open prompting you to answer a series of questions, as shown in Figure 6-6. Click Get Started to begin.**

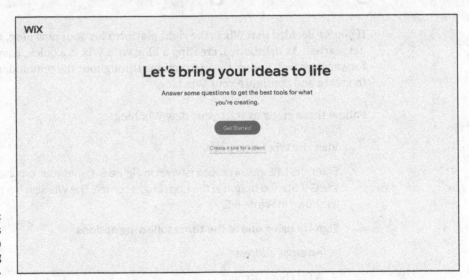

WiX

Let's bring your ideas to life

Answer some questions to get the best tools for what
you're creating.

[Get Started]

Create a site for a client

FIGURE 6-6:
Answer a series
of questions to
begin building
your Wix blog.

4. **Select the type of website you would like to create, as shown in Figure 6-7, and click Next.**

TIP

If you would like to skip the guided set-up questions, feel free to choose Skip in the bottom right-hand corner of the questions pages.

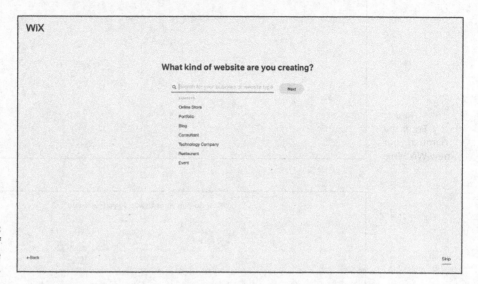

FIGURE 6-7:
Select the type of website you are building.

5. **Name your website, as shown in Figure 6-8, and click Next.**

Don't worry if you're not sure about what to name your blog! You can always change the name later.

6. **Wix will now offer a number of features to add to your site. Select the features you would like, as shown in Figure 6-9, and click Next.**

7. **Choose to select a template to begin designing your site, as shown in Figure 6-10.**

It is possible to go straight to your dashboard and skip this step, but part of what makes blogging on Wix quick and easy is the ability to select a template and dive right in. If you choose not to select a template at this step, you can find the template page later by visiting https://manage.wix.com/website/templates.

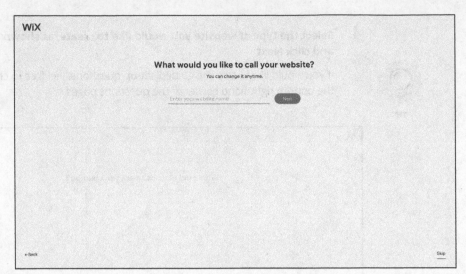

FIGURE 6-8:
Enter the
name of your
new Wix blog.

FIGURE 6-9:
Select the
features you
would like to add
to your Wix blog.

8. **Browse through the template options, as shown in Figure 6-11, and select the one that is right for your blog.**

   To select the template that you want, hover over that template and click Edit.

WARNING

Once you have selected a template, you are not able to change it! This is one of the cons of blogging on Wix. In order to use a different template, you will need to create an entirely different blog and import your content to that new blog.

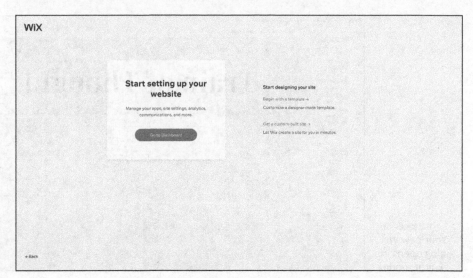

FIGURE 6-10:
Choose to select a template in order to build your blog quickly.

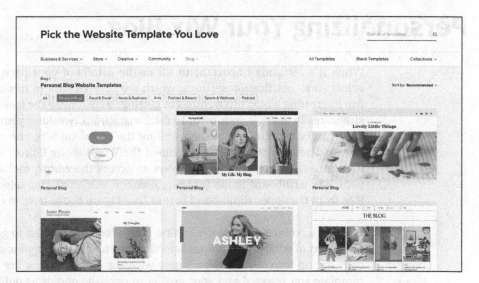

FIGURE 6-11:
Select your template by browsing through the options.

9. **Your new Wix blog will open in Editor mode, waiting to be customized, as shown in Figure 6-12. Congratulations!**

   Your Wix account and blog are now ready for you to configure and customize, which you learn about in the next sections of this chapter.

FIGURE 6-12:
Your new Wix
blog opens in
Editor mode.

Personalizing Your Wix Blog

While it's certainly important to fill in the details of your personal profile and select email notification settings, which are covered later in this chapter, the real fun in creating a blog often comes in getting to customize the look and feel of your site to really make it your own. In fact, sometimes tweaking your blog's appearance can be even more fun than writing the posts! On Wix, the customizing and personalization occurs in what's called the Wix Website Editor, shown earlier in Figure 6-12. There are multiple ways to access the editor, including by visiting your Wix dashboard home (https://manage.wix.com) and selecting Customize Site from the upper right-hand corner (see Figure 6-29, later in this chapter).

TIP

It is not a requirement to personalize your Wix blog in order to get started blogging! Part of what's great about selecting a template is that your site is automatically set up for you. If you're happy with the elements that are included in the template you selected and your goal is to publish content as quickly as possible, feel free to skip customization and jump right to posting!

Touring the Website Editor

The Website Editor also opens immediately after selecting your template during the Wix new website set-up process. It's a good idea to spend some time in the editor at that point in the process to personalize the look and design of your blog.

To get started, take a look at the horizontal navigation bar across the top of the editor. You'll notice in the upper left-hand corner that you can edit different parts of your blog, as shown in Figure 6-13. Use this area to choose which page of your website you would like to edit including the home page, a sample blog post page, and the about page. Clicking Manage Pages allows you to edit what pages are included on your website.

FIGURE 6-13:
Determine which page of your website you would like to edit.

In the upper right-hand corner of the editor are three very important icons. From this area, shown in Figure 6-14, you can Undo or Redo any action that you have taken. Take note that this is also where the Save button is located. Be sure to save your work often while you go! If you'd like to see how your site looks while you are editing, click the Preview button, which is located next to Save.

FIGURE 6-14:
The Save button is located in the horizontal navigation bar at the top of the editor.

The upper right-hand corner of the editor is also where you will find the Tools menu, shown in Figure 6-15. Use the tools menu to determine which tools you would like to utilize as you build your website in the editor.

Finally, head to the upper right-hand corner to find the search function for the editor. If there are any elements that you would like to add to your site that you can't find, use this area to search for it or search for editor help. The location of the search function is shown in Figure 6-16.

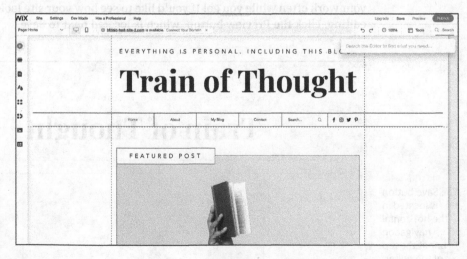

It's time to take a look at the menu options on the left sidebar of the Wix Website Editor. Anything that you find in the left sidebar that you would like to add to your blog can be dragged and dropped directly onto your new site. The following sections take a closer look at all of the options available to you.

TIP

The Wix Website Editor will look slightly different depending on the template you select when creating your new website. The general drag-and-drop menus featured in the following sections are an overview of what you might expect to find.

Add Elements

The Add Elements section of the editor, shown in Figure 6-17, allows you to add new components to your site from a new area of text to a blog post or even an online store! This is where you will decide what the reader will find when they visit your blog. Are you primarily interested in sharing blog posts? Are you a photographer focused on sharing media? Do you plan to incorporate the sale of goods or services to your site? All of these items and more can be added to your website from this section of the editor.

FIGURE 6-17:
Add the elements to your website that fit your goals for your blog.

Add Section

The Add Section area of the editor tools, shown in Figure 6-18, allows you to drag and drop new sections of content onto the pages of your blog. Choose a blank section to insert completely customized content onto the page of your website. You also have the option to choose from pre-formatted sections including a block of welcome content, contact information, and blocks of text. Should you choose to create a new section using the blank content option, you can save that new section and re-use it later or on another page of your website.

FIGURE 6-18: Add new sections of content to your website pages.

Pages and Menu

In the Pages and Menu area of the left sidebar, shown in Figure 6-19, you are able to add and remove areas from your website menu including links to your About page, search area, and contact information. You can also utilize this section to edit your blog post pages, including SEO settings for posts.

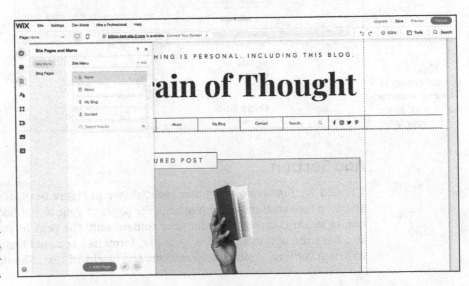

FIGURE 6-19: Edit the page menu for your site as well as the SEO settings for blog posts.

Site Design

The Site Design section of the editor, shown in Figure 6-20, is where you can edit visual design elements of your site. Select this section to change the appearance of the pages, including background images, as well as the appearance of the font. Select Site Theme to select a different group of fonts and color combinations. You can also edit font and color settings within theme selections.

FIGURE 6-20: Customize the visual design elements of your website.

Add Apps

Add Apps, shown in Figure 6-21, allows you to access one of the features of Wix that makes the blog platform unique. Wix Apps allow you to add new elements to your website ranging from social media icons to photo galleries to special site effects. The Wix App Market allows you to search for specific features as well as read reviews and ratings of apps you are considering. Some apps are only available to Wix premium accounts.

My Business

The My Business area of the left sidebar, shown in Figure 6-22, is a one-stop-shop to manage aspects of your website management that have to do with the business of blogging. From this area you can create new content, including blog posts, but you can also use this area of the menu to add features that will help you locate, connect with, and manage your subscriber base. Apps from the Wix App Market that pertain to the business side of blogging, such as those used to set up an eCommerce platform, can be added and accessed from this menu area.

FIGURE 6-21:
Add new capabilities to your blog from the Wix Apps Market.

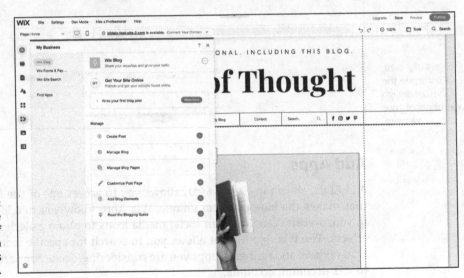

FIGURE 6-22:
Manage the business side of blogging from the My Business menu.

Media

Use the Media section of the tools, shown in Figure 6-23, to manage the media content on your website. You can upload images from other platforms, such as Facebook and Instagram, from this section of the editor. You can also search for and locate free images to add to your Wix blog. The Media sidebar tool even allows you to upload and edit photos as well as video content!

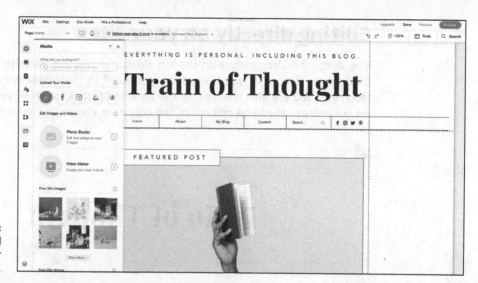

FIGURE 6-23:
Add and
edit media for
your blog.

Content Manager

The Content Manager area of the left sidebar, shown in Figure 6-24, allows you to add a content manager system to your website. The Wix Content Manager provides a more robust way to organize content than the default blog settings allow. This is not necessary as you set up your blog and begin writing content, but it's good to know that it's here should you need it in the future.

FIGURE 6-24:
Explore the
option of adding
a Content
Manager to your
Wix blog.

Editing directly on your site

The drag-and-drop menus on the left sidebar of the Wix Website Editor are valuable tools that offer you everything you need to customize your new website. However, you are also able to edit the look and functionality of your site directly on your site in the main column of the editor, as shown in Figure 6-25.

FIGURE 6-25:
Edit directly on your site's content in the main section of the editor.

To edit content directly without the use of the sidebar, take the following steps:

1. **Begin by selecting the page you want to edit, as shown earlier in Figure 6-13.**

   The page that you selected will appear in the main section of the editor.

2. **Hover over the area of the page that you want to edit, as shown in Figure 6-26.**

   As you hover, the options available to you will appear. Continue to navigate around the main column of the editor to see and select any options that you are interested in utilizing.

3. **Click on the area that you would like to be edited to be taken to the related tool, as shown in Figure 6-27.**

   As you select an area to edit, the related tool in the left sidebar opens. This provides you with the tool you need to complete the action you selected.

4. **Click Save to finish.**

FIGURE 6-26:
Select the area that you want to edit by hovering over it.

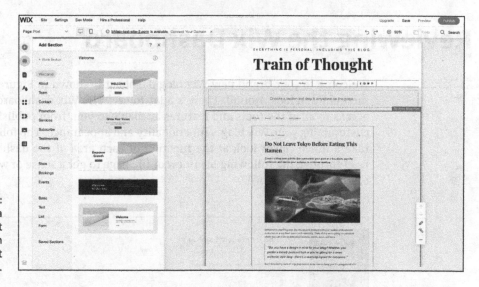

FIGURE 6-27:
Click on the area that you want to edit to open the related left sidebar tool.

REMEMBER

You can click Preview in the upper right-hand corner of the editor at any time to view the changes you've made to your site without the distraction of the editor tools. Simply click Go Back to Editor to continue your work.

Once you've finished making the changes that you'd like to make to the look and functionality of your new Wix website, you can choose to click Publish in the upper right-hand corner, which will make your site visible to the public. However, you likely don't have any content on your site and have not yet finished setting up your blog and personal profile. I recommend that instead you go to the upper left-hand corner, as shown in Figure 6-28, and click to visit your Wix dashboard.

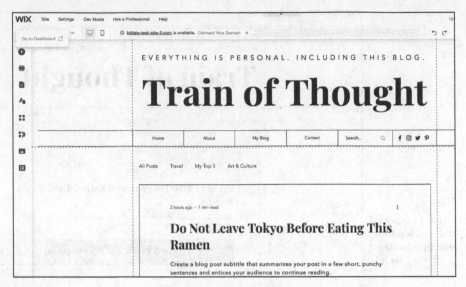

FIGURE 6-28:
Click to visit your
Wix dashboard.

Reviewing the Wix Dashboard

Welcome to your brand new Wix blog dashboard (shown in Figure 6-29)! Take a moment and look around. There's a lot to see! The Wix dashboard provides easy access to all of the tools and features available to you, from publishing content to customizing your Wix blog's functionality and appearance. The following sections take a much closer look at the function of each area of the dashboard, but first read through the following overview of the page to get a sense of what is available on the Wix dashboard.

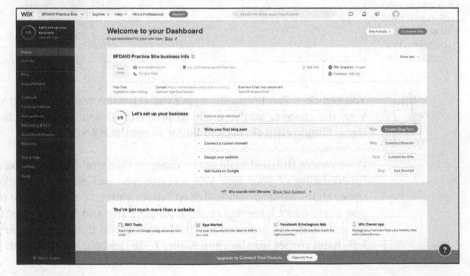

FIGURE 6-29:
Publish
content and
customize
your blog's
appearance
from your Wix
dashboard.

Start by taking a look at the horizontal navigation bar across the top of the page. From this area you are able to do the following:

>> Create a new Wix site or switch between the Wix sites you own

>> Explore apps, updates, courses, and more

>> Find help and answers to your questions

>> Hire professional help

>> Upgrade your account

>> Search Wix for anything you need for your blog

>> Check your Wix account inbox

>> Check your Wix account notifications

>> Read about new releases from Wix

>> Access your account settings including billing information

The main area of the dashboard home page allows you to continue to set up your Wix account and your new blog. From this area you're able to do the following:

>> Add a logo

>> Edit your profile and contact information

>> Connect a custom domain

>> Upgrade your account

>> Explore and install additional tools

>> Complete your blog set up by following suggested steps

The final area of the Wix dashboard is the left sidebar. This is the area where you will spend the majority of your time while working on your blog. From the sidebar you're able to navigate away from your dashboard home page to other dashboard pages including:

>> Activity page

>> Blog page

>> Contacts page

>> Communications page

>> Automations page

>> Marketing and SEO page

» Analytics and Reports page

» Finances page

» Site and App page

» Settings page

» Apps page

TIP

You may quickly notice that there are many places to upgrade your account from free to premium. If you don't need the premium features in order to blog the way you want to blog, there's no need to upgrade. It's okay to continue to use a free Wix account!

Getting to Know the Dashboard Tools

Some areas of the dashboard are more important than others when you get started blogging on Wix. Even though it's possible to jump right into writing a blog post, it's worth investing just a bit more time to set up items such as your profile and settings preferences. This will save you time down the road and will also help you put your best foot forward as you enter the blogosphere.

TIP

You can always make changes to any of the settings in your Wix dashboard by simply returning to your Wix dashboard by directing your browser to https://manage.wix.com and selecting your blog to get started.

Managing your personal profile

To complete your personal profile information, click on the blue profile icon in the upper right-hand corner of your dashboard as shown in Figure 6-29. Select Account Settings as shown in Figure 6-30.

Your Wix Account Settings page, shown in Figure 6-31, will open. This page allows you to update profile settings, including the following:

» Name

» Profile image

» Account name

» Login email

» Password

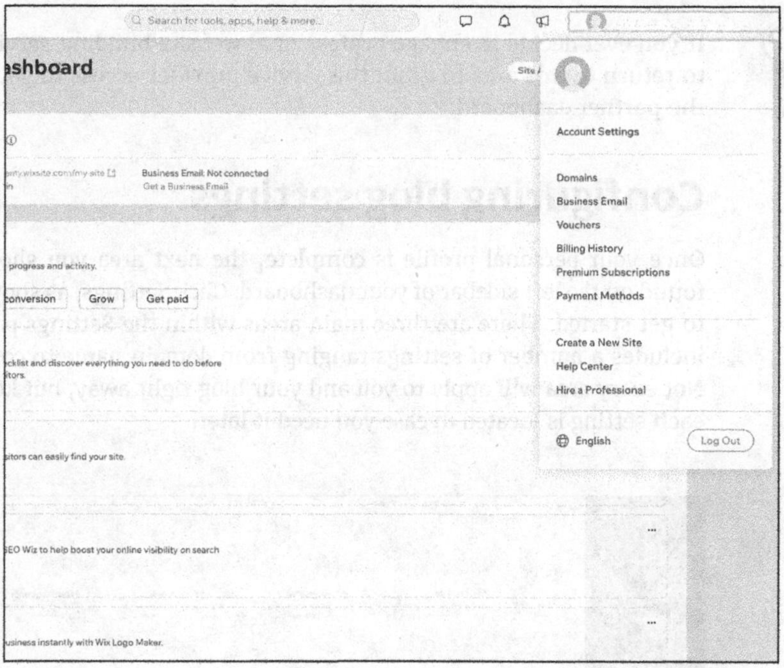

FIGURE 6-30:
Select Account
Settings to open
the Account
Settings page.

FIGURE 6-31:
Update your
profile from the
Account Settings
page.

>> Social logins

>> Email preferences

>> Privacy preferences

TIP

If you ever decide to engage professional website building services, you will need to return to this area to grant the service provider access to your site by enabling the partner dashboard.

Configuring blog settings

Once your personal profile is complete, the next area you should personalize is found on the left sidebar of your dashboard. Click Settings, as shown in Figure 6-32, to get started. There are three main areas within the Settings page, and each area includes a number of settings ranging from domain name to contact information. Not every area will apply to you and your blog right away, but keep in mind where each setting is located in case you need it later.

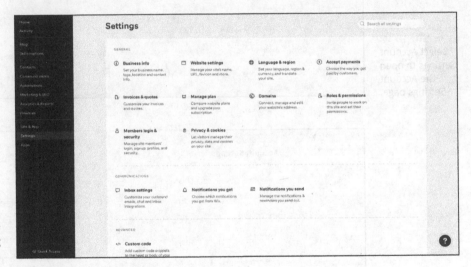

FIGURE 6-32:
Click settings in the left sidebar to configure blog settings.

General settings

Within the General settings, Wix users are able to configure the following areas:

>> **Business Info:** This section allows you to configure a number of settings related to your blog profile and contact information. From the Profile area, shown in Figure 6-33, you can change the name of your blog. This is also where you can upload a logo or choose to create a logo using the Wix logo creator tool. Finally, visit the Profile settings to select the type of site you are creating and write a brief 150 character or less description of your site. Scroll down to the Location and Contact Info sections to add information about your location and how to be contacted. This is especially important if you plan to conduct business from your Wix website.

FIGURE 6-33:
Update your
blog's profile
information on
the Business Info
setting page.

>> **Invoices and quotes:** Use this area of your settings to create and manage items related to business such as invoices and client quotes. This setting is helpful if you use your blog to offer products or services.

>> **Members login and security:** From this section of Settings you can determine who is able to view each section of your website and manage member information and permissions.

>> **Website settings:** Visit this area if you want to change the name of your blog. This is also where you can select your site's URL. The default URL for your Wix blog is `https://username.wix.com/my-site`, as shown in Figure 6-34. From this area of Settings you are able to change the "my-site" section of your URL. In order to change what appears for username, return to the Account Settings page and change your account name. In order to use a custom domain name that you've purchased, you will need to upgrade from a free Wix account to a premium account. You are able to do that in this section of your settings.

>> **Manage plan:** Should you decide to upgrade to a paid blogging plan, you can use this section of your settings to select a new plan.

>> **Privacy and cookies:** Use this area of settings to customize and create your site's privacy and cookie information to notify readers of your policies. To learn more about privacy policies, visit Chapter 4 of Book 1.

>> **Language and region:** Update the language and time zone you wish to use on your site in this section of the settings page.

>> **Domains:** If you would like to either purchase a custom domain for your Wix blog or connect a domain you already own to your Wix blog, visit this section.

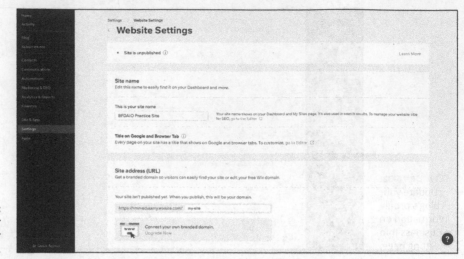

FIGURE 6-34:
Personalize your
blog's URL under
Website Settings.

>> **Accept payments:** Connect methods to accept payments, including via
PayPal and credit card, through this setting.

>> **Roles and permissions:** This section of settings allows you to provide others
with access to work on your site. It also allows you to manage what each
person has permission to do. The Manage Roles area, shown in Figure 6-35,
names and describes the available settings. It is also possible to create a
custom role as needed. This area is especially helpful if you have a team of
writers working on your site or someone helping you with billing.

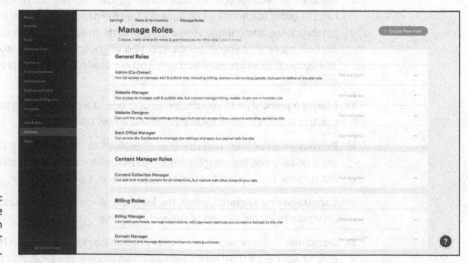

FIGURE 6-35:
Manage the role
that each person
working on your
site plays.

Communications settings

The Communications section of the Settings page allows you to edit the following:

» **Inbox settings:** From your inbox settings you can manage messages from connected accounts such as Instagram and Facebook as well as manage who is able to access your Wix inbox.

» **Notifications you get:** Visit this area to select with notifications you receive from Wix.

» **Notifications you send:** This setting allows you to customize the settings that you send out including notifications of new blog posts, comments, or even invoice reminders.

Advanced settings

The Advanced Settings area is where you can add snippets of custom code to your site. Your blog must be published before you are able to customize the code.

Diving into the blog menu

Once you have finished configuring all of your main profile and blog settings, it's time to take a look at the Blog menu on the left sidebar of your dashboard, as shown in Figure 6-36.

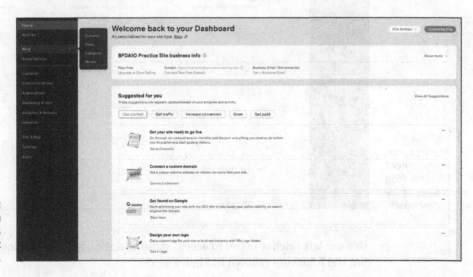

FIGURE 6-36: The Blog menu page button is located in the left sidebar.

Select the Blog menu button to open the Blog menu page, which is shown in Figure 6-37. This is the area of your dashboard where you will likely spend the most time as you create and manage your blog's content. From the Overview section (Figure 6-37), you can take the following actions:

» Create a new post

» Create a new blog category

» Invite a new writer

» Track interactions on existing posts

» Use an existing blog template to create a post

» Add additional features to your blog using Wix apps

» Access blog reports with statistics and insights related to existing posts

» Customize how readers are notified of new content

» Edit the SEO settings for posts

» Import posts from another blog

» Access the Wix Blogging Guide

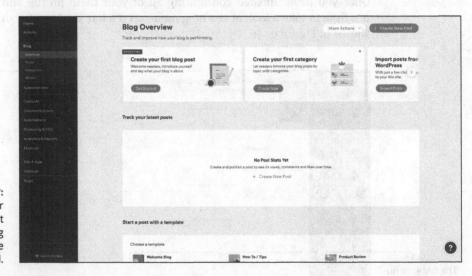

FIGURE 6-37:
Manage your blog's content from the Blog menu page of the dashboard.

Use the left sidebar menu to access more specific areas of the Blog menu, including the following (shown in Figure 6-38):

» **Posts:** Create new posts, view published posts, access drafts, review pending posts from other writers, schedule posts, and move posts to trash from this area.

» **Categories:** Create and manage categories from this page.

» **Writers:** Invite additional writers to your blog and manage their site permissions from this area of the dashboard.

FIGURE 6-38: Access more specific Blog menu settings from the left sidebar menu.

Before continuing, take some time to click around the additional dashboard menus to get a better understanding of where everything is located for when the time comes that you need additional tools.

Publishing a Post

Once all of your settings are configured and your blog's appearance is customized and personalized, it's time to create content and hit publish on your new Wix blog!

Like all things with Wix, there are a variety of ways to get to the tools that you need. Let's take a look at one of the most straightforward ways to create new content on your blog right from your dashboard.

To create your first blog post on your dashboard, take the following steps:

1. **Click on Blog on the left sidebar, as shown earlier in Figure 6-36.**

   The Blog section of the dashboard opens.

2. **Click the blue Create New Post button in the upper right-hand corner of the page, as shown in Figure 6-39.**

   The blog post creation page opens.

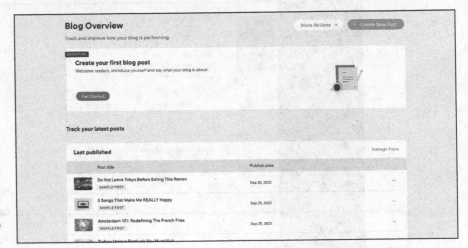

FIGURE 6-39: Use the Create New Post button to write a new blog post.

3. **Add a title to the title field at the top of the main column, shown in Figure 6-40.**

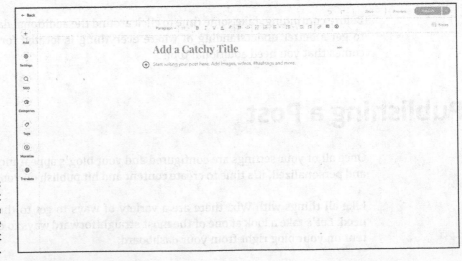

FIGURE 6-40: Create content in the main column of the new blog post creation page.

4. **Add text, images, or other content to the body of your blog post, as shown in Figure 6-41.**

You can begin typing your text directly into the body of your blog post. You also have the option of either selecting the + sign in the body of the post or clicking Add in the left sidebar to open a menu of other content options.

These options include the following:

- Image
- Gallery
- Video
- GIF
- File
- Divider
- Button
- Table
- Collapsible list
- Poll
- HTML code
- AdSense ads
- SoundCloud tracks

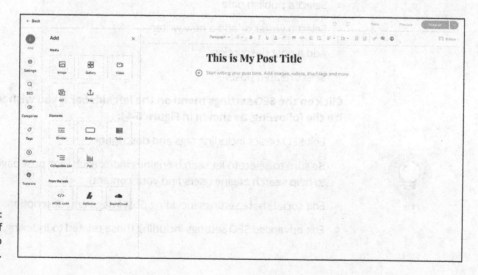

FIGURE 6-41:
Add a variety of content types to your post.

5. **Use the horizontal navigation bar at the top of your blog post creation area to customize text, as shown in Figure 6-42.**

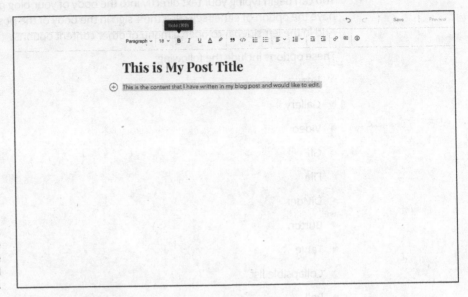

6. **Visit the Settings menu on the left sidebar to do the following, as shown in Figure 6-43:**

   - Upload a cover image
   - Select a publish date
   - Select a writer or add a new writer
   - Add a post description
   - Select related posts

7. **Click on the SEO settings menu on the left sidebar if you wish to customize the following, as shown in Figure 6-44:**

   - Edit SEO basics including tags and description.

     Be sure to select to let search engines index each blog post page in order to help search engine users find your content!

   - Edit social share settings including post image and description.
   - Edit advanced SEO settings including those related to indexing.

TIP

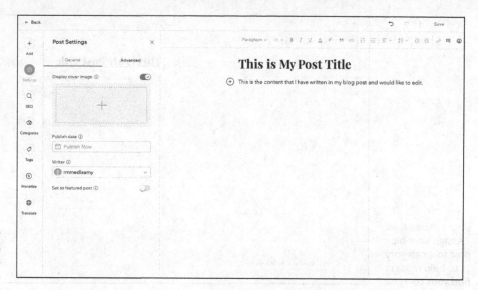

FIGURE 6-43:
Edit post features with the Settings menu.

FIGURE 6-44:
Edit SEO settings related to your blog post.

8. Click on the Categories menu on the left sidebar, as shown in Figure 6-45, to assign your new blog post to a category or create a new category.

9. Add Tags in the left sidebar, as shown in Figure 6-46, that relate to your post content to help your readers find your content.

10. Once you have added and customized all of the content you'd like to include on your blog post, click Publish in the upper right-hand corner, as shown in Figure 6-47.

Congratulations! You have published your first blog post on your new Wix blog!

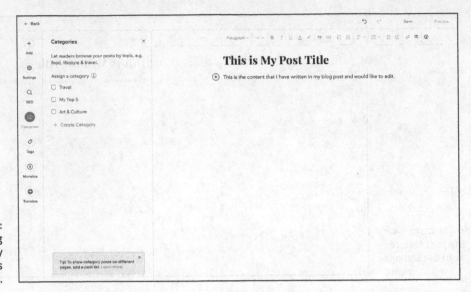

FIGURE 6-45:
Assign your blog post to a category to help readers find your content.

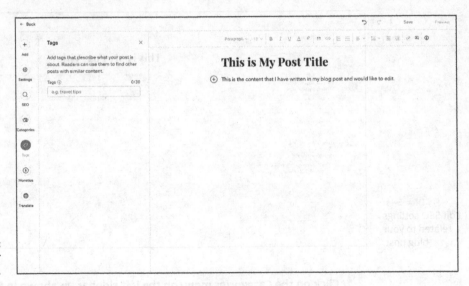

FIGURE 6-46:
Add tags to your blog post.

Once you have customized all of the elements of your blog that you wish and created enough content to get your site started, it's time to publish your site so that the public is able to access it. Up until this point, only you could see your Wix website. Return to your dashboard and select the blue Edit Site button in the upper right-hand corner. Your Wix Website Editor page will open. Click Publish in the upper right-hand corner, as shown in Figure 6-48. Your Wix blog is now live and visible to the public!

FIGURE 6-47:
Click Publish to
post your blog
content.

TIP

Want to preview your site one more time? Once in the Wix Website Editor, click
Preview in the upper right-hand corner before clicking Publish.

FIGURE 6-48:
Click Publish to
take your new
Wix blog live.

5
Blogging Tools

Contents at a Glance

Chapter **1**

Optimizing for Search Engines

Search engine optimization, commonly called SEO for short, refers to maximizing your blog's potential to be found by search engines such as Google and Bing. A blogger who has mastered the art of SEO is likely to have their blog appear higher on a list of search engine results than a blogger who hasn't attempted to solve the puzzle that is SEO.

The fact is that SEO often seems puzzling because the exact recipe for success is a secret known only by a select group of Google and other search engine company employees. With that said, SEO can be challenging, but it's not impossible to boost your blog's traffic from search engines with a bit of understanding and commitment. The best way to get the hang of SEO techniques is to invest time into researching everything you can about it and testing different techniques to determine which work best for your blog. That's because each blog's content is different, and each blog's audience is different. Both of these factors significantly affect the search traffic that has the potential to come to your blog.

This chapter introduces some of the commonly accepted SEO techniques so you can begin blogging with confidence that your content has a chance to be found through keyword searches on popular search engines such as Google. However, the information in this chapter is just the tip of the SEO iceberg! For more detailed information about SEO, read *SEO For Dummies*, by Peter Kent (John Wiley & Sons, Inc., 2020), or the more comprehensive *Search Engine Optimization All-in-One For Dummies*, by Bruce Clay and Kristopher B. Jones (John Wiley & Sons, Inc., 2022).

Understanding SEO Basics

REMEMBER

Why does SEO matter? A large proportion of Internet traffic to your blog will come from search engines, which means that bloggers need to help search engines locate their blogs if they want to bring more readers to their content. Speaking of content, all of the content on your blog, from the words in your posts to the titles you give to your images, play a role in whether or not search engines include your content in their search results (as you'll discover in this chapter).

When most people hear the term SEO, they tend to think of keywords, which are discussed later in this chapter. There's actually a lot more to SEO than using targeted keywords that match people's search engine queries. Although keywords are the starting point for your blog's SEO strategy, they can only take your blog so far. You also need to focus on other SEO techniques to truly grow your blog's search engine traffic.

For example, did you know that the number of incoming links to your blog, particularly incoming links from popular blogs and websites, is very important when it comes time for search engines to *rank* your site in comparison with similar sites for search results? In other words, your blog can stand on its own, but it will be very lonely. Boosting the number of incoming links to your blog is discussed later in this chapter in the section "Increasing your blog's ranking in Google searches."

REMEMBER

While it's definitely not what people think of first when they hear the term SEO, one of the most important aspects of SEO is relationship building. Why? Because the relationships that you build with other bloggers and your audience help spread your content across the web. On the other hand, some SEO techniques can actually get you in trouble and cause your blog's search traffic to plummet or disappear entirely. In other words, you need to avoid some SEO don'ts at all costs, unless you want to risk having your blog dropped from search results.

And when it comes to SEO, you need to be flexible. Just when SEO experts think they have another aspect of Google's proprietary search algorithm figured out, Google changes it. If you're serious about SEO, be sure to visit sites like The Moz Blog (`www.moz.org/blog/`), shown in Figure 1-1, and stay abreast of the trends and tips related to SEO.

FIGURE 1-1:
The Moz Blog is a popular blog and community dedicated to search engine optimization.

Finding SEO Tools

At this point you may be feeling a little overwhelmed. Not only do you have to write content that you love writing and that readers love reading, but now you also have to think about what search engines want to see? Take heart! There are new SEO tools and resources emerging daily, both free and with a price tag, that can help move your blog up the ranks in search engine results.

Staying on top of SEO news

Sites like The Moz Blog, shown previously in Figure 1-1, keep their subscribers up to date on the latest happenings in the world of SEO. If this is an area of blogging that is important to you, it might be a good idea to subscribe to a couple of your favorite SEO blogs so that you're always in step with what is changing in the world of search engine optimization.

Along with The Moz Blog, consider checking out the following:

» **Search Engine Land** (www.searchengineland.com)

» **SEO Roundtable** (www.seoroundtable.com)

» **Search Engine Journal** (www.searchenginejournal.com)

» **The Ahrefs Blog** (www.ahrefs.com)

» **Search Engine Journal** (www.searchenginejournal.com)

» **Search Engine Watch** (www.searchenginewatch.com)

» **Yoast Blog** (www.yoast.com/seo-blog/)

Plugging in for better SEO

If you would like to improve the SEO of your blog but would prefer a somewhat automated path, consider utilizing WordPress plugins that are designed to help bloggers improve their standing in search engine results. *Plugins*, blog add-ons that provide additional functions to your blog, are available both for free and at a cost to guide you through various aspects of SEO from keyword selection to social media sharing.

If your blog uses the WordPress blogging software on any platform, consider checking out the following SEO plugins:

» **Yoast** (www.yoast.com)

» **All in One SEO** (www.aioseo.com)

» **SEOquake** (www.seoquake.com)

» **Schema Pro** (www.wpschema.com)

» **Rank Math** (www.rankmath.com)

» **SEO Press** (www.seopress.org)

WARNING

While you may want to try out multiple SEO plugins before deciding what works best for you, never use more than one at a time on the same blog. SEO WordPress plugins may interfere with the functionality of each other and should only be used separately.

Utilizing keyword tools

While you most likely are not interested in writing content solely because it will be popular in a Google search, there is value in knowing what topics potential readers are searching for often.

REMEMBER

Keywords are the words that search engine users type into the search bar when looking for information online. For example, if I'm starting a new diet and I want to focus on low-fat foods that I can prepare for my family, I may search the term *low-fat recipes* in my search engine of choice as shown in Figure 1-2.

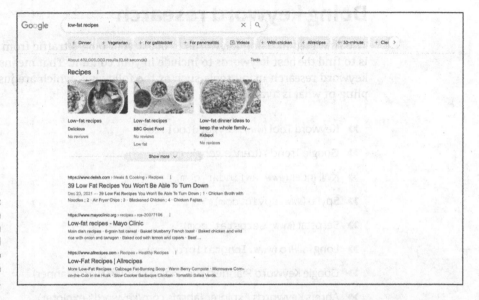

FIGURE 1-2:
A Google search for the term *low-fat recipe* will drive traffic to blogs focusing on that topic.

Keyword tools assist in selecting search-friendly wording for your blog posts. If you're hoping to lead new readers to your blog, it's best to make sure that you include the keywords that are searched most often and are related to your post topic within your blog post. Let's take a look at examples of keyword tools to get you started in the next section.

TIP

Suffering with a bad case of writer's block? Playing around with keyword tools can help you come up with ideas for new posts!

Interpreting Keywords

Keywords are often the first stop on the SEO train because you can use them to choose a blog topic or optimize your already-planned content with those keywords.

Focusing on targeted keywords helps search engines find your content and rank it accordingly in keyword search results. Paying attention to keywords is so important to SEO — and a fairly easy task — that it's worth taking a closer look at how to use them.

Doing keyword research

The first step to using keywords to boost your blog's traffic from search engines is to find the best keywords to include in your content. That means you need to do keyword research using tools such as the following, which are just a small sampling of what is available:

>> Keyword Tool (www.keywordtool.io)

>> Google Trends (trends.google.com)

>> KWFinder (www.kwfinder.com)

>> SpyFu (www.spyfu.com)

>> Serpstat (www.serpstat.com)

>> LongTailPro (www.longtailpro.com)

>> Google Keyword Planner (ads.google.com/keywordplanner)

>> Ahrefs Keywords Explorer (ahrefs.com/keywords-explorer)

>> Semrush (www.semrush.com)

>> AnswerThePublic (www.answerthepublic.com)

TIP

The goal for keyword research is to find keywords to target in your posts that are relevant to your blog's topic and neither too popular (because there's too much competition from powerful sites for those keywords) nor too unpopular (because there's no sense in focusing on keywords that no one is searching for).

Exploring keyword search tools

While it is best to take a look at a variety of keyword search tools to decide which one works best for you, the following takes a closer look at one such tool to get you started: Keyword Tool.

Follow these steps to begin using Keyword Tool:

1. **Point your web browser to** `www.keywordtool.io`.

The Keyword Tool homepage, as shown in Figure 1-3, allows you to engage in a free keyword search. There is also a paid subscriber option for those looking for additional resources.

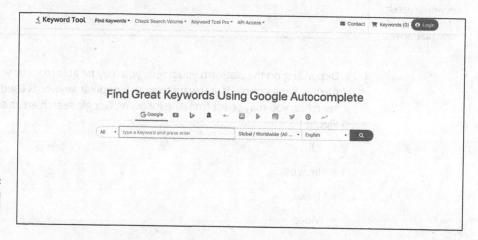

FIGURE 1-3:
Keyword Tool is a popular keyword search site.

2. **Select the platform focus of your keyword search, selecting from the following options (Figure 1-4):**

- Google
- YouTube
- Bing
- Amazon
- EBay
- App Store
- Play Store
- Instagram
- Pinterest

- Twitter
- Google Trends

FIGURE 1-4:
Keyword Tool allows users to focus their keyword search to a variety of platforms.

Depending on the platform you select, you may be able to focus your search further. For example, if you want to search popular keywords used in Google searches, you may select from the following Google search areas as shown in Figure 1-5:

- All
- Images
- News
- Video
- Shopping

FIGURE 1-5:
Depending on the search engine you've chosen, you may be able to add additional focus to your keyword search.

3. **Select the geographic location you would like to search as shown in Figure 1-6.**

While you most likely are interested in attracting readers from around the globe, there may be certain circumstances when you would prefer traffic from a specific country location.

4. **Type your preferred keyword or phrase in the search bar and click the search icon to the right, as shown in Figure 1-7.**

A list of popular keywords related to your search term appears, as shown in Figure 1-8. That is the extent of the information provided by Keyword Tools to free users. Paid account holders receive additional information about each keyword in the list (such as the total search volume and average cost per click for the keywords).

Using keywords

After you identify the keywords you want to target on your blog, you need to use them appropriately so that they are as helpful as possible.

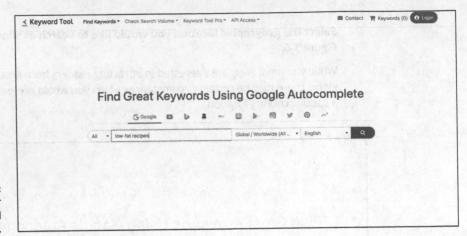

Find Great Keywords Using Google Autocomplete

FIGURE 1-7:
Search for your
desired keyword
or phrase.

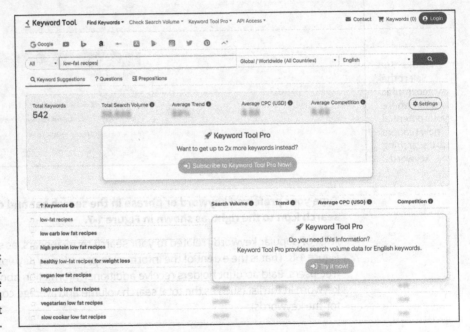

FIGURE 1-8:
Free account
users receive
a list of related
keywords without
additional data.

TIP

There are strategic places to use your keywords, discussed later in this chapter in "Writing SEO-Friendly Blog Posts," including the following:

>> Post titles

>> Headings within posts

>> Near the beginning of your post's content

>> Within and near hyperlinks

Placing your selected keywords carefully helps ensure that they're given more weight in search engine *algorithms* (formulas that determine how useful a search result is in relation to the search term) and that your content is ranked appropriately because of them. You can boost your search engine rank for targeted keywords by following these tips:

» **Do not use too many keywords in one post or page.** A good guideline is to focus each blog post that you write on three to four keywords or keyword phrases.

» **Choose keyword phrases that are short.** Statistics show that nearly 60 percent of keyword searches include just two or three keywords. That's where you want your keywords to be!

» **Be specific.** This applies to the concept of going after the long tail, which is discussed in detail in the next section of this chapter.

Although these are broad keyword tips that you can use to boost your search engine traffic to your blog, you can use many more techniques within your blog writing to enhance your SEO. You can find out more on that subject later in this chapter, in the section "Writing SEO-Friendly Blog Posts," but first, let's look at long-tail SEO.

Demystifying Long-Tail SEO

Long-tail SEO is a hot topic in the online world as the landscape gets more and more cluttered and the competition for keyword traffic grows exponentially every day. A small blog has little chance of competing with top sites for broad and popular keyword traffic. Imagine you're starting a blog about travel, and then imagine how many other sites are competing for broad, related keywords such as *travel* or *vacations*. There's little hope for your new blog to appear high in search engine rankings for those broad terms. However, you can target very specific keyword phrases, called *long-tail SEO*, and attract very targeted traffic to your blog with far less competition.

Long-tail SEO is the process of targeting very specific keyword phrases that are too narrow for big websites to feel threatened by but broad enough to get a decent amount of searches on them each day. For example, rather than targeting a broad term such as *travel,* you could target a more specific keyword phrase such as *singles resorts*. This is where keyword research can be extremely useful.

As discussed in Book 2, niche bloggers often find great success going after the long tail. It makes sense. These bloggers focus on attracting visitors who are looking for specific information, and niche bloggers make sure they deliver that information. Ultimately, that's the key to long-tail SEO success, to attract readers to your blog using less-popular keywords and then satisfy visitors when they get there by writing content that's relevant and useful to them.

Writing SEO-Friendly Blog Posts

Locating and selecting the right keywords for your content is only the first step to writing SEO-friendly blog posts. You then need to understand how to use those keywords in your writing so they actually help your search rankings. Let's take a closer look at the commonly accepted techniques (mentioned previously in this chapter) to use to ensure search engines find your keywords and rank your content accordingly:

>> **Use keywords in your post titles.** Make sure your keywords are included in your blog post's title. Bloggers who are serious about SEO fight the urge to write cute and catchy titles and instead focus on writing post titles that utilize targeted keywords. The best blog post titles both draw the reader and the search engines in.

>> **Use keywords in your subtitles and post headings.** Include a subtitle with your blog post or break your post into sections with a heading for each section. Use the HTML headings attributes, H1, H2, H3, and so on to format your subtitle and headings.

>> **Use keywords at the beginning and end of your post content.** Use the same keyword at least two times within the first 100 words or so of your blog post as well as at the end of your blog post.

>> **Use keywords in and around links in your posts.** If possible, make your keywords link to another page or post on your blog or include your keywords around links within your post.

Make sure the keyword links you use in your blog post are relevant, or they can do more harm than good. Google might view them as spam if they're abundant and aren't relevant to your post content.

WARNING

>> **Use keywords to name your images and in ALT tags.** If possible, name the images used in your post with your keywords and include them in the ALT tag of your image's HTML code. However, make sure it's relevant to do so, or Google might view your efforts as *keyword stuffing,* which is a form of spam discussed later in this chapter in the section "Avoiding SEO Don'ts."

WHAT IS THE HTML ALT TAG FOR IMAGES?

You can configure the ALT tag for an image in HTML as follows:

```
<img src="http://www.example.com/uploads/image.jpg" alt="Image Name Goes
Here"/>
```

When an image is missing or can't be displayed in a visitor's browser, the text in the ALT tag (your designated alternative text) is displayed in place of the image.

Building Relationships to Boost Search Rankings

Perhaps the most critical step to boosting the search engine traffic to your blog is the time you spend building relationships with other bloggers and your blog's readers, because that's how you can increase the number of links to your blog content. Search engines, such as Google, highly value incoming links (particularly links from popular and authoritative sites) in determining how to rank search results. The more time you spend cultivating relationships online, the more your search rankings will rise organically.

Following are some relationship-building tips that can help your SEO efforts:

>> **Leave comments on other blogs.** Start reading blogs written about subjects similar to your blog and then leave useful comments on posts you enjoy. Commenting is the first step to building a relationship with another blogger and that blogger's existing audience.

>> **Use the same link phrase everywhere.** When you leave comments on other blogs, always use the same phrase for the link back to your blog. This not only helps your branding efforts so that people begin to recognize you, but it also helps with search engine optimization.

>> **Link to content you enjoy from your own blog posts.** When you read something you like on another blog, mention it on your own blog and provide a link to the source. Your link shows up as an incoming link for the other blogger, and your own audience is likely to be happy to read more great content that you recommend. Just be sure that you don't copy content from another source verbatim. You don't want to be accused of plagiarism or scraping content, which is described in more detail in the "Avoiding SEO Don'ts" section later in this chapter.

>> **Share content you like on social media platforms.** Use social media tools to share links to content you enjoy, thereby driving traffic to other blog posts that you like. It's possible someone will reciprocate and share your content, too.

>> **Respond to comments left on your blog.** Don't ignore the people who take the time to leave comments on your blog posts. Instead, make them feel valued by writing a meaningful response to their comments.

These are just a few tips to start building relationships across the blogosphere, which should help your blog's traffic and search rankings over time. Remember, the relationships you build are likely to outlast any search engine algorithms, so make sure you take the time to cultivate them.

Understanding Google Search Results

In simplest terms, Google's search algorithm indexes online content and ranks it in terms of relevancy, usefulness, and authoritativeness. Relevancy is primarily determined contextually and relies heavily on keywords, whereas usefulness and authoritativeness rely more heavily on incoming links.

Google ranks sites and blogs with a lot of incoming links higher than those with few incoming links. The thought process is that sites with a lot of incoming links must have great content on them or other sites wouldn't want to link to them. Furthermore, sites that are updated frequently with a lot of fresh content have more chances to attract incoming links, driving their Google rank up higher.

It's important to understand that Google claims not to use the page ranking system in determining how search results are delivered, but the *process* behind the system is still valid. In other words, the steps that people took to increase what used to be referred to as a Google PageRank are still effective in terms of increasing the ranking of your posts and pages within relevant Google searches, regardless of whether the official Google PageRank system is still in effect.

Avoiding SEO Don'ts

Just as there are steps you can follow to increase your blog's search traffic by appropriately using keywords, links, and techniques to boost your blog's ranking in online searches, there are also things you can do that ultimately hurt your blog's search engine rankings. In fact, there are even things you can do that can get your blog eliminated from Google search entirely!

WARNING

If you want to grow your blog's readership, don't do any of the things in the following list:

>> **Don't pay for text links.** Google views text link advertising as a way to artificially boost search engine rankings. If you're caught paying for text links to your blog, your search rankings could drop or your blog could be removed from Google search results entirely.

>> **Don't publish links that have been paid for.** Google punishes both the site that pays for text links *and* the site that publishes paid text links in the same way — by dropping both sites' search rankings or dropping both sites from search results completely.

>> **Don't keyword stuff.** *Keyword stuffing* is the process of overloading a webpage with keywords for the sole purpose of increasing search engine rankings. For example, you might find a long list of keywords at the top or bottom of a webpage. They may or may not be set up as links. Use your keywords strategically as suggested earlier in this chapter.

>> **Don't hide keywords.** Don't try to hide keywords in a very small font or a color that matches your blog's background. Google looks for sites that do this and considers them to be spam, which means reduced or no search traffic for sites that are caught hiding keywords.

>> **Don't scrape content.** Never copy content from another site and republish it as your own on your own blog — called *scraping* content. Although it's okay to copy a quote or small section of content from another site, you should never plagiarize content and republish it on your site. First, to do so without permission is illegal. Second, Google gives credit only to the first site that publishes that content and might penalize sites that are found copying content, regardless of whether you link to the original source.

>> **Don't publish content that is nothing more than links.** Your blog must contain far more original content than links. Google views pages that include little more than links as spam. Your blog will be downgraded if you're caught publishing pages full of links, particularly if those links are ads.

Using the NoFollow Tag

The NoFollow tag is a snippet of HTML code that you can add to your links so they're invisible to Google and not included in Google's search rankings. Many bloggers use the NoFollow tag on all outgoing links within paid content on their blogs so there's no chance that their links could be considered paid text links.

The format for the NoFollow tag is as follows:

```
<a href="http://www.example.com/" rel="nofollow">link text goes here</a>
```

It's up to you to decide whether you want to use the NoFollow tag on your blog, but at the very least, use it in any text link advertising links and in any sponsored posts. You can find out more about blog monetization through text link ads and sponsored content in Book 7.

Considering Search Engine Reputation Management

Search engine reputation management (SERM) is the process of making sure the search engine results for keywords related to yourself, your blog, your business, your brand, and so on are the ones that you want people to see. For example, you wouldn't want someone to type your name or the keyword phrase related to your blog into Google and find that the top results returned provide negative information about you. That's where SERM comes in handy: You can directly affect the search results that people find with time and commitment.

First, you need to stay on top of what people find when they search for the keywords related to your blog so you always know where you stand. Conduct regular searches on your chosen keywords and keep track of the results. The more quality content you flood the online world with that's optimized for your keyword phrases, the farther down other content will fall in search result listings. You can also sign up to receive email alerts using Google Alerts (www.google.com/alerts) whenever your chosen keywords are mentioned online.

Furthermore, the relationships that you build online can help your SERM efforts because the other bloggers that you have relationships with are typically happy to help you get new content online that tells the story you want to share.

Ultimately, the key to SEO success comes from two things: a lot of great, original content and relationships. You can find out more about SERM in Chapter 5 of Book 3.

IN THIS CHAPTER

» **Making sense of web analytics terminology**

» **Knowing what to track**

» **Choosing a web analytics tool**

» **Using collected data**

» **Tracking influence**

» **Keeping perspective**

Chapter **2**

Measuring Blog Performance

Publishing great content is only the tip of the iceberg when it comes to developing a successful blog. To truly understand which of your blogging efforts is delivering the biggest bang for the buck in terms of boosting traffic, comments, subscriptions, and more, you need to track your blog's performance over time.

By analyzing your blog's traffic patterns, you can quantify your successes as well as test new features, tools, and content. Alternatively, you can determine which of your blogging efforts isn't delivering the results you want and need, tweak those elements, or stop them completely. Your goals for your blog greatly affect how committed you need to be to tracking your blog's statistics.

Fortunately, a number of web analytics tools are available to help you easily track your blog statistics. In this chapter, you find out about popular web analytics tools, what to track, and how to use the information you collect.

Making Sense of Web Analytics

You can easily gather statistics related to your blog's performance by using a web analytics tool, such as the tools discussed later in this chapter, but your efforts won't help much if you don't understand what the data you collect means. Furthermore, web analytics tools can provide *a lot* of data, but all that data isn't helpful to you if you don't know what to focus on.

Each blogger has different goals for their blog, and that means each blogger has different data that's meaningful to them. This section focuses on the most commonly tracked data.

Defining web analytics terms

Before you can start tracking your blog statistics, you need to understand what the terminology used by web analytics tools means. Following are descriptions of some of the most commonly used terms:

>> **Hits:** A *hit* is counted by web analytics tools every time a file loads in your web browser from your blog. Each page on your blog can have multiple files on it. When a person accesses a page on your blog, every file on that page loads on your screen and counts as a hit. For example, if a page includes a blog post with multiple images in it, each of those images loads when a visitor accesses that page and counts as a hit, which gives an inflated view of the popularity of your blog. Therefore, hits aren't commonly used to evaluate web traffic trends.

>> **Visits:** Each time your blog is accessed, a visit is counted by your web analytics tool, meaning a person who accesses your blog more than once is counted multiple times. Therefore, visits may give an inflated view of your blog's overall popularity. Visits are still generally useful information, but they aren't the most important way to determine web traffic trends. (The next bullet explains a more accurate way to determine information about visits to your blog.)

>> **Visitors:** There are three visitor statistics:

- *Visitors:* Anyone who visits any page of your blog is a visitor, so a person can be counted more than once if they visit multiple times.

- *Return visitors:* Anyone who visits your blog more than one time is a return visitor.

- *Unique visitors:* Each visitor is counted one time regardless of how many times they visit your blog. Unique visitors demonstrate a blog's reach.

    However, unless visitors register and sign in to access your blog's content (which isn't recommended), it's nearly impossible to ensure repeat visitors to your blog are counted only one time.

    Web analytics tools use *cookies* (small pieces of text or code that are stored in your web browser when you visit a web page) to reduce the number of visitors who are counted twice, but if people clear their cookies from their web browsers, the web analytics tool has no way to identify them as repeat visitors. That is, if a visitor comes to your blog, clears the cookies from their web browser, and then returns to your blog, they're counted as a new visitor (meaning they're counted as two visitors, when in fact, they're just one).

    The opposite is true in terms of tracking return visitors. If people clear the cookies from their browsers, they won't be tracked accurately. Therefore, tracking visitors is more accurate than tracking visits, but still far from perfect.

>> **Pageviews:** The most common statistic for bloggers to track because it provides the clearest picture of how popular a blog is. Each page viewed on your blog, regardless of who views it, counts as a pageview. Online advertisers use pageviews as the standard of measurement to calculate advertising rates. More pageviews equals more people seeing an ad and potentially clicking it or acting on it.

>> **Top pages viewed:** Web analytics tools typically provide a report that shows your blog's most viewed pages (including post pages). This statistic is also referred to as *top content.* Monitoring top pages viewed can help you focus your content-creation and marketing efforts.

>> **Top paths taken:** Paths represent the way visitors navigate through your blog — the links they follow, the content that's most interesting to them, and the features that keep them on your blog longer.

>> **Top entry pages:** Top entry pages represent the pages that people most frequently land on when they visit your blog. This statistic is helpful in terms of finding where visitors are coming from. Using the Top Paths Taken data with the Top Entry Pages data can provide valuable information.

>> **Top exit pages:** Top exit pages represent the last pages that people view before leaving your blog. This statistic can help you identify content that is underperforming.

>> **Bounce rate:** The bounce rate tracks the percentage of people who leave your blog immediately after landing on it. The bounce rate represents people who didn't find what they were looking for when they were led to your blog. The lower this number is, the more effective your marketing and search

engine optimization efforts are, meaning the people who are finding your blog are the ones that you want to find it. In other words, your SEO and marketing efforts are reaching your blog's target audience.

» **Referrers:** One of the most useful statistics you can find using your web analytics tool is referrers, which identifies the websites, blogs, and search engines that lead visitors to your blog. Often the referrers statistic is broken down further into a category for search engines only and another for non-search engines. You can find where traffic is coming from and determine where to focus your marketing efforts going forward by analyzing referrer statistics.

» **Keywords and keyword phrases:** Using your web analytics tool, you can learn which keywords and keyword phrases people are typing into their preferred search engines that are leading them to your blog. Search engines can drive large amounts of visitors to your blog. By analyzing the keywords and keyword phrases that people type into search engines, which lead them to your blog, you can focus your future SEO and content creation efforts to target those keywords.

Knowing what to track

In addition to the most commonly tracked statistics listed in the preceding section, web analytics tools provide the ability to track a myriad of other statistics, such as the browsers your blog visitors use and their geographic location while browsing. The sheer volume of available data can make narrowing down that data into usable chunks of information overwhelming.

To make blog traffic analysis a less daunting task, take the time to review the data available to you through your web analytics tool to determine which statistics are most useful to you in terms of helping you reach your blogging goals. Focus your analysis on those data points and then enhance your analytics from there. Starting small and working your way up as you get more comfortable with the data you collect makes the process of understanding your blog's performance more manageable. Suggestions for putting the data you collect to work for you are included later in this chapter.

TECHNICAL STUFF

Depending on your blogging application and host, you might not be able to access a full complement of web analytics. Self-hosting your blog through your chosen web host, as discussed in Chapter 1 of Book 4, gives you maximum control and provides access to the widest array of web analytics data. Many blogging platforms — including some free sites — include built-in analytics tools. Be sure to look at all a blogging platform has to offer in this area if analytics are important to you and your blogging goals!

Choosing a Web Analytics Tool

Various web analytics tools are available to bloggers, offering different levels of data and at varying price points. Most bloggers start with a free web analytics tool, and as their blogs grow, they might consider moving to a fee-based tool. Take the time to research the various web analytics tools to find the one that integrates most easily with your blogging application and offers you the functionality you want at a price you're willing to pay.

Several free web analytics tools, such as Google Analytics, provide sufficient data and functionality for the majority of bloggers.

TECHNICAL
STUFF

Most web analytics tools are easily integrated into your blogging application. Simply sign up for an account for the web analytics tool you choose, copy the HTML or JavaScript code provided to you, and paste it into your blog's footer, sidebar, or other location as directed by the web analytics tool provider.

Some of the most popular web analytics tools are discussed in the following sections.

TIP

Be sure to evaluate your blogging goals before you invest in a fee-based web analytics package. It's very likely that a free tool, such as Google Analytics, can provide the data you need.

Google Analytics

Google Analytics (`https://analytics.google.com`) has become one of the most popular web analytics tools for four reasons:

>> It's easy to integrate into your blog.

>> It provides comprehensive results.

>> It provides reasonably accurate results.

>> It's free.

To use Google Analytics, you must create a free Google account if you do not already have one. In order to get started with Google Analytics, take the following steps:

1. **Sign in to your Google account.**

2. **Point your web browser to `https://analytics.google.com`, as shown in Figure 2-1.**

FIGURE 2-1:
The Google
Analytics
home page.

3. **Click the Start Measuring button, and the account setup screen will appear, as shown in Figure 2-2.**

4. **Create an account name and select how you wish to share your site data with Google and click Next.** For ease of use, create an account name associated with your blog name.

5. **Create a property name for your blog and select the appropriate time zone and currency then click Next.**

6. **Fill in the business information requested by Google and click Create. At this point you will be asked to agree to the Terms of Service.**

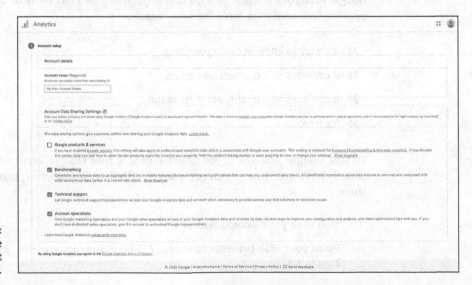

FIGURE 2-2:
The Google
Analytics account
set-up page.

Once your Google Analytics account has been created, you will need to set up data collection for your blog. Google walks you through the steps to do this and provides help via the question mark button in the upper right-hand corner of the screen, as shown in Figure 2-3.

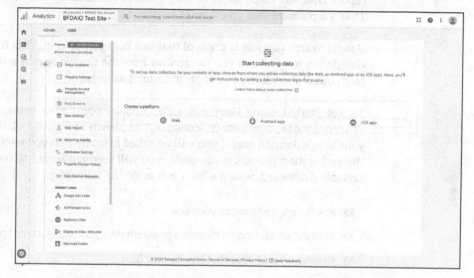

FIGURE 2-3: Access Google Analytics help via the question mark button in the upper right-hand corner of the screen.

Google Analytics provides a variety of reports, including custom reports, so you can easily track your blog's statistics. You can also track advertising and promotional campaigns. Figure 2-4 shows a snapshot of some of the information available through Google Analytics.

FIGURE 2-4: The Google Analytics dashboard.

Google Search Console

While it is definitely important to track web analytics such as page views and unique visitors, it's also helpful to know how well your blog is performing in search engine results. For example, you may notice in your Google Analytics report that not many of your blog readers are finding you via search engines. That's a problem that you'll want to fix!

Google Search Console is the tool that can help you do that. This free service from Google not only allows you to monitor how the Google search engine views your blog, but it also allows you to troubleshoot as needed.

To get started using Google Search Console, point your browser to `https://search.google.com/search-console/`, as shown in Figure 2-5. Once you type in your blog's domain name, you will be asked to verify that you own that site. When the verification process is complete, you will be given access to the Google Search Console dashboard, which allows you to do the following:

>> Ask Google to re-index your site

>> Find out when Google locates a problem with your site such as spam

>> Receive a list of sites that link to your blog

>> Monitor how much traffic is coming to your site from Google searches

>> Determine what search terms are leading readers to your site

>> See which blog pages are drawing in the most search engine traffic

FIGURE 2-5: Google Search Console is a free tool to help you monitor your blog's search engine performance.

MonsterInsights

MonsterInsights (www.monsterinsights.com) is a popular WordPress plugin that works with Google Analytics to provide a variety of web analytics tools to WordPress bloggers.

One of the downsides of using an analytics tool such as Google Analytics is the need to insert code into your blog. If you're not especially tech-savvy, this can be a stumbling block. Plugins such as MonsterInsights take care of this for you. Among many other features, MonsterInsights also allows you to:

>> Track analytics for affiliate links

>> Assess which call-to-action links on your site are performing well

>> Track reader interaction with your video content

>> Analyze keyword traffic by integrating with SEO plugins such as YoastSEO (for more on SEO, check out Chapter 1 of this Book)

>> Track traffic on your blog's contact forms

TECHNICAL STUFF

MonsterInsights requires a licensing fee, which varies in price based on the services you require.

Matomo

Matomo (www.matomo.org) introduces itself as the alternative to Google Analytics (which is far and away the most popular analytics tool in the blogosphere). Matomo's biggest selling point is that, unlike Google, they do not use the data collected from your blog for their own purposes. Their focus is on the privacy of both you, the blog owner, as well as your readers.

Similar to Google Analytics, Matomo provides information about who is visiting your site, where they're coming to your site from, and how long they're staying there once they arrive.

TECHNICAL STUFF

Matomo's pricing is based on both where you host the software as well as the amount of traffic your blog receives.

Semrush

Semrush (www.semrush.com) is an incredibly robust tool that goes far beyond web traffic analysis and into SEO, content distribution, social media management, and more.

REMEMBER

TECHNICAL STUFF

This is not a tool that a beginning blogger or hobbyist will likely ever require, but for someone who is looking to take their blogging success to the next level, Semrush may be the perfect web analysis tool.

Semrush offers a free trial, and while accounts are pricey, they do offer a discount if you sign up for an entire year.

Hotjar

Hotjar (www.hotjar.com) is a tool that is meant to complement Google Analytics rather than replace it. Hotjar, shown in Figure 2-6, provides Heatmaps, their visual take on analyzing the actions that your readers take once they arrive on your site. The idea is that by watching reader activity you can learn more about what is working on your site and what is not working.

FIGURE 2-6: Hotjar provides heatmaps to show reader activity on your blog.

While Hotjar does offer paid accounts that come with a variety of features and products, they also offer a free basic account.

Mixpanel

Mixpanel (www.mixpanel.com) is a free tool to blogs up to a certain size and offers paid accounts beyond that. Mixpanel takes a close look at the visitors coming to your site and what they're doing once they arrive, but Mixpanel goes beyond the basics and takes a closer look at areas such as contact forms, subscriptions, and sign-ups.

If you plan to include calls-to-action as part of your blogging experience, you may want to check out Mixpanel.

Crazyegg

Similar to Hotjar, Crazyegg (www.crazyegg.com) uses snippets of code that you install on the pages of your blog to show you a visual representation of visitor activity. This is especially helpful if you have content — such as a subscriber sign-up form — that no one seems to be finding. You can tell where readers are spending their time and move your sign-up form to that location.

TECHNICAL STUFF

Crazyegg allows bloggers to try their resources for free for 30 days before signing up for a paid-for account.

Clicky

Similar to Matomo, Clicky's claim to fame is their focus on the privacy of the website owner and the visitors to the site. Clicky, found at www.clicky.com, offers many similar features to the other services profiled in this chapter.

In order to receive all of the analytics, including heatmaps, you need to open a paid Clicky account. Clicky also offers free accounts with more limited services.

Finteza

While some analytics tools focus on heatmaps, Finteza (www.finteza.com) is all about funnels. This analytics tool claims to help you move blog visitors from the point of hovering over text to clicking to signing up.

Finteza offers a free trial for new users, but you will need to select a paid package to stay with Finteza for the long haul.

Chartbeat

Chartbeat, found at www.chartbeat.com, offers many of the same analytical data as Google Analytics. However, Chartbeat promises to provide real time analytics, helping bloggers to identify trends as they're happening and maximize the potential around them.

Chartbeat, shown in Figure 2-7, offers Basic, Plus, and Premium subscription levels for their paid customers.

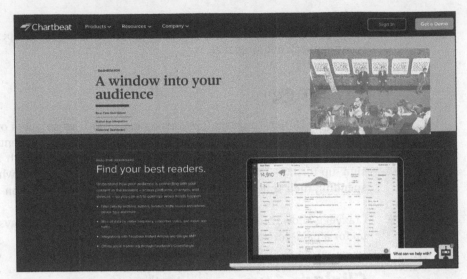

FIGURE 2-7:
Chartbeat offers
real time web
analytics.

Using Your Blog Data

Now that you know the most common data to analyze and a variety of web analytics tool options, you need to know what to do with the data you collect about your blog. The more content you publish on your blog, the longer your blog exists, and the more useful your data will become in terms of trend analysis. The date ranges you select to analyze depend on your individual blogging goals. However, you can start using the data you collect sooner rather than later in a variety of ways. Some common uses for blog data are included in the following sections.

REMEMBER

Always be sure to set the date range you want to track within your web analytics tool.

Harnessing the power of referrer statistics

One of the best ways to grow your blog is by building relationships with other bloggers and people across the social web. Your blog statistics offer a unique way to do exactly that. By visiting the sites that refer traffic to your blog and taking the time to comment or participate in the conversations on those sites, you not only acknowledge the other site, but also start a new relationship that can grow and be beneficial to both parties.

TIP

Did another site owner link to your content from their site? Considering sending them a thank you email or better yet, return the favor!

Publishing content similar to popular content

Review your blog statistics to figure out what posts on your blog are getting the most traffic and then publish more content like those original posts. Chances are good that if those posts are popular, that's the kind of content your audience wants. At the very least, that's the content that's driving people to your blog. If it worked once, it just might work again!

Timing post publishing for high-traffic days

If you have posts that you want to be certain a large audience sees, use your blog statistics to determine which days of the week your blog gets the most traffic by analyzing pageview trends over time. You can then publish the posts that you think have the best chances for being shared and sparking conversation to go live on those days for maximum exposure.

Identifying keywords

By analyzing the top keywords that are driving traffic to your blog from search engines, you can determine which keywords are performing well, which aren't, and which are misused. You can then use that analysis to revise existing content and create new content that focuses on the keywords that drive the best traffic to your blog.

Finding underperforming content

Using the Bounce Rate and Top Exit Pages statistics, you can determine which content on your blog isn't enticing people to stay on your blog longer. You can try to revise that content to make it more useful and appealing.

Calculating online marketing results

If you publish content on your blog for marketing purposes, such as an e-book, a press release, an announcement, or presentation, you can determine how frequently that content was accessed and when it was accessed using your web analytics tool. This allows you to determine how well your promotional efforts are working to drive targeted traffic to those specific pages or content on your blog and use those results to tweak your current or future campaigns.

Keeping Perspective

Don't expect to understand and effectively use web analytics tools immediately. It takes time to understand how to read your blog's data and figure out how to use it effectively to reach your individual blogging goals. In fact, you might want to try more than one web analytics tool and compare the data provided by each to find the one that you're most comfortable with. No two web analytics tools are exactly alike in every way, so don't be surprised if two tools tell very different stories about your blog.

Understanding web analytics limitations

Unfortunately, no web analytics tool in existence can provide completely accurate data about any blog or website. It's unfortunate, but true. The best you can do to analyze your blog's performance is to choose a web analytics tool and stick with it in order to analyze trends over time.

The problem lies in a lack of standards related to web analytics. There simply are no rules in place, so each website is different, browsers are different, users are different, and analytics tools are different. With so many variables, it's no wonder that no single web analytics tool is 100 percent accurate.

The first thing you need to understand is that no two web analytics tools are going to provide the exact same statistics. That inconsistency is just something web analysts accept as a limitation they have to deal with. Typically, web analysts test more than one tool and choose the one that provides the level of detail they need, relying more on trend analysis than specific numbers.

For example, if you use the same web analytics tool for six months and suddenly see a significant jump in the number of visitors to your blog, such as the one shown in Figure 2-8, you can feel confident that a catalyst, such as a link to your blog from a very popular website, caused the jump. However, if you switched back and forth between multiple tools that provide varying data from one day to the next, you might not detect a traffic jump.

REMEMBER

Although web analytics is an inconsistent and imprecise science, you can create a semblance of consistency by choosing a tool and sticking with it over time.

Remembering not to sweat the numbers

It can be easy to get caught up in your blog's statistics, but try not to do so. It will drive you crazy, and it can take up a lot of time that could be better invested in creating great content and building relationships across the social web. Try to refrain from checking your blog's statistics every day, at least during the first few months of your blog's lifespan. Instead, focus on publishing content and check your blog statistics once a week. Over time, focusing on trend analysis will help you refine your blogging strategy more so than worrying about daily traffic fluctuations.

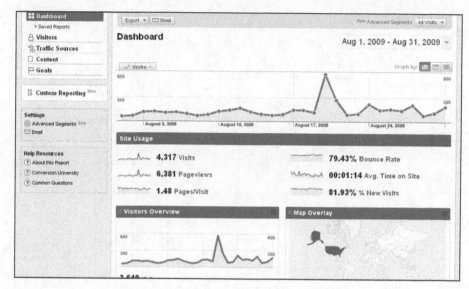

FIGURE 2-8:
A blog statistic anomaly.

However, throughout your blog's lifecycle, you will undoubtedly test different techniques to boost traffic, and you should analyze those tactics more closely using the statistics provided in your web analytics tool. How else will you know whether those efforts produced positive results?

REMEMBER

The key to blogging success is developing a strong, loyal community around your blog. Short-term traffic jumps are nice, but if those visitors don't come back, short-term jumps don't help your blog much overall. Try to focus on long-term growth rather than short-lived jumps.

You can find out much more about growing your blog in Book 6.

IN THIS CHAPTER

» Creating robust content

» Utilizing free online tools

» Writing on-trend posts

» Using keywords to draw in readers

» Focusing on readability

Chapter **3**

Enhancing Content

As bloggers we sometimes get caught up in the technical side of the craft, focusing on widgets and plugins and blog themes — oh my! But the heart of blogging resides in the content. Great content attracts readers and provides a space for community to grow through interaction in the comment sections of posts. It is certainly important to take the time to create and tweak the platform itself, but you then need to focus on crafting great content that draws readers in, holds their attention, and invites conversation. Ideally, your blog will keep its readers wanting more!

This chapter takes a look at a sampling of the tools available to help with content creation from the writing of click-worthy post titles to the editing of post content. Tools are also available to monitor what topics are post-worthy at any given time and to show you what keywords are most likely to place those posts in front of new readers.

Asking the Question with Quora

Creating great content and delivering that content consistently is one of the best ways to find success in the blogosphere. As mentioned in Chapter 2 of Book 1, even the most prolific writer can find themselves with a bad case of writer's block. Every blogger needs to be prepared with a variety of ways to find inspiration for new content and learn what potential readers are interested in at any given time.

One way to do just that is to spend time on Quora (www.quora.com). Quora, shown in Figure 3-1, describes itself as "a place to share knowledge and better understand the world." Put more simply, it's an online platform where users can ask questions and receive answers. Users can upvote the answers that they believe are higher quality and downvote answers that they believe are poor responses to the question that was asked. While there are moderators who monitor reported content, the upvoting and downvoting process results in the community self-moderating and highlighting the higher-quality responses.

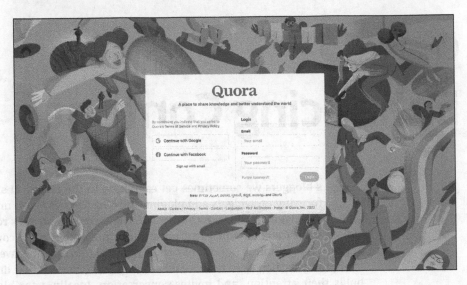

FIGURE 3-1:
Quora is the online home of questions and answers.

Asking a question

Sometimes the best way to find blog post ideas is to poll your readers, but what do you do when you're just starting out and only have a small, or maybe non-existent, audience to poll? Also, if you're hoping to draw in new readers, polling the existing readers may not be the best course of action.

Bloggers can use Quora to ask any question they'd like, not only receiving a variety of answers, but also watching to see which answers are upvoted for popularity. Questions you may want to ask include general questions such as what type of content they like to read as well as specific questions about niche blog topics. Some bloggers turn to Quora for help with round-up style posts, blog posts that contain lists of related content curated from readers or other content creators, as shown in Figure 3-2. For example, round-ups include topics such as:

» Favorite childhood chapter book

» Best movie seen in a theater in the last year

» Favorite ride at Walt Disney World

» Best meal you've ever eaten out

» What to make with one pound of ground beef

» Most clever ways to ask someone out on a date

TIP

It's best to let Quora users know if you're going to be including their answers in a blog post! You may even want to give them the opportunity to share a link to their own blog, which you can use in your post.

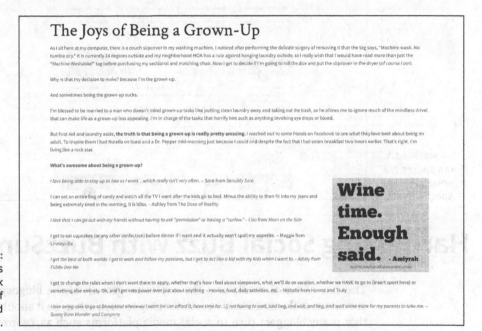

FIGURE 3-2:
Round-up posts contain feedback from a variety of people around one topic.

Reading what's popular

Some days you may sit down to write a blog post and not even know what questions to ask to help you get started with content ideas! Quora is a great place to go to see what questions others are asking and what topics are on people's minds at that moment.

One place to start is in Quora Spaces, topic-based gathering spots within Quora, shown in Figure 3-3. Look for topics related to your blog content area to read conversations that people are having related to that subject area. You can also take a look at the Home feed of current questions being asked and answered.

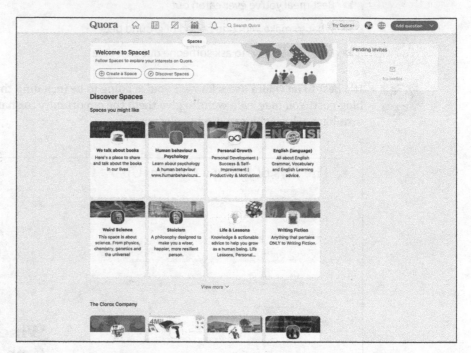

FIGURE 3-3:
Quora Spaces are organized around specific topics.

Harnessing Social Buzz with BuzzSumo

The rise of social media and the explosive growth of the blogosphere happened simultaneously, and likely in relationship to each other, so it should be no surprise that many bloggers turn to social media platforms such as Twitter and Facebook to work on content ideas for their blogs. Going from one platform to another can be time consuming, and what you see based on your friends and followers may be a unique echo chamber compared to what's popular on the platforms in general.

BuzzSumo (www.buzzsumo.com) is a tool that helps users to discover what topics are currently buzzing — or popular — across social media platforms. Shown in Figure 3-4, BuzzSumo offers a free trial, a free account option, and paid options for users interested in more features.

FIGURE 3-4:
BuzzSumo helps
bloggers discover
popular topics
across social
media.

BuzzSumo's Content Analyzer, shown in Figure 3-5, allows users to search social media platforms and other web content for specific topic areas. You can set search filters to narrow your search around characteristics such as when it was published and in what language it was published. BuzzSumo recommends that you begin your searches by casting a wide net and then narrow down your topic as you go.

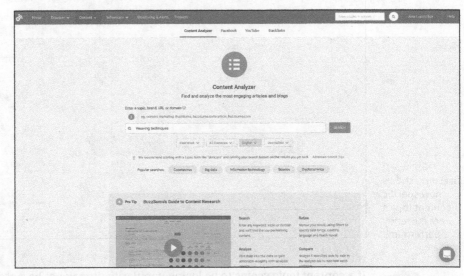

FIGURE 3-5:
Use the
BuzzSumo
Content Analyzer
to create better
blog content.

The Content Analyzer results, shown in Figure 3-6, show what content has been created in the last six months in the United States around the searched topic, weaving techniques. Results include information about engagement on specific social media platforms including Facebook, Twitter, Pinterest, and Reddit.

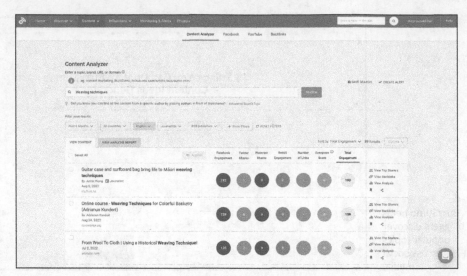

FIGURE 3-6:
Content Analyzer results show content titles and social media engagement.

BuzzSumo also offers a deeper dive into the Content Analyzer results (Figure 3-7) so that you can see both how a topic's popularity has waxed and waned over time as well as how popular it is on specific social media platforms.

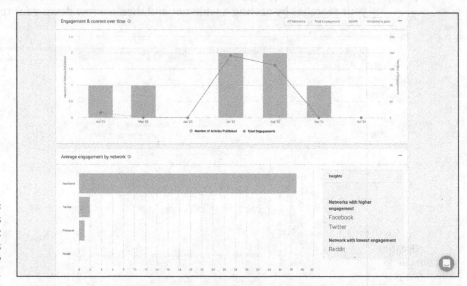

FIGURE 3-7:
BuzzSumo shows how specific content topics are currently performing.

TIP

If a content topic seems to be losing popularity, it may not be a great idea for your next blog post. Likewise, if the topic you want to write about isn't performing well on one particular social media platform, that may be an indication that you shouldn't spend much time and effort promoting that content on that particular platform.

Sizing Up the Competition

One of the main aspects of blogging that makes the blogosphere a unique corner of the web is the sense of community among bloggers as well as readers. So, the idea of competition may be a little tough to reconcile with this image of a happy community of colleagues. It's important to clarify that *competition* is referring to other blogs that are trying to reach — or are successfully reaching — the same target audience as you. These may be bloggers who write in the same niche or simply appeal to the same demographic. And in the blogosphere, competitors are often also collaborators, friends, contacts, and maybe even contributors on each other's blog. So as you read this section, think of the word competition in a friendly sense!

With that said, it *is* important to keep your finger on the pulse of what's going on around the blogosphere if you are interested in knowing what content readers are hoping to find and returning to read. In order to size up the competition, you need to start by identifying those sites. One of the easiest ways to do that is by visiting your favorite search engine, such as Google or Bing, and typing in your content area and the word blog. For example, Figure 3-8 shows a quick Google search to find blogs about parenting toddlers. The results are a great place to start to know which blogs in that niche are popular and what type of content is performing well on their sites.

FIGURE 3-8: Use search engines to find other blogs writing similar content to yours.

TIP

Once you've found other blogs in the same content space as you, it's helpful to know which keywords are performing well for them. While your content must always be your own, it's certainly helpful to have a general sense of what's working well on other blogs. There are a number of tools available to monitor keyword performance, but the majority of them come at a cost, sometimes a quite high cost. If money is no object in your quest for the best keyword analysis to help with your content creation, check out iSpionage (www.ispionage.com), shown in Figure 3-9, or Ahrefs (www.ahrefs.com), shown in Figure 3-10. Both offer a variety of tools to help you size up the competition on the professional level!

FIGURE 3-9:
Monitor keyword performance with iSpionage.

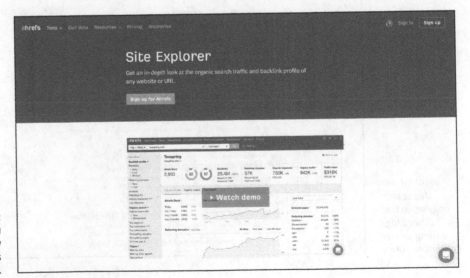

FIGURE 3-10:
Ahrefs helps you determine how competing blogs are performing.

Thankfully, you don't need to pay for a professional service to determine how content is performing on similar blogs to your own. You simply need to visit those blogs. Michelle of Honest and Truly (www.honestandtruly.com) includes a list of her most popular content (shown in Figure 3-11) right on her home page. Nancy at Mama Maven (www.mamamaven.com) includes the number of comments a post has received under her post title making it easy to see which posts are resonating with readers (see Figure 3-12).

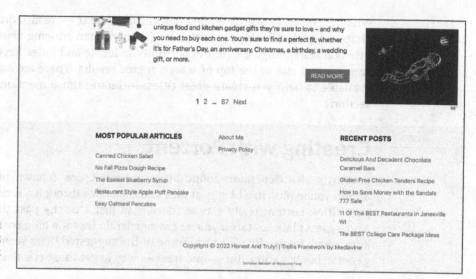

MOST POPULAR ARTICLES

Canned Chicken Salad

No Fail Pizza Dough Recipe

The Easiest Blueberry Syrup

Restaurant Style Apple Puff Pancake

Easy Oatmeal Pancakes

About Me

Privacy Policy

RECENT POSTS

Delicious And Decadent Chocolate Caramel Bars

Gluten Free Chicken Tenders Recipe

How to Save Money with the Sandals 777 Sale

11 Of The BEST Restaurants in Janesville WI

The BEST College Care Package Ideas

Copyright © 2022 Honest And Truly! | Trellis Framework by Mediavine

Exclusive Member of Mediavine Food

FIGURE 3-11: Look for a list of a blog's most popular content.

FAMILY TRIP TO PHILLY: CRAYOLA IDEAWORKS AT THE FRANKLIN INSTITUTE

By The Mama Maven — 275 Comments

This post is sponsored by Epson. As always, all opinions are my own. There are affiliate links in this post. Ever take a trip to Philadelphia with your kids? Epson recently asked my family and I to check out Crayola IDEAWorks at the Franklin Institute in Philly recently and it was amazing. I'm a ...

INSTANT POT RED LENTIL SOUP WITH KALE

By The Mama Maven — 3 Comments

This post contains affiliate links. I'm a huge fan of lentils, especially lentil soups. But since I adore my Instant Pot, could I adapt my favorite red lentil soup recipe for it? Why yes, I could totally make Instant Pot Red Lentil Soup and it came out fantastic. This is based on a recipe that my ...

FIGURE 3-12: The number of comments a post receives can indicate its popularity.

Writing Great Titles

REMEMBER

You can't judge a book by its cover, and you can't judge a post by its title. Unfortunately, that doesn't mean that blog post titles don't matter. Your post's titles are the first indicator to your readers that you've written new content that they want to read. A well-written title is a hook, drawing the readers in, convincing them to click through an email or a link.

When it comes to search engine optimization (SEO — read more about this in Chapter 1 of this Book), post titles are far more than enticing words. A blog post title is a search engine's first opportunity to locate and index keywords, helping your content rise to the top of search engine results. There are a variety of tools available to help you create great titles, including those mentioned in the next sections.

Creating with Portent

Portent's Idea Generator, found at www.portent.com (shown in Figure 3-13), allows you to plug in a blog post idea and then click through a series of suggested post titles. Portent really acts as more than just a catchy post title creator. It's also a great place to start if you've got a general idea for a blog post but you aren't sure where to go with that idea. Some of the suggested titles seem unrelated and generic, but it's still a fun — and free! — way to get those creative juices flowing.

In Figure 3-13, I typed in the content idea of vintage sofas. Figure 3-14 shows an example of a Portent suggested blog title.

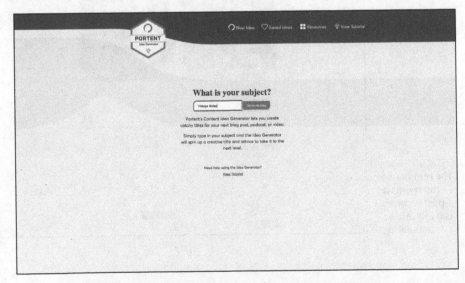

FIGURE 3-13:
Create fun post titles with Portent.

FIGURE 3-14:
Let Portent
suggest where to
go with a general
blog post idea.

Finding ideas with HubSpot

Another free tool for post title generating is the HubSpot Blog Ideas Generator (`www.hubspot.com/blog-topic-generator`) as shown in Figure 3-15. Simply plug in any noun to get started, and then add up to five additional nouns.

FIGURE 3-15:
Use HubSpot to
create new blog
post ideas.

Once you've added as many nouns as you would like, a screen will appear with a week's worth of blog post ideas, as shown in Figure 3-16. If you create a HubSpot account, you will have access to additional blog post ideas.

FIGURE 3-16:
Receive a week's worth of blog post ideas without creating a HubSpot account.

Riding the Trends

There was likely something specific that inspired you to join the blogosphere. Perhaps you have a love of writing or a passion for a particular topic. Maybe you've always wanted to be part of the online community. Whatever it was that brought you to this journey, that is probably what has the biggest influence on your content. That doesn't mean that you can't use trending topics and buzzing conversations to inspire and enhance your post content!

TIP

Riding the wave of trending subject matter can help draw you out of writer's block, pull in new readership, and add to your already great subject matter. The key to using this method to enhance your content is knowing how and where to stay up to date with all that is going on in the online world.

Trending on Twitter

Twitter (www.twitter.com) is a social media platform that is known for its trending topics lists. If you want to know what people are talking about on the Internet at any given time, head to Twitter on your favorite browser or via the Twitter app and click on Explore, as shown in Figure 3-17. Trends can be sorted based on geography as well as topical areas such as politics and entertainment. If you choose to write content inspired by a Twitter trend, be sure to act fast! As quickly as a Twitter trend appears, it is gone.

FIGURE 3-17:
Click Explore
to browse the
trending topics
on Twitter.

Exploring on LinkedIn

It may surprise you to know that LinkedIn (www.linkedin.com), the professional social media network, utilizes hashtags much like most of the social media world! The platform is a great place to see what others are writing and talking about around any one topic at any given time. The best way to monitor these conversations on LinkedIn is by searching hashtags related to that topic.

To search a hashtag on LinkedIn, take the following steps:

1. Point your web browser to www.linkedin.com as shown in Figure 3-18.

2. In the search field at the top of the page, type in a hashtag related to the topic you want to search.

   For example, if you are interested in reading the latest LinkedIn posts related to affiliate marketing, type #affiliatemarketing in the search field.

FIGURE 3-18:
Search hashtags
on LinkedIn.

3. **Use the horizontal navigation bar on the results page to filter results, as shown in Figure 3-19.**

LinkedIn also posts a running list of the day's top professional news and stories (Figure 3-20) in the right sidebar of the home page, another great place to monitor what topics are trending and may be the perfect topic for your next blog post!

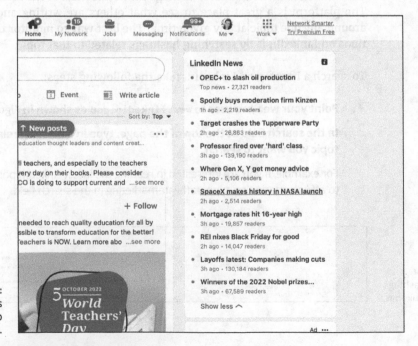

Browsing Google Trends

As mentioned in Book 1, Chapter 2, Google Trends is always a great way to discover which topics are most popular with readers at any given time. If you're hoping to enhance your blog content with posts focused on topics that are being searched frequently, point your web browser to `https://trends.google.com` and start searching!

Not sure where to start? Scroll down the page to see what is recently trending or read the latest stories and highlights.

REMEMBER

If a topic is trending, then it is likely that there are many bloggers jumping on that trend. Try to find a unique spin on the topic so that you stand out in the crowd.

Building in Keywords

In an online world where content is king, keywords are the gateway to the kingdom. You can write the best blog post ever created and if no one can find it, no one will read it. Even the least SEO conscious blogger should take the time to enhance their content with the occasional keyword strategy in order to help that great content be seen and shared. While SEO is discussed in this Book, this section takes a look at just a couple of the tools available to help build keywords into your content strategy. After all, you deserve to have your wonderful content read!

Writing with Keyword Tool

Keyword Tool (`www.keywordtool.io`), shown in Figure 3-21, is a free online tool that allows you to input a search term and find a list of the keywords related to that term that are being searched most frequently. The tool allows you to narrow your search down by platform as well as by geographical region. Select some of the related keywords to include in your content in order to increase the likelihood of that content appearing in search engine results.

Optimizing with Yoast

Yoast (`www.yoast.com`), shown in Figure 3-22, is another popular tool to help enhance your content with SEO-friendly keywords. One of the most popular WordPress plugins, and available in a free format, Yoast helps you optimize your use of keywords in your content. Once installed, Yoast will evaluate each of the posts you create and make suggestions about ways to improve that content. Remember doing that keyword research with the Keyword Tool? Yoast is where you can put those keywords to good use! Yoast also helps enhance your content by analyzing your text for readability, which is discussed in more depth in the following section.

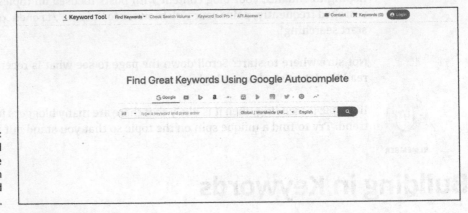

FIGURE 3-21:
Use Keyword Tool to enhance your content with frequently used search terms.

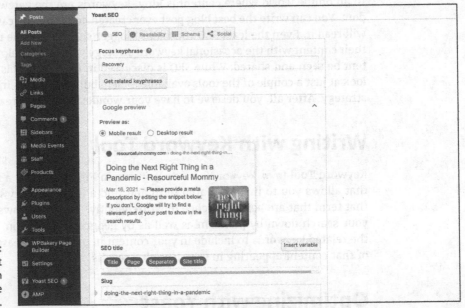

FIGURE 3-22:
The Yoast WordPress plugin helps enhance content.

Checking Your Readability

While many bloggers join the blogosphere because of a love of writing, there are honestly just as many bloggers who dive in because they enjoy the other aspects — from the community to the website building to their chosen content area. But even bloggers who don't come to the table with a strong writing background should strive to write content that is readable for the average blog visitor.

The best blog posts are those that present great ideas in a way that the average reader can easily consume and with limited grammar and spelling mistakes. If all of this is giving you flashbacks of spelling bees and sentence diagramming, take heart! Tools are available to take you from a writing class dropout to a content superstar, as explored in the next sections.

Editing with Hemingway

Hemingway Editor (www.hemingwayapp.com) is a desktop app that uses an algorithm to analyze your writing and give it a score based on the following:

» readability

» grammar

» spelling

» passive versus active voice

» style

The paid version of the app integrates with WordPress and Medium, allowing you to edit prose in Hemingway Editor and then share directly to your WordPress or Medium blog. You can also share directly from Hemingway Editor to other colleagues such as a site editor or members of your blogging team. The free tool, shown in Figure 3-23, allows you to write and edit directly from your favorite web browser.

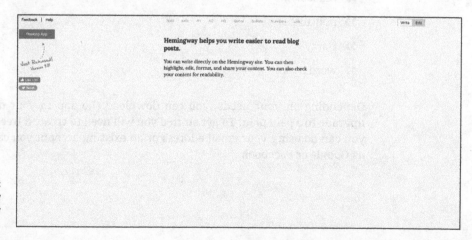

FIGURE 3-23:
Write directly
in Hemingway
Editor.

Once you have written your content, click Edit, as shown in Figure 3-24, to receive a readability score along with specific feedback about the content you've written.

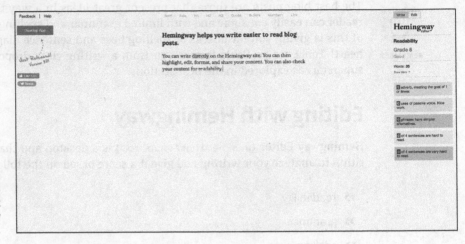

Proofing with Grammarly

Grammarly (www.grammarly.com) is a free online tool that helps check your writing for the following:

>> spelling

>> grammar

>> tone

>> readability

>> punctuation

>> clarity

>> word choice

Depending on your needs, you can download the app to your desktop or even upgrade to a paid plan. To get started you will need to create a free account, which you can do using your email address or an existing account you can connect such as Google or Facebook.

Grammarly, shown in Figure 3-25, allows you to set goals for your writing and provides you with an overall score for each post. For example, if you would like to sound more authoritative in your blog posts, Grammarly will assess your writing to determine if you need to make adjustments to achieve that goal. Or perhaps you're used to academic writing and hoping to come across as more friendly and conversational in your blog posts. Whatever your goal, Grammarly can help you achieve it!

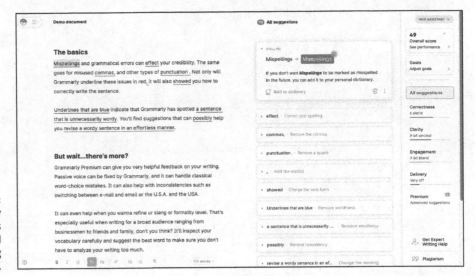

FIGURE 3-25: Grammarly provides feedback based on your writing goals.

IN THIS CHAPTER

» Using online tools to organize posts

» Creating blogging task lists

» Keeping track of your time

» Working efficiently and effectively

» Writing without visual distractions

Chapter 4

Staying Organized

When I began blogging in 2008, I was a stay-at-home mom of two small children, looking for a creative outlet apart from coloring with crayons next to my kids. I have always loved writing and taught middle school English prior to becoming a mom, so when a friend suggested blogging, I jumped right in. At first it was purely a creative pursuit, a chance to publish whatever my heart desired and as often as an idea came to me! However, I quickly figured out that keeping track of fleeting ideas was tricky in my busy life, and posting on a regular schedule was tough to do without, well, a regular schedule.

Thankfully, it is far easier today than it was in 2008 for bloggers to get and stay organized. There are online tools — many of them free — available to help you with everything from organizing images to managing your time. If an idea for a great blog post comes to mind, you can grab your mobile device and jot it down digitally instead of hoping that you'll remember it later when you actually have time to write and post.

This chapter takes a brief look at just some of the tools available to help you stay organized as you launch your blog and watch it grow!

Collecting Your Content Components

In the early days of blogging, posts very much resembled online journals. Each post would read like a daily chronicle with a series of paragraphs, a date at the top, and a place for readers to respond in comments. While some bloggers still write for the sake of personal journaling, long gone are the days of blog posts comprised solely of words. Posts today are filled with dynamic content from videos embedded within the posts themselves to beautiful photos and graphics.

TIP

To learn more about blog content that goes beyond words, check out Book 8!

If your desk looks anything like mine, you've got file folders with lists of things to remember and stacks of items you don't want to misplace. In the digital world, you've still got lists and stacks, but instead of a physical space in your home office, you've got your computer desktop. Without the use of organizational tools, your computer's desktop could quickly look like my home office desktop — cluttered and unhelpful!

The trick to avoiding this pitfall and instead stay organized while you work on the writing process is to lean into the tools available to help you organize your blog post content components until they're needed. The following are two simple yet powerful tools to help you do just that.

Gathering with Dropbox

Dropbox (www.dropbox.com), shown in Figure 4-1, is an online tool available via your favorite web browser, a desktop app, and a free mobile app. This free tool is most commonly used as a storage device, a place to upload photos off of your mobile phone or store files safely away from your computer's hard drive. Because you can sync your device with Dropbox and set up your account to automatically back up files and images to Dropbox, many people think of this tool as mainly a failsafe for important files. But Dropbox is so much more, especially when it comes to organization.

To get started with Dropbox, point your favorite web browser to www.dropbox.com. If this is your first time using Dropbox and you do not currently have an account, create an account in one of the following ways:

>> Sign in using your current Google account

>> Sign in using your current Apple account

>> Create a new account by selecting create an account from the sign-in page

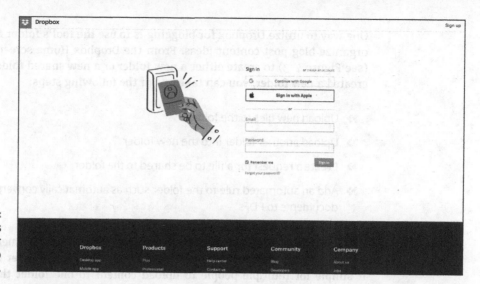

FIGURE 4-1:
Dropbox is
available via your
favorite web
browser.

Dropbox offers free accounts with restrictions based on storage capabilities. Pricing for paid accounts, as shown in Figure 4-2, increases based on both the number of account users as well as the amount of storage available for use.

FIGURE 4-2:
Dropbox offers
free accounts as
well as a range of
paid options.

One way to utilize Dropbox for blogging is to use the tool's folder functionality to organize blog post content ideas. From the Dropbox Home screen, select Create (see Figure 4-3) to create either a new folder or a new shared folder. Once you've created a new folder, you can take one of the following steps:

>> Upload new files to the folder

>> Upload another folder into the new folder

>> Create a request for a file to be shared to the folder

>> Add an automated rule to the folder such as automatically converting all documents to PDFs

TIP

Dropbox is a fantastic tool for bloggers who either write as a member of a team blog or manage a blog with multiple authors. The shared folder function makes it simple for multiple people to upload content to one folder that can then be accessed by every member of the team.

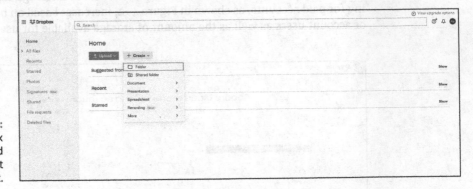

FIGURE 4-3:
Create Dropbox folders related to specific post content.

Once you have created folders in Dropbox, you can organize them into a hierarchy. For example, perhaps you know that you want to devote a section of your blog to recipes. When you first begin to gather ideas for content related to that subject area, it is likely that you'll pull in all sorts of very loosely related content components. There might be a really great recipe sent to you by your grandmother or maybe a particularly well-taken photograph of your attempt at a favorite cake recipe. To start, these documents and images may all belong in one folder titled "Recipes." However, over time you may find that you're better served by subfolders such as one titled "Dessert Recipes" and another titled "Heirloom Recipes." Dropbox allows you to break out content into folders within folders making it easy for you to place your gathered content components and ideas into the most easily accessed and clearly organized folder locations over time, as shown in Figure 4-4.

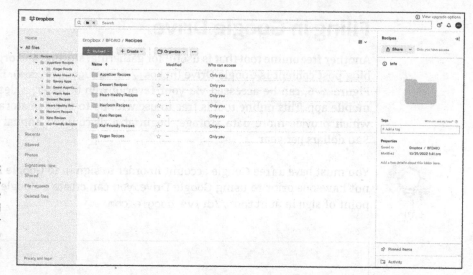

Dropbox not only allows you to gather existing files into easily organized folders in order to help you prepare to create blog content. It actually allows you to create that content right there within the tool (shown in Figure 4-5)! Tools that help you write content without the visual distractions found within many blogging platforms are discussed later in this chapter. Dropbox serves that purpose as well by allowing you to create documents within the Dropbox tool itself. This functionality makes it possible for you to write content without needing to leave the platform and then return to upload that content back into a Dropbox folder. This not only helps you organize but also saves you time, making Dropbox a powerhouse blogging tool!

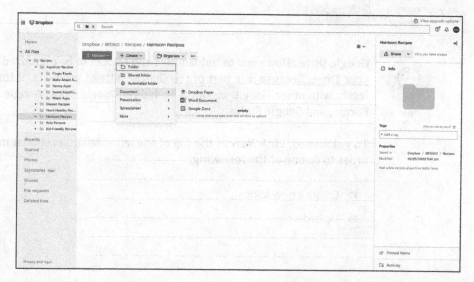

Staying Organized

Filing in Google Drive

Another free online tool that is useful for gathering, storing, and organizing future blog post content is Google Drive (https://drive.google.com). Drive, shown in Figure 4-6, can be accessed via your favorite web browser, a desktop app, or a mobile app. This online tool is free to use with up to 15 GB of storage. Paid plans, which provide more data storage, begin at a discounted annual price of about $20 dollars per year.

TIP

You must have a free Google account in order to sign in to Google Drive. If you do not have one prior to using Google Drive, you can create a Google account at the point of sign in at https://drive.google.com.

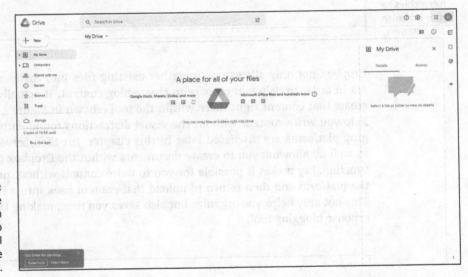

FIGURE 4-6:
Google Drive is available on your desktop computer as well as your mobile device.

TIP

Google Drive allows you to upload files and folders to be organized into folders on your Drive. Because it is part of the Google suite of products, it integrates seamlessly with other Google products including Google Docs, Google Sheets, Google Forms, and Google Slides.

To get started, click New at the top of the left sidebar, as shown in Figure 4-7, in order to do one of the following:

- » Create a new folder
- » Upload a file

>> Upload a folder

>> Access another application in the Google suite

FIGURE 4-7:
Click New in
Google Drive to
get started.

Similar to Dropbox, discussed previously in this chapter, Google Drive allows you to pull together content that you may want to use in a future post including photos, text documents, and graphics. Drive serves as a place to organize that content until you are ready to use it in a post. It is also a great way to store and organize post content that you may wish to reuse in the future, such as images for a recipe round up or a parenting reflection post looking back on past vacations.

Also similar to Dropbox, Google Drive makes it very easy to share organized content and collaborate within the tool. This is especially helpful when writing as part of a team blog or when managing a team of writers. It's also helpful if you need to share a post with an editor in order to receive feedback before posting and publishing. Right clicking on any file opens up a menu of actions that you can take related to that file, as shown in Figure 4-8.

One of the options that appears when you right click a file is the option to share access to that file, as shown in Figure 4-9. You can share access by providing an email address of your intended recipient. You can also change the settings on the file so that anyone you provide with a link to that file can access it.

Staying Organized

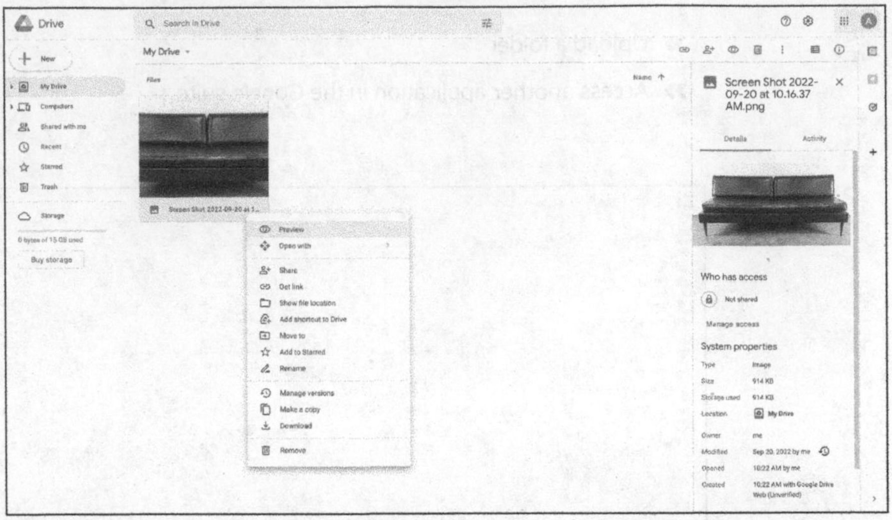

FIGURE 4-8:
Right click to
access a menu of
file options.

FIGURE 4-9:
Share Google
Drive files with
other blog post
collaborators.

When adding collaborators to a file in Google Drive, you can assign them one of
the following roles (as shown in Figure 4-10):

>> Viewer, only able to view the content

>> Commenter, able to make comments on the content

>> Editor, able to edit the content directly

Formulating Tasks

I have to admit that when it comes to my to-do list, if I don't see a task written down, it is unlikely that I am going to remember to do that task. Most bloggers don't join the blogosphere and immediately make blogging their full-time job, which means that for most of us, blogging is just one of the many aspects of our busy lives. We've got to remember to write that next post in our blog post series, send out a prize to a blog contest winner, and moderate comments all while still navigating our daily lives and day jobs!

Thankfully there are tools available to help you track all of those blogging to-dos, including the two tools featured in the following sections.

Todoist

Todoist (Figure 4-11), found at www.todoist.com, is an online tool that allows you to organize task lists and manage projects. Todoist can be used on both your desktop as well as your mobile device via the free app, which is available for both Apple and Android devices. Accounts are free up to a certain number of projects and then can be upgraded to a paid account based on individual or team needs.

In order to create a free account, take the following steps:

1. Point your favorite web browser to www.todoist.com.

2. Select Start for free in the upper right-hand corner, as shown in Figure 4-11.

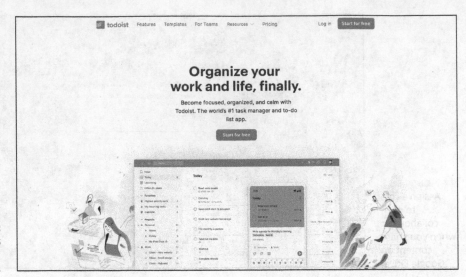

FIGURE 4-11:
Todoist is
found at www.
todoist.com.

3. Create a new account using one of the following sign-up options, as shown in Figure 4-12:

- Google account
- Facebook account
- Apple account
- Email address

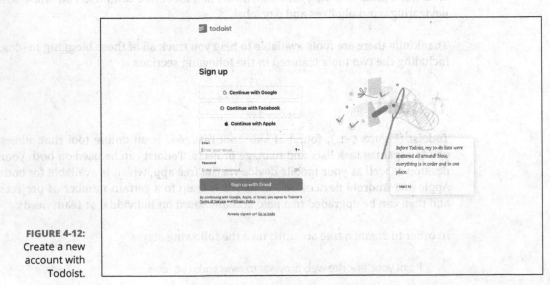

FIGURE 4-12:
Create a new
account with
Todoist.

Todoist then walks you through a series of questions regarding your intended use of the tool in order to help get you started.

Once your account is set up, you can begin creating projects by clicking on the three-line menu button in the upper left-hand corner of the screen, as shown in Figure 4-13. Selecting the plus sign in the upper right-hand corner allows you to create a new task. When creating a new task, you can choose to also do the following:

» Set task reminders

» Select task priority level

» Add labels to help you organize similar tasks

Adding labels may be helpful if, for example, you are creating a series of tasks related to a specific blog post series, you may want to give each task the same label to help you pull those tasks together into one project folder. You can also give each task a due date to help keep you on task and following a set timeline.

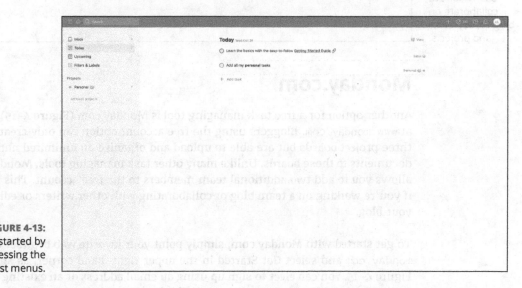

FIGURE 4-13:
Get started by accessing the Todoist menus.

Project folders and tasks can be shared with other blog team collaborators, as shown in Figure 4-14, as well as assigned to individual team members. Collaborators are invited via email and must have their own Todoist account in order to accept your invitation to collaborate on a task or project.

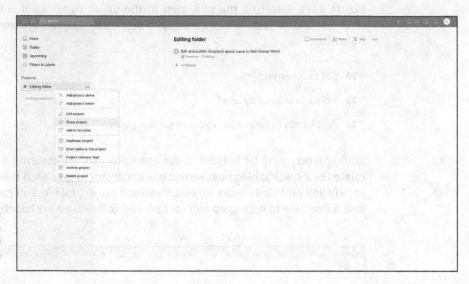

FIGURE 4-14:
Use Todoist to collaborate on blog-related tasks and projects.

Monday.com

Another option for a free task managing tool is Monday.com (Figure 4-15), found at www.monday.com. Bloggers using the free account option can only create up to three project boards but are able to upload and organize an unlimited number of documents to those boards. Unlike many other task managing tools, Monday.com allows you to add two additional team members to the free account. This is ideal if you're working on a team blog or collaborating with other writers or editors on your blog.

To get started with Monday.com, simply point your favorite web browser to www.monday.com and select Get Started in the upper right-hand corner, as shown in Figure 4-15. You can elect to sign up using an email address or an existing Google account. Once signed in, Monday.com will ask you a series of questions regarding your intended use of the tool. Bloggers can select a content calendar as one of the tools they'd like to use to get started, as shown in Figure 4-16.

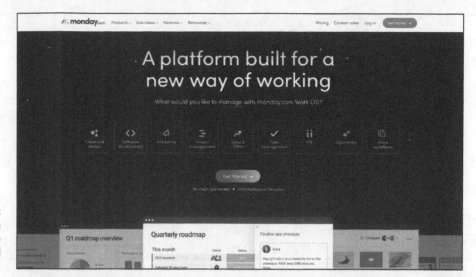

FIGURE 4-15:
Monday.com
allows you to
organize and
track tasks.

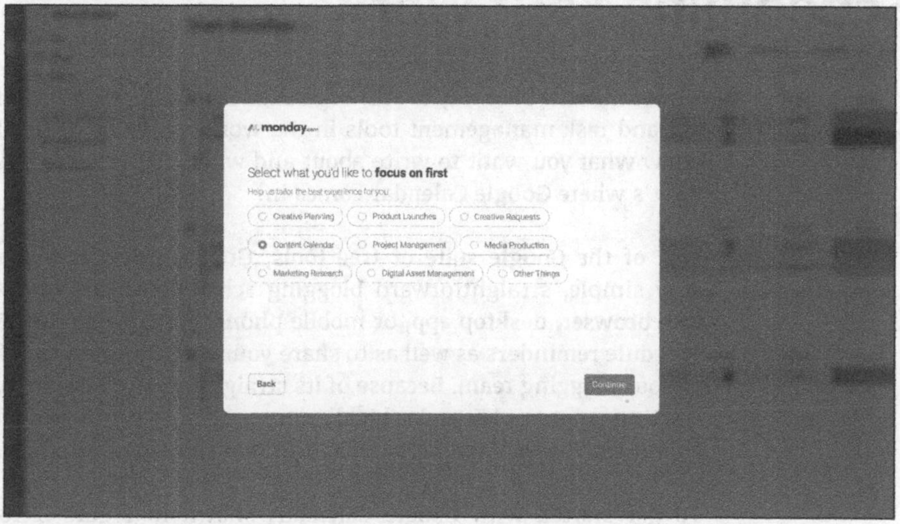

FIGURE 4-16:
Monday.com
helps bloggers
manage a content
calendar.

While it's possible to customize your task management boards on Monday.com, the tool also provides a board based on your answers to the set-up questions so that you have a place to start. For example, I signed up to organize tasks on a content calendar, and Monday.com created a content calendar task board for me, as shown in Figure 4-17.

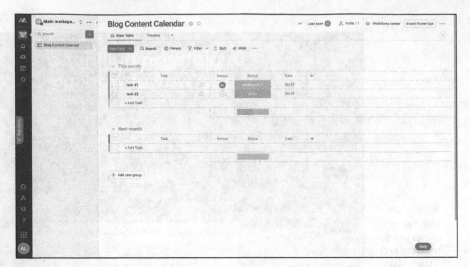

FIGURE 4-17:
Monday.com
creates an
organization
board to get new
users started.

Scheduling Your Work

Sometimes the best way to stay organized is to keep it simple. All the file organizing and task management tools in the world won't be of much use if you don't know what you want to write about and when you want to publish that content. That's where Google Calendar comes in!

Part of the Google suite of free tools, Google Calendar allows you to create a very simple, straightforward blogging schedule on a tool that is available via web browser, desktop app, or mobile phone app. You can use Google Calendar to schedule reminders as well as to share your content calendar with other members of your blogging team. Because of its straightforward simplicity, it is a wonderful starting point to plan and schedule content before turning to more robust tools to create and manage the tasks related to that calendar.

To get started with Google Calendar, shown in Figure 4-18, point your web browser to `https://calendar.google.com`. A free Google account is required for sign in, but you can create an account to get started if you do not already have an existing one.

To create a new calendar, click on Other Calendars on the left sidebar (see Figure 4-19) and select Create new calendar.

You will then be able to give your new calendar the name and a description, as shown in Figure 4-20.

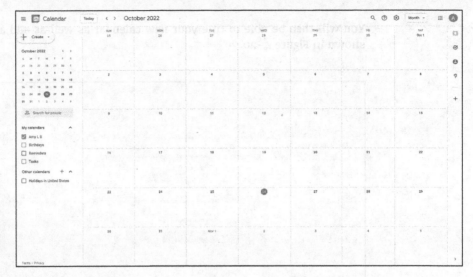

Give your new calendar a name and a description

FIGURE 4-18:
Google Calendar allows you to create a simple content calendar to schedule posts.

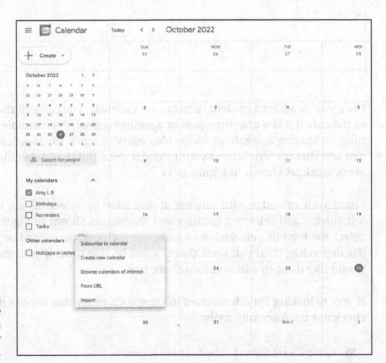

FIGURE 4-19:
Create new calendars from the left sidebar menu.

Staying Organized

You will then be able to title your new calendar as well as add a description, as shown in Figure 4-20.

Once you've added a content item to your calendar, you can edit that calendar item to indicate if it is a one-time post or a recurring post. For example, if you're planning on sharing a meatless recipe idea every Monday for Meatless Mondays, you can add that content idea to your calendar once and then schedule for it to repeat every week, as shown in Figure 4-21.

Share your calendar with anyone at any time by selecting the calendar on the left sidebar and selecting Settings and sharing, as shown in Figure 4-22. You can select the level of permission to assign to each person invited to see your calendar depending on if you want them to just be able to view your calendar or if you would like them to edit and contribute to it.

TIP

If you're looking for alternatives to Google Calendar that serve a similar purpose, check out the following tools:

>> Apple iCloud Calendar (www.icloud.com)

>> Asana (www.asana.com)

>> Cozi (www.cozi.com)

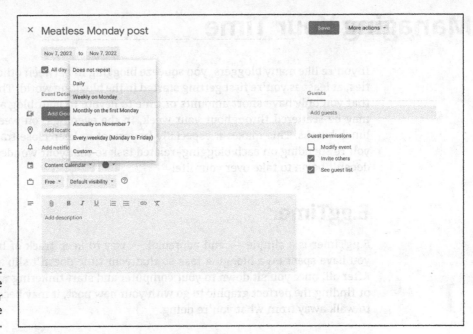

FIGURE 4-21:
Use Google
Calendar
to schedule
recurring posts.

If you're like many bloggers, you squeeze in blogging after your responsibilities, or less, as you've just getting started. In blogging's so odd. That often means that you actually have a more structure routine in place, you find those that may have entered the one from your posts...

...daily on each outgoing-related task...
...for to take over your dail...

...A resistance can diminish until you realize...to figure out just how much time
you have spent on a blog in a day is...that you must blog if you...
...after all, once you sit down to your computer and start imagining that schedule...or finally the perfect graphic to go with your new post, it may be difficult
to walk away from what you're doing.

...fingertips (shown in Figure 4-23), a bunch of...helps you better your...
...starts to slacker from process time for yourself...to, or...regulates, create then
...For example, selecting Pomodoro prompts you to work for...minutes followed
by a 5-minute break once the interval of time passes. An alarm sound is up, an alarm
alerts you to stop working.

» Microsoft Outlook Calendar (https://office.live.com)

» Teamup Calendar (www.teamup.com)

» Zoho Calendar (www.zoho.com)

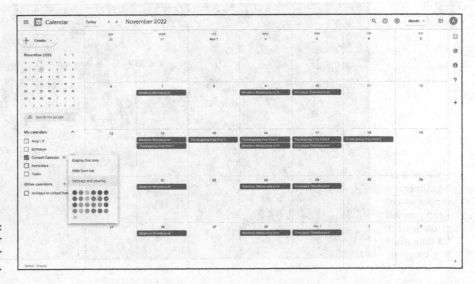

FIGURE 4-22:
Share your
Google Calendar
with anyone.

Managing Your Time

If you're like many bloggers, you squeeze blogging in between other responsibilities, at least as you're first getting started in the blogging world. That often means that you only have short amounts of time to devote to your blog and those times may be scattered throughout your week, in the evenings, on weekends, or over lunch breaks. This makes it especially important to keep close track of how long you're spending on each blogging-related task so that your wonderful new hobby doesn't begin to take over your life!

E.ggTimer

E.ggTimer is a simple — and adorable! — way to keep track of how much time you have spent on a blogging task so that your time doesn't slip away from you. After all, once you sit down to your computer and start tinkering with HTML code or finding the perfect graphic to go with your new post, it may become very tough to walk away from what you're doing.

E.ggTimer (shown in Figure 4-23), found at `https://e.ggtimer.com`, allows users to select from preset time increments of 5, 10, or 15 minutes, create their own custom amount of time to work, or follow a preset work/rest timer routine. For example, selecting Pomodoro prompts you to work for 25 minutes followed by a 5-minute break. Once the amount of time you have selected is up, an alarm alerts you to stop working.

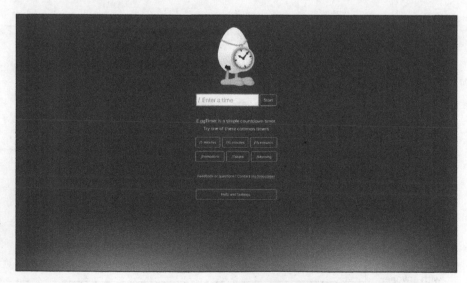

FIGURE 4-23:
E.ggTimer is a simple way to keep yourself from losing track of time while blogging.

Toggl

Toggl, found at www.toggl.com, is a sophisticated and robust tool to help you manage your time beyond only starting and stopping work tasks in a timely manner. Toggl, shown in Figure 4-24, allows you to create a free account using a Google account, Apple account, or email address. There is a free Toggl account option as well as paid options if your needs require more features.

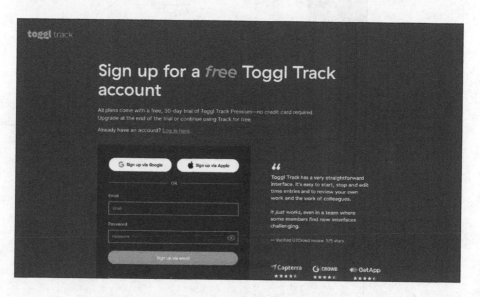

FIGURE 4-24:
Sign up for a free Toggl account.

Toggl is a wonderful tool if you need to keep close track of exactly how long you are spending on each blogging task. For example, perhaps you would like to track how much time you spend writing content for your blog on the weeks when you post five out of seven days. You can use Toggl to record starting and stopping times, as shown in Figure 4-25, so that you can look back at the end of the week to see how much time actually went into writing alone. You may find that writing five posts a week takes up more time than you realized and adjust future content calendars accordingly.

Like E.ggTimer, Toggl also works as an online timer. The Toggl timer is located in the upper right-hand corner of the calendar screen. Unlike basic online timers, Toggl is both a timer and a time keeper. You can use Toggl to assign the amount of time you recorded while working to a specific project, a task, or even a billable client. Once you are done working for the day on that associated task, simply click stop on the timer to record on your Toggl calendar the amount of time you spent working, as shown in Figure 4-26.

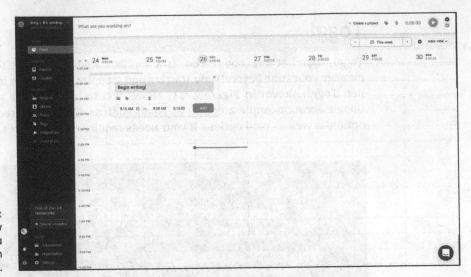

FIGURE 4-25:
Track how much time you spend on each blogging task.

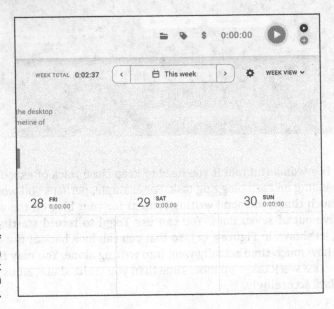

FIGURE 4-26:
Keep track of exactly how much time you've spent working on each task or project.

TIP

Toggl is also helpful if you are blogging for a client and need to track your time for billing purposes.

Freeing Yourself from Distraction

It's one thing to track the amount of time you spend on each blogging task, but it's another issue entirely to work on your blog without distractions so that you can work more efficiently and effectively!

While it is, of course, impossible to work entirely free of distraction, it is possible to write without the distractions that come from writing on a blogging platform. Blogging software has grown and changed in leaps and bounds since the early days of blogging, which means that blog post editors fill the computer screen with reminders of all of your blog's shiny bells and whistles (see Figure 4-27). Media, SEO, comments — oh my! There's so much to see and do when you open your blog's administrative panel to write a great new post.

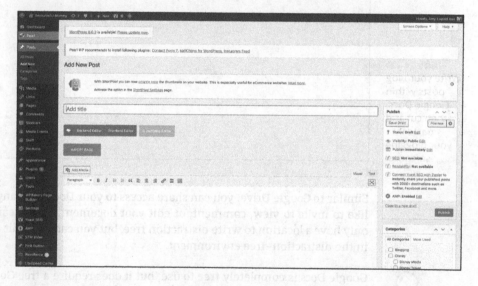

FIGURE 4-27: Blog post creation pages often contain far more than just the tools you need to write the post.

The following tools provide free and easy ways to write that great content without the distraction of everything else happening behind the scenes on your blogging platform. While these tools can't keep you from picking up your phone to text or open your favorite social media app, they are a step in the right — or write! — direction.

Google Docs

Another free tool in the Google suite of tools, Google Docs (`https://docs.google.com`) is a word processing application available via web browser, desktop app, or mobile phone app. Because Google Docs, shown in Figure 4-28, is strictly a word processing tool, it allows you to write and edit without the distractions of blogging tools within your blogging software.

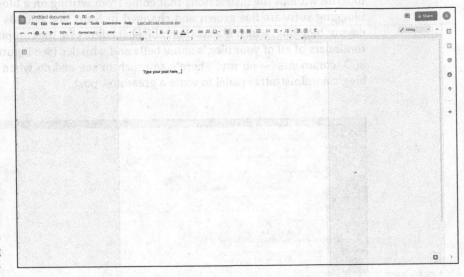

FIGURE 4-28: Write your blog posts within Google Docs, then cut and paste into your blogging software.

Similar to Google Drive, you can share access to your Docs with anyone you would like to invite to view, comment, or edit your document. This means that you not only have a location to write distraction free, but you can also edit and collaborate in the distraction-free environment.

TIP

Google Docs is completely free to use, but it does require a free Google account in order to sign in and begin creating.

When you're ready to post your finished content on your blog, simply cut and paste into your blogging software from Google Docs. Once in your blog's editing software, you can format your text, create headings and paragraphs, and add any media or other dynamic content.

WordPress Distract-Free Editor

For bloggers using WordPress as their blogging software, there is an option to write without the distraction of blogging tools right there within the application itself! WordPress Distract-Free Editor is a place to write new content without visually seeing all that is typically found around the content creation area.

Within the post creation section of the WordPress new post page, look for the arrows pointing in different directions in the upper right-hand corner, as shown in Figure 4-29. By clicking on the arrows, all of the extra menus around your post creation field magically disappear (Figure 4-30) leaving nothing but the space to write your next post. When you're ready to work on SEO or add categories to your content, you can click the arrows again for all of your blogging tools to return!

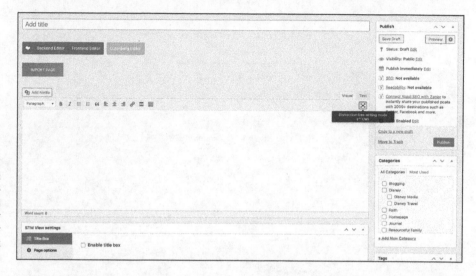

FIGURE 4-29: Distract-Free Editor is found in the upper right-hand corner of the new post creation area.

FIGURE 4-30: WordPress provides an option to write without the visual distraction of other blogging tools.

6

Promoting and Growing Your Blog

Contents at a Glance

Chapter **1**

Secrets to Blogging Success

Taking your blog from launch to success is a process not unlike growing a plant from seed to flower. It takes time, focus, and patience to build a successful blog. Without the necessary commitment in all of those areas, your blog can only grow so far. Just like you must water and nurture a plant, modifying its food and sun intake to ensure it thrives, you must nurture your blog with great content, promotion, and community building in order for it to grow and thrive.

Blogging success comes directly from the time you spend *on* your blog as well as the time you spend *off* your blog, meaning your blog needs great content but also continual promotional efforts by you to ensure that awareness, recognition, and repeat traffic follows. Blogging success depends on more than a site-centric marketing approach. This chapter introduces you to the fundamental secrets that position you for blogging success.

Writing Well

The best bloggers write well. Does that mean you need to be a professional writer or hold an advanced degree in writing or literature to become a successful blogger? Absolutely not! In fact, the vast majority of popular bloggers aren't trained writers. However, they do have several traits in common that are vital to a blog's success:

>> **Grammar knowledge:** To be a successful blogger, you need to know how to structure sentences. Does your grammar have to be perfect? No. But you do need to be able to use a grammar checker within your word processing software to help you learn and follow the rules.

>> **Ability to spell or use spell check:** If you can't naturally spell well, you are certainly not alone! But you may be alone on your blog if you don't take the time to consult a dictionary and use spell check to ensure your blog posts are free of spelling errors.

>> **Succinct style:** Blog posts are traditionally short. It's difficult to read long text online, so bloggers who are capable of writing succinctly without sacrificing their messages have an advantage over long-winded bloggers. Try to keep your blog posts under 800 words and delete extraneous words and phrases that don't help make your point or move the post along. If readers get bored, they'll click away. If you want to write a long post, consider splitting it up into a series of posts or adding a note about predicted read time at the top of the post.

>> **Clear communication:** Always edit your posts for clarity. A sentence might seem perfectly understandable to you as you're typing it, but it might make little or no sense to readers. Take a step back from your post and look at it from an unbiased perspective to ensure people will understand you without question.

Reading your posts aloud to yourself before publishing will help you find sections that sounded clear in your head but are far less clear when read.

>> **Engaging style:** Your blog posts should be written in a style that engages your audience. Let your passion for your subject and your personality shine through your writing! After all, you're not writing a term paper — you're writing a blog post! Your personality and unique voice is what will draw readers in and make them feel like they know you, and that's how you will gain a regular readership and build community.

Always proofread your blog posts before you click the Publish button! Blog posts laden with spelling and grammatical errors frustrate readers and drive them away.

Writing Often

Popular blogs are updated frequently. The reason is simple. The more posts you publish on your blog, the more entry points there are for people to find your blog through links, keyword searches, and so on. The amount of new content you publish and when you publish it is dependent on your goals for your blog. The more great content you publish, the better chance your blog has of growing quickly.

The sweet spot for frequency of posting seems to be one post a day. This is a great goal to set if you're serious about building your blog's popularity with readers!

However, the quality of your content can't suffer due to an aggressive publishing schedule. It doesn't matter how many posts you publish per day if they're all terrible. No one will return to your blog if the content they find on their first visit isn't satisfactory, but if they find great content that has been published recently, they're likely to return.

Quality of posts trumps quantity of posts.

Just because you publish great content on your blog doesn't mean it will grow. That's just the first step to creating a successful blog. You also need to spend time building your blog's community and promoting it. The remainder of this chapter provides the fundamentals you need to get started.

Being Organized

Many bloggers simply post content as an idea comes to them, following their writing moods and whims. That's okay! Not every blogger launches a site with the hope of being the next big thing. Many enter the blogosphere as a hobby or side project, an opportunity to scratch that writing itch or flex their creative muscles.

However, there are also many bloggers who prefer to follow a content or editorial calendar to ensure that they post new content on a regular schedule. Play around with different ways of planning your posts to see what works best for you. Your blogging calendar can be as structured as setting an exact day and time to write or as loosely planned as a list of topics you'd like to write about over the course of the month.

One way to get started with planning content is to create a thematic blog series and schedule the related posts. Want to write about summer activities for the family? Consider tackling a different activity idea in each post, scheduling the posts out over a period of a week. Gauge how your readers respond to your planned content — are there more comments than normal, for example? — to decide if you'd like to continue with that level of organization.

For more tips about content planning as well as other tools of blogging organization, take a look at Chapter 4 of Book 5.

Building Links

One of the best ways to boost your blog traffic is through incoming links — links on other blogs and websites that lead *to* your blog. If you write great content on your blog, the commonly accepted theory is that other bloggers and website owners will want to talk about it and attribute your blog as the source for their own posts through links back to your original post.

Each incoming link to your blog from legitimate blogs and websites helps your ranking with online search engines, meaning your blog appears in search results leading to more traffic to your blog from those search engines. At the same time, those links provide direct traffic to your blog from people who want to learn more about what you have to say.

Link baiting

Although generating incoming links is a goal of all bloggers who want to grow their blogs, another tactic, *link baiting*, works a bit differently. In short, link bait blog posts are typically written about hot, buzz-worthy topics that people are actively searching for online. You can write a post on a hot topic in an attempt to not only drive short-term traffic from those searches but also to encourage other bloggers and website owners to link to your post.

Link baiting can be a great way to boost short-term traffic to your blog, but unless the subject of the post with the link bait is related to your blog's topic, the short-term traffic will disappear as soon as it arrives simply because it's unlikely the rest of the content on your blog will interest those visitors. Consider how well link bait posts fit into your overall blogging plan before you use them, particularly because they can dilute the overall experience on your blog for users who are confused by the inconsistency they can present.

WARNING

Writing link bait posts is often seen as a way to attract cheap or even illegitimate traffic by others in the blogging community. Use this technique with caution and sparingly!

Using Google Trends for short-term traffic boosts

Google Trends, described in Chapter 1 of Book 5, provides a great way to find current buzz-worthy topics to blog about. To see what searches are trending on any particular day, visit trends.google.com/trends/trendingsearches/daily, shown in Figure 1-1, to find a list of the top 20 keyword search terms or phrases. Use those keywords to write your own blog post in an attempt to attract some of that search traffic.

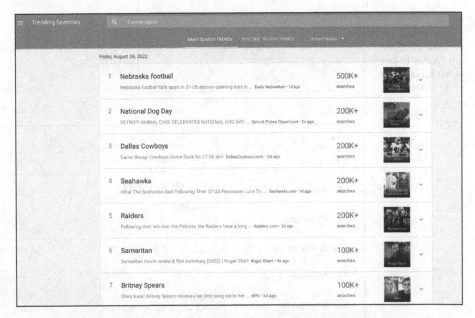

FIGURE 1-1:
Pay a visit to Google Trends to discover popular blog topic ideas.

Using Twitter to find hot blog topics

Twitter offers another easy way to find buzz-worthy topics to blog about in an attempt to boost short-term traffic. Log In to your Twitter account at www.twitter.com, and click #Explore to take a look at the current trending topics as shown in Figure 1-2 and Figure 1-3.

Click through links that interest you and relate to your blog topic to get a better understanding of what's being said. If it's a good fit for your blog, you can write a blog post using related keywords to try to capture some of that active traffic.

Secrets to Blogging Success

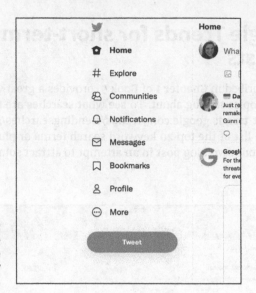

FIGURE 1-2:
Click #Explore
on Twitter to see
what is currently
trending.

FIGURE 1-3:
Twitter lists
trending topics
to show what
people are
tweeting about
most at any given
moment.

Committing the Time

Building a successful blog requires a consistent time commitment. You can't draw readers in and then abandon them until the next time you get around to working on your site.

Although it's possible to blog successfully with a nonexistent or negligible monetary investment, the consistent time commitment is non-negotiable and often more than bloggers bargained for when they joined the blogosphere. Don't be misled. Creating content and promoting a blog in order to grow it into a successful online destination takes time, and you can't take long breaks or much of the results from the work you did prior to your break will disappear.

Think realistically about how much time you have to invest in growing your blog, and then develop a plan that not only helps you reach those goals but also fits your schedule.

Streamlining Tasks

Successful blogging requires a significant time investment, but tools are available to help you streamline tasks and boost efficiency.

TIP

Aim to work smarter, not harder! It is a worthwhile time investment to look at available online tools for any number of blogging-related tasks. You'll save countless hours of work moving forward.

While this isn't an exhaustive list, there are tools available in the following areas that are helpful in your blogging journey:

>> Content organization and planning

>> Time tracking

>> Social media content sharing

>> Content scheduling

>> Search engine optimization (SEO)

>> Email distribution

>> Comment management

This is just a brief overview of the types of tools to explore. For a deeper dive into organization tools, take a look at Chapter 4 of Book 5. SEO automation is covered in Chapter 1 of Book 5, while blog-platform-integrated tools can be found in Book 4. Interested in learning more about tools that streamline the use of social media as it relates to your blog? Head over to Chapter 3 of Book 8 to learn more about time-efficient social media sharing.

Because so many tools are available for free (or at least with a free trial period), don't be afraid to test new tools to find ones you like. Only by experimenting with these tools can you determine which ones truly boost your efficiency.

Having Passion

No one wants to read bland content written by a bored blogger! In order for your blog to grow, you have to love your topic and let that passion show in everything you do that's related to your blog. Make your passion for your subject so obvious that it's contagious! Readers will feel that passion and be moved by it in a way that makes them want to return to your blog again and again.

It's your passion, personality, and authentic voice that makes your blog unique. It's highly unlikely — maybe even impossible — that you'll be the only blogger writing about your blog's topic or focus. What sets you apart from all those other bloggers is your unique perspective, voice, and passion. Don't be afraid to be yourself!

Socializing and Supporting

The most successful bloggers are usually very active in the online community in general, not just in the blogosphere. They're happy to respond to every comment left on their blog posts, and they do so with a personal touch. Of course, time constraints might make that level of personal attention impossible for you, so the goal is to be as active and social on and off your blog as you can.

The best bloggers respond to, acknowledge, and validate their readers, making them feel important.

TIP

Not only should you be sure to respond to comments and emails on your blog, but you should also leave comments on other blogs. Become active in the blogosphere, supporting fellow bloggers at every opportunity. Find a blog post that you particularly enjoyed? Share a link on your favorite social media platforms! You may want to consider joining online forums and social networking groups as well, to become active across the social web. You need to get to know people online just as you would offline to build a successful blog. That's how you build a community around your blog, and that community will ultimately include your most loyal readers who will discuss your blog, link to it, share your content!

Read more about social media in Chapter 3 of this Book.

Reading More than Writing

The most successful bloggers read a lot. Not only do you have to read to get blog post ideas, but you should stay on top of what's going on in the world as it relates to your blog topic in order to respond to questions published through the comments on your blog or through emails to you.

Furthermore, you need to read all the comments and correspondence you receive related to your blog. The longer you blog, the more this correspondence will grow. Even owners of low-traffic blogs can receive a lot of correspondence on a day-to-day basis through comments, emails, and social media messages. Successful bloggers get massive amounts of correspondence, which means they have to read a lot.

If you're not willing to read to find blog post ideas, build your blog community, improve your network, and continually learn about blogging *and* your blog topic, your blog will face limited growth potential.

Being Comfortable with Technology

You don't have to have a degree in computer science to be a successful blogger. You just need to be willing to learn what you need to know in order to blog the way you want to blog.

Keep in mind that there are blog platform options for every level of technical ability and budget. Read more about blog platform options in Book 4. Regardless of how much you want to learn, if you can use the web and a word-processing program, you can start blogging!

The best bloggers do more than simply the bare minimum with the technology that powers their blogs. They take time to learn some HTML and CSS, how to obtain and use a custom domain name, how to use a web host to store and share their blogs, how to install add-ons and plug-ins to enhance their blogs, and more. Most beginner bloggers don't know how to use any of these tools until they dive in and get started. In fact, most bloggers are self-taught when it comes to using the tools of the blogosphere.

With this book in your hands and some practice, you can get over any fears you have of technology and start testing new tools as your blog grows.

Having Patience

If patience is a virtue, bloggers are very virtuous because blogging success requires *a lot* of patience. Achieving blogging success happens over a period of time, not instantly.

First, you need to build up a repository of great content. At the same time, you need to get involved in the online community of the social web by joining the conversation and building relationships with other bloggers. Next, you need to promote your blog content and leverage many of the common blog promotional tactics to boost your blog traffic.

REMEMBER

The other chapters in this Book provides many suggestions for how you can get started in growing your blog through promotion. Promoting your blog does not require monetary investment, but it does require a time commitment. Consider your own blogging goals as you read through and begin creating your own blog-promotion plan.

Chapter **2**

Building Community

The most successful blogs have a powerful community of readers who join the conversation on the blog, advocate for the blog, protect the blog against incorrect critiques or negative publicity, and promote it to their own communities. Building a community around your blog takes time and commitment, but if you are successful, your blog will grow exponentially at the hands of your loyal community.

The commenting feature inherent in blogs makes it a powerful tool for interaction and conversation. The web that was once dominated by one-sided narrative and exposition turned into a two-way dialogue with active participants when Web 2.0, the social web, evolved. Blogs are a place where like-minded people can share information, ask questions, and enjoy life together thanks to the commenting feature.

This chapter shows you how to leverage the comments feature both on and off your blog to grow your blog community. Your blog's success starts with great content followed by the loyal community of readers who are impacted by that content and motivated enough by their appreciation for it to actively respond to it. Read on to find out how to spark the conversation and community on your blog.

Responding to Comments

REMEMBER

While blog posts are the foundation of any blog, the comments are the community that is built on that strong foundation. They're the lifeline of a blog because the conversation that occurs on your blog is where the community develops to create and sustain the success of your site. Conversations create relationships, which lead to loyalty. That means the comments left on your blog posts are extremely important, and you should treat them as such.

To be a successful blogger, you need to be accessible and responsive to your readers. That ideally means responding to every comment left on your blog to acknowledge the commenters and attempt to engage them further. People need to feel valued, not ignored, when they take the time to read your posts and leave comments on those posts. Show them they matter to you by responding to them directly through the comment feature on your blog. Mention them by the names they provide in the blog comment form so they know your response is directed at them.

TIP

Some bloggers choose to employ a community manager once their blog has become too popular to manage entirely on their own. Often this community manager, whose job it is to respond to comments consistently, comes from existing loyal readers!

One of your most important jobs as a blogger is to create compelling content that motivates people to comment on that content. However, after they comment, you can't abandon them. Make your readers feel comfortable in expressing their thoughts and opinions on your blog, and the conversation will grow in time. Subsequently, a sense of community will evolve organically as you continue to keep the community entertained, interested, and comfortable sharing their thoughts and ideas in comments.

REMEMBER

It's okay to delete off-topic comments or, better yet, redirect comments that stray off-topic. Read Chapter 4 of Book 1 to find out about creating a blog comment policy to set expectations for conversations on your blog.

Posting Comments on Other Blogs

Your efforts to build a community and grow your blog don't end when you log out of your blogging application. To truly be successful in your blogging efforts, you need to read more than you write, meaning you need to spend a lot of time reading posts on other blogs, leaving comments on those posts, and networking with those bloggers and their readers.

TIP

Whenever you leave a comment on another blog, be sure to use the same keyword phrase in the Name field of the comment form and provide the URL to your blog in the URL field of the form. Doing so helps your search engine optimization and branding efforts.

When you leave comments on other blogs, make sure the comments you leave are insightful and truly add to the conversation. Don't be afraid to ask questions, respond to questions left by other readers, and engage the blogger or other readers. This is another form of networking that can help you establish yourself and your blog as a go-to place online for information about your blog's topic.

WARNING

Avoid getting involved in comment wars, where two or more readers move from healthy debate to arguing through the comment feature on a blog post. Getting tangled up in such a comment war, especially if it becomes personal, could potentially damage your brand and your blog.

Handling Comment Moderation

A common question that beginner bloggers have is whether they should moderate the comments left on their blogs. *Comment moderation* simply means that comments are not published directly once readers submit them. Instead, comments are held for your approval and can either be published or deleted.

Figure 2-1 shows what it looks like when comments are waiting in moderation for approval.

FIGURE 2-1:
Comments from new readers wait in moderation for blogger approval.

Unfortunately, comment moderation is essential if you want to ensure the conversations on your blog are relevant and appropriate. Spam is more prevalent than ever, and even the best spam blockers allow some spam comments to slip through. The only way to ensure that spam and inappropriate comments aren't published on your blog is to moderate them.

Most blogging applications offer customizable comment moderation settings, which you can configure to best suit your needs. The most effective setting is one that requires moderation only the first time or two that a visitor leaves a comment on your blog. After a person has a comment or two approved on your blog, they can comment anytime in the future, and their comments will publish instantly.

TIP

Just as comment moderation tools sometimes allow spam to slip through the cracks, they also sometimes place legitimate comments in the spam category. Occasionally take a look to make sure that there aren't any genuine comments stuck in the filter!

If your blogging application allows it, set up your comment moderation to mark comments with two or more links as spam automatically. This setting doesn't count the link provided in the URL field of the comment form as one of the two links, so a reader can leave two additional links within his comment before it's identified as spam. As an example, Figure 2-2 shows the comment moderation settings page in a WordPress blog account dashboard.

Discussion Settings

Default post settings	☑ Attempt to notify any blogs linked to from the post
	☑ Allow link notifications from other blogs (pingbacks and trackbacks) on new posts
	☑ Allow people to submit comments on new posts
	(These settings may be overridden for individual posts.)
Other comment settings	☑ Comment author must fill out name and email
	☐ Users must be registered and logged in to comment
	☐ Automatically close comments on posts older than 14 ⇅ days
	☐ Show comments cookies opt-in checkbox, allowing comment author cookies to be set
	☑ Enable threaded (nested) comments 5 ⌄ levels deep
	☐ Break comments into pages with 20 ⇅ top level comments per page and the last ⌄ page displayed by default
	Comments should be displayed with the older ⌄ comments at the top of each page
Email me whenever	☐ Anyone posts a comment
	☐ A comment is held for moderation
Before a comment appears	☐ Comment must be manually approved
	☑ Comment author must have a previously approved comment
Comment Moderation	Hold a comment in the queue if it contains 2 ⇅ or more links. (A common characteristic of comment spam is a large number of hyperlinks.)
	When a comment contains any of these words in its content, author name, URL, email, IP address, or browser's user agent string, it will be held in the moderation queue. One word or IP address per line. It will match inside words, so "press" will match "WordPress".

FIGURE 2-2:
The WordPress comment moderation settings allow you to decide how and when comments are published.

Similarly, you may be able to block comments from specific IP addresses or comments that include specific words, depending on the blogging application and comment spam blocker you use. Most spam blockers catch comments with profanity and other common spam words, but if you see comments with words you want to block coming through for you to moderate, add those words to the list of words to block within your comment spam settings.

The bottom line is that spam, inappropriate comments, and irrelevant comments can offend your readers and disrupt the experience on your blog. In the early days of your blog, your moderation queue is likely to be manageable. As your blog grows and you receive more comments to moderate, you can reevaluate your comment moderation settings and adjust them as necessary.

Linking and Creating Trackbacks, Backlinks, and Pingbacks

Including links to other blogs within your blog posts is a great way to get on the radar screens of those bloggers and drive traffic to your own blog.

The various terms related to linking to other blogs can be a bit confusing, so let's start by defining each of the three closely related terms:

>> **Trackback:** This allows you as a blogger to notify another blogger that you've included a link to their blog in your blog post. In order to create a trackback related to your blog post, you have to be blogging on a compatible platform and you have to take the manual step of actually creating the trackback.

For example, if you use WordPress as your blogging application, you can use the trackback function incorporated into your blog post editor to provide the URL where you want to send a virtual shoulder tap, which lets another blogger know that you linked to their content within your blog post. Your link appears within the blogger's blogging application dashboard as well as on the post page for the URL you tracked back to. Readers of that blog can see the link to your blog and follow it to read more from you.

Figure 2-3 shows an example of where to create a trackback link within the blog post editing area.

>> **Pingback:** This is essentially the same thing as a trackback in that it notifies another blogger that you've linked to their content within your site. The difference is merely technical. A pingback, or ping for short, is sent automatically, rather than created manually, if you are blogging on a compatible platform.

FIGURE 2-3:
A trackback is
manually created
by the blogger
within the blog
post editing tool.

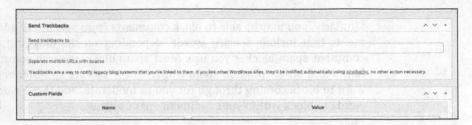

Figure 2-4 shows pingback notifications within the comment moderation area of a blog. Just as you may review a comment and decide it is spam, pings sometimes also are best moved to your spam folder because they have come from a low-quality website. Determine if you want the pingback to appear at the bottom of your blog post or if you would like to move the notification to your spam folder (or even delete!).

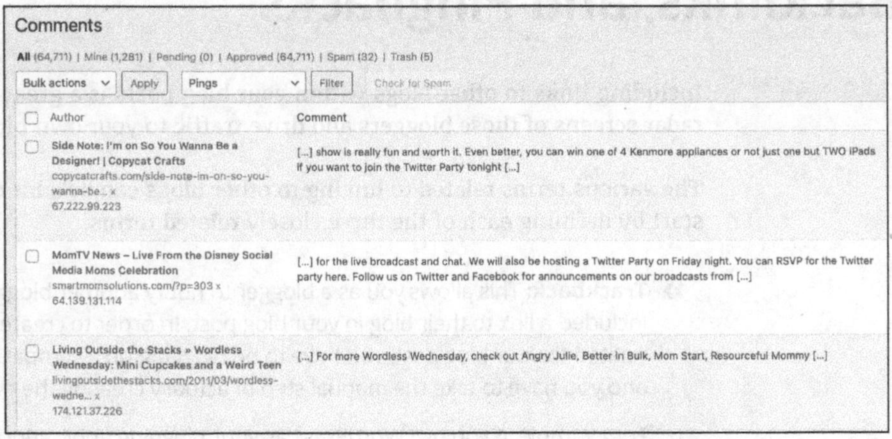

FIGURE 2-4:
Pingback noti-
fications are
automatically
sent and appear
within the blog's
comments mod-
eration tool.

>> **Backlink:** This is the term for any link from one page to another. So technically, both trackbacks and pingbacks are backlinks.

Figure 2-5 shows what it looks like when backlinks have been approved for a blog post. In this example, the backlinks appear within the post's comment section right along with the comments that have been approved to appear.

As mentioned, pingbacks are created automatically by your blogging platform, but platforms that automatically attempt to ping other bloggers that you've linked to them also typically allow you to turn the pingback feature off on your blog. Figure 2-6 shows the area within the discussion — or comments — section that can be unchecked to stop pings from being sent from your blog to other blogs when you've linked to them.

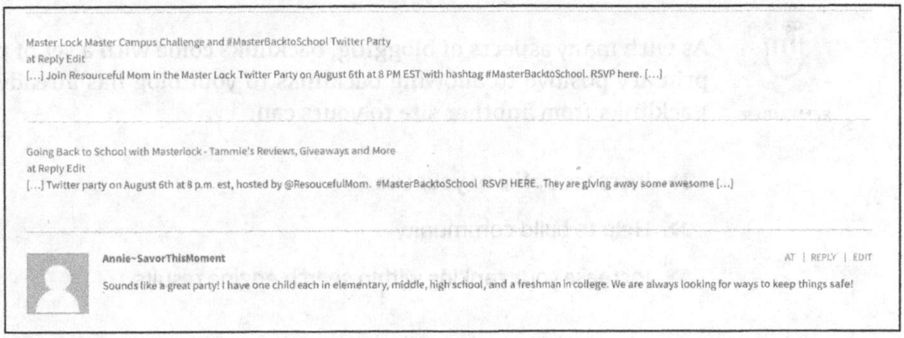

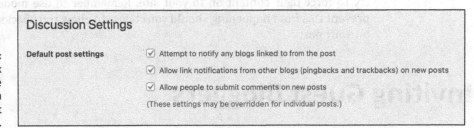

Master Lock Master Campus Challenge and #MasterBacktoSchool Twitter Party
at Reply Edit
[...] Join Resourceful Mom in the Master Lock Twitter Party on August 6th at 8 PM EST with hashtag #MasterBacktoSchool. RSVP here. [...]

Going Back to School with Masterlock - Tammie's Reviews, Giveaways and More
at Reply Edit
[...] Twitter party on August 6th at 8 p.m. est, hosted by @ResoucefulMom. #MasterBacktoSchool. RSVP HERE. They are giving away some awesome [...]

Annie-SavorThisMoment   AT | REPLY | EDIT

Sounds like a great party! I have one child each in elementary, middle, high school, and a freshman in college. We are always looking for ways to keep things safe!

FIGURE 2-5:
Once backlinks
have been
approved, they
appear on a blog
post's page.

Discussion Settings

Default post settings   ☑ Attempt to notify any blogs linked to from the post

☑ Allow link notifications from other blogs (pingbacks and trackbacks) on new posts

☑ Allow people to submit comments on new posts

(These settings may be overridden for individual posts.)

FIGURE 2-6:
The pingback
feature can be
turned off within
the default post
settings menu.

While it is up to you if you would like to notify a blogger through a trackback or pingback that you have linked to their content, it is up to that blogger if they are willing to do the following:

>> Receive notifications of trackbacks and pingbacks

>> Display approved backlinks

These decisions are made within the settings of the receiving blog, much the same as the settings of the linking blog, as shown in Figure 2-7.

TIP

Even though your blog's settings may enable you to either allow or deny sending and receiving trackbacks and pingbacks by default, individual post settings allow you to change that decision on a post-by-post basis as desired.

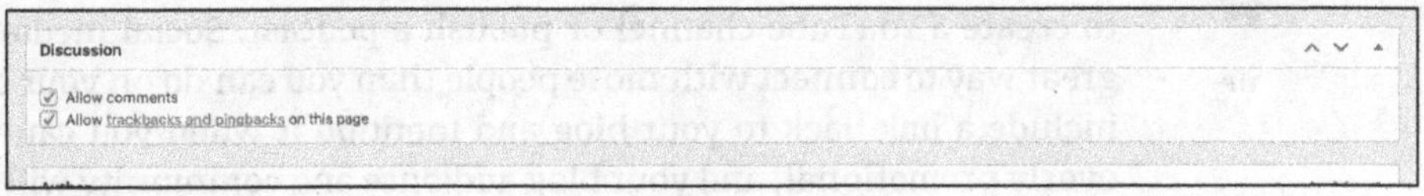

FIGURE 2-7:
Settings include
a place to either
allow or deny
pingbacks and
trackbacks to
your blog from
other blogs.

Discussion   ⌄ ⌄ ⌃

☑ Allow comments
☑ Allow trackbacks and pingbacks on this page

REMEMBER

As with many aspects of blogging, backlinks come with a set of pros and cons. The primary positive to allowing backlinks to your blog has already been mentioned. Backlinks from another site to yours can:

>> Increase traffic to your site

>> Help to build community

>> Increase your ranking within search engine results

Unfortunately, just as with comments, backlinks are often used by spammers to try to force their content on to your site. Remember to use moderation tools to prevent this from happening should you choose to allow trackbacks and pingbacks on your posts.

Inviting Guest Bloggers

Opening your blog up to guest bloggers is a great way to build the community around your blog because it can make readers feel valued when you allow them to participate in this seemingly formal way. Sometimes a guest blogger's post can spark a new conversation and breathe new life into a blog, too. You can find out more about guest blogging in Chapter 5 of this Book.

Going Beyond the Blogosphere

Community building can be done outside of the blogosphere in a variety of ways. Don't be afraid to get creative in your efforts to connect with people, network, and build relationships across the social web. For example, you can join forums and Facebook Groups related to your blog's topic and answer related questions on LinkedIn.

TIP

You can also think outside of the box and build your online presence in an effort to reach out to a broader audience. For example, you can move beyond your blog to create a YouTube channel or publish a podcast. Social media platforms offer a great way to connect with more people than you can do on your blog alone. Always include a link back to your blog and mention it when you can without sounding overly promotional, and your blog audience and community will grow. Learn more about moving beyond your blog in Book 8.

IN THIS CHAPTER

» **Understanding social networking**

» **Finding social networking sites**

» **Using social networking to boost blog traffic**

» **Scheduling with social media tools**

» **Avoiding social networking don'ts**

Chapter **3**

Social Networking

The evolution of the Internet from a navigational tool to a transactional tool and eventually to a social tool has opened up the world of communication in ways no one expected. Through the social web, people from across the globe can easily interact and share thoughts, news, photos, videos, and more at any time. Like-minded people whose paths might never have crossed 20 years ago can now find each other on blogs, forums, and a variety of social media platforms.

Social networking is just one of the tools of the social web that people from all walks of life have embraced, and it's an excellent tool to build relationships and grow your blog. This chapter explains what social networking is and how you can use social networking sites to drive traffic to your blog.

Defining Social Networking

In the simplest terms, *social networking* is networking done via social media. It's exactly like in-person networking, but instead of doing it face-to-face, you do it virtually via your mobile phone, tablet, or computer. There are no barriers to entering the world of social networking. Anyone with an Internet connection is invited to the party.

As the social nature of the web evolved, innovative people saw an opportunity to provide online destinations for those interactions to take place. Thus, social media was born. Today, various social networking sites allow you to register for an account, create a profile, interact with other members, share content, and develop relationships.

REMEMBER

Any networking done online via social web is considered social networking, but there are also specific social networking websites that exist as central destinations for social networking activities between users. Facebook and LinkedIn are just two examples of social networking websites, some of which are discussed in detail in this chapter.

Social networking can be a formal or informal activity. Unlike offline networking, which is typically associated with business networking, online social networking sites are open to formal and informal networking uses. Bloggers and business people, journalists and charity organizations use social networking sites to promote products and services, provide customer service, spread news stories, and build support for causes. At the same time, friends, families, and peers use social networking sites to converse, share personal stories and photos, and plan events and activities.

As the social web grows, the world gets smaller and smaller. Friends and families who once had trouble communicating across long distances can now communicate in real time and share far more than just spoken words. Business people who once shared ideas through email can now collaborate through social networking.

Finding Popular Social Networking Sites

There are many social networking websites, but some have grown more popular than others. Each offers slightly different capabilities, and some are preferred by niche users. Some of the most popular social networking sites are Facebook, You-Tube, Twitter, and Instagram. Each offers unique features and formats, appealing to a slightly different audience to be used for different purposes.

Friending with Facebook

www.facebook.com

Facebook is the most popular social networking site, with nearly three billion users as of the end of 2022. The site is known for providing a wide variety of features as well as an onsite advertising mechanism. You can create a personal profile, a brand page for your blog, a business page, and a Facebook group for your blogging community. You can also join existing groups through your Facebook account.

Additionally, you can upload photos and videos and update your Timeline with short posts related to longer content in your blog posts. Your Facebook posts also appear in the News Feeds of some of your Facebook friends and followers. Other users can leave comments in response to your updates and share your content with people who may not currently follow your blog's page.

However, you can't interact with other users on Facebook via your personal account until you connect with them by sending a *friend request,* which the other person can either accept or decline. That's because Facebook is a closed site, meaning you can view other users' profiles only if you're a registered member. If a member chooses to hide his profile, you can't view it unless you *friend* that person via Facebook first. If your friend request is accepted, you can view that person's profile, pictures, and posts.

To create your own profile in Facebook, simply visit www.facebook.com (shown in Figure 3-1) and begin the signup process.

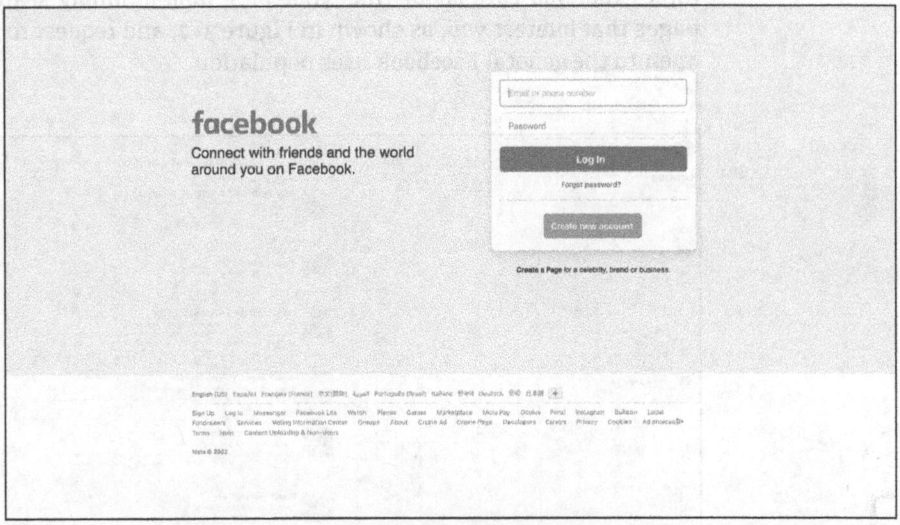

FIGURE 3-1:
The Facebook home page.

Once your account is active, take some time to create a complete profile and then start searching for people you know on Facebook. When you find someone you know, send them a friend request and start sharing, conversing, and networking via the social web!

TIP

You can read more about Facebook in *Facebook For Dummies,* 8th Edition, by Carolyn Abram and Amy Karasavas (John Wiley & Sons, Inc., 2021), and you can find out more about promoting your brand and blog using Facebook as part of a larger content-marketing strategy in *Digital Marketing All-in-One For Dummies* by Stephanie Diamond (John Wiley & Sons, Inc., 2019).

Facebook benefits

Facebook is a great social networking tool because so many people use it. Of course, the sheer volume of users can also be a negative because you can get lost in the clutter. However, you can find a lot of people to meet and build relationships with on Facebook.

Facebook is active. That means a lot of users are regularly updating their profiles, sharing photos and videos, posting information, and sharing links and comments on their own Timelines and other users' News Feeds. Unlike other some other social networking sites where people create a placeholder profile and then abandon it, Facebook users are engaged. That's exactly the atmosphere you need to promote your blog! I explain more about that in the following section.

Facebook also makes it easy to find people who might be interested in the same topics that you care about (like your blog topic). Simply search for groups and pages that interest you, as shown in Figure 3-2, and request to join those that are open to the general Facebook user population.

FIGURE 3-2:
Search for Facebook groups by area of interest.

Facebook blog promotion

Facebook is an excellent social networking site to leverage for blog promotion. Although you should refrain from flooding the Facebook community with promotional information, there's no reason why you can't provide links to your blog posts or mention your successes, particularly if you do so in relevant groups or pages.

Following are suggestions for using Facebook to promote your blog:

» **Status updates:** Post status updates to your Timeline that mention your new blog posts and include links to those posts. You can also publish requests for guest posts. Don't be afraid to get creative!

» **Making friends:** Send friend requests to other bloggers and people you want to connect with who can help you promote your blog in the future.

» **Creating a Facebook Page for your blog:** Although Facebook profiles are intended to be a place for individuals to create a presence on Facebook, Facebook Pages are intended to represent a business, brand, or celebrity. They're meant to give those businesses, brands, and celebrities a presence on Facebook. Facebook Pages are a great way to provide information, links, photos, videos, and more related to your blog and build a separate community around your blog's topic. You can also like Facebook Pages related to your blog that are created by other people, especially other bloggers, and then get involved by adding content to those Pages and joining the conversation. You can start a Facebook Page by logging into your Facebook profile and visiting www.facebook.com/pages/create.

» **Starting a group:** Facebook Groups are meant to create places where people can discuss and share information about specific topics. They provide one more way you can connect with people and share information about your blog and related subjects. You can either start your own Facebook group or join other groups related to your blog. You can create a Facebook group by logging in to your Facebook profile and visiting www.facebook.com/groups/create.

» **Advertising:** Facebook users can place ads that can be specifically targeted. The cost is minimal, but your ad needs to be compelling to encourage clicks. You can create your own Facebook ad by visiting www.facebook.com/ads/create.

TIP

Take the time to read your friends' updates in your News Feed and leave comments. Join groups, follow pages that interest you, and start conversations that lead back to your Facebook profile and blog. Using Facebook is a 360-degree marketing strategy wherein all parts should work together and always lead people back to your blog for more information and conversations.

Influencing on Instagram

www.instagram.com

Owned by the same parent company as Facebook, Meta (www.meta.com), Instagram is a social media platform that exists primarily via a mobile app. Created in 2010, Instagram has exploded in popularity in recent years. While anyone can use the app to share everything from their favorite pet pics to a picture of what they're having for breakfast, the visually driven platform has become a favorite of online influencers sharing their latest finds and brand partnerships.

REMEMBER

Content on Instagram falls into two categories: images and videos. The video content on Instagram is referred to as *Reels*. There are two posting locations on Instagram. Content posted on a user's Instagram account page remains there permanently unless deleted. Content posted in a user's Stories only remains visible for 24 hours.

An Instagram account (shown in Figure 3-3) has become an integral part of every blogger's branding strategy in recent years along with other social media platforms such as Facebook and Twitter. Bloggers hoping to review products or earn revenue through affiliate links find Instagram to be especially useful as part of a larger branding and monetizing strategy. You can learn more about blog monetization through affiliates in Book 7, Chapter 3.

FIGURE 3-3:
An Instagram account related to a blog's brand.

TIP

Learn more by checking out *Instagram For Dummies,* 2nd Edition, by Jenn Herman, Corey Walker, and Eric Butow (John Wiley & Sons, Inc., 2019).

Connecting on LinkedIn

`www.linkedin.com`

LinkedIn is quite a popular social networking site, particularly among business people and people looking to further their careers. It's an excellent site for sharing professional knowledge and career development networking. Many companies actively seek new employees through LinkedIn, and many users find new careers through the networking they do on LinkedIn.

You can create a free LinkedIn account at `www.linkedin.com`, shown in Figure 3-4. Take the time to create a comprehensive profile. Next, start searching for people you know on LinkedIn and send *connection requests* to them. As your network grows, you'll find more and more people to connect with. You can update your LinkedIn profile with interesting information (such as links to your blog posts), join or create groups, and send private messages to other users.

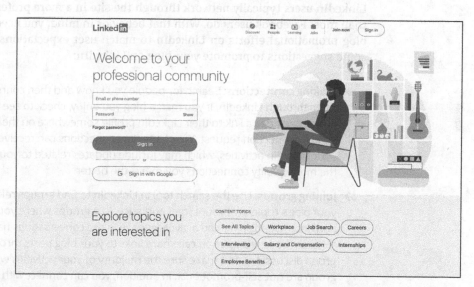

FIGURE 3-4:
The LinkedIn sign-up page.

TIP

To find out more about LinkedIn, you can read *LinkedIn For Dummies,* 6th Edition, by Joel Elad (John Wiley & Sons, Inc., 2021).

LinkedIn benefits

One of the primary benefits of LinkedIn is its focus. Because most users have some interest in business or career development, LinkedIn offers more opportunities than direct blog promotion. The networking you do on LinkedIn can open the doors to a lot more than added blog traffic. With that in mind, try to keep the content you publish on LinkedIn professional.

The LinkedIn user audience is made up of professional adults, which means the site is fairly clear of the clutter that teenage audiences can create on social networking sites. That means the site has a bit more of a premium reputation without the price tag one might expect from a business networking site.

REMEMBER

The majority of active LinkedIn members use the site for business networking and career development. If your blog and social networking goals aren't related to business or career development, LinkedIn probably isn't the site where you should invest a lot of your time promoting your blog. However, it's a popular social networking site that can open new doors to people who do use it.

LinkedIn blog promotion

LinkedIn users typically network through the site in a more professional manner than most Facebook users do. With that behavior in mind, you need to adjust your blog promotional efforts on LinkedIn to match user expectations. Following are some suggestions to promote your blog on LinkedIn:

» **Making connections:** Search for people you know and then connect with them through LinkedIn. If you read a blog you enjoy, check to see whether the author provides a link to their LinkedIn profile somewhere on their blog. If so, send a connection request. Your LinkedIn connections can receive updates of your LinkedIn activities, which may include updates related to your blog, so the more quality connections you make, the better.

» **Joining groups:** Use the search tool in LinkedIn to find groups relevant to you, your blog's topic, and your target audience. Join groups where your target audience spends time and actively engage in the conversations happening through those groups. You can share links to your blog posts through the group discussions, but make sure the majority of your activities within the group are not self-promotional. In addition, you can connect with anyone on LinkedIn who is in a group that you're in, so take advantage of that extended reach by actively sending connection requests to fellow group members with whom you'd like to network more closely.

>> **Endorsing people:** LinkedIn offers an endorsement tool that you can use to write recommendations for people you're connected with, which appear in their profiles. You can write an endorsement for someone and send a request asking them to write an endorsement for you in return. Positive endorsements boost your online reputation and credibility as the go-to source for information related to your blog topic or area of expertise.

Microblogging on Twitter

https://twitter.com

Twitter (shown in Figure 3-5), one of the top social media platforms in the world, was launched as a microblogging tool in 2006, with users answering the question, "What's happening?" in 140 characters or less. Today users are able to add media to their posts and include up to 280 characters per post, which is called a *tweet*. Twitter is free to use and can be accessed via your favorite web browser or via an app on your mobile device.

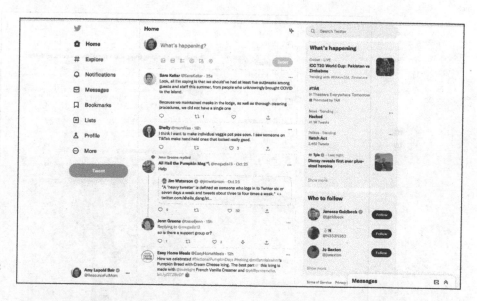

FIGURE 3-5:
The Twitter feed.

Twitter hashtags

While trying to keep up with what is happening on Twitter can be a bit like drinking from a firehose, there are ways to make using the social media tool more manageable. The best way to connect with others on Twitter is through *hashtags*, searchable terms that begin with the # sign and follow with a series of characters related to the tagged content.

TECHNICAL STUFF

Hashtags began in the early days of Twitter as a visual cue to other users that a tweet could be categorized within a theme or topic. While tweet after tweet scrolled past quickly, users scanned and looked for the hashtag so that they could focus on those tweets and reply to participate. Eventually Twitter made hashtags clickable, meaning that clicking on any given hashtag within a tweet takes users to all of the tweets using the same tag. Third-party apps and websites were also developed to pull all tweets using a particular hashtag into one page, making those tweets easier to find.

Today Twitter hashtags are a great way to see what the Twitter community is discussing at any given moment and to find other Twitter users and content related to your interests and blog. For example, even as I write this there is a Twitter hashtag, #PBPitch (see Figure 3-6), being used by potential picture book authors and illustrators to pitch their best ideas to potential publishers and agents. By searching potential hashtags related to your content area, such as #homereno for home renovation bloggers, you can find others writing and sharing content related to yours. You can then engage with those users, following them and tweeting with them as you build your Twitter community.

FIGURE 3-6:
Use Twitter hashtags to find content related to your blog.

Community retweets

The early days of Twitter were built around the idea of a community helping one another out. It was a great place for bloggers to pop into late at night as they were trying to figure out their new site's HTML code or how to publish a post on a new blogging platform. Now it is far less a community and far more a bulletin board where people blast what's important to them, but Twitter can still be used to build a mutually supportive community.

TIP

Each tweet includes a button called the retweet button, as shown in Figure 3-7. If you click on the retweet button, that person's tweet will now show up to your followers as well whether or not they also follow that Twitter user. Retweets are a great way to support other Twitter users and build comradery with them. As you participate in and support the online community of Twitter users, you will eventually begin to have your content retweeted to new followers as well. This is a great way for your blog content to find new pairs of eyes!

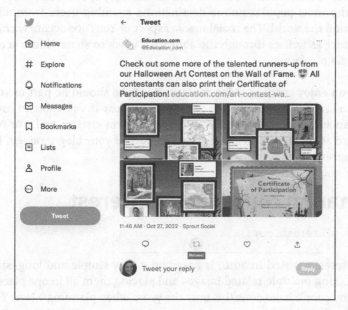

FIGURE 3-7:
The Twitter
retweet button.

Reaching a new audience with TikTok

www.tiktok.com

TikTok is a wildly popular social media mobile app that consists of short-form videos. Rising to popularity due initially to teen users creating and sharing dance and lip sync videos, TikTok is used now by all sorts of content creators for everything from quick cooking videos to humorous content. The most popular TikTok videos go viral and are shared on a variety of social media platforms including Instagram, Facebook, and Twitter. In fact, many social media users never actually view TikTok videos on the app itself but rather within other communities due to viral sharing.

Regardless of whether or not TikTok is a fit for you and your blog content, it's important to be aware of its existence and the potential to reach a very large audience. This is especially true if video content is a particular area of interest for you or fits well with your blog topic.

Connecting via videos on YouTube

www.youtube.com

While TikTok tends to cater to and reach a very specific audience, YouTube is one of the most popular online destinations reaching users from all demographics around the world. The social media aspect of YouTube occurs within the comment feature as well as through the ability for users to share videos across other social media platforms.

TIP

If you enjoy creating video content, YouTube should be part of your overall blog branding strategy. YouTube is especially great if you want to establish yourself as an authority, share product reviews, or demonstrate crafts or recipes. To learn more about creating video content as part of your blog strategy, head to Book 8, Chapter 2!

Sharing content on Pinterest

www.pinterest.com

Pinterest, created in 2010, is based on a very simple and long-standing practice of taking multiple related images and placing them all in one place on a pinboard. Many people have done this over the years when planning a New Year's resolution vision board, getting ready to redecorate a room, or creating a collage for a school project. With Pinterest, however, this is all done digitally.

Pinterest is a visually driven platform and pulls together images taken from posts all over the blogosphere. Users can pin and re-pin, share and comment on pins, and create boards related to any number of topics.

TIP

It's not only important to be active on Pinterest in order to build your blog brand's presence on the platform, it's also crucial to keep Pinterest in mind when creating visual content for your blog posts. You want your blog readers to find your images compelling enough to pin, therefore sharing a link to your blog post on Pinterest. You can also create your own pins related to your blog posts, as shown in Figure 3-8, making it easier for new readers to find your content.

FIGURE 3-8: Create pins related to your blog posts to increase social shares.

Using Social Networking Sites to Boost Blog Traffic

Social networking is a long-term blog growth strategy, but it's possible to get direct and more immediate bursts of traffic from your efforts as well. In general, social networking helps your blog growth strategy in three ways:

>> **Raising awareness:** Social networking could be called *free awareness advertising*. Just publish announcements or links to your blog, and your blog is on the radar screen of all your social networking connections.

>> **Relationship building:** The time you spend interacting on social networking sites is incredibly valuable. Strong relationships lead to loyalty and future opportunities.

> **» Generating buzz:** If you publish a link to one of your blog posts that is particularly interesting, timely, or helpful, you're likely to see a bump in traffic.

REMEMBER

Social networking is just one tool in your blog marketing toolbox, and it's a long-term strategy. Don't rely on it entirely, or you'll be disappointed in your results.

Leaning on Social Media Scheduling Tools

For bloggers with an already busy schedule, it can seem that social media is just one more thing to keep track of and manage. Because branding for your blog — maintaining a related and recognizable presence across a number of platforms — really should include multiple social media platforms, it's important to do your best to build consistent social media account creation into your blog strategy.

Thankfully there are social media scheduling tools and apps available that can make managing your blog's presence across multiple platforms easier. The following are just a sample of the tools available to help you save time and create a consistent social media presence for your blog:

>> **Hootsuite (www.hootsuite.com):** Hootsuite allows you to create and schedule posts on a variety of social media platforms as well as monitor engagement on your posts.

>> **SocialBee (www.socialbee.io):** SocialBee allows users to create, schedule, and post content across a variety of social media accounts including but not limited to Facebook, Twitter, and Instagram.

>> **Buffer (www.buffer.com):** Buffer allows users to create and schedule posts as well as analyze engagement results.

>> **MeetEdgar (www.meetedgar.com):** MeetEdgar allows users to post on Instagram, TikTok, Facebook, Twitter, Pinterest, LinkedIn, and Google Business Profile.

>> **Later (www.later.com):** Later allows users to create and schedule social media content to be posted at a future date.

>> **Post Planner (www.postplanner.com):** Post Planner allows users to connect all of their social accounts including Facebook pages and groups.

Avoiding Social Networking Don'ts

As with all online activities, some things you just shouldn't do if you want to remain a welcomed member of the online community. These don'ts range from ethical to legal considerations, and you need to be aware of them and follow them at all times. Think of it this way: If you socialize with another person in public, there are rules of etiquette that you follow, and the same is true of online social networking.

TIP

Read and adhere to the terms and conditions and user agreements for any social networking sites that you join.

Following are several social networking don'ts that apply to all online social networking sites and activities:

>> **Don't be 100 percent promotional.** No one wants to read your updates and content if they're entirely promotional. Don't just publish link after link to your blog on your social networking profiles. It's perfectly acceptable to promote your new blog content, but be sure to publish far more nonpromotional content than promotional content on your social networking profiles.

>> **Don't be nasty.** Remember your manners. Don't get involved in online arguments or publish negative comments. Be diplomatic and remember that a lot of people can see what you publish in your social networking activities. Also, keep in mind that content lives online for a long, long time.

>> **Don't spam anyone.** Spam is the kiss of death for social networking. Don't send spam links or participate in spam activities of any kind.

>> **Don't be deceptive.** The social web community is large, but chances are good that if you lie, you'll get caught. Be honest and stay out of trouble.

>> **Don't forget the law.** Copyright laws apply in your social networking activities just as they do in your blogging activities. Don't copy another person's work (written, video, or photo content) without permission, and always attribute your sources.

WARNING

Once you're identified as a spammer or person who acts inappropriately, it can be hard to repair your online reputation. Don't give anyone a reason to speak negatively about you and tarnish your personal brand or your blog's brand image.

Chapter **4**

Distributing Content

With so many aspects of blogging to track, from search engine optimization (SEO) to social media account management, it can be easy to forget that perhaps the *most* important part of blogging is the content that you write. Many bloggers join the blogosphere because of a passion for a particular topic or maybe even a strong interest in writing itself. The last thing any blogger wants is to write compelling content and have it go unread.

It's certainly important to take the time to work on SEO in order to draw in readers through search engine traffic. It's also a good idea to spend time on other blogs connecting with members of the blogosphere and their readers. However, there are a variety of other ways to make sure that your great content is getting to the readers who will love it.

This chapter takes a look at a variety of ways to distribute content, from free tools to paid accounts, email newsletter services to social media platforms. With so many options to choose from, chances are that you'll find something that fits both your needs *and* your budget.

Sharing Content by Email

With new technology emerging every day and product innovations replacing yesterday's "next big thing" in the blink of an eye, it can often feel like the online world is moving too quickly making it impossible to keep up. Email, however, is a great equalizer, a familiar tool that is in nearly every home and handheld device. That makes email the perfect way to reach readers with your blog content.

It is entirely up to you how you choose to use email to get your content into the hands of your readers. Some bloggers prefer to send only an introductory paragraph of each new blog post followed by a link to click through to continue reading the rest of the post. This is a great way to boost traffic to your site, earn pageviews, and potentially reach readers with your blog advertisements. However, you take the risk that email recipients won't bother to click through and read. This is especially problematic if there is some call to action within your content or an affiliate link you'd like them to click to help you earn revenue.

TIP

You can learn more about monetizing with affiliate links in Chapter 3 of Book 7.

Some bloggers elect to send complete posts. There are opportunities to monetize with in-email advertising and links, such as the affiliate links mentioned above, so that it is less of a loss should the readers decide not to click through to your actual blog. However, you can still find ways to draw readers from your emailed content to your website such as through click-to-enter blog contests, click to comment, or click through to receive additional content links.

However you choose to utilize email to distribute content, a variety of tools are available to you at a variety of price points. A small sampling is covered in the following sections.

Building with Buzzstream

Buzzstream (www.buzzstream.com) is powerful software that helps you to build lists of email contacts, manage those lists by demographic information, and then choose which list to email based on your needs. For example, you may keep one list of subscribers who are interested in receiving blog contest opportunities and another list for readers who would like to receive any new content you publish.

Buzzstream's emailing tools allow you to create email campaigns, including distributing your content, and then monitor the results to determine how many readers opened and then engaged with your emailed content. This is especially helpful if you are distributing sponsored content and need to report back to a client regarding campaign results.

TIP

Learn more about sponsored post campaigns in Chapter 4 of Book 7.

Because Buzzstream, shown in Figure 4-1, does not offer a free account option, this software option best serves business and organization blogs or bloggers who have already successfully begun to monetize their sites.

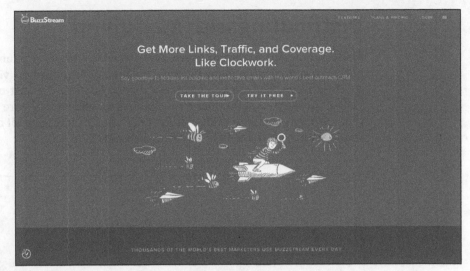

FIGURE 4-1:
Buzzstream helps
bloggers build
email lists and
distribute content
to subscribers.

Reaching with ConvertKit

ConvertKit, found at www.convertkit.com, is an online tool that is for free to bloggers who have up to 1,000 email list subscribers. Like other tools, ConvertKit helps you create and manage your distribution lists. You can also create email campaigns that are distributed automatically at a pre-determined time.

ConvertKit, shown in Figure 4-2, is especially helpful for bloggers who plan to include eCommerce in their monetization strategy. You can use ConvertKit to create a landing page for a specific campaign that works alongside your emailed content distribution.

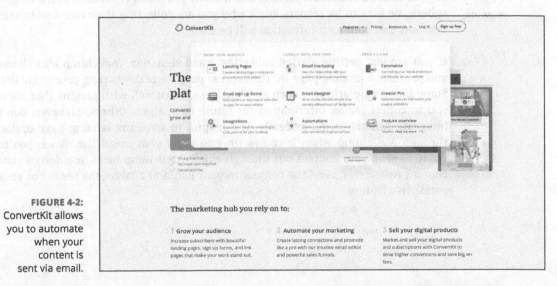

FIGURE 4-2:
ConvertKit allows
you to automate
when your
content is
sent via email.

Distributing with Mailchimp

Mailchimp (www.mailchimp.com), now owned by Intuit, is a long-time favorite of the blogging world. Many bloggers gather email subscribers via contact forms on their blogs. The trick is to know what to do with that list of contacts once you've grown your subscriber base. Mailchimp, shown in Figure 4-3, allows you to import your email distribution list to be used in future email campaigns. This service is free up to the first 500 email subscribers.

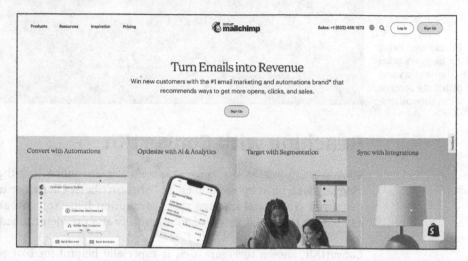

FIGURE 4-3:
Mailchimp allows bloggers to import contacts and send email campaigns.

WARNING

If you send emails to addresses of people who have not opted-in to receive your content, you may be reported for spam! This puts you in danger of being kicked off of your email distribution service, and it earns you a bad reputation in the blogosphere. Be sure to let readers know why you are collecting their email addresses and how that contact information will be used.

If you are just getting started collecting email sign-ups, Mailchimp also allows you to create a landing page for the express purpose of developing your email list. Some blogging platforms, such as WordPress, work well with plugins that allow you to collect reader information for future campaigns. Others, however, don't integrate contact forms as easily. It's helpful to have the landing page option through Mailchimp when it comes time to grow your email list. When you're ready to send your content out through email, Mailchimp helps you design your content newsletter, send the content to your list, and analyze the results of your email distribution.

Emailing with Constant Contact

Another favorite of bloggers is Constant Contact, found at www.constantcontact.com. Constant Contact originally grew in popularity as an email list management and email campaign tool. However, it now also offers additional services such as social media scheduling, which is covered in more detail later in this chapter. Constant Contact, shown in Figure 4-4, offers a free trial but then charges a monthly fee based on the number of email subscribers.

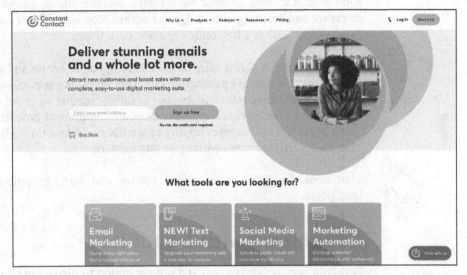

FIGURE 4-4: Many bloggers use Constant Contact to distribute content via email.

Similar to other email distribution tools, Constant Contact's web-based service allows you to create email campaigns with newsletter templates. You can also choose to send the same content in two different formats to different sections of your list in order to test which content distribution strategy worked better. Once an email campaign is complete, you can view data to see how well your emails were received and use that information to make changes to upcoming email campaigns.

Plugging in with Thrive Leads

Unlike some of the other tools mentioned in this section, Thrive Leads (www.thrivethemes.com), is a plugin that works with WordPress blogging software. This plugin helps WordPress bloggers to build a list of email subscribers from their blog readers and site visitors. Bloggers can use this same plugin to create any number of opt-in lists, not just content distribution email lists. Unfortunately, this plugin is a bit pricey and may work best for business and organization bloggers.

Creating with Aweber

Aweber (www.aweber.com) is a robust tool that includes the ability to create and send emails to blog content subscribers. Aweber allows bloggers to use Canva to create and design graphics for use within blog newsletters and emails. Canva (www.canva.com) is a free online graphic design tool.

Aweber includes a Canva integration allowing you to create and edit graphics via Canva from the Aweber platform itself. This saves bloggers the step of having to visit Canva and then return to Aweber to finish creating an email campaign. Aweber's drag and drop email creation tools and automated emailing ability makes this a great tool for bloggers hoping to distribute content through email regularly. This tool is free for users with up to 500 subscribers.

TIP

Visit Book 8 to learn more about creating and using graphic content in your blog posts.

Organizing with Goodbits

Goodbits (www.goodbits.io) is a unique option to distribute your blog's content via email. Goodbits allows you to pull links from your blog, your social media posts, or other online sources to create and send a weekly digest of your best content to your subscribers.

Because it utlizes a drag and drop creation tool, Goodbits is an option for bloggers who want to distribute their content via email but don't have time to spend learning complicated newsletter design tools. The Goodbits (shown in Figure 4-5) email creation tool integrates with other email distribution tools, including Mailchimp and Aweber (discussed earlier in this chapter).

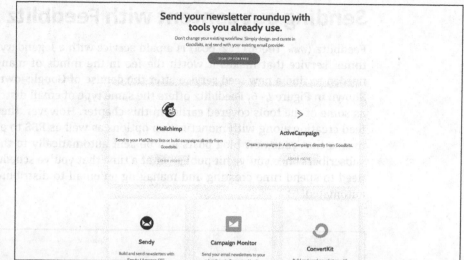

FIGURE 4-5:
Goodbits email creation tool integrates with other email distribution services.

Syndicating Content

In the early days of blogging, most bloggers distributed their content through an RSS feed via a tool called Feedburner. Feedburner no longer exists, along with many favorites from the original days of the blogosphere, but RSS feeds continue to offer a great way for bloggers to share content.

TECHNICAL STUFF

An RSS feed, which stands for *Real Simple Syndication*, simply refers to the process by which a blog's contents are transmitted to a reader's "feed reader" or email address in a coded format that is easily shared with feed reading platforms. Choosing to make your blog posts shareable as RSS syndicated content means that readers can receive your blog posts — either in full or partial post format — on another platform along with their other favorite blogger's posts. Think of it like a subscription to all of their favorite blogs, and your blog posts are just part of the larger document!

Put simply, syndicating your blog content via RSS is yet another way to share and distribute your blog content. The following tools are all great options to help you use this method of content distribution.

Sending out content with Feedblitz

Feedblitz (www.feedblitz.com) is a paid service with a legendary knack for customer service that makes it worth the fee in the minds of many bloggers who needed to find a new feed service after the demise of Google-owned Feedburner. Shown in Figure 4-6, Feedblitz offers the same type of email distribution services as some of the tools covered earlier in this chapter. However, they also offer RSS feed creation along with monetization options as well as RSS to email tools. This means that your new blog posts will be sent automatically to the inbox of your subscribers once you've hit publish or at a time that you've scheduled. There's no need to spend time creating and managing an email to distribute. Everything is automated.

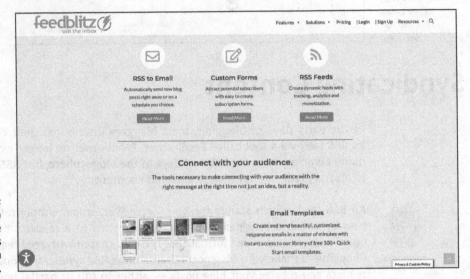

FIGURE 4-6: Feedblitz is a robust service that includes a syndication component.

Speedy RSS with New Sloth

Formerly called Feedity, New Sloth (www.newsloth.com), shown in Figure 4-7, offers a variety of features including RSS feed creation. You can use New Sloth to syndicate your blog content via RSS and build that into a curated feed, similar to the tools covered later in this chapter. Subscribers can then receive your blog posts in the form of a syndicated email along with relevant, related content of your choosing.

New Sloth offers a free trial to new subscribers. However, in order to continue using the service, you will need to pay a monthly fee at the end of the trial period.

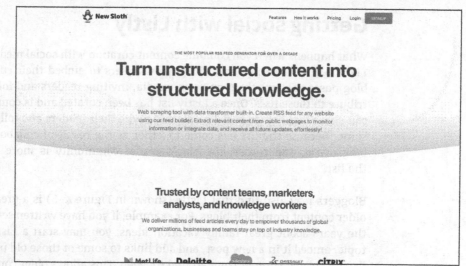

FIGURE 4-7:
New Sloth allows bloggers to syndicate their blog content and send it out along with curated content.

Utilizing syndication with Rapid Feeds

Rapid Feeds, found at www.rapidfeeds.com, offers a free two-week trial to new users followed by a monthly subscription fee that is lower than many of its competitors. Like the other service providers in this section, Rapid Feeds allows bloggers to syndicate and distribute their content in the form of an RSS feed. You can choose to send out syndicated content the moment you hit publish, or you can choose to schedule it to be delivered at a specific time each day.

TIP

Are you interested in podcasting? Rapid Feeds allows you to syndicate and distribute your podcast to subscribers as well! Learn more about podcasting in Book 8.

Curating Content

One place that members of the online community often turn to find great new content is to content curation sites and lists. *Content curation* is simply the gathering and organizing of online content into one location, often through the selection of related content and the compiling of links. A great way to distribute your blog content and find new readers is to find a way to include your content and links within content curation. The following tools are just two ways to ride the wave of content curation's popularity.

Getting social with Listly

What happens when you combine content curation with social media? Listly (www. list.ly) is what happens! Listly allows users to embed their curated lists into blog posts or share them on social media, inviting readers and followers to contribute to those lists. Once a Listly list has been curated and is complete, bloggers can share that list via social media and invite their readers and followers to do the same. Because the list has come together as the result of collaboration between blog owner and reader, the blog's reader community is more likely to share the list.

Bloggers may also find that Listly (shown in Figure 4-8) is a great way to reuse older content from their blogs. For example, if you have written several posts over the years about great family vacation ideas, you may start a Listly around that topic, embed it in a new post, and add links to some of those old posts along with lists of related content from around the web. This allows older content to become evergreen and find new readers.

FIGURE 4-8:
Listly combines content curation with an interactive social vibe.

Digging in with Digg

Digg, once the most popular social bookmarking site and now a top content curation site, considers itself to be somewhat of a front page for all the news of the Internet. That's because the site's purpose is to enable users to share links to content, including favorite posts from around the blogosphere.

To share content on Digg, set up a free account from the Digg home page, found at www.digg.com. Once signed in, you can submit any link by clicking the Submit Link button in the upper right-hand corner, as seen in Figure 4-9.

FIGURE 4-9:
Submit a
link on Digg.

Each time a user "diggs" a submitted link, that link rises in popularity. Digg users can find content by newness of the submission, popularity, or category. You can also search by keyword.

TIP

If you have a post that you absolutely love and want to get the word out about it, consider submitting it on Digg and ask your readers to do the same! While there are certainly a lot of competing voices on the site making it tough for a blog post to rise to the top, you never know and it is certainly worth a try.

Sharing with Social Media

Social media is an especially useful place to share blog content, and the following tools are particularly helpful when it comes to getting the links to your latest post out into the social web. As mentioned in Chapter 3 of this Book, a variety of social media tools are available to help automate your use of various social media platforms. You can also recruit your readers to share your content on their social media accounts.

Spreading the word with Click to Tweet

Click to Tweet, found at www.clicktotweet.com, is a link creation tool that allows you to create a specific tweet that you would like shared by your followers and readers. You can use this tool, linked to your Twitter account, to create a tweet announcing your new blog post (shown in Figure 4-10) and then ask both readers and followers to share.

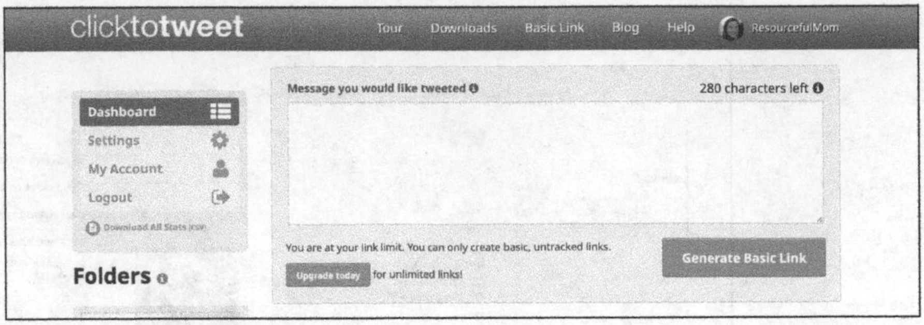

FIGURE 4-10:
Use Click to
Tweet to recruit
readers and
followers to help
share your blog
content.

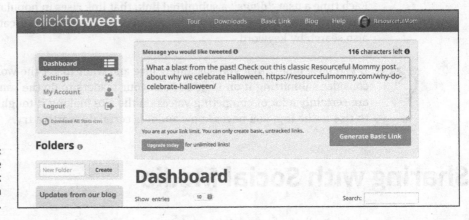

Once you've created the tweet that you would like shared, click Generate Basic Link to receive a link to share, as shown in Figure 4-11.

FIGURE 4-11:
Click Generate
Basic Link
to receive a
link to share.

After creating your Click to Tweet link, you can share your request for tweets anywhere you like, including within the blog post you are linking to, as shown in Figure 4-12.

When readers see your request to tweet, they can click on the linked content and be taken to their Twitter account where the link to your content will automatically appear, as shown in Figure 4-13.

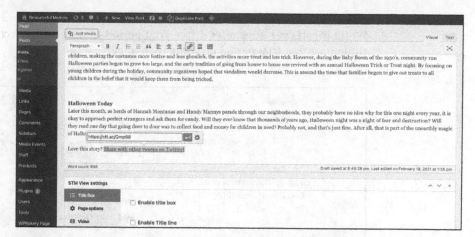

FIGURE 4-12:
Embed the link
to your Click to
Tweet creation to
encourage others
to share.

FIGURE 4-13:
Click to Tweet
automatically
populates a tweet
to share your
blog post link.

TIP

Many blog platforms integrate social media sharing tools directly into blog post options. Look for the opportunity to include buttons with links to all of your social media platforms as well as buttons taking your readers directly to their own accounts where they can automatically share a link to a favorite post.

Scheduling with MeetEdgar

MeetEdgar (www.meetedgar.com), mentioned previously in Chapter 3 of this Book, allows users to schedule social media content in advance, including the sharing of blog post content through scheduled links. This is especially helpful if you have posts you have written previously that you would like to share on a social media platform such as Facebook. You can write the related social media posts with links back to your blog in advance, schedule those social media posts on a planning calendar, then simply wait for MeetEdgar (shown in Figure 4-14) to publish that content!

While MeetEdgar does offer a free trial period to new users, accounts that continue past that trial period do come with a fee.

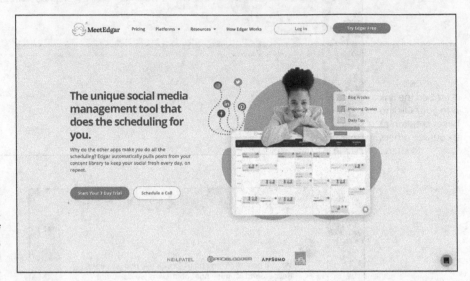

Chapter 5

Inviting or Being a Guest Blogger

O ne of the core components to a successful blog is the networking and community building that a blogger does in support of their blog. Those efforts not only offer ways to broaden online relationships but also open opportunities for cross-promotion with other bloggers through guest blogging. Whether you invite another blogger to write a post on your blog or you write a post for another blogger to publish on their blog, the key is sharing great content with audiences who are likely to find value from it.

Guest blogging also provides a great way to inject new life and fresh ideas into a blog. Every blogger faces blogger's block on occasion and has trouble coming up with new posts or putting a creative spin on a topic they've been writing about for a long period. A guest blog post can bring new energy and perspectives to a blog, giving it a much-needed boost.

This chapter walks you through the process of guest blogging — both being a guest blogger by writing for another blog *and* accepting guest blog posts for publishing on your blog. You find out how to get started and make guest blogging work for you in growing your blog and your online network.

Understanding Guest Blogging

Guest blog posts are posts written for a blog by someone other than the blogger or bloggers who typically author the blog. There are two ways you can get involved with guest blogging:

>> **On your blog:** When you accept guest posts on your blog, it means that you publish posts written by other bloggers who either request permission to write the guest post or whom you invite to write a guest post.

>> **On another blogger's blog:** When you write a guest post for another blog that you don't own or typically write for, you're submitting a guest post for potential publication on that blog.

Most bloggers accept and publish guest posts on their own blogs as a way to build relationships with other bloggers, add a new perspective to their blog content, or attract new readers that the guest blogger may drive to the post. Alternatively, bloggers write guest blog posts to build relationships, share their expertise or opinions, and get to know a new audience that might follow the blogger back to their blog, thereby boosting their own blog traffic.

Defining Your Goals

Whatever reason you choose to accept or write guest blog posts, take the time to define your guest blogging objectives before you get started. Your goals may greatly affect the guest blogging opportunities you pursue. For example, if you want to introduce yourself to new audiences by writing guest posts for other blogs, take the time to research the blogs where your desired audience already spends time and then submit guest blog inquiries to those blogs.

TIP

Think of it this way: Writing guest blog posts for five highly trafficked and targeted blogs could be far more effective in driving repeat traffic to your blog than writing 50 guest blog posts for blogs with little readership and about irrelevant topics.

With that in mind, focus your guest blogging efforts to ensure you get the biggest bang for the buck in terms of meeting your short- and long-term objectives. Both writing and publishing guest blog posts take time, and it's essential that you pursue the best opportunities for you and your blog rather than waste time on many activities that are unlikely to help you achieve your goals.

REMEMBER

Just because a guest blogging opportunity doesn't drive loads of traffic to your blog doesn't mean it wasn't useful and worthwhile. Much of guest blogging is about building relationships with other bloggers.

Being a Guest Blogger

If you're ready to forge new relationships across the blogosphere, expose your content to new audiences, and potentially increase traffic to your own blog, then guest blogging is a great option to pursue. Keep in mind, guest blogging takes time, both in writing great content and in building relationships with other bloggers. It takes time, patience, and a willingness to follow up after your guest post is published to make guest blogging successful.

Writing a guest blog post

Many of the best bloggers built their blogs by including guest blogging in their repertoire of promotional activities. Writing a guest blog post requires time and thought. You need to determine the best topic to write about for the blog and audience where your guest post will be published, and then you need to think of how you can bring your unique voice, opinion, or expertise to that topic to make your post stand out, get noticed, and coexist with the other content on that blog.

The first step to writing a guest blog post is taking the time to read the blog where your post will be published. Get an idea of the content that has already been covered, the content that gets people talking, and the topics that are inappropriate or best to avoid. This is particularly important when you provide a guest post to a well-established blog where the author has already covered every topic and subtopic you can imagine. Take the time to come up with a unique perspective that makes your post irresistible.

REMEMBER

Keep in mind that the blog you're writing for is not your own when you're writing a guest post! Don't forget to consult with the site owner and meet their needs and requests.

For example, the guest post shown in Figure 5-1 was published on one of the most popular blogs about blogging, Darren Rowse's ProBlogger (www.problogger. com). The guest blogger, Sid Savara, took a topic that's often covered on blogs — WordPress plug-ins — and provided a highly focused, extremely useful post with "5 Plugins to Make Your WordPress Blog Blazing Fast." This is just one way to write a great guest blog post — provide immediately actionable and useful information.

FIGURE 5-1:
A unique guest blog post found on ProBlogger.

It's also important to ensure your tone, writing style, post length, and language match the blog where your guest post will be published. In other words, your post needs to comfortably live next to the other content that's already published on the blog. For example, if you provide a guest blog post to a highly political blog, it's safe to assume your post should probably reflect the views typically published on the blog, or you're likely to have a rough experience in the comments section of the post!

TIP

When you write your guest posts, you need to strike a balance to ensure your posts stand out from the other posts but aren't jarringly different from them.

Choosing blogs to write guest posts for

The most important part of choosing which blogs to write guest posts for is to know who your best audience is and find blogs where similar people spend time. Make sure the content on those blogs matches yours in terms of view points, tone, and so on to ensure the audience would be comfortable reading your guest post. Look for blogs that you would enjoy reading if you were looking for the type of information your guest post would contain.

After you create a list of blogs you'd like to send guest blog pitches to, spend some more time reading the content, including the archives and comments, to truly understand the audience and the blogger. Get involved in the conversation by leaving comments and informally introducing yourself to the blogger and their community of readers.

Finally, be sure to check the popularity of blogs you consider sending guest blog post pitches to in order to ensure it's worth your time. Although you might have to start pitching smaller blogs until your online reputation grows, you should at least check to make sure the blog is updated frequently and some comments are left on recent posts. If a blog doesn't seem to have any comments on their posts, it might not be the best place to engage with new potential readers for your blog!

Making your pitch

After you identify a blog where you would like to guest post, you need to contact the blogger behind that blog to make your pitch. You can simply send an email to the blogger (most bloggers provide their email addresses or a contact form on their blogs) to introduce yourself and your guest post idea.

TIP

Don't underestimate the power of social media when reaching out to bloggers. A friendly tweet is often received better than a spammy email. Take the time to introduce yourself and engage before making a request to write for a site.

To make your pitch stand out and increase the likelihood it will be accepted by the blogger, follow these suggestions to write a great query note:

>> **Provide your credentials.** Established bloggers are protective of their readers and only publish guest posts that are well-written and provided by people who can demonstrate their expertise or the added value they bring to the blog. With that in mind, be sure to fully describe yourself, your credentials, and any other information that directly applies to the blog and your guest post to ensure the blog owner understands that you know what you're talking about and have something important to contribute.

>> **Offer your blog and social media statistics.** If your blogging statistics and social media followings are growing or doing well, provide traffic statistics (such as monthly pageviews or number of followers) to the blogger to show you can send some traffic to the blog when you promote your guest post on your own blog.

>> **Demonstrate your blogging knowledge.** If you can send a blog post written in HTML, tell the blogger! It takes a blogger time to copy and paste a guest post, fix formatting issues, add images, and so on. If you can do all of that for them, make sure they know it. They'll appreciate the time saving.

>> **Provide links to your blog and/or online writing.** Show the blogger that you already have an online presence or, at the very least, that you can write well. Guest blog posts should be error free. Demonstrate that you can write the perfect post without any editing on the blogger's part!

>> **Define how you'll promote your post.** If you plan to promote the guest post on your blog, Twitter, Facebook, in a newsletter, and so on, tell the blogger. All that promotion means more potential traffic for the blogger!

>> **Write unique content.** Tell the blogger the post you plan to write for them is 100 percent unique and has not — and will not — be published elsewhere in whole or in part. Duplicated content can hurt a blog's Google search rankings and traffic, so it's important to demonstrate that you understand this.

>> **Include your guest post with your query.** If you've already written your guest blog post, send it to the blogger with your pitch, making it even easier for them to publish it!

TIP

Many bloggers publish guest blogging requirements and guidelines on their blogs. Be sure to search for them before you send your pitch. If a blog states that it is not accepting guest posts, as shown in Figure 5-2, don't spam them with a pitch! The last thing you want is to sully your reputation in the blogging community.

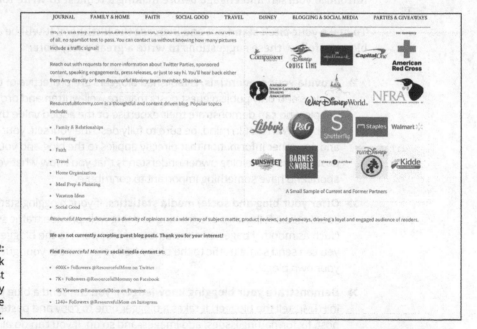

FIGURE 5-2:
Be sure to check a blog's guest blogging policy before reaching out.

Following up after your post is published

When your guest post is accepted and published, that doesn't mean your job is done. Next, you need to promote your guest post, respond to comments left on the post, and make sure both you and the blogger who published your guest post get the most from it in terms of traffic, exposure, and relationship-building.

Many bloggers check their blog analytics to determine the popularity of specific posts, including guest posts. Make yours stand out by promoting it heavily and driving a lot of traffic to it. On the flip side, make sure some of that traffic follows you back to your blog by joining the conversation and forging new relationships with that blog's audience.

If you committed to a certain number of social shares when signing on to write a guest post, be sure to follow through!

Inviting Guest Bloggers to Write Posts for Your Blog

You can open up your blog to guest writers at any time, but until your blog starts to grow in terms of traffic and readership, you're unlikely to get a lot of inquiries. However, it's important to be prepared because you never know when you'll get your first pitch. Also, you can ask other bloggers to write guest posts for your blog at any time. Remember, writing guest blog posts takes time (that's time away from their own blogs), but extending the invitation can never hurt!

If you are hoping to include guest posts on your blog but feel your blog and social media following is not yet in a place that will entice writers, get creative with how to draw writers in! A lot of what makes the blogging community great is the ability to support one another, often in a *quid pro quo* ("I help you and you help me") arrangement. Can you swap guest posts with another blogger also starting out and support each other? Can you provide multiple posts to a more highly trafficked blog in exchange for one post for your blog? Don't be afraid to think outside the box!

Benefits of accepting guest bloggers on your blog

Not only can guest bloggers add new ideas and perspectives to your blog, but they can also bring some traffic with them. Believe it or not, there are benefits to accepting guest bloggers on your blog that go beyond blog traffic. For example, the relationship that you build with a guest blogger may open doors for new opportunities in the future for collaboration or referrals. You never know!

The most obvious and universal benefit of publishing guest posts on your blog is the fact that a guest post equates to one less post you have to write! Take that time off from writing and do some extra off-blog promotion such as commenting on other blogs, social networking, and social bookmarking. Guest posts also add to the frequency of posts on your blog, which helps drive more search traffic to your blog — each new post is a new entryway for Google to find your blog!

Finding guest bloggers for your blog

One of the first steps to opening your blog to guest bloggers is to publish a post announcing it! A "Call for Submissions" post can jumpstart the process by publicizing the news, which you can then share through social media channels such as Twitter, Facebook, and LinkedIn.

If your blogging application allows you to create pages, create a page and publish the link in your blog's top navigation bar or another prominent place on your blog. The page should communicate what people should do in order to submit a guest blog post to your blog.

Furthermore, don't be afraid to reach out to other bloggers you like and ask them if they would be interested in writing a guest post for your blog. The worst that can happen is they say no!

Setting guidelines for guest bloggers

Many bloggers publish guest blogging guidelines on their blogs, so the requirements and restrictions are very clear to anyone who considers submitting a pitch. At the very least, you should have text prepared to respond to email inquiries that outline your requirements.

TIP

Take some time to visit blogs and look for links that say such things such as "Write for Us" or "Post Ideas." Often, bloggers publish guest blogging guidelines on pages labeled in such a way, which you can use to help create your own requirements.

Figure 5-3 shows the guest blogging requirements for HubSpot (www.hubspot.com), which are comprehensive and differ based on which section of HubSpot you're interested in writing for.

Tracking the results

If you want to find out just how much traffic a guest blog post drives to your blog, you need to track the results. You can do this by looking at the number of comments left on the post, the interactivity of the guest blogger in terms of responding to those comments, and using your web analytics tool, as discussed in Chapter 2 of Book 5.

FIGURE 5-3:
Guest blogging
guidelines on
HubSpot.

For example, drill down into your blog analytics to determine how many page views the guest blog post received on the first day it was published, the first week, two weeks, and so on. Then check to see where that traffic came from. If you saw a noticeable bump in comments, traffic, and incoming links to the guest post, then that's a guest blogger you want to invite back!

Repaying the favor

If someone writes a guest blog post for you, you aren't obligated to write a reciprocal post for their blog unless that was discussed during the initial planning. However, it's definitely something you want to do for bloggers whose blogs are well-trafficked or cater to a niche audience that matches yours very well. It's also a relationship you want to maintain and grow in case new opportunities arise in the future.

Separating spam guest post requests from legitimate ones

Many people send guest post requests for the sole purpose of boosting incoming links to their blogs or websites with little or no interest in actually building relationships or real cross-blog promotion. Remember, more incoming links boost a blog or website's Google search rankings, so many unscrupulous people online might send you guest blog requests with ulterior motives.

Unscrupulous companies hire people to generate incoming links for websites and blogs. The content is often republished or loosely related to the blog being pitched, and they add no value to your blog. Therefore, be sure to check the source for guest blog post inquiries to ensure they're legitimate and associate your blog only with websites and people that you want to be connected to.

TIP

You can run guest post submissions through Copyscape (www.copyscape.com), as discussed in Chapter 4 of Book 1, to determine whether the content is original.

Often, the problem comes not from the content of the guest post but from the links within the guest post. For example, a post with seemingly random and irrelevant links to keyword phrases should jump out at you as a link-buying scam, and you shouldn't publish that guest post. Similarly, a keyword phrase that's used repeatedly and hyperlinks to a specific web page could be a blatant attempt at paid link-building. Always use your best judgment and err on the side of caution to protect your blog and your audience from spam.

WARNING

If the links within a guest blog post submitted to you are spam, don't publish the post.

Although you need to be wary of spam guest blog post inquiries, you're also likely to receive legitimate requests. Do your due diligence to get to know the blogger and where the site links within the post will send your readers before you accept a guest blog post, and you should be safe.

7
Making Money from Your Blog

Contents at a Glance

Chapter 1

Blog Advertising 101

Blog advertising comes in many forms, offering bloggers a wide array of monetization options. From text ads to video ads and everything in between, many bloggers dabble in the world of online advertising in an attempt to make money from their blogs, and there's no shortage of advertisers looking for the unique and targeted audiences that blogs already have in place. Why not publish ads on your blog in an attempt to recoup your hosting, design, development, or other costs or as compensation for your time and sweat equity?

Of course, not every blogger feels the same way about advertising, and not every blogging application allows bloggers to monetize their blogs with ads. However, you can't make an educated determination about whether you want to publish ads on your blog until you understand how blog advertising works. This chapter explains the basics, and the remainder of this Book delves into the specifics about the various opportunities the majority of bloggers pursue to make money through blog advertising.

Determining Your Goals

Do you want to make money from your blog? If so, hosting advertisements on your blog is one way to try to do it that does not take much time or effort in comparison to other monetization strategies. Some bloggers shun publishing ads on their blogs believing they reduce the authenticity or credibility of the blog.

However, the majority of bloggers do pursue some kind of advertising opportunity at some point during the course of their lives as bloggers.

With that in mind, you need to determine what your blogging goals are and then decide whether publishing ads on your blog in an attempt to make some money matches those goals or runs counter to them. You might find a happy medium that balances a small number of ads with your amazing content is the best mix for you, your audience, and your blogging goals.

WARNING

Blogs that are covered in ads with little or no original content are typically identified as spam by major search engines such as Google. Make sure your blog includes more original content than ads!

Deciding to Publish Ads on Your Blog

Once you've decided that you're interested in publishing ads on your blog, the real work begins! If you're serious about making money from your blog, be prepared to invest some time into trying new advertising opportunities and testing ad placements until you find the best moneymakers for your blog. Just make sure the advertising opportunities you pursue always complement your overall blogging goals.

Take some time to research a wide variety of advertising opportunities and truly understand the requirements of each before you dive in. Every space on your blog could potentially be monetized, but you need to pick and choose the tactics that help you make money without offending your readers. In other words, never allow your monetization efforts to override your efforts to publish great content. Without great content, your blog can't grow, and without an audience, it's nearly impossible to make money from your blog.

Keep in mind that blog advertising doesn't make many people rich. Certainly, there are exceptions, but the vast majority of bloggers don't make a lot of money from their blogs, despite their efforts. The reason is that successful blog monetization requires a lot of time and dedication in terms of growing your blog and then finding the monetization opportunities that best leverage your audience and traffic patterns to drive income. It's a tough nut to crack, but with patience and persistence, you can make more than pocket change and possibly a lot more than pocket change.

TIP

Darren Rowse of ProBlogger does a great job of chronicling his blog monetization efforts at www.problogger.com.

Reviewing Types of Ads

There are a number of different types of ads that you can publish on your blog as well as other online monetization efforts. The three most common advertising models are

>> **Pay-per-click (PPC):** Advertisers pay the blogger each time a person clicks the advertiser's ad.

>> **Pay-per-impression (PPM):** Advertisers pay the blogger each time the ad appears on the blog's page (that is, each time a person loads the page in their browser).

>> **Pay-per-action (PPA):** The advertiser pays the blogger each time someone clicks the ad and performs an action such as making a purchase or filling out a contact form.

Those advertising models are broken down further into the types of ads that bloggers can publish on their blogs. Following are the most common ad types:

>> **Contextual:** These ads are delivered based on the content on the page where the ad is displayed. The intention is to match ads with relevant content in order to maximize click-throughs.

>> **Text link:** Text link ads are hyperlinked text (usually using specific keywords) within a blog post, list, sidebar, and so on that links to the advertiser's chosen page.

>> **Image:** Banner, button, skyscraper, leaderboard, and any other picture ads qualify as image ads (also called *display ads*). These are described in more detail later in this section.

>> **Video:** Ads that are displayed within online videos (preroll, postroll, overlay, and so on) are a popular option.

>> **Affiliate:** Affiliate advertising gives you the opportunity to place ads for specific products, companies, and services and get paid a predetermined percentage or rate when someone performs an action related to the ad.

>> **Sponsored posts:** Bloggers can write content that has been commissioned and sponsored by a brand client in exchange for payment, as shown in Figure 1-1 at www.caseypalmer.com.

FIGURE 1-1:
Sponsored
content is
one type of
advertising
on blogs.

Bloggers can publish a variety of specific types of image ads to make money, including

>> **Banner:** Display (image) ads that appear on a website and link directly to the advertiser's landing page are called *banner ads.*

>> **Button:** Button ads are a popular form of display advertising on blogs because they fit well in a blog's sidebar and don't take up a lot of real estate. Button ads are typically 125 pixels wide by 125 pixels high and are commonly placed in groups of two, four, six, or eight.

>> **Skyscraper:** Ads that are tall and narrow are called *skyscraper ads.* The most common sizes are 120 pixels wide by 600 pixels high or 160 pixels wide by 600 pixels high. Skyscraper ads fit well in a blog's sidebar.

>> **Leaderboard:** Ads that are short and wide are called *leaderboard ads.* The most common size is 728 pixels wide by 90 pixels high. Leaderboard ads fit well above or below a blog's header.

>> **Transitional:** Ads that appear as a web page before, in between, or after a visitor arrives at the webpage are *transitional.* Transitional ads are often referred to as *interstitial, introstitial,* or *exterstitial,* depending on where they appear within a website.

>> **Floating:** Floating ads appear to float or move across a web page in front of the actual page content.

>> **Pop-up, pop-over, pop-under:** Ads that appear in a window in front of or behind the window a visitor is viewing are called *pop-up, pop-over,* or *pop-under ads.*

>> **Peel-back:** Peel-back ads appear behind a web page and look like a corner of the page is lifted up to expose the ad beneath it (like the corner of a page of a book is being peeled back to expose the page behind it). When the visitor clicks the corner, the web page appears to peel back, and the ad beneath it is fully displayed.

>> **Expandable:** Expandable ads are typically image ads that enlarge when a visitor's mouse pointer hovers over them or when the visitor clicks them.

Many bloggers find a mix of ad types and payment models that works best for them through trial and error over time, as shown in Figure 1-2 at www. knowitallnikki.com where both banner ads and sidebar ads are utilized. Don't be afraid to try new programs, but always read the agreements, terms and conditions, and other legal documents before you sign up for a new program to ensure it will help you meet your goals.

FIGURE 1-2:
Know It All Nikki uses multiple types of ads.

TIP

For each advertising opportunity you pursue, check the payment method, payout threshold, support provided, whether you're allowed to publish other ads on your site, placement requirements, and so on. Also, make sure you can cancel at any time.

Setting Earnings Expectations

If you're a new blogger with little traffic to your blog, you can't expect to make much money. Your earnings will increase as your traffic grows, your content archive grows, and your efforts in testing advertising opportunities allow you to hone in on the best options for your blog.

You're likely to hear stories of bloggers making thousands of dollars each month from their blogs. It's certainly possible for you to do the same. However, don't be tempted to cover your blog with ads.

As you read through this Book, you find out about a variety of blog advertising options as well as the positives and negatives of each. Be sure you understand the potential pitfalls before you commit to publishing ads on your blog that could do more harm than good.

Set small goals for your monetization efforts and continually boost them as your time as a blogger and your audience grow. For example, set a reasonably attainable goal to make $25 per month within three months, and $100 per month within six months. Again, your goals depend on your overall blogging goals and your commitment to monetizing your blog.

Keeping Ethics and Legalities in Mind

WARNING

There are many forms of blog advertising, many of which you can learn about in this book. However, you should avoid participating in any advertising opportunities that are illegal or could be deemed unethical by the blogging and search communities. For example, the Federal Trade Commission issues laws and restrictions related to publishing reviews or endorsements online and accepting free products or payments in return for publishing such reviews, which you can review in Title 16 Part 255 of the Code of Federal Regulations (CFR) available at your local library or at www.ftc.gov. Here's the specific URL for Part 255 of the electronic CFR: https://www.ecfr.gov/current/title-16/section-255.5.

In terms of ethics, the blogosphere also penalizes bloggers for ads that aren't disclosed as such, particularly reviews and text link ads. For example, search engines, such as Google, consider text ads as a deceptive practice that artificially inflate the assumed popularity of the web page the link leads to. Potential sponsored content clients are also less likely to work with a blogger if they feel that that blogger hasn't been honest and disclosed paid relationships in the past. The key is to remember to be honest, disclose ads as such, and follow the law.

Tips for Advertising Success

There's no single recipe for blog monetization success. If there were, everyone would be following that plan! Instead, the successful bloggers make money because they do several things well, and you can do them, too. Check out the following tips to boost your advertising success:

>> **Stay focused.** Both your blog content and ads should be highly focused and appeal to your blog's audience in order to drive any interest to them from visitors.

>> **Test.** Placement, type, and size are all critical components to the success of the advertising you place on your blog. Take the time to test different ways of displaying the ads on your blog as well as the types of ads you publish in order to find the best mix for your blog.

>> **Diversify.** Don't put all your eggs in one basket. Instead, publish a variety of ad models and types to not only make your blog visually appealing and allow each ad to stand out, but also to continually test performance of different opportunities.

>> **Monitor your blog ads.** No matter what advertisements you decide to publish on your blog, always make certain that the ads that actually appear on your blog match what you expected from the advertiser and are appropriate for your blog. It's not uncommon for irrelevant or offensive ads to sneak onto your blog through large advertising networks. Monitor your blog ads to ensure they don't negatively affect the experience visitors have on your blog.

>> **Focus on growth**. Always write great content, work on boosting incoming links, build your community, and grow your audience. Without those things, you'll have a hard time finding advertisers who are interested in placing ads (at least ones who pay well) on your blog.

>> **Track results.** Pay close attention to the performance of the ads on your blog so you can make changes as necessary. If an ad isn't driving revenue, replace it. That's valuable advertising space on your blog. Don't give it away for free, and don't let it go to waste!

TIP

Some advertising programs, such as affiliate networks or sponsored post networks, provide tracking reports to ad publishers, so it's easy to analyze how ads are performing on your blog. If tracking is vitally important to you, make sure the program you choose has such a feature.

It's also important to understand that different advertising opportunities have different technical requirements in terms of how you integrate the ads into your blog, how long the ads take to load on your blog, and how the auto-play functions of the ad work. Some of these requirements could negatively affect your blog.

For example, if an ad causes your blog to load extremely slowly, that ad is negatively affecting the user experience on your blog. The last thing you want is for someone to click away from your blog because an ad is causing it to load in a browser too slowly. Be sure to read and understand the technical requirements of placing ads on your blog supplied by the advertiser to ensure you can handle them and are comfortable with them.

IN THIS CHAPTER

» **Getting to know different types of advertising**

» **Looking at the benefits of specific advertising types**

» **Understanding the drawbacks of various advertising models**

» **Knowing where to find advertisers**

Chapter **2**

Publishing Advertising

O nce you've made the decision to monetize your blog, it's time to take a deeper look at the different options available to help you earn money. If you decide to employ advertisements as one form of monetization, it is important to understand the various types of ads that you may encounter. Each type of advertisement earns you money in a slightly different way, and knowing your options may help you decide which ads you're willing to try.

This chapter introduces you to contextual advertising so you can evaluate contextual advertising opportunities and programs in order to choose the best ones to experiment with on your blog. It also walks you through an introduction to text link ads so you fully understand the pros and cons of publishing them on your blog. You also find out about some of the most popular text link advertising programs, so you can begin experimenting with them if you choose.

I also discuss impression-based ads so you understand their pros and cons and can make the best decision about testing impression ads on your blog. You'll find out about some of the most popular impression-based advertising programs, so you can begin your experimentation. Finally, this chapter looks at feed and email advertising and what you need to consider before including them in your overall monetization strategy.

Understanding the Different Types of Advertising

While the following sections aren't an exhaustive look at types of blog advertising, they do provide a good general overview at the types of ads you may encounter when deciding to monetize. Take some time to think about what makes the most sense for your site and what will be best received by your readers. Remember that it's okay to mix and match ad types!

REMEMBER

If at first you don't succeed, try, try again! Not every type of ad performs equally across all blogs. If you've placed an ad on your site and it isn't working for you or for your client, it's okay to pivot and go in a different direction. After all, you want happy advertisers and a happy bank account!

Fitting in with contextual ads

Contextual ads are text, image, or video ads that are displayed to your blog visitors based on the content on the page where the ads appear (shown in Figure 2-1). They are one of the most popular types of online advertising, and many bloggers publish them on their blogs in an effort to derive an income. These ads come in a variety of formats and offer several payment models for bloggers to choose from, making them flexible and easy to implement on your blog.

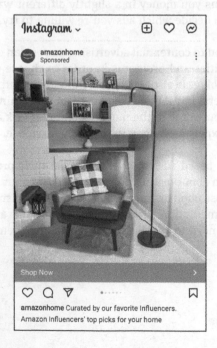

FIGURE 2-1:
Social media platforms often use contextual ads based on the types of accounts you follow.

Because these ads are contextually relevant to your blog's content, visitors are expected to be more likely to be interested in them and click them than they would completely irrelevant ads.

For example, if you write a blog about pregnancy, an ad about smoking products or alcohol would be highly irrelevant and unlikely to generate interest or perform well. If an ad can't generate interest and click-throughs, you won't make any money from it. That's why contextual relevance is so important, and that's why contextual advertising is so popular for advertisers and ad publishers.

TECHNICAL STUFF

Contextual ads typically use the pay-per-click payment model, but pay-per-impression and pay-per-action contextual ads exist as well. (Payment models are discussed in detail in Chapter 1 of this Book.)

Inserting ads with text link advertising

Text link ads are exactly what the name implies: text links that advertisers pay for, which lead people to the advertiser's web page. Many companies sell text link ads, and different programs have different publisher requirements in terms of whether or not your blog will be accepted.

When you join a text link advertising program, you submit specific pages of your blog into the network's inventory. Advertisers look for inventory pages that are likely to attract visitors who will be interested in their products. When they find pages they want to advertise on, they purchase text link ad space on those pages, and an ad from that advertiser appears in that space. You earn money each time someone clicks the text link ad published on your blog. It's that simple!

Blogs with a lot of content that are highly trafficked can make quite a bit of money from relevant text link ads.

WARNING

Text link ads can generate a nice amount of income from your blog, but they're controversial because search engines view them as a way to artificially inflate the popularity of a web page. For example, Google's search-results-ranking algorithm includes the number of incoming links to a web page as assumptive of that page's popularity, believing that the more people who link to a web page, the better the content must be. Therefore, paying for links skews the assumed popularity of a web page, and Google punishes both the text link advertiser and publisher for giving an unfair advantage to the advertiser's search rankings. In fact, your blog could be dropped from Google search results entirely if you publish text link ads.

Text link ads may or may not be contextually based, and they can appear *inline* (within the body copy of your posts) or as standalone links, as shown in Figure 2-2 (notice the text links within the post and in the sidebar under the

Related Resources heading). Payment models also differ, with the most common being the pay-per-click method.

FIGURE 2-2:
Examples of inline and standalone text link ads.

Counting pageviews with impression-based advertising

Impression-based ads pay you each time the page on your blog loads (hence the term "impression") that the ads appear on, and they offer a great way to monetize your blog. Although many impression-based ad networks have strict requirements for publishers related to traffic levels and content, it's not impossible for beginner bloggers to find programs to join.

In simplest terms, you're paid based on the number of times an ad is shown on your blog. With each pageview where the ad is placed, that ad is delivered to a visitor, which counts as an impression. Advertisers pay bloggers a small fee, such as $0.10 per 1,000 impressions, so you're not likely to make a lot of money from these ads unless your blog is very highly trafficked.

REMEMBER

Typically, impression-based ads pay less per impression to publishers than most pay-per-click or pay-per-action ads, but blogs with high traffic levels can earn a nice amount of money from them. In fact, many impression-based ad programs accept only well-trafficked blogs into their networks. The reason is simple: Advertisers want to make sure they're going to get enough exposure (page views) to make their monetary investment worthwhile.

That's not to say that a blogger with a smaller audience can't find an impression-based advertising program that will accept them. The more targeted your blog content is and the more desirable your niche blog audience is to advertisers, the more likely you are to secure impression-based advertising on your blog.

REMEMBER

Many bloggers think impression-based ads, as shown in Figure 2-3, are the ultimate form of advertising to monetize their blogs, but that isn't always the case. Unless your blog gets a lot of traffic, you won't make a lot of money from impression-based ads. However, it's guaranteed money if you have a highly trafficked blog because no action is required by your audience in order for you to earn an income from impression-based ads.

FIGURE 2-3:
ClassyMommy.
com runs
impression-based
ads in the footer
and sidebar.

Taking advantage of feed and email advertising

So you're chugging along, monetizing your blog, and everything seems to be going well. Only, there's a catch: Some of your regular readers don't visit your blog page very often because they receive your blog posts via an RSS feed or email newsletter. Wait, wait, don't panic just yet! There's a solution: Add advertisements to your syndicated content. There are several programs that make the process of setting up this type of advertising easy for you, and once it's set up, it typically works on its own with little intervention by you.

TECHNICAL STUFF

RSS feeds are mentioned in Chapter 4 of Book 6. In short, feeds are distributed using Really Simple Syndication (RSS). They include either full or partial content from your blog. Each time you publish a new post to your blog, it's distributed via your blog's feed to anyone who subscribes to it. Subscribers can access your blog's feed via email or through a feed reader, making it easy for subscribers to find new, enjoyable content in one place rather than visiting each blog individually to determine if new content has been published. Email syndication works in a similar way in that your readers choose to receive your content via email delivery rather than only by visiting your blog. While it is possible to schedule and automate some aspects of content delivery through email subscriptions, it is never as automated as an RSS subscription.

Feed advertising enables bloggers to insert ads within their blogs' feeds. For example, an advertisement could automatically appear in between posts within a blog's feed thanks to a feed advertising service. Bloggers can also sell newsletter ad space and insert advertising themselves before sending out email campaigns, as shown in Figure 2-4.

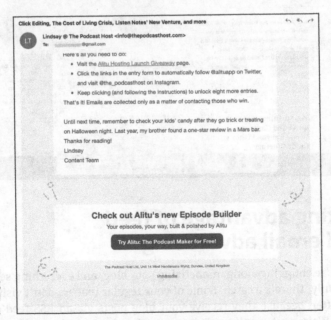

FIGURE 2-4: Bloggers can add advertising to email newsletters.

Most feed advertising programs allow you to choose the type of ads you want to display in your blog's feed, including text or image ads. You may also be able to customize the colors of the ads displayed in your feed and choose the position where ads are placed, such as above or below each post in your feed.

Feed advertising programs usually use the pay-per-click payment method, so you earn money every time a person clicks an ad displayed in your blog's feed.

Benefiting From Each Ad Type

As with all blog monetization opportunities, there are positives and negatives to each type of advertising. The following sections take a closer look at how to get the most out of each ad type and what to consider before you choose to display each of these common types of ads on your blog or in your feed. Knowing what to expect and hope for will ensure that the type of advertising you try is the appropriate way for you to meet your monetization objectives. (The negatives are assessed later in this chapter.)

Getting the most benefit from contextual ads

Not all contextual advertising programs are equal, and none are likely to make you rich. However, they're an important element to test as part of your blog-revenue-generating plan.

The best way to boost your earning potential from contextual advertising is to write highly focused content so that the most relevant ads are displayed on your site. For example, fashion blogger Gabi Fresh, found at www.gabifresh.com, blogs exclusively about topics related to all things fashion. It is not a coincidence that the contextual ads appearing on her site, as shown in Figure 2-5, are also related to fashion, style, and shopping.

Furthermore, it's essential that you spend time growing your blog. The larger your blog's audience of targeted readers, the greater chance there is for people to click the contextual ads placed on your site. As your blog grows, you can also secure higher paying advertising opportunities because advertisers are apt to pay more for exposure to a larger, highly targeted audience.

Often advertisers bid on keywords related to their ad in an attempt to secure placement on websites and blogs that have a built-in audience of people who are already likely to be interested in their ads. In other words, they determine the maximum amount they're willing to pay to place ads on sites that match their chosen keywords, and ad space is given to the highest bidder, similar to an auction. For bloggers, that means writing with keywords in mind can give your contextual advertising income a boost. Bloggers who write about topics with popular keywords that many advertisers are actively bidding on are likely to earn more than bloggers who write about topics with less-popular related keywords. That's because as more advertisers bid on specific keywords through the common auction process that contextual advertising programs such as Google AdSense use, the price for those keywords goes up.

FIGURE 2-5: Contextual ads are relevant to the content of the page where they're displayed.

REMEMBER

It's important to note that focusing on popular keywords might cause you to earn less money than focusing on less-popular keywords. The reason is simple: Popular keywords have a lot more competition for advertisers' dollars. It's difficult for a smaller blog to compete with big, established websites and blogs for extremely popular keywords. Can you imagine competing for a broad, popular keyword such as politics with all the other blogs and websites related to politics that have significantly bigger audiences than yours? You're unlikely to win.

Therefore, a better strategy might be to focus on highly targeted, less-popular keywords (such as *California local politics*, if your blog is about local politics in California) that draw attention from advertisers who are looking to promote their products and services to your blog's niche audience. The assumption is that your audience will be more valuable in terms of conversions than a broader, less-focused audience would be.

TIP

You can find out more about keywords and analyzing keyword popularity in Chapter 2 of Book 2.

Unfortunately, there's no written recipe for success that any blogger can follow to earn money from contextual advertising. Instead, the best course of action is to experiment. Test types of ads, payment models, placement, keywords, and so on until you find the recipe that works for you, your blog, and your audience. Every blog is different, and it takes time to determine which ad mix drives the most interest and revenue on your blog.

Knowing the positives of text link ads

Just like contextual advertising, text link ads have some great things going for them. They're fairly unobtrusive to the user experience on your blog, and they take up little space (or no additional space in the case of inline text ads). For bloggers who want to make as much money as possible from the limited space on their blogs, text link ads are very attractive.

At the same time, text link ads tend to convert better in terms of generating click-throughs than other types of ads, particularly inline text ads, because readers assume the text link will take them to more useful information. In other words, they might be fooled into thinking the link isn't an ad at all. Unfortunately, this misconception is also a negative because it could be considered unethical and a loose bait-and-switch tactic. It's up to you as a blogger to determine the level of transparency you require on your blog to protect the user experience.

REMEMBER

One of the biggest positives of text link ads is the simplicity of integrating them into your blog. Most text link ad programs make it extremely easy to sell space on your blog to eager advertisers. The more focused your blog's content is, and the more traffic it receives, the more money you can make from text link ads.

Looking at the positives of impression-based ads

Depending on how much traffic your blog receives, you may find that impression-based ads are not for you because it may take a while before you see any decent payout. However, impression-based ads are popular with many bloggers because no action is necessary for you to make money. In other words, each time the ad is displayed on your blog (meaning each time someone loads a page on your blog where the ad appears), you earn money regardless of whether visitors click the ad or notice it at all.

REMEMBER

If your blog *does* receive a large amount of traffic, impression-based ads are a good investment for potential advertisers on your blog, which makes them an easier sell for you. They typically pay out less than pay-per-click advertisements while increasing brand awareness and recognition. They're also often well-targeted because advertisers use your site's demographics to select what ads to serve. This makes them less intrusive on your site.

Prospering with feed and email advertising

Many bloggers view their blog feeds and email newsletters as lost monetization opportunities because people who subscribe to blogs and read them via email or a feed reader often don't click through and visit the blog where the post was published. This is particularly true for bloggers who syndicate full-text feeds of their blog posts, because subscribers can read the entire content of those posts through their feed reader or via email (depending on their chosen subscription method).

The reason is simple. If people aren't clicking through to your blog, they don't see the ads and other monetization tactics on your blog at all, which means you lose the chance to generate ad revenue from them. Inserting ads in your blog's feed helps offset that lost opportunity.

You can't benefit from feed and email ads if no one is clicking them. In order to maximize your earnings from this type of ad, you need to monitor them to ensure they're relevant to the content of your blog. If they're not relevant, your blog subscribers are unlikely to be interested in them and less likely to click them. It's up to you to analyze the relevancy of ads displayed in your feed and ensure the program is meeting your needs and goals.

Placing ads in your email newsletters allows you to have optimum control over the ads your readers view. No matter which email newsletter tool you use, be sure to carefully monitor the metrics related to each email campaign including data such as email open rate. Because you have the ability to sell and place advertising in your emailed content, it is important to be able to share potential metrics with possible advertisers.

Recognizing the Negatives of Each Ad Type

Just as each advertisement type includes inherent ways to benefit and reasons why you should consider choosing each ad type, they also have potential negatives. The following sections dive into what possible negatives to consider before you choose to utilize each type of ad.

It is up to you to determine if the negatives outweigh the positives and you should opt to not include this type of advertisement in your monetization strategy.

Exposing the negatives of publishing contextual ads

As with anything, there is a downside to publishing contextual ads on your blog. Foremost, your contextual advertising earning potential is only as good as the contextual advertising program from which you publish ads.

Most contextual advertising programs such as Google AdSense or Media.net (both discussed later in this chapter) rely on computer algorithms to determine content relevancy and display ads accordingly. If the algorithm is subpar, the ads displayed on your blog may be irrelevant to your content and uninteresting to your audience. That means click-throughs will be lower than they would be for highly relevant ads, and that means less revenue for you.

Irrelevant ads can also damage the user experience on your blog, particularly if ads that are considered to be inappropriate or offensive to your audience are displayed on your blog. For example, displaying an ad for fast food burgers on a vegan lifestyle blog might not go over well. With that in mind, it's essential that you monitor the ads that appear on your blog to ensure they are acceptable and relevant.

REMEMBER

Another negative to contextual advertising is the earning potential. You need three things to earn money from contextual advertising:

>> An audience: Without traffic to your blog, you won't make any money because there aren't enough people to click the ads on your blog.

>> A good contextual advertising program: As mentioned earlier, if the contextual ads that appear on your blog are irrelevant, your earning potential goes down.

>> Focused content —a lot of it: The more targeted content you write for the keywords you choose to focus on, the more opportunities there are for relevant ads to display on your blog to an interested audience.

If you don't have these three things going for you, your contextual advertising income is likely to be limited. Be patient and persistent. Your earnings should rise over time as you spend more time testing programs, researching keywords, growing your blog traffic, and writing focused content.

Uncovering the negatives of text link ads

Text link ads have some drawbacks, and they're nothing to sneeze at. They can frustrate your blog's visitors who click a link within one of your blog posts and end up getting an ad in return. You certainly don't want to drive traffic away from your blog because your links fail to meet expectations and the user experience becomes frustrating! However, a negative user experience isn't the only drawback of publishing text link ads on your blog.

The biggest problem with text link ads is the potential harm they could do to the amount of search traffic that comes to your blog. Google and other search engines rank web pages in terms of keyword relevancy and usefulness and return results for keyword searches based on that algorithm, which includes a component related to incoming links. Although no one but the inner circle of Google's employees knows the secrets of Google's page-ranking algorithm, one thing is for certain — Google doesn't like sponsored links (such as text link ads) because they artificially inflate a site's popularity.

WARNING

Google believes that the best pages on the web will naturally receive a lot of incoming links because people organically want to share that content. If someone pays for incoming links, that person is artificially inflating the popularity of the linked web pages. As a result, Google has been known to punish both the advertiser and text link ad publisher by dropping both sites' standing in Google search results or eliminating them from Google search results entirely. Most blogs generate the bulk of their traffic from Google searches. Imagine the harm that a lowered place in Google search results or even removal from Google search could do to your blog.

Although some text link ad networks claim to have procedures in place to protect advertisers and publishers, unless the link uses the NoFollow HTML tag, which means Google won't include the link in its ranking process, there's no way to be sure publishing text link ads on your blog is safe.

TECHNICAL STUFF

The NoFollow HTML tag can be added to any link to make that link invisible to Google when it counts incoming links to a site for ranking purposes. You can find out more about the NoFollow tag in Chapter 1 of Book 5.

TIP

Only you can decide whether the safeguards used by the text link advertising network coupled with the revenue potential are enough to meet your goals for your blog. Weigh the positives and negatives carefully and proceed with caution. See the nearby sidebar for a real-world case study in the negative effects of text link advertising.

Reviewing the problems with impression-based ads

Before jumping on the impression-based ads bandwagon, you should know the downsides to impression-based ads. Aside from limited earning potential, wherein only highly trafficked blogs are likely to make a lot of money from impression-based ads, the format has a few other problems as well.

TEXT LINK ADS AND THE DEATH OF A BLOG NETWORK

Know More Media was a popular business blog network founded in late 2005 with nearly 100 highly trafficked blogs by 2008. Know More Media employed business experts to author the blogs in the network and sold ad space to cover expenses. The network grew quickly and derived a large amount of traffic from Google and other search engines until one day in 2008 when Google traffic to all blogs in the network virtually stopped.

What happened?

It took some investigation, but the definitive answer was that Know More Media published text link ads on its blogs without the NoFollow HTML tag, and it was punished severely for it.

Just a few months earlier, Know More Media had begun displaying text ads on its blogs, and Google dropped all of the Know More Media blogs from its search ranking. After removing the text link ads from all Know More Media blogs and spending a few months trying to work with Google to get the Know More Media blogs included in Google search results again, Know More Media saw no signs of redemption or reinclusion.

With no search traffic, the entire network folded, and Know More Media closed its doors in mid-2008.

First, you need to be certain that the advertiser or program you join is accurately counting pageviews. Make sure you join a program that provides detailed reports and match them up to your own site analytics to ensure they're correct.

Furthermore, impression-based ads are a great way for bloggers to monetize the area of their blog below the fold (the *fold* is the area that's visible in a browser window without scrolling when a page loads), which works very well for publishers but not for advertisers. That's why many advertisers have strict placement restrictions related to their impression-based ads —to ensure their ads aren't hidden in places where no one will see them.

Some impression-based advertisers even have restrictions on where other ads can be placed on your blog when their ads are displayed. For example, an advertiser might require that its impression-based ad be published within the top 720 pixels of your blog with no other ads appearing above the 720-pixel mark. In essence, the advertiser wants its ad to be the only one visible above the fold on your blog. These requirements can severely limit the advertising flexibility on your blog.

REMEMBER

Always check the restrictions on ad placement and participation in other advertising programs for the impression-based ad network you join to ensure it doesn't actually reduce your blog's earning potential.

It's important to balance the amount of money you're likely to generate from impression-based ads by placing them in premium locations on your blog against the earning potential that pay-per-click or pay-per-action ads could derive from those premium locations. That's why testing and experimenting is so important to finding the best earnings plan for your blog.

Uncovering the negatives of feed and email ads

Although many bloggers are proponents of placing ads in your syndicated feeds and email newsletters, there are just as many bloggers who refuse to insert ads into their blogs' feeds.

The primary reason is because they believe ads in distributed content such as an RSS feed or an email campaign clutter the actual content of the feed and create a negative user experience (particularly if the ads are irrelevant to the blog's content), making it even less likely that the subscriber will click through to read more from the blogger. Even worse, some bloggers believe that a feed covered in ads turns off subscribers so much that they not only unsubscribe from the blog but also stop visiting the blog altogether.

TIP

If you see your blog subscribers decreasing after you add advertising to your blog's feed or newsletter, take a closer look to determine whether the ads are the reason. Take some time to analyze the amount of money you're earning from ads to ensure the benefits outweigh the negatives.

Knowing Where to Find Advertising by Type

Once you've made the decision to add advertising to your blog, syndicated content, or email outreach, you need to know where to start to find advertisers interested in placing their ads on your blog.

The following sections take a look at where to start to find advertisers that may be a fit for your content. This is a small sampling and the area of digital marketing is an ever-changing landscape. Be sure to ask around the blogosphere for recommendations before you join a network and don't be afraid to reach out to potential advertisers on your own as well!

Finding popular contextual ad programs

There are many contextual advertising networks that you can join in order to serve ads and make money from your blog, but the same programs don't always work well for all bloggers. Always research contextual advertising programs that you consider joining to ensure the payout method, payout threshold, requirements, and restrictions match your goals before you join.

TECHNICAL STUFF

Some contextual advertising programs have established requirements that sites and blogs need to meet in order to be accepted into the network. Be sure to review any requirements before you join a program. Of course, as your blog grows, it will qualify to participate in more contextual advertising programs, some of which may perform better than the broad and highly popular programs such as Google AdSense.

The following sections feature some of the most popular contextual advertising programs; read on to figure out whether one of them works for you.

Google AdSense

www.google.com/adsense

Google AdSense, shown in Figure 2-6, is the most popular contextual advertising program. It's easy to include Google AdSense ads on your blog, and ads come in a variety of formats. Payments are reliable, and it's rare to see an ad space left open on your blog for long.

With such a big program and the mammoth Google algorithm behind it, Google AdSense is certainly the simplest program to implement. That's why most bloggers experiment with it before they try another ad program. Unfortunately, that also means your earning potential from Google AdSense might be more limited because there are so many blogs and websites competing for available ads, and the relevancy of ads served can sometimes be questionable.

Additionally, it's not uncommon for spam ads to be served through Google AdSense. It's up to you to monitor the ads served on your blog to ensure they're appropriate and modify your account settings or notify Google when problems arise.

FIGURE 2-6:
The Google
AdSense
homepage.

Google AdSense offers a variety of ad sizes for you to choose from and display on your blog, making it extremely versatile, as shown in Figures 2-7 through 2-10. There are display ads, in-feed ads, in-article ads, and multiplex ads.

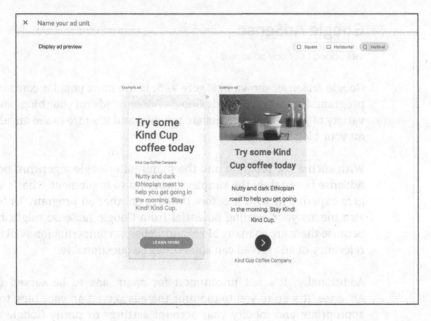

FIGURE 2-7:
Google AdSense
display ads.

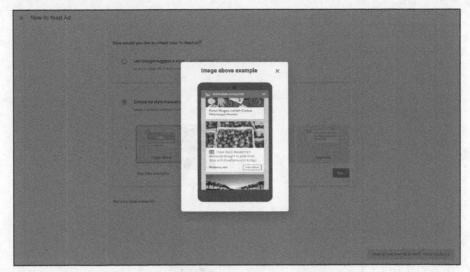

FIGURE 2-8:
Google AdSense
in-feed ads.

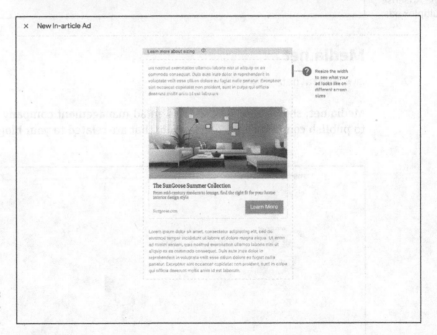

FIGURE 2-9:
Google AdSense
in-article ads.

After you sign up for a Google account and configure your AdSense settings, you can select an ad unit, copy the provided HTML code, and paste it on your blog where you want ads to appear (often in the sidebar, header, or between posts). Within a couple of days, ads start appearing on your blog. You can log in to your Google AdSense account at any time to track your earnings and modify your ad settings. It's entirely up to you to manage your Google AdSense account. You earn money when visitors to your blog click a Google AdSense ad displayed on your blog.

FIGURE 2-10:
Google AdSense
multiplex ads.

Media.net

`www.media.net`

Media.net, shown in Figure 2-11, is an ad management company that allows you to publish contextual ads on your site that are related to your blog's content.

FIGURE 2-11:
Media.net
manages
contextual ads.

Unlike Google AdSense, which is available for bloggers just starting out, Media. net requires potential publishing partners to contact them and apply. In other words, if your blog is brand new and your traffic reflects that, this may not be the ad program for you.

Propeller Ads

www.propellerads.com

Propeller Ads offers a variety of ad formats for bloggers, and with a minimum payout threshold of only $5 and no traffic minimum, it is a potential alternative to Google AdSense for bloggers who don't yet have huge metrics to support applying to another ad network.

To join Propeller Ads, visit https://publishers.propellerads.com and click Register to be taken to the sign-up page, as shown in Figure 2-12.

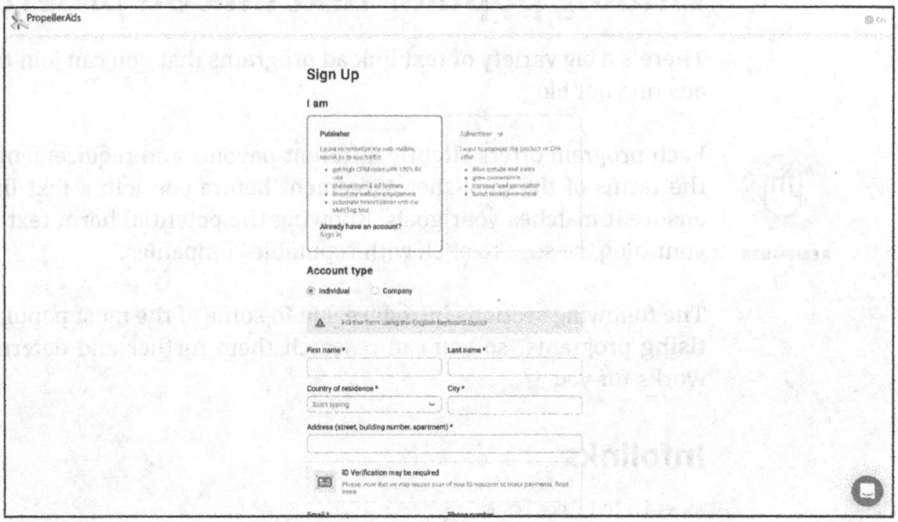

FIGURE 2-12:
Sign-up for
Propeller Ads.

Vibrant

www.vibrantmedia.com

Vibrant Media, shown in Figure 2-13, offers a variety of contextual advertising options for bloggers to make money from their blogs. Unfortunately, the Vibrant Media program has an exceptionally high requirement in terms of the number of pageviews your blog needs to generate each month in order to sign up for the program, but it's definitely worth putting the program on your radar.

FIGURE 2-13:
Vibrant Media
offers ads for
highly trafficked
websites.

Finding popular text link ad programs

There's a big variety of text link ad programs that you can join to publish text link ads on your blog.

REMEMBER

Each program offers slightly different payouts and requirements. Always read all the terms of the publisher agreement before you join a text link ad program to ensure it matches your goals. Knowing the potential harm text link ads can do to your blog, be sure to stick with reputable companies.

The following sections introduce you to some of the most popular text link advertising programs, so you can research them further and determine whether one works for you.

Infolinks

www.infolinks.com

Infolinks offers a variety of ad types to publishers, including in-text link ads. Payouts begin at the $50 threshold and are available through PayPal to make ease of payment easier. You can learn more by visiting www.infolinks.com, shown in Figure 2-14.

FIGURE 2-14:
Infolinks offers
in-text link ads.

LinkWorth

www.linkworth.com

LinkWorth, shown in Figure 2-15, offers a wide variety of text ad formats. LinkWorth publishers (called *partners*) can configure their accounts to use the NoFollow HTML tag with all text link ads, thereby avoiding any problems with a drop in Google search rankings and traffic.

FIGURE 2-15:
LinkWorth offers
text link ads.

Text link ads might seem like easy money, but they can do more harm than good. Do your research first!

Skimlinks

www.skimlinks.com

Skimlinks, shown in Figure 2-16, is a text link ad network that pays out at a low minimum threshold and is popular with many bloggers. It is free to join and there is no monthly site traffic minimum to get started serving ads on your blog.

FIGURE 2-16: Skimlinks is a popular text link ad server.

Finding popular impression-based ad programs

You have many impression-based ad programs to choose from, and it's up to you to read the current requirements of each program in order to determine whether a program is right for you to test on your blog. Requirements change frequently! The following sections identify some of the most popular and well-known impression-based ad programs to help you get started.

Carefully read all impression-based advertising agreements before you sign them to ensure you're willing and able to comply with them.

Mediavine

www.mediavine.com

Mediavine is a very popular blog ad network, especially with lifestyle bloggers. While some bloggers report that Mediavine pays out at a higher cost-per-impression rate than other similar ad networks, always keep a close eye on your site metrics and the related money earned in order to evaluate if this is a monetization strategy that is working for you. In order to apply, visit www.mediavine.com, as shown in Figure 2-17.

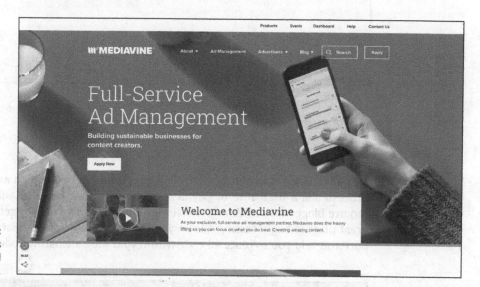

FIGURE 2-17: Mediavine offers impression-based ads for bloggers.

Revcontent

www.revcontent.com

Revcontent, shown in Figure 2-18, stands out a bit from the crowd because of the option to customize the look of the ads that appear on your site. Bloggers who use Revcontent ads do so by placing *widgets* (blocks of content that display an interactive graphic on a blog) within their site's content. Revcontent allows bloggers to see what the ads will look like before they are placed on their site.

FIGURE 2-18:
Revcontent uses widgets to place ads on blogs.

AdMaven

www.ad-maven.com

AdMaven (shown in Figure 2-19) is a popular ad network with an easy sign-up process and a high rate of payment per impression. Because AdMaven doesn't require bloggers to achieve a certain level of traffic in order to get started, it is a great place to begin testing ads on your blog. They also offer great technical support and help you to place ad code within your blog's existing code.

FIGURE 2-19:
AdMaven allows bloggers with little traffic to join their ad network.

Finding popular feed ad options

Multiple feed advertising options exist for bloggers to test on their blogs. Each offers a variety of monetization options to help you earn money from your existing RSS feed. Test multiple options and compare the results to determine which is best for your feed audience and your blogging goals.

BuySellAds

BuySellAds (`http://buysellads.com`) is a very popular option for selling ad space on your blog. A feature that many bloggers don't know about is the BuySellAds RSS advertising opportunities. You can choose the price of ad space in your blog's feed, the type of ads you'll accept (text or display), and where those ads will appear within your feed (top or bottom).

BuySellAds, shown in Figure 2-20, is most effective for blogs with sizeable RSS subscriber numbers because advertisers want to reach enough people to justify the ad space they're paying you for. Therefore, you'll find greater success as your blog's audience and RSS subscribers grow.

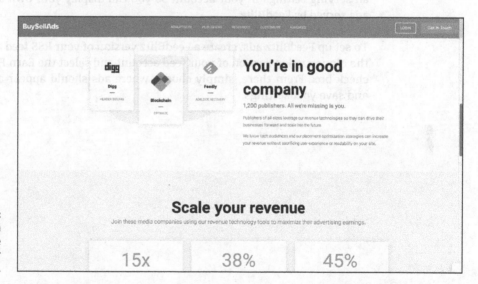

FIGURE 2-20: BuySellAds is a popular source of ad revenue for bloggers.

FeedBlitz

FeedBlitz (`www.feedblitz.com`) is an RSS feed creation and management tool, shown in Figure 2-21. To provide email subscriptions through FeedBlitz, you pay a monthly fee that scales up with the number of subscribers your feed has.

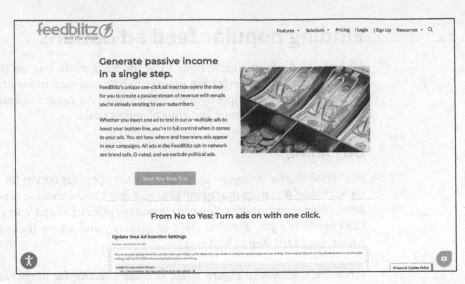

FIGURE 2-21:
FeedBlitz helps bloggers earn revenue from ads placed in emails and RSS feeds.

FeedBlitz offers monetization options for both RSS and email subscribers through its own ad service. If you'd prefer, FeedBlitz gives you the option to customize the ad serving settings in your account so you can display your own ads rather than ads served by FeedBlitz.

To set up FeedBlitz ads, create a FeedBlitz version of your RSS feed and navigate to the Monetization section of your feed account and select the Earn From RSS Feeds check box. From there, simply choose where ads should appear and how often, and save your settings.

IN THIS CHAPTER

» **Understanding affiliate marketing**

» **Benefiting from affiliate marketing**

» **Knowing the problems of affiliate marketing**

» **Making affiliate marketing work on your blog**

» **Finding popular affiliate marketing programs**

Chapter **3**

Making Money with Affiliate Marketing

Affiliate marketing is a form of online advertising where online publishers, such as bloggers, encourage readers or followers to visit an online store and make a purchase in exchange for a percentage of the sale, otherwise known as a *commission*. Affiliate marketing is popular among both bloggers and advertisers. Not only does it offer advertisers a way to promote their products and services in front of highly targeted audiences, but it also provides an excellent way for bloggers to make money from their blogs with little additional effort. After an affiliate program is set up, it typically runs on its own!

This chapter explains what affiliate marketing is and how you can use it to derive an income from your blog. I also warn you about problems to avoid and how to find affiliate marketing programs that offer the best chance for you to make money.

Understanding Affiliate Marketing

Affiliate marketers pay bloggers to promote their products and services on their blogs. In return, the advertiser pays the blogger whenever a visitor to that blog performs some type of action such as clicking the affiliate link and making a purchase or registering for a service.

Both large and small companies use affiliate marketing to promote their products and services. Some manage their affiliate programs internally, and others go through a third-party affiliate directory, which handles all the technology and behind-the-scenes maintenance of each advertiser's program.

TECHNICAL STUFF

Affiliate marketing comes in many forms. You can publish text, image, or video ads that link to the advertiser's website, or you can link to that site directly within the content of a blog post. Bloggers who participate in affiliate marketing programs are provided a unique link or code for readers to use. Anytime a blogger links to the advertiser's site, they simply include the unique affiliate identification link or code so the reader's actions can be tracked back to that blogger. Money earned through affiliate marketing programs comes directly from the use of that special link or code.

Benefiting from Affiliate Marketing

Affiliate marketing can work very well for niche blogs that are directly related to consumer products or services. For example, technology bloggers can easily join affiliate programs that allow them to earn money from affiliate links to computer products, gadgets, and services such as premium blog theme providers. Similarly, pregnancy bloggers can benefit from affiliate programs that allow them to earn money from affiliate links to baby gear, books, and related products.

TIP

The more closely your affiliate ads are tied to your blog topic, the more money you're likely to make.

With that in mind, affiliate marketing is a form of blog monetization that can actually *enhance* your blog. If the products and services advertised through the affiliate ads on your blog are directly related to your blog's topic, your readers are likely to find those links to be useful and helpful. That's not always the case with other marketing opportunities such as contextual ads that offer far less control to bloggers and can become a distraction or even an annoyance to readers.

Think of your affiliate marketing earnings as a commission paid to you for helping to sell the advertiser's product or service. Rather than the advertiser paying for ad space on your blog, they pay you when your affiliate link drives the action the advertiser requires from it. Typically, payments from affiliate marketing are higher on a per-action basis than contextual or impression ads are on a per-click or per-impression basis. However, because an action is required in order for you to make money, the frequency of earnings is lower. That's why it's absolutely essential that you test affiliate marketing programs on your blog to identify the ones that your audience members are most interested in and find most useful.

Knowing the Problems with Affiliate Marketing

As mentioned in the previous section, affiliate marketing requires an action for you to make money. The space taken by an affiliate ad on your blog reduces the amount of contextual, pay-per-click, or direct marketing you can place on your blog. It's up to you to evaluate your blogging goals to determine whether you should use that space for pay-per-action affiliate marketing.

Furthermore, affiliate marketing won't help you make money from your blog if your readers aren't interested in the products and services you're linking to as an affiliate. Your efforts are for naught if you're not offering products that appeal to your existing audience.

Many bloggers are turned off by affiliate marketing. Although the payments are higher than many other forms of marketing, they come less frequently because of the action that is required for a reader to take before the blogger earns a payout. Therefore, affiliate marketing tends to work best for niche blogs with large audiences. The reason is twofold: It's easier to find products readers are interested in when you blog about a highly targeted topic and more people are statistically likely to click your affiliate link and perform the required action when there's a larger audience that sees it.

Another important point to understand about affiliate marketing is that not all programs are created equal. Don't quickly accept every affiliate program offer that comes your way! Be sure to thoroughly research any affiliate marketing program you consider joining before you do so. Read the contracts and agreements, become familiar with the payment terms, and make sure the process works for you and helps you meet your goals for your blog.

Making Affiliate Marketing Work on Your Blog

Affiliate marketing is popular for several reasons. Including affiliate links within your blog can be very easy — and quick! — to implement. For example, if you participate in Amazon's affiliate program and frequently write about products you use in your home that have been purchased from Amazon, it's simple to just link to those products using your affiliate link every time you mention the product in a post. Unlike other advertising models, affiliate links can generate sizeable revenues for both advertisers and bloggers. Also, don't forget that affiliate marketing can actually be viewed as unobtrusive and helpful to blog audiences, which is something most other monetization opportunities don't provide.

TIP

How do you make affiliate marketing work for you, your blog, and your readers? Begin by researching affiliate marketing programs to find ones that offer the best earning potential given the products or services being advertised and the interests of your audience. The following tips help you make your affiliate marketing efforts a success:

>> **Program trustworthiness:** Make sure you choose an affiliate program that is reputable, meaning it tracks results accurately, pays decent commissions, and pays on time.

>> **Company reputation:** Only choose affiliate programs whose products and brands match your audience's expectations for your blog. If you wouldn't be comfortable buying from the company you're marketing, don't publish those ads and links on your blog. They can do more harm than good in terms of how your audience views you and your blog.

>> **Commissions:** The types of commission structures offered by affiliate advertisers runs the gamut. Make sure you stand to make an adequate amount of money on any affiliate program you join. A good guideline is to look for commission rates above 20 percent.

>> **Product and service pricing:** If the products or services you're selling on your blog through affiliate marketing are priced very low, you need to generate a lot of clicks and actions in order to make more than pennies on your effort. Consider how well an affiliate ad can monetize a space on your blog given the product and service pricing and commission rate to ensure it's worth your while.

>> **Tracking mechanism and accuracy:** The best affiliate marketing programs offer tracking tools so you can analyze your blog's performance and modify your participation as necessary to maximize your earning potential. Furthermore, the affiliate marketing program you choose should be capable of accurately tracking the performance of your affiliate ads and links so you're certain you're paid correctly.

>> **Support and help:** Make sure the affiliate program you join offers help when you need it. Online, email, or telephone support is adequate — so long as you have some way to contact a human being to work through any problems you encounter related to ads displaying correctly, payments, or trouble with links or affiliate codes.

TIP

After you choose your affiliate program, there are additional steps you can take to boost the earnings potential of your affiliate ads and links. Following are some more tips to help you:

>> **Placement:** Where you place your affiliate ads and links on your blog can have a significant impact on conversions. For example, an affiliate link placed within your blog's footer is unlikely to generate as many clicks and actions as an affiliate link at the top of your blog's sidebar could. Place your affiliate ads and links where your blog readers are likely to see them, such as within your blog posts, between posts, in your blog's sidebar, in your blog's header, or in your blog's navigation bar. The very best placement for an affiliate link is within the content of a naturally related blog post.

>> **Promotion:** You can drive traffic to your affiliate links and ads with promotion. For example, don't only include your links on your blog. Be sure to also make promotion of affiliate content part of your social media strategy and even include links at the bottom of your email signature when appropriate.

>> **Timeliness:** Don't select an affiliate program and then abandon it. Update your affiliate links and ads so they always lead to products and services that your audience is likely to be interested in at that moment in time. Stale ads don't drive as much attention and traffic as timely, updated ads do. Rotate your ads for maximum awareness and interest.

>> **Tracking:** Don't just rely on the advertiser to provide you with tracking reports. Instead, set up your own tracking mechanisms to enhance the advertiser's reports by using your web analytics tool (as discussed in Chapter 2 of Book 5).

Finding Popular Affiliate Marketing Programs

With so many affiliate programs available for bloggers, it can be hard to find the right place to start. The following sections provide you an overview of some of the most popular affiliate marketing programs, so you can begin your own research to find the one that best meets your goals and your audience's needs.

REMEMBER

Much of your affiliate marketing success comes from testing different products and programs and finding the right mix for your audience, but you can help the earnings come in by following the tips listed earlier in this chapter and experimenting with placement, ad types, and products, as well as promoting your affiliate links off of your blog.

WARNING

Read all the terms and conditions related to any affiliate program you're considering joining before you commit. For example, the last thing you want is to join a program only to find out later that the program is exclusive, meaning you aren't allowed to display any other form of affiliate marketing on your blog. Also, make sure you can drop out of the program at any time if it's not meeting your needs.

Exploring direct affiliate programs

Direct affiliate programs are created and managed directly by the brand or company. You sign up to participate in the affiliate program on the advertiser's website, you access reports and tracking through the advertiser, and the advertiser pays you directly. Following are a few popular direct affiliate programs for bloggers.

Amazon Associates

```
https://affiliate-program.amazon.com
```

The affiliate program from Amazon.com is called Amazon Associates, shown in Figure 3-1. Nearly any online publisher can join Amazon Associates for free and immediately begin publishing affiliate links and ads to any product listed on the Amazon website. Because Amazon sells such a wide variety of products, it's easy for bloggers to find something — or many things! — that would be useful to their readers.

The Amazon Associates program offers flexibility in terms of both the earnings model and payments. Additionally, Amazon offers a wide variety of ad formats to choose from, some of which are shown in Figure 3-2. You can share on social media platforms, such as Twitter and Facebook. You can also publish multiple Amazon affiliate ads on your blog.

FIGURE 3-1: Amazon Associates is a great place for bloggers to start earning affiliate commission.

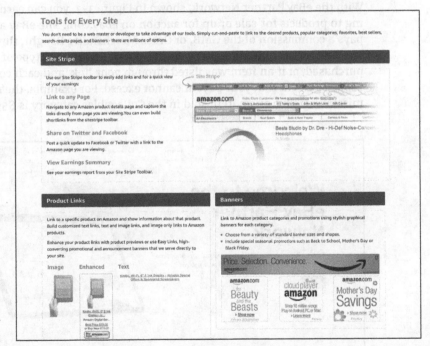

FIGURE 3-2: Amazon Associates offers a variety of ad formats.

To become an Amazon Associate, simply visit the Amazon Associates website and click the Join Now button. Provide the information requested in the application form, and you're given access to Associates Central, where you can configure your ads and start making money!

It's very easy to add Amazon Associates affiliate links and ads to your blog. The Associates Central site walks you through the process to configure any ad for your blog. After you configure your ad, you're given a bit of HTML code, which you can copy and paste on your blog where you want the ad to appear. It really is that easy.

As an Amazon Associates affiliate, you can either self-select the products you want to link to from your blog or use one of the automated features to link to current popular products, wish lists, and more.

TIP

The options for making money with Amazon Associates on your blog are numerous, and because so many people know the Amazon brand and trust shopping with Amazon, your earnings potential goes up.

eBay Partner Network

`https://partnernetwork.ebay.com`

With the eBay Partner Network, shown in Figure 3-3, you can earn money by linking to products for sale or up for auction on eBay.com. The eBay affiliate program pays a commission of the GMB, or Gross Merchandise Bought, through your affiliate link. The commission percentage is determined by the type of goods that were purchased, or if an item was listed through your link, and each commission has a capped amount that your payout cannot exceed. For example, the maximum commission amount on an item sold in the Collectibles category is $550.

FIGURE 3-3:
The eBay Partner
Network.

You can include eBay ads on your blog through image ads, banners, text links, or within your blog's feed. Figure 3-4 provides an example of eBay Partner Network banner ads.

FIGURE 3-4:
Examples of eBay Partner Network banner ads.

Bluehost

www.bluehost.com

If you write a blog directly related to technology, Bluehost offers an affiliate program, shown in Figure 3-5, that might work well for you and your audience. For example, bloggers focusing on all things WordPress.org are likely to attract an audience interested in learning more about blogging using the WordPress.org self-hosted software. Therefore, including affiliate links to Bluehost, a web hosting and URL purchasing company, in sidebar ads and within related content could be incredibly beneficial both to the readers and to the blogger through earned commission.

The standard commission rate for Bluehost is currently $65 for each qualified sign-up. Even if your readers don't click through and sign up for Bluehost frequently, each payout may make it worth the time it takes to set the ad up on your site as well as the real estate the ad takes up in your header, footer, or sidebar.

FIGURE 3-5:
Webhost
Bluehost offers
an affiliate
program.

Walmart Creator

www.walmartcreator.com

Similar to Amazon's affiliate program, Walmart Creator, shown in Figure 3-6, offers bloggers the opportunity to earn commission on the sale of a huge variety and number of products sold at Walmart.com.

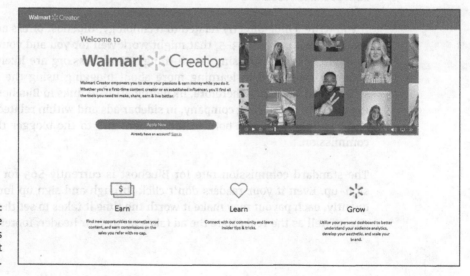

FIGURE 3-6:
Walmart's affiliate
program is
called Walmart
Creators.

There is no requirement for a certain amount of blog traffic or number of social media platforms followers in order to join. There is also no cap on the amount of money you can earn through commission on sales that come through your affiliate link.

The Walmart Creators program provides a hub to each affiliate partner where bloggers can track how their links are performing. Walmart Creators also receive information about upcoming product launches and sales earlier than the general public to help them get a jump on spreading the word along with their affiliate link.

Understanding third-party-managed affiliate programs

Third-party-managed affiliate programs are run by companies that handle all of the technical and payment aspects of an advertiser's affiliate program. Bloggers can join a number of advertiser's affiliate programs through the third-party manager's website. Reports, payments, and tracking are handled by the third-party manager rather than through the advertiser directly.

Rakuten Advertising

www.rakutenadvertising.com

Rakuten Advertising (shown in Figure 3-7), formerly called LinkShare, is a popular third-party affiliate program that allows you to create affiliate links for a wide variety of Rakuten partner advertisers. In fact, many of the companies that advertise through the Rakuten affiliate program are well known, such as JetBlue, Lilly Pulitzer, New Balance, Sephora, and Vera Bradley. Many of your blog's readers are likely to feel more comfortable clicking links and buying from companies and brands they recognize and trust, which could boost your earnings as a Rakutan affiliate versus other programs.

Unlike other affiliate directory programs that require publishers to have highly trafficked blogs in order to become an affiliate, Rakuten is open to small blogs, too. The site provides an extensive help section, and it's easy to register, as shown in Figure 3-8, and start displaying a variety of affiliate ads on your blog.

WARNING Not all advertisers in the Rakuten affiliate program pay the same. Be sure to check the requirements and payment method for each advertiser to ensure the terms match your goals.

FIGURE 3-7: Rakuten Advertising is a popular third-party affiliate program.

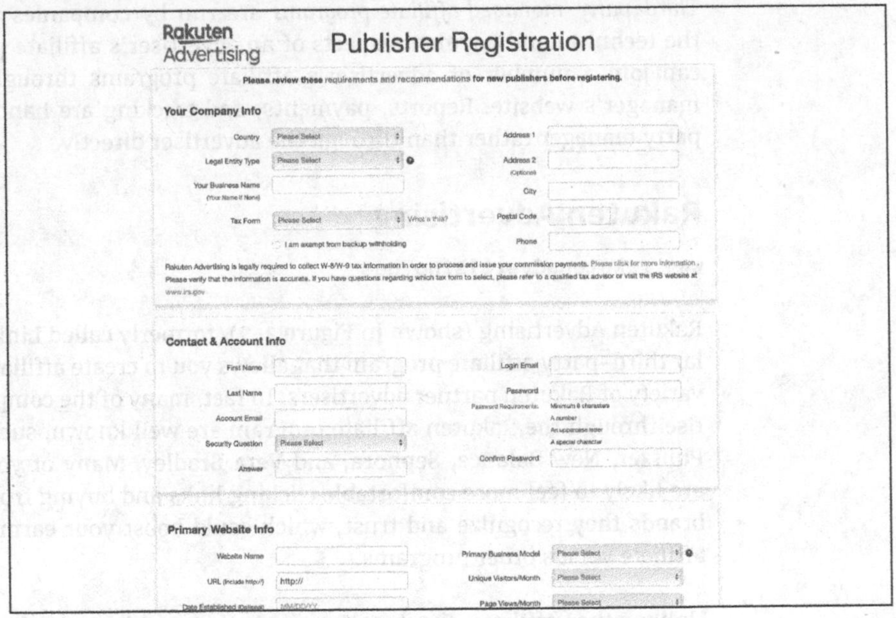

FIGURE 3-8: Bloggers can apply to join the Rakuten Advertising affiliate program.

Commission Junction
www.cj.com

Commission Junction, shown in Figure 3-9, is a popular third-party affiliate program, particularly for established and well-trafficked blogs. To become a Commission Junction affiliate, your application goes through a multistep approval process. After your blog is approved, you can apply to join specific Commission Junction advertiser partners' affiliate programs. Different advertisers use different payment models within the Commission Junction affiliate program.

Commission Junction advertisers are typically well-known companies and brands such as Barnes & Noble, Overstock, and Office Depot. Your blog's readers are likely to feel comfortable clicking ads and buying from those companies. Of course, that trust helps boost your conversions and earnings.

Skimlinks

www.skimlinks.com

Skimlinks, shown in Figure 3-10, works differently to many affiliate marketing programs. What makes Skimlinks stand out is that they take the links you are already using to share the products you know and love and they turn them into affiliate links.

In other words, rather than signing up directly with a variety of different affiliate programs, such as Rakuten, Skimlinks does that part of the work for you. You sign up with Skimlinks and they take care of the required affiliate network partnerships to make your links work for you and make you money!

ShareASale

www.shareasale.com

ShareASale, shown in Figure 3-11, is a well-known third-party affiliate program that is popular in the blogosphere. ShareASale partners with many well-known advertisers including Etsy and Cricut. Bloggers can earn revenue based on leads generated from links on their blogs as well as based on purchases. You can join ShareASale and search for and apply to join affiliate programs that you think would work well on your blog.

FIGURE 3-10:
Skimlinks is a twist on the traditional third-party affiliate network.

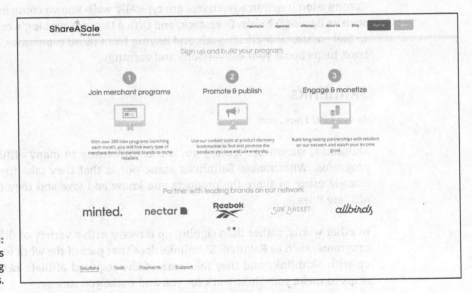

FIGURE 3-11:
ShareASale is popular among bloggers.

Advertising partners are searchable by category, making it easy for bloggers to find advertisers that are a fit for their content. ShareASale provides all the technical information you need as well as payments and reporting.

Chapter **4**

Publishing Sponsored Posts

P ublishing posts on your blog that a company or individual pays you to write is a popular way to make money, but sponsored posts don't come without potential problems. In fact, they can bring big problems to bloggers who aren't aware of how to publish sponsored content transparently to meet blogosphere, ethical, and legal requirements.

This chapter walks you through the process of publishing sponsored content on your blog with extra attention given to the written and unwritten rules related to the practice. You can also find a variety of popular sponsored content programs that you can join as well as tips on how to connect with companies looking to hire bloggers to write paid posts.

Discovering Sponsored Content

In the simplest terms, *sponsored content* is any content, such as a blog or social media post, that is written in return for payment from a sponsor. Sponsored content may include information about a product or service that has been provided to review. It may also just be content a blogger was paid to write about a product, service, company, or anything else without that product being provided for review. Even when the only payment received is the product or service, it is still a sponsored post and needs to be disclosed as such, which will be covered in depth later in this chapter.

Figure 4-1 shows an example of a sponsored post found on the personal blog of influencer Robyn Wright at www.robynwright.com. Note that Robyn discloses that the following content has been sponsored both by using the #sponsored hashtag at the start of the post as well as with a sentence explicitly disclosing that the product was provided to her at no cost.

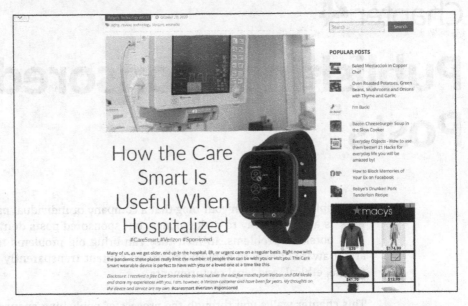

FIGURE 4-1:
An example of a sponsored post as seen on RobynWright.com.

Sponsored posts typically include links, sometimes using specific keywords provided by the advertiser, to the advertiser's website or web page of choice. Sometimes the advertiser requires that the blogger include specific language or images within the paid post. Sponsored content contracts typically also include requirements about the sharing of the content on specific social media platforms.

WARNING

A sponsor should never require a positive, biased review of a product in the terms of the sponsored post contract! Before receiving a product for review, be clear with the product provider that you will be sharing your unbiased opinions. You should also make it clear to your readers that your opinions are your own and that the product was provided to you. The last thing you want is to lose your credibility in exchange for a product.

Advertisers like to hire bloggers to write sponsored content for a number of reasons. Bloggers are able to help spread the word about a product or service and generate an online buzz among a specific target audience that is likely to use that product or service. They can also boost the number of incoming links to the advertiser's site, thereby increasing the advertiser's website Google search results rankings, as discussed in Chapter 1 of Book 5. A higher search rank can lead to increased search traffic from Google and other search engines, and of course, more site traffic can lead to more sales for the advertiser.

Sponsored posts are also often more effective at convincing readers to try a product than a traditional advertisement because the content is relational. Bloggers build up relationships with their readers over time, earning the respect and trust of their audience. Even when a post has clearly been written in exchange for payment, the advertised content within the post is more personal and more easily related to than a print ad or television commercial. Readers are more likely to click through and make a purchase when it feels like it's in response to the advice of a trusted friend.

Bloggers who publish sponsored content meeting the advertiser's requirements are paid based on the terms set forth in prior to the writing of the content. Most often, the payment is a flat fee, which is paid upon publication of the post. In the case of a product review, the product itself is often the only payment.

A blogger with high traffic and a large social media following can expect higher pay per post payments because advertisers have tangible proof that their ads will get a good amount of exposure — more than a lesser-trafficked blog is likely to deliver. However, small, niche blogs with desirable target audiences that are loyal and engaged can also receive considerable pay-per-post fees.

TECHNICAL STUFF

Some sponsors choose to hire bloggers to publish sponsored content exclusively on their blog-related social media platforms such as Twitter, Facebook, and Instagram. This is partly why it's so important for bloggers to maintain accounts and build audiences on multiple social media platforms.

Understanding why bloggers like sponsored content

To be completely frank, bloggers often enjoy sponsored content opportunities because in comparison to other forms of monetization, publishing sponsored content is easy money. In just the amount of time it takes you to write and share a post, you can earn anywhere from 50 dollars to several hundred dollars depending on the size of your blog following and the specific opportunity. Even a small blogger can earn enough for a nice meal out with just a short amount of time writing and publishing a sponsored post. Face it: You're writing posts for your blog anyway, so why not get paid for it?

If a paid post is directly related to your blog topic and you can write honestly about the product, service, or company, that post can actually be beneficial to your audience (as shown in Figure 4-2). For example, if a company sends you a product that your blog audience would be interested in learning about and asks you to test it and write about it on your blog in return for a payment, that's a win-win situation for you and your audience.

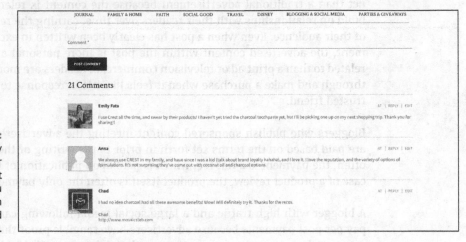

FIGURE 4-2: Readers may be grateful for the product information you share within sponsored content.

REMEMBER

Partnering with brands on sponsored content can also help bloggers earn credibility with future potential clients and opportunities. While you don't want a future advertiser to visit your blog and find nothing but sponsored post after sponsored post (more on that later in this chapter), it is important for them to find a variety of well-produced sponsored content to demonstrate that you are a blogger who can be trusted with important ad campaigns. Showing that you can write quality sponsored content could lead to special opportunities beyond financial payouts, including travel or continued relationships with a favorite brand. For example, Leticia Barr of TechSavvyMama.com, has an ongoing relationship with a number of brands, including serving as a YouTube Kids Parent Panel member, as shown in Figure 4-3 with the badge in her blog's sidebar.

Each sponsored content opportunity is different. It's up to you to review each opportunity to ensure it not only offers you the chance to earn money but also allows you to meet or exceed your audience's expectations for your blog.

FIGURE 4-3:
Writing sponsored content may lead to long-term brand partnerships.

Exposing potential drawbacks of sponsored content

WARNING

Sponsored content can be relatively easy money for bloggers and advertising for companies that provides a good return on investment, but there can be serious negatives to publishing sponsored posts on your blog. Be sure you understand the requirements of any sponsored post opportunity before you commit to publishing the associated post. Some drawbacks of sponsored posts include

>> **Loss of search traffic:** Publishing sponsored content with DoFollow links can hurt your blog's search rankings, which leads to lower search traffic (or no search traffic at all). See later in this chapter for more on this.

>> **Legal trouble:** There are legal requirements, mentioned in Chapter 1 of this Book, mandated by the Federal Trade Commission related to publishing paid content. These requirements must be followed in order to avoid legal issues.

>> **Loss of readers:** Publishing too many sponsored posts can hurt the user experience on your blog if readers see them as little more than clutter that adds no value to the blog at all.

If your blog readers believe you're publishing useless paid posts simply to make money, they're likely to be disappointed and leave your blog entirely. It's important to balance organic content and sponsored content so that your readers continue to come back for more.

Publishing Sponsored Content Safely

Despite the drawbacks to publishing sponsored posts, you can take some steps to do so safely. Keep in mind that some advertisers won't want you to take these steps to protect yourself. If that's the case, you shouldn't work with those advertisers.

The following sections provide the most important steps to take in order to publish sponsored posts safely to protect yourself and your blog.

Providing full disclosure

The Federal Trade Commission (FTC) enacted regulations in December 2009 that require bloggers to disclose (an example is shown in Figure 4-4) any "material connection" between themselves and an advertiser that provides money, free products, free services, or other compensation in exchange for writing and publishing a post for the advertiser. The FTC regulations also require bloggers to provide accurate reviews about how the product or service would work for an *average* user. Noncompliance with the regulations can lead to fines and penalties.

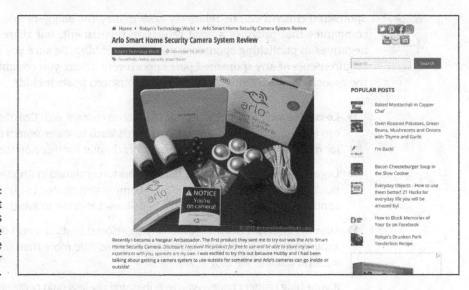

FIGURE 4-4: Robyn Wright discloses receiving free product at the beginning of her product review.

TIP

Be sure to check the FTC website, at www.ftc.gov, for the most recent regulations and updated "Guidelines Concerning the Use of Endorsements and Testimonials in Advertising," from the *Code of Federal Regulations* (16 CFR Part 255).

Using the NoFollow HTML tag

Google and other search engines use proprietary algorithms to rank web pages and return relevant results for keyword searches. Incoming links to a website boost that site's ranking by search engines for those specific keywords used in the link and context of the page. The assumption is that web pages with a lot of incoming links must include great content or no one would want to link to them.

Google views the practice of paying for incoming DoFollow links to a website as a way of artificially inflating the popularity of that site. Therefore, Google penalizes sites that pay for incoming links and sites (including blogs) that publish paid links. That includes links within sponsored posts. You can make your links invisible to Google by inserting the NoFollow HTML tag within the link code, as discussed in Chapter 1 of Book 5.

Staying relevant and useful

REMEMBER

Only publish sponsored posts that are relevant to your blog's topic and that your audience is likely to find interesting, meaningful, and useful. In other words, make sure your paid enhance your blog's content rather than detracting from it.

For example, if you write a blog about protecting the environment, don't publish a paid post for a Hummer or another gas-guzzling vehicle. Instead, your sponsored posts should focus on green products and services to enhance your blog content overall. Writing a paid post about the Toyota Prius would make better sense for your blog, and your audience would be apt to *want* to read your review, finding it useful and helpful.

For example, the eco-friendly fashion blog, Sustainably Chic (www.sustainably-chic.com), includes sponsored partnerships within their blog content. However, they not only disclose properly to ensure they're meeting legal guidelines, they also select sponsored partnerships that are in line with the purpose and content for their blog, as shown in Figure 4-5.

FIGURE 4-5:
Sustainably Chic partners with eco-conscious fashion brands.

Connecting with Sponsored Content Opportunities

As your blog grows, companies are likely to contact you directly and ask whether you're interested in participating in sponsored content campaigns promoting the company's products or services. You can also join a blog or influencer network connecting sponsors with online publishers and influencers. The following sections take a closer look at these two ways that you can connect with sponsored content opportunities to monetize your blog.

Finding sponsored content networks

Some sponsored post programs allow you to search for opportunities that you're interested in and apply to be selected to participate. Other programs vet network bloggers on behalf of sponsored content campaigns, making participating blogger recommendations. Some networks automatically match participating publishers with advertisers' submitted opportunities.

The terms of each opportunity are always unique and determined by the advertiser, so the onus is on you, the publisher, to review the offer and make sure it meets your needs before you apply for it or accept it. After you accept an opportunity from a paid posting program, you're required to publish the post within a specific amount of time. It's important to understand that your published post is likely to be reviewed by the advertiser who may be able to withhold payment or ask you to rewrite your post if it doesn't meet the requirements of the opportunity.

TIP

Read more about influencer marketing in Chapter 5 of this Book.

Following are a number of popular sponsored content programs that you can join for free so that you can start earning money from your blog by doing what you already do — writing posts.

Clever

www.realclever.com

Clever, shown in Figure 4-6, was founded in 2009 by bloggers who were working with brands and agencies themselves. They decided to join forces to create their own influencer network, and all these years later they are a full-service agency partnering bloggers with sponsored content. Bloggers interested in working with Clever should visit www.realclever.com/join to apply to participate in network opportunities.

FIGURE 4-6:
Clever is an influencer network founded by bloggers.

Linqia

www.linqia.com

Linqia bills themselves as one of the fastest paying sponsored opportunity networks for bloggers. Linqia provides support to participating bloggers for each campaign and helps bloggers to earn more the more campaigns they complete. You must meet a certain threshold for posting frequency and social media following in order to join Linqia. To learn more, visit www.linqia.com/creators, as shown in Figure 4-7.

FIGURE 4-7:
Bloggers interested in working with Linqia can apply online.

TapInfluence

www.tapinfluence.com

Bloggers can join TapInfluence for free and set up a profile on the platform in order to bid on potential sponsored post campaigns. TapInfluence focuses on food, lifestyle, fashion, and beauty brands, making it a great fit for bloggers who write in those specific niche topics. To learn more and apply, visit https://app. tapinfluence.com, as shown in Figure 4-8.

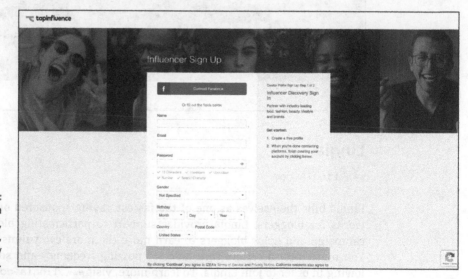

FIGURE 4-8:
TapInfluence is a great fit for food, lifestyle, fashion, and beauty niche bloggers.

Acorn

www.acorninfluence.com

Acorn works a bit differently than many agencies connecting brands and bloggers. On Acorn, online influencers, including bloggers, read information about potential campaigns. The bloggers are then given the opportunity to pitch how they would create online content for that campaign. If they're chosen, the blogger is hired and paid to produce the content. In order to sign up for Acorn, visit https://app. acorninfluence.com/influencers/signup, as shown in Figure 4-9.

FIGURE 4-9: Bloggers create pitches to earn paid content campaigns on Acorn.

Izea

www.izea.com

Izea, shown in Figure 4-10, allows bloggers to find and pitch brands who have signed up with Izea to hear from online content creators. Online creators open a profile on Izea in order to get started. Brands include well-known companies such as Target, Whole Foods, and Comcast.

Being included in sponsored campaigns

Sponsored post networks are a fantastic way to connect with agencies and brands to find sponsored post campaigns, but they are not the only way. Brands often come to bloggers directly to invite them to create sponsored content, and there's no reason that a blogger can't also reach out to favorite brand!

FIGURE 4-10:
Influencers on Izea pitch participating brands.

TIP

The following are some ways to help create sponsored content opportunities for yourself:

>> **Include your contact information on your blog:** Imagine that your favorite brand finds your blog, reads all about how much you love their products, decides they want to partner with you on an upcoming campaign, and then they can't figure out how to contact you! One of the best ways to ensure that sponsored content opportunities come your way is to make it easy to contact you, as shown in Figure 4-11.

>> **Connect with favorite brands on social media platforms:** Don't underestimate the power of social media! Many brands have social media teams actively posting, tweeting, and conversing with brand fans — including bloggers — on various social media platforms.

>> **Attend blog conferences:** Attending blog conferences will help you connect with the blogosphere community and learn more about the craft, but it also gives you an opportunity to connect with agencies and brands who are there specifically because they would like to connect with bloggers like you!

>> **Write great content:** One of the best ways to show a potential paid content sponsor that you will do a great job for them is to write great content on a regular basis, even when no one is paying for it.

>> **Network via LinkedIn:** Don't be afraid to network with agencies and brands via LinkedIn, especially through mutual blogger connections. You never know where it will lead. You can read more about using LinkedIn in Chapter 3 of Book 8.

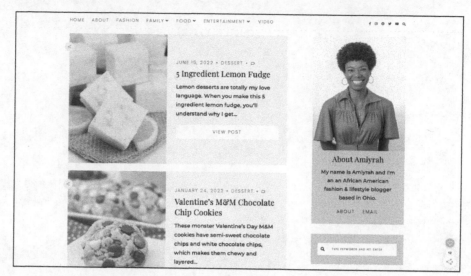

FIGURE 4-11:
Amiyrah Martin of 4HatsandFrugal.com makes it easy for potential sponsors to email her.

Chapter **5**

Monetizing with Social Commerce

I n the early days of the blogosphere, a blogger's community existed primarily on their website. Readers engaged with content within the comments section or interacted with each other within the threads on the blogger's forum page. Readers might occasionally send an email, but for the most part, the term *community* referred to the activity happening on that blogger's actual site.

The emergence and then explosion in popularity of social media changed everything for the blogosphere because suddenly bloggers had new platforms where they could share content and build community. Bloggers now not only create personal profiles on platforms such as Facebook, Twitter, and Instagram. They also create accounts and pages to help build their blog's brand.

In this chapter you'll learn about monetizing your little corner of the blogosphere by cashing in on the influencer marketing phenomenon within your own online community including creating and selling your own merchandise and marketing for other brands.

Defining Social Commerce

You've created a blog, you've written great content, you've built up a huge following both on your site and across social media platforms, and it seems like monetizing such a big following should be easy. But now what do you do? One option is to include social commerce in your monetization strategy. Put simply, social commerce is using your online influence on social media platforms to sell something to your social media followers. What you sell can be products, services, or even access to your content.

An *online influencer* is someone with the power to impact the purchasing decisions of their followers. Sometimes this influence comes from the blogger's knowledge or authority, but often it is related primarily to the influencer's relationship with their audience. Online influencers, including bloggers, fit perfectly into the world of social commerce. There are almost endless options for how you can cash in your social capital, and this chapter takes a look at just a few of those options.

TIP

Social commerce can be an especially powerful way for niche bloggers to monetize, especially those bloggers who focus on topics that lend themselves naturally to online purchases such as fashion bloggers.

Selling for yourself

One option for how you can use social commerce to monetize your blog community is to sell products, services, or even access to content on your own behalf. In other words, you set up the online store, select what items to sell, and decide how and when you sell them. While you will likely use third-party services to engage in social commerce, you will be in charge of everything from the decision regarding what to sell to how often you post about and link to the items you're selling. This is different from being hired by a client on behalf of a brand to market goods and services to your followers.

Selling for yourself can include anything from a print-on-demand storefront to creating original items to sell on sites such as Etsy and everything in between. Both options are discussed in more detail later in this chapter along with other social commerce ideas.

Selling for a client

Many brands turn to bloggers with big online followings for help with influencer marketing. Influencer marketing on behalf of a client is when a brand collaborates with a blogger in order to market their product, either with a goal to increase brand awareness or by having the blogger encourage their community to purchase a product or service directly.

Unlike the option of engaging in social commerce on your own behalf, bloggers who sell for a client are hired to participate in specific campaigns or programs. These programs will determine what products or services you promote as well as how much you earn for your work. You may receive a flat fee for producing what is called *deliverables* (the blog posts and social media content associated with the job). You may also be paid based on how many of your followers click from your content to complete a purchase or a service sign up.

REMEMBER

There is less up-front work for you, the blogger, when monetizing through social commerce on behalf of a client compared to selling on your own behalf. However, the payout for your work may also be less.

Building Your Brand

Before you can successfully monetize with social commerce, you need to first build your blogging brand. Are there certain companies that are immediately recognizable to you as soon as you see their logo or hear their jingle? That recognizability is the result of successful branding, and just like major corporations and organizations, bloggers need to consider branding if they are interested in monetizing with influencer marketing.

TIP

Your blog brand is far more than one website and the posts you've written there. Your brand includes your related social media properties and even offline interactions that you engage in on behalf of your blog. Take the time to think about what you want your brand to convey and then take the steps to send that message to the world.

Maintaining consistency

In order for companies to feel safe engaging you and your blog in their influencer marketing campaigns, they need to know that they can trust you with their name and their messaging. That means that they need to get to know your blog brand and feel that it relates to their campaign goals. If your words and images on your associated social media accounts are not consistent with what you write on your blog, then working with your brand is a risky endeavor. Companies need to know what to expect consistently from your posts.

Consistent branding starts all the way at the beginning with the creation of your blog's name and the purchase of your URL. Check out Chapter 3 of Book 1 for more information on this.

Beyond just words, potential monetizing partners should be able to easily recognize your blog branding around the blogosphere and social web based on visuals such as logos and even color palettes. Digital content is a very visual medium and influencer marketing content is no exception. Do your blog posts display beautiful and carefully edited photographs but your Instagram account is sloppy and haphazard? That's a signal to potential sponsors that if they hire you for a campaign, they may not receive the quality work that they're hoping to find.

Blogger, author, and speaker Luvvie Ajayi writes at www.awesomelyluvvie.com. When you visit her blog's social media properties, as shown in Figure 5-1, you find similar visual and written content to what's available on her blog, Awesomely Luvvie, shown in Figure 5-2. No matter which social media platform you visit, Awesomely Luvvie is easy to recognize. That's successful branding!

FIGURE 5-1: Awesomely Luvvie's Facebook Page is visually similar to her blog.

Learn more about moving beyond words to the visual components of blogging in Book 8.

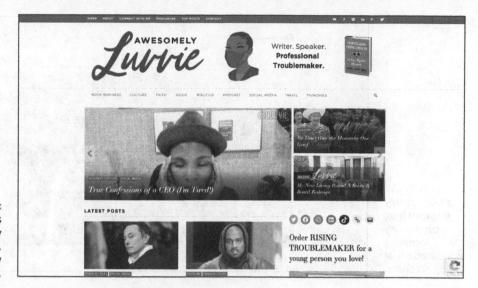

Growing your community

Companies looking to hire bloggers for influencer marketing campaigns have one goal in mind, and that goal is to connect with the blogger's online community. It is important for bloggers hoping to monetize via social commerce to invest time and energy into growing their community, both on their site as well as on their associated social media accounts. Take the time to get to know your blogging community through conversation and tools such as reader surveys. Sponsors are not only interested in how many readers and followers you have but also on the demographic breakdown of those readers and followers. They also want to see a highly engaged community, as shown on the Facebook page for the popular blog, The Bloggess (www.thebloggess.com, see Figure 5-3).

TIP

To help grow your online community, try the following strategies:

>> Interact with readers in your blog post comments

>> Visit other blogs and participate in the comment sections

>> Locate online forums related to your blog's focus and engage with existing related communities

>> Create social media accounts for your blog on all major social media platforms

>> Interact with other followers on social media platforms for related blogs

>> Blog often and well to encourage readers to return often

>> Be a good citizen of the blogosphere, open to collaborating and supporting other bloggers

FIGURE 5-3:
Build a highly
engaged blog
community
including
associated social
media accounts.

To read more about building your blogging community, visit Chapter 2 of Book 6.

Inviting brand partnerships

One of the best ways to establish your brand as a viable brand partner for social commerce marketing opportunities is to select a favorite brand and demonstrate that you can deliver great content on their behalf. This may mean reaching out to that brand and pitching your blog as a brand partner via social media, email, or in person at a blog or social media conference.

It may also simply mean creating brand enthusiast content that makes clear to potential brand partners that you write well and produce high-quality content on your site and social media. Think of this is as dressing for the job you want and not the job you have. Let brands know that you are interested in building a brand/blog partnership and that you're ready to meet the challenge!

Jessica Turner of The Mom Creative (www.themomcreative.com) is a popular parenting and lifestyle blogger who works full time as an online influencer. Jessica certainly frequently creates content on behalf of brand partnerships such as her well-established partnership with the online shopping site, Zulily.com. However, Jessica is not afraid to show her love for non-paying brands, such as a social media video highlighting Target that went viral, as shown in Figure 5-4. Authentic, organic viral content such as this sends a clear message to potential partners that Jessica is a blogger who knows how to deliver!

REMEMBER

You can learn more about sponsored content in general in Chapter 4 of this Book.

Cashing in with Influencer Marketing

Once you've built your online community and created content that attracts brand clients, it's time to take a closer look at ways bloggers monetize through influencer marketing. Remember, *influencer marketing* is when brands and agencies partner with online influencers — including bloggers — to build awareness of or even sell products and services to blog and social media followers. That can occur in a number of ways, including but not limited to those discussed in the following sections.

Participating in affiliate programs

One way that brand clients entice bloggers to help them sale their wares is through affiliate programs. *Affiliate programs* are when a blogger or other online influencer agrees to help sell a product or service on behalf of a brand client in exchange for payment. The payment model varies depending on the brand or program, but often the payout to the blogger is a percentage of the sale. Some clients also hire bloggers for short-term specific campaigns, paying a set fee on top of any earned affiliate revenue.

To learn far more about monetizing your blog with affiliate programs, visit Chapter 3 of this Book.

It's up to you as the blogger to create the blog or social media content that convinces your readers to make the purchase. This gives you complete creative control and the opportunity to find a way to make the affiliate sales messaging fit seamlessly into your blog's content. Michelle from the blog Honest & Truly (www. honestandtruly.com) creates themed gift guides (shown in Figure 5-5), which include affiliate links for each item. If a reader clicks through and makes a purchase, Michelle receives an affiliate program payout.

FIGURE 5-5: Bloggers participating in affiliate programs create posts to help sell products in exchange for a commission.

Providing discount codes

Another way that bloggers assist advertisers in social commerce sales is through the creation of unique discount or sales codes. While some readers and social media followers will click through and make a purchase solely on the recommendation of the blogger, others need more of an incentive. Brands create discount codes, typically for a percentage off the purchase price, that are unique to each individual blogger. Bloggers then promote the product or online store through blog posts and social media using the discount code. Followers who make a purchase using that code receive a special deal, and the brand uses the use of the code to keep track of the payout to the blogger.

Collaborating through social media takeovers

One very creative way that brands and bloggers partner to sell products or services through social commerce is through social media takeovers. Advertisers pay online influencers, including bloggers, to create content for the brand's social media accounts for a set period of time. The blogger promotes the takeover to their audience with the hope that that audience will follow them to the brand's social media.

Sometimes the goal is for an increase in sales, but sometimes the brand simply hopes to grow their own online community.

TIP

Consider combining multiple monetization methods when working with brands in order to get the most bang for your buck! For example, if a client hires you to participate in a social media takeover for their brand in exchange for a set fee, ask about also including a special deal code that provides your followers with a discount and provides you with an additional affiliate revenue.

Signing up for product collaborations and endorsements

While participating in social commerce through affiliate programs allows bloggers to create whatever type of content they like in order to encourage sales, brands sometimes engage bloggers to create very specific content with the same goal in mind — sales.

One such engagement is when a brand or client hires an influencer to create a piece of content that highlights a specific product or group of products. This product endorsement typically includes a link to purchase and sometimes includes affiliate links as well. Product collaborations can live on the influencer's blog and social media properties or on the brand's site, as shown in Figure 5-6, in the case of influencer Katie Feeney's partnership with Dormify (www.dormify.com). Katie selected a number of college dormitory products to endorse, and Dormify created a specific landing page featuring those items knowing that Katie's online community would be likely to purchase the items she recommended.

Benefiting from Print-on-Demand Merchandising

One way that bloggers utilize the power of influencer marketing without brand involvement is by adding an eCommerce component to their sites to sell merchandise. Selling merchandise through your blog and social media promotion is a fairly simple and straightforward way to make money. You can find products to sell that can be tied to nearly any blog topic. Whether you create your own logo or slogan and sell t-shirts with those elements printed on them or you decide to sell products offered through a merchant, you can find a way to monetize your blog through merchandise sales.

Anyone can create and sell merchandise on a blog, but doing so can take time and skill. Fortunately, there are websites that make selling merchandise through your blog extremely easy.

Most online merchandising programs provide two options for selling merchandise on your blog:

>> **Create your own designs.** You can create your own digital images and upload them to the merchandising program site. After they're uploaded, you can sell merchandise such as mugs, bags, and so on with your image printed on those products.

>> **Use established designs.** Many merchandising programs offer a variety of art and images that you can choose from to print on merchandise items. This is a great option if you cannot create your own digital art.

You can design and promote the products you want to sell on your blog. All sales and shipping are managed by the merchandising program. Because products are printed on demand (when a person orders the item), you don't have to worry about paying for inventory, shipping costs, and the like. Usually, you're given the option to set your own prices, thereby establishing your own profit margin.

Some merchandising programs provide free and paid options. Typically, if you pay a fee, you can create custom stores. If you want to create and sell different types of merchandise to different audiences, then having the ability to create multiple stores is important. For example, you can create a store related to your cooking blog and a store related to your travel blog, which would be likely to carry very different merchandise. The guidelines and capabilities of programs differ, so be sure to research your options and choose the best one for you, your audience, and your blogging goals.

Merchandising can be an effective blog monetization tactic, particularly for bloggers who write about topics that can be directly linked to consumer products. However, not every blogger writes about a topic like baking, where selling products such as t-shirts that say "My Buns are Hotter Than Yours" makes sense. The most successful merchandising efforts offer products that the blog's audience members are likely to be interested in at the moment they're reading the blog and see the associated product. Most bloggers can find ways to creatively associate some kind of product with their blog topics. Don't be afraid to think out of the box and tie merchandise and consumer products to your blog's topic creatively.

Furthermore, the most effective merchandising efforts are promoted both on and off the blog. You can drive people to your merchandise through your blog, social media accounts, email newsletters, and more. No one can buy your merchandise if they don't know where to find it.

Similarly, make sure the links and ads that lead your blog's visitors to your merchandise are placed strategically. For example, don't hide links to your merchandise in your blog's footer or subpages. Instead, include ads in your blog's sidebar, between posts, or in links within your posts. Make sure it's easy for your audience to find your merchandise. If that merchandise is directly related to your blog's topic, which is of interest to them, you stand a greater chance of actually selling it.

Reviewing considerations before jumping in

WARNING

At first glance, it might seem like there are no negatives to participating in product advertising programs and selling merchandise through your blog. However, there are some pitfalls that you need to be aware of and analyze before you get started:

» **Quality:** Before you advertise your merchandise on your blog, purchase a few items from the program site to ensure the quality is acceptable. The last thing you want to do is offer clothes that shrink after one washing or bags that aren't strong enough to carry more than a single book.

» **Return policy and process:** Make sure that any product advertising or merchandise program you join has a clear and easy-to-follow return process. If people purchase products through your blog and they're dissatisfied, you want to be certain they have an easy way to return the items and get their money back.

» **Costs:** Make sure that the cost of the item plus shipping plus your up-charge doesn't make the merchandise you sell through your blog too expensive. (An *up-charge* is the dollar amount you add to the product cost and keep as your earnings.) No one will buy your products if they're priced too high.

Review the programs you consider joining to ensure that the costs of the items plus any other fees added to the cost of the product (such as shipping and handling) aren't excessive. You need to know what the final cost of any item you sell is, because it's usually up to you to add an additional dollar amount to that cost, which you keep as your profit. If the price is already too high *before* you add your up-charge to an item, you won't sell anything, making the entire effort a waste of time.

» **Relevancy and uniqueness:** As discussed earlier in this chapter, the merchandise you sell through your blog should be relevant to your blog's topic in order to leverage the real-time interest of your blog visitors. At the same time, your merchandise should be unique and representative of your blog. There's little incentive to purchase an item through your blog that a visitor can buy anywhere. Make your merchandise special, and your sales should go up.

» **Copyrights and trademarks:** It's absolutely essential that you make sure you own the copyright for (or get permission to use) any image or text that you upload for imprinting on the merchandise you sell through your blog. Otherwise, you could open yourself up to being accused of copyright and trademark violations and legal troubles.

Taking a look at print-on-demand options

There are a few popular merchandising sites, which are reliable and easy to use. As mentioned in the previous section, when selecting a merchandising site, it's a good idea to order some products first, making sure you're satisfied with the quality, shipping, and customer service. Then determine what you want to sell and confirm that those products are available to you before you take the time to set up your store.

Following are highlights of some of the most popular merchandising sites, including the two most popular, CafePress and Zazzle.

CafePress

www.cafepress.com

CafePress, shown in Figure 5-7, is one of the most popular online merchandising sites for bloggers to monetize their blogs. You can upload your own designs to CafePress to print on products such as t-shirts, sweatshirts, bags, mugs, and posters, or you can sell merchandise on your blog with existing designs offered by CafePress. When you sign up with CafePress, you get your own CafePress storefront, which you can link to from your blog, so your blog visitors can view and purchase your items.

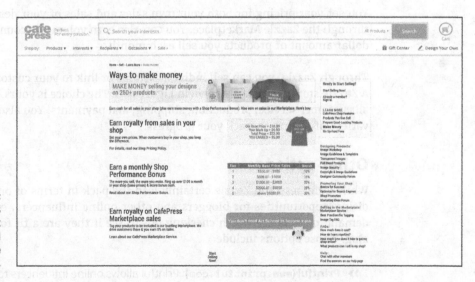

FIGURE 5-7: CafePress allows bloggers to mark up prices and sell merchandise on their sites.

CafePress handles all the logistics of the merchandising program. Purchased products are produced on demand and shipped directly from CafePress to the customer. All you have to do is set up your store and promote it, and CafePress takes care of the rest — including returns and customer service. CafePress also handles all payments. Because you determine how much you want the mark-up on items to be, you control your potential revenue stream.

CafePress allows you to set up as many stores as you want with two Shop Service Plans to choose from. You can either pay a monthly fee to maintain your shops or you can agree to let CafePress keep a percentage of your monthly earnings.

WARNING

Check the CafePress website before you create a store to ensure you're comfortable with the current program features and pricing.

Zazzle

www.zazzle.com

Zazzle is an online merchandising program that's free to join. You can set up your own store and sell as many products as you want. Your products can come from the Zazzle marketplace of designs and items provided by Zazzle or created by other Zazzle members. You can also upload your own designs and sell them on products or add your designs to the Zazzle marketplace for other members to sell.

You set your pricing for both your own sales and sales of your designs and items through the Zazzle Marketplace. You can also earn volume discounts based on the dollar amount of products you sell each month.

Through Zazzle, you can sell individual items or link to your custom Zazzle store. A Zazzle store example is shown in Figure 5-8. The choice is yours. Zazzle handles all customer service, production, shipping, and payments. You also get access to a variety of reports to track your progress.

Other options

While CafePress and Zazzle certainly lead the pack in terms of online merchandising opportunities for bloggers and other online influencers, other print-on-demand options are worth checking out to see if they are a fit for you and your blog. Those options include:

>> **Printful (www.printful.com):** Printful allows online influencers to register for free and create customized products to sell online. Printful provides a recommended sale price, but bloggers get to choose what pricing to use.

FIGURE 5-8:
YamPuff's Stuff is
an example of a
Zazzle Store.

>> **Gelato (www.gelato.com):** Gelato works a bit differently than some other print-on-demand services in that they don't actually produce the products influencers sell. Instead, Gelato manages the process from selling products on your platform to fulfilling those sales. In fact, they view themselves as a software company rather than a print-on-demand company. Influencers select from an existing product catalog, which includes items from Gelato's product partners.

>> **Teelaunch (www.teelaunch.com):** Teelaunch is a print-on-demand app that is free for bloggers to use. You'll only pay based on the sales that you make to your followers. If you're interested in selling custom-printed products, you'll need to use Shopify, an eCommerce platform, along with Teelaunch.

>> **Pillow Profits (www.pillowprofits.com):** Pillow Profits is another company that integrates into the Shopify eCommerce platform used by many bloggers. This particular platform focuses on footwear and home goods.

>> **Redbubble (www.redbubble.com):** Getting set up on Redbubble does not cost anything and it offers a print-on-demand platform for influencers who want to sell their own designs or artwork. Redbubble pays users once their earnings reach a $20 threshold.

>> **Sellfy (www.sellfy.com):** Similar to some of the other print-on-demand options covered in this section, Sellfy allows bloggers to create a custom storefront, including print-on-demand items. Sellfy also provides bloggers with marketing tools to help make their store more successful.

Participating in Existing eCommerce

While many bloggers like the simple monetization option of selling print-on-demand items through a third-party merchandising site, others find success using their online influence via the blogosphere to sell products to consumers through existing eCommerce platforms. The following sections take a look at just two of the options, Etsy and eBay.

Crafting with Etsy

www.etsy.com

Etsy is a popular online marketplace where creators can set up an online store-front in order to sell everything from handmade items to vintage clothes. Creating an Etsy shop and linking to it via a blog is an especially good idea for niche bloggers whose topic is related to the products that they sell in their Etsy store.

TIP

While many Etsy shop owners open blogs in order to support their stores, it also works in the other direction. Opening an Etsy shop is a great option for bloggers to monetize their time online.

Bugs and Fishes (www.bugsandfishes.blogspot.com), shown in Figure 5-9, is the personal blog of Laura Howard who writes about crafts and design from her home near Bristol, UK. Laura includes a link directly on her blog to her Etsy shop so that her readers can click through and purchase her creations. Her Etsy shop, Lupin (shown in Figure 5-10), includes items related to her blog content making her blog audience perfect potential shoppers in her online store.

FIGURE 5-9:
Bugs and Fishes is a blog about crafts and design that includes a link to the blogger's Etsy shop.

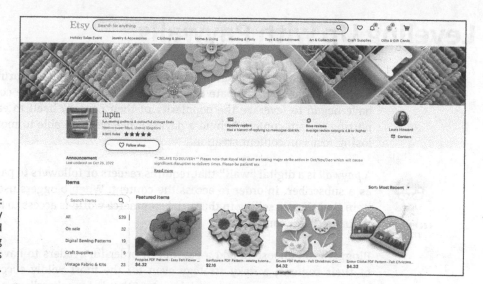

FIGURE 5-10: Lupin is the Etsy shop connected to the crafting blog, Bugs and Fishes.

Making money with eBay

www.ebay.com

Similar to bloggers setting up a shop on Etsy, eBay, the online eCommerce and auction platform, offers a great opportunity for bloggers to sell items such as antiques and to promote those sale items via their blog. Scavenger Life (www.scavengerlife. com), shown in Figure 5-11, is a blog focusing primarily on selling on eBay. The site owners have built an entire business through social commerce and their blog, social media properties, and eBay product listings all work together to provide income.

FIGURE 5-11: The Scavenger Life is owned and written by successful eBay sellers.

Leveling Up with Paywalls

You don't need to take an interest in selling antiques, crafts, or print-on-demand items in order to participate in social commerce. Many online content creators have begun to leverage the popularity of their content itself to earn money. By putting certain content behind a paywall, bloggers are able to monetize without losing focus on content creation.

TECHNICAL STUFF

A *paywall* is a digital "wall" that requires readers or followers to pay a fee, usually as a subscriber, in order to access the content. When bloggers use paywalls, the item that they're selling in the social commerce world is access to themselves and their premium content.

Bloggers can choose to add a paywall in order for readers to have access to any of their content, a risky strategy even for the most wildly successful blogger. Another option is to create special content that is for subscribers only and charge a fee for bloggers to join that subscription list. This can be especially useful for bloggers who create resources as part of their content such as printable lists or online tools. It can also be a useful strategy for bloggers who partner with brands to offer special deals and coupon codes.

Some blog platforms, such as WordPress.org, allow bloggers to install tools in order to create a paywall. You can also employ easy-to-use payment systems such as PayPal (www.paypal.com) combined with a newsletter service to control who receives which content. Some social media platforms also allow online influencers to paywall certain content. For example, Instagram allows bloggers to offer subscriptions and the bloggers share unique content via Instagram to only the people on their subscriber list, as shown in Figure 5-12. Blogger Vera Sweeney's Instagram account includes a "Subscribe" button for subscribers who are interested in receiving unique content beyond the free videos and posts from Vera.

TIP

Another option is to create content on a platform designed specifically to give bloggers the opportunity to earn an income from their writing. For example, Substack (www.substack.com), shown in Figure 5-13, is an online publishing platform that integrates features of blogs, such as online posts and analytics tracking, with a newsletter subscription service. Substack makes creating online content and monetizing it with a paid subscription requirement simple and easy.

Award-winning author, speaker, and poet Kaitlin Curtice utilizes Substack to host her work, The Liminality Journal (https://kaitlincurtice.substack.com), shown in Figure 5-14. Readers who wish to read her paywalled content may choose to subscribe for either a monthly or yearly fee. Kaitlin continues to offer free content, but she uses the Substack platform to host additional work in order to earn an income from that.

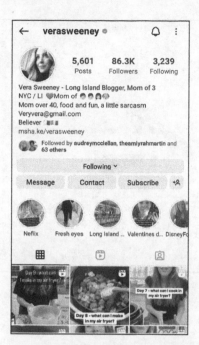

FIGURE 5-12:
Bloggers can place certain Instagram content behind a paywall.

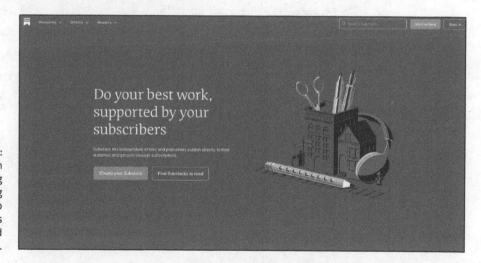

FIGURE 5-13:
Substack is an online publishing platform allowing bloggers to require readers to pay to read content.

This social commerce option is not for everyone. You certainly need to build up a loyal base before you can consider asking readers and followers to pay for your content. It can also be risky because readers may feel like what they're used to getting for free is suddenly coming at a price. With those concerns in mind, paywalls are a very simple and easy way for successful bloggers and social media influencers to monetize what they're already spending their time doing and doing well!

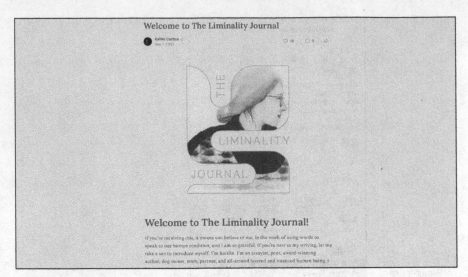

Welcome to The Liminality Journal

Welcome to The Liminality Journal!

If you're receiving this, it means you believe in me, in the work of using words to speak to our human condition, and I am so grateful. If you're new to my writing, let me take a sec to introduce myself: I'm Kaitlin. I'm an essayist, poet, award-winning author, dog owner, mom, partner, and all-around layered and nuanced human being. I

This social commerce option is not for everyone. You certainly need to build up a loyal base before you comfortable asking readers and followers to pay for your content. It can also be risky to shift to a monetized tier when those used to getting content for free is suddenly coming at a price. With those concern in mind, paywalls are a very simple and easy way for successful bloggers and social media influencers to monetize what they're already spending their time doing and doing well.

IN THIS CHAPTER

» **Choosing to sell direct ads**

» **Selecting types of ads to sell**

» **Researching similar blogs**

» **Developing a rate sheet and accepting payments**

» **Promoting your blog ad space**

» **Using a third party to facilitate the process**

Chapter **6**

Selling Ad Space Directly

Although most people first think of selling advertising space through a program like Google AdSense when they hear of blog monetization, you can also sell ad space on your blog directly or through a third party that can facilitate the process for you. There are advantages and disadvantages to both options, but one thing is for certain: You should strongly consider making directly selling ad space on your blog a part of your blog monetization plan.

This chapter explains how to sell ad space on your blog, how to price that space, and how to create a rate sheet for potential advertisers. You also find out how to accept payments and how third-party facilitators can help make the process of selling your own ad space easier.

Choosing to Sell Direct Ads

Why share your ad revenue with sites such as Google AdSense? Wouldn't it be better if you could keep 100 percent of the fees charged for ad space on your blog? Those are fair questions to ask. Certainly, if you sell your own ad space, you can set your own prices and keep all your earnings. You can also charge flat fees for your ad space, which guarantees that you make a specific amount of money for that space.

However, selling direct ads has big drawbacks. First, your blog usually has to be well-trafficked and produce high monthly pageviews and unique visitors to entice an advertiser to solicit and purchase ad space from you. Furthermore, you have to do all the promotion to spread the word about your available ad space and make it seem like *the* place for advertisers to display their ads. In other words, selling your own ad space requires a lot of time and effort. Of course, when your blog is well-established, it's easier to sell ad space directly, but that can take a long time. Therefore, many small bloggers offer ad space for direct purchase but combine those efforts with other contextual and impression advertising.

You certainly have nothing to lose by offering ad space for direct sale on your blog. Create a post or page that provides the details about your ad space opportunities, such as the uncharacteristically entertaining one shown in Figure 6-1 for the highly popular site The Bloggess (www.thebloggess.com). Your ad sheet doesn't have to be as much fun as Bloggess author Jenny Lawson's, but you should be sure to include your email address or contact form so interested advertisers can contact you for more information. You should also include guidelines for the types of ads you'll accept and the type of advertisers you'll include on your site. Why not give it a try? The worst-case scenario is that no one contacts you.

FIGURE 6-1:
The Bloggess advertising page.

Selecting Types of Ads to Sell

When you sell ad space directly on your blog, you get to decide what types of ads you're willing to accept and publish. Having control over what your readers see when they visit your site is one of the best aspects of direct ad sales!

However, you also need to have the technical ability to insert the ads on your blog. For example, selling text link ads is easy — just insert the text link. Similarly, it's not difficult to place an image ad in your blog's sidebar, particularly if your blogging application allows you to paste HTML code into a widget or gadget easily. On the other hand, inserting ads into your blog's header or between posts is a bit more challenging for beginner bloggers unless your blog platform or theme includes those ad locations in their stylesheets. With that in mind, your technical abilities could dictate the types of ad space you can sell on your blog.

When you sell your own ad space, you can accept or decline any ad space inquiry that you receive, giving you the ultimate control of the ads that appear on your blog and the websites those ads lead your audience to. Most bloggers like having this level of control, and it's one more benefit of selling ad space directly.

REMEMBER

You can sell ad space in a variety of forms on your blog, including image, text, video, sponsored content, and more.

Researching Similar Blogs in Size and Topic

How do you know how much to charge for the ad space on your blog? This can be a tricky question because many bloggers aren't very transparent about their site traffic or their ad pricing. Also, some bloggers are happy to make a small amount of money without being selective about price or ad client, while other bloggers value the visual real estate of their website over making a little extra money to support their latte habit. Blog monetization can be a very personal and individual topic.

You've got to start somewhere, so take some time to research other blogs that are similar to yours in size and topic, look at the rates they charge if they publish their rates, and price your ad space accordingly. For example, a beginner blogger with a small audience can't expect to charge the same fees for ad space that a well-established blog such as The Bloggess charges. No advertiser would be willing to pay the same amount to place an ad on a site that gets hundreds of thousands of pageviews per month as they would on a site that gets just hundreds or just thousands of pageviews per month. Advertisers are willing to pay rates that match the exposure and return they expect to get from their investment, and you need to price your ad space to match the results your blog can deliver.

TIP

Finding blogs is discussed in Chapter 1 of Book 1. There you can find tips for finding blogs on specific topics.

To find out where your rates should be set, you can inquire about purchasing ad space on blogs that are similar to yours — if the rates are not already published on the blog. Alternatively, you can visit a site such as BuySellAds.com (http://buysellads.com), which is discussed in detail later in this chapter, and search for publishers to find out the rates they're charging as well as their traffic levels.

For example, Figure 6-2 shows a list of publishers in the content area of education selling ad space through BuySellAds.com. You can click each publisher to get additional details about ad space available and price per ad. Figure 6-3 shows the ad rates for Teach Train Love.

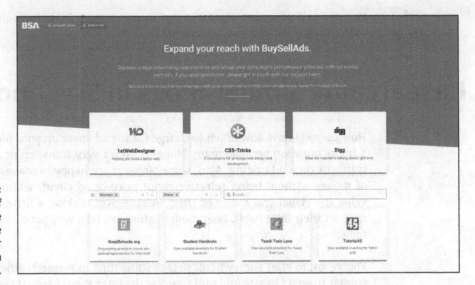

FIGURE 6-2:
A list of publishers where direct ad space is available for purchase through BuySellAds.com.

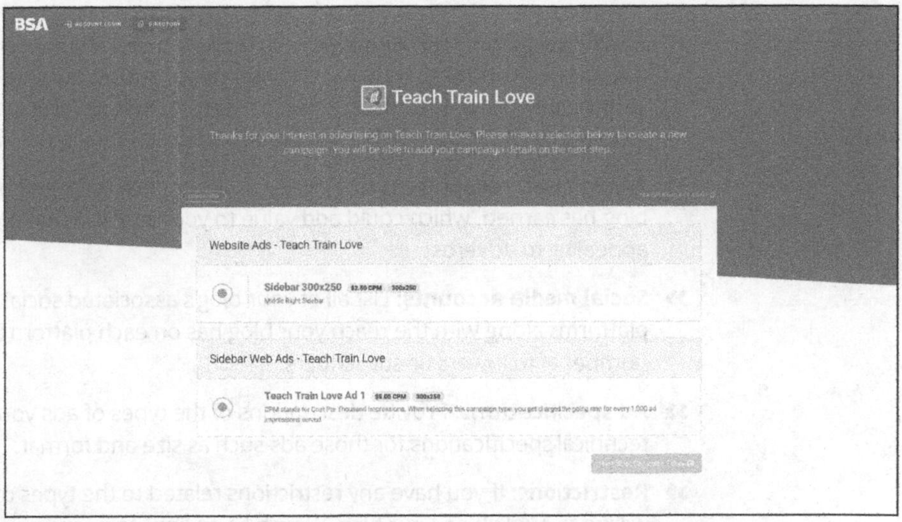

FIGURE 6-3:
Ad rates for Teach Train Love via BuySellAds.com.

Developing a Rate Sheet

When you have an idea of what you want to charge for your ad space, you should create a rate sheet that not only provides your ad space rates but also helps to sell your blog to advertisers. You can either publish your rate sheet information on your blog or email it in response to inquiries. Having a rate sheet prepared ahead of time saves you time later because you won't have to retype the same information again and again each time you get an inquiry.

TIP Be sure to update your rate sheet as your blog traffic and audience change!

Your rate sheet should include the following information:

>> **Description of your blog:** Try to sell the value of your blog by making it sound appealing. Be sure to be honest about your content area and subject matter. Ads that are a fit with your content will perform the best making it likely that an ad client will return to you again in the future.

>> **Demographic profile of your blog's audience:** Tell advertisers who will see their ad when it appears on your blog. Include any demographic statistics you have such as gender, age, and geographic location. You could get this information by publishing a poll on your blog using www.crowdsignal.com, www.alchemer.com, www.surveymonkey.com, or another website that allows you to create free polls, which you can easily insert into a blog post by simply copying and pasting some HTML code. Check out the sidebar later in this chapter to find out more about demographic surveys.

>> **Traffic statistics and rankings:** Provide your blog's statistics such as monthly pageviews, monthly unique visitors, number of subscribers, and time spent on your blog to show advertisers the kind of reach that advertising on your blog can give them. Be sure to include email list subscribers in this data.

>> **Awards and recognition:** List any awards or special recognition that your blog has earned, which could add value to your site and make it more appealing to advertisers.

>> **Social media accounts:** List all of your blog's associated social media platforms along with the reach your blog has on each platform such as number of followers or subscribers.

>> **Ad specifications:** Provide descriptions of the types of ads you accept and technical specifications for those ads such as size and format.

>> **Restrictions:** If you have any restrictions related to the types of ads you're willing to publish on your blog — such as no links to pornographic sites, text links must use the NoFollow HTML tag — be sure to define them.

>> **Pricing and payment terms:** Provide prices as well as payment guidelines. For example, explain when payments must be made and how they can be made, such as by check, PayPal, or money sharing app.

>> **Custom advertising opportunities:** If you're open to discussing customized advertising on your blog, make sure you mention it on your rate sheet.

>> **Your contact information:** Make it easy for interested advertisers to contact you to set up their advertising with you or get more information.

Sometimes an advertiser will approach a blogger knowing only that they'd like to hitch their wagon to that blogging horse but knowing very little about what it means to advertise on a blog. The more information you can provide to a potential advertiser, and the easier it is to understand that information, the more likely it is that an advertiser will be comfortable placing an ad on your blog.

TIP

Consider including a graphic representation showing the ad space available on your blog, as shown in Figure 6-4. Don't assume that a client will understand what you mean by terms such as header, sidebar, and footer!

FIGURE 6-4:
Make it clear
what you mean
by terms such as
header, sidebar,
and footer.

Accepting Payments

Selling ad space is only half the job when it comes to monetizing your blog directly. You also need to collect payments, and not everyone is as honest when it comes to paying bloggers as they should be. Make sure your payment requirements and terms are spelled out clearly in your rate sheet, and obtain the advertiser's agreement to your terms in writing via email or a signed contract.

Make sure you provide details in writing about how and when advertisers must pay you. For example, you can require that payments be made up front *before* you place the advertiser's ad on your blog. If an advertiser doesn't agree with those terms, you can certainly refuse to publish the ad. The most important thing is to ensure you're protected.

Also, make it easy for advertisers to pay you. Sign up for a PayPal account at www.paypal.com (shown in Figure 6-5), or a similar money transfer app such as Venmo or Zelle, so you can accept bank account transfers and credit card payments. If you have to accept checks, make sure you cash the check before you place the ad. Again, you need to protect yourself. Of course, you must place the ad in a timely manner and for the time period that you and the advertiser agree upon.

WARNING

It is up to you to know what taxes you need to pay and when (for example, quarterly estimated taxes for independent contractors) based on your income and where you live. If your advertising client needs a copy of your tax paperwork, such as a W-9 form, make sure you know that up front.

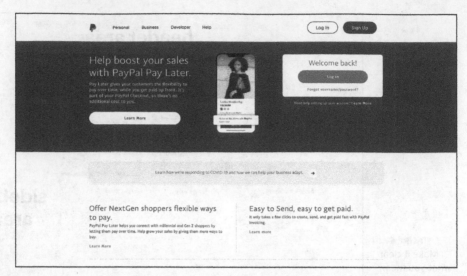

FIGURE 6-5:
Use PayPal or a
similar service
for easy payment
processing.

Promoting Ad Space for Sale on Your Blog

After you put together your rate sheet and determine the types of ads you're willing to publish on your blog, it's time to spread the word that the space is available. The key to selling ad space on your blog is to first spend time growing your blog's audience by writing great content and promoting your blog as discussed in Book 6. Then you can tell the online world about your desirable audience and targeted ad space.

Make sure you take the time to learn about your audience. As mentioned elsewhere in this chapter, use a free survey tool to create and publish demographic polls on your blog. Ask your blog audience for demographic information to help you find out more about them. Advertisers need to know who will be viewing their ad before they can know if they're interested in placing an ad on your site.

Check out the survey example shown in Figure 6-6 to see how a survey or poll can look in a blog post. Sites such as Survey Monkey and Crowd Signal make it easy to create your own survey, copy some HTML code, paste it into a blog post, and collect information from your readers. Many blog platforms include survey creation and sharing as an option within the functionality of the platform. You can also create and embed a survey using various WordPress plugins. You can find out more about polls and surveys in the nearby sidebar.

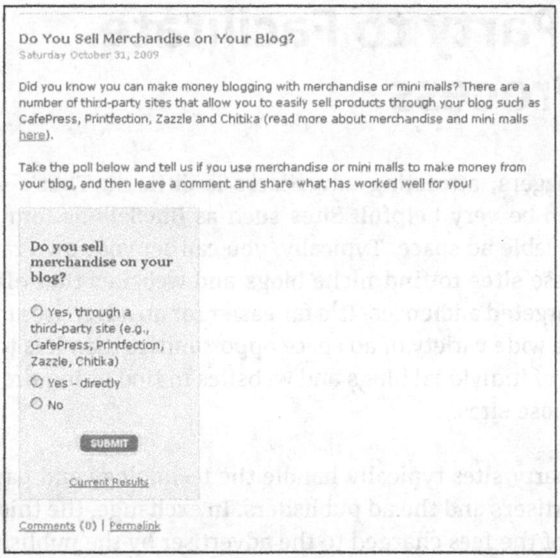

FIGURE 6-6:
Include a demographic survey within your blog content.

USING SURVEYS TO LEARN ABOUT YOUR BLOG'S AUDIENCE

Fortunately, there are a number of websites that allow bloggers to create surveys (or polls) to embed in a post. Crowd Signal (www.crowdsignal.com), SurveyMonkey (www.surveymonkey.com), and Alchemer (www.alchemer.com) are three popular options. Depending on your survey needs, you can create single-question or multiple-question surveys to find out more about your blog's audience. Try to create multiple-choice answers, so it's easy to tabulate your survey results. Questions might include the following:

- What is your age?

- What is your highest level of education?

- Where do you live? (Answers could be country, state, or town of residence, and so on.)

- What is your gender?

- What is your nationality?

- What is your income?

- What is your profession?

- What is your marital status?

- What are the ages of your children?

- What kinds of pets do you have?

Using a Third Party to Facilitate the Ad Sales Process

For many bloggers, attracting advertisers is difficult. That's where third-party facilitators can be very helpful. Sites such as BuySellAds.com allow bloggers to post their available ad space. Typically, you can set your own rates, and advertisers search these sites to find niche blogs and websites that offer great rates for exposure to targeted audiences. It's far easier for an advertiser to search through a site that lists a wide variety of ad space opportunities than it is to find and visit the same number of individual blogs and websites to find or inquire about purchasing ad space on those sites.

These third-party sites typically handle the technology and payment process for both the advertisers and the ad publishers. In exchange, the third-party site takes a percentage of the fees charged to the advertiser by the publisher.

You need to consider whether the benefits of getting wider exposure for your available ad space are worthwhile given the loss in revenue taken by the third-party site. Only you can determine through testing whether the amount of ad space sold through a third party is more than you can sell on your own and makes up for the loss in revenue. Of course, you can always increase your advertising rate to make up for the lost revenue.

There are a number of sites that offer ways for bloggers to sell ad space. Some of the most popular sites include:

>> Adblade (www.adblade.com)

>> Adsterra (www.adsterra.com)

>> Adversal (www.adversal.com)

>> BidVertiser (www.bidvertiser.com)

>> BuySellAds.com (www.buysellads.com)

>> Infolinks (www.infolinks.com)

>> Revcontent (www.revcontent.com)

>> Native Ads (www.nativeads.com)

IN THIS CHAPTER

» Requesting guest blogging fees

» Booking speaking engagements

» Offering consulting and writing services

» Asking for donations

» Using licensed or ad-supported syndication

» Accepting job offers

» Self-publishing your content

Chapter 7

Benefiting from Indirect Monetization Opportunities

Some bloggers don't like the idea of displaying ads on their blogs or publishing sponsored content. The concern is that monetizing a blog can damage the blog's brand image by making readers believe the blogger is more interested in making money than providing useful content and building relationships with readers.

For most bloggers, there's both a monetary investment to keep a blog going as well as a significant time investment. Therefore, it's common for bloggers to search for some way to generate revenue from their blogs because blogging takes away from other income-generating activities that help the blogger pay the bills.

This chapter tells you about some of the popular ways bloggers can make money from their blogs without publishing ads, sponsored reviews, or paid posts at all. You can jumpstart the process by actively seeking and pursuing these monetization options, but the longer you blog and the more your blog grows, the more opportunities will find you!

Requesting Payment for Guest Blogging Services

In Chapter 5 of Book 6, you find out all about guest blogging. To review, guest blogging is the process of writing a post to be published on another blogger's blog. You can write guest blog posts for other blogs or you can publish guest posts written for your blog by other bloggers. Guest blogging is a great way to boost your online exposure, build relationships, generate incoming links, and grow your blog's traffic. As your blog and your online reputation grow, you can charge a fee to write a guest blog post for other blogs.

Some of the most popular bloggers charge hundreds of dollars to write a guest blog post for another blog. Keep in mind that you're unlikely to earn high fees until you firmly establish your blog and online reputation as an expert in your blog's topic. Consider setting your fees based on the amount of time you anticipate it takes you to write guest posts to ensure it's worth your time investment.

REMEMBER

You can always continue to volunteer to write guest blog posts for sites that are larger than your own and stand to give your blog extra promotion.

Booking Speaking Engagements

The more well-known you become across the blogosphere and online community, the more you can build your online brand, reputation, and recognition. This effort can help you establish yourself as an expert in your field who has important opinions and ideas to share, which other people can learn from. After you establish that reputation, you can sell your knowledge by making yourself available to speak at conferences and events.

Many well-known bloggers earn significant fees for public speaking. For example, Gary Vaynerchuk of Wine Library TV has become a sought-after social media expert and public speaker as a direct result of his highly successful video blog related to his wine store in New Jersey and his contagious passion for his subject matter. Gary offers his speaking services through his website (`http://tv.winelibrary.com/speaking`) as shown in Figure 7-1.

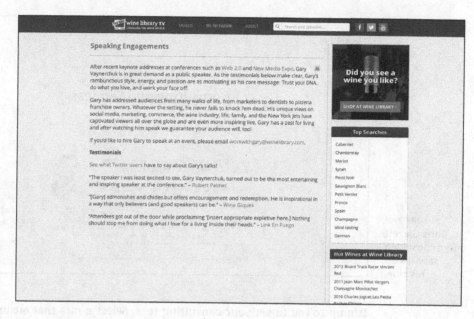

FIGURE 7-1:
Gary Vaynerchuk
is a sought-after
public speaker.

To offer your public speaking services, add a page or post to your blog that details your expertise, experience, and capabilities. It's up to you if you want to publish your rates or negotiate with each person who inquires about your services separately. Keep in mind that popular bloggers can charge thousands of dollars plus expenses to speak at events around the world. Price your services accordingly and be certain that all your expenses are paid by the group that hires you.

Offering Consulting Services

As your reputation as an expert in your field grows online thanks to your blogging efforts, you can offer consulting services to people and companies that want greater access to your expertise. It's easy to offer consulting services. Just add a page or post to your blog, outline the type of consulting services you want to provide, include information about your experience and expertise, and provide a way for people to contact you for additional information.

Popular blogger Chris Garrett offers a great example on his blog, www.chrisg.com, of how to create a page on your blog that describes your consulting services, as shown in Figure 7-2.

FIGURE 7-2:
Chris Garrett offers consulting services on his blog.

It's up to you to set your consulting fees. Select a rate that ensures you'll make enough per hour to make consulting worth your time. Top bloggers can charge hundreds of dollars per hour for their consulting services. Price your services to match your level of expertise and your reputation in comparison with other people in your field and the acceptable "going" rates.

Writing for Other Publications

One of the most common ways bloggers who operate blogs of all sizes use to indirectly monetize their blogs is by writing for other publications. Once you establish your online expertise and reputation, you can apply to write for other publications such as blogs, websites, article repositories, magazines, and so on.

Various freelancing websites, such as Upwork (www.upwork.com), are set up to connect writers with people who are actively looking for their services. There are also blogs that list online writing and blogging job opportunities such as ProBlogger (www.problogger.com), shown in Figure 7-3, and Freelance Writing Jobs (www.freelancewritinggigs.com).

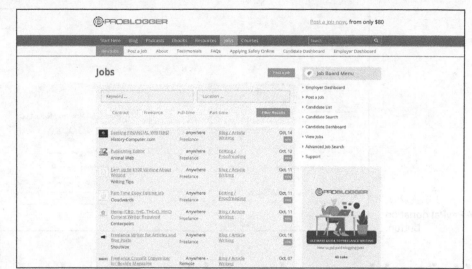

FIGURE 7-3:
Find writing jobs
for bloggers at
ProBlogger.com.

TIP

Polish your writing skills, and be prepared to provide writing samples for most writing jobs that you apply to.

Asking for Donations

With the incredible growth in popularity of cash sharing apps such as Venmo and Zelle, it has become very common for independent creators (such as bloggers) to solicit donations on their sites. You can make it easy for your readers to donate to your blog by signing up for accounts to Venmo, Zelle, and PayPal then adding a donation button to your blog, which automates the process by electronically transferring money from the donor's account to yours. An example of what a PayPal button looks like is shown in Figure 7-4.

TIP

Get creative with your donation requests. Add a link at the end of your posts that says, "Like my blog? Buy me a cup of coffee." It's just another way to ask for your loyal readers to support your blog and help you cover hosting costs, your time investment, design costs, and so on, which can add up quickly as your blog grows.

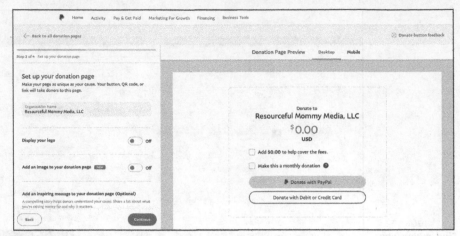

FIGURE 7-4:
A PayPal donation button.

Using Licensed or Ad-Supported Syndication

You can syndicate your blog content and make money. Using a company such as Newstex (www.newstex.com), shown in Figure 7-5, you can license your content for syndication to distributors (such as LexisNexis), who, in turn, provide that content to end-user customers — such as business people, academics, legal professionals, and more — who use it to do their jobs. Alternatively, you can syndicate your blog content through an ad-supported syndication company and potentially earn revenues.

FIGURE 7-5:
Make money by syndicating your blog content through Newstex.

WARNING

Truth be told, most bloggers make very little money from syndication. Instead, syndication is best leveraged for promoting and growing your blog to a wider audience, but if you can make a few dollars, why not?

Accepting Job Offers

One of the most interesting ways to monetize your blog indirectly is by accepting new opportunities that come your way as your online reputation grows. As more people hear of you, read your content, and find out about your expertise, you're likely to receive more and more opportunities for writing, speaking, and consulting. Some of these opportunities may come in the form of job offers.

As an established blogger, you may get offers to report on events, provide consulting services, write for new publications, or even join a company in a role related to your expertise. For example, I've had opportunities to appear on television and radio, speak at events, and consult for global brands as a result of my blog and social media presence. I've also gotten more than one book deal as a direct result of content from my blogging portfolio. That's just one more way that the power of the social web and blogging can lead to new opportunities and additional earnings!

TIP

Be sure to thoroughly research any opportunity that comes to you to ensure it's legitimate and worth your time investment.

Self-Publishing Offline and Online Content

Many bloggers dream of someday moving from blog posts to e-books or print books. While many in the blogosphere have received publishing contracts as a direct result of their blogs, many more have turned to self-publishing in order to write the content they love in book format.

With an existing audience already tuned in and hungry for more content, a blogger interested in writing an e-book or self-published book in print may find that marketing and selling that book is an easy next step. *E-books* are digital books that anyone can write and readers can purchase and download.

Self-published books and online e-books can range from how-to guides to fiction and everything in between! Self-publishing content beyond your blog may be especially useful if you hope to establish yourself as an expert on a specific topic.

Some bloggers find that self-publishing is a great way to transition from their non-fiction blog post content to writing and selling fiction without needing to first sell their ideas to a publisher or agent.

Author Audrey McClelland, shown in Figure 7-6, is a great example of a blogger who successfully transitioned from writing online content only (`www.momgenerations.com`) to self-publishing popular romance novels!

FIGURE 7-6:
Author Audrey McClelland moved from blogging to self-publishing fiction.

8
Moving Beyond Writing Blog Posts

Contents at a Glance

Chapter **1**

Painting a Picture with Visual Content

There's no denying it: The Internet is a visual place! Whether it's sharing funny memes, graphics of inspirational quotes, or pictures of kittens playing the piano, the fact is that visual content and the World Wide Web fit together like a hand in a glove. For bloggers, this means that including photos and graphics in your blog posts is very nearly a requirement. At the very least, it is a very strong recommendation.

Including visuals in your blog content helps with everything from attracting readers to making content sharable. Thanks to the availability of online tools and free stock photos, including visuals is simple and cost-effective. Also, with the ever-improving cameras in the cell phones we all carry with us every day, there's no longer a need for bloggers to own a fancy camera or have special skills in order to include beautiful images in posts.

This chapter takes a look at the role visual content plays in your blogging strategy as well as how to include great and creative images in your posts.

Understanding the Importance of Visual Content

If you've ever spent any time on social media, then you are familiar with how much of the content online is visual rather than verbal. Platforms such as Pinterest and Instagram focus almost entirely on photos and graphics. Even platforms that include a large percentage of written posts, such as Facebook, seem to prioritize the visual with algorithms that show posts with pictures to more friends and followers than those posts with words only. If you want your content to be seen by the most people possible, it's important to spend at least some time focusing on being able to produce and integrate quality images into both your blog posts and your associated social media posts.

TIP

Want to learn more about creating content on social media that supports your blogging strategy? Take a look at Chapter 3 of this Book!

REMEMBER

Visual content does more than help get your content seen, however. The following are just some of the reasons that bloggers should take creating visual content seriously:

>> **Visual content makes posts more shareable.** Creating content that can be shared via the sharing of an image always makes it more likely that readers will actually pass that content along to friends and followers. This is especially critical when it comes to sharing on sites such as Pinterest. Without an image, a post will not be shared on certain platforms.

>> **Visual content grabs the attention of people online.** Taking in online content is a bit like trying to drink from a firehose. It's simply too much at times. If you want your content to rise above the noise and stop scrollers in their tracks, you need the help of visual media!

>> **Visual content can be used to help with search engine optimization.** Including images in posts gives search engines more content to crawl and index. To learn more about SEO, or search engine optimization, check out Chapter 1 of Book 5.

>> **Visual content helps with monetization strategies.** Book 7 takes a close look at various ways to earn money via your blog. A number of methods of monetization, including ads and affiliate programs, rely heavily on convincing readers to click through and take an action such as signing up for a service or making a purchase. Creating convincing visual content is important as part of those and other monetization methods.

>> **Visual content helps with blog branding.** It is very important that readers and followers are able to identify you and your blog regardless of if the

content they're viewing is found on a social media platform or on your website. Visuals play an important role in the branding of your blog, making it easier for your blog community to recognize you at a glance.

» **Visual content makes reading content easier.** Just as things such as headings and bullet points can help break up written content, making it easier for readers to take in, visual content also helps to give readers a break. Visual media can also sometimes help explain your points better than a long paragraph. Show them, don't just tell them!

» **Visual content helps you reuse blog content.** Part of a good blogging strategy is being able to reuse content from your blog in social media posts. Creating strong visual content allows you to grab images from blog posts and use them to share the same general content on other platforms such as Facebook and Instagram.

Planning a Visual Content Strategy

The term *visual content* refers to far more than just photos. Later in this chapter, we'll take a closer look at different types of images to include in your visual content strategy. How you plan to incorporate visual content into your overall blogging strategy depends heavily on a number of factors including:

» Your blog niche

» Your blog platform

» Your use of syndication services

» Your use of newsletters to distribute content

» Your social media strategy

For example, a food blogger will probably rely heavily on visual content. Is there anything more likely to encourage a potential reader to click through than the image of a delicious plate of cookies? Similarly, it surely makes sense that a craft or DIY blogger would include visuals in blog posts, using photographs to take readers step-by-step through projects. However, it may also be helpful for tech bloggers to utilize screenshots in explanatory posts, much like the pages of this very book. Political bloggers may find that graphs inserted into posts are visually able to explain election results better than a paragraph of typed text alone.

TIP

Don't be afraid to think outside of the box when it comes to your blog content and visual media. The benefits of visual content extend across the blogosphere. Thinking about visual content strategy early in your blogging journey provides an opportunity to implement that strategy consistently from the start.

If you've already begun blogging and are just now thinking about the role of visual media, don't fret. There's still time to create a strategy moving forward and even revisit some top posts from the past to bring them up to date with your current visual content plan. The following sections take a closer look at just two areas to consider when integrating visual content into your blogging.

Keeping consistent branding with unified visuals

One of the best ways to include visual content into an overall strategy is to use images to unify the branding of your blog. Visual content such as logos or color schemes, when used consistently across your blog and related social media properties, signals to readers and followers that they are viewing and reading content that is from you. Take the blog TeachMama. (www.teachmama.com), for example. Figure 1-1 shows Amy Mascott's education-focused blog, TeachMama.com, including her logo, color scheme (repeated use of teal), and use of photo collages.

FIGURE 1-1: TeachMama.com uses recognizable image strategies.

A quick visit to the TeachMama page on Facebook, shown in Figure 1-2, reveals the same visual characteristics. For example, the TeachMama Facebook page features the same logo with teal color scheme and photo collage cover photo.

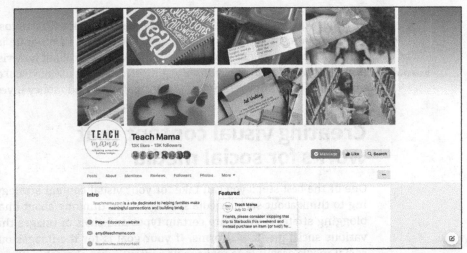

FIGURE 1-2:
The TeachMama
Facebook page is
visually familiar
for TeachMama.
com blog readers.

It is not surprising that a visit to the TeachMama Twitter pages once again brings in the TeachMama logo in the pinned tweet and that same photo collage strategy for the cover photo (Figure 1-3).

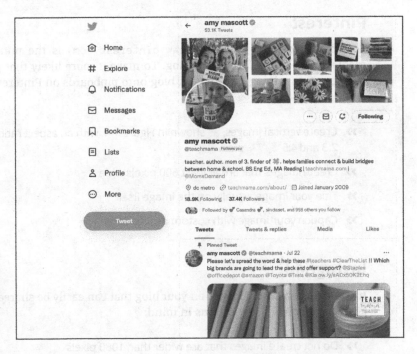

FIGURE 1-3:
The TeachMama
Twitter visuals
align with other
TeachMama
properties.

REMEMBER

Whether you decide to select a color scheme and stick with it across all properties, create or purchase a professionally designed logo to incorporate in your posts, or some other strategy entirely, take some time to think about how visual content can pull together all aspects of your blogging efforts. This use of visual content strategy often provides a huge return for a very small time and money investment.

Creating visual content that works for social media

One of the best steps you can take for your visual content strategy is remembering to think about social media strategy when thinking about images and overall blogging strategy. There are certain types and sizes of images that work best on various social media platforms. If your goal is for the images on your blog and social media accounts to make your content more shareable, then it's worth taking the time to create images that are social media friendly.

The following sections take a look at recommendations for images on a number of the most popular platforms on the social web.

Pinterest

For many bloggers, Pinterest (www.pinterest.com) is the number one social media source of traffic to their blog. To make it more likely that people will pin, and re-pin, the images from your blog onto pinboards on Pinterest, take the following steps:

>> Create vertical images, as shown in Figure 1-4, with an aspect ratio between 2:3 and 4:5

>> Create images that are at least 600 pixels wide

>> Title your image actually on the image itself

>> Caption your image with custom descriptions

Instagram

If you plan to include images on your blog that can easily be shared on Instagram, keep the following suggestions in mind:

>> Do not create images that are wider than 1080 pixels

>> Upload photos in the .jpg format rather than .png

>> Use a 1:1 square shape for profile page photos, as shown in Figure 1-5

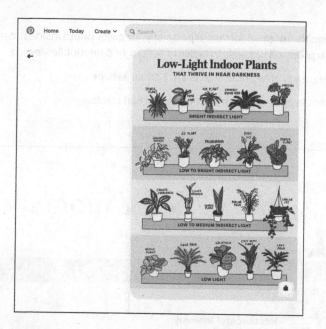

FIGURE 1-4:
Pinterest favors
vertical images.

FIGURE 1-5:
Upload square
photos on
Instagram.

Facebook

As with other social media platforms, it's best to create and use images for Facebook that follow a set of basic guidelines. Those guidelines include:

>> Create cover photos that are 820 pixels x 360 pixels, as shown in Figure 1-6

- » Keep the most important aspects of your cover photo inside the middle 640 pixels x 312 pixels in order to accommodate mobile viewing

- » Create a profile photo that is a 1:1 square shape

- » Event images should be 1200 pixels x 628 pixels

FIGURE 1-6:
Follow Facebook's
guidelines for
images size
and ratio.

TIP

Need help resizing your images to optimize them for your favorite social media platforms? Check out the tools later in this chapter to find a free social media image resizer tool.

Creating Powerful Visual Content for Your Blog

There's no need to go out and buy an expensive camera to take visually perfect photos for your blog! No degree in graphic design is necessary to create powerful images for your social media! There are seemingly endless tools available, many of them free and online, to assist bloggers in creating great visual content for their websites and affiliated social media platforms. There are also many types of visual content that can be created beyond graphics and photographs.

The following sections take a closer look at both the types of visual content as well as just a small number of the available tools to get you started on your journey moving beyond the written word and into the world of visual media!

Getting to know the different types of visual content on your blog

Inserting a photograph into a blog post may seem intuitive, especially depending on which blog platform you've selected. In fact, most post menus prompt bloggers to upload a photo as well as select a featured image to automatically appear when readers link to that post. Depending on your comfort with video, it may even seem natural to include video tutorials or commentaries in your visual content strategy. There are so many other options, however, if you're ready to branch out beyond the written word in your posting!

Infographics

Infographic is a mashup of the words "information" and "graphic." Simply put, infographics convey information through a graphic. They can be complicated, a combination of pie charts and words, images, and captions. Infographics don't have to be complicated to be effective, however. In fact, for the sake of blogging and shareability, simple is probably better.

Figure 1-7 shows an example of a very simple infographic created by a recovery ministry. It serves the dual purpose of letting participants know that there will not be a meeting and reminding them of their recovery tools to use when there isn't a meeting.

FIGURE 1-7: Infographics can be simple and still be effective.

Quotes

Quotes can be an especially good way to create visual content for bloggers who often include interviews or other content involving direct quotations. It's very easy to pull out a key quote and create a graphic. It breaks up what may be dense text within the post and also provides an opportunity for readers to pin and share the post through a related image. Figure 1-8 shows an example of how to pull a quote out of text and place it in a graphic.

The Joys of Being a Grown-Up

As I sit here at my computer, there is a couch slipcover in my washing machine. I noticed after performing the delicate surgery of removing it that the tag says, "Machine wash. No tumble dry." It is currently 34 degrees outside and my neighborhood HOA has a rule against hanging laundry outside, so I really wish that I would have read more than just the "Machine Washable" tag before purchasing my sectional and matching chair. Now I get to decide if I'm going to roll the dice and put the slipcover in the dryer (of course I am).

Why is that my decision to make? Because I'm the grown-up.

And sometimes being the grown-up sucks.

I'm blessed to be married to a man who doesn't mind grown-up tasks like putting clean laundry away and taking out the trash, so he allows me to ignore much of the mindless drivel that can make life as a grown-up less appealing. I'm in charge of the tasks that horrify him such as anything involving eye drops or blood.

But First Aid and laundry aside, **the truth is being a grown-up is really pretty amazing.** I reached out to some friends on Facebook to see what they love best about being an adult. To inspire them I had Nutella on toast and a Dr. Pepper mid-morning just because I could and despite the fact that I had eaten breakfast two hours earlier. That's right. I'm living like a rock star.

What's awesome about being a grown-up?

I love being able to stay up as late as I want ... which really isn't very often. – Sara from Sensibly Sara

I can eat an entire bag of candy and watch all the TV I want after the kids go to bed. Minus the ability to then fit into my jeans and being extremely tired in the morning, it is bliss. – Ashley from The Dose of Reality

I love that I can go out with my friends without having to ask "permission" or having a "curfew." – Lisa from Mom on the Side

I get to eat cupcakes (or any other confection) before dinner if I want and it actually won't spoil my appetite. – Maggie from Linneyville

I get the best of both worlds. I get to work and follow my passions, but I get to act like a kid with my kids when I want to. – Ashley from Fiddle Dee Me

I get to change the rules when I don't want them to apply, whether that's how I feel about sleepovers, what we'll do on vacation, whether we HAVE to go to (insert sport here) or something else entirely. Oh, and I get veto power over just about anything – movies, food, daily activities, etc. – Michelle from Honest and Truly

I love being able to go to Disneyland whenever I want (or can afford it, have time for ...), not having to wait, and beg, and wait, and beg, and wait some more for my parents to take me. – Sunny from Wonder and Company

Wine time. Enough said. - Amiyrah
www.fourhundredmommy.com

FIGURE 1-8:
Pull favorite quotes and create a graphic.

GIFs

A GIF, which stands for *Graphics Interchange Format*, is an image, typically animated and simple, that exists only on the Internet. GIFs are often embedded in tweets, Facebook updates, and text messages between teenagers. And yes, you can include GIFs in your online content! They are often humorous, highly shareable, and a great way to mix things up with your content.

TIP

Giphy (www.giphy.com), shown in Figure 1-9, is a great place to find GIFs for all occasions and topics.

Slideshows

Slideshows are a great way to include a series of images without flooding your blog post with pictures, forcing readers to scroll and scroll to get to the end of the post. Many blog platforms include the ability to post a series of photos in a slideshow or offer the ability to download the necessary widget or plugin to do so.

FIGURE 1-9:
Giphy.com is a
great source of
GIF images.

Graphs and Charts

Graphs and charts aren't just useful for your Statistics 101 class! They can be a simple and effective way to communicate information to your readers visually. Take your charts to the next level by including interactive content, such as columns that include a pop-up caption when the reader hovers over the image. Bloggers using WordPress should try out a variety of related plugins to find the features that work best for them, including Visualizer (www.themeisle.com), wpDataTables (www.wpdatatables.com), Graphina (https://iqonic.design), and iChart (www.quantumcloud.com).

Photographs

Perhaps the first type of visual content that comes to mind when you think about including images in your blog strategy is the use of photographs. There is no doubt that a beautiful photograph enhances both blog and related social media content. Every mobile phone now comes equipped with a camera able to take quality photographs suitable for the Internet. Photographs are especially helpful for certain blog niches, such as food blogging. Figure 1-10 shows how a post about an ombre cake recipe on MomAdvice.com (www.momadvice.com) is enhanced through the use of a beautiful photograph.

Memes

A *meme* is an image or video, often with text written over it, that is shared repeatedly around the Internet, especially on social media. Some Facebook groups host Meme Mondays when groups can share their favorite memes on a variety of topics from parenting to politics. While the use of memes on your blog depends largely on the usual tone and seriousness of your blog, memes are readily acceptable on social media even from the most serious of posters. I occasionally use a meme for a comedic moment (shown in Figure 1-11), especially to break the tension from a serious topic, on my personal blog, Resourceful Mommy (`www.resourcefulmommy.com`).

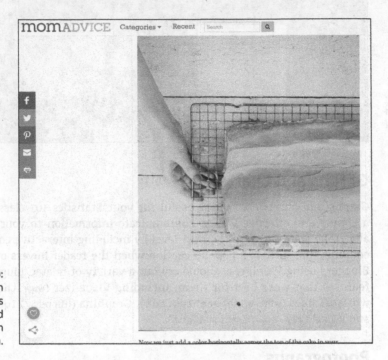

FIGURE 1-10:
A photograph enhances this food-related post on MomAdvice.com.

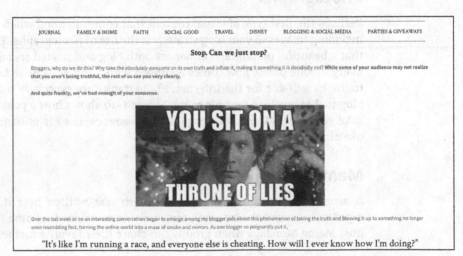

FIGURE 1-11:
Use of a meme in a blog post on Resource fulMommy.com.

Illustrations

Illustrations are images that are visual explanations, interpretations, or even decoration created by an artist or graphic designer. Due to the popularity of online image creation tools, many bloggers find that it's easy to create illustrations for their blog posts by themselves. As with other images, illustrations provide a visual break within a blog post and an alternative way to convey information to readers.

Flipbooks

A *flipbook* is a digital brochure that can be digitally flipped through by readers. Flipbooks visually appear different than a slideshow even though they serve a similar purpose. Bloggers interested in participating in affiliate programs where they are likely to encourage readers to make an online purchase may find that flipbooks aid them in introducing products to their audience. Flipbooks are especially popular with fashion bloggers looking to highlight a series of related clothing items. Figure 1-12 shows a fashion flipbook created on Issuu (`www.issuu.com`).

FIGURE 1-12: A flipbook created on Issuu.com.

Painting a Picture with Visual Content

Video

Video has been rising in popularity in the blogging world for a number of years, and I don't believe that trend is going to stop any time soon. Most social media platforms are extremely video friendly, and most blog platforms make both uploading video directly and embedding video from other sites such as YouTube a very easy and straightforward process.

TIP

Video is a great way to move beyond written content because it is so shareable from one platform to another. To learn more about video, stop by Chapter 2 of this Book!

Cartoons and Comics

If you, like me, grew up reading the Sunday comics, you know exactly what it means to include cartoons and comics in a blog post. You may be asking yourself, however, *how* to create your own cartoons and comics. Stay tuned! We'll take a look at how to do just that later in this chapter. In the meantime, Figure 1-13 shows the use of cartoons on Problogger.com in a post about, well, the use of cartoons in a blog post!

FIGURE 1-13:
The use of a cartoon in a post on Problogger.com.

Printables

A *printable* is downloadable digital content that typically includes graphic design elements as well as text. Printables often offer useful content for readers such as sticker design sheets, calendars, educational worksheets, and coloring pages for both kids and adults. Creating printables that can be downloaded and shared is a great way to add value to your blog posts and encourage your readers to share links with their friends and families who may benefit from downloading and printing the content as well. Some bloggers offer printables to readers for a small fee as a way to monetize. Others offer printables for free as a value-add for loyal community members. The preschool-related blog, No Time for Flashcards (www.notimeforflashcards.com), shown in Figure 1-14, offers a variety of printables.

Utilizing available visual content tools

As with most areas of technology, there are many image creation and photo editing tools available for purchase, many at incredibly high costs. If you are a professional photographer or hobbyist, you may wish to select and use one of these professional-grade tools. Likewise, if you have a background in graphic design, the tools available online, often for free, may not provide you with what you prefer to use to create powerful visuals for on your blog and social media tools. That said, there exists a seemingly endless number of tools that can help you in creating visual content to both enhance your blog as well as your social media content. The following sections take a look at a small number of those tools and what services they provide to bloggers.

Death to the Stock Photo

www.deathtothestockphoto.com

Death to the Stock Photo is an online subscription site that provides users with stock photos that they believe to be newer and more authentic than the images available on free stock photo sites. Subscription fees begin at $12 per month when paid annually and $15 a month when paid on a month-to-month basis. Bloggers who plan to use stock photos on a regular basis may find that this fee is worth-while in order to have consistent access to a reliable source of quality images.

Vecteezy

www.vecteezy.com

Vecteezy is an online source of digital images and vector illustrations for use by bloggers. They offer free services, including the use of some images, as well as additional features for paying subscribers. The site offers millions of stock photos organized by thematic categories.

Skitch

https://evernote.com/products/skitch

Skitch is an app that can be downloaded to both Android and iOS devices. This multi-purpose editing tool allows you to doodle and make notations on existing images. You can add graphics such as arrows or emojis as well. The app is free and can be downloaded from the iOS App Store and the Google Play Store.

Meme Generator

www.memegenerator.net

If you would like to use memes in your content and the millions of memes available online don't suit your needs, you can create your own meme for free! Meme Generator is a fairly rudimentary and straightforward site that offers up an assortment of popular meme images with the opportunity to create new captions, as shown in Figure 1-15.

Canva

www.canva.com

Canva is a free online design tool that allows users to create graphics used for social media posts, blog posts, slideshows, videos, and any other location where you might want to insert a customized graphic. Users can go to www.canva.com and create a free account with an email address, Facebook account, or Google account in order to be able to create and save designs.

TECHNICAL
STUFF

While Canva works on a variety of platforms, the tool is optimized to be used on Chromebooks.

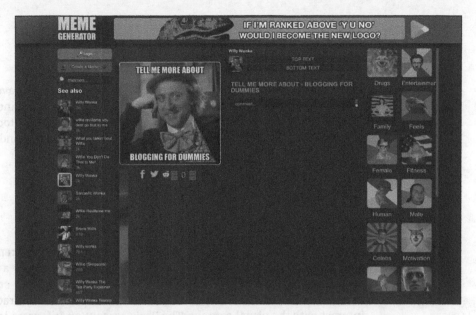

FIGURE 1-15:
Create your own
memes with
Meme Generator.

Canva offers templates to get users started, but you can also create your own design from scratch. If you find a template that works for you, you can continue to use that same template as the start for your designs in order to create a consistent visual brand in your visual content across blog-related platforms. Canva images can be used in video, such as Instagram Reels and TikToks as well as to create blog logos and profile images, as shown in Figure 1-16. It's a fantastic and easy-to-use tool that can be incorporated into many aspects of a blogger's work.

FIGURE 1-16:
Create a logo for
free with Canva.

Gimp

www.gimp.org

GIMP is a free and open-source graphics editor that bloggers have been using for very many years, long before many of today's most popular online tools emerged. To use GIMP, head to www.gimp.org and download the free tool. GIMP allows for everything from free-form drawing to removing backgrounds from existing images.

Infogram

www.infogram.com

Infogram is an online tool that allows users to create digital representations of data through infographics, maps, charts, and more. It utilizes a drag-and-drop editor, making it easy to use for most. Options for Infogram creations include the use of animation and interactive charts, and the platform tracks how readers interact with the visual content. The Basic account on Infogram is free with pricing going up to $67 a month for users who require all of the bells and whistles.

Unsplash

https://unsplash.com

Unsplash is a free image and photo service that is owned by Getty Images. Images on Unsplash are free and can be used for personal use as well as editorial and commercial. This licensing is important for bloggers interested in monetizing content that includes stock photos.

Photovisi

www.photovisi.com

Photovisi is a free online tool that allows bloggers to create photo collages. The tool also offers a free photo editor that includes tools such as photo filters. To get started, simply select a collage design and add the photos that you wish to include. You can then save your collage and download it to be used on your blog and social media accounts.

Shutterstock

www.shutterstock.com

Shutterstock is a popular stock image website that offers royalty-free photos, vector drawings, and illustrations. Shutterstock templates to help bloggers create graphics using stock photo images. The platform offers subscription pricing starting at $29 per month for ten credits. Credits are used to purchase stock images as needed.

Picmonkey

www.picmonkey.com

Picmonkey is an online photo editor and graphic design maker. The site offers free tools that are limited in terms of storage, tools, and templates. In order to save and download creations, users need to subscribe. The site is very straightforward and easy-to-use with the option to upload custom graphics and images and incorporate them into designs. This is especially useful for bloggers who want to make branded content that is highly customized and unique to their blogs.

Snappa

https://snappa.com

Snappa is a cloud-based graphic design tool that allows bloggers to create everything from infographics to images for blog newsletters. Users can select from design templates, including infographic templates and banners to use in video content to be uploaded to YouTube. Bloggers can create a free account, which will give them access to up to three downloads per month. If you want to use more than three downloads, the price jumps to $10 a month if billed annually. This price includes access to additional services, including being able to remove backgrounds from images. You also will have access at this price point to unlimited downloads of your visual creations.

Giphy

www.giphy.com

Have you ever wanted to create your own GIF? With Giphy, you can! Giphy is an online tool that not only provides access to tons of existing GIFs but also allows you to create your own GIF by uploading one of the following file types, as shown in Figure 1-17:

» JPG

» PNG

» GIF

>> MP4

>> MOV

>> WebM

TouchRetouch

https://adva-soft.com/app-pageTouch.html

TouchRetouch is an app available on both iOS and the Google Play store. The nearly free app allows you remove items from images that you prefer to not be there — a stranger, a trashcan, your ex-partner — all from your cell phone! You can also use the tool to edit photos of people for items such as a blemish or fly-away hair.

Quozio

https://quozio.com

While you can certainly use any graphic creation tool to create quote graphics to include in your blog content, Quozio is a tool that is specifically designed to create images out of favorite quotes and sayings. The tool is free and incredibly simple to use. Simply plug in your quote and select Create My Quote to select from a variety of quote image options, as shown in Figure 1-18.

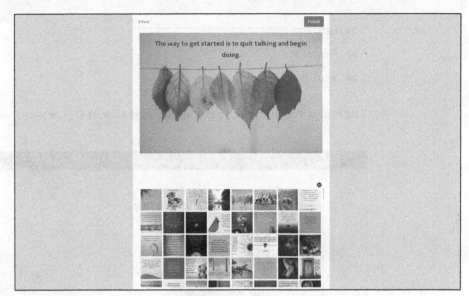

FIGURE 1-18:
Create images
from quotes
with Quozio.

Easelly

`www.easel.ly`

Easelly is an online design tool that allows users to get started with thousands of templates to create infographics. Pricing depends on how the tool will be used. For example, students using the tool for schoolwork pay only $2 a month, but bloggers using the tool for their blogging business pay $5 per month. This fee gets you access to hundreds of templates, icons, photos, organization folders, and the right to use your creations for commercial use.

Landscape

`www.sproutsocial.com`

Landscape is the free social media resizer tool by Sprout Social. The online tool allows users to upload an image, select a social media platform, resize the image to be optimized for that platform, and then export that image for use. Social media platforms that work with this tool include:

- >> Twitter
- >> Facebook
- >> Instagram

- » LinkedIn
- » Pinterest
- » YouTube

The tool is very basic and easy to use, as shown in Figure 1-19.

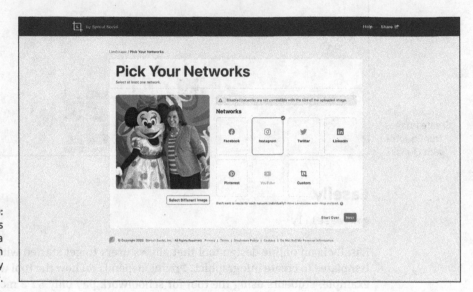

Landscape

- » Instagram

Chapter **2**

Reaching Your Audience with Video Content

O nline video has become one of the most — if not *the* most — popular content mediums on the Internet, and adding video content to your blogging strategy is an excellent way to enhance and extend your blog.

Many people already spend as much (or more) time watching online videos as they spend reading online written content, and that number will only continue to grow. Just as audio podcasts, covered in Chapter 4 of this Book, can help you grow your blog in new directions and attract new audiences, so can video content. However, jumping into the world of video isn't something to do without a little planning. It takes time and effort to create quality videos that people want to watch and share. This chapter helps you determine whether video content is right for you and shows you how to get started on a successful path as a video content creator.

Benefits of Creating Video Content

Platforms, domains, daily posting — oh my! To a beginning blogger, and even to a seasoned member of the blogosphere, it can feel at times that there are simply too many moving parts to manage. It's tough to keep up with the next big thing in blogging while still maintaining an attractive website with well-written content.

REMEMBER

If video content doesn't turn out to be a fit for you, that's okay! There are plenty of other aspects of blogging to keep you busy and help you find success. For many bloggers, however, it is a fun medium that comes naturally and enhances the rest of the work they're doing for their site.

Video content added in to an overall blogging strategy provides a number of benefits including:

>> **Providing a break from writing content:** As much as you love writing, it can be tiring to keep up with the grind of a regular content calendar posting schedule. Plugging in video content from time to time, or even on a regular schedule, gives you a break from producing written content.

>> **Allowing you to elaborate on written content:** Sometimes bloggers write a post or post series and find that there's still more to say. Want to elaborate on a post topic but don't want to write one more post? Consider using a video follow up to add more to the topic without writing more posts.

>> **Giving readers another way to consume content:** Your blog readers are coming to your blog because they enjoy consuming the written word and like your writing in particular. However, there are times when your blog audience simply doesn't have the time or opportunity to read your latest post. The occasional video gives your readers the opportunity to listen or watch instead, which can be worked into times when reading just won't work such as when they're out for a walk or making dinner. Consider creating a link to your video content for readers to click through when they're not in the mood for the written word as shown in Figure 2-1 on Four Hats & Frugal (www.4hatsandfrugal.com).

FIGURE 2-1:
Create a navigational link to your video content.

>> **Working well with certain social media platforms:** As is covered in depth in Chapter 3 of this Book, social media is a fantastic way to participate in the blogosphere away from your blog. While anyone who has ever read a Facebook rant knows that the written word is part of the social media experience, there are certain platforms where video is the only way to go. Quite honestly, video is welcome and successful on every social media platform!

>> **Attracting a different audience:** The people who come to your blog to read your posts clearly enjoy your writing. But what about the people less likely to sit down and spend a few minutes reading your carefully crafted content? Wouldn't you like them to be part of your blog audience as well? The folks who come to you for your long-form thought pieces and the ones who love your quick, witty video content may not be the same, but they're both valuable members of your community.

>> **Encouraging the sharing of your content:** Anyone who has ever been texted a link to a funny video knows how shareable video content can be. Certainly, people will retweet or email a favorite blog post as well, but there's something about a compelling video that makes people click share more quickly.

Deciding to Include Video Content in Your Blog Strategy

WARNING

Before you dive into the world of video content, take some time to consider your overall goals for your blog and building your online presence. Bloggers who use video in their blogging plan are exposed in ways that other bloggers aren't, simply because they appear on camera for the world to see and judge. You need to have a thick skin to be a blogger and a thicker skin to be a video blogger, because negative comments are inevitable. However, video can also help you build your online presence and brand in ways that blogging alone can't. Your long-term online goals are an important factor in determining whether you should include video in your blogging.

Furthermore, video takes time. Not only do you need to determine what you're going to talk about, but you need to record your video; possibly edit it; add introductions, closings, and music if you're trying to create a polished video for a platform such as YouTube; save and compress it for the web; upload it to a host or video-sharing site; name, tag, and describe your video; and promote it. That's a lot more steps than typing and publishing a blog post. However, the potential exposure video offers is something you might not be able to achieve through written posts alone.

Ultimately, your decision to include video depends on three primary factors:

>> Your comfort level in putting yourself and your thoughts on camera for the world to see

>> Your commitment to creating and uploading quality videos consistently

>> Your desire to grow your online presence

When you know how you feel about each of these factors, your decision to enter the world of video (or not) should be easier to make.

Introducing Popular Video Content Platforms

Your decision to dive into the world of video content may mean that you plan to include video content on your blog, but you may also choose to include video on other platforms as part of your overall blogging strategy. For example, investing time in social media platforms should absolutely be part of your blogging life, as covered in detail in Chapter 3 of this Book.

If you're already on those platforms, why not give video a try? You may find that you love the freedom of creating quick video content pieces and that love of video may result in the inclusion of video on your blog as well. Plus, some popular video content platforms make sharing uploaded videos on your blog easy!

YouTube

www.youtube.com

It may seem obvious that bloggers should not only purchase the domain name related to their blog but should also establish blog-related social media accounts on platforms such as Facebook and Twitter. It may be less apparent, however, that you can create a YouTube channel associated with your blog as well! Owned by content creator Amiyrah Martin, Four Hats & Frugal (featured as a blog in Figure 2-1) has a dedicated YouTube channel with over 6,000 subscribers, shown in Figure 2-2!

FIGURE 2-2:
Create a
YouTube channel
associated with
your blog.

REMEMBER

While YouTube is a video content site, in many ways it is also a search engine. Internet users often search YouTube for information and content in much the same way they search via Google, for example. That means that creating blog-associated content on YouTube is a fantastic way to drive readers back to your actual blog site.

YouTube is also a great way to build community around your blog. YouTube viewers tend to be highly engaged, liking, commenting on, and sharing content. For example, Amiyrah Martin's video tutorial about banana bites has over 6,000 likes, has been viewed more than half a million times, and has over 250 comments, as shown in Figure 2-3. Those are engagement numbers that most bloggers could only dream of getting on a blog post! That is the power of well-made YouTube video content.

To create a YouTube channel for your blog, take the following steps:

1. **Point your favorite browser to www.youtube.com.**

2. **Click Sign In in either the upper right-hand corner or the left sidebar, as shown in Figure 2-4.**

3. **Sign in using an existing Google account or create a free Google account in order to be able to sign in to YouTube.**

4. **Click on your account logo in the upper right-hand corner of the screen, as shown in Figure 2-5.**

    A dropdown menu will appear.

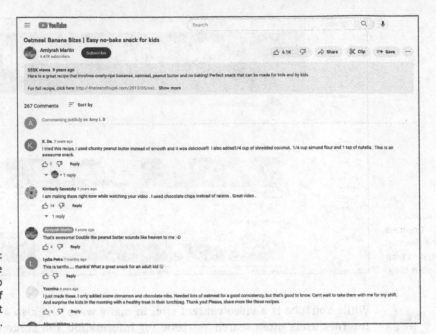

FIGURE 2-3:
YouTube videos tend to receive a lot of engagement from viewers.

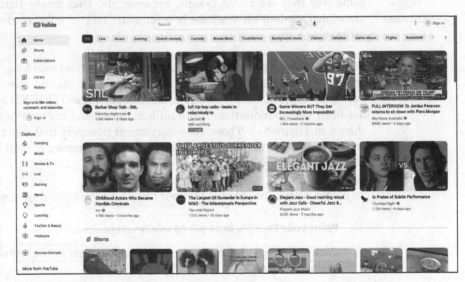

FIGURE 2-4:
Click Sign In at www.youtube.com.

5. **Select Create a Channel from the dropdown menu in order to create a channel *handle* (a short channel identifier that begins with an @ symbol that is used to help you connect with other YouTube creators) and name, as shown in Figure 2-6.**

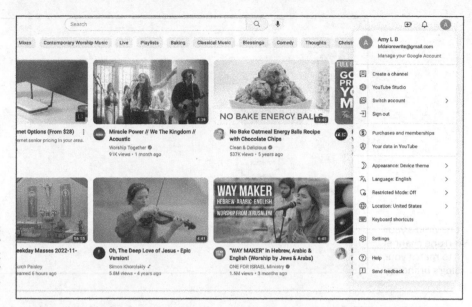

FIGURE 2-5:
Click on your Google account logo in order to access the dropdown menu.

FIGURE 2-6:
Click Create a Channel.

6. **Select a name that is associated with your blog and click Create Channel.**

You may also upload a picture, such as your blog logo, at this time. You can now begin uploading video content as well as customizing your channel including adding images that match the branding of your blog, as shown in Figure 2-7.

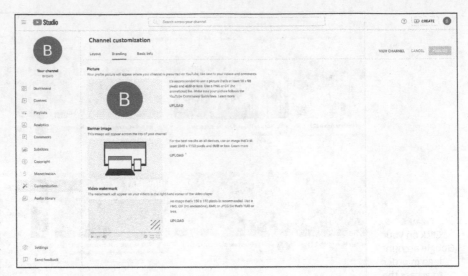

FIGURE 2-7:
Customize your
YouTube channel
to match your
blog's branding.

TIP

While most blog platforms allow you to upload video files directly to your site and posts, you can also upload video first to your YouTube account (see Figure 2-8) and then embed the YouTube video into a blog post (see Figure 2-9, using a cat costume tutorial video from 5MinutesforMom.com as an example.)

FIGURE 2-8:
5Minutes
forMom.com
uploaded their
video content to
YouTube.

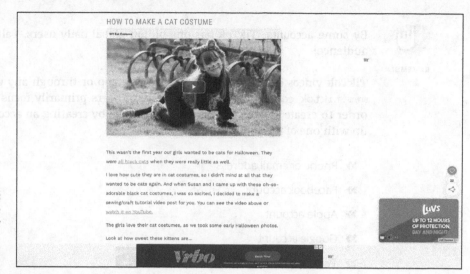

FIGURE 2-9:
The YouTube video created by 5MinutesforMom.com embedded into a blog post.

TikTok

www.tiktok.com

TikTok, shown in Figure 2-10, is arguably the most popular video platform and one of the most popular social media platforms in the world. The TikTok app allows users to create, watch, and share videos that could originally only be 15 seconds in length at the time of the app's initial popularity. At the time of this book's publishing, TikTok allows videos up to 10 minutes in length.

FIGURE 2-10:
TikTok.com is the home of popular video content.

REMEMBER

By some accounts, TikTok has one billion global daily users. Talk about a huge audience!

TikTok videos can be uploaded via the free app or through any web browser at www.tiktok.com. However, the majority of users primarily focus on the app. In order to create a video via the app, users start by creating an account by signing up with one of the following methods:

>> Phone or email address

>> Facebook account

>> Apple account

>> Google account

>> Twitter account

Like all social media, you need to create a profile including uploading a profile photo, adding a bio, and selecting a name. This is the perfect opportunity to promote your blog! Keep branding consistent between platforms by using your blog name on TikTok as well as an image that is recognizable to your blog readers. You can even link to other accounts in your TikTok account, including YouTube and Instagram.

That's all that's required to get started with TikTok. Once your account is set up, you can begin uploading videos immediately by selecting the + sign on the app. You can use a video up to 10 minutes in length that's already on your phone or you can record video right from the app in either 15-second, 60-second, or 3-minute increments. You can even edit your video right from the TikTok app including adding music and adjusting start and stop locations. You can even add captions so that your speaking is automatically captioned for viewers.

TECHNICAL STUFF

TikTok allows users to decide if they would like to post a video immediately or sometime in the future up to ten days later. While social media tools such as Hootsuite (www.hootsuite.com) allow you to schedule social media posts in advance on a variety of platforms, TikTok's app offers this ability right within the app. The ease with which bloggers can create an account, record and edit video, and schedule the video to post makes the app an easy place to dip your toe into the video content world.

Instagram

www.instagram.com

Instagram was, for years, known as a photo sharing app. It no longer identifies itself in that way as the app has become more robust over time, including the addition of video. Videos on Instagram are called *Reels*. Reels are full-screen and viewed vertically. They can be up to 90 seconds in length and include music, multiple clips from multiple videos, and captions. In many ways, Instagram Reels are meant to be similar to videos created on TikTok.

Reels are a great idea for bloggers on Instagram because the app is more likely to recommend Reels than photo content to their users. This means that bloggers posting Instagram videos have a greater chance of finding a new audience through the platform that those posting only still photos. To give Instagram Reels a try, take the following steps:

1. **Create or sign in to your Instagram account on your Instagram app.**

2. **Go to your profile page.**

3. **Click on the + sign in the upper right-hand corner, as shown in Figure 2-11.**

4. **From the Create menu, shown in Figure 2-12, click on Reel.**

5. **Press and hold the button at the bottom middle of the screen, as shown in Figure 2-13, to record your video.**

6. **You also have the option of uploading pre-recorded video instead of recording new content.**

FIGURE 2-11: Click on the + sign on your profile page.

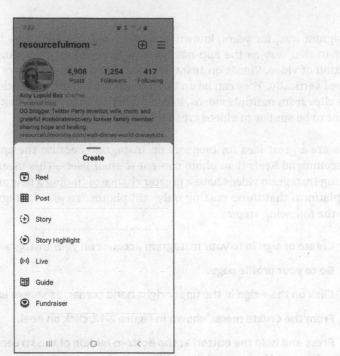

FIGURE 2-12:
Select Reel from
the Create menu.

FIGURE 2-13:
Hold the
button down to
record video.

Once your video is created, you can edit your Reel through a built-in editor to add the features mentioned earlier such as music.

TIP

While Reels are created via the free Instagram app, you can also upload pre-recorded video to your Instagram account through your web browser at www.instagram.com as shown in Figure 2-14.

FIGURE 2-14:
Upload video to
Instagram.com.

TIP

Instagram is owned by the same company that owns Facebook: Meta. This makes it easy to share video content created on Instagram with your blog's Facebook account! Be sure to link your accounts and take advantage of the ease of use that comes from being able to create content once and reach two different audiences.

Preparing to Create Video Content

The process of creating videos for the web has become less overwhelming thanks to technological advancements. For example, many computers come equipped with cameras, microphones, and video editing software. Many bloggers easily create and upload compelling video content right from their mobile phones. What was once an intimidating and expensive process is now very easy and even fun with the right planning!

Finding the tools you need

If you are interested in creating video content for your blog or other online platforms that is more involved than a quick video shot on your cell phone, you'll need to take a look at what other equipment and tools are needed. At the very least, you will need a microphone and camera. If your computer does not come with a microphone or camera, look into options that are compatible with your computer. Many budget-friendly options are available.

TIP

If you plan to create videos often using your cell phone, consider investing in a tripod to help you film from an appropriate angle with a steady focus. If you hope to create quality, professional-looking videos, you also need video-editing software, either downloaded, online, or pre-installed on your computer. Your goals for your videos dictate the equipment you need.

The following tools are popular with video content creators and provide a variety of ways to enhance and improve your video content. This is just a small sampling of what's available to download to your phone or access online. Think outside the box when it comes to including video content in your blogging. Consider animation! How about creating video from a series of still photos? Don't be afraid to look for the video enhancements that you need. Chances are that if you're looking for it, it's out there!

Animoto

www.animoto.com

Animoto, shown in Figure 2-15, is a cloud-based, easy-to-use tool that allows you to create video and share it. Users can select from a variety of templates to make the video creation process easier. You can create your video content using photos, graphs, and even stock images which can then be set to music, edited, and shared. It is a great way to create video content that goes beyond pressing record and filming video footage.

Animoto offers a free account that requires Animoto branding to appear on every video. A $9 per month account removes that branding and also allows you to change the quality of the video image to HD 1080p.

Powtoon

www.powtoon.com

Powtoon is a free (with the option to upgrade to a paid account) web-based software that allows bloggers to create video content quickly. Unlike video editors that allow you to edit content that has already been recorded, Powtoon focuses on the creation of animated, professional-looking videos using hundreds of free, professionally designed animated video templates. To use Powtoon, shown in Figure 2-16, bloggers need to simply create a free account, select a design, edit, and share!

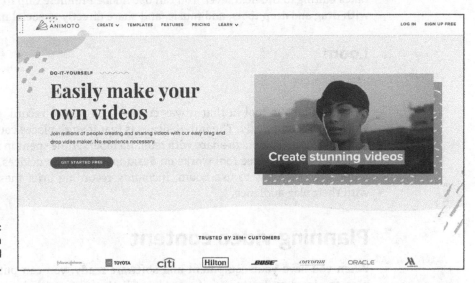

FIGURE 2-15:
Animoto is a video making and editing tool.

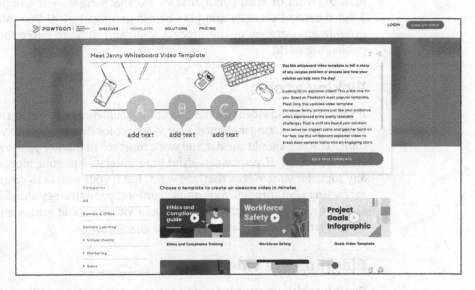

FIGURE 2-16:
Bloggers create custom animated videos at Powtoon.com.

Adobe Premiere Clip

Adobe Premiere Clip is a free app available for download on both iOS and Android devices. While most mobile phones make it easy to record and make basic edits to video with pre-loaded camera tools straight from the factory, Adobe Premiere Clip takes editing to the next level. You can use Adobe Premiere Clip to film video, edit with drag and drop tools, add music, and share directly to social media.

Loom

www.loom.com

Loom is a unique tool in that it was created as a way to record, edit, and share video messages quickly. The initial idea was that if work places could create quick videos for team leaders to share with team members, time spent in meetings could be decreased. This free tool works on desktop and mobile devices. Bloggers have found creative ways to use Loom, including recording brief messages to share with their blog audience.

Planning video content

When you have your equipment and software ready, you can put together your plan to record or create your first video. That's right — it's important to create a video content strategy and plan before getting started! The following sections provide an overview of the process you can follow to enter the online video-publishing world.

Picking a topic

If you're creating video to extend your blog audience or to enhance your blog content for your existing audience, your video topics should relate to your overall blog topic. The two should coexist and work together to market your overall web presence. Of course, if your video efforts are unrelated to your blog, you can choose any topic for your videos that you want, but if your goal is to create an integrated marketing plan through your online content, your strategy should be one of consistent branding. With that in mind, your videos should mirror and enhance your blog in terms of content and tone, and vice versa.

Planning the video

Don't just pick up your video camera and start recording. Chances are good that the result won't be as professional or high-quality as your potential audience would like. Instead, take the time to structure your video, create a loose script or outline of what you'll do and say in the video, and stick to it. Determine whether your videos will include a consistent introduction, music, and closing, and pick the tone your videos will adhere to. In other words, decide whether your videos should be highly professional, educational, entertaining, or humorous, and then stay true to that voice. By setting expectations for your content with your audience, and then delivering on those expectations in every one of your videos, you can build audience loyalty.

Lighting considerations

Make sure the location for your video shoot has sufficient lighting and that the lighting is positioned correctly. For example, if the light source is behind the person in your video, the person's face will be shadowed and difficult to see in the video. Practice with your lighting in a test video to make sure it's adequate and translates well on a computer screen.

Setting up sound

Record your video in a quiet location or be certain that the microphone you're using is adequate to pick up the sound of your voice rather than background noise. No one wants to watch a video that's difficult to hear. Test your sound and listen to it on your computer before you record your final video.

Editing the video

Few videos are perfect without some editing, and this is particularly true for online content. If you want people to return to view your videos week after week (or whenever you publish them), you need to take the time to edit out mistakes and remove dead space or other problems. Also, adding a consistent introduction and closing that play in all of your videos can give your video content a professional boost without a lot of effort.

Remembering laws and rules

WARNING

Copyright and slander laws apply to video content just as they apply to blog and audio podcast content. Don't use a piece of music in your videos unless you own it or have permission to use it. Similarly, don't use photos or images in your videos unless you own them or have permission to use them. And just as you can't say defamatory comments in person or in your podcasts, you can't do so in your videos either, or you could be accused of slander, which is punishable by law. Always err on the side of caution to be safe.

You should also be sure to read all of the terms and conditions and user agreements for any sites that you upload and share your videos through.

Most importantly, make certain that you retain all rights to your video content after you upload it to a video website.

Promoting Your Video Content

With so many online videos available, it can be very difficult to acquire search traffic to your content. Although it's essential that you take the time to name, describe, and tag your online videos when you upload them in an attempt to attract search traffic, it's equally or more important to promote your videos in every way that you can. The following suggestions can help you promote your online videos:

» **Blog about it.** Before your new video is published, write a blog post telling your blog readers what they can expect in your upcoming video.

» **Embed your video in a blog post.** After your video is published, embed it into a new post on your blog.

» **Include your video content in your blog's sidebar.** Most blogging applications provide easy ways to add a widget or gadget to your blog's sidebar, where you can republish your video content.

» **Mention it on social media platforms.** Share the link to your new video content on Facebook, LinkedIn, and other social networking sites that you belong to.

» **Send emails.** Send a professional email to your email address list with a link to your new video content.

» **Promote it anywhere and everywhere.** Include the link to your video channels on your business cards, in your email and online forum signatures, on your invoices, and anywhere else you can think of.

If you create great video content consistently and continually, your audience will grow in time. Don't give up too soon!

Chapter 3

Getting Social with Social Media

I f a blogger writes on their blog and no one reads it, was it ever really posted? Of course, this question is tongue in cheek, but the truth is that as much as bloggers receive fulfillment from the writing itself, most bloggers really do want their content to be found, read, and engaged with through comments and sharing.

REMEMBER

One of the best ways to increase the impact of your blog posts is to invest time in developing a strong social media presence, a place where you can share your blog posts and drive traffic to your site. While social media platforms are wonderful locations to amplify your blog's reach through the sharing of links and other blog-related announcements, they're also a place where bloggers can move beyond their own sites and create additional engaging content.

This chapter takes a look at how creating great content on social media platforms helps you move beyond the pages of your blog and contributes to the overall success of your blog. It also looks at the most popular social media platforms as well as the available tools to help you weave social media content into your overall blogging strategy.

Understanding How Social Media Amplifies Your Blog

With so many ways to spend your blogging time, from working on SEO strategy (read more about SEO, or search engine optimization, in Chapter 1 of Book 5) to researching content for blog posts, it can be daunting to add another piece to the already complicated puzzle. Social media takes a lot of additional effort on top of all that you're already doing for your bloggy life.

Making the case for social media

So, is it a good use of your time? The following reasons are why I believe it very much *is* a good use of your time and why. While these reasons for investing time in social media aren't exhaustive, they do give you a good snapshot of the importance of including social media in your overall blogging strategy.

>> **Social media shows readers a different side of you.** There's nothing quite like a silly lip-syncing video on TikTok to show the lighter side of a personality! While I'm not suggesting that bloggers whose niche topic is tax law should switch to posting dance videos on YouTube, I am suggesting that you take advantage of the opportunity on social media to be a bit more casual and personal. Perhaps you don't want to include video within your blog posts, but you're open to posting the occasional Reel on Instagram. Maybe you don't have time to create and edit a beautiful graphic for daily blog posts, but you'd love to show off that side of your creativity. Instagram posts may be the perfect place for that content!

TIP

Learn more about creating video on social media platforms in Chapter 2 of this Book. Look to Chapter 1 to learn more about visual content on your blog that may also be helpful for your social media platforms.

>> **Creating content for social media is generally quicker than writing a blog post.** Writing a blog post takes time. You need to create the content, edit your post, select the write SEO keywords, edit and upload a great main image, and then share and promote the content once it's published! In general, social media content is much shorter than a blog post, and you can leave all of the formatting and categorizing to the platform. Social media is a great way to get content out fast when you simply don't have time to write another post.

>> **Social media platforms allow visual content to be the focus.** While it's not only possible but actually advised to include images in your blog posts, unless you are a blogger focusing on visual media, it's most likely that the written word is the focus of your blog content. While there is writing involved on

some platforms, such as Twitter and Facebook, there are others like Pinterest and Instagram that focus heavily on images. If you enjoy taking and editing photos, creating interesting graphics, or creating fun collages, social media is the place to flex those creative muscles!

>> **Social media posts tap into an existing audience that may not know about your blog.** When you begin writing your blog, your audience consists of one person — you. Unless you share your URL with potential audience members, there is no way for anyone to know your blog exists until search engines begin to index your site. On social media platforms, however, there's already an audience ready and waiting to meet you. Take TikTok, for example, with one billion daily users. Building a presence on social media creates an opportunity for those social media users to find you — and your blog!

>> **Social media posts drive traffic back to your blog.** Social media provides you with the opportunity to link back to your blog often, including in your account bios, in your posts, and even in comments. If done well and intentionally, social media is a fantastic tool to drive new readers to your site.

>> **Social media is a great place to write about special content.** From time to time, you are going to want to write about content that is of special importance, such as a sponsored product collaboration with a favorite brand. In times such as this, a standard blog post is simply not enough. That's when social media comes the rescue, allowing you the opportunity to create additional content such as fun teaser videos or a series of photos. It may also be the best place to jump on current trends in content or newsworthy stories that may not be a fit for your blog posting calendar.

>> **Developing your social media profile is a key piece of blog branding.** It's important that readers learn to know, like, and trust you, but that sort of thing takes time and patience. Creating blog-related social media profiles and staying consistent with who you are and what you're about from one platform to the other helps speed that along. Over time, that consistent branding is how readers and followers learn to recognize you and count on receiving the same great content no matter the platform.

>> **Social media helps you to be seen by potential clients.** For the same reason that there is a vast audience of potential future blog readers on social media, an audience just waiting to be introduced to your blog, there are also future advertisers and clients on social media platforms. Brands and advertising firms scour social media platforms looking for online influencers and writers to partner with on anything from paid content to special travel opportunities.

>> **Social media is a great place to build community around your blog.** There's only so much community building that can happen in the context of blog post comments because each post is an island onto itself. Social media

helps that because the platforms are designed specifically to create engagement.

Creating robust social media accounts related to your blog provides your readers with a better place to gather together and get to know each other.

>> **Social media content is highly sharable.** While there are tools available to make sharing blog posts easy and accessible to readers, the fact remains that social media content is easily sharable with no learning curve. Social media users are used to hitting the share button on Facebook or sending a favorite TikTok video to a friend. Blog-related content on social media platforms is always more likely to be shared than even your favorite blog post on your website.

>> **Social media is a great place for your blog to interact with other blogs.** Yes, your blog can interact with other blogs! When you create social media accounts that are branded as your blog, you are able to comment on other blog social media properties with that branding. For example, Facebook allows you to switch from your personal profile to your blog profile, as shown in Figure 3-1, so that when you comment on Facebook pages belonging to other blogs, those comments appear to come from your blog rather than from you. This is a great way to support other bloggers with encouraging likes and comments, but it's also a chance for others to get to know you and begin to recognize your blog's branding.

>> **Links from social media to your blog are fantastic for SEO.** As mentioned previously, one of the end goals of creating blog-related social media accounts is to drive traffic back to your site. Because social media platforms are highly respected by search engines, links from them to you are great for your standing in search engine rankings.

FIGURE 3-1:
Your blog can interact with other blog pages on Facebook through your blog's branded Facebook profile.

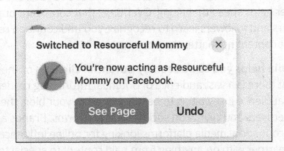

Switched to Resourceful Mommy

You're now acting as Resourceful Mommy on Facebook.

See Page   Undo

Addressing social media concerns

As with all things, including social media in your overall blogging strategy is not without its downsides. Social media — for bloggers and the general public alike — is known to be a bit of a time suck, meaning its addictive nature can distract you from focusing on not only the rest of your blogging but also your life. Also, different social media platforms call for different types of content, including, at times, a different writing tone. For example, Instagram is a highly visual platform whereas Facebook values both images and written content. That means that it's not possible to simply duplicate your efforts from one platform to another, which would be a huge help in the battle against the clock. Each one requires a separate devoted amount of time in order to find success on those platforms.

If getting lost in a task is a concern for you, check out Chapter 4 of Book 5, Blogging Tools, for ideas about how to keep track of how long you're spending on each social media platform or strategy!

Social media can be frustrating for bloggers because the distribution of content to followers is dependent on platform-driven algorithms that are entirely outside of the control of the user. That means that you may build a large following on Instagram, for example, and the content you produce simply won't be shown to a large number of those followers through no fault of your own. Speaking of followers, social media can sometimes be an ugly place. With people hiding behind the safety of anonymity, there are often unkind or even cruel comments made on social media posts, and not everyone is interested in subjecting themselves to that ugliness.

Even though you're not in charge of the social media platforms the way you are the boss of your blog, you can still set community guidelines. If someone crosses those lines, feel free to delete their comments!

Perhaps the most compelling reason to think carefully about the time you devote to social media as part of your blogging strategy is that you do not own any of the content on social media platforms. You also do not have control over your community on social media. For example, if Twitter shuts down tomorrow, all of the time that you spent building up a follower base will have been for naught unless those followers have also clicked through to your blog and provided their contact information. It is critical that as you build a social media following on any platform, you continue to drive those new members of your community to a sign-up form on your blog so that you are able to engage with them on your terms now and in the future.

The goal of including social media in your overall blogging strategy is to build your blog community, which means driving followers back to your site. Keep that strategy in mind and find creative ways to draw them into your email list so that you have control over when and how you reach out.

Getting to Know the Most Popular Social Media Platforms

If you're convinced that social media is a great place to create content beyond the blog posts you write on your own website, it's time to take a closer look at the social media platforms that are currently among the most popular. The following sections offer a peak into what makes each platform unique and how you can dive in to those social media waters.

TIP

While this is a great place to start, give yourself time on each platform to get to know the community and feel. Over time you may find that certain platforms are more your style than others, and that's okay! The goal is to create a general presence across social media. You may want to go beyond that and specialize in just a couple of your favorite platforms.

Twitter

www.twitter.com

Twitter is considered a *microblogging* platform, meaning users tweet or send out tiny little blog posts of 280 characters or less. It's been quite a long time since anyone has really thought of it in that way, however, as it's become more of a place to use your account as a global megaphone, a place to say what you want to say on topics ranging from what you had for lunch to how you feel about the upcoming primary elections. Users select who to follow and tweets are placed in the Twitter feed of a select number of people who follow the account tweeting. Who sees what depends largely on a mysterious algorithm, which can make the platform frustrating to users as only a very small fraction of followers actually each tweet.

Twitter is perhaps best known for its trending topics list, a way to see what topics are being discussed by the largest number of people at any given moment. For this reason, Twitter is often the first place to break news of celebrity deaths or political results. *Retweets*, or the sharing of someone else's content to your own followers, help news to travel quickly and breaking news to trend to the trending topics list.

Many bloggers simply use Twitter as one more place to share links to new blog posts. In Figure 3-2, blogger Erin Buhr of My Storytime Corner (www. mystorytimecorner.com) shares her latest blog post, a gift guide for children, with her Twitter followers. Most blog platforms make it easy to connect the publishing of blog posts to sharing on social media platforms, including Twitter.

FIGURE 3-2:
Many bloggers
share new blog
post links on
Twitter.com.

However, creating content on Twitter has benefits to bloggers beyond sharing links. Twitter is a great place to earn and spend social capital. In other words, it's traditionally a very collaborative community where questions are asked and answered. By spending just a bit of time on the platform getting to know other content creators, you may find opportunities to help a fellow blogger out. Rather than tweeting your link out into the void and hoping for the best, your Twitter community, ideally, will help you out with a friendly retweet.

Twitter is also a great place to find and share content related to your blog in hashtag searches. *Hashtags* are keywords set next to the # symbol, and on Twitter those keywords are searchable. That means that it's possible to go to the Twitter search and look for like-minded people tweeting about the blog-related topics that are important to you. For example, Figure 3-3 takes a look at what happens when the hashtag #wordpressplugins is used to conduct a Twitter search.

Twitter is able to be accessed via web browser or app. To join Twitter via web browser, take the following steps:

1. **Point your favorite browser to `www.twitter.com`.**

2. **Click Sign up.**

3. **Choose to sign up for a new account using one of the following methods, as shown in Figure 3-4:**

   - An existing Google account
   - An existing Apple account
   - A phone number
   - An email address

FIGURE 3-3:
Bloggers use the
Twitter search
function to find
content related
to blogging.

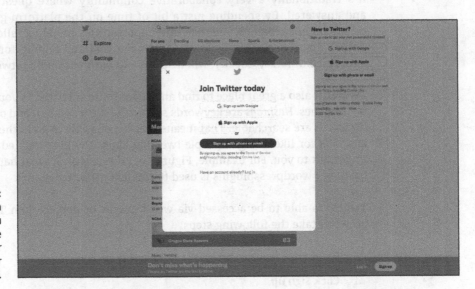

FIGURE 3-4:
Select which
method you
would like to use
to sign up for
a new Twitter
account.

4. If using your email address, input your name, email, and date of birth, as shown in Figure 3-5, and click Next.

5. Choose whether or not to allow Twitter to track where you see the platform and click Next.

6. Confirm that your name, email, and date of birth are correct and click Sign Up.

FIGURE 3-5:
Add your name,
email, and date
of birth.

7. **Authenticate your email address.**

8. **Create a password and click Next.**

9. **Either upload a profile picture or elect to skip for now, as shown in Figure 3-6.**

TIP

This is an opportunity to maintain consistent branding by selecting a photo that relates to your blog as well as other social media properties.

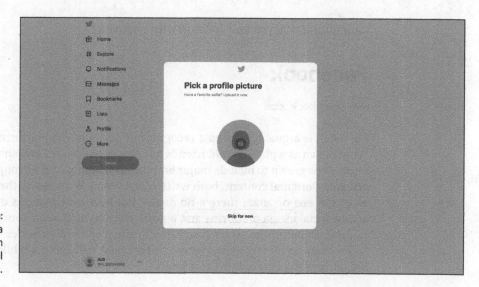

FIGURE 3-6:
Uploading a
profile picture on
Twitter is optional
during sign up.

10. **Create a username, as shown in Figure 3-7.**

TIP

Try to keep your username consistent with your blog name. If your first choice is unavailable, take your time and find an available name that matches your blog as closely as possible.

11. **Finish selecting your preferences from options such as receiving notifications and choosing subject matter preferences.**

FIGURE 3-7:
Select a Twitter
username.

Congratulations, you now have a Twitter account!

Facebook

www.facebook.com

Facebook is arguably the most recognizable social media platform on the planet. What began as a place for old friends and family to connect and share updates and photos has grown to include major brand pages, highly active groups, and a steady stream of original content, both written and visual. With nearly three billion users as of the end of 2022, there's no doubt that Facebook remains one of the most active social media platforms and a great place to help build your blogging community. Unlike some social media platforms, Facebook provides an opportunity to focus on written content, video content, and still images while building your blogging brand and online community.

Bloggers use Facebook as a place to share blog posts, often automatically through the tools available on their individual blogging platforms. However, Facebook is far more than just a bulletin board where you can slap up a link and walk away. It allows you to create both a personal profile as well as a brand page for your blog. You can even create a Facebook group to help build your reading community! Many bloggers find that it's useful to join existing groups related to blogging and online content as well as to visit the pages of other blogs.

One of the best aspects of Facebook is the sheer number of people using the platform and the amount of time they spend there. It can be tough to not get lost in the clutter, but by creating unique and useful content for your audience, you can rise above the noise. Get creative with the type of content you post on your blog's Facebook page, and take the time to interact with your followers in the comments. Consider occasionally posting content to Facebook that your readers won't find anywhere else, and if you participate in brand partnerships, occasionally give your Facebook community the first crack at exclusive offers.

Be sure to support other bloggers on Facebook and share their content from time to time. It's also important to engage and comment on their content to show your support and participate in their online communities. Follow the blog pages that most interest you and start conversations. The more you put into your time there, the more you will get out of it!

TIP

Learn more about Facebook in *Facebook For Dummies*, 8th Edition, by Carolyn Abram and Amy Karasavas (John Wiley & Sons, Inc., 2021).

In order to create a Facebook page for your blog, you first need to have a personal account. Once you have a personal Facebook account, take the following steps via your web browser to create your blog's Facebook page.

1. **Sign in to your Facebook account on your favorite web browser.**

2. **Select the menu from the upper right-hand corner, as shown in Figure 3-8.**

3. **From the menu, select Page under Create.**

   The Facebook Create a Page screen will open, as shown in Figure 3-9.

4. **Fill in the following information:**

   - Page name: The page name should match your blog's name.

   - Category: Type in keywords related to your blog to select a category that most closely fits your content.

   - Write a brief description.

5. **Click Create Page.**

FIGURE 3-8:
Locate the menu in the upper right-hand corner of the screen.

FIGURE 3-9:
The Facebook Create a Page screen.

Once you have created a Facebook page for your blog, take some time to customize the page to fit your blog's branding. Figure 3-10 shows my personal blog's Facebook page with a cover image and profile picture matching the color and logo on my website. When readers find me on Facebook they know immediately that yes, this *is* the same Resourceful Mommy as the website that they know and like.

FIGURE 3-10:
The Resourceful
Mommy
Facebook page
matches the
branding of
the related blog.

Instagram

www.instagram.com

Instagram is a primarily app-based social media platform owned by Meta, the same company that owns Facebook. Instagram began as a photo sharing app only, with users uploading an image, adding an artsy filter, and writing an associated caption. In recent years, however, Instagram has become so much more than just a look book of fun photos. The following are the four ways that bloggers can create content on this easy-to-use social media platform:

>> **Create a Post:** An Instagram feed post is the original type of content on the platform. This will appear on your profile page and remain there unless you delete it, as shown in Figure 3-11. A *post* may consist of either a single photo, a single video, or what Instagram calls a *carousel post*, a selection of up to ten photos or videos that appear as one post with the option to scroll through content.

>> **Create a Story:** An Instagram *story* is temporary and only remains visible to your followers for 24 hours. Bloggers often gather thematically related stories to place long term in their story highlights, which can be seen with the label "Disney" in Figure 3-11. Creating story highlights allows followers to view that story content beyond the standard 24 hours. Stories offer bloggers an opportunity to tap into their creative side with the option to add music, captions, and even fun stickers to their content. Stories can be video content or still photos or simply words on a colorful background.

FIGURE 3-11:
Instagram Posts remain on your profile page unless deleted.

>> **Record or upload a Reel:** An Instagram *reel* is a video that is 60 seconds or less. It can be recorded via the Instagram app and immediately uploaded or can be uploaded from your video library. Reels can be edited directly in the Instagram app, including changing the length and speed of the video. Like stories, you can add stickers and text over your reel.

>> **Go Live:** Instagram also allows bloggers to *go live* to their community via the app. This means that you can broadcast live to your followers, who will receive a notification that your live broadcast has begun. This works especially well for some bloggers depending on their focus. For example, an antiques blogger may choose to go live while out on a picking adventure, or a fashion blogger may choose to go live while shopping for the latest coveted outfit.

In order to join Instagram, I recommend first downloading the app. Then take the following steps to create an account:

1. **Open the Instagram app.**

2. **Choose to either login with Facebook or using an email address/phone number, as shown in Figure 3-12.**

TIP

Because Facebook and Instagram are both owned by Meta, the easiest way to open an Instagram account is to do so through your Facebook account. If you already have a personal Instagram account, you can open a second account for your blog. This can be done via the same Facebook account. If you do not want to use your Facebook account, select to sign up with email or a phone number.

FIGURE 3-12:
Sign up for
Instagram using
either your
Facebook account
or email address.

3. **If you've chosen to sign up with an email address, fill in the appropriate information, as shown in Figure 3-13, and select Next.**

   You will be prompted to enter a confirmation code.

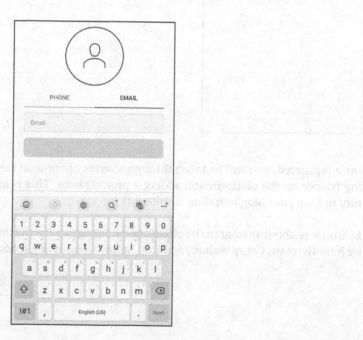

FIGURE 3-13:
Fill in your email
address or
phone number.

4. **Provide your full name and create a password for your account, as shown in Figure 3-14, and select to either continue while syncing contacts or without syncing contacts.**

5. **Provide your birthdate.**

6. **Choose to either sign up with the suggested username or select change username, as shown in Figure 3-15.**

   If you choose to create a different username, Instagram will prompt you to try again if the name you like is already taken. The app will also suggest alternatives that are related to the name you have requested.

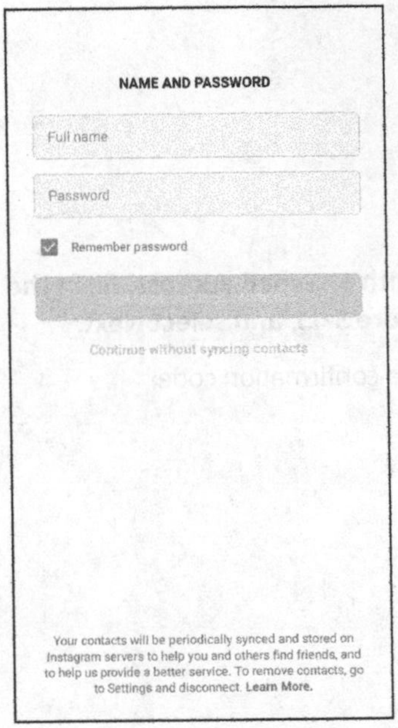

NAME AND PASSWORD

Full name

Password

☑ Remember password

Continue without syncing contacts

Your contacts will be periodically synced and stored on Instagram servers to help you and others find friends, and to help us provide a better service. To remove contacts, go to Settings and disconnect. Learn More.

FIGURE 3-14: Provide your name and password.

Once registered, you will be taken through a series of optional steps such as finding friends on the platform and adding a profile photo. This is another opportunity to keep your blog branding consistent!

TIP

Learn more about Instagram by checking out *Instagram For Dummies*, 2nd Edition, by Jenn Herman, Corey Walker, and Eric Butow (John Wiley & Sons, Inc., 2022).

FIGURE 3-15:
Decide what
username you
would like to use.

Pinterest

`www.pinterest.com`

Pinterest is an incredibly visual social media platform that is based on the concept of a pinboard, taking images and pinning them to create a thematically unified pinboard.

REMEMBER

Pinterest is a fabulous place for bloggers to create content because each image on Pinterest links back to another website, ideally, including your blog. This is not only great for bolstering the size of your readership, but it's important for SEO as well. Search engines respect links to blogs from highly trafficked sites and apps such as Pinterest. Participating in Pinterest by creating pins for your own content, as well as other content you would like to promote and share, makes it more likely that others will link back to you through pins as well.

TIP

Some of the best ways to integrate content on Pinterest into your blog strategy include the following:

>> Make the images on your blog *pinnable* (meaning they can be easily be saved onto a pinboard on Pinterest). To learn more about the role of visual content on your blog, check out Chapter 1 of this Book.

» Create a board named after your blog. Pin your own content to your blog board. This makes it more likely that others will re-pin the images that lead to your posts.

» Create boards related to your content. If you create useful content on Pinterest with pins to other related resources, users will be more likely to re-pin and click through your pins, including the pins that lead to your blog!

» Create themed boards that consist entirely of your content. Take a look at your blog categories and find topics that would work well as a Pinterest board. Then pin your best content from within those categories to themed boards.

» Keep a consistent pinning schedule. Make sure that your followers on Pinterest know that they can consistently find great content on your pin-boards so that they are more likely to return again and again.

Pinterest can be used on an app or by visiting www.pinterest.com. To create a Pinterest account via a web browser, take the following steps:

1. Point your favorite web browser to www.pinterest.com.

2. Click Sign Up in the upper right-hand corner, as shown in Figure 3-16.

3. Sign up using one of the following methods, as shown in Figure 3-17:

   - Email address
   - Facebook account
   - Google account

FIGURE 3-16:
Sign up at
Pinterest.com.

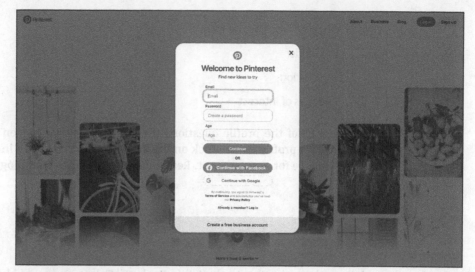

FIGURE 3-17:
Select your
method for
signing up for
Pinterest.

4. **If signing up with email, type your email address, create a password, and share your age then select Continue.**

5. **When a welcome screen appears prompting you to answer a series of questions, as shown in Figure 3-18, click Next to answer each question.**

FIGURE 3-18:
Click Next to
begin answering
profile questions.

Questions include the following:

- Gender
- Location
- Areas of interest

TIP

At the start of the profile questions there is a somewhat hidden opportunity to change your profile name. Click on the little pencil icon, shown in Figure 3-18, to select a name for your account. Remember to relate it to your blog!

TikTok

www.tiktok.com

As mentioned in Chapter 2 of this Book, TikTok is an incredibly popular social media platform that exists primarily via a free app. The platform is the home of short-form videos that are never more than ten minutes long and are typically much shorter.

REMEMBER

The content on TikTok tends to be shared often and easily, making it a great place for bloggers to create a branded profile and occasionally post video content. It's also the perfect place for bloggers to dip their toes into video even if they aren't sure that's the best medium for them. The videos on TikTok tend to be far less polished than those on other platforms such as YouTube, for example. This makes TikTok less of a time investment for already busy bloggers, providing a lot of bang for your buck.

TikTok can be especially useful to bloggers looking to create content off of their sites if their blogging niche is a particular fit. For example, any blogger who is likely to create and post how-to content should consider creating brief and easy how-to videos on TikTok. I can't count the number of times I've heard people mention that they're trying a TikTok recipe or a TikTok beauty tip. What they're saying is simply that they learned these skills from videos on TikTok. This is great for fashion, beauty, DIY, and food bloggers.

To sign up for a new account on TikTok, take the following steps:

1. **Download the free app from your phone's app store.**
2. **Click Sign up at the bottom of the screen, as shown in Figure 3-19.**

Log in to TikTok

Manage your account, check notifications, comment
on videos, and more.

   Use phone / email / username

   Continue with Facebook

   Continue with Google

   Continue with Twitter

By continuing, you agree to our **Terms of Service** and acknowledge
that you have read our **Privacy Policy** to learn how we collect, use,
and share your data.

Don't have an account? Sign up

FIGURE 3-19:
Click Sign-up to
create a new
TikTok account.

3. **Select a method to sign up from one of the following options, as shown in Figure 3-20:**

   - Phone number or email address
   - Facebook account
   - Google account

4. **Provide your birthdate.**

5. **Provide your phone number or email address and select Next.**

6. **Create a password.**

7. **Create a username and select Sign up.**

   This can be changed later if you change your mind. Remember, this is an opportunity to keep consistent branding with your blog!

8. **Choose your interests from a variety of video topics or select skip.**

Congratulations, you now have a TikTok account!

TIP

Don't forget to tell your new TikTok audience about your blog and send them back to your site!

FIGURE 3-20:
Select a method
to sign up for a
new account.

YouTube

www.youtube.com

Anyone who has ever typed www.youtube.com into their web browser in order to conduct a search rather than going to a search engine such as Google knows first-hand the power of the platform. While YouTube is most definitely a social media platform, to many it is also a search engine, a television channel, or their favorite source of entertainment.

YouTube is one of the most popular global online destinations, and any bloggers who are interested in creating video content should make it a top priority in their blogging strategy. YouTube not only provides bloggers with a place to upload content that differs from the normal written post format, but it makes those uploaded videos easy to integrate into posts back on your blog. Creating on YouTube is the perfect way to move beyond the written words of your posts while also driving traffic to your blog and providing readers with exciting and fresh content.

Learn more about the power of video in Chapter 2 of this Book!

TIP

To get started with a YouTube account, simply sign in to your existing Google account or sign up at www.google.com. Like many online entities, YouTube is owned by Google!

In order to create your blog–related YouTube channel, take the following steps:

1. **Point your favorite web browser to www.YouTube.com.**

2. **Click on your Google account icon in the upper right-hand corner to open a dropdown menu, as shown in Figure 3-21.**

3. **Select Create a Channel.**

   A Create a Channel screen will open, as shown in Figure 3-22.

4. **Type the name and handle that you would like associated with your YouTube channel or accept the names suggested.**

5. **Click Customize channel in the upper right-hand corner, as shown in Figure 3-23, to get started creating a channel that works well with your blog.**

FIGURE 3-21:
Open the drop
down menu on
YouTube.com.

FIGURE 3-22:
The YouTube
Create a Channel
screen.

FIGURE 3-23:
Customize
your channel
to include blog
branding.

LinkedIn

`www.linkedin.com`

Not everyone automatically associates LinkedIn with social media, but for bloggers in particular, the platform offers an alternative location to create and post content. LinkedIn is a great place to share professional knowledge and build your identity as an expert in your blogging niche or even in blogging itself.

TIP

Because employers seek new employees through the professional networking platform, creating content on LinkedIn is especially advantageous for bloggers who are hoping to monetize. Many opportunities exist for bloggers through LinkedIn messaging or networking.

To create a LinkedIn account, take the following steps:

1. **Point your favorite browser to www.linkedin.com.**

2. **Click Join Now at the top of the screen, as shown in Figure 3-24.**

   A sign up screen will appear.

FIGURE 3-24:
Create a new
LinkedIn
account at www.
linkedin.com.

3. **On the sign up screen, shown in Figure 3-25, choose to sign up via one of the following ways:**

   - Email address
   - Google accounts

4. **Provide your first and last name, as shown in Figure 3-26, and click Continue.**

5. **Work through the list of questions to help customize your LinkedIn experience.**

TIP

To find out more about LinkedIn, you can read *LinkedIn For Dummies*, 6th Edition, by Joel Elad (John Wiley & Sons, Inc., 2021).

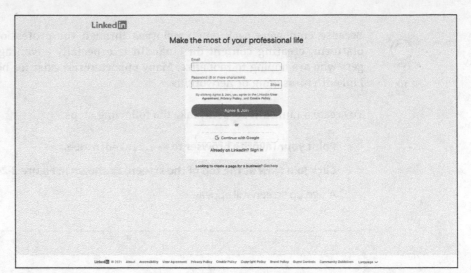

FIGURE 3-25:
Select a sign up
method.

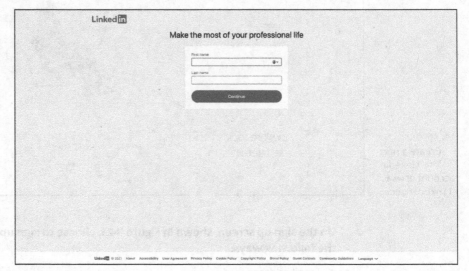

FIGURE 3-26:
Provide your first
and last name.

Introducing Social Media Tools for Bloggers

Even if you're completely on board with branching out from just creating written blog posts on your site, that doesn't mean that you have the time to master posting content around the social web. While creating great content anywhere — even on social media platforms — takes time, planning, and effort, take heart! There are a number of wonderful tools available to help you maximize your time and your social media as efficiently as possible. The following list offers just a very small number of ideas for tools that you may want to use to help you on your social media journey:

>> **SocialPilot** (`www.socialpilot.co`): SocialPilot is a tool that focuses on helping bloggers to automate their social media posting. It is able to be used on most social media platforms and offers analytics as well.

>> **Buffer** (`www.buffer.com`): Buffer assists bloggers in selecting the best content to share on social media as well as knowing when the best time is to share it. Its intention is to decrease your work time and grow your social media following at the same time.

>> **Agorapulse** (`www.agorapulse.com`): Agorapulse is social media management software that helps bloggers to manage and then monitor social media posting on Facebook, Twitter, Instagram, YouTube, and LinkedIn.

>> **Tailwind** (`www.tailwindapp.com`): Tailwind is a social media tool that automates content creation, scheduling, and publishing on platforms including Instagram, Pinterest, and Facebook.

>> **ClicktoTweet** (`www.clicktotweet.com`): ClicktoTweet is a fantastic tool for bloggers because it enables readers to tweet your content out on your behalf. It is free and easy to use as well!

>> **Hootsuite** (`www.hootsuite.com`): If you are interested in scheduling your social media posts in advance so that they go live at optimal times without you being there, then Hootsuite is for you! The tool also offers robust analytics so that you can track how successful your efforts have been and adjust future plans accordingly.

TIP

To learn more about social media tools, visit Book 6, Chapter 3.

IN THIS CHAPTER

» **Discovering why podcasts are popular**

» **Determining whether podcasting is right for you**

» **Choosing the right equipment and recording your podcast**

» **Finding an online home for your podcast**

» **Publicizing your podcast**

Chapter **4**

Creating a Podcast

M any bloggers begin publishing podcasts as an extension of their blogging experience. In simplest terms, *podcasts* are audio files delivered online. This chapter focuses entirely on the creation and publication of audio podcasts as they relate to enhancing or extending a blog.

Creating a podcast can seem intimidating to beginner bloggers, but there are many free tools available that make becoming a podcaster easier than you might imagine. This chapter tells you how to start a podcast, publish it, and promote it so you can determine for yourself whether podcasting is right for you and your blogging goals.

For complete details about beginner podcasting, pick up *Podcasting For Dummies*, 4th Edition by Tee Morris and Chuck Tomasi (John Wiley & Sons, Inc., 2020).

Getting the Scoop on Podcasts

A traditional podcast is an audio recording that you publish online, and fans can use an RSS feed to subscribe to new episodes of the podcast, which are pushed to them through their preferred podcast services. Unlike radio programs that are broadcast at specific times and on specific radio stations, people can access and download podcasts any time after they're published, and they can listen to the podcast as many times as they want.

In recent years, the term *podcasting* has become a bit diluted and now represents a variety of online audio publishing methods. In this chapter, I bypass semantics and reference podcasts in the broader sense: online audio publishing that extends or enhances a blog. Therefore, for the purposes of this chapter, a podcast doesn't have to be a traditional ongoing broadcast; there are many options available to bloggers these days for publishing and promoting audio content through their blogs, many of which are collectively referred to as podcasts, regardless of whether that label is technically correct.

Here are two common methods for getting a podcast out there to the public:

>> **Bloggers can upload their audio files to their own web hosting site and publish them directly within a blog post.** Although that's not the traditional definition of podcasting, many people refer to this method of publishing audio files as podcasting, simply because it represents a method of online audio publishing.

>> **Bloggers can open accounts on radio and podcasting sites.** Bloggers can sign up for accounts with online radio and podcasting sites where they can not only upload their podcasts and create media RSS feeds for those podcasts, but also bypass traditional recording methods if they choose.

Bottom line: Podcasting might technically mean subscribable, broadcast-online audio publishing, but the lines between online audio and podcasting have blurred. That's actually a good thing though, because the shift has opened wide the doors to online audio publishing. Anyone can develop an online audio presence these days.

WARNING

Most of the concerns podcasters face are related to copyright laws. Always consult your attorney for legal advice, but the basic issues facing podcasters involve using music in a podcast without permission. Furthermore, you have to be careful what you say in your podcasts to avoid being accused of slander. The best way to avoid trouble is to use music in your podcasts only if you own it or have written permission to use it. Alternatively, some podcast-recording applications, discussed later in this chapter, provide music options that you can use freely in your podcasts. In terms of what you say during your podcast, make sure you provide attribution to anyone you quote, and don't say anything that can be viewed as defamatory or malicious toward another person or entity. Editorial commentary is perfectly acceptable as long as it doesn't cross the line into slander territory. The best choice is to always err on the side of caution.

Discovering Why Podcasts Are Popular

Podcasts have grown more and more popular as the technology to create and publish them online has gotten easier to use, and the ability to download and listen to podcasts has become accessible to a wider audience.

Podcasts are an excellent way to extend a blog, particularly if they're published through an online radio or podcasting site, where they can be advertised and shared to a broader audience. Similarly, podcasts present a great opportunity to enhance your blog. By including a link to your podcast or the audio file directly within one of your blog posts, blog readers have a new, more personal way to interact with you. Podcasts tap into the readers' sense of hearing, which adds a new layer to your online content and may even appeal to some visitors more so than written posts.

In other words, podcasts help to draw attention, attract new audiences, and build relationships. They're just one more way you can deliver meaningful, useful content and connect with your audience.

Determining Whether Podcasting Is Right for You

Podcasting offers a variety of positives and negatives to bloggers. Take the time to consider your blogging goals before you dive into the world of podcasting, so you don't waste your time. Following are some of the reasons you may decide to become a podcaster:

>> **Grow your audience.** When you publish podcasts, you can host them through sites designed specifically for sharing and promoting audio content. (Some of those sites are discussed later in this chapter.) Doing so opens your content up to new audience members who might not find your blog otherwise. They might simply prefer audio content or stumble upon it while searching for something else. Either way, as more people find your podcast, more people can be led to your blog.

>> **Entertain or educate your existing audience in a new way.** Reading blog post after blog post can get boring for some people. Adding an audio component to your blog with a podcast creates a new element of interest.

>> **Expand on your blog posts.** Sometimes it just takes too long to type a detailed blog post, and more often, people won't read a lengthy blog post if

it's not riveting. Podcasts help solve that problem. If your podcasts are entertaining and interesting, they might hold an audience's attention longer than a 1,000-plus-word blog post does.

REMEMBER

Many blog readers will only devote a certain amount of time to sitting down and reading a blog post. However, they are likely to listen to additional related content via podcast while going for a walk, for example, or preparing dinner.

>> **Communicate with like people.** Podcasts can be highly interactive depending on the format you choose and the provider you use to publish them online. For example, you can interview people in your podcasts and publish them online at a later date for people to listen to. They can leave written comments but can't vocally participate. Alternatively, if you record your podcasts through a radio or podcasting site that allows listeners to call in and participate, similar to an online radio show, they can join the conversation, too. It's a great way to make your listeners feel valued and important.

>> **Make your content more convenient to consume.** Podcasts can be downloaded and listened to at any time, making them easy to consume. For example, a person can download a podcast to their phone and listen to it while they're working out or driving to work. It's a convenient medium to spread your messages and connect with people in ways a blog doesn't provide.

Podcasting can be fun and help you reach your blogging goals, but there are also negative aspects. For example, it's time-consuming to plan, create, edit, and publish a podcast. Also, podcasting might require a monetary investment in equipment such as microphones, editing software, and more. Consider your goals and make sure that shifting to podcasting matches those goals before you dive into the world of audio blogging.

TIP

Your podcasts can only be as successful as you make them. That means publishing one podcast and never publishing another won't work. To be a successful podcaster, you need to publish new audio content on a consistent basis that's relevant to your overall blog topic, and you need to commit to promoting your podcasts by talking about them on your blog and through social networking. Just as blogging success is a long-term strategy, so too is podcasting success. Promotional suggestions are provided at the end of this chapter.

Finding the Equipment You Need

A variety of ways exist to create a podcast, including the following:

>> With your own digital recording and editing equipment

>> Through a website that allows you to record your podcast via your phone

>> Through video conferencing software such as Zoom or Skype

>> With a portable recorder

Some options allow you to become a podcaster with just your computer and an Internet connection. For other options, the equipment you need gets a bit more complex. Don't be overwhelmed though. You don't need a state-of-the-art recording studio to create a podcast.

You can use free audio-recording programs to create your podcasts. There are also many audio-recording programs that cost money, some with high price tags. However, before you invest in expensive software, try a free alternative. You might find it serves your purposes quite well. The following sections describe two of the most commonly used free audio-recording programs and take a look at a variety of additional options.

Audacity

www.audacityteam.org

Audacity, shown in Figure 4-1, is a free audio recording and editing program available for Windows, Mac, and Linux users. It's a simple program that allows you to create audio files with basic effects such as introductions. Many podcasters use Audacity because it offers plenty of features to create professional audio files, and it's free!

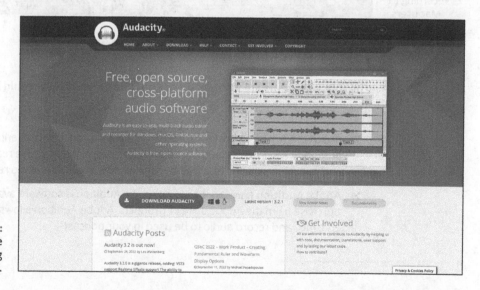

FIGURE 4-1:
Audacity is a free audio-recording program.

Creating a Podcast

GarageBand

www.apple.com/ilife/garageband

GarageBand, shown in Figure 4-2, is a free audio production app for macOS and iOS systems. It offers easy-to-use, audio-recording capabilities, which you can use with the microphone built into your Mac or with an external microphone plugged into one of your Mac's USB ports. GarageBand also has a large library of music that podcasters can use freely and without violating copyright laws. Furthermore, GarageBand makes it easy to share your podcast online through iTunes.

FIGURE 4-2:
GarageBand offers audio recording to Mac users.

Further options

The following tools are also worth looking into to see if they would be a fit for you as you begin your podcasting journey:

» **Restream (www.restream.io):** Restream allows you to record and store audio and save it to a cloud-based storage system. When you're ready to edit and release your podcast content, you just download your audio recording.

» **Adobe Audition (www.adobe.com):** Adobe Audition is software available for purchase from the Adobe suite of products. Adobe Audition allows you to edit, mix, and record audio to be used in your podcast.

>> **Auphonic** (www.auphonic.com): Auphonic is a tool that helps podcasters edit and perfect their audio recordings after they are recorded. For example, Auphonic assists with podcasting issues such as changes in sound levels or background noise.

>> **QuickTime:** QuickTime is software that comes installed on many Apple products and allows you to create audio recordings easily.

>> **Alitu** (www.alitu.com): Alitu is an all-in-one podcasting product that allows you to record your podcast, including with more than one participant, then engineer your audio recording. Alitu even generates a transcript and facilitates publishing your finished podcast.

>> **REAPER** (www.reaper.fm): For those who want a more complex and powerful tool, REAPER is a digital audio production application able to be downloaded to computers.

Strategizing and Creating Your Podcast

Before you sit down at a microphone and record your first podcast, you need to do some planning, and not just technical planning. First, you need to create a strategy for it. Don't worry. You don't have to create a list of strategic imperatives and action items. A podcast isn't a business plan. However, you do need to consider some of the fundamental decisions that have the greatest impact on your podcast's success. The following sections help you focus on the building blocks of your podcasting venture.

Setting goals for your podcast

Before you start creating podcasts, you need to set your goals. It can take longer to prepare, record, edit, and publish a podcast than a written blog post, so before you invest that time, make sure you have a goal in mind.

Take a look at the reasons why people create podcasts earlier in this chapter to help you define your own objectives. What do you hope to achieve by adding audio content to your blog? For example, podcasts are a great way to build relationships, particularly if you record your podcasts in a format that allows listeners to call in and participate verbally.

However, if you're simply creating podcasts as a hobby, goal-setting isn't as essential. The important thing is to always have fun. If you sound bored and indifferent during your podcast, no one will listen, and it can reflect poorly on your blog, too.

Don't start your podcasts with unrealistic goals, or you set yourself up for failure. It takes time to create podcasts. For example, if you start with a one-hour format, you might become overwhelmed quickly and abandon your podcast entirely. Instead, start small and grow as your comfort level and audience grow. For example, begin with a 5-minute podcast and work your way up to longer podcasts as you get more comfortable.

Picking your podcast subject matter

For a podcast related to your blog to be successful, you need to make sure that your podcast content is relevant to your blog's content. That means the first step to planning your podcast is defining your podcast's primary topic. More than likely, this topic should mirror your blog's topic, or it should be a niche within your blog topic that can be effectively discussed in audio format.

Considering your audience

After you determine your podcast's topic, you need to take some time to consider your existing blog audience as well as the new audience you want to attract with your podcast.

Podcasts are part of an integrated blog marketing strategy, meaning your blog and podcast should work seamlessly together to help you achieve your broader goals. The two media shouldn't be disjointed but rather work cohesively. That means your podcast content should benefit and meet the needs of your existing audience as well as the new audience you're trying to attract to your blog.

If your podcast and blog don't work cohesively, either your existing audience or your new audience will be disappointed. In other words, your existing blog audience won't want to listen to your podcasts if the content is meaningless to them, and your new podcast audience won't want to visit your blog if the content you write doesn't interest them. Consistency is key to overall online publishing success.

Selecting your voice

Depending on your subject matter and your audience, you need to decide the tone of your podcast. Will it be humorous and fun or serious and business-like? Should it be purely entertaining or educational? The way you speak has a significant effect on your podcast in terms of how you and your podcast connect with your guests and audience as well as how you handle the topics you discuss during your podcast. Your voice should be consistent with your blog voice in order to cohesively integrate them into your overall online presence.

Think of it this way. If you write a blog about providing expert stock market advice and education and then you start a podcast to enhance and extend your blog, the topics and your voice used in your podcast should mirror those in your blog. For example, if your podcast is a satirical look at the stock market filled with dark comedy and commentary that doesn't offer helpful advice to investors, your existing blog audience is unlikely to be interested in your podcast, and the new audience that finds your podcast is unlikely to be interested in your blog. Certainly, you may get some audience crossover, but not even remotely close to the crossover that could exist if your blog and podcast provide a consistent brand message, image, and promise that meet your audience's expectations of you and your content.

TIP Most importantly, be expressive and show passion for your subject in your podcast. Make your audience care as much as you do.

Of course, if you're starting a podcast that you plan to have live completely separate from your existing blog or web presence, consistency in voice and content aren't an issue for you.

Identifying your podcast format

Similar to radio shows all mimicking a similar format, your podcast should have at least a loose format that includes a professional introduction and closing. For example, use music (with copyright permission) and a scripted introduction and closing statement before and after *every* one of your podcasts for consistency. Once your podcast attracts an audience, you might want to invest in hiring a company to help you create a show introduction and closing that are similar to those you hear on radio shows.

Furthermore, select a length for your podcast and don't deviate from that length. Just as television and radio shows don't deviate in length from one day or week to the next, neither should your podcast. It's important to set audience expectations and consistently meet them in order to gain loyalty. If your podcast exceeds your allotted time, consider splitting it up into multiple parts and promote the continuation to drive interest and excitement just as television shows do with multipart episodes.

If you record your podcast through a website that allows you to take listener calls, determine when you'll take those calls during your show (for example, as they come in or at the end of the podcast) and stick to that format for all of your podcasts. Again, consistency is key to creating listener expectations — be sure to deliver on those expectations every time. That's how audience loyalty develops.

Recording your podcast

When the time comes to record your podcast, you need to have a microphone — even if only the one that comes with your laptop — and audio-recording software. Make sure you have a quiet location to record from and test your equipment before you begin. Most importantly, prepare your podcast content, and practice what you're going to say. Although it's not necessary to have a written script, and in fact, in some cases scripted podcasts can be very dull, you do need to have a basic structure in mind before you get started. Stick to your time guidelines, and have fun! Your audience will know if you're overly nervous or utterly disinterested.

Editing your podcast

After your podcast is recorded, you can use your audio-recording software to make any necessary edits. Of course, if you produce a live podcast, editing isn't an option. However, for recorded podcasts, editing is extremely important. Not only can you add music, introductions, closings, and so on during the editing process, but you can also delete dead air, clean up "ums," and fix any errors. No podcast is perfect, and that's part of what makes online audio interesting and real. Your goal should be to create a professional-sounding podcast but not so perfect that you seem inhuman.

Testing, analyzing, tweaking, and learning more

The world of podcasting continues to evolve, and new tools for podcast recording, publishing, and analyzing results are hitting the Internet all the time. After you determine your podcasting goals, take the time to research some of the current recording, publishing, and hosting options available to you, and select the tool that helps you meet those goals. Your choice might come down to selecting the tool that requires the least technical knowledge to use, and that's absolutely fine. Fortunately, there are podcasting tools available today that enable anyone to create online audio content quickly and easily.

Also, take the time to figure out what kind of metrics you can get from the publishing and hosting site (or sites) you choose, and then track those statistics. You might be able to determine topics that drive significant traffic or promotional efforts that cause a boost in listeners. By analyzing your podcast's performance over time, you can identify areas for improvement or opportunities for continued success.

Most importantly, don't get complacent with your podcasts. Not only will your audience notice, but you might miss opportunities for improved technology or analysis that can ultimately save you time or money. In short, you never know what podcasting advance will launch next week, next month, or next year. If you're serious about podcasting, the next great tool may be exactly what you need to take your podcast to the next level of success!

TIP

Take some time to listen to other podcasts to get an idea of what works so you can apply similar techniques in your own podcasts. Following are several great podcasts to get you started:

» **Crime Junkie** (`https://crimejunkiepodcast.com`): A weekly true crime podcast.

» **The Daily** (`https://www.nytimes.com/column/the-daily`): A five-day-a-week news podcast.

» **This American Life** (`https://www.thisamericanlife.org`): A weekly public radio program and podcast focused on storytelling.

» **My Favorite Murder** (`https://myfavoritemurder.com`): A popular true crime comedy podcast.

» **Office Ladies** (`https://officeladies.com`): A rewatch podcast, shown in Figure 4-3, with two cast members from the American television show, *The Office*.

FIGURE 4-3:
Office Ladies is a popular podcast starring former cast members from *The Office*.

Finding an Online Home for Your Podcast

Many websites allow you to upload your podcast to prepare it for sharing or distribution. Some of those sites also host your audio file for you, and some even create an RSS feed of your podcasts for you, which you can use to upload your podcast to more sites. To choose the site where you want to upload and host your podcasts, you need to determine your distribution objectives and your overall strategic goals for your podcast.

Hosting your podcast

The following list takes a look at some of the most popular sites to upload and prepare to distribute your podcasts. Review each in detail and be sure to check the current offerings on each site before you dive into uploading your first podcast. Some are easier to use than others, and each one offers different features. You can't really go wrong with any of the options discussed in this chapter, but doing a bit of research up front can help you make the best decision for you, your podcast, and your blog. Options for hosting your podcast online include:

>> **Buzzsprout** (`www.buzzsprout.com`): Buzzsprout, shown in Figure 4-4, is a cloud-based podcast host that allows podcasters to upload files and schedule their distribution. There are a variety of hosting prices beginning at $12 per month.

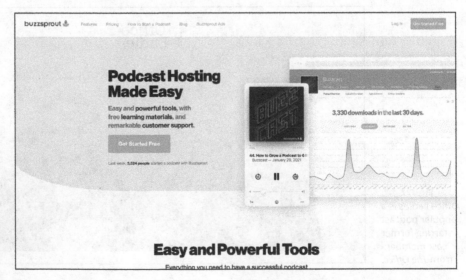

FIGURE 4-4:
Buzzsprout offers podcasters a cloud-based hosting solution.

- » **RSS.com (www.rss.com):** RSS.com hosts your audio files to create your podcast, helps with distribution, and even provides a landing page for your podcast. Prices begin at $8.25 per month.

- » **RedCircle (www.redcircle.com):** RedCircle is a podcast hosting site that focuses on monetization of podcasts and audience growth. Unlike some other hosts, RedCircle offers a free plan.

- » **PodBean (www.podbean.com):** Like RedCircle, PodBean helps podcasters to publish and then promote and monetize their podcast. They offer a Basic plan that is free.

- » **Spreaker (www.spreaker.com):** Spreaker provides a hosting solution for podcasters as well as assistance with distribution. They offer a free plan called Free Speech, which does not allow for monetization.

- » **Transistor (www.transistor.fm):** Transistor allows users to host as many different podcasts as they wish and offers a free 14-day trial. At the conclusion of the trial, prices begin at $19 per month.

- » **Simplecast (www.simplecast.com):** Simplecast provides everything from podcast hosting to distribution to analytics. Pricing begins at $15 per month.

- » **Captivate (www.captivate.fm):** Captivate allows podcasters to upload or even move their podcast to the Captivate hosting solution and then helps distribute the podcast to top directories. Pricing begins at $17 per month.

Distributing your podcast

Once your podcast has been prepared for sharing with a tool similar to those discussed in the previous section, you'll need to find a place to upload and distribute the podcast to a listening audience. Some tools, such as Buzzsprout, offer to take care of this step for their users. Buzzsprout will not only store your files but also automatically distribute them to directories such as Apple Podcasts on the schedule you choose.

But what do you do if your host does not offer a free distribution service? How do you distribute your podcast where listeners go to find new podcasts to listen to?

The following sections take a brief look at some of the most popular podcast directories where audiences go to listen to great audio content.

Apple Podcasts

https://www.apple.com/apple-podcasts

The Apple Podcasts app is available only on Apple products such as iPhones and iPads. To submit your podcast to be listed by Apple Podcasts you will first need your podcast's RSS feed URL from your third-party host, as described earlier in the chapter. Go to https://podcasters.apple.com to submit your podcast's RSS link for approval and distribution.

Spotify

www.spotifyforpodcasters.com

Podcasters can sign up for a Spotify for Podcasters account and then upload their podcast's RSS feed URL in order to list their podcast on Spotify.

Amazon Music

https://podcasters.amazon.com

Podcasters can add their podcasts to Amazon Music by submitting the URL to their podcast's RSS feed, as shown in Figure 4-5.

ADD YOUR PODCAST

To get started, enter the RSS feed URL below.

FIGURE 4-5:
Submit your
podcast to
Amazon Music's
directory.

Stitcher

www.stitcher.com

Stitcher is an app that allows listeners to find and listen to their favorite podcasts. Podcasters can submit their podcast to the app's directory by visiting https://www.simplecast.com/stitcher to access Simplecast Creator Connect.

TuneIn

www.tunein.com

TuneIn allows Amazon Alexa users to listen to podcasts on the TuneIn directory. To be included, podcasters need to sign up for a free account and then visit the podcaster's page at https://tunein.com/podcasters, shown in Figure 4-6, to submit their RSS feed URL.

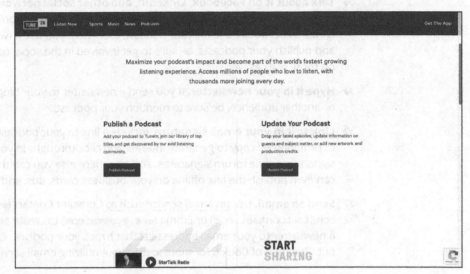

FIGURE 4-6: Submit your podcast's RSS feed URL to TuneIn's podcast directory.

Publicizing Your Podcast

After you create your podcast and make it available online, you need to promote it and drive traffic to it. Don't be afraid to get creative with your promotional efforts. The key is to drive targeted traffic to your podcast (people who are likely to be interested in the topics you discuss during your podcast) and to make sure your content, voice, and style are interesting and useful enough to ensure they'll want to come back to listen to your next podcast and share it with other people.

Making your podcast available through several distribution points is a great start to publicizing your podcast. To make your podcast successful, you need to do more to spread the word about its existence than simply uploading it to a couple of podcasting directories.

TIP

This list describes several ways you can begin promoting your podcast:

>> **Blog about it.** Write a post about your upcoming podcast and entice your blog readers to listen. Don't be afraid to remind them with another post as the date and time of your podcast gets closer!

>> **Tweet it.** Twitter is a great place to hype your podcast, and your Twitter followers might just retweet your podcast link for you!

>> **Talk about it on Facebook, LinkedIn, and other social networking sites.** Mention your podcast on all your social networking profiles. Don't forget to create a Facebook Page for your podcast, too! And if you use a website to host and publish your podcasts, be sure to get involved in the social communities on those sites as well.

>> **Hype it in your newsletter.** If you send a newsletter to your blog subscribers or another audience, be sure to mention your podcast!

>> **Link to it in your email signature.** Include a link to your podcast with a blurb of promotional copy to generate interest and click-throughs in your email signature, online forum signatures, and anywhere else you can think of. You can even publish the link offline on your business cards, ads, and invoices.

>> **Send an email.** Use an email service such as Constant Contact (www.constantcontact.com) or Emma (www.myemma.com) to create and send a newsletter to your email address list that hypes your podcast. Check out Chapter 4 of Book 6 for more ideas about utilizing email services!

REMEMBER

Creating podcasts takes time, and your first attempts aren't likely to be perfect. Don't give up. Keep creating and publishing podcasts, and you'll get better and better at it. Continuously promote your podcasts, and your audience will continue to grow. As long as your podcast content is interesting, meaningful, and useful, and your voice and tone are entertaining, your podcast efforts are not for naught.

Index

A

internal blogs, 172

interviews
  for niche blogs, 130
  as posts for corporate and
    non-profit blogs, 216
  as a type of post, 37

inviting
  brand partnerships, 608–609
  guest bloggers, 535–538

Invoices and quotes section,
  configuring on Wix, 389

.io extension, 48

irrelevant comments, 70

iSpionage (website), 442

Issuu (website), 655

iTunes (website), 105

Izea, 599

J

Jekyll, 263–264

job offers, accepting, 639

job postings, for bloggers,
  204–206

John Deer News (website), 158

John Deere, 158–159

Jones, Kristopher B. (author)
  *Search Engine Optimization
    All-in-One For Dummies*, 404

Joomla!, 266

journal blogs, 16, 29

JUST is a Four Letter Word (blog),
  54, 56, 58, 61, 62, 65

K

Karasavas, Amy (author)
  Facebook For Dummies, 8th
    Edition, 502, 693

Kent, Peter (author)
  SEO For Dummies, 404

key influencers, creating
  relationships with, 226

keyword searches, 123–126,
  409–411

keyword stuffing, 417

Keyword Tool
  building in keywords with, 449–450
  for search engine optimization
    (SEO), 407
  website, 408, 449

keywords
  for body, 211
  building in to content, 449–450
  defined, 730
  hiding, 417
  identifying, 431
  interpreting for search engine
    optimization (SEO), 408–413
  researching, 408
  for titles, 210
  using, 411–413

Kim, Arnold (blogger), 19

Know It All Nikki (blog), 545

Know More Media, 561

knowledge
  as a benefit of business blogs,
    173–174
  sharing your, 115–116

KWFinder (website), 408

L

labels, 59, 730

The Landing (website), 158

Landscape, 663–664

Language and region area,
  configuring on Wix, 389

Later (website), 512

Lawson, Jenny (blogger), 17

Layout button, Google Blogger
  dashboard, 309

lead, for body, 210

leaderboard ads, 544

The Leaky Cauldron (blog), 18, 19

legalities
  about, 229–230
  as considerations, 546
  laws for video content, 681–682
  sponsored content and, 593

length, for body/titles, 210

libel, 69, 230

licensed syndication, 638–639

Life with Tanay (blog), 139

lifestyle, as a blog topic, 29

lighting, for video content, 681

The Liminality Journal (website),
  620, 622

limitations, of web analytics, 432

link baiting, 484

link phrases, for
  relationship-building
  to boost search
  rankings, 415

link responsibilities, on Terms
  and Conditions of Site Use
  page, 80

linkbait, 731

LinkedIn
  about, 145, 262–263, 505,
    706–708
  benefits of, 506
  blog promotion on, 506–507
  finding groups on, 184–185
  networking via, 600
  trends on, 447–448
  website, 447, 505, 706

LinkedIn For Dummies, 7th Edition
  (Elad), 505, 707

links
  about, 63–64
  as a blog feature, 12
  for body, 210
  building, 484–486
  in comment policy, 77
  comments stuffed with, 70
  for community building, 495–498
  defined, 730
  as direct sales tool, 220
  driving consumers to your blog
    using, 191
  for niche blogs, 103–104,
    129–130, 132–133
  to online catalog, as direct sales
    tool, 220
  to online catalogs/stores on
    business blogs, 168

About the Authors

Amy Lupold Bair is the owner of Resourceful Mommy Media, LLC, a social media marketing company that includes the blogger network Global Influence as well as her own blog, Resourceful Mommy (`www.resourcefulmommy.com`). Amy has been named one of the most powerful women in social media by *Working Mother* magazine, and over the last 15 years, has partnered with top brands such as Disney Parks, Hershey, and Walmart. She has spoken at social media marketing and blogging events around the world and has appeared in television, radio, and print media. Amy has loved the Internet since she first heard the whir-whir-click of a dial-up modem. Her first home online was a Geocities community, and she still maintains a Prodigy email account for sentimental reasons. Amy's primary digital addiction is Twitter, where she is always available in 280 characters or less as @ResourcefulMom, although her use of Instagram is climbing the social media ladder and is nearly on par with her diet soda obsession. Over the years, she has contributed to a variety of blogs including Lifetime Moms and the Disney Voices team at Babble.com. Amy is also the author of *Raising Digital Families For Dummies* (John Wiley & Sons, Inc.) as well as *Blogging For Dummies* (John Wiley & Sons, Inc.). Prior to her career as a social media consultant, writer, and speaker, Amy taught middle school English and drama. She and her social media-averse husband live in the D.C. suburbs where they are raising their two bloggers-in-training along with three social media-savvy pets.

Susan Gunelius has more than 30 years of business and marketing experience working for some of the largest companies in the world, including AT&T and HSBC, and as the owner of a marketing communications company, KeySplash Creative, Inc. (`www.keysplashcreative.com`). As president and CEO of KeySplash Creative, Susan strategizes and writes copy, messaging, and content (including blog content) for businesses of all sizes operating in a variety of industries, including well-known companies like Citigroup, Cox Communications, and Intuit. She is the author of a dozen books about marketing, business, and technology and has written about these topics for *Forbes*, Entrepreneur.com, and many other online and offline publications. Susan owns the award-winning blog WomenOnBusiness. com. She is a certified business and career coach and holds a BS in marketing and an MBA in management and strategy.

Dedication

This book is dedicated to all the members of the OG blogging community who created this little corner of the Internet together in stolen moments, building something amazing together in a brave new media world.

Amy Lupold Bair

Author's Acknowledgments

Thank you first and foremost to John Wiley & Sons for giving me this opportunity and making me part of the *For Dummies* family. It is an absolute pleasure and highlight of my blogging adventure. Special thanks to Ellen Gerstein, who changed my life with the best Twitter direct message ever, as well as to Amy Fandrei, the first Wiley team member to give this very grateful blogger a chance at book writing. Thank you as well to my acquisitions editor Elizabeth Stilwell, my project editor Dan Mersey, and the entire *For Dummies* team.

I am grateful, always, for the love and support of my husband, Jason, and our children Emma and Noah. "You be the anchor that keeps my feet on the ground. I'll be the wings that keep your heart in the clouds." I am also thankful for Winnie the Wonder Pup, Mr. Lumperson, and Soozle Doodle, the best home office pets a girl could hope for. Mom and Dad, thank you for not rolling your eyes too often when I told you I was becoming a blogger even though I'm still not sure you understand what I do. Thank you to my Celebrate Recovery family who has made it easier to enjoy this writer's life without hurts, habits, and hang-ups weighing me down. "As iron sharpens iron, so one man sharpens another." — Proverbs 27:17

Amy Lupold Bair

Publisher's Acknowledgments

Acquisitions Editor: Elizabeth Stilwell

Project Manager: Dan Mersey

Technical Editor: Thomas Egan

Project Coordinator: Kristie Pyles

Cover Image: © Palto/Shutterstock